WILLIAM BLAKE

HIS PHILOSOPHY AND SYMBOLS

By S. FOSTER DAMON

MICHAEL AND SATAN *(p. 222)*

TO

MISS AMY LOWELL

POET, SCHOLAR, AND THEREFORE

A LOVER OF BLAKE

PREFACE

THE present study of the philosophy and symbols of William Blake was begun ten years ago, when Dr. Sampson's edition of *Blake's Poetical Works* made most of the texts accessible in their correct form. At first, the study was little more than an intellectual puzzle,—a sort of mosaic of other critics' interpretations. Soon, however, it became obvious that these interpretations were vague guesses, and that Blake's philosophy was yet to be explained. An examination of practically every book that mentioned Blake in its index, as well as of the majority of magazine articles concerning him, resulted only in the conclusion that the great part of this material was worthless.

Consequently, I fell back on tracing out Blake's very definite system of symbols, and on uncovering his literary sources; and these have proved the twin keys to his thought. By finding what books he had read, by determining the currents of speculation which had formed his philosophy, I was gradually enabled to interpret with a degree of certainty Blake's symbols as he meant them to be interpreted. He himself had systematized his thought so carefully that one clue led to another, until at last the general structure of each book was clear.

Then, in 1919, the Blake exhibition of the Grolier Club of New York gave me an unusual opportunity to examine and compare his books. It was my good fortune to help arrange these books; an opportunity which was repeated later when most of them were transported to the Fogg Art Museum of Harvard University, where the collection was augmented by a number of items from Boston. This opportunity for careful research proved invaluable. A year later, during a visit to London, I supplemented this study with an examination of the more important Blake items in England.

As might be expected, many of these chapters have been rewritten several times; none stands in its original form. At any moment, some obscure place in Blake's text would suddenly reveal itself plainly, and a great portion of my work would need thorough revision. This has been exciting, if laborious; but after ten years of it, I feel that at last my manuscript has reached something like a form which may be submitted to public challenge.

There are, of course, many places the meaning of which was undoubtedly clearer in Blake's mind than my own. When such a passage could not be definitely explained by cross-references to other passages in Blake's own works, or by checking with literary sources, I have felt it better to leave the passage as it is, with some indication of what I take to be its general meaning. But I feel convinced that my explanation of the fundamentals of Blake's works will prove to be essentially sound.

I wish to express my gratitude to Miss Amy Lowell, not only for giving me permission to reprint a letter in her possession, and for allowing me to examine her copies of Blake's books, but especially for her outspoken criticism of a very large part of the manuscript. Like all Blake scholars, I am also deeply indebted to Mr. W. A. White of Brooklyn, New York, for his generosity in allowing me to go leisurely through his remarkable collection, and for his courtesy in answering innumerable questions by mail. To Mr. Henry E. Huntington I am indebted for permission to publish extracts from the Thornton and the Watson marginalia, as well as for a description of the illuminated manuscript of *Genesis*. Mr. Grenville Lindall Winthrop of New York has kindly sent me versions of the inscriptions on the water-colours and drawings in his collection. I am indebted to Mr. W. E. Moss for permission to print part of the letter from William Blake to his brother James ; this, with Miss Lowell's letter, has hitherto been printed only in the *Bibliography of Blake*, published by the Grolier Club of New York, 1921.

Dr. Geoffrey Keynes of London was also extremely generous in sending me information about books and manuscripts in England ; needless to say, his studies for his very complete *Bibliography*, which has just been mentioned, made his assistance invaluable. Professor John Livingstone Lowes of Harvard University has been kind enough to listen to two chapters, with the result that one was much revised and the other discarded. Mr. John Brooks Wheelwright of Boston not only read my manuscript, but also gave me the fruits of his labours over the maps in *Jerusalem*. To Professor Vilhelm Grønbech of Copenhagen University, I am indebted for the information concerning translations of Blake into Danish, and also for assistance in regard to the Hebrew names. Professor M. Anesaki of Tokyo University sent me the account of the influence of Blake in Japan. Mr. Thomas Ollive Mabbott of New York furnished me with an inscription from a drawing, a literary parallel in Pope, and hints concerning the derivation of two names.

The *Introduction* has already appeared in *The Freeman*.

S. Foster Damon.

Cambridge, Massachusetts.

INTRODUCTION

THIS book is an attempt to give a rational explanation of Blake's obvious obscurities, and to provide a firm basis for the understanding of his philosophy. The public has been baffled so long with hints of mysteries and madnesses, that it has come to regard Blake's work as too eccentric and remote to repay personal investigation. This attitude is completely wrong. Blake's thought was of the clearest and deepest ; his poetry of the subtlest and strongest ; his painting of the highest and most luminous. He tried to solve problems which concern us all, and his answers to them are such as to place him among the greatest thinkers of several centuries.

The attitude of modern criticism towards Blake to-day is analogous to its attitude towards Beethoven not so long ago. The world at large then admitted that Beethoven had written many charming things in his younger days ; but that his last twenty years were matters for the maddest enthusiasts only. The poor man's complete deafness had cut him off so entirely from humanity, that theory overcame him : he was carried to the clouds by his hippogriff ; and whatever transcendental heaven he wished to express, the human ear was physically incapable of supporting his harmonic monstrosities.

And so with Blake. The *Songs of Innocence* are read everywhere ; yet we lack a correct text of *The Four Zoas* ! The lyrics are in every anthology ; yet professors of literature wonder if the epics are worth reading !

I confess frankly that when I began collecting comments on Blake, I thought him mad and the *Jerusalem* trash. But as the work went on, and plane after plane of sanity was opened, my conversion began. Now I firmly believe that the last of Blake's works are his greatest ; that the *Jerusalem* ranks with its contemporary, the *Inventions to Job*.

Neither taste nor opinion, however, is basis for criticism. The only possible method of judging is to find out : to find out, first, what the man tried to do ; secondly, whether or not he did it ; after which, in a mere coda, we may venture our individual decisions as to whether or not it was worth doing.

Blake was trying to do what every mystic tries to do. He was trying to rationalize the Divine (' to justify the ways of God to men '), and to apotheosize the Human. He was trying to lay bare the fundamental errors which are the cause of misery. These errors he sought, not in codes of ethic, nor in the construction of society, but in the human soul itself.

It is the fashion among a few enthusiasts to compare Blake with Shakspere. The absurdity is obvious. Great men can seldom be compared. Nevertheless, the two fit curiously together ; Blake was the complement of Shakspere. The Elizabethan recorded all the types of humanity but one—the mystic ; the Georgian recorded no other but the mystic. One saw individuals everywhere ; the other saw Man. The first hardly systematized human problems : he beheld situations only to whose solution he gave no clue ; the second saw problems everywhere, to be solved by Reason under the guidance of Inspiration. One hid himself, and identified himself so well with his creations that we can hardly say what Shakspere was like ; while from Blake's writings we could reconstruct his very features. Shakspere found our life a dream rounded by the sleep of death ; Blake found our life a dream to be followed by a more glorious awakening than we can possibly imagine. Both were poets who translated everything into the terms of humanity.

And here lies the root of Blake's greatness. His feet stride from mountain to mountain ; and if his head is lost among stars and clouds, it is only because he is a giant. His heaven is no abstract of metaphysics ; it is a map which charts the soul of every living individual. His God is not some dim and awful Principle ; he is a Friend who descends and raises Man till Man himself is a God. And by this dealing in universals Blake came to that point where such diverse temperaments as Milton, Fra Angelico, Nietzsche, El Greco, Paracelsus, Shelley, Michelangelo, and Walt Whitman may be invoked for fair comparisons. It is in a way not a bad sign of Blake's greatness that so many dissimilar sects claim him : the Revolutionaries, the Theosophists, the Vers Librists and their opponents, the Spiritists, and so on. We can treat of Blake as an Alchemist. There have been prominent Catholics who have welcomed many doctrines of this hater of priests !

But I have wandered far from my thesis. What Blake tried to do I have briefly described ; whether it was worth doing, we need not say. Whether he did it—just there is the centre of the critical vortex.

For Blake did not believe in unveiling the Truth completely. He always held something in reserve. He not only cried to mankind to ' put on intellect ' ; he made that faculty necessary if his works are to be understood. There never was a greater intellectual snob. He elaborated a marvellously woven veil for his Sanctuary, so heavy that none has moved it very effectually, so beautiful that none has refused some genuflection.

This was not due to cowardice or caution. When Blake spoke out, none could be bolder than he. Nobody in his own age approached him for boldness. Even now, we who recognize his purity hardly dare repeat some of his doctrines. There are poems printed with the asterisks of prudery ; there are drawings which have not been reproduced nor even described. We admit our own silliness, yet we lack courage, even after this lapse of a century and more, to repeat Blake's own words, safely dead as he is.

Can we then condemn his reticence ? Before we condemn, we must know that it was deliberate, and, furthermore, was in accordance with the most sacred traditions of all ages and races. Blake does not cry ' Procul, profani ! ' but he baffles all such by requiring that first they put on intellect. No swine can ever reach his pearls.

He charts us the road to Eleusis, he gives us the Keys of Paradise. But he conveys them in symbols whose meaning he stipulates we first learn. We *must* find the meaning. Too many in this world mistake the word for the thought : we juggle with terms as though they were magical formulæ. ' Hoc est corpus ' becomes Hokus-pokus ; and the Way is lost. Blake simply removed the word to preserve the meaning.

He had two methods of charting his way through the Inexpressible : these were Poetry and Painting. Herein he was far more fortunate than the average mystic, who has no means of grappling with the Ineffable. Poetry and Painting were the two torches which lit 'the fury of his course among the stars of God and in the abysses of the Accuser.' To be dazzled by those twin lights, to consider him as author and artist only, is an unfair shifting of emphasis. His arts were tools, not ends in themselves. That he paid immense attention to the perfecting of his tools is beside the point. He himself realized that the sweetness of his early lyrics seemed self-sufficient; so later he subordinated literary effect to higher aims. He wanted to rouse with thought, not to lull with beauty. He judged all art, all poetry, according to the magnitude of its conception; and so he expected to be judged in turn.

In order to fix Blake with reference to humanity, we seem at first to repeat the astronomer's difficulty of determining the curve of a comet. But Blake was not such an irrational and unrelated phenomenon. The Sea of Time and Space alone makes him appear a solitary island. I have tried to indicate his relationship to other great thinkers by inserting passages from those authors whom we know he read, and also by quoting parallels from entirely independent sources. This was done with no intention of establishing plagiarisms. Astonishing as many parallels are, especially in the case of Shelley, they are caused by similar methods of thought under similar circumstances. The identity of, say, Urizen and the Demiurge is neither accident nor coincidence.

There is a certain type of critic in whom the Will to Believe ousts the ability to judge Thought without bias. These have been content to point scornfully to these very parallels, in an attempt to brand Blake as anti-Christian. It is quite true that no history of what I may call 'Gnostic Christianity,' from Simon Magus to Eliphaz Lévi, could afford to ignore Blake. But Blake's great idea was to synthesize all these contradictions. He was not shocked to find in such philosophers more truth than had ever been admitted. He saw that no sincere thought could be wholly untrue, and therefore could not be wholly rejected.

But at heart, Blake is one of the great Christians. The strangeness of his language has often repelled the orthodox; his attacks on priesthood have irritated many sects; and his generosity towards all Truth-seeking has seemed heretical. Yet behind all this, we find Blake becoming more and more passionate, even dogmatic, over the essentials of the Christian Faith. His tenderest lyrics, his most turbulent vortices of design, his inexplicable nadirs of thought, all resolve eventually into one thing: Man in the arms of God.

The world has long since done its worst towards Blake; and he has emerged triumphant, with the twin crowns of Poet and Painter. But this is not enough. The modern Trismegistus must receive his third crown, that of Philosopher, before his permanent place among the great of this earth can be determined.

CONTENTS

COMMENTARIES

NOTE ON THE ILLUSTRATIONS

THE Frontispiece, *Michael and Satan*, is from a water-colour drawing in the Fogg Art Museum of Harvard University. It is based on *Revelation* xii. 7-9 ; but see also page 222.

The illustration facing page 250 is one of the famous Visionary Heads which Blake drew for the amazement of Varley. It is undoubtedly a satirical sketch of Blake himself. On comparing this profile with that in the *MS. Book*, page 67, we see that Blake has enlarged his own brow, has made his snub nose very snub indeed, has poetically developed his eye (just as Phillips had done in all seriousness), while the chin remains unchanged. Blake was born under the astrological sign of Cancer : hence the word ' Cancer ' is written above. This drawing is listed by Gilchrist under the title ' Cancer ' (*ed.* 1863, no. 57 ; *ed.* 1880, no. 63), where the resemblance to Blake is noted.

WILLIAM BLAKE: HIS PHILOSOPHY AND SYMBOLS

CHAPTER I

THE INEFFABLE SECRET

His spirit recovered its pristine liberty and saw through the mud walls of flesh and blood. Being alive, he was in the spirit all his days. While his body therefore was inclosed in this world, his soul was in the temple of Eternity, and clearly beheld the infinite life and omnipresence of God: having conversation with invisible, spiritual, and immaterial things, which were its companions, itself being invisible, spiritual, and immaterial. Kingdoms and Ages did surround him, as clearly as the hills and mountains: and therefore the Kingdom of God was ever round about him. Everything was one way or other his sovereign delight and transcendant pleasure, as in Heaven everything will be every one's peculiar treasure.—THOMAS TRAHERNE: *Centuries of Meditations*, iii. 95.

THE key to everything Blake ever wrote or painted lies in his mysticism. We must understand this thoroughly before we can pass to a consideration of his works.

The Mystic is one of the eternal Types of Humanity. Rare though he be, he has left such deep impresses upon history, that the modern psychologists have been particularly interested in the workings of his mind; especially since all mystics have a surprising sameness, no matter from what culture or creed they may have sprung.

The test by which the Mystic is positively recognized is the 'ecstasy.' During such moments, he enters a peculiar state of mental illumination, in which he is exalted above the world as we know it, into a supersensuous state, where he is violently united with Ultimate Truth. This 'Truth' he may call 'God,' 'Beauty,' 'Law,' or any other name; but it is always One and always Truth. This Union with the One combines pain and pleasure, emotion and knowledge, nature and supernature, body and soul, man and God. Those who have experienced it can imagine no higher state of existence; and generally their whole lives thereafter are devoted to revealing on earth this ineffable secret.

Blake was subject to these ecstasies, and he never seems to have emerged from one without wresting some great Truth from the Eternity which he had entered; for he was not of that type which is content to let slip what it has learned. The strange poem in the letter to his friend Butts (Oct. 2, 1800) describes such a vision: how by the sea one day his eyes expanded 'into regions of fire remote from desire'; how everything in the world appeared as 'men seen afar'; and how eventually they were all combined into 'One Man,' the Christ, on whose bosom Blake reposed. His epic, *Milton*, is the record of one instant of such vision. His *Invention of Job* shows the Just Man saved from his own justice by such a vision. Are all these literary fantasies?

If we choose to think so, we can still turn to Blake's copy of Sweden-borg's *Wisdom of the Angels concerning Divine Love and Wisdom*, in which he made curious notes.   On page 33 (¶ 40), the text reads : ' The human Mind . . . cannot investigate it, *without keeping the Understanding some time in spiritual light* ' ; Blake underlined the italicized words and added : ' this, Man can do while in the body.'   On page 200 (¶ 241), the text reads : ' Every one who consults his Reason, *whilst it is in the Light* . . .' ; and Blake again underlined the words here italicized.   Yet once more, on page 220 (¶ 257) Blake marked a phrase of Swedenborg's as of great importance : ' But still Man, in whom the spiritual Degree is open, comes into that Wisdom when he dies, and *may also come into it by laying aside the Sensations of the Body, and by Influx from above at the same Time into the Spirituals of his Mind.*'   Opposite these words Blake jotted two notes : ' this is while in the Body ' ; and ' This is to be understood as unusual in our time but common in ancient.'

The intensity of such an experience is extraordinary.   A flash—a second—fills even the most ardent persecutor (such as Paul) with the conviction of truth, and backs this conviction with immense strength to further the very religion which till then he has hated with his whole soul.

The experience is always the same, no matter in what land or level of civilization it occurs.   It is above all creeds, for experience must have authority over theory.   More than that, Mysticism is the source itself of every creed ; all the founders of the great religions were mystics ; and their religions are at heart attempts to bring the beatific state to every man.   Mysticism explains all religions, all antique mysteries, and perhaps even such exotic sects as those of the Alchemists and the Rosicrucians. Many parallels of theirs with Blake's ideas will be pointed out later ; since mystics, in telling of their experience, ' speak the same language,' even to using the same symbols.

The principal thing of which they are all convinced is that, whatever this material world may be, there is another, so much more real and more ecstatic, that words can only stammer about it.   Heaven is not a comfort-ing hypothesis nor an exterior reward for the unrewarded : it is an actual state within us.   The mystics have been there, and they know.   Naturally they try to show others the way, and they have left many fascinating maps.

Miss Evelyn Underhill [1] divides the Way into five stages : (1) the awakening to a sense of divine reality ; (2) the consequent purgation of the Self, when it realizes its own imperfections ; (3) an enhanced return of the sense of the divine order, after the Self has achieved its detachment from the world ; (4) the ' Dark Night of the Soul,' or the crucifixion of the Self in the absence of the divine ; (5) and the complete union with Truth, the attainment of that which the third state had perceived as a possibility.

Blake passed through these identical five states.   His complete works, which are an accurate record of his life, fall into these same divisions. The first three states are named by him ' Innocence,' ' Experience,' and ' Revolution.'   The fourth state was passed in silence ; while the fifth state was a return to ' Innocence ' with the added wisdom of ' Experience.' Blake had not yet reached the first state when he wrote the *Poetical*

---

[1] *Mysticism : A Study in the Nature and Development of Man's Spiritual Consciousness,* by Evelyn Underhill (4th ed., N.Y., 1912), p. 205.

Sketches, which were finished when he was twenty. They reveal practically no sense of the transcendent. One poem, *The Couch of Death*, which contains a vision of Heaven, sounds like a literary exercise ; and *Fresh from the dewy hill* describes only an earthly passion, however much it suggests Neoplatonic adoration. Neither does Blake's next work, the unfinished *Island in the Moon* (1786-1789) show any sign of illumination. But the *Songs of Innocence* (1789) are entirely inspired by mystical perception ; therefore between the last page of *An Island in the Moon* (after Feb. 1787) and 1789, the first illumination must have taken place.

Blake left no record of this first great moment ; but we can conjecture what happened, from what we know of this part of his life.

He was thirty, married, and thoroughly dissatisfied with himself. His only worldly recognition had come from a small circle of Blue-Stockings hunting culture and literary lions. Through them he had printed his first book, a small volume with which he was disgusted, for he could only see how derivative his verses were, and how much better they should have been. Naturally he could not envisage our historical perspective, by which we place that volume as one of the great milestones in the progress of English poetry.

He felt that he had not justified his existence. He had not yet found his predestined way of expressing himself. Such a moment occurs in the life of every author, and it is always abysmally melancholy.

Blake's discontent took the form of a satire against his friends the Blue-Stockings, whose superficiality he could not help despising. He burlesqued their conversations, their intellectual pretensions, and their literary tastes. Into their mouths he put song after absurd song.

But these songs turned into poetry, for all his intentions. From satire they became the real thing ; and Blake began to see that he might yet do something, that his gift for poetry was not a mere ferment of adolescence.

Then a very heavy blow fell. In February 1787 his beloved younger brother, Robert, whom he was teaching to draw and paint, died. Blake expended every possible effort to save him, watching day and night by his bedside. But he was useless. And at the end he suddenly saw his brother's soul ascending, ' clapping its hands for joy ' at the great release.

' Fear and Hope are—Vision,' Blake wrote later, under a picture of just such a death-bed.[1] At this moment, the conviction that there is a World of Eternity rolled irresistibly over his exhausted mind. His brother could not be dead ; he had only passed into a higher, happier life. Religion had been teaching this for centuries ; and now Blake himself had *seen*. Whereupon, absolutely worn out, he went to bed and slept for three days and nights.

And now his latent gift for poetry sprang of itself into expression. What he wrote he still added to *An Island in the Moon* ; but that satire had become inadequate and silly. He knew that his lyrics deserved better presentation than any ordinary printed book could give them, that they called for some unusual and beautiful setting. The problem challenged him ; and like all such problems, it remained working in his subconscious mind.

Can we wonder, then, that Robert, closer to Blake in death even than in life, should have come to him ' in a vision of the night,' bringing the

[1] *Gates of Paradise*, plate 13, the turning-point of the series. Cf. also *Job*, plate 13.

solution of the problem ?[1] Blake was instructed to etch the text and its decoration on a copper-plate, take impresses in coloured ink, and finally paint each page by hand.

As was his custom, Blake recorded this process in *An Island in the Moon* ; then, fired with his new idea, he abandoned the satire forever, for his new work. It was called *Songs of Innocence*, and has since taken its place among the most beautiful books of the world.

The Mystical Path always begins in the Garden of Eden. Shafts of transcendental light pour down and apotheosize visibly the entire world. ' When I went in the morning into the fields to work,' wrote another mystic after his conversion,[2] ' the glory of God appeared in all his visible creation. I well remember we reaped oats, and how every straw and head of the oats seemed, as it were, arrayed in a kind of rainbow glory, or to glow, if I may so express it, in the glory of God.' This same light saturates the *Songs of Innocence* and *The Book of Thel*. No mundane landscape ever glittered with such strange, ecstatic iridescences ; no actual children ever lived such heightened, untroubled existences. And ' Innocence '—sacramental perception—became for Blake one of the permanent ' states ' through which souls pass. The effect of this illumination never left him.

Many poets, among them Shelley, Wordsworth, and Walt Whitman, often attain to a mild sense of this splendour and unity of the universe. They seldom go farther ; Blake passed them all, exploring the whole extent of the Mystic Way.

Another fact about Illumination is important. It is more than a state of emotion ; it is a state of knowledge as well. A new truth is perceived. Most mystics are unable to express, or even to remember, what they have learned. Blake always wrested from his visions some transcendental theory which he recorded in his work.

This time he discovered that the Mystical Paradise is the same as that in which children dwell. Heaven *literally* ' lies about us in our infancy.'[3] This was the very Eden from which Adam, and all men, fell. ' That is heaven,' Blake said once, leading a friend to a window, and pointing to a group of children at play.[4] No doubt he remembered that his own ' visions ' began at the age of four.[5] Of course, he admitted, ' Some Children are Fools, and so are some old Men. But there is a vast Majority on the side of Imagination or Spiritual Sensation ' ; therefore it is not surprising that Blake wrote of his books, Particularly they have been Elucidated by Children.'[6]

[1] Gilchrist, ch. ix. J. T. Smith (*Nollekens and his Times*) simply says ' in one of his visionary imaginings.' Allan Cunningham (*Life of Blake*) is the most dramatic ; he says that Blake ' was made aware that the spirit of his favourite brother Robert was in the room, and to this celestial visitor he applied for counsel.' It is noteworthy that Blake's imaginings were especially apt to be active at night.

[2] Quoted by W. James (*Varieties of Religious Experience*) from Leuba. His two chapters on Conversion, as well as Miss Underhill's (*Mysticism*, Pt. II. ch. 2), are filled with case after case, all reporting this intense and very real sense of a new light. I must ask the reader to remember that I am not trying to prove any transcendental theories myself. I am only trying to show how Blake underwent certain definite psychological experiences recognized by science ; and that these experiences were the inspiration of his work.

[3] The ' hysterical rapture ' which Wordsworth's poem caused to Blake in his last years is recorded in H. C. R., Feb. 27, 1852.

[4] Palmer's letter in Gilchrist, ch. xxxiii.

[5] However, these were only the imaginings likely to occur to any sensitive child brought up in a religious household. [6] Letter to Trusler, Aug. 23, 1799.

Such seems to have been Blake's first illumination.

But after mystical joy follows reaction, the purgation. ' The world is evil,' says the mystic ; ' why ? ' And Blake, in a new book, remorselessly wrote against each of the best *Songs of Innocence* a *Song of Experience*. He substituted *The Tyger* of wrath for *The Lamb* of love ; *Infant Sorrow* for *Infant Joy* ; and so on. This state of cynicism he called ' Experience.' *Tiriel*, his first Prophetic Book, is of this period, preoccupied with the error of the world's way. *The Gates of Paradise* must also have been conceived about this time. Looking back upon the state, he wrote : [1]

> . . . . Terrors appeared in the Heavens above,
> And in Hell beneath, and a mighty and awful change threatened the Earth.

The change came, but it was for the good. The American and French Revolutions promised a better world ; and stirred Blake to a new enthusiasm, from which he deduced the theory that apparent Evil, such as War, is only Energy working against established order. This was a new perception of Truth ; all his problems seemed solved by it ; and he hailed the light triumphantly in another book, *The Marriage of Heaven and Hell* (1793). ' A new heaven is begun . . .'; and the third state of the Path was reached : the return of the sense of the transcendent. In the same year, urged perhaps by the expectation of death,[2] he began the series of Prophetic Books engraved at Lambeth (' Lambeth ! The Bride, the Lamb's Wife, loveth thee : Thou are one with her & knowest not of self in thy supreme joy,' he fondly wrote later [3]) ; and before the series was ended in 1795, two years later, the ' supreme joy ' of creation produced seven books of strange poetry and matchless decoration.

This period of inspiration meant a great deal to him. In *Milton*, he described this descent of the Poetic Spirit, Los ; and added a full-page illustration of the moment, a picture vibrating with metallic flames. The appearance of Los seems more than a figure of speech. Blake's words are filled with the physical sensation of actual presence :

> And Los behind me stood : a terrible flaming Sun : just close
> Behind my back : I turned round in terror, and behold,
> Los stood in that fierce-glowing fire. . . .

Los then enters into Blake, who at once beholds the eternal functioning of the Imagination throughout the Universe.

The tremendous creative energy which produced the Lambeth books is one of the three characteristics of the new illumination.[4] Of the other two, the first, the ' joyous apprehension of the absolute,' is undoubtedly signified by the many paintings of sunrises which Blake did at this period,[5] and his faith in the transcendental effects of Revolution ; [6] while the second characteristic, the ' cleansing of the doors of perception,' has itself been made famous by Blake's quatrain :

> To see a World in a grain of sand,
> And a Heaven in a wild flower,
> Hold Infinity in the palm of your hand,
> And Eternity in an hour.

---

[1] Letter to Flaxman, Sept. 12, 1800.
[2] ' I say I shant live five years. And if I live one it will be a Wonder. June 1793.'—*MS. Book.*   [3] *Jerusalem*, 12 : 41-42.   [4] Underhill, pp. 288-289.
[5] *Marriage*, plates 11, 21 ; *Visions, Argument* ; *America*, plates 2, 6, 7.
[6] See the last line of *America*.

But perhaps this is too 'poetical' to be trusted ; let us turn to a letter of the same period : [1]

I know This World is a World of Imagination and Vision. I see Everything I paint in This World, but Every body does not see alike. To the Eyes of a Miser, a Guinea is more beautiful than the Sun, and a bag worn with the use of Money has more beautiful proportions than a Vine filled with Grapes. The tree which moves some to tears of joy is in the Eyes of others only a Green thing which stands in the way. Some see Nature all Ridicule and Deformity, and by these I shall not regulate my proportions ; and some scarce see Nature at all. But to the Eyes of the Man of Imagination, Nature is Imagination itself. As a Man is, so he sees.

But the Lambeth books show an increasing pessimism. This is the familiar reaction. From the exultation of *America*, through the ominous vortices of *Europe*, to the terrible nadir of *Urizen* and the two books of *Los*, there is a direct descent, which ends with the wail of *Ahania*. To the blackness of Blake's thought was added presently the bitterness of artistic sterility, and the fourth stage, the 'Dark Night of the Soul,' passed in silence.

Before this Night set in completely, there was an illusory increase of light. In 1800 Blake moved to Felpham, to a cottage near the poet Hayley's 'Hermitage.' The change from city to seashore, the relief from monetary anxiety (for Hayley was giving him a lot of engraving to do), and the promise of a sympathetic friend, all conspired to make Blake believe that his mundane troubles were over. His poem *To Mrs. Flaxman* breathes with supernatural light. In a letter to her husband, Blake wrote : ' Heaven opens here on all sides her golden gates ; her windows are not obstructed by vapours ; voices of celestial inhabitants are most distinctly heard, and their forms more distinctly seen ; and my cottage is also a shadow of their houses. . . . And now begins a new life. . . .' To Thomas Butts a few days later, Blake wrote of his 'first vision of light,' the ecstasy which came over him on the beach.

But all this, as has been hinted, was illusory. Hayley was a gentleman, but also a fool, who kept Blake either busy engraving (' a work of magnitude,' said Blake), or miniature-painting—of all things ! What wonder that all Blake's inspiration for his own painting or poetry stopped completely !

One of his worst troubles at this time was the fear of poverty, by which Hayley seems to have held his nose to the grindstone. Blake could not make much money by his own poems and paintings, neither could he give up these 'treasures in heaven' just to make money by the nerve-racking work of engraving plates for others, work which often offended his deepest principles. But the greatest suffering he underwent came from the final conviction that the world was deaf to his messages. Even Hayley, the outward friend, despised them. But Blake *knew* his own worth ; and it was characteristic of him that he directed his appeal to the ' Young Men of a New Age,' rather than change his chosen mode of expression one jot. [2]

He complained to one friend only, Thomas Butts. Their letters during this period show only too clearly how Blake was tortured by the galling patronage of Hayley, the 'best-seller' in verse. Blake realized that

[1] Letter to Trusler, Aug. 23, 1799.
[2] See the letter to Butts, July 6, 1803 ; also the Preface to *Milton*.

Hayley was kind, that he was trying to help him along by giving him profitable work ; but ' Corporeal friends are spiritual enemies,' and finally Blake wrote Butts his sincere opinion of Hayley, adding : ' Indeed, by my late firmness I have brought down his affected loftiness, and he begins to think I have some genius,' and ends this sentence with an outburst of contempt : ' as if genius and assurance were the same thing ! '

This ' late firmness ' was a burst of wrath which began a series of events in Blake's spiritual life so far-reaching in results, that he recorded them in a fifty-page poem, the Prophetic Book *Milton*. The poem is entirely personal throughout ; it is one of the most important documents of mystical psychology in existence.

It describes Blake's return to mental illumination and his final awakening to the ' Unitive Life,' the last stage of the Mystic Way. Blake begins with an account of the ' firmness,' told as a spiritual act in Eternity ; Hayley (or rather, Hayley's type) being completely disguised, as Blake thought, under the name of Satan ! After various difficulties, Blake recognizes his spiritual enemy, and casts off all the intolerable obligations.

At last he is prepared for the final communion with the unseen world. His first vision is pictured on page 36, and is labelled, to prevent any doubt, ' Blake's Cottage at Felpham.' He is walking in the garden, and the angelic visitor, Ololon, descends. Other spirits follow, each apparition preceding a sudden understanding of some truth. Faster and faster the states of vision and of knowledge alternate, until at the last, Unity is achieved : a unity which is ' One Man, Jesus the Saviour, wonderful ! '

How ' real ' was this ? What did Blake actually see ? He told Crabb Robinson that he saw it ' in imagination ' ; and Blake generally was careful to describe all his visions as such ; but this cannot satisfy us. It was unmistakably a mystical vision ; what is a mystical vision ?

In anticipation of a future chapter, it should be explained that Blake never was known to show the slightest belief in the *objective* reality of any vision. ' *Where did you see all that, Mr. Blake ?* ' ' *In here* ' (*pointing to his forehead*) is a formula recurring again and again under various guises, in his poems as well as in his biographies.

And yet the violent reality of this vision is underscored. ' I turn'd round in terror . . . sudden I beheld . . . words distinct . . . . more distinct than any earthly . . . trumpets innumerable sounding articulate ' are a few of the phrases, showing his intimate participation in the visionary action. And finally, in a column of fire and a roaring of trumpets, the vision ends.

> Terror-struck in the Vale I stood, at that immortal sound.
> My bones trembled. I fell outstretch'd upon the path
> A moment ; & my Soul return'd into its mortal state. . . .
> And my sweet Shadow of Delight [1] stood trembling by my side.
> Immediately the Lark mounted with a loud trill from Felpham's Vales.

Such was the experience which abruptly swung Blake from the ' Dark Night ' into the raptures of the Unitive Life. It was marked outwardly by a farewell to Hayley and a return to London. He called it a ' Last Judgment,' a casting-out of error ; which explains his fondness for that

---

[1] Blake's wife.

particular subject.[1] In October 1804, he was even reconciled to the
' spiritual enemy ' Hayley, and wrote him :

O lovely Felpham, parent of immortal friendships, to thee I am eternally indebted for my three years' rest from perturbation and the strength I now enjoy.
Suddenly, on the day after visiting the Truchsessian Gallery of pictures, I was
again enlightened with the light I enjoyed in my youth, and which has for exactly
twenty years [2] been closed from me as by a door and by window-shutters. . . .
Dear Sir, excuse my enthusiasm, or rather madness, for I am really drunk with
intellectual vision whenever I take a pencil or graver into my hand, even as I used
to be in my youth, and as I have not been for twenty dark, but very profitable, years.

So at last Blake reached the Unitive Life, the ultimate stage of the
Mystic Way. What he had suffered, we can hardly guess. One picture
is surely a record : the Crucifixion in the *Jerusalem*, a Crucifixion which,
for its feeling, ranks among the greatest ever executed. The night is
completely black, in spite of a faint thread of light on the horizon. Hardly
more than apprehended is the upturned face of Man gazing upon his
tortured God. But the worshipper's faith is unshaken.

And now this was passed. Blake's faith was justified, his inspiration
had returned. His state may be verified by a comparison with Miss
Underhill's analysis of the ultimate stage.

There are three characteristics. The first is a complete absorption
in the interests of the Infinite. Blake devoted the rest of his life to
interpreting it by pen and graver. The second is the consciousness of
strength, of acting by Divine authority, with an invulnerable serenity.
This might well serve as an appreciation of Blake alone ! The third is the
expression of that strength in some kind of worldly activity. Paul established Christianity ; Jeanne d'Arc drove the English from France ;
Catherine of Siena dominated Italian politics ; St. Teresa reformed her
order ; Blake produced a series of books which reveal the incessant flow
of inspiration.

It is profitless to search here for facts about his subsequent spiritual
life. One or two facts show that even he could still be reached by cir-
cumstance. There is on the tenth page of the *MS. Book* a note : ' Tuesday
Jan. 20, 1807, between Two and Seven in the Evening—Despair.' There
was anger over two outrageous attacks in Leigh Hunt's *Examiner*. On
the other hand, the *MS. Book* contains a mysterious note dated May 23,
1810 : ' Found the Word Golden,' which has been conjectured to mean
' Found the Bible inspired,' though that was an already old doctrine
with him. Beyond these few items there seem to be no indications
of mental turmoil or change of attitude towards the world temporal or
spiritual.

As he lived, so he died, singing triumphantly upon his death-bed the
hymns which soared upward from his subconscious mind, confident that

---

[1] There is a picture in Blair's *Grave* ; one in *Job* ; a water-colour done for the Countess
of Egremont ; a fresco (since lost) ; an ink drawing owned by Mr. W. A. White ; plate 7
of *America* ; besides various sketches. The *MS. Book* contains a famous literary
description, with which should be mentioned the letter to Ozias Humphrey (1808) and
the climax of all three epics.

[2] ' Exactly twenty years ' is a misstatement of enthusiasm. In 1784 the *Poetical
Sketches* had been printed for a year, and the *Songs of Innocence* had not even been thought
of. Judging by Blake's own works, the terrible period of sterility had lasted only nine
years, beginning in 1795, after *Ahania* was engraved.

at last he was passing directly to that Union which he had already known in the flesh.[1]

Thus the five States of the Mystic Way were manifested in Blake's life and works. Naturally he tended to see everything in the same divisions. All history fell into this order : first there was the ' Innocence ' of unfallen Eternity ; then the ' Experience ' of the Fall ; next the appearance of the spiritual Revolutionist, Jesus ; whose doctrines were misinterpreted during the ' Dark Night ' of the following eighteen centuries ; which was, however, about to end in the new revelation of Truth and the redemption of Mankind.

One of Blake's most cryptic poems, *The Mental Traveller*, resolves into an analysis of the five States. In accordance with Blake's customary arrangement of composition, it does not begin with the first State, Innocence, because that is not self-conscious. Only in Experience does man begin to feel his separate selfhood. The recognition of errors and sufferings, whether interior or exterior, brings about an immediate reaction. This newborn reaction is ' The Babe,' who in the Prophetic Books is named Orc. The Babe is crucified by the Old Woman, Custom ; but this crucifixion, far from killing the boy, matures him. At last he breaks loose ; and the third State, Revolution, is reached. The Old Woman becomes the youthful bride of Orc ; Nature is subjected to the creative instinct. He establishes the Truth for which he has suffered ; his hearth welcomes all the outcast. But the fourth State is at hand. From his Truth springs Dogma (' the Female Babe ') who becomes so sacred that none dare touch her. Blake elsewhere named her Rahab. She sets up her tyranny, indulging her chance favourites, but driving out the very Truth from which she sprang. This is the Dark Night of the Soul. Orc, now aged, wanders through the desert of error, seeking for a new ideal, which is Freedom (Jerusalem). In his pursuit of her, he grows younger and younger again, until the last State is reached, the ultimate Union. Blake, believing that the States move in an eternal cycle, identifies the last and first. Man is now a Babe again in the delights of the first State of ecstasy. In the arms of Freedom he has re-entered Innocence. But it cannot last ; Freedom becomes aged into Custom ; the Babe again is crucified ; and the poem ends while the cycle continues.

This detailed emphasis upon Blake's mystical life is important. Many have ignored, and some few have even denied,[2] Blake's mysticism ; while those who mention it speak vaguely, as without knowledge of the matter. Mysticism was *always* the inner impulse of everything Blake wrote or painted, from the *Songs of Innocence* to his last works ; if we do not recognize this, we only wonder and aimlessly admire. It is the source of

[1] The three designs ending the three epics symbolize the moment of death as the mystical ecstasy. In each the soul is represented as a woman, since it is in the presence of God. The last sketch for *The Four Zoas* represents this soul leaping enraptured from the earth, which has become a tiny globe beneath its feet. The last plate of *Milton* represents the soul in adoration between two seraphim. But the last plate of *Jerusalem* is Blake's finest depiction of the ultimate union. God holds the soul tightly clasped ; and together they soar upwards in a region of pure fire.

[2] Theodore Maynard in *The Poetry Review*, 1916, vol. vii. p. 317. Irving Babbitt : *Rousseau and Romanticism*, 1919, p. 152. Professor Babbitt's contention that either Blake or Buddha could not be a mystic, because their doctrines differ, is as absurd as claiming that, of two men, one cannot be intoxicated because one goes to sleep while the other breaks windows open.

all his doctrines, for it was an actual experience which took precedence of the established faiths and theories. We become ridiculous in protesting against the authority which visions have over seers. Their answer is simply : ' I have seen ' ; and they will not argue as theory what they have known as fact.

But to us who are not seers, visions cannot be authoritative. Blake realized that ; and he expended his energy, not in apologizing for his visions, but in teaching the truths they revealed. These truths he intended to be self-justified ; they are propped by no appeals to supernaturalism.

The central task he set himself was :

> To open the Eternal Worlds, to open the Immortal Eyes
> Of Man inwards into the Worlds of Thought : into Eternity ;
> Ever expanding in the Bosom of God, the Human Imagination ; [1]

or, in other words, to teach all mankind how to reach the Paradise of Mysticism, the Garden planted in the brain.

Many other mystics have tried to tell the Ineffable Secret ; it is their great tragedy that they all have failed. Mystics, like poets, are born to their inheritance, and words of light mean nothing to the blind.

Among the great poets, only one other—Dante—has described the Mystical Path. Did he succeed ? It is hard to say. Dante limited himself for the most part to simple psychology described in terms of the established symbols. Yet even so, when he begins penetrating the abstractions of his Paradise, our interest rapidly vanishes. We are fitter to understand Hell. What we really enjoy in Dante is the poetry, not the fundamental ideas. Probably only one in a thousand understands Dante's Paradise ; the rest see nothing but the outward aspects of the images, never suspecting that they are only symbols of something very different, something esoteric.

Therefore Dante, for all his success as a poet, had no success in bringing his mystical message to any but the elect. Blake fails—and succeeds—in precisely the same way.

But Blake falls far below Dante in the literary presentation of the Mystic Way. Dante's lines always remain poetry, however occult his ideas ; Blake's do not always. And the contrast is made stronger by the fact that with Blake the general reader *knows* he does not understand, while with Dante he guesses vaguely at meanings, and puts the vital phrases aside as ' merely poetry.'

There is one more important aspect of Blake as a mystic. In him we find no rejections, no disgusting temptations, terrible starvings or lashings of mind or flesh, no cult of filth ; nothing morbid or ascetic whatsoever, not even a disposition towards solemnity or pitiful self-accusations. The normal life, *heightened*, was his ideal. He never lost his grip on this world. Even his ecstasies came uninvoked. He left no systems of meditation or magical ceremonies to invoke deity ; prayer was his sole method. And at the highest moments of the ecstasy, he puzzles in the back of his mind : ' How can I make other men see this ? '

It is the purpose of this book to uncover these mysteries of which he wrote. They are not morbid, unbalanced ravings ; they contain definite

---

[1] *Jerusalem*, 5 : 18-20. See also *Milton*, 3 : 7-8.

ideas expressed as Blake thought best. There is no need of any spiritual Illumination to comprehend these ideas, for they are self-explanatory, even to the non-mystical.

But is any one entirely non-mystical ? Blake, with his amazing psychological insight, decided not.[1] Indeed, how else can we account for such things as the wide response to the quatrain already quoted :

To see a World in a Grain of Sand ?

Judged from the purely rational point of view, this is nothing but nonsense.

There has been tremendous response to all Blake's work, both poetry and painting, in the past few years. To those who have known Blake's works intimately, they already have meant much, even with their principal messages undelivered. Is it not likely, then, that what remains may be equally human, equally worth hearing ?

[1] H. C. R., Dec. 17, 1825. See also W. R. Inge's *Philosophy of Plotinus*, ii. 144.

The Five Mystical States.	In Man.	In History.	Blake's Works.	'The Mental Traveller.'	'The Gates of Paradise.'
					[Plates 1-5 are concerned with pre-natal forces and the weaving of the elements.] Plate 6.
Innocence.	Childhood.	Eternity.	Songs of Innocence (1789). The Book of Thel (1789).	[Identified with the last State, in the great cycle.]	
Experience.	Manhood.	The Fall.	Tiriel (1789). Visions of the Daughters of Albion (1793). The Gates of Paradise (1793). Songs of Experience (1794).	Stanzas ii-v.	Plates 7-12.
Revolution.	The New Birth (Revolt).	The Life of Christ.	The French Revolution (1791). The Marriage of Heaven and Hell (1793). America (1793).	Stanzas vi-xi.	Plate 13.
The Dark Night.	Despair.	The Eighteen Christian Centuries.	Europe (1794). Urizen (1794). Song of Los (1795). Book of Los (1795). Ahania (1795).	Stanzas xii-xxi.	Plate 14.
The Ultimate Union.	Attainment.	The New Age.	The Four Zoas (1795-1804). Milton (1803-1809). Jerusalem (1803-1827). Job (1821-1825).	Stanzas xxii-xxiii.	Plates 15-16.

CHAPTER II

THE TEMPORAL BLAKE

But to himself he seem'd a wanderer lost in dreary night.
—*Milton*, 14 : 16.

HAVING placed Blake as one of the unchanging types of humanity, it remains to fit him into his century.

That century—the Eighteenth—was as queer and fascinating a century as ever existed. Reason was its God ; and never were charlatans so bediamonded as Cagliostro, St. Germain, Casanova,[1] besides hosts of alchemists, astrologers, geomancers, Rosicrucians, fortune-tellers, all mostly forgotten. Reason was exalted ; yet dull George III. went mad ; most of the poets could stand the strain no better than he ; and finally the whole world suffered a mental collapse in the French Revolution ! For the French king, to spite the English king, encouraged the revolt of the Americans—and lost his own throne and head as a result ! His executioners were quite as deluded ; they, too, erected an altar to Reason, and heaped it with massacred victims.

Everything turned out just the wrong way. When the century sought for peace and retirement, it did nothing but wage pointless wars. Reacting against the extravagances of the previous century, it looked for natural simplicity in all things ; yet never were hoops wider or coiffures higher. It gazed enviously at pastoral existences ; then powdered, rouged, and made love with shameless ease. It wrote more verses than any other age (not even excepting the present)—and produced less poetry.

Briefly, the usual paradoxes and human contradictions were in full swing ; and in the midst of all the artificial correctnesses appeared the sincere, enthusiastic, mystic Blake. His was a type which is never in tune with the times ; but one cannot imagine a century more definitely opposed, point by point, to everything in which he believed. The corollary is equally true, that no age needed him more. But, of course, it never heard him.

The reign of George III. covers fairly exactly the period of Blake's life, though Blake was born in 1757, three years before the coronation, and

---

[1] I am well aware of the modern tendency to rehabilitate these historic rascals, which is due solely to a discovery that there is ' something in ' occultism, after all, though rabbits can never actually be produced from high hats. To be sure, William R. H. Trowbridge, in his *Cagliostro, the Splendour and Misery of a Master of Magic* (London, 1910), has cleared Cagliostro very reasonably from the worst crimes attributed to him ; yet at the end he leaves his hero vastly differentiated from the obscure adepts of other centuries, who in the pursuit of their studies renounced everything which makes life seem valuable. St. Germain has also found defenders (I. Cooper Oakley, *The Comte de St. Germain*, Milano, 1912 ; and H. S. Olcott, *The Count de Saint-Germain and H. P. B.*, Adyar, Madras, India, 1918) ; but these attempts remain unconvincing. However, Casanova will rest forever a rascal by his own confession in his marvellous *Mémoires* : yet may not some one discover (as was very true) that he had greater belief in Magic than he was willing to admit ; and conclude that, thanks to these studies, he contrived his celebrated escape from the prison at Venice, etc., etc. ?

died in 1827, seven years after George. It was a long reign and a bad one from beginning to end.

In the first place, there were the wars which deranged all Europe. A year before Blake's birth, the 'Seven Years' War' began ; and after an interval, all during Blake's lifetime, were England's two wars with America, and the great war with the French. This last war alone covered practically a quarter of a century, and contained over one hundred and thirty pitched battles, having begun during the French Revolution and not actually ending until Waterloo. These wars invariably managed to revive old enmities and to force other nations from neutrality ; until the whole theory of monarchy, to which these evils seemed referable, began for the first time to be seriously debated.

Nor were the wars the only source of discomfort. England was then undergoing that complete social metabolism, the Industrial Revolution, which continues to our day. A series of labour-saving inventions threw huge numbers out of work ; the cost of labour sank to the nadir and the cost of living soared to the zenith (thanks to the wars) ; and as the burden of everything was thrown on the poor, social unrest was at a climax. The great result of these and many other causes was a new stratification of society : the division of capital and labour. And very soon all the characteristic evils appeared : sweating, unions, strikes, and sabotage.

Plenty of minor disturbances accompanied this great unrest. There were, for example, the anti-Catholic 'Gordon' riots, on one day of which thirty-six fires were to be seen blazing simultaneously. A Roman chapel was destroyed in Golden Square, Blake's birthplace ; and Gilchrist tells us that the young poet was caught in the mob which stormed Newgate. Rather more trivial, and far less disastrous, was the 'O.P. Riot' (1809), to restore the old prices at the New Covent Garden Theatre.

Heading (though not controlling) all this social convulsion was incompetent George III. and a thoroughly corrupt parliament. Every honest history records with more or less contemptuous amazement the chauvinism and stupidity of their activities. Unfortunate men ! ignorant of the elements of sociology and economics, they were chosen to guide their people through times whose problems they could not begin to analyse. They were unable to imagine why violence increased, though there were already over two hundred crimes whose punishment was death ! When the militia without warning sabred a mass-meeting (as it did in 1819 at Manchester), the authorities were sincerely puzzled to find public spirit unsoothed. They played up their army and navy as the glories and safeguards of England, but they allowed such unbelievable conditions that they had to resort to press-gangs and crimpage to fill the ranks and man the ships. And the more the authorities 'put their foot down' and disregarded human life and suffering, the more the people perversely followed their example. The result was a steadily increasing record of smugglers, highwaymen, extortions, pointless murders, poverty, bribes, imprisonments in filthy jails, floggings, and public hangings.

Let us give one example and have done. The slave-ships were one of the worst evils. Frequently before port was made, half the human cargo disappeared. In order that the loss might fall on the underwriters, captains regularly threw the negroes overboard when they were sick or when the ship in a storm needed lightening. In 1783 the underwriters brought a case to court : this time one hundred and thirty-two negroes had been so disposed of. And the court, fearful of interfering with existing trade-conditions, upheld the captain, claiming that his act was not murder, nor even anything punishable !

Yet bad conditions produce their own reaction. A great hope was growing in the world that these things need not be so always. Towards the middle of the century, authors began to take notice of the state of affairs and comment on them ; by 1794 a novel appeared whose avowed purpose was to show society how bad things were. This was Godwin's *Caleb Williams*. In 1787 a Society for the Suppression of the Slave Trade was formed, and the next year it submitted its schemes before Parliament ; though owing to the usual delay nothing was accomplished until 1807. In 1774 John Howard, having spent £30,000 and travelled 50,000 miles, exposed the horrible conditions of the jails : the fees necessary for all the essentials of life ; no beds ; no sanitation ; fetters ; jail-fever, which made even the courts dangerous ; innocent people awaiting trial for years ; at the end a hanging, or transportation (the planters in America paying twenty pounds apiece for their white slaves, whose bondage lasted for seven or fourteen years). But mere exposure of conditions was not enough. Society, openly convicted of its sins, still refused to plead guilty. John Howard could do very little. Half a century had to pass before his ideas soaked into the public mind.

Philanthropy meanwhile became thoroughly respectable and almost fashionable. It enrolled a few too many ' enthusiasts ' to please the aristocracy ; moreover, a certain bulk of bourgeois coin was necessary. So the Beau Monde generally limited itself to approval—perhaps at times heading subscription lists ; while among the middle classes Society after Society arose to improve or prevent this or that. Sunday schools, organized charities, and reforms of all sorts took up the time of the idle merchants' wives and daughters, and such things even lent new purposes to the meetings of the Blue-Stockings.

We can easily poke fun at all this frivolous bustle and discussion about such terrible matters. We can smile sadly over Arthur Young's denunciation of tea-drinking,[1] which was the one extravagance of the lower classes, and hence the obvious cause of the unbelievable increase in poverty. No doubt a very large percentage of the efforts of these good people was foolish, fruitless, and even harmful ; however, the harm was only temporary, while the good has been so firmly endorsed by all the succeeding generations, that our approval or disapproval suddenly loses significance.

All this philanthropy was due to the inevitable god—Reason. Reason, by undermining the supernatural, had gradually emphasized ethics to the exclusion of religion. The salvation of man—on this earth at least—depended upon a rational observation of natural laws, and the ordering of them until each man should have his due. Among the masses, the belief was all the stronger, since it was unformulated and subconscious. The two great names which furthered it were Voltaire and Rousseau. Voltaire's virulent attacks on the abuses of the Church also demolished much of its supernaturalism, thus clearing the way for a time when men could believe in decency apart from the Church's arbitrary ethics. He

---

[1] Modernists denounce gin-drinking.

was strongly reinforced by the Deists and the Encyclopedists. Rousseau completed Voltaire's negative work by the constructive theory of the inherent purity and nobility of man. Some echo from the world-wide myths of an original Eden or Arcadia produced in his mind a firm belief that man was corrupted by environment, not by anything inherent in himself. And if man once were given a chance to live his life as he naturally wished, all the meaningless madnesses—poverty, roguery, harlotry, superstition, courts (both royal and police), and fashions [1]—all would disappear forever !

Philanthropy, however, could not satisfy those who saw only its blindness and consequent ineffectiveness. There was a still better way of saving mankind, a way at once swift and thorough, besides being a direct expression of the people's will—Revolution ! Mob-consciousness was growing. What might it not do ? And sure enough, in 1776, the United States, headed by the obviously unselfish Washington, cast off the corrupt British Government. How the Radicals exulted ! How they anticipated their own emancipation from all horrible tyrannies ! And in 1789 the French continued the good work ! The Millennium was trembling on the horizon.

Then the refugees began to pour in with tales of horror. The Natural Man loosed in Paris was not following closely the pastoral virtues adumbrated by Rousseau. Somehow the old vices and miseries were increasing. Then came the September massacres of 1792, confirming the worst reports. *Such things might take place in London !* The reaction was complete, and needed only the threats of Napoleon to give England a Reign of Terror of its own.

In the midst of all this uproar, the Church of England was peacefully doing little. People were tired of purely intellectual metaphysics ; while the philosophy of the Deists seduced many by providing a practical basis for ethics. Meanwhile, neither the High Church, rich, Tory dignitaries, nor the poor, Low Church, Whig clergy could stir much enthusiasm—on the contrary, had not a Bishop announced that his duty was ' to preach the Gospel and put down Enthusiasm ? ' In other words, ' Enthusiasm ' was not ' correct.'

Much as we may smile at this (we who are almost equally intolerant of religious ' enthusiasm,' whose present name is ' fanaticism '), this attitude was a salutary self-correction of earlier excesses. People were discovering it better to have a number of religions and peace, rather than one religion and war. Then in 1773, the worst source of disturbance, the Jesuits, were finally suppressed by a Papal Bull, having already been expelled from most civilized countries. The result was an immediate sense of relief, a relaxation. ' Toleration ' became the fashion ; for once men were convinced that religious divergences would not touch their pockets nor blow up their king, they found they had no further interest in other people's views ; so they made a virtue of their indifference.

Thus in 1779, Protestant Dissenting ministers and schoolmasters were no longer required to sign the Thirty-nine Articles, but merely to declare

---

[1] It is curious to note, by the way, that the last of eighteenth-century artificiality to vanish was that of the fashions. Only when the French Revolution produced a certain amount of sentiment against extravagance, which caused in turn an affectation of careless boorishness in manners and dress, did hoops and high headdresses disappear. ' Natural hair,' in fact, came into fashion very suddenly, thanks to the shortage of flour and the high tax on hair powder in 1795.

themselves Christians, Protestants, and believers in both Testaments as the revealed will of God.   There was even some sympathy for the Catholics when the half-mad Gordon in the following year loosed a mob upon them—or rather upon London, which they sacked for six days.   In 1812 the Free Churches were kindly allowed to share with the Established Church its legal protection from disturbance.   In 1813 it was declared no blasphemy to deny the Trinity—which put all Unitarians much at their ease. And so the Church continued, gradually moving towards toleration and rational utilitarianism.

But this sort of thing could not satisfy those who needed more intimate religious experiences.   The exclusion—or at least the neglect—of supernaturalism left certain hypersensitive natures cold.   Inevitably various sects and heresies appeared, some extremely sensational, others merely freakish, all more or less cheaply mystical.   As the Church clung to Reason and cast out Faith, so these in their turn exalted Faith and rejected all Reason utterly.

One movement, at least, reached huge proportions, and won public respect, even awakening in the Church itself a sense of necessity of the very things which it was trying to rule out of life.   This was Methodism, as taught by John Wesley (1703-1791) and George Whitefield (1714-1770).

John Wesley, descendant of a line of clergymen, was brought up in a very devout family (where, significantly, occurred one of the most famous cases of a poltergeist).   At Oxford he and his friends reacted against the customary foppery and dissipation, winning the name of ' Methodists ' from their punctilious observance of rules and rituals.   In 1735 John and his brother embarked for Georgia to do missionary work among the Indians.   On the voyage they were much impressed by the courage of certain Moravians ; then, in the streets of Savannah, John met a Moravian pastor named Spangenberg.

' Do you know Jesus Christ ? ' asked Spangenberg.

' I know he is the Saviour of the world.'

' True, but do you know he has saved you ? '

' I hope he has died to save me,' was Wesley's orthodox reply.   But Spangenberg repeated :

' Do you yourself know ? '

Wesley said he did, and that evening decided he didn't.   And apparently for the first time in that century, an Englishman discovered that the drama of the Christ is repeated in every soul !   The would-be Converter was converted.

Meanwhile an Oxford friend of his, George Whitefield, began Revival Preaching in its most thrilling form.   Throughout his whole ministry he averaged ten sermons a week.   In New England he went so far as to become a public nuisance, dividing families, stirring up the servants against their ungodly masters, and railing against the ' unconverted ' clergy.   What wonder, then, that on his joining Wesley in England, the bishops began to protest and forbid ' enthusiasm ' ?   But it was too late. Denied a parish, John Wesley took the world as a substitute.   In 1742, refused the use of his father's pulpit, he preached in the churchyard from his father's tomb.   The meetings spread amid great excitement.   Often the preacher's voice was quite drowned by the cries and convulsions of the penitents. The uncontrollable sobs of a convert quickly infected all those nearby. Scoffing bystanders were suddenly struck to earth, where they rolled repenting in the mud. There were faintings, convulsions, possessions, ecstasies, and all the usual marks of religious hysteria. Orthodox pulpits and pamphleteers designated these meetings as legitimate sport for the mob; but Wesley always seems to have converted the foremost assailants before he was seriously hurt. Thousands gathered to see the excitement; and surprising proportions were overwhelmed by the discovery of a Voice in their own hearts.

It is not hard to believe these indubitable facts when we remember how unsatisfactory the Established Church was to all those who sought for supernaturalism. That instinct is ineradicable. The ultimate effect of Wesleyan Methodism was good; it brought into the Church a new life, a new care for individual souls, a new responsibility in the hierarchy, a new respect for 'enthusiasm,' and an interest in problems which were spiritual rather than intellectual.

Less spectacular, yet also enduring to this day, was the sect due to Emanuel Swedenborg (1688-1772). This prominent scientist began to have visions at the age of fifty-five, whereupon he devoted his life to the exposition of the doctrines which the spirits revealed. He developed various rare psychical gifts, such as telepathy and clairvoyance. Among other things, he taught that the Bible should be interpreted spiritually, not literally (developing an elaborate system of correspondences, by which all material objects were symbols of higher truths); that Jesus was the only God; and that in 1757 a spiritual Last Judgment took place, which restored moral freedom to mankind, being a New Dispensation.

There were many other sects: Behmenists, who studied the fascinating but obscure works of Jakob Böhme, a German cobbler of the early seventeenth century; the Irvingites; and innumerable sects of Illuminati, Thaumaturgists, 'French Prophets,' Kabalists, Philaletheans, Rosicrucians, Necromantists, and so forth; all of which were unbalanced and ephemeral. One of the last of the paranoiacs was the prophetess Joanna Southcott (1750-1814), who claimed to have experienced an Immaculate Conception, but her 'pregnancy' was discovered to be nothing but dropsy of which she died.

It may readily be seen that this age of wars, social disturbances, Materialism, offset by obscure false prophets, was no age for the arts. Painting, to be sure, was cultivated, for it catered to the rich through a series of fine portraitists: Reynolds, Gainsborough, Romney, Lawrence, and others. In 1768 the Royal Academy was founded, with Reynolds as president. The abominable poetry of the times must be dealt with in the ensuing chapter. As for music, in spite of Handel (1685-1759), it was no occupation for a gentleman. Fiddling, according to Lord Chesterfield, might be paid for, but certainly not practised. Even as late as 1840, an Oxford undergraduate was hissed from the stage for being so unmanly as to try to play the piano in public.

The times, in short, were absolutely against Blake, and he was not the man to submit to them. Rather than accept conditions as they were, he endeavoured to remodel them to his heart's desire, and this very attitude, predestined to failure, quickly cut him off from contemporary life. Here his mysticism aided him to create his own universe. So he may be roughly defined as a radical gradually finding himself through a powerful religious impulse.

His attitude towards war was typical. He was a born fighter ; and his *Poetical Sketches* contain some of the few good patriotic verses in English literature. *King Edward the Third* is entirely concerned with the glories of Crécy. *The Prologue to King John* and *A War Song to Englishmen* also celebrate the joys of just battle. But already some reaction is traceable. ' The Kings and Nobles of the Land have done it ! ' he protests ; and in another place : ' O what have kings to answer for ! '

His views of war at this early time resolve to this rather naïve formula : that man has always the right of revolt against tyranny, however horrible warfare itself may seem ; but war in the interests of tyrants is indefensible.

Then certain personal experiences began to develop doubts about any war whatsoever. Early in life he went on a sailing and sketching expedition to Upnore Castle on the Medway with the artist Stothard and a Mr. Ogleby. Some soldiers came upon them, insisted that they were mapmaking French spies, and detained them until they were identified by the Royal Academy. Such an incident could not fail to have some effect on any lover of liberty.[1]

Then about 1790 he got in with the radicals who centered round the publisher Johnson. At their literary dinners he met Tom Paine, Godwin, Mary Wollstonecraft, Dr. Priestley, and several others. Blake announced himself a ' Liberty Boy ' and sported a red cap in the streets to show his approval of the Americans and the French. Such an attitude was growing steadily more and more dangerous. Nevertheless he wrote a poem on *The French Revolution*, the first *Book* of which Johnson planned to publish in 1791. This was the year when all the radical societies banqueted on the 14th of July in commemoration of the fall of the Bastille. One result was an anti-radical four days' riot at Birmingham, in which Dr. Priestley's house was burned.

Then came the September Massacres in Paris, when 1085 prisoners were butchered. At once Blake's views swung definitely into Pacifism. He indignantly threw off the Red Cap and abandoned his poem, *The French Revolution*, since things were going just contrary to his Prophecy. A reign of terror swept over London, during which Blake's prompt common-sense saved Tom Paine's life by warning him to leave the country at once, without even returning to his lodgings. They never saw each other again.

From this year to his death, Blake firmly refused to admit any warfare but warfare of the mind. ' God never makes one man murder another, nor one nation,' he wrote in his annotations on Bishop Watson (1798). And much later, in the *Jerusalem* (43 : 41-43) he developed the idea :

> For the Soldier who fights for Truth calls his enemy his brother.
> They fight and contend for life, and not for eternal death ;
> But here the Soldier strikes, & a dead corse falls at his feet.

In 1793 all the thinkers were puzzling over the salvation of the world. Most of them, with admirable common-sense, sought it in an analysis of

---

[1] Mrs. Bray, *Life of Thomas Stothard, R.A.* (London, 1851), p. 20. This incident occurred between 1780 and 1782, for Blake met Stothard in 1780, and the Peace of Versailles was signed January 1783.

society ; but Blake, with less common-sense and more wisdom, sought it in the human soul itself. And sick as he was,[1] in this year began the famous series of the Lambeth booklets.

Five years later, Blake found his views still incompatible with those of the public. 'To defend the Bible in this year 1798 would cost a man his life,' he bitterly noted in his copy of Bishop Watson's *Apology for the Bible*. Johnson was then giving his weekly dinners in jail. What use to preach brotherly love when it was automatically denounced as treason ?

Two years later, in September 1800, when the Scarcity Riots were at their height, he moved from London to the seclusion of Felpham, by the ocean. Yet even here he was not safe ; for just after war was declared on Napoleon (May 18, 1803), Blake was forced to run a drunken soldier out of his garden. This soldier (named Scofield—a name we shall meet again in Blake's *Milton* and *Jerusalem*) with the customary arrogance and spite of the lowest of his class, entered a charge of sedition against him, claiming that Blake shouted all manner of treasons while running him out of the garden.

As a matter of fact, Blake by now had lost the last vestiges of sympathy for the militaristic French. We know this from his unfinished poem *Now Art has lost its mental charms* and a passage in the *MS. Book* inspired, no doubt, by Napoleon's theft of art-objects :

Let us teach Bonaparte and whomsoever else it may concern that it is not Arts that follow and attend upon Empire, but Empire that attends upon and follows the Arts.

Nevertheless Blake was in great danger. What court was to believe a citizen against a soldier, especially when the citizen was known to be an Enthusiast, a Radical, and a wearer of the hated Red Cap ? It is even quite possible that this was a trap laid by the Government in which to catch Blake ; indeed, he himself thought so. But Blake escaped after all. For the Great Man of the neighbourhood, Squire Hayley, appeared in court, though seriously inconvenienced by a fall from a horse (due not to bad horsemanship, but to the horse's fright at the sudden furling of the umbrella which Hayley always held over him when riding) ; and the testimony of the Great Man, backed by Blake's own earnest honesty, obtained an acquittal which the court-room applauded loudly.

Then Blake buried himself in London, to ignore wars and politics for the rest of his life. What though Napoleon projected an invasion of England in 1804 ! Hand-bills were posted ; volunteers were drilled ; clergy and poets combined in exalting patriotism ; societies were formed to listen to all public conversations and detect spies and traitors ; but Blake was concerned with greater matters, for he was beginning the engraving of his two epics, *Milton* and *Jerusalem*.

Blake even blamed Jesus for being concerned with politics. 'He was wrong in suffering Himself to be crucified. He should not have attacked the Government. He had no business in such matters.'[2]

Perhaps we should make exceptions. In 1805 Blake addressed the dedicatory verses of his illustrations to Blair's *Grave* to stodgy Queen

---

[1] 'I say I shant live five years. And if I live one it will be a Wonder. June 1793.'—*MS. Book*.　　　　　　　　　　　　　　[2] H. C. R., Dec. 10, 1825.

Charlotte. Like all such verses, they have nothing of the patroness in them ; and we might add that they were certainly the most beautiful things which ever were connected with her.

Moreover, we find evidences of a hidden indignation breaking out in private notes, or even in poetical passages. On the 96th page of the *MS. Book*, across the first sketch for the Creator, is copied (apparently from some Birmingham newspaper) a poem bitterly attacking the British for the bombardment of Copenhagen. Again, in transferring various lines from *The Four Zoas* to *Jerusalem*, he inserted the following protest against conscription and the press-gang :

> We were carried away in thousands from London, & in tens
> Of thousands from Westminster & Marybone in ships clos'd up :
> Chain'd hand & foot, compell'd to fight under the iron whips
> Of our captains, fearing our officers more than the enemy.

The Established Church was hardly more worthy of Blake's respect than the State.

Having been brought up under Swedenborgian doctrines, in 1789 he with his wife signed an affirmation approving the establishment of a New Jerusalem Church.[1] Then, a few years later, he cast Swedenborg off, in *The Marriage of Heaven and Hell* :[2]

Now hear a plain fact : Swedenborg has not written one new truth. Now hear another : he has written all the old falsehoods.

The same volume shows a peering into many other books which dealt with the cultivation of the mystical faculty. Gathering all evidence together, these seem to have been the *Bible*, the *Kabala*, the *Bhagvat-Geeta*, Plato, Porphyry, Hermes Trismegistus, Paracelsus, Cornelius Agrippa, Jakob Böhme, later Dante, St. Teresa, Madame Guyon, and probably the Gnostics, Henry More and Thomas Vaughan. Blake was, in short, a religious radical trying to find himself by communion with all the great dead. He was out of sympathy with the times, discovering error mixed with truth everywhere, until at last he established an individual religion of his own. He was always tolerant, even towards the doctrines he detested the most. One of these was Deism ; yet in the Watson marginalia we find him defending its most outrageous exponent, Tom Paine, against a bishop. And indeed, he himself accepted the Deistic views of prophets and miracles.

The manner of a miracle being performed is in modern times considered as an arbitrary command of the agent upon the patient, but this is an impossibility, not a miracle. Is it a greater miracle to feed five thousand men with five loaves than to overthrow all the armies of Europe with a small pamphlet [?] Look over the events of your own life & if you do not find that you have both done such miracles & lived by them you do not see as I do.[3]

---

[1] *Notes and Queries*, April 10, 1915. Their signatures are the thirteenth and fourteenth of the eighteen signatures in the MS. *Minute Book* of the Great Eastcheap Society, which had been meeting informally since Dec. 5, 1783.
[2] *The Marriage* is usually dated 1790, but for various reasons (discussed in a following chapter) I feel that it must have been written later. It hardly seems likely that in one year Blake favoured the establishment of a Swedenborgian church, and in the very next year uttered such pronouncements against its prophet.
[3] Marginalia to Bishop Watson's *Apology for the Bible*, pp. 12-13.

Voltaire was another Deist against whom Blake flung many harsh words ; yet what is eventually juster than his remark :

I have had much intercourse with Voltaire, and he said to me I blasphemed the Son of Man, and it shall be forgiven me. But they (the enemies of Voltaire) blasphemed the Holy Ghost in me, and it shall not be forgiven them.[1]

The cult of Classicism was another thing against which Blake violently protested ; yet again he summed up the situation in one just sentence :

If Morality was Christianity, Socrates was the Saviour.[2]

Even towards his friends Blake was keenly critical. Dr. Thornton, who had employed Blake as one of the illustrators for a new edition of Virgil, published *The Lord's Prayer, New Translated* in 1827. Blake was thoroughly disgusted with the materialism and lack of spiritual insight displayed by the scholar ; so, as usual, he covered the pages of the pamphlet with indignant annotations :

This is saying the Lord's Prayer Backwards, which they say Raises the devil.

Then he adds his own ' translation ' of Dr. Thornton's translation :

Dr. Thornton's Tory Translation translated out of its disguise in the Classical or Scotch language into the vulgar English.
Our Father Augustus Caesar, who art in this thy Substantial Astronomical Telescopic heavens,
Holiness to thy name or title & reverence to thy Shadow. Thy Kingship come upon Earth first & then in Heaven. Give us day by day our Real, substantial, money-bought, taxed Bread. Deliver [us] from the Holy Ghost so we can [? tax everything that] cannot be taxed forgive all debts and taxes between Caesar and us and one another.
Lead us not to read the Bible, but let our Bible be Virgil and Shakespeare, and deliver us from Poverty in Jesus that over one [? . . .].
For thine is the Kingship, or Allegoric Godship, and the Power, or War, and the Glory, or Law, Ages after Ages, in thy descendants, for God is only an Allegory of Kings and nothing else. Amen.

Not satisfied with the bite of this, Blake scattered here and there several other bits of indignant paraphrase ; then, fearing perhaps that some reader in the future might not understand, he inserted, by way of counterblast, his own intense version of the Lord's Prayer :[3]

Jesus our[s], to thee who art in thy Heavens call'd by thy Name the Holy Ghost, thy Kingdom on Earth is Not, nor thy Will done, but Satan's Will who is the God of this World (the Accuser. Let his Judgment be Forgiveness that he may be consumed on his own Throne).[4] Give us this Eternal Day our own right [? spiritual] Bread. [? Take] away Money, a Value or Price, or Debtor['s] Tax.[5] Leave us

---

[1] H. C. R., Feb. 18, 1826.

[2] Laocoon plate, repeated also in the Thornton marginalia.

[3] Mr. E. J. Ellis in *The Real Blake* (London, 1907) printed practically all the Thornton marginalia, but unaccountably omitted this. Perhaps he did this because the prayer is scribbled very illegibly in pencil, and is much smudged by time. Only with the greatest difficulty was I able to decipher some of the words. Moreover, certain phrases run up the side of the page, detaching themselves entirely from the rest of the text. Blake himself recopied two of the illegible lines. All the marginalia which I quote have been transcribed from the original pamphlet, with the kind permission of Mr. Henry Huntington, the present owner.

[4] All in the parenthesis is run up on the right-hand margin, apparently as an afterthought.

[5] Opposite, on p. 2, is another version of this sentence : ' Give us the Bread that is our due & Right by taking away Money or a Price or Tax upon what is Common to all in thy Kingdom.' The text of the Prayer (p. 3) here again runs up on to the margin, continuing : ' as a[n] hour all the time [? . . .]. Everything has as much right to Eternal

not in Parsimon[y], Satan's Kingdom ; liberate us from the Natural Man [1] of Satan's Kingdom. For Thine is the Kingdom & the Power & the Glory & not Caesar's or Satan's. Amen.

In his *Milton*, Blake had already summed up the ecclesiastic history of his times very characteristically :

> Remember how Calvin and Luther in fury premature
> Sow'd War and stern division between Papists & Protestants.
> Let it not be so now : O go not forth into Martyrdoms & Wars ! [2] . . .
> Milton's Religion [3] is the cause ; there is no end to destruction.
> Seeing the Churches at their Period in terror & despair,
> Rahab [4] created Voltaire ; Tirzah [5] created Rousseau :
> Asserting the Self-righteousness against the Universal Saviour,
> Mocking the Confessors & Martyrs, claiming Self-righteousness,
> With cruel Virtue : making War upon the Lamb's Redeemed :
> To perpetuate War & Glory, to perpetuate the Laws of Sin.
> They perverted Swedenborg's Visions in Beulah & in Ulro, [6]
> To destroy Jerusalem as a Harlot & her Sons as Reprobates,
> To raise up Mystery the Virgin Harlot, Mother of War,
> Babylon the Great, the Abomination of Desolation.
> O Swedenborg ! strongest of men, the Samson shorn by the Churches,
> Shewing the Transgresors in Hell, the proud Warriors in Heaven,
> Heaven as a Punisher, & Hell as One under Punishment :
> With Laws from Plato & his Greeks to renew the Trojan Gods
> In Albion : & to deny the value of the Saviour's blood.
> But then I [Rintrah] rais'd up Whitefield, Palamabron rais'd up Wesley, [7]
> And these are the cries of the Churches before the two Witnesses,
> Faith in God the dear Saviour who took on the likeness of men :
> Becoming obedient to death, even the death of the Cross,
> The Witnesses lie dead in the Street of the Great City :
> No Faith is in all the Earth : the Book of God is trodden under Foot ! [8]

Blake's meaning is clear. The cult of reason grew so powerful that even Swedenborg was overcome by it, and rewrote ' all the old falsehoods '; but at last the reaction came, and the Methodists proclaimed the authority of Faith. However, this approval of Methodism is qualified, for in this same book Blake inverted their whole classification of mankind, putting the Elect in the class of Satan, for ' they cannot Believe in Eternal Life Except by Miracle & a New Birth ! ' [9]

Blake's gradual process was towards catholicity, even towards Catholicism, though he always remained separated from it by several serious heresies. [10] In his old age ' he had a sentimental liking for the

Life as God who is the breast of Man. The Accusation. His Judgment shall be Forgiveness that he may be consumed on his own Throne.' The last sentence is evidently a repetition for the sake of clarifying the text.

[1] The Natural Man is Rousseau's Natural Man, the materialistic worshipper of Nature.
[2] *Milton*, 22 : 47-49.
[3] Milton, the only great religious poet of his century entirely without Mysticism, exalted Reason as the supreme authority over man.
[4] Rahab, the spirit of licence.   [5] Tirzah, the spirit of restriction.
[6] ' Visions in Beulah & in Ulro ' are his doctrines on the sexual life and the world of matter.   [7] Rintrah is the spirit of Wrath, Palamabron is Pity.
[8] *Milton*, 20 : 39-60.   [9] *Milton*, 25 : 33-34.
[10] This point has been made, then ingenuously over-elaborated, in Mr. Charles Gardner's *Blake the Man* (London, 1919). To the end, Blake rejected miracles and prophets (in the accepted sense), hated all outward ceremonies and priesthoods, believed that Creation was evil, caricatured the Pope, mocked at the Immaculate Conception, and in the Dante illustrations he represented Mariolatry as a most insidious error.

Romish Church ' because it was ' the only one which taught the forgiveness of sins.' [1]   But at the last he asked to be buried in the Church of England, which, after all, he seemed to have felt the nearest to him.

He had some sympathy for the religious cranks of the period, since they sincerely exalted Faith above Reason, but he never took them too seriously.   Of Edward Irving (1742-1834), founder of the ' Catholic Apostolic Church,' where ' pentecostal tongues ' were cultivated, Blake told Crabb Robinson : ' He is a highly gifted man—-he is a sent man— but they who are sent sometimes go further than they ought.'   On Joanna Southcott, Blake wrote one of his sarcastic and ambiguous epigrams. Two lines in the *Milton* (36 : 14-15) dispose of such psychopaths :

> They [Inspirations] could not step into Vegetable Worlds without becoming
> The enemies of Humanity except in a Female Form.

That is, when Inspiration descends into the world of matter, it must be productive (Female), or it is a great danger to the recipients.   Every one has seen queer people who have become so because they cannot express themselves.[2]

There was, however, one avowed Occultist, with whom Blake became very intimate.   This was John Varley, a delicate landscape painter and an ardent astrologist, whose predictions came true often enough to worry some people.   Varley was convinced that Blake was a medium.[3]   Blake, as was his custom, did not attempt to explain the nature of artistic inspiration to one who had not instinctively understood ; instead, he rather encouraged Varley's beliefs by drawing a series of Visionary Heads ' from invisible sitters.   The humour of the situation would be obvious enough, even without Linnell's sketch of the two,[4] which shows Varley in the midst of an exalted argument, while Blake sits back with a cryptic smile. Varley reproduced Blake's *Ghost of a Flea* in *A Treatise on Zodiacal Physiognomy* (London, 1828).   The effect he had on Blake's work is untraceable, except in a certain respect for astrology.

This covers briefly Blake's attitude towards Church and State.   What other minor points there were will be dealt with as they turn up in his writings.

---

[1] Gilchrist, ch. xxxv.

[2] *The Hill of Dreams*, by Arthur Machen (London, 1907), is an exquisite novel dealing with this very subject.

[3] Varley was perhaps the first, and certainly not the last, to think Blake a medium. The question will be dealt with in detail in Chapter xxviii.

[4] A. W. Story, *Life of John Linnell* (London, 1892) ; Keynes, p. 318.

CHAPTER III

IMPERISHABLE SKETCHES

The following sketches were the production of untutored youth, commenced in his twelfth, and occasionally resumed by the author until his twentieth year; since which time, his talents having been wholly directed to the attainment of excellence in his profession, he has been deprived of the leisure requisite to such revisal of these sheets as might have rendered them less unfit to meet the public eye. Conscious of the irregularities and defects to be found in almost every page, his friends have still believed that they possessed a poetical originality which merited some respite from oblivion. These, their opinions, remain, however, to be reproved or confirmed by a less partial public.
—*Advertisement to the ' Poetical Sketches.'*

In 1744 Pope died, leaving to the world what was considered a priceless poetic heritage. This heritage consisted mainly in neat formulae by which anything might be turned into verse. They conferred elegance upon the most homely subjects ; added a snap—almost a brilliance— to the dullest ideas ; were just stimulating enough to exercise the intellect without requiring too much of it ; and, best of all, gave the critics a great chance to justify their existence.

As a result, the Age of Prose was almost smothered in verse. The mob always rejoices in formulae ; the genius usually tries to escape from them. In vulgarizing poetic technique, Pope had created a school of verse predestined to extinction ; for none could rival his genius. He was the climax of the reaction from seventeenth-century irregularity. He had made hard, smooth, and glittering the colloquial and varied style of Dryden ; he had made elegant the familiar style of Swift and his period. He had written satire, didactics, critiques, and society verse so astonishingly well that no one could compete. Advance seemed wholly impossible ; therefore everybody tried imitation.

' Bring out number, weight, and measure in a year of dearth,' noted Blake dryly. Indeed, perhaps it was to be expected that the profound exuberance which had poured forth the various poetry of the two preceding centuries must some time be exhausted. But there were obvious causes for this cessation of inspiration. Besides the standardization of technique, there was something yet deeper : the denial of imagination, which is the source itself of poetic beauty. Reason was pre-eminent ; reason was establishing a great prose ; but reason was also doing its respectable best against verse of all kinds.

We are not surprised, then, to find that the majority of verse written in Pope's day and after was frankly derivative. Dryden had bravely tried his hand at bringing Chaucer, Shakspere, and Milton up to fashionable requirements ; and he had set a bad example. Translations from the classics, ' imitations ' of Milton, Spenser, and Pope himself, satires, critiques—all these depended on originals, and demonstrated the lack of poetic initiative.

25

Of such work, only satire accomplished much, and then only when it transcended its predecessor. Apparently the substitution of coffee-houses for Mermaid Taverns sharpened the wits, but left the inner spirit unstimulated. Yet *The Rape of the Lock* flies surprisingly near to a high place on Parnassus, and we are really not too much interested to learn who Belinda really was. We do not find it necessary to trace the originals of *The Dunciad*. A knowledge of Phillips is not essential to enjoy Gay's *Shepherd's Week* ; we are rather bored at the burlesques of classical quotations in his *Trivia*. There is something of real life in these things—human life, as distinguished from the accidents which inspired them. In prose, satire managed to break away completely : *Joseph Andrews* became a serious book. But in poetry, satire never was quite so completely emancipated. The realistic school of verse was not for this age.

Of course there were serious works written in verse ; but again the Georgian poets usually blundered fatally in selecting politics and didactics for major themes. Neither of these has ever been notable inspiration ; and satire was always close at hand to answer dull epic with mock-heroic, political panegyric was equally extravagant abuse. Yet none the less, the didactic school managed to produce *The Deserted Village*, the *Essay on Man*, and some poems of the melancholy school, notably the *Elegy in a Country Church-yard*.

It is difficult for us to realize how bad was the average run of verse in those days, because what we read of it has been carefully selected. During Blake's lifetime, there were four laureates : William Whitehead, Thomas Warton, Henry James Pye, and Robert Southey ; only two of whom are of any interest to scholars, and only one of whom is still read. Southey's verse has lasted a century—some of it ; yet the only thing of his which seems likely to attain immortality is a bit of prose which few people know he wrote—the nursery tale of *The Three Bears*.[1]

But it may well be objected that the laureateship was in disrepute, thanks to the gibes of Dryden and Pope, and consequently is no fair test of poetic merit those days. Turning from royal to popular approval then, we find two poets of Blake's own day highly lauded. They were Erasmus Darwin who, in spite of his *Loves of the Plants*, remains best known as a grandfather ; and William Hayley, whose *Triumphs of Temper* ran through an unusual number of editions, and yet who is remembered now merely because he was kind to Blake.

Of course, in spite of contemporary taste, there was still a certain cult of the imagination, and here we find the real poets. Gray, the Latinist, woke ' the Gothic Harp's terrific fire ' with various Scandinavian poems such as *The Fatal Sisters* and *The Descent of Odin*. William Collins, the Grecian, wrote an *Ode on Popular Superstitions of the Highlands*. Dr. Johnson found these two writers equally affected and unmoral ; and in echoing his times he perhaps explains why Gray ' never spoke out,' and why Collins, equally limited in output, finally went mad. Macpherson's *Ossian* revived primitive terrors and was denounced as forgery, though it swept all Europe ; Chatterton's poems were also denounced for the same reason—he committed suicide. Bishop Percy's *Reliques* escaped, largely as a curiosity. The saner romanticists (or rather, pre-romanticists)

---

[1] *The Doctor*, quarto ed., p. 327.

followed the example of the Wartons, one of whom affected the *Pleasures of Melancholy* and was fashionable, the other of whom politely praised Enthusiasm, only to be rebuked by laureate Whitehead in a counter-ode. The cult of melancholy indeed became popular in such efforts as Blair's dreary *Grave*, and internationally famous in Young's equally dreary *Night Thoughts*; but Enthusiasm was essentially incorrect—even Crabbe was censured for mentioning heaven and hell in his discourses.

By Blake's day it was clearly evident that the mistaken impulses which had made eighteenth-century poetry were already exhausted. The didactic had sunk to such feeble efforts as the *Triumphs of Temper*; the classical and realistic to the *Loves of the Plants*—a series of scientific notes copiously sprinkled with feeble goddesses; the rococo to such silly stuff as the productions of the Della Cruscan school. Naturally Blake turned from all this, and even from the period which preceded it. We may trace in his work a line of Gay's, a metaphor of Dryden's, a picture from Dyer; we feel Gray once or twice—Chatterton, possibly—Macpherson certainly; we catch echoes from the hymns of Watts and the Wesleys; but of the great Alexander himself there is absolutely nothing. Even when Blake takes up some form that Pope had polished particularly well—such as the heroic quatrains of *The Little Black Boy*—Blake does it with a naïve ignoring of his predecessor. In fact, Blake had a habit of doing things differently, which makes the tracing of his literary history somewhat difficult. He may take a subject from Gray or Goldsmith, but only to treat it in a wholly new way. Yet from his early poems, it is fairly easy to see what he had been reading.

In the very first of the *Poetical Sketches* we find the influence of Milton—an influence that Blake was to cultivate to the end of his career. Milton, poet and revolutionist! Milton, explorer of heaven and hell! In Blake's day, he was still remembered and imitated, but his verbal magnificence had become an involved pomposity, his intense and sensitive rhythms were smoothed out into correct decasyllabics. Blake reversed this by simplifying the verbiage and involving the metre. Shakspere (as was thought [1]) had abolished rhyme in the theatre; Milton had done the same for the epic; now Blake took the same step for the lyric, and wrote a number of pieces, Collinsian in substance, but neo-Miltonic in manner. So much for rhyme; but metre was a teasing thing: usually singsong, yet not easily abolished. Therefore Blake tried smoother and subtler metres which changed before one's eyes at the whim of the mood. And thus Blake was led back to the great lyricists of the seventeenth century: Ben Jonson, Beaumont and Fletcher, and William Shakspere. Shakspere was a real discovery of Blake's. Of course his name was perfectly familiar to the scholars, who had done their duty to the public in the form of various editions of the plays; but it was still possible to be ignorant that Shakspere wrote sonnets and other poems. Dr. Malkin in 1806 noted that ' these poems, now little read, were favourite studies of Mr. Blake's early days.' [2] But Blake did more than read them: he was the first to return to their way of seeing and feeling. He was the first

[1] Cf. Edward Bysshe's *Art of English Poetry*, § 7: ' Shakespear, to avoid the trouble-some Constraint of Rhyme, was the first who invented |blank verse].'
[2] B. H. Malkin, *A Father's Memoirs of his Child*, p. xxxiv.

to re-establish in literature the ecstasy, the fresh music of the imagination. And thus he was in the front rank of those who were to rescue English poetry from the decadence of the eighteenth century.

Less felicitous was the influence of *Ossian*. Nobody was able to escape *Ossian* in those days. Blake thought that he saw possibilities in subtilizing metre by following Macpherson's method of printing unrhymed metres as prose. Such an experiment was *The Passions*,[1] a work Blake never published; such were other bits which appeared in his first volume. But thereafter, though he retained the Ossianic septenary, Blake dropped the custom of printing it as prose. But aside from technique, the cloudy, raw supernaturalism was extremely appealing to Blake: it completely dominates a few of the early poems, and sometimes reappears for a brief instant in the first of the Prophetic Books.

Coincident with the decay of poetry in the eighteenth century had been the rise of the Blue-Stockings. On the last day of the year 1711, Addison had boasted in his *Spectator*: 'As, on the one Side, my Paper has not in it a single Word of News, a Reflection in Politicks, nor a Stroke of Party; so, on the other, there are no fashionable Touches of Infidelity, no obscene Ideas, no Satyrs upon Priesthood, Marriage, and the like popular Topicks of Ridicule; no private Scandal, nor any thing that may tend to the Defamation of particular Persons, Families, or Societies'; and half a century later this had become the ideal of many learned ladies. They were tired of being considered so far the inferiors of men that it was immodest to admit that they could read Latin; they were sickened by the interminable gambling and gallantry which dominated their homes. About 1750 Mrs. Vesey, daughter of a bishop, and wife of a member of the Irish Parliament, made the first attempt of her time to unite culture and society. She succeeded against all expectations; and soon the 'Blue-Stockings' (as they were called, from one gentleman's worsted hosiery) found followers everywhere. Mrs. Vesey's Blue Room became famous; still more so Mrs. Montagu's Chinese Room; and the eight-tongued Mrs. Carter fearlessly elaborated the conversation. Although cards could not be thought of, and wine was generally replaced by lemonade, tea, coffee, or orgeat, they managed to enjoy themselves frequently till past eleven, without the intrusion of politics or scandal. They cultivated geniuses: the 'Queen of the Blues,' Mrs. Montagu, was also dubbed 'the female Maecenas of Hill Street.' Nor were their efforts wasted: the great Dr. Johnson graced these 'petticoateries,' also Walpole, Burke, Hannah More, Fanny Burney, besides many others whose names are not yet forgotten.

During their best period, 1770-1785, William Blake was taken up by such a set. The once celebrated Mrs. Mathews and her husband, the Reverend Henry Mathews, held their circle at 27 Rathbone Place, in a strange room whose windows were painted in imitation of stained glass, and whose walls were decorated by the sculptor Flaxman 'with models in putty and sand, of figures in niches in the Gothic manner.' Even the furniture was entirely 'ornamented to accord with the appearance of

---

[1] Published in the *Monthly Review* for August 1903 and in E. J. Ellis's edition of *Blake*, vol. i. pp. xxv-xxx. In both these printings the prose form has been rearranged as verse. The nature of the imagery would suggest that this poem is earlier than anything in the *Poetical Sketches*; hence it must have been written prior to 1777, though it is usually dated later.

those of antiquity.'[1] Mrs. Montagu, Mrs. Carter, Hannah More, and all the rest were familiars ; and here came William Blake and his newly wedded wife, the ignorant Catherine, piloted by Flaxman. Here also came Nollekens Smith, then eighteen, who recorded hearing Blake sing various poems, while musical professors eagerly noted down the airs.

Mrs. Mathews was thrilled by these strange poems ; Flaxman was pleased at the success of his protégé ; and soon he and the Reverend Henry Mathews split the cost of printing the poems. The unbound sheets were given Blake to deal with as he liked ; and strangely enough, he never did anything with them ! The proofs were not carefully corrected ; the volume itself was never regularly published ; no critic ever seems to have received a copy ; and Blake himself never even put the title on his lists of Books for Sale. As a result, this volume is one of the prizes of book collectors.[2]

Why was it that Blake did not like his book ? The reason is simple : all the poems were ' the production of untutored youth, commenced in his twelfth, and occasionally resumed by the author till his twentieth year,' to quote the *Advertisement*. Why, then, did he allow them to be printed ? But what young poet could resist the opportunity of having his first book appear at no expense to himself ? No doubt he felt overpersuaded : the title *Poetical Sketches* and the modest *Advertisement* (when was Blake ever modest without meaning to be ?) all point this way. And seeing the poems in cold type, naturally he was all the more ' conscious of the irregularities and the defects to be found in almost every page ' ; and pleasant though the book might be as a souvenir of his boyhood, he could not forget how imitative much of it was, and how wilful still more of it must seem.

Another reason for the suppressing of his book lay in his quarrel with the Mathews circle. Poor Blake, who praised friendship so, lost far too many of his friends through his unyielding temper. Perhaps in this case, his ignorant wife was patronized by the intellectual ladies ; or still more likely, their mental pretensions were as irritating to Blake as Hayley's were later to be. At any rate, it would be quite characteristic of the man to refuse to profit by the gifts of those with whom he had quarrelled.

Blake did not foresee that in this volume he had boldly trodden through the marsh of contemporary verse, well into those mysterious hills where Keats, Shelley, and Tennyson were to follow. The domination of the seventeenth century obscured to him his anticipation of the nineteenth. His strange metrical experiments were not eccentric, but authentic, marking a new epoch of versification.[3] The volume, in short, remains one of the great milestones in the progress of poetry.

[1] Gilchrist, ch. vi. Mrs. Mathews was evidently following the fashion set by Walpole's impossible ' Gothic ' castle at Strawberry Hill and Beckford's still more absurd villa at Font Hill.

[2] An inscription by John Linnell, junior, in a copy of the *Poetical Sketches* now owned by Professor George Herbert Palmer, is perhaps worth preserving here : ' I found in Mr. S. Palmer's store room at Furze Hill House, 3 copies of this book (one not quite perfect). S. P. told me to take one for myself. I had this copy half bound in morocco—this is the copy. It should have been left untrimmed at edge. A. H. Palmer sold one of his copies for £20 (I believe as he told me).'

[3] A detailed discussion of Blake's versification is to be found in Chapter viii., *The Chariot of Genius*.

The scope of the book alone is astounding.   When the other versifiers were printing nothing but heroic couplets and sentimental quatrains, and calling them *Eclogues, Epistles*, and the like, Blake produced lyrics intended to be sung, the metre of which changes at will ; lyrical blank verse ; ballads ; a 'Gothic' story in verse ; a historical drama (or at least the beginnings of one) ; patriotic chants ; rhythmic prose (which is, however, fairly metrical) ; a superb bit of Augustan verse ; and experiments in the still stilted matter of rhyme !   The mental tone of the poems is no less interesting.   Though Blake still clung to the eighteenth-century impersonality. using capitalized abstractions (but in the best Collinsian manner), yet his book is exalted into a new ecstasy.   He delights in the purely sensuous.   He dares strange images : who else in his day would have had the courage to print such nonsense as :

> Speak silence with thy glimmering eyes !

Nothing like that had been given the public since Milton's even less famous

> Blind mouths ! that scarce themselves know how to hold
> A sheep-hook !

This sort of thing was not a careless use of imagery, or a mixed metaphor ; it was a deliberate use of sense-confusion.   Another example is to be found in *The Couch of Death* :

> On his majestic brow the voice of Angels is heard, and stringed sounds ride upon the wings of night.

Yet daring as he was, Blake was not yet expressing himself fully. There are hints only of symbolism and of his revolutionary thought ; and we can find no mysticism whatsoever.

Like all poems by boys of twenty, this book, as we have seen, shows clearly the influence of other poets.   Too much stress has been laid on these influences.   Being obvious, they are the things which critics stress. T. Sturge Moore, who was the harshest towards Blake, goes so far as to accuse him of ' direct thefts from Elizabethan poetry ' (p. 198).   However, he must have modified his attitude of stricture later, since he has recently admitted borrowing lines for his own use.[1]   Blake did not borrow lines ; but he did utilize images, besides copying thoughts and cadences.   Yet even this is, in one way, notable and a matter for praise.   Blake was the first to bring back into poetry the spirit of the newly discovered Elizabethans.   While the scholars were correcting texts, Blake lived the old ecstasy, rather than copied it.   The resulting poems are still completely beautiful and authentic ; and we should care little whether he or an Elizabethan wrote them.

As a matter of fact, these influences are not important ; and they are entirely outweighed, though not cancelled, by Blake's own originality.

And thereafter even such influences vanished from his work.   When his next volume appeared, he was entirely detached from the outside world of letters, and stayed so to the end of his days.   Whatever few borrowings can be traced are invariably quotations, cross-references, which are intended to be recognized ; with the possible exception of a few lines half-remembered from Milton.

---

[1] Letter to *The London Mercury*, April 1920.

Blake was the first, but not the only, Pre-Romanticist.[1] If these poems, as the *Advertisement* states, were written before 1777, they antedated the publication of Chatterton's collected poems (1777), Cowper's first volume (1782), and Burns's (1786). Not until 1793 did Wordsworth's *Evening Walk* appear, and the *Lyrical Ballads* followed five years later. During Blake's lifetime Burns, Shelley, Byron, and Keats were born and died ; while Coleridge, Wordsworth, Crabbe, and Cowper did their best work ; yet all of them left him untouched. Born a Romanticist too soon, when the great time came, he had already discovered the farther world of mysticism, and never returned from it.

Finally, I should like to point out that the Rev. Henry Mathews made a slight misstatement in the *Advertisement* which he prefixed to the *Poetical Sketches*. If these poems were written before 1777, Blake could not have seen Chatterton's *Miscellanies* (June, 1778) ; yet Chatterton's *Godred Crovan, A Poem*, must, with Percy's *Reliques*, have been responsible for *Gwin, King of Norway*. *Gwin* was hastily written, and is not at all in the style of the rest of the book. It seems likely that this was a late piece included with Blake's earlier poems ; and the Rev. Mathews out of kindness—perhaps (we shudder to think) ignorance—ignored six months for the sake of the round number ' twenty ' ; which is, at worst, a small matter.

[1] Some objection may be raised here, in favour of Gray, Thomson, and others. The question of classifying them is not new. I can only add that, considered apart from their century, their ' Romanticism ' is at best incidental, and would seem strongly reactionary if dated a century later. None of them was possessed to the core by Romanticism, as were Blake, Burns, Chatterton, and the others.

CHAPTER IV

LUNAR BURLESQUE

> . . . . the lunar sphere,
> Since all things lost on earth are treasured there.
> There heroes' wits are kept in pond'rous vases,
> And beaux' in snuff-boxes and tweezer-cases.
>
> —POPE: *The Rape of the Lock*, v.

BLAKE, the young poet, naturally came into contact with all the freakish personalities that live in the suburbs of the arts and philosophies. London at that time was full of revolutionists, magicians, materialists, Deists, atheists, Grub Street poets.

There was, for example, Thomas Taylor 'the Platonist.' He first made a noise by his demonstration of a Rosicrucian perpetual lamp, which snuffed itself out so speedily and spectacularly that it all but destroyed the Freemasons' Tavern. He was an intelligent person, however, and was taken up by Flaxman, at whose house he delivered twelve lectures on Plato. Blake must have been there. Intellectually intoxicated by his reading in the Neoplatonists, Taylor preached stubbornly the glories of ancient philosophy, of which Christianity was but a 'bastardized and barbarous' imitation. This philosophy, he claimed, was brought to Greece from Egypt by Orpheus (whose existence Taylor never seems to have doubted); his disciple Aglaophemus taught it to Pythagoras; and from the Pythagoreans, Archytus and Philolaus, Plato learned it. Plato concealed the mysteries from all·but the elect in his poetical embellishments, Aristotle in his crabbed style. (Taylor also cultivated an unnecessarily crabbed style—knowing, perhaps, that he was no poet.) After these philosophers there was a break in the tradition, until Plotinus exposed it openly for the first time, his teachings being seconded by Porphyry, Iamblichus, and Proclus. Finally it was crushed out by its inferior rival, Christianity. The Platonists taught the pre-existence of the soul, its shameful fall into generation, and its salvation by an inner communion with the Light which streams from the Archetypal World. Taylor insisted that all this was really true; he knew; he had experienced personally the divine communion.

Blake, we imagine, was alternately shocked and delighted at this 'philosophical polytheist'; but at first he could only laugh.

Another person who seems to have amused him mightily was Dr. Priestley, Socinian, materialist, and revolutionist, whose experiments in 'different kinds of air' were rewarded with the discovery of a 'dephlogisticated air'—since renamed oxygen. As a citizen of the French Republic, he later earned the disfavour of the Birmingham mob, and eventually ended his days in America.

The young Blake, vastly amused by such people, began [1] a prose

---

[1] Dr. Sampson (1905, p. 51) dates it *circa* 1784, because Blake broke off relations with the Mathews' circle (whom he is supposed to be satirizing here) on December 20, 1784. But

satire entitled *An Island in the Moon*, which we may translate 'Lunatic England.' Taylor appeared as 'Sipsop the Pythagorean'; Priestley as 'Inflammable Gas the Wind-finder'; his wife as 'Gibble-Gabble'; and Blake himself (in the last chapter at least) as 'Quid the Cynic.' The other characters are unmistakably real people; perhaps some were frequenters of the Mathews circle; it is quite possible that they may all be yet identified.

There is no particular plot; indeed, how could there be, in dealing with such eccentric people? They gather and talk Art, just as pseudo-intellectual circles do to-day; they try scientific experiments which fail; get tipsy; sing songs; make coarse jokes; attack and defend religion.

But the most interesting thing about the manuscript is that towards the end, in the eleventh chapter, after 'they play'd at forfeits & tryed every method to get good humour,' they began to sing some quite poetic songs, three of which (*Holy Thursday*, the *Nurse's Song*, and *The Little Boy Lost*) were to be included in the *Songs of Innocence*. Then there is missing at least one page—perhaps the most important of all: for on the next and last page, Quid the Cynic is just ending his account of the invention of Illuminated Printing. Did that missing page tell the true story of Robert's apparition? Or was there something too coarse for Mrs. Gilchrist to let live?

There the manuscript abruptly ends. I imagine that Blake, bored by Bohemians and Blue-Stockings, and not sure of his own possibilities, suddenly had discovered that his old poetical powers (lost since he was twenty) had returned. He was writing the *Songs of Innocence*, puzzling meanwhile how he could print them appropriately. The answer to that question came; what then was more natural than that he forgot his satire, which now seemed worthless and foolish, to work on what he wanted to be the loveliest book in the world?

Blake's humour stands just half-way between Sterne and Carroll. The one might well have written Chapter iv., the other Chapter v. Personal as the work is, it yet escapes from the individuals to the types that they represent, thus avoiding satire's greatest danger. Indeed, we need not know the originals at all to enjoy it, for to-day we are surrounded by exactly the same people.

This age, however, being what it is, has not always been able to stomach the *Island in the Moon* because of a few boyishly coarse passages of the mildest Rabelaisean flavour. Blake, one of the most decent people that ever lived, like the Elizabethans saw no harm in using coarseness where it belonged. His Lambeth poem on Klopstock is famous; and finally, his comments on Dante's Goddess Fortune (plate xvi) show that he never changed his attitude. However, several critics of our times fall from the violent ecstasy induced by the poems into equally stupendous indignation at the prose. That side by side with some of the poems Blake should have placed jokes which have since gone out of style makes

it should now be clear that Blake was satirizing far more important people—none of the Mathews' circle may be concerned at all. Therefore we are free to date the manuscript between 1787 and 1788 for the following reasons: (1) Robert Blake, whose ghost is supposed to have given William the idea for his new printing (described on the last page) did not die until February 1787; (2) this manuscript seems to have been written before his first experiment, which took place in 1788. At any rate, the *Island* seems to have been written very shortly before the *Songs of Innocence*, which appeared in 1789.

Mr. J. P. R. Wallis (p. 184) use the alarming adjective ' inexpiable ' ; while Mr. Hubert J. Norman, in the *Journal of Mental Science* (April 1915, p. 204) goes dangerously far : ' The association of these charming poems with the fatuous nonsense and utter vulgarity of the remainder of this fantastic performance is sufficient evidence of the chaotic mental state in which Blake was at this period.   There is a marked lack of cohesion, and such an irregular sequence of ideas as are characteristic of pronounced states of excitement ; [1] while the lack of the sense of proportion which allows of the juxtaposition of refined and delicate poetic utterances and indecent and ribald expressions is almost as suggestive of a morbid brain state.   It is certain, therefore, that at the time when Blake wrote this curious medley he must have been in an abnormal mental condition.' This is a sad example of a man ridden by his own hobby.   Mr. Norman might apply this test of ' abnormal mental condition ' to Herrick's *Hesperides* and many another masterpiece, with precisely the same deduction.   As a matter of fact the humour, while coarse, is certainly not obscene, and is even remarkably *pure* for a generation brought up to respect Swift, Fielding, Smollett, and Sterne (the latter of whom certainly influenced the style).   Indeed, if we compare Blake's coarseness with the verses reprinted in Charles Welsh's *On Some Books for Children of the Last Century* (London, 1886), we realize how ignorant all such critics are, who virtuously write of ' this morass of scurrilous abuse and plebeian coarseness ' (Selincourt, p. 10).   Or closer yet, take Taylor's satire on Paine and Mary Wollstonecraft.   Taylor probably did not find the Londoners as sympathetic to Platonism as he wished, yet he was being identified with them.[2]   Therefore in 1792 he published anonymously *A Vindication of the Rights of Brutes*, in which he twits Paine for cowardice and Mary Wollstonecraft for her love-affairs, and fills up his real argument (for vegetarianism) with the most pompous nastinesses.

But indeed, we need not invoke the eighteenth century at all in defence of Blake ; for here he anticipates the century to come.   His coarseness in this and other scraps of manuscript was no worse than passages in Keats's letters, or Burns's poems, and rather better than *Don Juan*.   We can leave it at that, for it is absurd to demand Victorian standards in the days of George III.

---

[1] Or characteristic of any imitator of Sterne.—*S. F. D.*

[2] See, for example, *Orpheus. Priest of Nature, and Prophet of Infidelity* (London, 1781). On p. 6 Taylor is called ' old Hypocrisy,' while later, long lists of prominent Deists are given, as though Platonism and Deism were identical.

CHAPTER V

ORIGINAL CONCEPTIONS

'I am certain of nothing but the holiness of the heart's affections and the truth of imagination.'—KEATS: letter to Benjamin Bailey, Nov. 22, 1817.

An Island in the Moon ended abruptly, having been tossed aside at the threshold of a new plane of life. Blake at last had found again the poetic faculty which he thought he had lost at the age of twenty. He also had invented a unique and exquisite method of printing,[1] which would give his works the artistic setting that they deserved.

Dr. Sampson describes this process as follows : 'The text and surrounding design were written in reverse, in a medium impervious to acid, upon small copper-plates, which were then etched in a bath of aquafortis until the work stood in relief as in a stereotype.' Impressions were then taken in coloured inks, which Blake made himself. Sometimes these were touched up with pen and ink ; sometimes they were sold just as they were ; sometimes they were completed with a wash of the same colour (or nearly the same) as the ink. But usually Blake coloured them with water-colours, or other mediums whose processes he invented. This colouring varies from the lightest tinting of the designs, to the most elaborate repainting, when the whole design was considerably altered. There seems to be no way of judging whether the more elaborate copies of his work are later or earlier, for Blake made each copy as individual as possible, changing the order of the plates when he could, and almost always using a new system of colouring. He could do this, since he finished copies as they were ordered, in some compliance with the taste of the purchaser. A good remuneration would stir him to unusual artistic efforts. At times he would try for very rich effects, using gold, silver, and other metallic paints ; but on the whole these are not among his most successful efforts.

In general the *Songs* and *Thel* are coloured very simply, though towards the end of his life the *Songs* are very elaborately done. In the *America* Blake generally reached the height of clear brilliancy of tone. *Europe* and *Urizen* are keyed to entirely different effects : of corrosion, where the colour chords are far more sophisticated, and placed, as it were, in the lower gamuts. On the other hand, the illustrations to Milton's poems, and to Job, are subdued almost to pallor. Examples of Blake's books completed with a wash are not common ; but I have seen a *Songs of Innocence,* a *Europe,* and a *Jerusalem* so finished ; which proves that Blake practised this all his life.

Before Blake began his new book, the *Songs of Innocence,* he experi-

[1] Dr. Keynes, alas ! has discovered what is at least a previous discovery of the same process, in a letter from George Cumberland to his brother Richard early in 1784. There is, however, no evidence that Blake knew Cumberland at this date.

mented by making plates of various mystical aphorisms. These he collected into two tractates, *There is No Natural Religion* and *All Religions are One*. The two tractates are tinted very gently. The printing itself is rather roughly done, and the decorations are exceedingly minute. In fact, these little books are the smallest as well as the first examples of Blake's illuminated printing. There is a question whether these two tractates together do not form one complete work ; [1] but as the first is known from several copies, while the second exists only in one set of sheets, this may be left an open question.

These tractates are the first record of Blake's mystical experience which was to be expressed so finely in the *Songs of Innocence* and *Thel*. At first, however, Blake was not concerned with the ' spiritual sensation,' but with the truths which mystical vision revealed to him.

THERE IS NO NATURAL RELIGION

' Natural Religion ' was Blake's name for the Deistic religion, which taught that, while God existed, he kept himself aloof from this world, interfering in no way whatsoever. Man's code of conduct (for to this the religion was necessarily reduced) was to be drawn from the laws of nature. A rational observation of causes and effects should indicate the mode of life best calculated to bring about a maximum of Good and a minimum of Evil.

Blake must have had plenty of arguments about Natural Religion, since among his radical friends were the most prominent Deists : Tom Paine, Dr. Priestley, and Godwin. Blake, who had recently known the ineffable communion in his own person, could only look upon this religion as blindly judicial and mechanistic. According to him, man was not a product of nature, but an immortal being fallen to the halfway station between the natural and the divine. God, to be sure, did not dwell in nature ; but he did dwell in man ; indeed, he had no other habitation. Morality, or the division of the universe into Good and Bad, was an artificial and acquired classification of the world ; and this classification was in itself the cause of the original Fall, the eating of the fruit of the Tree of the Knowledge of Good and Evil. Nature itself is only an illusion, created by the Poetic (Divine) Instinct in man, and therefore seems continually to transcend itself.

The *First Part* of the tractate has for *Argument* : ' Man has no notion of moral fitness but from Education.' Education is bad, being the imposition of one mentality upon another, by which means the error of Morality is repeated down the ages. ' *Naturally*, he is only a natural organ, subject to sense.' To this the Deists would have agreed, ignoring Blake's implication that therefore man must be something more than an Educated Natural Organ. So Blake sets out to prove his implication, and comes logically to the point that ' Man's desires are limited by his perceptions ; none can desire what he has not perciev'd,' and that ' the desires & perceptions of man, untaught by any thing but organs of sense, must be limited to objects of sense.' This is the *reductio ad absurdum*, for man's desires are infinite, and how could he desire the Infinite if he had not perceived it ? No mystic could deny this. ' Few will believe

[1] *Grolier Club Catalogue*, 1919.

the soul to be infinite,' wrote Thomas Traherne a century before, ' yet
Infinite is the first thing which is naturally known. Bounds and limits
are discerned only in a secondary manner.' [1] This part of man is the
Poetic, or Divine, Character ; were it not for this, ' the Philosophic &
Experimental would soon be at the ratio of all things ; & stand
still, unable to do other than repeat the same dull round over
again.'

The *Second Part* contains Blake's rebuttal of the Deistic arguments.
Man's perceptions are *not* bound by his natural organs ; or, as Coventry
Patmore later put it : ' Those who know God know that it is quite a
mistake to suppose that there are only five senses.' [2] Reason itself,
which is only a summary of what we know, changes and expands as it is
led by the ' Poetic Character ' ; for man rebels against any limitations.
' The same dull round, even of a univer[s]e, would soon become a mill
with complicated wheels.' But man's true cry is not for ' More ! ' it is
for ' All ! ' ; and if he could not possess it, he is necessarily damned to
eternal despair. He is not damned : ' The Desire of Man being Infinite,
the possession is Infinite, & himself Infinite. He who sees the Infinite
in all things sees God. He who sees the Ratio only, sees himself only.' [3]
And this in turn leads to the heart of Mysticism : ' Therefore God becomes
as we are, that we may be as he is.' [4] In the Crucifixion of God is the
Resurrection of Man. Blake's sentence is one of the greatest voicings of
the greatest truth.

ALL RELIGIONS ARE ONE

This tractate, which exists only in Mr. Henry Huntington's copy,[5]
has for title a plate printed in a different colour, with *There is No Natural
Religion* in a new design. The substance of this tractate is repeated in
The Marriage of Heaven and Hell, especially in the second *Memorable
Fancy*. In the tractate Blake, with a customary reticence, leaves the
reader to assume that the ' Poetic Genius ' is God ; in *The Marriage* he
goes a little farther and claims the ' Poetic Genius ' is the greatest of the
gods. This ' Poetic Genius ' exists as a Universal, also as the central core
of each man's personality.

He begins by stating that from this individual Poetic Genius the outward form of a man is derived. In other words, the soul forms the body.
' As all men are alike in Outward Form ; so with the same infinite variety,
all are alike in Poetic Genius.' [6] A Universal Poetic Genius also exists,
from whom the Poetic Genius in each man is derived, and from whom all
religions and philosophies flow, differentiated by the varied needs and
tastes of the various nations. The voice of this Genius is sincerity, which
of itself makes its utterances true. Prophets are merely poets in this

---

[1] *Centuries of Meditations*, ii. 81.   [2] *Aurea Dicta*, 143.
[3] This is the pantacle of Trithemius in his *De Septem Secundis*, as described by Eliphas
Lévi, *Histoire de la Magie*, v. ii.
[4] This may have been suggested by lines 21-22 of Henry More's *Hymn upon the Nativity
of Christ* (*Divine Dialogues*, ii. 496) :
> The Son of God thus Man became,
> That Men the sons of God might be.'
[5] Reproduced in facsimile by Keynes, p. 94.
[6] Cf. Lavater's opening *Aphorisms* : ' 1. Know in the first place, that mankind agree
in essence, as they do in their limbs and senses. 2. Mankind differ as much in essence
as they do in form, limbs, and senses—and only so, and not more.'

sense.[1] The two Testaments are directly derived from the Poetic Spirit (*i.e.* are ' inspired ') ; but are derived only (are not infallible and completely expressive) owing to the incapacity of ' bodily sensation,' of which all writings must appeal, to describe ' spiritual sensation.'

[1] ' There is not throughout the whole book called the Bible, any word that describes to us what we call a poet, nor any word that describes what we call poetry. The case is that the word *prophet*, to which later times affixed a new idea, was the Bible word for poet, and the word *prophesying* meant the art of making poetry. It also meant the art of playing poetry to a tune upon any instrument of music.'—Thomas Paine, *The Age of Reason*, ch. vii.

CHAPTER VI

THE INITIAL EDEN

The corn was orient and immortal wheat, which never should be reaped, nor was ever sown. I thought it had stood from everlasting to everlasting. The dust and stones of the street were as precious as gold: the gates were at first the end of the world. The green trees when I saw them first through one of the gates transported and ravished me, their sweetness and unusual beauty made my heart to leap, and almost mad with ecstasy, they were such strange and wonderful things. The Men! O what venerable and reverend creatures did the aged seem! Immortal Cherubims! And young men glittering and sparkling Angels, and maids strange seraphic pieces of life and beauty! Boys and girls tumbling in the street, and playing, were moving jewels. I knew not that they were born or should die; But all things abided eternally as they were in their proper places. Eternity was manifest in the Light of the Day, and something infinite behind everything appeared: which talked with my expectation and moved my desire. The city appeared to stand in Eden, or to be built in Heaven. The streets were mine, and so were the sun and moon and stars, and all the world was mine; and I the only spectator and enjoyer of it. I knew no churlish proprieties nor bounds, nor divisions: but all proprieties and divisions were mine: all treasures and the possessors of them. So that with much ado I was corrupted and made to learn the dirty devices of this world. Which I now unlearn, and become, as it were, a little child again that I may enter into the Kingdom of God.—THOMAS TRAHERNE: *Centuries of Meditations*, iii. 3.

THE *Songs of Innocence* was the first great fruit of Blake's first mystical insight. The Mystic Way begins in the Garden of Eden. Blake identified at once the ecstasy of the revelation with the state of mind of a child, believing deeply that ' of such are the Kingdom of Heaven.' All of us can recollect the time when every common sight seemed ' apparell'd in celestial light, the glory and the freshness of a dream '; when our feet were never tired of investigating the mysteries that lay beyond each rise of meadowland; and when we were intimate, as we never can be again, with every bend of the brooks for miles around. Then we accepted the world without suspicion of its troubles. What sorrows came to us disturbed only the surface of things, and passed away ' like little ripples down a sunny river.'

In just the same way the world seems entirely simple and happy to the newly initiated mystic. Intuition tells him all things; he reasons little more than does a child. Innocence is free, as it needs no laws. It is happy, since it is unsophisticated. It enjoys the most spontaneous communion with nature, readily perceiving the divine in all things. When trouble comes to others, it is ready with the completest sympathy, though without understanding. Its own sufferings are felt to be only temporary; they will be followed by some still greater happiness. All help each other, as the glowworm lights the lost ant home; and even when the wolves break in on the sheep, the lions are there to guard the slain lambs in the immortal home. Our bodies are a brief cloud, a coffin which an angel will soon unlock. The only God is Christ, the kind father, to whom children were always dearest. It is the Golden Age.

This Christian Arcadia is not limited to childhood. Any person who has not undergone an embittering contact with the world is yet innocent. Blake seems to have conceived the state of Innocence as ending generally with the passing of youth. Thel is still in the state of Innocence; and many of Blake's shepherds seem aged (if we dare age such immortal beings!) about eighteen. Job, Blake's extreme example, was an old man before his Experience came.

Thomas Traherne of the preceding century was perhaps the only other mystic who celebrated Innocence with Blake's enthusiasm. Having once appreciated it, he devoted the rest of his life to recapturing the first rapture, whose technical name, for him, was 'Felicity.' What it meant to him may be surmised from the following quotation:

All appeared new and strange, at first, inexpressibly rare and delightful and beautiful. I was a little stranger, which at my entrance into the world was saluted and surrounded with innumerable joys. My knowledge was Divine. I knew by intuition those things which, since my Apostasy, I collected again by the highest reason. My very ignorance was advantageous. I seemed as one brought into the Estate of Innocence.[1] All things were spotless and pure and glorious: yea, and infinitely mine, and joyful and precious. I knew not that there were any sins, or complaints or laws. I dreamed not of poverties, contentions, or vices. All tears and quarrels were hidden from mine eyes. Everything was at rest, free and immortal. I knew nothing of sickness or death or rents or exaction, either for tribute or bread. In the absence of these I was entertained like an Angel with the work of God in their splendour and glory. I saw all in the peace of Eden; Heaven and Earth did sing my Creator's praises, and could not make more melody to Adam than to me. All Time was Eternity and a perpetual Sabbath. Is it not strange, that an infant should be heir of the whole world, and see those mysteries which the books of the learned never unfold?

St. Francis also remains as one of the supreme examples of the state of Innocence, though he was also much more. Wordsworth's most famous Ode was only a lament that the state is lost so early.

Innocence, Heaven though it be, is not perfect. The child contains seeds of error, which must grow until they can be weeded out. 'Man is born a Spectre or Satan,' Blake wrote in his *Jerusalem* (52). 'To be an Error and to be cast out is part of God's design,' he explained still further in his *Last Judgment*. So Thel, ignorant of the world, is drawn irresistibly from her Eden. For, after all, Ignorance is not a means of Salvation; 'the fool shall not enter into heaven, let him be ever so holy.'[2] But Innocence knows nothing of this; and such thoughts do not appear in this first volume of *Songs*.

Yet there is one hint that Innocence is not everything. In the introductory poem, the Piper pipes his song about the Lamb twice: and the second time the Poetic Genius 'wept to hear.' Blake meant to indicate that Innocence had its 'Contrary State,' which later he was to call 'Experience.'

Blake, then, in writing about Innocence, was describing a mystical state, rather than childhood; but he identifies the two so closely that his poems seem to be spoken by the very children themselves. He does not

[1] Thomas Traherne, *Centuries of Meditation*, iii. 2. All mystics speak the same language. Blake could not have seen this passage, for Traherne died eighty-three years before Blake's birth, and his mystical works were not published until the present century.
[2] *Last Judgment* (MS. Book).

contemplate children, in the manner of Wordsworth, Hugo, and Long-
fellow ; he actually enters into their souls and speaks through their own
mouths.   Only Stevenson repeated the feat ; and even his children are
conscious and prim beside Blake's.   Blake's poems illustrate his own line
in *Milton* (30) : ' How wide the Gulf & Unpassable ! between Simplicity
& Insipidity.'   For Blake is sweet without being sentimental, graceful
without being weak, moral without being didactic, simple without being
obvious.   He dared the worst failures—those of triviality and affectation ;
and yet he always avoided them as completely as though they did
not exist.

The *Songs of Innocence* are generally recognized as Blake's highest
achievement as poet.   A great deal of this opinion is due to the obscurity
which increasingly overwhelms one in all his later work.   Everybody can
understand Innocence ; but we do not willingly admit the facts of
Experience ; while the remote world of mystical knowledge is beyond the
comprehension of most of us.   Moreover, Blake's technical experiments
in his later books tend to make many readers uneasy.   But whether or
not this is his most perfect work, it is unquestionably one of the most
perfectly beautiful books of the world.

When Blake found himself at last, all the influences of other writers
seemed to vanish.   Both thought and form are completely his own.
Watts is the only author we can positively name whose writings may have
affected these *Songs* even slightly.   Strictly speaking, Blake has even
turned from the immediate future of the literary world ; for he is now
thoroughly a Mystic, rather than a Romanticist.   The whole external
world, whether literary or historical, had vanished, or left but the dimmest
traces.   Who could imagine from Blake's book that the French Revolution
was then roaring its way into every one's soul ?

But there were two general literary influences which deserve attention.

The Pastoral had always been one of the great traditions of English
verse.   From the days of the Elizabethans, it had passed through *Lycidas*,
and was to reappear in such a masterpiece as *Adonais*.   In the eighteenth
century the pastoral had become almost wholly a matter of affectation.
Hogarth had expelled it from painting, but the other arts still preserved
it.   Good old *Mother Goose* thus satirized the popular taste :

> Dear Sensibility, O la !
> I heard a little lamb cry, baa !
> Says I, ' So you have lost mamma ? '
>   ' Ah ! '

> The little lamb, as I said so,
> Frisking about the fields did go,
> And, frisking, trod upon my toe.
>   ' Oh ! '

Blake gave the tradition an entirely new turn.   He employed all the
pastoral properties as symbols of Innocence, and cast a mystical aura over
the landscape.   The result was that he made the pastoral something
completely his own ; infused it with artlessness and freshness—with
spontaneity, in short—which completely differentiated his work from
both that of his predecessors and his followers.   It was as though a Fra
Angelico, under the influence of St. Francis, had written poetry at the

dictation of children ; yet this does not wholly describe Blake's verses, for through them all blow the clear winds of April.

The second literary influence upon the *Songs* is more doubtful. Was Blake, in writing his poems of children, affected by their books ? At the moment a new interest in the literature for children was already producing excellent results. The public was reacting from the hell-fire tales, the books of martyrs, and the like, which had been the usual reading given to children ; and they found even Bunyan's absurd *Divine Emblems* not wholly appealing. So a new literature was springing up, which already included such immortals as *Mother Goose, Goody Two-Shoes,* and *Sanford and Merton.* Perrault's tales were translated, and old English legends were being revived from their chap-book existence. John Newbery won his niche in fame by giving these books a decent form : good English, good printing, good wood-cuts, and unforgettable Dutch paper-covers. All these books (with the one exception of *Mother Goose*) were still primarily moralistic, but they had wholly cast away the morbid elements of the earlier books. The children had to wait for the great Victorians before they could read wholly unmoral books, like *Alice in Wonderland* and Edward Lear's *Nonsense Book.*

The *Songs of Innocence* must have been influenced at least slightly by this new spirit in children's books. Blake sustained the same moral tone in just the same way as his contemporaries, though it is subdued to a minimum. But the question goes farther than that : was Blake's own ear responsible for his original and instinctive cadences (which were quite unlike anything in the poetry of his day), or was he imitating the queer, yet satisfactory, metres of *Mother Goose* ? Already in *An Island in the Moon* Blake had quoted *The Froggy would awooing ride* ; and in the *Jerusalem* (of all places !) we find an unmistakable reminiscence of *Fa, fe, fi, fo, fum* !

> Boys and girls, come out to play,
> The moon does shine as bright as day

is strangely parallel in spirit to the *Nurse's Song*. Certainly, nothing in Blake's day approaches his *Songs* metrically, except *Mother Goose*.

But we can find neither real predecessors nor imitators. The *Songs of Innocence* remains one of the unique, inimitable achievements in books, whether it be considered from the poet's or the painter's standpoint. And the miracle seems the greater when we remember that Blake was always childless.

CHAPTER VII

REACTION

When the Lion dies the Crow is born.
—GEORGE STIRK : *An Open Entrance to the
Closed Palace of the King*, chap. xxv.

THOUGH the *Songs of Experience* was not Blake's next book, yet it should be considered here, since it is actually the second half of the single volume anticipated in the *Introduction* to the *Songs of Innocence*. Blake issued very few separate copies of the *Songs of Experience*. Most commonly the two groups appear in one binding, with a general title-page besides the two separate ones.

The second stage, both of the Mystic Way and the life of man, is Disillusionment. 'Shades of the prison-house begin to close upon the growing Boy' early ; he can readily be led astray by any false light, as we saw from the last two poems of the *Songs of Innocence*. So the Fall continues until that day when he is completely steeped in materialism ; and he realizes 'that there has passed away a glory from the earth.'

In the *Songs of Innocence* a child sang ; now the voice of the man is heard. Blake, who had been so responsive to the ecstasy of his early life, felt the change particularly keenly. To him the State of Experience was especially bitter. For a long time he wrestled with it, and found no satisfactory solution, though he tried again and again in the early Prophetic Books. But the solution came, about 1793, when he began *The Marriage of Heaven and Hell*. Meanwhile there was nothing to do but record the truth as he felt it. That he once had found intense happiness was true ; that he now found the exact reverse was equally true. He was too honest to close his eyes sentimentally upon the facts.

Therefore, in contrast to many of the *Songs of Innocence* he wrote antitheses. Against *The Lamb* stands *The Tyger* ; against one *Nurse's Song* there is another ; *Infant Joy* is offset by *Infant Sorrow* ; and so on. It is rare to find any one with such courage of despair ; rarer yet when such people do not allow the pessimistic present to cancel the happy past. Blake was certainly not trying to reverse the lesson he had so beautifully taught ; instead he retained them both, carefully labelling them, to prevent misconstruction, 'the Two Contrary States of the Human Soul.'

The child knew no problems, and hardly felt suffering. The man sees problems everywhere, which he cannot solve. For this very reason (and this reason alone, as far as I can discover), the *Songs of Experience* are apt to seem not so good from the literary standpoint. The human mind curiously refuses to receive pessimism whole-heartedly ; it must reject such uncomfortable thoughts, or else disguise them under a Byronic romanticism. Good folk are shocked by Blake's 'cheap anti-clericalism and perverse antinomianism.' [1]   They cannot put away childish things when Innocence had been expressed so wonderfully.

Another cause for a feeling of discomfort with the *Songs of Experience* rises from Blake's increasing use of symbolism.   We knew instinctively what *The Lamb* represented ; but we have to think if we wish to find the meaning of *The Tyger*.   Lines occur, such as

> The starry floor,
> The wat'ry shore,
> Is giv'n thee till the break of day,

which require, not only thought, but wider reading in Blake, before we know their exact meaning.   (Blake is apt to fascinate and irritate us together by *invariably* having an exact meaning.)   There are still to be found poems like *Ah ! Sunflower*, whose exquisite music lulls the average reader past any caring as to occult thought ; but when he glances over *To Tirzah*, he suddenly realizes that he has been led into a far country whose language he does not know.   So he retreats hastily to his own land, from whose bulwarks he has only too often proved himself apt in shouting ' Madman ! '   But no book containing *The Tyger, Ah ! Sunflower*, and *London* need fear such timorous attacks.

The literary influences upon the *Songs of Experience* are remarkably hard to find.   Those which can be positively named are the Bible, Spenser, Milton, and Gray.

[1] Percy H. Osmond, *Mystical Poets of the English Church*, p. 281.

CHAPTER VIII

THE CHARIOT OF GENIUS

Execution is the Chariot of Genius.
—BLAKE's Marginalia to Reynolds.

THOUGH Blake is supposed to have been a careless, even an automatic writer, in reality he was one of the great technicians. He had all the tricks at his finger-tips, and we cannot doubt that every line he ever wrote was tested at least semi-consciously by his inner ear.

A radical in philosophy, religion, and painting, he was also a great innovator in metrics. His earliest poems show an attempt to transcend rhyme, which he finally rejected. In metre, he sought constantly for lines which were at once freer and more accurately expressive. It was characteristic of him that the line he finally adopted for its easy ability to say all things was a line two feet longer than the norm accepted by Shakspere and Milton ; and this expansive line, the iambic septenary, was a line which no one before or since has been able to use with any fluidity or variety.

Blake did not, however, have a sense of the larger *forms* of poetry. He could build up charming and unique stanza-forms eight lines long ; but more elaborate patterns seem to have been outside his interest. He could not even tell a long story well. Yet his epics are saved from total chaos by the rather automatic device of being poured into a set number of pages : fifty in *Milton*, and four sections of twenty-five each in *Jerusalem*. In short, his larger efforts are designed, rather than composed ; plateresque, rather than organic.

Historically, his metrics were evolved by his reaction from the formalities of the eighteenth century's technique : its impeccable heroic couplets and quatrains, its syllabic blank verse, and its angular odes. He found a better tradition of expressiveness in the easy lyrics of the Elizabethans ; but his own car so refined, strengthened, and compressed them, that soon he went far beyond them in the solution of prosodic problems, and finally anticipated, in some form, all the most modern techniques.

The eighteenth century generally wrote in iambs, which are, after all, the most natural foot of English versification. Blake, however, tried other feet : the trochee, of which he became very fond ; and the anapest, whose expressive qualities he seems to have been the first man to discover. Dactylic lines occur very rarely, and then only accidentally.

The trochee was used in several of the most famous *Songs*, such as *Piping down the Valleys Wild*, *The Lamb*, *The Tyger*, and *A Poison Tree*. These titles alone show the contrasting effects which Blake extracted from this foot.

The music latent in the anapest had never been appreciated before Blake's time. The Elizabethans hardly suspected its existence ; and when they stumbled upon it, curious jingles, such as some of the dialogues in *Love's Labour's Lost*, II. i, were their best results—results which never became fashionable. Gradually the anapest stretched its limbs into a canter well suited to drinking songs and hunting choruses, but for nothing else. The eighteenth century seems to have thought that this trumpery effect was the only possible variation from the iamb. But Blake, who was trying to extend poetic expressiveness in all metres, discovered that as rare and rich a music lay in the anapest as in any other metre. By shortening the usual tetrameter to a dimeter, he evoked the light laughter of *The Ecchoing Green*. His greatest success in lyrical anapests, however, was in the tragic *Garden of Love* and the strangely exotic *Sunflower*.

> Ah, Sunflower ! weary of time,
> Who countest the steps of the sun ;
> Seeking after that sweet golden clime
> Where the traveller's journey is done.

Poe later was to obtain the same effect in his *Ulalume* ; but he found it necessary to repeat lines as a refrain, in order to retard the ordinary rush of the anapests. In his later poems, such as *The Land of Dreams*, Blake retarded the anapest by substituting iambs here and there.

This mixture of feet was characteristic of Blake's aesthetics. ' Bring out number, weight & measure in a year of dearth,' he wrote scornfully of purists. Practically never did he hesitate to introduce a variety of feet, so long as he did not overwhelm the general effect of the fundamental foot. In the very first quatrain of *The Tyger* he boldly inserted an iambic line :

> Could frame thy fearful symmetry.

The added syllable becomes still more emphatic in the terminal line :

> Dare frame thy fearful symmetry.

Obviously, such an effect was not accidental.

Sometimes Blake alternated anapests and iambs so freely that we cannot say what the fundamental foot is : as in the *Laughing Song* and the two *Chimney-Sweepers*. Sometimes he juxtaposed two metres, as in *Night* (*Songs of Innocence*), whose stanza is composed of two iambic septenaries followed by four anapestic dimeters. He also devised the scheme of changing gradually from one metrical pattern to another. The first and most famous of these is the *Mad Song* of the *Poetical Sketches*. This poem, according to Saintsbury, marks the beginning of all modern prosody. Other examples are *I laid me down upon a bank*, and *The Voice of the Ancient Bard*, which moves from iambic trimeter to anapestic pentameter.

Finally Blake's theory of immediate expressiveness through constant variation developed so far, that he actually denied the basis of metre entirely, and thus he wrote the first Manifesto of Free Verse :

When this Verse was first dictated to me, I consider'd a Monotonous Cadence like that used by Milton & Shakspeare & all writers of English Blank Verse, derived [? delivered] from the modern bondage of Rhyming, to be a necessary and indispensible part of Verse. But I soon found that in the mouth of a true Orator, such monotony was not only awkward, but as much a bondage as rhyme itself. I therefore have produced a variety in every line, both of cadences & number of syllables. Every word and every letter is studied and put into its fit place ; the terrific numbers are reserved for the terrific parts, the mild & gentle for the inferior parts ; all are necessary to each other.[1]

---

[1] *Jerusalem*, 3.

Blake never quite achieved this complete liberation. Metres were always humming somewhere in his head. However, as we shall see, he did his best to eliminate them.

He treated lines with the same freedom that he treated feet. He tried all lengths from the dimeter to the septenary, and individualized each of them.

He used two-beat and three-beat lines fairly often. The dimeter appears in such contrasting poems as *Spring*, *The Ecchoing Green*, *The Fly*, and *The Sick Rose*. The trimeter appears in *My Silks and Fine Array*, *Memory*, *Come Hither*, *Ah! Sunflower*, *The Garden of Love*, *The Little Girl Lost and Found*, *Silent, Silent Night*, and many others.

But Blake's favourite line for lyrics was the tetrameter. The contrasting *Lamb* and *Tyger* show what he could do with it.

What dread hand forged thy dread feet ?

seemed to Saintsbury a climax in the use of the trochaic tetrameter. *My Spectre around me* is the extreme variation of a form which can still be accurately designated as iambic tetrametric quatrains rhymed in couplets. *The Everlasting Gospel* is just as free as Coleridge's famous *Christabel*, and its freedom is based upon precisely the same prosodic principle ; yet its effect is curiously different. Blake does not consciously pass from one species of foot to another ; he mingles them at the instantaneous prompting of his ear, and consequently his effect is far less academic.

It might be worth noting that the *Mad Song* was written before 1777 and was printed in 1786 ; the Preface to *Jerusalem* was dated by Blake 1804 ; *The Everlasting Gospel* is calculated to have been written about 1810 ; while *Christabel* was not published until 1816. Coleridge, it appears, knew Blake.[1] It would be a fine feather in Blake's cap could it be proved that Coleridge privately took over the older poet's theory of versification, and thus turned the current of Romantic metre. But unfortunately the dates are against this. For *Christabel* was begun in 1797 ; in 1818 Coleridge returned the *Songs of Innocence* to Tulk with a note which gave no hint of any personal knowledge of Blake ; and not until 1826 did Crabb Robinson write Dorothy Wordsworth that Coleridge had met Blake. So evidently the two poets developed their versification quite independently, while to Coleridge belongs the credit of giving it to the world.

Although the pentameter is the commonest line in English verse, Blake managed to use it individually. From *The Little Black Boy* it would be very difficult to know that Dryden and Pope had existed. Yet Blake's only obvious variation from the standard heroic quatrain is the 'Saying' of the nineteenth line, which stands in the place of the first unaccented syllable.

Blake's most interesting work with the pentameter, however, lies in his blank verse. The *Poetical Sketches* show a very high and subtle appreciation of its possibilities. Blake already knew, no doubt, from reading Shakspere and Milton, that the great principle in blank verse is

---

[1] ' Coleridge has visited Blake, and, I am told, talks finely about him ' (Crabb Robinson's Letter to Dorothy Wordsworth, postmarked Feb. 20, 1826 ; quoted in *Notes and Queries*, Feb. 17, 1906). ' Blake and Coleridge, when in company, seemed like congenial beings of another sphere, breathing for a while on our earth ' (*London University Magazine*, 1829 ; quoted in *Notes and Queries*, Feb. 3, 1906).

the *variation around* the iambic pentameter. His *King Edward the Third*
shows all the Elizabethan tricks, regulated somewhat by the eighteenth-
century restrictions, yet breaking out now and then into effects entirely
Blake's own. We must confess that a line sometimes needs re-reading,
to get the right cadence ; but this cadence is often truly admirable,
always interesting, and never a mistake. The very opening lines challenge
one with their perverse beat :

> O thou to whose fury the nations are
> But as dust, maintain thy servant's right ! . . .
> When confusion rages, when the field is in a flame,
> When cries of blood tear horror from heav'n . . .

Startling as these seem, they can readily be paralleled by lines from
accepted masterpieces. However, Blake was generally more felicitous.

> Let those that fight, fight in good earnestness

contains a simple yet inevitable juxtaposition of accents. The profusion of

> Flowers of heaven's growth over the banquet table

is subtler, but equally effective in its way.

Blake's great triumph with blank verse, however, was in using it for
actual lyrics. This was a feat not to be paralleled until the nineteenth
century. The poems to the seasons, to the evening star, and to morning
anticipated Poe's second poem *To Helen* and Tennyson's *Summer Night.*
Fair Elenor and the Minstrel's song at the end of *King Edward the Third*
are arranged in quatrains ; nevertheless they are blank verse, and not
unrhymed iambic pentameters, which puts them in another classification
from Tennyson's *Tears, Idle Tears.*

After the *Poetical Sketches,* Blake wrote only one other bit of blank
verse. This is the passage of the 77th plate of *Jerusalem.* While it is
far more radical and varied than the blank verse of the contemporary
Romanticists, it is nevertheless smooth enough to disturb no one, even at
the first reading.

Blake never was sufficiently interested in alexandrines to make whole
poems out of them ; indeed, he used them almost entirely as a variation
of his ' Prophetic ' septenaries, which, as his most interesting extension
of the bounds of poetic expressiveness, will be discussed later.

His lyrical septenaries, however, are of comparatively little interest.
The first *Holy Thursday* appears to be his only use of this line in his early
poems ; but as a matter of fact, *Gwin, King of Norway,* the two *Nurse's
Songs, The Divine Image,* and *The Little Boy Lost and Found* are septenary
couplets divided at the caesura into quatrains. Blake's freedom in their
use is characteristic, but never striking.

Before discussing the metres of the Prophetic Books, it will be best to
finish our consideration of the lyrics.

Blake, like every good poet, invented several lyrical patterns of his
own ; which, as we have seen, are very lovely, but not complicated.
These patterns can easily be reduced to technical formulae ; however,
such descriptions would not be of great interest or importance here.

There was, nevertheless, one form entirely his own, in which he made
several experiments, whose true value could not be appreciated until the
present day. This was his metrical ' prose,' which is very like Paul

Fort's ' polyphonic prose,' from which Amy Lowell's elaborate compositions developed.

Blake's original idea was to vary blank verse so much that it would be presented most smoothly as a solid block of prose. Ossian had treated septenaries in the same way, so Blake did it with blank verse.

The *Prologue to King John* was the first of these experiments, judging by the form.

> The trembling sinews of old age must work
> the work of death against their progeny ;
> for Tyranny hath stretch'd his purple arm,
> and ' Blood !' he cries ; ' the chariots and the horses,
> the noise of shout, and the dreadful thunder of battle heard afar !'
> Beware, O proud ! thou shalt be humbled.[1] . . .

This is obviously blank verse with variations which many an Elizabethan might have written. But this was only Blake's starting-point. In *Contemplation* the variations are far greater, and made with the sympathetic rhythm in mind.

> Vain, foolish man, that roams on lofty rocks,
> where, 'cause his garments are swollen with wind,
> he fancies he is grown into a giant !

The windy rhythm of the second line is obvious. But in the following quotation we are losing sight of blank verse very quickly.

> The brook stretches its arms along the velvet meadow,
> its silver inhabitants sport and play ;
> the youthful sun joys like a hunter roused to the chase,
> he rushes up the sky,
> and lays hold on the immortal coursers of day ;
> the sky glitters with the jingling trappings.

In fact, such non-metrical rhythm is simply Free Verse.

Samson, the last in the book, is far more regular, yet differs from all the other experiments. Blake evidently was trying to improve on the broken, yet metrical, cadences of Milton's *Samson Agonistes*. Blake's cadences are perfectly clear. Early editors yielded to the temptation of fixing it up into respectable blank verse ; but in doing so they changed Blake's effect. He deliberately eliminated overflow and all the effects which come from the conflict of the iambic pentameter with the surge of the words themselves. Such an effect is Miltonic, but it is not Blakean. A single specimen, arranged with reference to the cadences, should prove this beyond dispute.

> Call thine alluring arts and honest-seeming brow,
> the holy kiss of love, and the transparent tear ;
> put on fair linen that with the lily vies,
> purple and silver ;
> neglect thy hair,
> to seem more lovely in thy loose attire ;
> put on thy country's pride, deceit,
> and eyes of love decked in mild sorrow ;
> to sell thy lord for gold.

[1] Humbled : trisyllabic after the Elizabethan tradition. Blake used the word twice again in the same way, in *Gwin, King of Norway*, lines 12 and 30.

The most varied of all these bits of metrical prose is *The Couch of Death*. Its most regular passage is the following :

> Sorrow linked them together ;
> leaning on one another's necks alternately—
> like lilies dropping tears in each other's bosom—
> they stood by the bed like reeds bending over a lake,
> when the evening drops trickle down.
> His voice was low as the whisperings of the woods
> when the wind is asleep,
> and the visions of Heaven unfold their visitation.

Another influence appears : the inevitable influence of the Bible. The parallel cadences of Hebraic poetry find an echo in the following :

> My hand is feeble, how should I stretch it out ?
> My ways are sinful, how should I raise mine eyes ?
> My voice hath used deceit, how should I call on Him who is Truth ?
> My breath is loathsome, how should He not be offended ?
> If I lay my face in the dust, the grave opens its mouth for me ;
> if I lift up my head, sin covers me as a cloak.

The influence of Blake's ' polyphonic prose ' upon Coleridge's *Wanderings of Cain* (1798), and so upon the whole family of Prose Poems in English, is possible, even likely ; but if it be so, Blake's work was misunderstood. The Pro e Poem is actually prose, and is not written with the unifying effect of rhythm constantly in mind. We find nothing like Blake's work until Paul Fort began writing in Paris, who conceived that prose and poetry were simply two ends of the same instrument, which he united, playing upon all the intermediary stages. It must be confessed that his transitions are not so subtle as they might have been : on the whole we find the narrative portions fall into unrhymed or rhymed alexandrines, and that occasionally some moment may blossom into a lyric, while the conversations are pure prose. It remained for Amy Lowell to use all rhythms easily in one compact form.

Blake's use of rhyme in his lyrics was quite as sophisticated and free as his use of lines. He was dissatisfied with it because its automatic tinkle had become meaningless. At first he considered abolishing it altogether, and the *Poetical Sketches* open with lyrics freed entirely from the ' modern bondage of rhyming.' In this he was justified by Milton's translation of Horace's *Fifth Ode* (Bk. i.) and by Collins's *Ode to Evening*. But Blake soon realized that he was eliminating an effect which had its place. His more elaborate stanza-patterns allowed fresher echoes of sound, but this was not enough. He wished to transcend rhyme, to produce subtle and strange chimes in the inner ear. This was not easy to do, as he discovered.

At first he was contented with false vowel-sounds. These were not the conventional rhymes for the eye, which are still considered perfectly allowable. Scoffers should be reminded that Blake's new rhymes are even harder to produce consistently than regular rhymes. Blake found this out in his *Fresh from the Dewy Hill*, whose first four stanzas are rhymed entirely in his radical way, but whose last two stanzas are rhymed impeccably. It is obvious that Blake's technique failed him. He falls into rhyme, not out of it.

There are also several cases of false terminal consonants. *Dawn–scorn* is to be found twice : in the *Mad Song* and in *Fresh from the Dewy Hill* ; although the merest novice would know enough to substitute *morn* for *dawn*. *Vault–fraught* may be made to rhyme by adopting the early pronunciation of *vaut*. But such combinations as *girl–small* (*Spring*) and *lambs–hands* (*Holy Thursday*) are not to be explained away.

This use of false rhymes gradually found its place marvellously. *Love and Harmony Combine* (rhymed *aaaa*) obtains a very pleasant effect by the use of one false rhyme per quatrain, which breaks up an effect which otherwise would be angular and monotonous. The variation of the less prominent rhymes is very successfully done, as in *When Old Corruption first begun* and the *Introduction* to the *Songs of Innocence*.

Eventually Blake produced three or four poems which seem perfect, yet which depend on these false rhymes. *Lamb–name*, though used twice in one stanza, has never been considered a blot on *The Lamb*. *Am–name* is equally successful in *Infant Joy*, though the economy of rhyme there is remarkable. *Hum–home* is a perfectly satisfactory termination to *A Dream*. *Spring* is hardly more than a string of these false rhymes, in two of the three stanzas. Why these rhymes are so delightful, while the experiments in the *Poetical Sketches* are not, is very difficult to say.

Blake had other interesting tricks which he played with rhyme.

There are a few cases of internal rhyme, besides the entirely conventional ones which are almost always found in septenaries. *The Garden of Love* (rhymed *abcb*) changes its pattern without warning in the last stanza, and, by the internal rhymes of the last two lines, ends the poem appropriately with the dull and heavy effect of a tolling bell. The first two lines really do not rhyme at all, but the impetus from the preceding stanzas fools us.

> And I saw it was filled with graves,
> And tomb-stones where flowers should be ;
> And priests in black *gowns* were walking their *rounds*,
> And binding with *briars* my joys and *desires*.

Another case where the impetus of the pattern carries over the effect of rhyme is in the fourth stanza of *Earth's Answer* (*abaab*), whose terminal words are *joy, grow, sower, night, plough*. The pattern is corrected by the fifth stanza.

But to return to internal rhymes, sometimes we find that Blake will infuse a rhyme sound throughout several lines. Thus *or* runs riot through the eighteenth and nineteenth stanzas of *Gwin, King of Norway*. Far more successful is the first stanza of his poem *To The Queen* in his edition of Blair's *Grave*, where the coldness of the sepulchre is invoked by all the *ol*'s.

> The Door of Death is made of *gol*d,
> That mortal eyes cannot beho*l*d ;
> And when the mortal eyes are c*l*os'd
> And c*ol*d and pale the limbs repos'd,
> The s*ou*l awakes ; and, wond'ring, sees
> In her mild hand the go*l*den Keys ;
> The Grave is Heaven's Go*l*den Gate,
> And rich and poor around it wait ;
> O Shepherdess of England's *fol*d,
> Beho*l*d this Gate of Pearl and Gol*d* !

Once in a while Blake used what might be called idea-rhymes, where the antithesis alone produces the desired effect.   Thus in *Gwin, King of Norway* we find *seas–skies*, and in *The Little Vagabond*, *cold–warm*.

Sometimes he repeated words, instead of using rhymes.   In *The Little Vagabond* (immediately after *cold–warm*) he repeated *well*, and seemed to think it satisfactory.   *Appear* is used in the same way in *The School-Boy*.   Coleridge did the same thing quite as consciously in the couplet from *Christabel* :

> Is the night chilly and dark ?
> The night is chilly, but not dark.

Blake was most successful with his repetitions when he used them as a sort of refrain.   *The Lamb* is the best-known example of this.   Another example occurs in *On Another's Sorrow* :

> No, no ! never can it be !
> Never, never can it be !

Leaving the lyrics for Prophetic Books, Blake at once encountered a new problem.   Instead of modelling miniature thoughts and moods into exquisite patterns of words, he was now concerned with extensive, rather than intensive, expression.   He had to find a line which could be repeated indefinitely with the least possible monotony, a line so flexible as to express the greatest number of thoughts and emotions.   Such a line would be the quintessence of English versification, the perfect length, and the natural beat.   Blake's predecessors had found it in the iambic pentameter ;   Marlowe, Shakspere, and Milton had already used it gloriously ;   but Blake found it too restricted to contain his expansive soul.   As we have noticed, he used it but once after the *Poetical Sketches*.   So, abandoning their ‘ Monotonous Cadence,’ which was ‘ not only awkward, but as much a bondage as rhyme itself,’ he turned to Macpherson's *Ossian*, which he, like all his contemporaries, greatly admired.

Ossian was printed as prose ;   but in fact the greater part of it falls into frightfully dull blocks of septenaries, with caesuras placed regularly after the fourth foot.   The alexandrine is freely interspersed, for it is a peculiarity of that line that it can be thrown in anywhere among septenaries without interrupting the rhythm.   The alexandrine breaks so violently in the middle that this break seems to count as the extra beat.   A specimen from the *First Book* of *Fingal*, arranged as verse, will illustrate the Ossianic septenary.   The fourth line is an alexandrine.   Metrically, it was far rougher than any other verse Blake knew, which undoubtedly accounts for much of his love for it.

> When did I fly, replied the king, from the battle of many spears ?
> When did I fly, son of Arno, chief of the little soul ?
> I met the storm of Gormal when the foam of my waves was high ;
> I met the storm of the clouds, and shall I fly from a hero ?
> Were it Fingal himself, my soul should not darken before him.
> —Rise to the battle, my thousands ; pour round me like the ecchoing main.
> Gather round the bright steel of your king ; strong as the rocks of my land ;
> that meet the storm with joy, and stretch their dark woods to the wind.

This, then, was the model after which Blake began to write his Prophetic Books.   But he understood perfectly how monotonous and limited Macpherson's effects were, so he practised varying the septenary more and more, till from the gentle meander of *Thel* we pass eventually to the choral tempest of *Jerusalem*. He also seems to have realized that many people did not feel the rhythm of *Ossian*, obvious as it was, so he printed his own lines as verse.

Later, another influence seems to have crept in for brief moments. This was the classical hexameter. Such lines as the following from *Milton* (20 : 50-52) are unmistakably, if accidentally, reminiscent of the classical metre :

> O Swedenborg ! strongest of men, the Samson shorn by the Churches:
> Shewing the Transgressors in Hell, the proud Warriors in Heaven,
> Heaven as a Punisher, & Hell as One under Punishment.

Needless to say, the ' Prophetic ' septenaries are quite different from the lyrical septenaries, which are not only rhymed, but are always broken at the obvious place, after the fourth beat.

The earliest septenaries, those of *Tiriel* and *Thel*, were written 1788-1789. They are treated almost as intellectually as the eighteenth century treated its blank verse. The caesuras are carefully yet easily varied ; extra light syllables are slipped in unobtrusively ; a few feet are inverted ; and there is no awkward overflow whatsoever. Occasionally unaccented syllables are omitted. In *Thel*, Blake scatters light accents in some profusion, to make his verbal music fit the text. *Tiriel*, being of rougher fibre, is more roughly treated. Blake's only really radical treatment of the line is the occasional interpolation of octameters, or, more rarely, alexandrines. These become especially noticeable toward the end of the poems ; Blake reserved his greatest irregularities for the climax. The excitement lashes itself, in the agony of expression, to stronger, more brutal cadences.

The most interesting feature, however, is Blake's tendency to interpret by the cadence the movement of the action. It sometimes goes so far that, while the seven fundamental beats are definite enough, they are distributed almost at random.

> Shout, beautiful daughter of Tiriel ! thou singest a sweet song ! . . .
> Westwardly journeying, till Tiriel grew weary with his travel.

One line is particularly interesting, since by the omission of one beat (which I take to be omitted after the word *refuse*) the following beat is felt with double force :

> Shall fail. If thou refuse . . . *howl* in the desolate mountains !

The terminal lament in *Thel* is suddenly and potently irregular. Its ten lines contain one pentameter, one octameter, and three alexandrines !

The next period of Blake's septenaries is dated 1793-1794 ; it includes the *Visions of the Daughters of Albion*, *America*, and the narrative parts of *Europe*. The development is marked. Still the lines are smooth enough ; the percentage of alexandrines and octameters has not increased ; but the greater turbulence of the subject-matter with Blake's growing familiarity with his medium produce sudden effects that once in a while puzzle us for the moment. Nevertheless, practically all of them are thoroughly successful.

One of the effects which Blake was developing was the omission of unaccented syllables, so that several accents may stand together. This had been done before in *Tiriel* :

> Rise from the centre, belching flames & roarings, *dark smoke*. . . .
> Some fled away : but Zazel *stood still*, & thus begun :—
> *Bald ty*rant, Wrinkled cunning, listen to Zazel's chains !

Also in *Thel* :

> Till to her own grave-plot she came, and there she *sat down*.

In the *Visions of the Daughters of Albion*, this effect is used rather more successfully :

> And thus I turn my face to where my *whole soul seeks*.

In *Jerusalem* the wilder metre allows much more of this sort of thing, as in 57 : 4—

> Of the Atlantic, which poured in impetuous *loud, loud, louder* & louder.

In *Milton* (31 : 31), Blake places five accented syllables together :

> He leads the Choir of *Day : trill, trill, trill, trill !*

Another effect, which might seem puzzling, is Blake's stretching of words, until they cover an extra syllable. This is done generally for emphasis. It was a custom with the Elizabethans, but had not been considered correct by the eighteenth century. In *Tiriel*, line 47, we find ' rememberance ' ; in the *Visions*, line 112, ' lamentati-ons ' ; in *America*, line 150, ' visi-ons,' ; and in *Europe*, line 107, ' fi-res ' (or rather, ' fi-yers ').

Sometimes the mere excitement packs the lines full of syllables :

> The lustful joy shall forget to generate, and create an amorous image. . . .
> Where the horrible darkness is impressed with reflections of desire.

Sometimes the drama itself affects the cadence :

> Heads deprest, voices weak, eyes downcast, hands work-bruis'd . . .
> The strong voice ceas'd ; for a terrible blast swept over the heaving sea. . . .
> Fury ! rage ! madness ! in a wind swept through America.

And once in a long while we encounter a line which seems to have broken loose completely from any metrical basis, as in Oothoon's outburst :

> I cry : Love ! Love ! Love ! happy happy Love ! free as the mountain wind !

In *Europe*, Blake, somewhat dissatisfied with the septenary, used other kinds of line for the speeches of the characters. In the remainder of the minor Prophetic Books, he tried a completely new experiment. But he returned to the septenary for his three epics.

It is hard to judge of the metre of *The Four Zoas*, since only fragments of it have been published accurately. The two complete reprints have been practically rewritten, with the avowed purpose of correcting Blake's versification. Neither the Manifesto at the beginning of *Jerusalem*, nor the pride which rings out in the very first lines of *The Four Zoas*, about

> . . . . the march of long-resounding, strong, heroic Verse,
> Marshall'd in order for the day of Intellectual Battle,

could deter the editors from clipping Blake's magnificent exuberance of utterance.

An examination of the manuscript, however, shows that *The Four Zoas* (1797-1804) represents the transitional stage from the minor Prophetic Books to the two later epics. The following passage is a fair sample of the usual septenaries (v. 114-142) : [1]

His limbs bound down mock at his chains for over them a flame
Of circling fire unceasing plays to feed them with life & bring
The virtues of the Eternal worlds ten thousand thousand spirits
Of life lament around the Demon going forth & returning
At his enormous call they flee into the heavens of heavens
And back return with wine & food. Or dive into the deeps
To bring the thrilling joys of sense to quell his ceaseless rage
His eyes, the lights of his large soul contract or else expand
Contracted they behold the secrets of the infinite mountains
The veins of gold & silver & the hidden things of Vala
Whatever grows from its pure bud, or breathes a fragrant soul
Expanded they behold the terrors of the Sun & Moon
The Elemental Planets & the orbs of eccentric fire
His nostrils breathe a fiery flame. his locks are like the forests
Of wild beasts there the lion glares the tyger & wolf howl there
And there the Eagle hides her young in cliffs & precipices
His bosom is like the starry heaven expanded all the stars
Sing round. there waves the harvest and the vintage rejoices. the Springs
Flow into rivers of delight. there the spontaneous flowers
Drink laugh and sing. the grashopper the Emmet and the Fly
The golden Moth builds there a house & spreads her silken bed
His loins inwove with silken fires are like a furnace fierce
As the strong Bull in summer time when bees sing round the heath
When the herds low after the shadow & after the water spring
The numerous flocks cover the mountains & shine along the valley
His knees are rocks of adamant & rubie & emerald
Spirits of strength in Palaces rejoice in golden armour
Armed with spear & shield they drink & rejoice over the slain
Such is the Demon Such his terror on the nether deep.

There are long passages, such as the description of the redeemed Vala in *Night the Ninth* (386-506), which are as smooth and iridescent as anything in *Thel* ; but at other times the variation around the septenary is so extreme as to produce such a line as this (viii. 444) :

Oh lovely, terrible Los, wonder of Eternity ! O Los, my defence & guide !

Alexandrines and octameters are not merely interspersed ; they may hold their own for several lines, as in Orc's War-Song :

Sound the War-trumpet terrific, Souls clad in attractive Steel !
Sound the Shrill fife, Serpents of war ! I hear the northern Drum
Awake ! I hear the flappings of the folding banners !
The Dragons of the North put on their armour ;
Upon the Eastern Sea they take their course. . . .
The northern Drum ! Now give the charge ! bravely obscur'd
With darts of wintry hail ! Again the black bow draw ;
Again the elemental Strings to your right breasts draw ;
And let the thund'ring Drum speed on the arrows black ! [2]

[1] I must be pardoned for quoting the whole of this beautiful passage. I have left the capitalizing and punctuation as Blake wrote it.
[2] *Night VII*, first version, 145-149, 153-156.

Pentameters appear (as in the fourth and fifth lines of the foregoing quotation) and even nonameters. Once in a while the anapest is substituted for the iamb, as in the first line quoted above, also in the following lines from Enion's lament (ii. 621-623) :

While our olive & vine sing & laugh round our door, & our children bring fruits &
   flowers,
Then the groan & the dolour are quite forgotten, & the slave grinding at the mill,
And the captive in chains, & the poor in the prison, & the soldier in the field.

There is far more rush in the verse. Blake evidently let himself be carried away by his ear, and became entirely careless of the academic aspect of his work. As he had one of the finest ears for verse that any poet has ever possessed in English, the results are for the most part entirely satisfactory.

Before passing to *Milton* and *Jerusalem*, mention should be made of the septenaries in the letter to Flaxman on September 12, 1800. These eleven lines are in rough anapests, all septenaries (if we make sure to read the two first syllables in each line as light syllables ; which is difficult when the lines begin with such words as ' angels ' and ' Ezra '), except for the last line, which is an alexandrine.

Milton and *Jerusalem* are both dated 1804 on the title-page ; but that date indicates only the time when the engraving was begun. Many changes and additions were made during the course of the engraving. The *Jerusalem* at least was not finished until Blake's last years. These two poems, then, represent Blake's ultimate experiments in poetic technique.

Still we find long passages of iambic septenaries ; but lines of different length have invaded the poems more and more, until we get such tough passages as the following (*Milton*, 11 : 18-29) :

But Lucifer refus'd to die, & in pride he forsook his charge :
And they elected Molech, and when Molech was impatient
The Divine hand found the Two Limits : first of Opacity, then of Contraction.
Opacity was named Satan, Contraction was named Adam.
Triple Elohim came ; Elohim, wearied, fainted ; they elected Shaddai :
Shaddai angry, Pahad descended : Pahad terrified, they sent Jehovah,
And Jehovah was leprous ; loud he call'd, stretching his hand to Eternity.
For then the Body of Death was perfected in hypocritic holiness,
Around the Lamb, a Female Tabernacle woven in Cathedron's Looms.
He died as a Reprobate, he was Punish'd as a Transgressor :
Glory ! Glory ! Glory ! to the Holy Lamb of God !
I touch the heavens as an instrument to glorify the Lord !

In contrast to this, yet equally daring, are these lines from *Jerusalem* (49 : 50-53) :

Rush on ! Rush on ! Rush on ! ye vegetating Sons of Albion !
The Sun shall go before you in Day : the Moon shall go
Before you in Night. Come on ! Come on ! Come on ! The Lord
Jehovah is before, behind, above, beneath, around.

The septenaries at times vanish, as in this accidental passage of pentameters (*Jerusalem*, 40 : 15-20) :

Those who give their lives for him are despised !
Those who devour his soul are taken into his bosom :
To destroy his Emanation is their intention.

Arise ! awake, O Friends of the Giant Albion !
They have perswaded him of horrible falshoods !
They have sown errors over all his fruitful fields !

The climax of *Jerusalem* is very largely in solid blocks of octameters :

And every Man stood Fourfold, each Four Faces had, One to the West,
One toward the East, One to the South, One to the North, the Horses Fourfold.
And the dim Chaos brighten'd beneath, above, around ! Eyed as the Peacock.
According to the Human Nerves of Sensation, the Four Rivers of the Water of Life.

Overflow, which had been used sparingly before, now becomes very common. In *Thel* we find the following passage :

For I walk thro' the vales of Har, and smell the sweetest flowers,
But I feed not the little flowers : I hear the warbling birds ;
But I feed not the warbling birds ; they fly and seek their food.

In *The Four Zoas*, the enjambement has become more daring, but still quite regular :

Four Mighty Ones are in every Man ; a Perfect Unity
Cannot Exist but from the Universal Brotherhood of Eden,
The Universal Man, To Whom be Glory Evermore. Amen.
What are the Natures of those Living Creatures, the Heavenly Father only
Knoweth : No Individual knoweth, nor can know in all Eternity.

But in *Milton* and *Jerusalem*, such restraint is often cast aside. The following passage (*Jerusalem*, 17 : 51-55) is not unusual :

First as a red Globe of blood trembling beneath his bosom
Suspended over her he hung ; he infolded her in his garments
Of wool : he hid her from the Spectre, in shame & confusion of
Face ; in terrors & pains of Hell & Eternal Death, the
Trembling Globe shot forth Self-living & Los howl'd over it.

It should now be quite clear how Blake meant these ' Prophetic ' septenaries to be read. They are to be poured out in a great flood of oratory, stressing the natural accents, and passing rapidly over the unaccented syllables. The ' syllabic ' tradition, which weighs every syllable with great care, is to be completely ignored. Each line represents a breath ; and this breath is the real metrical unit, around which all the variations are formed.

Let us now return to the other kinds of verse to be found in the Prophetic Books.

A Song of Liberty was arranged in prose verses, to resemble the topography of the Bible. But this was only to conceal the metrical basis of the poem. It is not ' of course, lyrical prose,' as one eminent critic described it ; it is really in alexandrines, with regular caesuras, but with a foot that varies from anapest to dactyl, with interpolated iambs and trochees. Arranged according to this scheme, the opening lines appear as follows :

The Eternal Female groan'd. / It was heard over all the earth.
Albion's coast is sick, silent. / The American meadows faint !
Shadows of Prophecy shiver / along by the lakes and the rivers,
and mutter across the ocean. / France, rend down thy dungeon.
Golden Spain, burst / the barriers of old Rome !
Cast thy keys, O Rome ! / into the deep, down falling,
even to Eternity / down falling, and weep.

To read these metrically, great violence must be done to the normal accent of the words. This was a new scheme of Blake's to transcend ordinary metres ; an experiment which he varied many ways in his minor Prophetic Books, before he discovered his ideal in the irregular septenaries of *Milton* and *Jerusalem*.

In *The French Revolution* he applied the same principle to anapestic septenaries. Customarily poets begin with lines absolutely according to pattern, in order that the pattern may be established ; but Blake, in direct defiance of this, is apt to begin with variations, so that the metrical basis may be less obvious. Just so he began *King Edward the Third* ; so now he begins *The French Revolution*.

The dead brood over Europe ; the cloud and vision descends upon chearful France ;
O cloud well appointed ! Sick, sick, the Prince on his couch ! wreath'd in dim
And appalling mist ; his strong hand outstretch'd, from his shoulder down the bone,
Runs aching cold into the sceptre, too heavy for mortal grasp—no more
To be swayed by visible hand, nor in cruelty bruise the mild flourishing mountains.

So it seems clear that Blake meant his metre to be overrun by the violence of the expression. *The dead brood* is not a good anapest. *Sick, sick*, comprise two accents, with compensating pauses. Blake substitutes spondees and paeons so freely, he packs the line according to its movement so often, and wrenches the accents so viciously, that the metre is fairly pummelled into expressiveness. As a result, we often puzzle over the number of beats intended in certain lines. How are we to scan—

His strong limbs ; from court to court curs'd the fierce torment unquell'd ?

Is this an alexandrine ? Or a pentameter ? By accenting *strong* as well as *limbs* ; and *curs'd* as well as the preceding *court*, we can make it conform to the septenary.

Were forg'd smaller as the flesh decay'd : a mask of iron hid the lineaments.

This line resolves easily to the pattern. But soon we discover that longer lines are being used.

Sleeping at midnight in my golden tower, the repose of the labours of men
Wav'd its solemn cloud over my head. I awoke ; a cold hand passed over my
    limbs, and behold !

The first of these lines is a septenary, whose first syllable is accented. Accenting the first syllable of the next (which is rarely done) we get a nonameter ; accenting the third instead, we get an octameter. Which is it ? Before we answer, it is as well to know that nonameters are unmistakably present :

To a bed of straw ; the seven diseases of the earth, like birds of prey, stood on the
    couch.

After this, Blake seems to have realized that the anapest, in which, as we have seen, he was much interested, was too big a foot for the septenary. He (or his publisher) suppressed this poem, and the next experiment was in anapestic trimeter, which forms the basis of *Urizen, Asia, The Book of Los*, and *Ahania*. The shortening of the line slowed the rush of the verse. Otherwise Blake observed the same principle of wrenching accents away from the metrical base.   He uses all his old tricks, but with much more sobriety.   The result is excellent.

> Lo, a shadow of horror is risen
> In Eternity ! Unknown, unprolific,
> Self-clos'd, all-repelling.   What Demon
> Hath form'd this abominable Void,
> This soul-shudd'ring vacuum ?   Some said
> It is Urizen.   But unknown, abstracted,
> Brooding, secret, the dark Power hid.

Reading this according to the metrical scheme, it is almost as uncomfortable verse as was ever written ; but reading it according to the natural cadence of the words, we find it ordered and final.   Sometimes the measure becomes iambic for a series of lines :

> From the caverns of his jointed Spine
> Down sunk with fright a red
> Round Globe, hot, burning, deep,
> Deep down into the Abyss ;
> Panting, Conglobing, Trembling,
> Shooting out ten thousand branches
> Around his solid bones—
> And a second Age passed over,
> And a state of dismal woe.

How flexible Blake's versification was to become is demonstrated by the inclusion of this and yet more lines from *Urizen*, iva, in *Milton* 5*.

> Deep sunk with fright a red round Globe, hot, burning, deep,
> Deep down into the Abyss, panting, conglobing, trembling ;
> And a second Age passed over, & a State of dismal woe.

Thus trimeter becomes septenary !

Besides these anapestic verses, Blake made yet another line of experimentation in the freer forms.   This was a continuation of the ' prose ' in the *Poetical Sketches* ; for Blake needed some more lyrical form in order to deal with the more songful moments.   Conventional lyrics, like the *Songs of Innocence and Experience*, would have been woefully out of place : his Eternals could never express themselves in such fragile patterns.   So Blake turned back to his early experiments with metrical lines of uneven lengths, and finally reached something very like some of our modern Free Verse.

The first example of it is the *Argument* to *The Marriage of Heaven and Hell*.   The lines are entirely iambic (with a few truncations), and vary from six to two feet in length.

In *Europe*, the same irregularities are observed in those passages which do not deal directly with narration, but with the invocations of Spirits and with the actions of Los and Enitharmon.   The opening lines of the *Prophecy* are influenced in rhythm as well as thought by Milton's *Hymn to the Nativity*, while *Samson Agonistes* also has its influence, especially in lines 21-22, which are a rhymed trimeter couplet, quite in Milton's style. Los's first speech swells from tetrameter to alexandrine.

Africa (Song of Los) is written in the same iambic lines of lengths varying from dimeter to septenary.

Blake also tried arranging these iambic lines into stanzas of a set pattern. The *Preludium* of *Europe* contains seven stanzas of four lines each, the first, second, and fourth of which are septenaries, and the third a trimeter. In *The Four Zoas*, Enitharmon's Song over Los (ii. 551-586) consists of seven iambic stanzas of five lines each, arranged 7, 3, 7, 4, 7. The lament of Urizen in the same poem (v. 190-241) might also be mentioned here, though its thirteen iambic quatrains are entirely in septenaries. There are a few variations in these lyrics from *The Four Zoas* : in Enitharmon's song, the second line twice is made a tetrameter, and the first one a pentameter ; while in Urizen's lament, the third line shows a very definite tendency to become an octameter. In none of these lyrics, however, did Blake reach again the freedom which he had shown in the ' prose ' of the *Poetical Sketches*.

This completes our survey of Blake's prosody. Besides his experiments in rhyme, he extended the expressiveness of practically all the boundaries of versification. In particular, he discovered the substitution of one foot for another, he brought out for the first time the true music of the anapest, and he developed as none have before or since the longest and most difficult lines in English verse. He was not a purist : he did nothing towards perfecting set forms like the sonnet or the hexameter ; what he did was to search for freer and newer forms. Guided by an excellent ear, he went so far as to anticipate most of the prosodic discoveries of the nineteenth century, and to lead directly toward those of the twentieth century. Indeed, at some moments he seems to have reached a complete liberation from metre in favour of the cadence ; at any rate, in most of his later work, cadence was certainly predominant.

CHAPTER IX

THE END OF THE GOLDEN STRING

> Sad task and hard, for how shall I relate
> To human sense th' invisible exploits
> Of warring Spirits ; how without remorse
> The ruin of so many glorious once
> And perfect while they stood ; how last unfould
> The secrets of another world, perhaps
> Not lawful to reveal ? yet for thy good
> This is dispenc't, and what surmounts the reach
> Of human sense, I shall delineate so,
> By lik'ning spiritual to corporal forms,
> As may express them best, though what if Earth
> Be but the shaddow of Heav'n, and things therein
> Each to other like, more then on earth is thought ?
>
> —*Paradise Lost*, v. 563-576.

BEFORE we can discuss Blake's method of literary presentation, we must appreciate his intentions. We must know what he was trying to do, before we examine how he did it.

Blake considered himself to be one of the race of the ancient Prophets ; and for that reason he called his books ' Prophetic Books.' By the word ' Prophet ' he did not mean one who foretells the future. He believed that true Prophets were simply poets who beheld the eternal truths by power of Imagination. In their moments of inspiration they became ' soothsayers,' expressing their discoveries in the obscure clothing of symbolism, knowing that the wise would penetrate its meaning, and not caring whether the fools understood or not. At such moments, the prophets *might* be led to forecast the future (Blake tried it himself, with strange results, in his *French Revolution*) ; but if the events should not follow the prediction, the prophet was not in the least to be discredited. The Fact was not to disprove the Truth. In the Watson marginalia, Blake became very explicit :

Prophets in the modern sense of the word have never existed. Jonah was no prophet in the modern sense, for his prophecy of Nineveh failed. Every honest man is a Prophet : he utters his opinion both of private & public matters.

This conception of the function of Prophets and Prophecy was derived from the Deistic doctrine. Tom Paine, whom Bishop Watson was attacking, had already declared that—

There is not throughout the whole book called the Bible, any word that describes to us what we call a poet, nor any word that describes what we call poetry. The case is, that the word *prophet*, to which later times have affixed a new idea, was the Bible word for poet, and the word *prophesying* meant the art of making poetry. It also meant the art of playing poetry to a tune upon any instrument of music.[1]

---

[1] *The Age of Reason*, ch. vii. This view was repeated, with much evidence, by the American poet and student of the *Kabalah*, Thomas Holley Chivers, in the Preface to his *Memoralia*.

It was thus, then, that Blake intended his own books to be considered. He imagined that his conception of prophecy was so obvious that it would soon be universal ; but the lapse of the century since has played him false.

His books were not intended for his unworthy contemporaries ; he avowed his purpose ' to speak to future generations by a sublime allegory.' He believed (with Swedenborg) that just so the inspired books of the Bible were to be read, besides all such works as the *Bhagvat-Geeta* and the *Timaeus*. He saw a sequence of similar writings throughout the ages, written with precisely this purpose of speaking to the select and keeping silence before the uninitiate : such as the works of St. John, of Trismegistus, Dante, Paracelsus, Jakob Böhme, Milton, and Swedenborg. He intended to continue this series, and he seems to have been its last exemplar.

All these writers dealt either with the progress of the individual soul, or with the history of human development. Blake tried to do both at once, to combine the two as mutual symbols ; for he believed that the whole history of creation is repeated in each individual. The advantage of this theory of Macrocosm and Microcosm is obvious. We care comparatively little about the remote history of the past ; but when we learn that it has a living, present significance, we cannot afford to ignore it. Therefore we find Blake's books—at least, the Lambeth books—fitting together.

The first three of the Lambeth books (ignoring the actual order of composition) deal with the events of Eternity ; the other four deal with the history of the world. The symbolism of these numbers is obvious, since Three is the number of God, and Four the number of Man, the sum of the two being the sacred number Seven.

The first three books deal with the Fall. *The Book of Urizen* and *The Book of Los* tell the same story from the opposing standpoints of Reason and Poetry (Urizen and Los) : while *The Book of Ahania* continues the story with an account of mystical Revolt and further Fall, ending with the rise of civilization in Asia.

Then recorded history begins, whose entire course is briefly described in four books, each named after a continent. The first two, *Africa* and *Asia*, are combined under one title, *The Song of Los*. They describe the degeneration and enslavement of man, up to the moment of the American Revolution. *America*, of course, follows ; then *Europe*, which describes the outbreak of the French Revolution. Here Blake ended the series of the Lambeth books, for the cycle seemed complete : Eternity was practically reachieved in the liberation of mankind.

Later, he revised and combined all this material, with a great deal of rewriting and additions, into one long epic, *The Four Zoas*.

Before he wrote the Lambeth books, he had composed several others, which must be considered separately. The first, *Tiriel* (which never got beyond manuscript form), represents the decay of a false religion ; *Thel* deals with the problem of individual incarnation ; *The Gates of Paradise* with man's life in this world ; the *Visions of the Daughters of Albion* with the social problem of love ; *The French Revolution* with contemporary history ; and *The Marriage of Heaven and Hell* with any number of philosophical problems, particularly those of Evil and Good and of the nature of God. Of the two epics which followed *The Four Zoas, Milton* is a bit of autobiography, while *Jerusalem* is a study of the cruelty of man to man.

Such were the purposes and the subject-matter of Blake's Books. But his method of presentation was so strange that it has caused a vast amount of censure.

The chief charge is that it ruined him as a literary artist. This charge is usually over-emphasized, but there is certainly some truth in it. *Jerusalem*, as pure poetry, is obviously inferior to the *Songs of Innocence*. But is it fair to judge a man by other standards than his own ? *Blake was not trying to make literature*. His message was far more important to him than its presentation. While the *Songs of Innocence* are exceedingly lovely, they contain only a very small amount of doctrine, as compared with *Jerusalem*. Blake's whole progress was towards the Ineffable. It is his subject-matter, rather than his method of writing that is to be blamed. Great poet though he was, his interest lay only secondarily in poetry. When he would record some splendid aphorism, such as ' Energy is Eternal Delight,' he was stating it as a fact, not as a thrill. Truth, not pleasure, is the object of all his writings.

And just here, our difficulties begin. Blake, curiously enough, believed that the Truth should not be told too plainly. The Rev. Dr. Trusler once objected to this idea, and Blake answered him as follows :

You say that I want somebody to Elucidate my Ideas. But you ought to know that what is Grand is necessarily obscure to Weak men. That which can be made Explicit to the Ideot is not worth my care. The wisest of the Ancients consider'd what is not too Explicit as the fittest for Instruction, because it rouzes the faculties to act. I name Moses, Solomon, Esop, Homer, Plato.

He might have named many more. Iamblicus, in his *Life of Pythagoras* (ch. xxiii.), wrote :

The mode of teaching through symbols was considered by Pythagoras as most necessary. For their form of erudition was cultivated by nearly all the Greeks, as being most ancient. But it was transcendently honoured by the Egyptians, and adopted by them in the most diversified manner.

The knowledge of this tradition never died out. The first kind of ' phrensie ' which Agrippa classified came ' from the Muses ' (*Occult Philosophy*, III. xlvi.). Sir Philip Sidney, in his *Apologie for Poetrie*, noted :

There are many mysteries contained in Poetrie, which of purpose were written darkely, least by prophane wits, it should be abused.

His *Arcadia* ever since has been searched for an inner meaning. Defoe claimed that *Robinson Crusoe* was an allegory. But Blake got his theory of obscure writing from Swedenborg, who announced the principle in the *Arcana Coelestia* :

The most ancient manner of writing was that of representing things by persons and by words, by which was understood something altogether different from what was expressed. In such manner, indeed, that nothing was literally true just as it was written, but under these narratives something allegorical was understood. . . . This method of writing they [the writers of the Bible] derived from the most ancient people, who lived before the flood, and who represented to themselves things heavenly and divine, by such as are visible on the earth and in the world, and thus filled their minds and souls with joyous and delightful perceptions. The most ancient people, as they had communication with spirits and angels, had no other speech than this . . . in every expression of which there was a Spiritual sense.

Blake, like any other person with common-sense, was relieved to learn that the story of Adam and Eve was something more than an impossible myth ; in fact, it was an incident in the life of every man. Turning from the Bible, in search for other books which dealt with Illumination, he found many from all ages. These books invariably described the same mystical experience ; and thus often evolved the same symbols. It is a curious fact that the majority of these books yield unexpected meaning when interpreted by Blake's own symbols !

The fascination of this method of writing grew upon Blake. The first examples of it are to be found in the *Poetical Sketches* : in *Gwin, King of Norway*, and in the Minstrel's song at the end of *King Edward the Third*. The *Songs of Innocence* contain poems which are full of an obscurity, which itself is concealed, though *The Little Boy Lost* and *The Little Boy Found* surely invite the thinker to look more deeply. The *Songs of Experience* include one frankly symbolic poem, *To Tirzah* ; while *A Little Girl Lost* begins with an invocation to ' Children of a Future Age.' All the Prophetic Books are obviously intended for the ' young Men of the New Age ' ; and in the last of them, *Jerusalem*, Blake warns the reader :

> I give you the end of a golden string,
> Only wind it into a ball ;
> It will lead you in at Heaven's gate,
> Built in Jerusalem's wall.

It should now be entirely clear that Blake, in concealing the highest meanings of his writings, was neither crazy, nor even unique. Whether or not we approve, we can at least understand his theory. It is too late now for critics to put aside his work as unbalanced because they cannot understand it. (A list of the names of those who have already made this mistake would be entertaining, were it not so long !)

Blake's method of concealing his ideas is known as Symbolism. It is not an arbitrary replacing of one word by another : for that is hardly more than a stupid trick of certain writers whom Blake condemned severely ; and in extreme forms is called aphasia. Symbolism is a development of the very nature of Poetry itself.

It is the highest degree in the poetic scale. The Peter Bell of poetry, the literalist (who is the lowest type), copies photographically what he sees or feels. He may arrange his material in the most pleasing of combinations, but the sensation to which he always appeals, whether knowingly or not, is the Pleasure of Recognition. His great ideal is to heighten the individual object or experience to its most beautiful or most typical form.

The escape from such literalism is through the simile. The poet who uses this compares his object to some other object, and thus obtains some sort of connection (though a weak one) with the rest of the universe. Moreover, he can invoke all sorts of things as contributory effects to his main sensation.

Higher yet is the metaphor, which, by eliminating the conjunctive words, ' like to ' and ' as,' practically identifies the object with its emotional equivalent.

The symbol, however, uses this identity, yet discards the named object for the Eternity which is thus invoked.

Practically the whole existence of poetry consists in this imposing of human values upon natural objects. ' Quant aux comparaisons . . . ce sont les nerfs et tendons des Muses,' wrote Ronsard, in his preface to *La Franciade.* ' [Poetic] language is vitally metaphorical,' echoed Shelley in his famous essay ; and in the preface to *Julian and Maddalo* : ' Strong passion expresses itself in metaphor, borrowed from objects alike far and near.'

Symbolism is the recognition and fixation of these values. It is the highest form of that process usually performed by the weaker metaphor and the still weaker simile. The simile states a resemblance, the metaphor states an identity, and the symbol assumes the identity without direct statement. In the first case, love would be likened to a rose ; in the second case, Love would be called a rose ; and in the third, the Rose would appear unexplained.

There is a rung still higher in this Jacob's Ladder : the rung popularly known as Prophecy. Here the Rose would indicate some particular act in the past, present, or future. A specific, temporal significance is thus imposed upon the Symbol, which hitherto dealt with Eternities. Nostradamus and Paracelsus, among others, experienced this abnormal state of mind.[1] It may be induced artificially, as the records of the ancient oracles prove. To-day the North American Indians use the drug peyote for this very purpose. But here we have passed beyond the province of poetry, and have wandered far from Blake.

Let us return, then, to the symbol. Blake, of course, knew perfectly well what he was doing. He deliberately interpreted objects to show their relation to, and their expression of, mankind. Everything he saw revealed to him its inner essence, which was in turn the revelation of a truth. Only through this method could Truth be approached. Isis cannot be seen unveiled, for the mortal eye itself is her vesture. The great secrets cannot be told ; the very syllables are their mask. Even Beauty may be an additional barrier ; for example, much in Shelley which we take to be pure fantasy is really faithful description of mystical facts. Blake himself must have known that the music of *The Sunflower* (as an instance) lulled the reader into intellectual somnolence. Therefore he deliberately destroyed the surface meaning of his later works, hoping to force open the interior eyes of his audience. ' Allegory addressed to the intellectual powers, while it is altogether hidden from the corporeal understanding, is my definition of the most sublime poetry. It is also somewhat in the same manner defined by Plato,' he wrote in 1803 to Thomas Butts. And thus we learn a strange fact : that the clearer, the more precise, Blake's writings become, the more obscure they seem. The trouble is not with Blake, it lies in our own inability to understand. The fires of Hell still seem like torment and insanity to us, the Angels. Therefore Blake cried so fiercely : ' Go ! put off Holiness, and put on Intellect ! '

This practice soon became an integral part of Blake's philosophy.

---

[1] The curious may consult Charles A. Ward's *Oracles of Nostradamus* (London, 1891) and the *Prophecies of Paracelsus*, translated by J. K. (London, 1915).

Everything must be interpreted in terms of humanity because it is actually a part of humanity. 'Man anciently contain'd in his mighty limbs all things in Heaven & Earth' (*Jerusalem*, 27). The Rose is not really a symbol of Love, it *is* Love, though now separated from the human mind, and given a visible exterior form. Nature is nothing but Man's mirror. The world as we see it is but an outward manifestation of inward truths.

> Listen : I will tell thee what is done in the caverns of the grave.
> The Lamb of God has rent the Veil of Mystery, soon to return
> In Clouds & Fires around the rock & thy Mysterious tree.
> As the seed waits Eagerly watching for its flower & fruit,
> Anxious its little soul looks out into the clear expanse
> To see if hungry winds are abroad with their invisible array.
> So Man looks out in tree & herb & fish & bird & beast,
> Collecting up the scatter'd portions of his immortal body
> Into the Elemental forms of everything that grows.
> He tries the sullen north wind, riding on its angry furrows,
> The sultry south when the sun rises, & the angry east
> When the sun sets, when the clods harden, & the cattle stand
> Drooping, & the birds hide in their silent nests. He stores his thoughts
> As in a store house in his memory ; he regulates the forms
> Of all beneath & all above ; & in the gentle west
> Reposes where the Sun's heat dwells ; he rises to the Sun
> And to the Planets of the Night & to the stars that gild
> The Zodiac & the stars that sullen stand to north & south ;
> He touches the remotest pole & in the center weeps
> That Man should labour & sorrow & learn & forget & return
> To the dark valley whence he came and begin his labours anew
> In pain he sighs, in pain he labours in his universe
> Sorrowing in birds over the deep & howling in the Wolf
> Over the slain & moaning in the cattle & in the winds
> And weeping over Orc & Urizen in clouds and flaming fires
> And in the cries of birth & in the groans of death his voice
> Is heard throughout the Universe—wherever a grass grows
> Or a leaf buds, the Eternal Man is seen, is heard, is felt,
> And all his Sorrows, till he reasumes his ancient bliss.
>
> —*The Four Zoas*, viii. 548-576.

Of course, the immediate accusation is that Blake, in using Nature as a symbol, was really out of touch with Nature. Nothing is more absurd. That Blake preferred to endow Nature with imaginative qualities is beside the point. 'Some see Nature all ridicule and deformity, and by these I shall not regulate my proportions ; and some scarce see Nature at all. But to the eyes of the man of imagination, Nature is Imagination itself. As a man is, so he sees,' Blake wrote in his famous letter to Trusler.

'I assert for myself,' he continued, in his *Vision of the Last Judgment*, 'that I do not behold the outward creation, and that to me it is hindrance and not action. "What !" it will be questioned, when the sun rises, " do you not see a round disc of fire somewhat like a guinea ?" Oh ! no, no ! I see an innumerable company of the heavenly host crying, " Holy, holy, holy is the God Almighty ! " I question not my corporeal eye any more than I would question a window concerning a sight. I look through it, and not with it.'

But Blake never confused the flaming disc with his choirs of chanting angels ; he merely preferred the angels. When he wished, he could describe Nature as well as any one else ; and his exhortations to 'copying' as the only practice for the beginner in painting have only too often been overlooked. His poetry is full of little touches that show a keen eye for landscape :

> Thus he sang all day
> Over the new-mown hay,
> Till the sun went down,
> And the haycocks looked brown.

Other times we find long passages that show a Whitmanesque love for the pageant of nature :

> The barked Oak, the long-limb'd beech ; the Chesnut tree ; the Pine,
> The Pear tree mild, the frowning Walnut, the sharp Crab, & Apple sweet.
> The rough bark opens ; twittering peep forth little beaks & wings,
> The Nightingale, the Goldfinch, Robin, Lark, Linnet & Thrush,
> The Goat leap'd from the craggy cliff, the Sheep awoke from the mould,
> Upon its green stalk rose the Corn, waving innumerable,
> Infolding the bright Infants from the desolating winds.

This, but for the last line, is pure description. The transition from this sort of poetry toward the symbol is nicely illustrated by a paragraph in one of his letters. Blake had arrived at Felpham, and was sure that at last he could do a lot of creative work. The sea air was fairly vibrating with inspiration ; and all objects became highly charged with splendid meaning. In writing of his hopes to Thomas Butts, he recorded :

> Work will go on here with God-speed. A roller and two harrows lie before my window. I met a plough on my first going out at my gate the first morning after my arrival, and the ploughboy said to the ploughman, ' Father, the gate is open.'

And thereafter, the instruments of agriculture became symbols of the cultivation of the best in mankind throughout the great stretches of history.

But we must not deduce from this that Blake's symbols are only to be explained by accidental occurrences of his life. He began by using all the conventional symbols : the Lamb, the Rose, the Lion, the Lily, and so on. But these symbols were not sufficient. Every one knows that the Lamb represents God's Love ; but what represents God's Wrath ? Blake adapted the Tiger for his purpose. The Tiger is not immediately understood ; but the context explains him at once. Blake then beheld the Sunflower ; and the pathos of its (reputed) following the sun forever with its gaze seemed to him, as it had seemed before to the Greeks, a symbol of the soul yearning for Eternity, yet bound to Earth by its very nature.

And so the entire material world came to symbolize various aspects of humanity. Blake looked at the world perpendicularly, and what was the result ? The lowest things he saw were the caves in the earth, representing those hopelessly buried in materialism. This symbol had already been made famous by Plato (*Republic*, vii.). The ocean was the symbol of the sterile waters of Matter—this time Blake used a symbol both Greek and Christian. On the shores grew forests, which are the growths of error. Here the true path is hidden by the many theories, and the sun is obscured. In this very same forest Dante lost himself at the beginning of the *Inferno*. Above the forests rise the mountains, which are the high places of thought, though still of this earth.   Higher yet are the birds, which can leave the earth completely for a while ; they are the geniuses, the messengers to and from Eternity.   Higher yet are the stars which, from the old theories of astrology, Blake took to repre- sent the laws of Reason, which move immutably in their meaningless circles, and whose light is scattered and ineffectual.   Here in the star- light dwells Lucifer ; he is himself the 'army of unalterable law.'   Above this realm, and untouched by it, moves the Moon, which came to represent Love, for it is a beautiful and endurable reflection of the true light, the Sun, the Eternal Light of Poetry itself.

Such is the perpendicular view of the world.   Blake also looked at it horizontally—as a map.   He took the North, which we instinctively think of as the highest, for the region of the Spirit.   From Galilee, in the North, Jesus came to Jerusalem.   The North is now frozen solid, since the Fall has taken place.   Opposed to the North is the South, the region of the Reason.   Mt. Sinai, where the terrible 'Thou-Shalt-Nots' were pro- mulgated, lay south of Jerusalem.   The West had two meanings for Blake—that of Liberty (for America lay there, and towards the West the Sun always moves to his repose), and that of the Body (since the West —to the English at least—is closed by the cold Sea, which represents Matter).   The last point, the East, was the region of Passion, since here Day always began.   In using these compass-points Blake freely intro- duces names of places in the Holy Land, whose significance is determined by their position in regard to Jerusalem.   Later Blake took London as the centre, in an unfortunate outburst of patriotism, and utilized the eighteenth-century suburbs with the same meaning.

These symbols remain fairly consistent throughout Blake's entire works, and they are the key to all his poems and to all the minor Pro- phetic Books.   But Blake had a horror of fixed symbols ; he did not wish his works to be translated with the aid of an easy key.   These things were to be *felt*, not to be reasoned over.   Therefore, being a poet, he introduced a number of other symbols whose meaning varies with the context.   Fire, for example, may mean wrath, inspiration, or annihilation ; while clouds may be focusses of power, or obscurers of the truth.

These unfixed symbols sometimes varied with the growth of his ideas. The word 'devil' is an excellent example.   In the *Poetical Sketches* the word is used with its ordinary meaning.   The next meaning appears in the poem, *I heard an Angel Singing* ; where the Devil is merely the conventional cynic, who sees the world all evil.   Thirdly, in *The Marriage of Heaven and Hell*, we find that Blake has been developing his ideas of evil, which is, it seems, only the energy revolting against the established order of the world.   Devils, therefore, are simply the Geniuses, among whose ranks is to be found the poet Milton ; they are the manifestation of the higher good !   But evil was not so easily explained away ; and Blake finally came to the decision that evil was a false system of thinking ; therefore in *Jerusalem* we find the statement : 'Devils are false religions.' Meanwhile the idea that the original thinkers were devils had clung ; but Blake applied a milder word to them : 'Demons.'

Had Blake gone no farther than this with his symbolism the world would never have quarrelled with him.   But he soon came to the point where there were no terms to express his ideas.   He wished to represent the history of certain phases of the human soul.   These were not virtues and vices, but various States : Reason, Revolution, Wrath, and the like. If he called them by such obvious names as these, their meaning was solidified past any fidelity to actual psychology, and their tremendous dramas lost all vitality.   Therefore he invented names for them, and endowed them with all the human attributes, except subjection to the laws of cause and effect, of time and space.

'These Gods,' Blake wrote in his *Descriptive Catalogue*, 'are visions of the eternal attributes, or divine names, which, when erected into gods, become destructive to humanity.   They ought to be the servants, and not the masters, of man or of society.   They ought to be made to sacrifice to Man, and not man compelled to sacrifice to them ; for, when separated from man or humanity, who is Jesus the Saviour, the vine of eternity ?   They are thieves and rebels, they are destroyers.'

Their names were created at random.   Some were anagrams ; some were found in strange books, such as Agrippa's *Occult Philosophy* ; some came from Ossian ; one from the *Bhagvat-Geeta* ; but the majority were invented for the sake of the sound alone.

These characters appear and disappear unaccountably ; they are born of various parents ; they die many times ; they suffer obscure crucifixions ; they are apotheosized, or sacrifice themselves for others; they war ; love ; exult ; lament.   Again Blake was smitten with a fear that these shifting forces of the soul of man would be mistaken for actual gods ; therefore he made a theogony absolutely impossible.   He was quite right in this.   Anger, for example, is the result of a variety of causes ; to give Anger only one set of parents would be absurd.   Consideration for the reader was not among Blake's intentions.

However, it is quite simple to outline the character of the main actors in these supersensual dramas.   The great hero is Los, who represents the Poetic Instinct.   He is the ruler of Time, the Sun God (his name being an anagram of Sol).   Blake often calls him 'the Eternal Prophet,' because Time is the prophecy of Eternity.   Before the Fall, in the days of Eternity, he was Urthona, the Spirit ; but in this world, Poetry is the great manifestation of the Spirit.

Associated with him is his wife, or 'emanation,' Enitharmon.   She rules the moon, and is Goddess of Space.   She represents in particular Spiritual Beauty, or Poetic Inspiration.   Her name is an anagram of Enarithmon ('numberless').   High as her place is, she (like indeed all these Gods) may be subject to error ; and not uncommonly we find her fleeing from her consort.

The great opponent of **Los** is Urizen, who represents Reason.   His name is easily remembered, because it is simply a combination of the words 'Your Reason.'   His great ambition is to rule the Universe, and he is constantly trying to invade the North, where the Spirit dwells. Whenever he succeeds, he blights everything, issuing tyrannical laws and prohibitions, establishing false religions, and in general petrifying the Invisible into the Visible.   It is he who is responsible for the Creation, and Blake cheerfully identifies him with the Jehovah of the Pentateuch, and also with Satan.   He is the God falsely worshipped by this world.

Another great character is Orc, the spirit of Youth and of Revolt. His name is an anagram of Cor ('heart').   He is the child of the Poet

(Los) and of Inspiration (Enitharmon).   He is crucified for a while by his own parents ; but eventually he breaks loose and directs the American and the French Revolutions.

There are many other characters, large numbers of whom appear for a moment only, and then are lost to sight forever.   Such are Tiriel, Thel, and Fuzon.   Others recur a number of times, but very obscurely.   It will be better to consider each of these as he or she appears.

It should now be clear that the great difficulty in interpreting Blake is not that he had a fixed system of symbols, but just the reverse.   Underneath his ideas are completely lucid.   Blake *never* falls into contradiction, however he may develop his theories.   He conceals his philosophy under the veil of poetry, which must be read as such.   A sympathetic intuition, not a glossary, must be our guide.   Blake's only divergence from the usage of all other poets is merely in the breadth of application of his symbols.   He went to the normal extreme in turning all Creation into a symbol of the Invisible.

His only fault lies in that he did not always remember that symbols may have different connotations to different people.   Why should not clouds be fructifiers ?   It is easy to extend the list of such questions.

In defence of Blake, we may state that none who wrote as he did are half so clear or so absorbing.   In how many households are the volumes of the Alchemists to be found ?   Nor is the comparison inapposite ; for Blake was actually the last of the Alchemists.   Jakob Böhme, one of his spiritual masters, threw off the pretence of dealing in an impossible chemistry, but nevertheless retained many of their symbols, for lack of better terms.   Blake followed Böhme's method of writing, but discarded the alchemical terms for new symbols of his own.[1]

However, there is no need to defend Blake ; he has uttered his own defence well enough.   He realized that his ideas were too valuable to be disregarded when the time came ; and since he could not live until that time, he probably took a savage delight in his own obscurities.   It is too late now to protest.   The treasure is there, and we must dig, lamenting meanwhile that Blake ever thought of saying :

> I must Create a System, or be enslav'd by another Man's.
> I will not Reason & Compare : my business is to Create.

---

[1] Since writing this passage I have had reason to change my own views as to the nature of true alchemy.   But I do not feel that this is the place to advance personal theories. I have left this and other portions of my text unchanged because, ever since Böhme, mystics have read alchemical books as mystical symbols, and so Blake apparently read them.   Therefore I have tried to refer to them as such, and to quote those passages which Blake may have thought mystically significant.

CHAPTER X

THE FIRST ESSAY ON BLINDNESS

This then is hypocrisy—not simply for a man to deceive others, knowing all the while that he is deceiving them, but to deceive himself and others at the same time.—J. H. NEWMAN : *Parochial Sermons*. i. 127.

TIRIEL was Blake's first Prophetic Book, yet it is by no means the simplest. Already his symbolism is deeply involved. Apparently he wrote it to please himself at a time when he was working hard to make a living by his other books ; and he felt rightly that he had complicated it beyond the intelligence of the public. Later, after he had given up all hope of appealing to his own generation, he may have considered engraving it when he was not occupied with his three epics ; but if he did consider it, he found his ideas had advanced too far, so the poem remained in manuscript until 1874, when W. M. Rossetti included it in the Aldine edition of Blake's poems.

Tiriel is Blake's best *story* (though it is somewhat pointless without the inner meaning). so Blake's commentators have generally expressed a doubt about its being a Prophetic Book at all. This opinion has been strengthened by the fact that the symbolism of *Tiriel*, being early, has not too much in common with the later books. But Blake imagined he had forestalled any such literal interpretations by concluding the poem with a frankly symbolic section (a trick repeated in *Thel*). The climax, being a direct growth from the esoteric meaning. should lead the thinker back to Blake's real thought.

Tiriel himself represents a very old religion, or way of thinking, which is about to die. Once he and his wife were the dominant powers in freeing the material world (the West) ; but as they grew old, their offspring (other sects, divided from them in body and in spirit) rebelled and took their place. So Tiriel, refusing to be subservient where he once ruled, prefers to wander, an outcast, though his vision is darkened. His wife, Myratana, dies at this moment, for she is his Inspiration. But the baleful influence of the religion itself does not die.

Tiriel, defined more closely, is the religion of hypocrisy that rules by power of the Curse. He can tolerate no other power but himself. He cast his brother Zazel out of the palace to wander ; he allowed his own children to live only because he expected them daily to be destroyed by fires from heaven or the torrents of the sea. Now it is too late ; they have become stronger than he. His vision has vanished, and his only remaining strength is the unreasoning curse.

So he wanders aimlessly, until he reaches the Vales of Har. Har represents degenerate poetry. He is degenerate, for he lives in a valley, though he is essentially a mountain (' Har ' in Hebrew means ' mountain '). His wife, Heva, is degenerate painting.[1] Only in such a state could the

---

[1] Blake of course had married poetry and painting. Later he allowed music to be a third means of conversing with Paradise.

arts receive Tiriel. They have entered a second childhood, ' playing with flowers and running after birds,' and singing in a cage. (Here the symbolism obtrudes a little too much ! Har in his cage represents, of course, poetry in the conventional metres which Blake was now casting off.)

To protect them is Mnetha, a woman aged but strong. From her skill in the weapons of war, and her position as the protectress of arts, plus the near-anagram of her name, we may assume that she is a Blakean transmogrification of Athena, goddess of Reason. Mnetha is zealous in watching her charges, but she does not understand them.

So Tiriel is received by Har and Heva. At first they are afraid of this strange Way-of-thinking ; but as soon as they see he is harmless, they welcome him. (Could anything be more scathing than this ?) Tiriel hypocritically realizes that in such a place it is best to conceal his true name (as all didacticism is apt to masquerade as poetry). He claims to come from the North, the spiritual region, though his rule had actually been only over the West, or the body and its sensations. Nor will he admit that he actually is a child of poetry himself, though all living things, especially all religions, are descendants of the Poetic Genius.[1]

Meanwhile they smile upon him, and give him food, which is new strength. But naturally Tiriel, being a tyrant, cannot be satisfied with such a habitation, however pleasant. No religion can be contented with the arts. Tiriel is self-driven to wander out into the forests of the errors of theory. But on the way he meets his mad brother Ijim, who represents the religion of the common people. Ijim is a religion of fear, thinking that all the terrible natural forces are God, or rather his brother Tiriel, who is the religion he mistakes for God. Therefore, seeing his brother dethroned, Ijim cannot understand the fall of omnipotence ; so he forces Tiriel back to the palace, where he intends to destroy this masquerader (as he thinks him) before the true ruler. In other words, the common people cry out against this change of thought in those whom they have been taught to respect as spiritual leaders, and force them—outwardly, at least—to accept the old error.

Ijim, though fortunately he does not know it, is the strongest of them all. No weapon can hurt him. All Tiriel's children cannot drive him away, much less answer his accusation. And he, seeing that his unthinkable treachery in the high places is true, cannot understand, nor act, but goes wandering himself in the secret forest, the desolate places of sterile thought.

Rejection of a religion does not kill its force ; and now the rejected force recoils. Tiriel pronounces his curse upon his offspring. (His sons represent the arts and sciences, his daughters the five senses.) His daughters protest bitterly ; but before morning four of them are dead (to the Infinite), while the fifth, Hela,[2] is left to guide Tiriel back to the Vales of Har. Of his sons, one hundred die ; thirty alone survive ' to wither.'

Tiriel now wishes Hela (Sex) to be reconciled with him, which can

[1] ' The Religions of all Nations are derived from each Nation's different reception of the Poetic Genius, which is everywhere call'd the Spirit of Prophecy.'—*All Religions are One*, Principle 5.
[2] Touch, or Sex. For the elaborate cross-references proving her identity and the significance of this whole episode, see the Commentary on line 236. Also see Chapter xv., *The Fifth Window*.

readily occur if she will only be obedient.   But it is not in her nature ;
she will lead her father to the Vales of Har only in the hope that there,
where truth and justice should be found, his curse will be returned upon
him.   Angered by her attitude, Tiriel pronounces a curse upon her also,
and at once her hair—the glory of womanhood (1 *Cor.* xi. 15)—is changed
into serpents.   Thus sex is cursed for rebelling against the established
religion.

In her agony Hela passes with her father through the forests of error
(to her, sexual aberrations and social evils) hoping that the tigers, or the
wrath of God, will destroy her.   But even God's wrath is terrified at her
cries of anguish ;   and Tiriel himself promises that the curse will be re-
mitted.

So at last the miserable couple reach the Vales of Har and Heva.
Tiriel now announces his true name, and finally realizing the mistake of
his anguished existence, he dies.   Error recognized expires of itself.

The age of experience is ended, but the rebirth is shown only by Tiriel's
death.

CHAPTER XI

THE PROBLEM OF DESCENT

Self is death and truth is life. The cleaving to self is a perpetual dying, while moving in the truth is partaking of Nirvana which is life everlasting. . . . There is a spirituality in all existence, and the very clay upon which we tread can be changed into children of truth.—BUDDHA.

MEANWHILE Thomas Taylor's mysticism, frigidly intellectual though it was, and his violent antibibliolatry were working in Blake's brain. Was it not likely that there might be spiritual truth in other books than the Bible ? Must we not respect the intelligence of such supermen as Pythagoras and Plato ? Could not their teachings be harmonized with those of the Gospels ? Is it not more logical to believe that we have always existed ? And in the Bible Blake no doubt came across texts like *Jeremiah* i. 5, *Wisdom of Solomon* viii. 20, *Mark* viii. 27-28, and *John* ix. 2, which would seem to indicate a belief in pre-existence. At any rate, Blake then accepted, once for all, the doctrine of the eternal existence of the soul, of its fall into the Sea of Generation, and its ultimate return to the Perfect World. And this drama is the basis of all the plots of all his future works.

Blake's first poem on the subject, *The Book of Thel*, was to be an allegory of the descent. It was to be veiled in the Platonic style, yet the climax should say strange things calculated to hint to the alert reader that 'more was meant than meets the eye.' The unfallen soul, Thel, was at first to appear merely as a maiden bewailing her coming death. This death from eternity would be the birth into this world, which Blake now assumed to be the lowest point in the universe ; and death here is the glorious rebirth so often promised.

For Socrates once said, in the *Gorgias* : ' And perhaps we are in reality dead. For I have heard from one of the wise that we are now dead, and that the body is our sepulchre.' And Philolaus of the fifth century B.C. also recorded : [1] ' The ancient theologists and priests testify that the soul is confined to the body through a certain punishment, and that it is buried in this body as in a sepulchre.'

Both Blake and the ancients admitted a redemption from this Hell : Blake, through the death of Jesus, which mercifully changes our own death into sleep ; and the ancients, through the initiations of their Mysteries. Virgil's famous ending of the 6th book of his *Aeneis* gives us a hint concerning the release, and a very Blakean hint. There are two gates ; Aeneas returns to the upper world *through the ivory gate of dreams* —that is, through his own imagination.

But Blake did not endorse the antique idea that we are incarnated as a punishment for some celestial sin. On the contrary, we fall simply through error. Blake denies vigorously elsewhere that there is anything

---

[1] Quoted by Clemens Alexandrinus, *Stromat*, iii.

to be gained by a Fall. Eternity is perfection ; to perfection we return, having gathered at the most some knowledge of the possibility of error. In the epic *Milton*, he shows us that poet descending to redeem his own errors and to sacrifice himself for his Emanation ; but ' this was never known before,' Blake warns us ; and elsewhere he laments ' that Man should . . . forget and return to the dark valley.' [1]

Thel, then, is a spirit not yet generated. She lives in the Innocence [2] of Eternity, and has still to learn of Experience by a descent into this world. Such a descent seems like Death to her, as it must seem to all dwellers in Eternity ; [3] and some premonition of this fate has come to her.

Therefore she wanders away from her sisters, to lament in solitude. She ponders over the evanescence of all things. Why is there such a thing as Death ? One by one, the Lily of the Valley, the Cloud, and the Clod of Clay answer her : the Cloud dies for the Flower, and the Flower for the Lamb. This is the Mystic Death, the sacrifice of oneself (one's Self) for another, at once the cause and the explanation of Life—Change—in the Universe.

Thel is somewhat comforted by this ; and the ' matron Clay ' invites Thel to enter into this world of ours to see her destiny, and then to return unharmed.

Thel accepts. She passes into this world through the northern gate of the imagination and sees the sorrows of all mortal dwellers. Finally she comes to her own ' grave-plot ' or body (Blake carries even so far his paradox of calling *death* what we call *life*) ; and from the flesh she hears a voice lamenting over the dangers and limitations of the senses. Suddenly terror comes upon her—the terror that lies in wait on any psychic threshold—and shaken with horror at the thought of descent into generation, she flies back to the realm of Eternity.

Blake found the Greek writers full of tempting symbols which appealed strongly to his poetic sense, and which might well reinforce the symbols he had already devised. Taylor made much of Porphyry's commentary *On the Cave of the Nymphs*, wherein were elaborate accounts of the Northern and Southern Gates. Through the Southern Gate the souls descend from Eternity ; through the Northern Gate they reascend after death. So Blake borrowed these Gates : knowing that when his source was discovered, the meaning of his poem should also be plain. For Thel is actually the Queen of Hell, Persephone, as yet free from the embrace of Dis. Her time approaches ; and a vague disquietude steals over her. Though she hardly knows it, she is being lured by the inaudible voice of Eros. She resents her fate ; beholds it in imagination ; and escapes for the time. But Blake does not assure us that she will escape forever. Should she ever yield to love, her fate is sealed.

> Nor can any consummate bliss without being Generated on Earth. [4]

Thus Blake, without knowing it as yet, had actually rewritten the first act of the Eleusinian Mysteries. It is curious (and perhaps only too human) that he should have attacked the Greeks so harshly and so

[1] *The Four Zoas*, viii. 567-568.   [2] Symbolized by her pastoral qualities.
[3] Cf. *Milton*, 12 : 14 : ' I go to Eternal Death.'
[4] *Jerusalem*, 86 : 42. See also *Jerusalem*, 69 : 30-31.

constantly, when he drew so much from them.   Everywhere we find the influence of Plato and Pythagoras.   But Blake no doubt felt justified, since he added both height and depth to the Greek breadth.   They lacked mysticism in the strict sense of the word.   They were mainly concerned with virtues and vices, misconceived the nature and place of poetry, had few prophets, and ignored God.   Blake used their symbols and systems at pleasure ; but invariably he transcended them.

The Book of Thel is generally and justly admired as one of Blake's best literary productions.[1]   It is the simplest and the loveliest of any of his Prophetic Books.   He wrote it when he was trying to reach the world through his writings, and he knew this was as appealing a long poem as he had ever written.   Therefore he simplified the symbolism as much as his conscience allowed,[2] and limited his decorations to literal illustration.

Yet even so, the book was commercially a flat failure ; and Blake, stubbornly setting his jaw, determined that since he was right, he would continue in the path he had chosen, unhampered henceforth by a public that would not read things it neither enjoyed nor understood.

As the second act of the drama of Persephone, Blake later wrote the *Visions of the Daughters of Albion*, which begins with the plucking of the fatal flower, and then reveals the state of woman in the Hell of this world. Thel has become Oothoon.

The third act, Persephone's redemption, was never written.

---

[1] Of course there are always those who disagree ; and Blake has had fully his share of ' common-sense ' critics who are impatient with anything they cannot understand.   Thus T. Sturge Moore (p. 200) asks : ' Is it not insipid ? '   Oswald Crawfurd (*New Quarterly Magazine*, 1874, p. 486) is the harshest : ' not very far from the confines of the namby-pamby . . . not in truth very different from the sort of mild goodliness of certain modern entertainers of simple youth.'   Cestre (p. 209) complains ' his vaticinations become incoherent ' ; and his fellow-countryman Milsand (*Littérature Anglaise*, p. 339) even finds the voice from the tomb to be ' the unbalanced note which announces coming madness ' ; but of the three Frenchmen, Berger, who ranks among the best Blake scholars, calls *Thel* ' one of the most beautiful elegies in the whole range of English poetry ' (p. 328), and the majority of critics echo him.

[2] In two copies (the Bodleian and that owned by Miss Amy Lowell) lines 126-127 are obliterated and painted over by Blake himself ; apparently an attempt to erase two innocent lines which might possibly have been thought offensive.

CHAPTER XII

THE UNFULFILLED PROPHECY

> The Earth has had her visitation.   Like to this
> She hath not known, save when the mounting waters
> Made of her orb one universal ocean,
> For now the Tree that grew in Paradise,
> The deadly Tree, that first gave Evil motion,
> And sent its poison through Earth's sons and daughters,
> Had struck again its root in every land ;
> And now its fruit was ripe—about to fall—
> And now a mighty Kingdom raised the hand,
> To pluck and eat.   Then from his throne step'd forth
> The King of Hell, and stood upon the Earth :
> But not—as once—upon the Earth to crawl—
> A nation's congregated form he took,
> Till, drunk with sin and blood, Earth to her centre shook.
> —Washington Allston.

At the end of the eighteenth century the French Revolution was the vortex of all European thought.   No political concept could remain unchanged in the dizzying whirl of those dangerous days.   The Radicals were especially delighted, since all their dreams seemed coming true at last.   Almost inevitably, Blake wrote an epic upon it, seven books long, which his friend, Johnson, promised to publish.   Johnson approved highly of that sort of thing.   In 1790 this same publisher had already brought out a poem in twelve books, with a similar title, *The Revolution*, which dealt, however, with the upheaval of 1688, when the Prince of Orange came to the English throne.   The moving spirits of the action were supernatural beings with such names as Japhetiel, Terzillia, and Ombruliel, their manifestations resembling those of traditional witchcraft.[1]

Perhaps this book suggested to Blake the idea that he could treat contemporary events in the same way.   His epic, *The French Revolution*, was to have appeared anonymously in the following year.   What happened to it, no one knows.   Not a copy has survived ; it was never reviewed ; nothing at all remains for us except the page-proofs of *Book the First*. These belonged to John Linnell, who showed them to Gilchrist, Swinburne, and William Rossetti.   Then they disappeared for some years, but were eventually recovered among Linnell's papers, and are now in the possession of Mr. Henry Huntington.   In 1913 this fragment was finally published by Sampson in the Oxford edition of Blake's *Poetical Works*.

The *Advertisement* stated : 'The remaining Books of this Poem are finished, and will be published in their Order.'   What became of them ? We can only conjecture.   Perhaps the growing danger to all Radicals

---

[1] See an account of this book in *The Monthly Review* for 1791 (vol. v. pp. 375-382) ; the Rev. William Pow being suggested as the author.   Blake certainly had nothing to do with it.

suggested discretion in publishing ; [1] moreover, Blake was about to lose all sympathy for the excesses of the French. We may be certain, at any rate, that events in France did not follow as Blake had forecast, so that the poet, through his only Prophecy (in *our* sense of the word), found himself in the position of Jonah when Nineveh was *not* destroyed.

Blake treated his subject with all the freedom of an epic poet. He compressed, magnified, and rearranged the action to suit himself. He simplified and idealized historical characters to represent aspects of humanity, rather than literal personalities ; and he created other characters at will. Indeed, in those times when press-reports were crowding in, contradicting each other day after day, it would have been impossible for any one to be strictly loyal to facts. As it is, Blake's poem remains among the most unbiassed of contemporary accounts which tried to do justice to both sides.

The *First Book* deals with the events from May to the middle of July, 1789, compressed into the action of a single day. The Commons are convening in the Hall of the Nation, ' like spirits of fire in the beautiful Porches of the Sun.' Meanwhile the King and his nobles are holding a separate meeting, greatly alarmed at the independent attitude of the Commons. The King, frankly incapable of controlling affairs, is racked by the memories of his glorious ancestors, but can suggest no remedy but self-obliteration. The Duke of Burgundy, however, is a sterner character :

Then the antientest Peer, Duke of Burgundy, rose from the Monarch's right hand, red as wines
From his mountains, an odour of war, like a ripe vineyard, rose from his garments,
And the chamber became as a clouded sky ; o'er the council he stretch'd his red limbs,
Cloth'd in flames of crimson, as a ripe vineyard stretches over sheaves of corn,
The fierce Duke hung over the council ; all around him croud, weeping in his burning robe,
A bright cloud of infant souls ; his words fall like purple autumn on the sheaves.[2]

The Duke represents the Intoxication of War—a favourite idea of Blake's, which reached its climax in the famous description of ' the Wine-Press of Los ' in the twenty-fourth plate of *Milton*. The Duke easily sways the King to approval of force, and at once Necker, the people's idol, is dismissed. The Archbishop of Paris (the Priest, as the promoter of War) confirms the King's attitude with a vision of the decadence of the Church's glory under democracy ; and he, too, calls for military law against the Assembly. In the midst of the excitement, the Abbé de Sieyès, representative of the National Assembly, is announced. The liberal spirit of Henry IV. at once sweeps into the council ; but the dukes of Bourbon, Bretagne, and Bourgogne draw their swords for war, and find but one man to stand against them : Orléans, ' generous as mountains.' Orléans's words are those of Blake : he denies that one class can really thrive at the expense of another, nor will he allow that any judgment should be made

---

[1] Cf. ' I have been commanded from Hell not to print this as it is what our Enemies wish.'—Watson Marginalia.

[2] I have quoted this one passage, for curiosity's sake, just as Johnson printed it, except for his use of long s's. Dr. Sampson's reprint corrects the spelling, punctuation, and the capitalizing in a way which clarifies Blake's meaning considerably.

without a sympathetic appreciation of the feelings and thoughts of others.

Can the fires of Nobility ever be quench'd, or the stars by a stormy night ?
Is the body diseas'd when the members are healthful ? can the man be bound in sorrow
Whose ev'ry function is fill'd with its fiery desire ? can the soul, whose brain and heart
Cast their rivers in equal tides thro' the great Paradise, languish because the feet,
Hands, head, bosom, and parts of love follow their high breathing joy ?
And can Nobles be bound when the people are free, or God weep when his children are happy ? . . .
But go, merciless man, enter into the infinite labyrinth of another's brain
Ere thou measure the circle that he shall run. Go, thou cold recluse, into the fires
Of another's high flaming rich bosom, and return unconsum'd, and write laws.
If thou canst not do this, doubt thy theories, learn to consider all men as thy equals,
Thy brethren, and not as thy foot or thy hand, unless thou first fearest to hurt them.

At this moment, Sieyès enters, and the spirit of Henri IV. departs, indignant at the opposition to Orléans. Sieyès, symbol of the people's ideals, describes the spiritual plight of France ' o'erclouded with power,' prophesies a sublime future, and ends his speech with an appeal for the withdrawal of the army from Paris, which is the necessary preliminary to the millennium.

Then the valleys of France shall cry to the soldier : ' Throw down thy sword and musket,
And run and embrace the meek peasant.' Her Nobles shall hear and shall weep, and put off
The red robe of terror, the crown of oppression, the shoes of contempt, and un-buckle
The girdle of war from the desolate earth. Then the Priest in his thund'rous cloud
Shall weep, bending to earth, embracing the valleys, and putting his hand to the plough,
Shall say : ' No more I curse thee ; but now I bless thee : no more in deadly black
Devour thy Labour ; nor lift up a cloud in thy heavens, O laborious plough.'

Naturally, this is not acceptable to the aristocracy. Burgundy answers with the King's refusal, saying that when the National Assembly can remove the Bastille by a command, then, and no sooner, will the King order the army to leave Paris.

But the moment when this contemptuous reply reaches the National Assembly, it defiantly votes for ' the removal of war ' ; Lafayette gives the command ; and the noise of the army's departure brings horror to the Louvre, while the morning rises.

Blake's deviations from the actual course of events are obvious and unimportant. In the first place, the army did not leave Paris until the 16th of July, two days after the Bastille had fallen : and then it went by the King's own command. Blake was evidently reserving the Fall of the Bastille for the *Second Book* ; since he had worked up to that event so carefully. Lines 19-51 describe the prison and its celebrated seven prisoners ; but Blake quite properly ignores the historical persons (who were unimportant forgers and the like), and symbolizes them as the seven high types of men subjected by the feudal condition of France. They are the poet, the prisoner of state, the religious radical, the person who denies the power of the State over the Church, the believer in free speech, the good man now become parasite, and the patriot. This passage, which is elaborated with much symbolic ingenuity, stands in a prominent place near the beginning; while the book ends with the Birnam-Wood-like defiance of Burgundy:

Seest thou yonder dark castle, that moated around, keeps this city of Paris in awe?
Go, command yonder tower, saying: 'Bastille, depart! and take thy shadowy
    course;
Overstep the dark river, thou terrible tower, and get thee up into the country ten
    miles,
And thou black southern prison, move along the dusky road to Versailles; there
Frown on the garden '—and, if it obey and depart, then the King will disband
This war-breathing army; but, if it refuse, let the Nation's Assembly thence learn
That this army of terrors, that prison of horrors, are the bands of the murmuring
    kingdom.

The unexpected fulfilment of this command must have followed.

A second important change in the actual facts was the creation of the Duke of Burgundy, to represent the Intoxication of War. The title really had been obsolete since 1761. To Blake, the suggestion of wine in the word 'Burgundy' was sufficient excuse for the introduction of this character, though he probably also had Charles the Bold in mind.

There are many other changes, which would interest only a pedant. Blake was entirely within his rights as an epic poet in modifying characters and events for a better presentation of the essential drama.

Since this work was not published until 1913, critics have had comparatively little to say about it. Their judgments divide into two opposed attitudes. On the one hand we have Swinburne, who calls it 'the only original work of its author worth little, or even nothing; consisting mainly of mere wind and splutter.' All the other English critics but one have dutifully followed Swinburne; the exception being Saintsbury, who, however, limits his approval to saying that he is 'utterly at a loss to understand how Mr. Swinburne, especially considering his general opinions at the time, could have thought it " mere wind and splutter." ' [1] Against the general English attitude is that of the French critic, Berger. He says: ' The poem, if complete, would rank among the most important of Blake's works. As it is, the first book is of the greatest interest. . . . In this work, as a whole, Blake had reached one of the highest summits of human poetry. He had accomplished what Victor Hugo was to plan on in his mind without having time to finish it: the legend of the Revolution, represented in his works only by a few chaotic and powerful fragments, mixing, as Blake does, visible and invisible things, and by the titles of unwritten poems. Like Victor Hugo, Blake could, at that moment, see in the development of mankind its historical and legendary aspects (Hugo, *Préface* to the *Légende des Siècles*). It was the latter that the imagination of both poets grasped most firmly, the "concentrated historical reality" which constitutes the epos of Man ' (pp. 330-337). In his enthusiasm, Berger also invokes for comparison Homer, Virgil, Carlyle, and Hardy.

[1] *Prosody*, iii. 23-25.

The truth, of course, lies between these two extremes. Blake's conception is a very high and difficult one. His intensely emotional theories of the salvation of man made the French Revolution seem (as it seemed to so many then) the climax of all history, the great initiation of European liberty. Ever since the original Fall from Innocence, man had steadily retrogressed into more and more complicated slaveries ; but now, at last, he had seen his degradation, and was victoriously casting off all his errors. Therefore the entire universe, invisible as well as visible, plays its part. The very landscape is affected : ' Sick the mountains ! and all their vineyards weep.' And when the army finally leaves Paris, presaging universal peace and the brotherhood of man : ' The bottoms of the world were open'd, and the graves of archangels unseal'd : The enormous dead lift up their pale fires and look over the rocky cliffs.'

Another mark of Blake's greatness of conception is that he practises the sympathy which Orléans preaches. Blame is laid nowhere ; the entire evil springs from the nature of man's mind and the whole course of history. This is the more surprising, since we know how Blake hated kings, warriors, and priests. Impotent Louis XVI. is what he is, because the sceptre has become ' too heavy for mortal grasp.' Burgundy's militarism is a real intoxication ; it has all the nobility and virile magnificence which could be desired. We cannot help sympathizing with his attitude, though we know he is wrong :

Shall this marble-built heaven become a clay cottage, this earth an oak stool, and
    these mowers
From the Atlantic mountains mow down all this great starry harvest of six thousand
    years ?
And shall Necker, the hind of Geneva, stretch out his crook'd sickle o'er fertile
    France,
Till our purple and crimson is faded to russet, and the kingdoms of earth bound in
    sheaves,
And the ancient forests of chivalry hewn, and the joys of the combat burnt for
    fuel ;
Till the power and dominion is rent from the pole, sword and sceptre from sun and
    moon,
The law and gospel from fire and air, and eternal reason and science
From the deep and the solid, and man lay his faded head down on the rock
Of eternity, where the eternal lion and eagle remain to devour ?

Only in the case of the Archbishop of Paris does Blake's wrath burst forth ; and then only for a moment, when the serpent is suggested. The Archbishop's speech puts his case quite fairly and even enthusiastically.

But there are two great faults with the poem, which prevent the execution from equalling the conception.

The first of these faults is the metre, which has already been discussed in Chapter VIII. It is an experiment of great interest, but an experiment not generally successful. Some of the lines are admirably cadenced, others are simply awkward. It is significant that Blake never used it again.

The other great fault lies in the poetic imagery. Blake packs every passage with mountains, fires, thunders, vineyards, fogs, and reptiles, until we cannot help being annoyed. They are the Ossianic imagery used to excess, but with a difference ; for Macpherson's imagery is purely atmospheric, while Blake's often passes over into symbolism. Over and over again Blake pours out some great image poised exquisitely between colour and meaning; then he falls into an enormous preciosity. The good and the bad alternate in the following lines :

He sat down : a damp cold pervaded the Nobles, and monsters of worlds unknown
Swam round them, watching to be delivered—when Aumont, whose chaos-born soul
Eternally wand'ring, a comet and swift-falling fire, pale enter'd the chamber.
Before the red Council he stood, like a man that returns from hollow graves.

The absurdity of the monsters, and the Ossianic adjective ' red,' are only intensified by the two fine images describing Aumont.

The chief offender among the images is the word ' cloud.' There are no less than thirty-six of them in the three hundred and six lines of the poem ! Blake attached no important and occult meaning to the word ; it means, quite simply, a focus of power—but not always even that. We have clouds of war, of Voltaire or Rousseau, clouds of wisdom, of power and dominion, of repose ; the cavalry is like clouds, the nobles sit round like clouds, and once Blake speaks excellently of ' the cloudy drum.' Eight years before, in the ballad *Gwin of Norway*, Blake had lapsed into the same overuse of the same word.

The French Revolution, then, is a very uneven work. Tremendous in conception, and containing several magnificent passages, it is spoiled by an unfortunate, if interesting, metre, and a flow of imagery which too often is careless and ill-advised. It never flags ; on the contrary, it suffers from too much badly-directed energy.

It remains unique among Blake's works in several ways. It was Blake's only ' prophecy,' in the accepted sense of the word ; it was the only Prophetic Book which even approached ordinary print ; it is Blake's most extended story, and hence his truest epic ; and (aside from some of the *Poetical Sketches*) it was his one attempt to set a historical scene with human characters ; and, what is perhaps strangest of all, it seems to have produced no illustrations or decorations of any sort.

CHAPTER XIII

THE GATES OF PARADISE

Ah ! luckless Babe, borne under cruell starre,
And in dead parents balefull ashes bred,
Full little weenest thou what sorrowes are
Left thee for porcion of thy livelyhed ;
Poore Orphane ! in the wide world scattered,
As budding braunch rent from the native tree,
And throwen forth, till it be withered :
Such is the state of men !

—Spenser : *Faerie Queene*, ii. ii. 2.

THE idea of expressing a sequence of thought by a series of pictures is not at all new. Many of the Alchemists tried it,[1] but Blake need have gone back no farther than to the *Divine Emblems* of Quarles (1635).

The Gates of Paradise was Blake's first attempt to outline in this way the spiritual life of man. It belongs to the stage of 'Experience,' for while Blake teaches that we will reach happiness, yet this happiness is in the world beyond, not this world ; and only by foreknowledge, to be gained by some vision, can we find contentment here. Later, of course, Blake discovered the secret of happiness here.

Yet he always was very fond of this book, since he issued it three times, adding the verses in the second version, and correcting them in the third. He undoubtedly felt that this book was true, in its limited way, and might comfort those unprepared for his later doctrines.

Above the title he added the words ' For Children,' by which he meant those whose vision was still undimmed by materialism.[2] In the second issue he changed these words to ' For the Sexes,' meaning those in this world of generation.

The *Prologue* repeats the familiar idea that the forgiveness of sins— *our* forgiveness of the sins of *others*—is the gate to happiness. This is against the desire of Satan, the Accuser. Jehovah wrote the stone table of law (always evil to Blake), then repented and hid this dead thing in the Mercy Seat of the sacred Ark.[3] Blake concludes—

O Christians ! Christians ! tell me Why
You rear it on your Altars high ?

After this *Prologue* follows the series of pictures.

Frontispiece. ' What is Man ? ' He is a baby in a chrysalis on a leaf. Here Blake uses the old Greek symbol of the body as a cocoon from which the soul (psyche) will be reborn as the butterfly. But Blake adds to the symbol. In the upper left-hand corner is a caterpillar feeding on a

[1] See the modern reprint of *The Hermetic Museum*, London, 1893.
[2] In a letter to Dr. Trusler (Aug. 23, 1799) Blake tells how children instinctively understood his Prophetic Books, which older people found incomprehensible.
[3] ' Man is the ark of God : the mercy seat is above. upon the ark ; cherubim guard it on either side : and in the midst is the holy law.'—Blake's Marginalia on Lavater.

leaf. This is a symbol of man in this world. It is a worm which feeds upon error (this vegetable world) and produces others like it.[1] This is a state of sorrow :

> The Catterpiller on the Leaf
> Reminds thee of thy Mother's Grief.[2]

To this plate Blake adds :

> The Sun's Light, when he unfolds it,
> Depends on the Organ that beholds it.

In other words, things are as they are perceived ; [3] man as a worm cannot perceive the true light.

1. 'I found him beneath a Tree.' Under a weeping willow, a woman pulls a child (as a mandrake) from the earth, while she holds another. Blake's explanation is :

> My Eternal Man set in Repose,
> The Female from his darkness rose ;
> And She found me beneath a Tree,
> A Mandrake, & in her Veil [4] hid me.

That is, when an inhabitant of Eternity falls into the sleep of this world [5] (as Adam slept in Eden) his Self is divided into two sexes (as Eve was created). The Female then gets the child beneath a tree (symbol of generation—our 'vegetative' body) ; and this child is excellently symbolized as a Mandrake, the vegetable which traditionally has sex, which springs from the degeneration of corpses, and which is plucked in anguish, endangering the life of the one who gathers it.[6]

So children are born, almost accidentally, as a result of the Fall. The child's life follows :

> Serpent Reasonings us entice
> Of Good & Evil, Virtue & Vice.

In Blake's early symbolism, the Serpent always means the materialistic priest, whose dogmatizings on right and wrong merely repeat the error of the Tree of Knowledge of Good and Evil (*Gen.* iii. 5).[7]

The mental struggles of the child are represented by the four elements.

2. Water. 'Thou Waterest him with Tears,' or

> Doubt Self-Jealous, Wat'ry folly.

3. Earth. 'He struggles into life.'

> Struggling thro Earth's Melancholy.

---

[1] The 179th water-colour of Young's *Night Thoughts* shows a whole plague of cater-pillar-babies devouring the last leaves of a tree.

[2] Cf. 'The sexes rose to work and weep' (*To Tirzah*). Blake repeats the caterpillar couplet in the *Auguries of Innocence*, and explains it in the 55th *Proverb of Hell*: 'As the catterpiller chooses the fairest leaves to lay her eggs on, so the priest lays his curse on the fairest joys.' In other words, the work of the sexes is a matter of sorrow, one which will not be repeated in Eternity, where the sexes disappear.

[3] Cf. the 8th *Proverb of Hell* : 'A fool sees not the same tree that a wise man sees.'

[4] The Mundane Shell, which will be discussed later in this chapter.

[5] Cf. *Jerusalem*, 99 : 3-4 : 'Into the Planetary Lives of Years, Months, Days, & Hours, reposing / And then Awaking into his Bosom in the Life of Immortality.'

[6] See Sir Thomas Browne's *Pseudodoxia*, Bk. II. ch. vi., for an account of the super-stitions about Mandrakes.

[7] Cf. H. C. R., Dec. 10, 1825: 'There is no use in education. I hold it wrong. It is the great sin. It is eating of the tree of knowledge of good and evil.'

4. Air. ' On Cloudy Doubts & Reasoning Cares,'[1] or

> Naked in Air, in Shame & Fear,

finally ending with inward revolt and agony, as—
5. Fire. ' That end in endless Strife,'[2] or

> Blind in Fire, with shield & spear,
> Two-horn'd Reasoning, Cloven Fiction,
> In Doubt, which is Self-contradiction,[3]
> A dark Hermaphrodite We stood—
> Rational Truth, Root of Evil & Good.[4]
> Round me [5] flew the Flaming Sword ;
> Round her [6] snowy Whirlwinds roar'd,
> Freezing her Veil, the Mundane Shell.[7]

6. ' At length for hatching ripe he breaks the shell.'[8] At last the child becomes a man ; the coming of sex being a new birth of the personality.

> I rent the Veil where the Dead dwell :
> When weary Man enters his Cave,
> He meets his Saviour in the grave.
> Some find a Female Garment there,
> And some a Male, woven with care ;
> Lest the Sexual Garments sweet
> Should grow a devouring Winding-sheet.

In the cave, or grave, which is this body, the sexes are formed, that desires may be gratified ; otherwise the stagnation of death would overcome us, and we should be doomed forever to the flesh. The use of sex in reaching Eternity was an important matter with Blake, discussed in the chapter on *The Fifth Window*. Here, too, in the grave of the flesh, the Saviour descends ; and by his power—the Imagination—we can rend the veil, or break this Mundane Shell.

7. ' Alas ! ' But sex can be abused. In the garden of love a youth chases a fairy—a natural joy—with his hat, disregarding the one he has already killed. ' What are these ? the Female Martyr. Is She also the Divine Image ? '

> One Dies ! Alas ! the Living & Dead !
> One is slain & One is fled.

8. ' My Son ! My Son ! ' Yet for all his sins, the youth is cruel towards the sins of age. He condemns his parents by their own moral

---

[1] Cf. ' While clouds of doubt bewilder the true sky ' (T. L. Beddoes, *Romance of the Lily*). This is a repetition of this same symbol, but not a plagiarism, for there is no reason to imagine that Beddoes knew of Blake.

[2] The four lines in quotation marks describing the Elements compose a quatrain.

[3] Cf. ' Reasoning upon its own dark fiction / In doubt which is self-contradiction.'— *The Everlasting Gospel*, 95-96.

[4] The state of dominant Reason, unilluminated by Imagination, is a state of error.

[5] The Male restrained.   [6] The Female restrained.

[7] The Mundane Shell, this hard coating of matter which separates us from Eternity, is a symbol often repeated in the water-colours to Young's *Night Thoughts*. Design 142, for example, shows the Saviour weeping over it.

[8] This is repeated in Young's *Night Thoughts*, design 16: ' We burst the Shell / Yon ambient, azure shell, and spring to Life ' (Night 1, 131-132), and even more closely in design 13.

laws. He is seen rushing past his father, threatening him with a dart.
The old man, though sword in hand, averts his head.

> In Vain-glory hatcht & nurst,
> By double Spectres, Self-Accurst,
> My Son ! my Son ! thou treatest me
> But as I have instructed thee.

9. ' I want ! I want ! ' Nothing seems too high for the youth. He
now tries to climb to the moon by a ladder through space, while two
lovers watch him.[1]

> On the shadows of the Moon,
> Climbing thro Night's highest noon.

10. ' Help ! Help ! ' The result of pursuing shadows and false light
is obvious ; the man falls into the Ocean of Materialism, and meets his
spiritual death.

> In Time's Ocean falling, drownd.

11. ' Perceptive Organs closed, their Objects close.' As the result of
his materialistic life, the man becomes ' Aged Ignorance.' Spectacles on
nose, for his eyes no longer perceive the Infinite in anything, he clips the
wings of those younger than himself.

> In Aged Ignorance profound,
> Holy & Cold, I clipd the Wings
> Of all Sublunary Things.

12. ' Does thy God, O Priest, take such vengeance as this ? ' In this
state he becomes dogmatic, or ' holy,' calling himself an authority on the
things to which he really is blind, and starving spiritually all who oppose
him. This plate represents Count Ugolino, his two sons, and two grand-
sons, starving to death in their dungeon.[2]

> And in depths of my Dungeons
> Closed the Father & Sons.

13. But ' Fear & Hope are—Vision.' By the death-bed of a friend
he sees the ascending soul of the corpse.[3] This is his spiritual rebirth, the
opening of his eyes to the transcendent.

> But when once I did descry
> The Immortal Man that cannot Die—

14. ' The Traveller hasteth in the Evening.' He looks forward with
eager confidence to his own death.[4]

> Thro evening shades I haste away
> To close the Labours of my Day.

---

[1] The Moon often represents ' Beulah,' the ideal marriage, to Blake, and this may
be the meaning here. At any rate, the man is trying to climb left foot first ; and the
left foot, according to traditional iconography (developed later by Blake) represents
material means. Naturally the man is doomed to failure, for spiritual aims are never
reached in this way.
[2] Dante's *Inferno*, xxxiii. 13 *seq.* Blake used this design again as plate 68 of his
Dante, with the addition of two weeping angels above.
[3] So Blake himself had his first illumination when he saw the soul of his beloved brother
Robert rise from the death-bed, clapping its hands for joy at the release.
[4] This idea is repeated in the *Night Thoughts*, design 113 (Night IV, 19-20).

15. ' Death's Door,' the design repeated in Blair's *Grave* and the 14th plate of Blake's own *America*.

> The Door of Death I open found.

16. ' I have said to the Worm : Thou art my mother & my sister.' [1] And the man, confident in his vision, now gladly casts off this body, leaving it to the worms.

> And the Worm Weaving in the Ground :
> Thou 'rt my Mother, from the Womb ;
> Wife, Sister, Daughter, to the Tomb ; [2]
> Weaving to Dreams the Sexual strife,
> And weeping over the Web of Life.

So the series of pictures ends. Following the pictures are two plates with the verses which here are quoted after each description of the plate. Those in quotation marks are under the pictures themselves.

At the end is an *Epilogue*. A man dreams of a demon whose wings contain the luminaries. The poem is dedicated ' To the Accuser who is The God of this World,' *i.e.* to Satan.[3] Here Blake says that Satan is stupid, thinking to corrupt the soul through the body, when the essential personality can never be changed.[4] And though Satan is worshipped under divine names (being still the God of this World), yet, after all, he is only ' the lost Traveller's Dream under the Hill,' or the mistaken ideals of those still wandering in the wilderness of life ; and at best, in spite of himself, he is Lucifer, the Son of Morn, who heralds the coming of the Sun, the true light, in which he, and the mundane shell with him, will fly away and disappear forever.

[1] *Job* xvii. 14.

[2] All feminine : a part, but a minor part, of man, existing only from birth to death, from womb to tomb. The body is feminine to the soul, which in turn is feminine toward God (as in the last plates of *The Four Zoas, Milton,* and *Jerusalem,* also throughout Blair's *Grave*). This couplet was evidently inspired by *Romeo and Juliet,* II. iii. 9-10 :

> The earth that 's nature's mother is her tomb ;
> What is her burying grave, that is her womb.

[3] Cf. ' Satan . . . who is the God of this World, the Accuser. Let his Judgment be Forgiveness that he may be consumed on his own Throne.'—Blake's Marginalia on page 3 of *The Lord's Prayer,* by Dr. R. J. Thornton, 1827.

[4] ' Every Harlot was a Virgin once, / Nor canst thou ever change Kate into Nan.' Kate, of course, was the name of Blake's own wife. Cf. *Jerusalem,* 61 : 52 : ' Every harlot was once a Virgin : every Criminal an Infant Love.'

CHAPTER XIV

THE NEW SYNTHESIS

'Heaven and Hell are born together.'
—BLAKE's Marginalia to Swedenborg.

SWINBURNE called *The Marriage of Heaven and Hell* 'the greatest of all Blake's works ; and . . . about the greatest produced by the eighteenth century in the line of high poetry and spiritual speculation.'[1] Perhaps more has been written, and will be written, upon this small volume of twenty-four engraved pages than upon any other of Blake's Prophetic Books.

Yet it is really little more than a scrap-book of Blake's philosophy, containing, as it does, metaphysical outlines, literary criticism, revolutionary proverbs, and several fantastic anecdotes of symbolic vision. The only fundamental unity in the book is that of the author's coherence of doctrine.

Curiously enough, it is this same fragmentary character which has placed *The Marriage* so high among Blake's works. He states so very little in comparison to what he suggests that the reader readily responds, passing over for future elucidation whatever is not immediately understood. Each sentence seems to give the mind a push, and then leave it moving. In the later, more complex works, Blake's elaborate system of metaphysics must be grasped to a certain extent before the reader can be freely stimulated. Blake's thought then imposes itself, and will not allow the individual to deviate from it. He must guess and flounder until he finds Blake's solution. But this is not necessary with *The Marriage*.

This book marks a new epoch in Blake's life. He begins it with the statement that now 'a new heaven is begun, and . . . the Eternal Hell revives'; and it is perfectly obvious that at last he has emerged from the state of 'Experience' into a clearer world. His concepts of life are rapidly crystallizing into satisfactory if fantastic doctrines ; and he is dancing with enormous delight at the spectacle.

The particular influence from which Blake was struggling was that of Swedenborg. Brought up in a household which had accepted the Swede's dream of the New Jerusalem, Blake and his wife, as late as 1789, had been among the founders of the Great Eastcheap Swedenborgian Society. But now Blake had become convinced that Swedenborg, for all his visions, had relied too much on the appeal to Reason, and therefore had repeated all the old errors, and added not a single truth to the wisdom of the centuries. He had rejected Hell without comprehending it. As a result, his writings were a recapitulation of all superficial opinions, the Contents or Index of already published books, stopping with a mere analysis of the more sublime. At the same time, he was as much above the churches as a man above

---

[1] All the other critics, with two exceptions, have enthusiastically repeated Swinburne's opinion. The schismatics are W. W. Ireland (*Through the Ivory Gate*, 1889), who was interested mainly in Blake's 'insanity' ; and J. L. Robertson (*History of English Literature*, 1894), who had the amazing ignorance to write that this extraordinary volume remains only a name.'

a monkey ; and in his writings were preserved the secret of vision during the materialistic age.

What particularly impressed Blake was that Swedenborg had announced a new spiritual dispensation beginning in 1757. That was the year of Blake's birth ; so he appropriated the statement as applying to his own divine mission. It is not likely that he applied it very seriously, however.

Blake's philosophy, as it had now developed, is that Poetry (Imagination) is the father of all great thought, and Reason is its limiter. Reason has petrified Man's instinctive life into an arbitrary code of false moral values, known as Good and Evil. The great mind rejects these, for he sees that Good is only the established conventions of life, and Evil the energy working without regard to those conventions. All the greatest men, including Jesus and Milton, have been Evil in this meaning of the word. These men act according to their own impulses, ignoring all established laws of morality ; for all such generalized laws are oppression, since each man is an individual. They follow every instinct to the most complete form of self-expression, lest they breed reptiles of the brain. No extreme should be avoided. Excess leads to wisdom ; the folly of one generation is the wisdom of the next.

All men, however, are not capable of such a life. There are two great classes of mankind, the wise men and the fools. These latter are exalted and considered wise, for the sake of disciplining their superiors and of receiving the excess of vision—the paintings and writings—which overflow from the great. Several of Blake's *Memorable Fancies* are dialogues between the Angels (the fools) and the Devils (the wise).

Blake also attacked current religious thought. God is neither a remote deity nor a pantheistic manifestation. He acts and exists, but only in men. His prophets are poets pure and simple, who have the courage to take their imaginings as truths. Real worship consists in honouring God's gifts in such men, each according to his genius, and loving the greatest men best : those who envy or calumniate great men hate God ; for there is no other God. But Blake does not identify God with Man ; God is simply immanent in humanity.

As the true dualism of Eternity is not that of Good and Evil, but of Wisdom and Folly, so the true analysis of Man is not that of Soul and Body, but of Energy and Reason. The body is nothing but a part of the soul—that outward part perceived by the five senses. However, it is degraded in this age, and has become like a cave in which man is shut off from the pure light of Eternity. This fall took place when the original leader of the heavenly hosts, Desire (*i.e.* Satan, or Lucifer), was dethroned by Reason. But in his fall he 'formed a Heaven of what he stole from the Abyss.' The salvation of all men (a salvation which the wise already enjoy in part) is the dethronement of the usurper Reason by the purification of the senses until the infinite is perceived in everything. Eventually the whole material world will be destroyed by this process, and the reign of the true God, Imagination, will begin.

In the phrasing of Blake this sounds like a very revolutionary heresy, but in reality it reduces itself to the most catholic doctrine that Faith should dominate Reason. And in truth, Reason can only work upon axioms which no man can prove, and which he accepts and believes without possibility of demonstration.

The Marriage of Heaven and Hell can be divided into certain sections. The passages up to the first *Memorable Fancy* form a unit which develops Blake's theory of Contraries (Restraint *v.* Energy, or ' Good ' *v.* ' Evil '). Then come the *Proverbs of Hell.* Plates XI-XV relate the birth and growth of Formal Religion, the nature of the True God and Vision, and the salvation of man, ending with a description of the Genius's psychology. Plates XVI-XVII revert to the nature of God and the two classes of mankind ; this is followed by the fourth *Memorable Fancy*, which tells of a futile argument on religion between representatives of the two classes. Plate XXI breaks away to attack Swedenborg. *The Marriage* ends with the fifth *Memorable Fancy,* which, over the plot of the conversion of an Angel to Hell, describes the true worship of God and the revolutionary character of the historical Jesus.

It is obvious that these dogmas weave themselves into a coherent system, yet the arrangement of the plates themselves is quite unsystematic, and capable of much alteration—which, in fact, Blake performed in a few cases.

However, let us consider them, plate by plate.

Skipping the first plate, which is the title-page, we come to plate II, *The Argument*, which, if we exclude the ' prose ' in the *Poetical Sketches*, just misses being the first piece of Free Verse in English.[1] It describes the usurpation of the Just Man's Eden by the hypocrite.

Once the Just Man in meekness followed the ' perilous path,' the way of true holiness, through this world, the ' vale of death ' ; and in all the barren places of Nature the beauties of Eternity appeared. The roses of love bloomed, and the bees of liberated instinct gathered the essence of their sweetness. Every cliff and tomb—every high, hard aspect of matter and every pronouncement of the mighty dead—became sources of the Waters of Life ; and the skeleton to which man had shrunk in his Fall was clad in living flesh. It was the Garden of Eden, the Earthly Paradise.[2]

Then the serpent entered, the hypocritical imitator of the Just Man's ways. Liberty became misinterpreted and burlesqued into arbitrary codes of morality, until the Just Man was oppressed and driven from his rightful path into the wilds where the lions (guardians of the Lamb) roam aimlessly. For the hypocrite pretended to mild humility, making the Just Man rage in self-protection and appear different from what he really was.

So Wrath, materializing as the storm of Revolution, hangs heavily over the world.

The only ambiguity in this beautiful poem comes from Blake's mixture of tenses.

Plates III-VI (up to the first *Memorable Fancy*), as we have seen, are a unit in themselves. Plate III announces the present redemption of the outcast Just Man to the new Heaven and Hell, which is brought about by Blake's doctrine of the synthesis of contraries and the rejection of good and evil. The branding of evil was in itself the cause of the Fall, the story of which is told from two opposing points of view (which agree in all essentials) in *Paradise Lost* and the *Book of Job*. Various prophecies are recalled as proof that the regeneration was to be expected. The revival

[1] Thomas Traherne's *Serious and Pathetical Contemplation of the Mercies of God* (1699) contains some *vers libres* imitations of the Psalms.
[2] Blake always represented the Fall as beginning long before creation with the fall of Lucifer. In this he was following Jakob Böhme.

of the Eternal Hell is this regeneration itself, for it is the freeing of all the great forces in man. From the strife of this Hell with the established Heaven spring the false moral values which the religious call Good and Evil. Good is really a passive quality which obeys Reason, and which produces an inferior, negative mode of living. Evil is the active, the aggressive, springing from Energy, and is not Bad at all, but rather the exact contrary. It is the highest mode of life, and seems bad only to weak inferiors, since it acts without regard for established laws of society. Heaven, therefore, is the abode of the fearful and conventional people, who live in the state of Reason. Hell is the abode of geniuses who move among the flames of poetic creation, living in the state of Intuition. Angels and devils throughout this book are therefore the Bourgeois and the Artists (using those terms in their broadest sense).

Then Blake, on the strength of his doctrine of Intuition, rejects all established beliefs to set up his own.

The first error to be destroyed is the doctrine that man's soul and his body are separate things. Blake contradicts this, claiming that the Body is only that outward portion of the soul which is perceived by the five senses.

The second error is that Evil (Energy) is the product of the body only ; and that Good (Reason) is of the Soul only. Blake's contradiction is that Energy is the only life, spiritual as well as physical, and Reason is merely its restrainer (circumference).

The third error is that Eternal Punishment awaits the man who gives himself up to the intuitive life. On the contrary, this is not torture, but Eternal Delight, the true Paradise itself.

The two remaining plates of this section (v-vi) deal with Reason as the cause of the Fall, by limiting man's eternal life. Self-restraint is weakness of desire, not strength of will ; and in such a case, the restrainer Reason usurps Desire and governs the unwilling. The process ends by Desire's becoming passive, only the shadow of itself. Blake then compares the treatments of this doctrine as it is symbolized in *Paradise Lost* and *Job*. The non-mystical Milton tells the story truthfully, but upside down ; for, though a defender of Reason, he was a true poet, and ' of the Devil's Party without knowing it.' Milton merely misplaced his adoration, taking the true God for Satan. For in his epic ' the Father is Destiny, the Son a Ratio of the five senses,' while the Holy Ghost never appears at all ! On the other hand, the original commander of the Heavenly Host is called the Devil or Satan, though, as every one knows, he is the true hero of the book.

This is not whimsical quibbling at all ; it is excellent criticism. Shelley wrote later to precisely the same purpose : ' Milton's Devil as a moral being is as far superior to his God as one, who perseveres in some purpose which he has conceived to be excellent in spite of adversity and torture, is to one who in the cold security of undoubted triumph inflicts the most horrible revenge upon his enemy, not from any mistaken notion of in- ducing him to repent of a perseverance in enmity, but with the alleged design of exasperating him to deserve new torments.' [1] Blake went even farther, for he remarked that the same spiritual attitude which Milton called the Messiah is recognized in the *Book of Job* as Satan, the Accuser.

---

[1] *Defence of Poetry.*

Plates VII-X contain the *Proverbs of Hell*, which are short aphorisms varying from pithy maxims of common-sense to gnomic epigrams and paradoxes of the highest order. They were inspired no doubt by the *Aphorisms* of Lavater and Fuseli, and possibly by Poor Richard's *Almanacks* and Bishop Hall's *Meditations*; but the difference is tremendous. Lavater's *Aphorisms on Man* (dedicated to Blake's friend, Henry Fuseli, Zürich, Oct. 13, 1787) are mild, shrewd sentences consigning true Christians to Heaven and condemning the intemperate in thought or action as vipers to be stamped upon. Blake reacted very violently from Lavater's insistence on the conventional virtues of moderation, humility, and self-denial ; nor could the book's complete lack of mysticism and poetry have been soothing. Yet its sincerity outweighed these faults ; and Blake wrote at the end of his copy : ' I say that this Book is written by consultation with Good Spirits, because it is Good.'

Blake used the stimulating form of these apothegms to teach his own doctrines, which were radically different in feeling and thought. Even when Lavater allows himself to make such a moral overstatement as : ' 456. An Insult offered to a respectable character were often less pardonable than a precipitate murder,' Blake outpasses this rather surprising statement with a note of real passion : ' Sooner murder an infant in its cradle than nurse unacted desires.' The difference is amusing : we cannot imagine Lavater either insulting respectable characters or committing precipitate murders ; and while we should doubt Blake's capability of infanticide, yet *The Marriage* would seem to put ' unacted desires ' beyond Blake's possibilities. Blake was a Revolutionist, Lavater was not. Therefore Blake casts over all Lavater's moral virtues as entirely wrong, preaching in their stead protests against oppression spiritual and physical, exhortations to the completest self-expression, and contempt for the unworthy. He iterates the Truth of the Imagination, the sanctity of every form of life, the wisdom of folly, and the danger of restraint.

We must remember, however, that Blake praised excess not for itself, but because it led to wisdom. ' Too much ' is only the second choice, after ' Enough.' In *The Four Zoas* he insisted still more strongly on the essential balance of life :

> If Gods combine against Man, setting their dominion above
> The Human Form Divine, Thrown down from their high Station
> In the Eternal heavens of Human Imagination, buried beneath
> In dark Oblivion, with incessant pangs, ages on ages,
> In enmity & war first weaken'd, then in stern repentance
> They must renew their brightness, & their disorganiz'd functions
> Again reorganize, till they resume the image of the human,
> Cooperating in the bliss of Man, obeying his Will,
> Servants to the infinite & Eternal of the Human form.[1]

Plate XI gives a history of anthropomorphic religion. The ancient poets, with their ' enlarged ' senses—ours being narrowed at present—perceived the character of each natural object ; [2] to these characters they gave names, although such characters obviously existed only as human perceptions. The characters became deities ; a system arose ; and finally the priesthood abstracted these ' Mental Deities ' from their objects, ' choosing forms of worship from poetic tales. And at length they

---

[1] *The Four Zoas*, ix. 364-372.   [2] *I.e.* its ' spiritual form.'

pronounc'd that the Gods had order'd such things. Thus men **forgot** that All Deities reside in the Human Breast.' Nor is Jesus an exception to this rule.

Plates XII–XIII. The second *Memorable Fancy* develops this theory of Deity in much the same words of the tractate *All Religions are One*. God is the Imagination, or the Poetic Genius ; from this First Principle all other Gods were derived—as Blake had already demonstrated in the preceding plate. By a capable imagination or a 'firm perswasion,' anything can be performed, in confirmation of which Blake refers to *Matthew* xvii. 20 : ' . . . If ye have faith as a grain of mustard-seed, ye shall say unto this mountain, Remove hence to yonder place, and it shall remove ; and nothing shall be impossible unto you.' The Jews always believed that all nations would at last be subject to them ; which, like all firm persuasions, is come to pass : 'for all nations believe the Jews' code and worship the Jews' God, and what greater subjection can be ? '

' I know what is true by internal conviction. A doctrine is told me—my heart says it must be true,' Blake told Crabb Robinson on December 10, 1825 ; which means quite simply that poets work intuitively. God is Truth ; and such convictions are his voice : for in this way and no other, God (who resides in the human breast) reveals himself. The traditional idea of ' finite, organical ' apparitions is false. Imagination, and this alone, is truth. And having reached this point, we find that Blake has explained the astounding appearances of Isaiah and Ezekiel at his supper-table through the very words he makes them utter ; for they, too, were present only in Blake's imagination.[1]

The ages of imagination, however, are now past. People no longer discover the infinite in everything : ' many are not capable of a firm perswasion of anything.'

The *Memorable Fancy* ends with a defence of all eccentricity of conduct which may draw man's attention to truth. This little touch shows that Blake was already justifying himself on that point.

Plate XIV is concerned with the Resurrection of Man. Blake saw the fulfilment of an ancient prophecy in the American and French Revolutions; these uprisings were the flames which were to accompany the Advent and to destroy the material world, leaving all pure spirit.[2] This destruction was to be accomplished by the disarming of the Cherub (Reason) who till then had been keeping mankind from the Tree of Life (Love). Free indulgence in love was to open the senses ; such an opening would reveal the infinite in everything, and destroy the material world simply by exposing it as a delusion. Of course the body is not separate from the soul ; and as long as people separate the two, and degrade one to exalt the other, they only degrade both. The indulgence in love would lift the body from its material aspect, elevating the whole of man at the same time. Blake uses his own peculiar method of printing as a symbol of the process.

---

[1] The mere fact that Blake called these anecdotes *Fancies* should have warned many literalists of the nature of this dinner-party. General E. A. Hitchcock, on pp. 119–124 of his *Swedenborg, A Hermetic Philosopher* (N.Y., 1858), describes a face-to-face talk with the spirit of Swedenborg, intending to demonstrate his belief that Swedenborg's ' visions ' were merely a mode of presentation of imaginative experience. In short, Hitchcock interpreted Swedenborg's visions exactly as Blake interpreted his own, which leads us to believe that Blake's *Fancies* were not really satires on Swedenborg (as has often been asserted) but interpretations of their nature.

[2] Cf. the end of *America*.

The third *Memorable Fancy* (plate xv) describes under strange symbols 'the method in which knowledge is transmitted from generation to generation,' or, in simpler terms, the psychology of the Genius. The sexual instinct opens the senses; Reason limits them; but the poetic inspiration reveals the infinite; just wrath turns revelation into fluid form; unknown spiritual forces fix the result into concrete form; and finally the men who receive it contract it into book-form, and classify the books into libraries.

Plates XVI-XVII contain a disquisition on God and the two classes of mankind. The great spiritual forces which manifest themselves in nature, and which now seem to be controlled by the average man's will-power, are really controlled by cunning, not courage.[1] There result two kinds of 'being': the Prolific (Genius), who lives in harmony with these forces; and the Devourer (Reasonable Man), whose great function is to 'receive the Prolific's excess of delights.' Genius, in short, needs some form of appreciation, although its audience never realize how little of the original ecstasy is transmitted to it.

God, the Poetic Instinct, is 'the only Prolific'; but he simply 'Acts and Is in existing beings or Men.'[2] This is Blake's clearest statement of his doctrine of God. In the *Everlasting Gospel* he repeated it:

> Thou art a Man; God is no more;
> Thine own Humanity learn to adore.

The plate ends with a few terminal notes. Formal Religion endeavours to reconcile the two classes of Imaginative and Reasonable men; while Christ (as evidenced by *Matthew* x. 34 and xxv. 33) endeavoured to separate them. The Reasonable Man then is the Lost Soul! In the last sentence Blake identifies his Giants (Energies or Desires) with the Antediluvians (*Genesis* vi. 4) who perished in the Deluge of Time and Space. This Sea of Time and Space later is to become one of Blake's most expressive symbols.

The fourth *Memorable Fancy* (plates XVII-XX) is the longest and most delightful of them all. It is a fantastic account of Blake's argument on religion with an 'Angel,' a wholly conventional person.

The Angel, warning Blake that he is on the road to damnation, takes him through a stable (of the tamed 'horses of instruction'), a church (of restraint), its nether vault (of dead passion), to a mill (the unproductive processes of Reason). Thus they reach the Cave (man's brain); and in the roots of the trees (the principles of this 'vegetable' life) they hang over a monstrous void; Blake resting comfortably in the twisted roots of an oak (a living and stubborn error—he has come there only on false premises), while the Angel hangs in a fungus, 'the parasitic blind form of some formula in which he finds repose.'[3]

The Abyss is filled with the flames of wrath; a black sun shines (giving heat—wrath—but no light, or truth, one assumes[4]); and everywhere are black and white spiders who war upon each other over their miserable prey. Thus Blake reinterprets the old pictures of Last Judg-

[1] Cf. 'Those who restrain Desire, do so because theirs is weak enough to be restrained; and the restrainer or Reason usurps its place and governs the unwilling' (plate v).
[2] Blake does not say simply 'in Men' but 'in existing beings or Men,' thereby admitting all those 'uncreated,' like Thel and Rintrah. For God does not exist solely in this world.
[3] EY, ii. 72.
[4] Cf. the Commentary on *America*, 28.

ments, where we see angels and devils fighting for the souls of men. These forces of good and evil differ, of course, only in colour. Man, their prey, is 'sprung from corruption,' *i.e.* as a result of the Fall.

As the two watch this enormous combat, they see the Leviathan approaching dangerously near them from the East. The Leviathan [1] is the Serpent of Nature ; the East is the realm of the passions. The Angel, about to be lost by this domination of Materialism, is driven from dogma (the fungus) to argument (the mill) ; but Blake, having dislodged him, remains to confront Leviathan alone.

The Angel once having retreated, nothing remains of all this warfare but a moonlit [2] bank beside a river (the shrunken form of the Sea of Time and Space, where the Leviathan was bred), while a bard sings : ' The man who never alters his opinion is like standing water, and breeds reptiles of the mind '—the unaltered opinion being the established dogmas, and the reptile, Leviathan himself.

So Blake returns to the argument (mill), having proved, to himself at least, that where Conventionality sees ' torment and insanity,' Genius is unperturbed and thoroughly at home. Now he insists on showing the Angel the Blakean conception of Infinity. They fly westerly (towards freedom, that ' glorious clime ' where the true light dwells), and fling themselves directly into the sun (mental illumination). Purified (clothed in white), they take Swedenborg's books (the Baedekers of the spiritual world) and pass beyond the planets. Here, between these wandering luminaries and the fixed stars is man's present place, half-way between the Temporal and Eternal. Again they pass through the stable to the Church, and Blake, opening the Bible, shows the Angel the true aspect of Established Religion ; for the Seven Churches are only seven filthy monkey-houses, where the sexes prey upon each other. Here the skeleton of one devoured body turns out to be Aristotle's *Analytics*.

As might be imagined, the Angel departs in wrath at having been led so far, and Blake retorts that it is a waste of time to argue with one ' whose works are only Analytics.'

Plates XXI-XXII deal with all such Angels, who ' have the vanity to speak of themselves as the Only Wise. This they do with a confident insolence sprouting from systematic reasoning,' for they reject all vision as completely as the Angel in the foregoing *Memorable Fancy*.

Swedenborg himself, deceived by his superiority to the monkey-churches, thought he was discovering new truths, though, according to Blake, he had not written one new truth, nor even destroyed one old error. His works are ' only the Contents or Index of already publish'd books ' such as any man of mechanical talents may produce from Paracelsus, Böhme, Dante, or Shakspere. But these compilers only hold candles in the sunshine.

The fifth and last *Memorable Fancy* (plates XXII-XXIV) describes an Angel's conversion to Hell. The Devil repeats Blake's theory that God exists only in men, and extends it by saying that God is to be worshipped only by the honouring of his gifts in men ; while hatred of great men is hatred

---

[1] The Leviathan is a sea-beast, by which Blake was referring to this world as still drowned in the Deluge of the Sea of Time and Space. Hobbes's *Leviathan* furnished him with this symbol. In his political paintings of Pitt and Nelson; in *Jerusalem*, 91 : 38-39; and in the 15th Illustration to *Job*, Blake used both Behemoth and Leviathan to symbolize natural forces.

[2] *I.e.* not the true light, though a pleasant reflexion of it.

of God.[1] Then the Angel appeals to the orthodox conception of God as the Law-Giver ; but when the Devil explains that Jesus, who ' was all virtue, and acted from impulse, not from rules,' violated at least vicariously whatever of the Ten Commandments opposed him, the Angel is converted, his material aspect is consumed, and like Elijah, he rises into Eternal life as a Devil.

And with a final proverb against the tyranny of Law, the *Marriage of Heaven and Hell* is consummated.

This book is usually dated 1790, though there is no date upon the title-page. However, I am convinced that it belongs to a later year. It marks so obviously the beginning of a period of new religious insight, that if there be anything in psychological development, this book must be the first of the series which culminated in the Lambeth books. *Thel* obviously belongs to the period of ' Innocence ' ; it was a poem inspired by the memory of the ecstasy of youth. *Tiriel, The Gates of Paradise,* and even the *Visions of the Daughters of Albion* are of the period of ' Experience,' when Blake saw the world was wrong, and could only conjecture how to set it right. *The French Revolution* at least presaged the new light. Then, in a burst of clean-sweeping vision, there followed *The Marriage of Heaven and Hell, America,* and *Europe.*

This new illumination, however, was mainly a co-ordination and synthesis of ideas with which Blake had already been playing. The tractates *There is No Natural Religion* and *All Religions are One* had already formulated with more or less clearness his ideas of God and the mind of man ; and traces of other ideas are to be found in all the earlier Prophetic Books. But suddenly all these ideas fitted together, glowed with each other's light ; and Blake saw the distinct path to Salvation, along which he had been blindly groping.

And yet it seems that this scrap-book (for such it really is) was composed at intervals. Blake was working on it after he finished *The Gates of Paradise* and during the composition of the *Visions of the Daughters of Albion* (1793). He put no date on the title-page (the only book not so dated) because he began it at no definite time, and finished it fairly late. This theory is supported by an examination of the *MS. Book,* in which appear all the sketches for *The Gates of Paradise* and several for the *Visions of the Daughters of Albion* ; after which, on the 44th page, is to be found the spirited sketch for the Nebuchadnezzar (the last plate of *The Marriage*) with the enthusiastic inscription above it : ' Let a Man who has made a Drawing go on & on & he will produce a Picture or Painting but if he chooses to leave it before he has spoil'd it he will do a Better Thing.' So it is obvious from the *MS. Book* that *The Marriage* at least could not have been finished until 1793, whenever it was begun. The psychology of the book points to 1793 or later, for it not only is of the new temper which followed *The Gates of Paradise* (1793), but is advanced both in symbolism [2] and general philosophic concept beyond *The French*

---

[1] These lines are repeated almost verbatim in *Jerusalem,* 91 : 7-12. Cf. also Blake's account of Voltaire's apparition : ' I blasphemed the Son of Man, and it shall be forgiven me. But they (my enemies) blasphemed the Holy Ghost in me, and it shall not be forgiven them.'—H. C. R., Feb. 18, 1826.

[2] The symbols in *The French Revolution* are very confused and indefinite ; to none of them seems to be attached one definite meaning. See, for example, the many meanings of the cloud-symbol (Chapter XII.). Aside from the early symbols of mountains, plains, etc., and a few animals, there are practically none of Blake's own peculiar symbols, of which *The Marriage* is full.

Revolution (1792). Moreover, the *Song of Liberty*, which never appeared but as a final chorus to the book, is also subsequent to *The French Revolution* and is printed so in Dr. Sampson's edition.

Against my theory stands one fact, which I do not think important. Blake begins his text with the phrase : ' As a new heaven is begun, and it is now thirty-three years since its advent. . . .' This reference can only be to the date of Swedenborg's new dispensation (1757), especially since Swedenborg is mentioned in the very next sentence. 1757 was the date of Blake's birth. Thirty-three years, the third of a century, and the length of Christ's life, brings us to 1790, which consequently is the accepted date of *The Marriage*.

But the objection at once arises that Blake was too fond of round numbers such as these. Over and over again we find him frankly adding or subtracting years in order to make some date seem significant and memorable. He allowed it to be printed that all the *Poetical Sketches* were written before his twentieth year, which would date them 1777. Yet at least one of the poems was influenced by Chatterton's *Miscellanies* (June 1778). In the letter to Hayley of October 23, 1804, Blake talked of *exactly* twenty years of spiritual darkness, though he meant only nine. According to *Milton*, 3 : 17, that poet had been dead a century, which was thirty years too short. In *Europe* (1794) Enitharmon had slept 1800 years, although her sleep obviously had lasted only 1794 years. And finally, Blake makes any number of references to the 6000 years of the world's allotted existence, which was then ending.[1] Now according to the accepted tradition, the world was created in 4004 B.C., and as Blake referred most often to world's ending in A.D. 1804, we can see that he had anticipated the event by 192 years.

Since Blake falsified so many dates for literary effect, I fail to see how we can attach much importance to this one. An additional grain of evidence against the date 1790 comes from the fact that as late as 1789 Blake had been instrumental in formally founding the Great Eastcheap Society of Swedenborgians. It is difficult to believe that, in one short year, even he could swing from complete approval of the New Jerusalem doctrines into such an abrupt rejection of them.

Finally, no copy of *The Marriage of Heaven and Hell* is water-marked earlier than 1794. So on the whole I think it far safer to date it 1793, between the completion of *The Gates of Paradise* and the *Visions of the Daughters of Albion*.

A Song of Liberty

This brief poem is almost always found at the end of *The Marriage of Heaven and Hell*, and does not exist in a separate form. It introduces us to new characters, whose names we learn only from later books, and describes that part of the Fall which leads direct to Revolution and Regeneration.

After a few lines describing the ominous condition of Europe, Revolt is born of Inspiration, and immediately cast out by Reason. But his fall into the West (America) entails the fall of Reason into ' Urthona's dens ' (the lower part of the spirit). There the two opponents attack each other, and the terminal chorus anticipates the complete liberation of man.

[1] ' Six Thousand years are pass'd away. the end approaches fast.'—*Milton*, 22 : 55.

CHAPTER XV

THE FIFTH WINDOW

> The cherub with his flaming sword is hereby commanded to leave his guard
> at [the] tree of life, and when he does, the whole creation will be consumed and
> appear infinite and holy, whereas it now appears finite & corrupt.
> This will come to pass by an improvement of sensual enjoyment.
> —*The Marriage of Heaven and Hell*, plate 14.

No aspect of Blake's teaching has been so completely misunderstood as
his theory of the sexes. The boldness of his words has shocked most
commentators into an abrupt rejection of his attitude, while a few have
hailed with delight what they supposed was a justification of illicit ways.
Nobody seems to have guessed that a secret lay behind his frankness (for
Blake invariably holds something in reserve) ; and only a few have been
puzzled by the apparent inconsistency of his rash doctrines with his
exemplary life.

His attitude towards sex was determined not by any aberrations of
temperament, but by a search for the highest ideal, which became an
essential part of his philosophic system. When he attacked this greatest
of problems (whose terms remain practically unchanged to our own day),
he answered it as he answered all such problems : that the ideal is the
broadest possible freedom of thought and action which is consistent with
the happiness of all. This, however, is an ideal to be attained only in
the future.

But the problem went far deeper than matters of social deportment.
Sex, involving the profoundest instincts of man, is rooted in eternity ;
and the proper directing of it is a solution of more problems than the
ethical one. For this reason so many of his poems (*Ah ! Sunflower* and
Earth's Answer, for example) terminate unexpectedly with invocations to
love, which contain the concealed answer to the questions asked by the
first lines.

We cannot insist too strongly that Blake, one of the most pure-souled
of men, wrote as he did, not because he was over-erotic, but because he
was trying by the sheer power of thought to unknot the world's weightiest
enigma, and to place it definitely in the eternal harmony of the universe.
He was among the very first to celebrate the decency—the holiness—of
sex ; and his doctrine was sadly needed in the eighteenth century. Even
now there is a strong tendency to consider love as divided into two aspects,
one good and one bad, the spiritual and the physical. Blake recognized
both, called them both good, and insisted on their union. The physical
act, he claimed, was entirely clean ; while its spiritual results were greater
than any one imagined.

This emphasis on the spiritual at once distinguishes him from all those
who practise illicit ways for the sake of immediate satisfaction and
nothing more. That type was particularly common in his day, nor has it

vanished yet. Blake tolerated such people, but took pains to conceal from them what sex meant to him, mindful of the Saviour's injunction about pearls cast before swine. And he concealed his beliefs so well that never before have they been exposed.

In considering his theories of sex, the first thing to remember is that he was ideally married. Mrs. Blake was a wife of the Pauline and Miltonic type, one entirely submitted to her husband, as he in turn was submitted to his God. More than that, she could assist him actively in his work, doing the less important things like stitching the books, taking impresses, and even at times colouring some of the pages.[1] Blake taught her to cultivate her imagination : and both used to sit staring into the fire in which they saw figures. Gilchrist tells us that her visions were quite different from his.

Blake was more than profoundly grateful for this ideal wife, without whom he could never have devoted so much of his time to his own concerns ; he adored her with the whole force of his passionate nature.

As a consequence, he believed that such felicity as his was the right— and the *possible* right—of every living person.

He was not discouraged by the little consideration given marriage in his time. He was merely the more indignant that people did not think clearly about their own real happiness. In the aristocracy he saw vice at its very dullest. In the middle classes, marriages were apt to be business affairs, it being understood that the husband would seek his pleasure wherever he wished. But in the lower classes the conditions were indescribable. Prostitution flourished unchecked, spreading poverty and disease. Every one professed the most enlightened cynicism, and tolerated with indifference the miserable purlieus of popular vice.[2]

The idealizing thinkers of the times saw the dangers—the absurdities— of the situation. Blake's set of radicals centred about the publisher Johnson. There he met Godwin, Mary Wollstonecraft, Tom Paine, and others. They, too, agreed not only in condemning conditions as they were, but in planning better things, which they believed entirely possible.

It seems to be a law of human nature that the worse existing conditions become, the more radical and impracticable are the reactions of the thinkers. Whether the circle agreed in their theories cannot be said ; but Blake, for one, took very extreme views, which at least two others tried to put into practice. We shall hear of them later.

Believing that every man was entitled to the ideal union, and following his beloved Milton in condemning any marriage which might hinder such a union, Blake taught and wrote, as emphatically as he could, that couples should live together and separate at pleasure. Even a plurality of paramours was not to be condemned.

This is Free Love, nothing else. Blake believed it was justified by the Bible,[3] since it was allowed among the patriarchs. After hinting at it in many lyrics, he finally expressed his theory quite clearly in the

---

[1] Several copies of the *Night Thoughts* seem to have been coloured by her ; and I have seen a *Songs of Innocence and Experience* which Blake himself could never have coloured. But we must be careful not to use Blake's wife as his scapegoat.

[2] John Cleland, a minor poet, was driven by poverty to write the first purely erotic book in English, the *Memoirs of a Lady of Pleasure* (1747). which gives an exact enough picture of the times. Hogarth's *Harlot's Progress*, however, is more commonly met with.

[3] H. C. R., June 13, 1826.

Visions of the Daughters of Albion ; and as long as he wrote, he continued teaching the same theory.[1]

Yet he admitted that Free Love was not practical ! Mary, in the poem of that name, is rejected by her friends as a result of her frankness in avowing a passion. Oothoon, on the title-page of the *Visions of the Daughters of Albion*, is pictured fleeing over the Sea of Time and Space from spiky-flamed Retribution ; and in the text itself she suffers enormous tortures.

But this condition of suffering will not last forever, Blake declared with equal vehemence. When human society has reached a higher stage of development, then sins will be forgiven and not punished ; and mankind can profit by its mistakes, aiding and comforting all those who fall. Blake describes the ideal state in his discussion of Mary's Conception (*Jerusalem*, 61), where he accepts the theory that an unknown man was the father of Christ. Nothing, he felt, could be more beautiful or immaculate than Mary's spontaneous act. The only matter for regret was that she could not be permanently united to the man for whom she must have felt such love.

At this moment we may pertinently inquire what Blake's own experiences were in such matters.

There is absolutely no evidence of any sort (beyond his own theories) that he ever was unfaithful to his wife, or she to him. We do know that he deliberately shocked Crabb Robinson by upholding in theory a plurality of wives ; but since ' Thought is Act ' (*Matthew* v. 28), he also accused himself of many murders ! So we must understand such speeches as characteristic of Blake, but in no way true to fact. There is also a legend, for which no authority can be found,[2] which tells how he wished to introduce a concubine into his household, but that Mrs. Blake cried, so he gave up his project. This seems to be pure scandal—exactly the sort of anecdote which begins from just such indiscreet remarks as he made to Robinson.

But there is one poem which seems to be autobiographical. This is *William Bond* (Pickering MS.). ' William B—— ' is quite near ' William Blake,' and ' Bond ' is just the sort of punning name which Blake often used. However, William Bond's true love is not his wife, nor is her name ' Catherine B—— '; it is a fiancée named ' Mary Green.' In this poem the hero falls in love with another than his betrothed. The latter, seeing his distress, is willing to give him up ; and at the effort, she falls in a swoon, and is laid beside her sick lover. Thereupon, William suddenly discovers that as soon as all obstacles to the satisfaction of his impulses are removed, he has no more desire for the new inamorata ; so he returns to his generous betrothed.

Such is the evidence of Blake's domestic relations ; and neither history, legend, nor quasi-biographical poem (if it be so) tells of infidelity. So we may assume that he was blameless, according to our own ideals (which, incidentally, were not those of Blake's time).

But there was one person at least who tried to practise what Blake preached (though Blake should not be blamed for her conduct). This was his acquaintance, Mary Wollstonecraft. She had two or three liaisons, one in particular with Gilbert Imlay, and an attempt at one with Blake's

---

[1] *Milton*, 11 : 38 ; *Jerusalem*, 61. [2] Symons, p. 73 *seq.*

close friend, the painter Fuseli ; then finally she married William Godwin (against the principles of both) for the sake of an expected child. It is not incurious to learn that she died bringing forth this child, a girl also called Mary ; and that this child later married Shelley.

The unhappiness of Godwin's temperamental wife is so obvious that we can hardly begrudge her what little happiness she found. The account [1] of her attempt to enter Fuseli's household inspires one with vague amusement at her persecution of the irascible Swiss, and an equally vague pity for her dignified retreat when she found she was unwanted. Surely Blake pitied and forgave her ; and I think it was she who gave him the idea for his poem *Mary*.

Blake's ethical teachings on the subject of sex resolve, then, to this : that every one is entitled to the most ideal union which he or she can find ; that marriage should be no restriction ; indeed, that any restriction is very dangerous ; [2] and that such unions some day will be quite possible. What prevents their possibility now is the jealousy of the lover, the hypocrisy of the beloved, and the persecution of society. These, and not the sex-impulse, are the true crimes, the real causes of suffering.

It is hardly necessary to point out the fallacies of Blake's theories. Jealousy is a part of man's nature and cannot be cut away ; so, too, ' hypocrisy ' (or ' modesty,' as he was equally likely to call it) is a form of self-protection in such matters, and is as ineradicable as jealousy.

So we must be content to leave Blake's ideals—as he did—for a future age.

But sex had transcendent meanings to Blake which underlie all his social ideals, and which he was too shy, or too cautious, to expose as plainly. Whether he felt they were too sacred to be revealed, or whether he felt that they would not be understood, and therefore mocked, I cannot say. But it is certain that he held these theories, and hid them in his writings ; and until now they have never been explained.

They concern the world of Eternity, not the future of society.

The first important theory was that in Eternity the lover and loved are literally one (*Matthew* xxii. 30). The fall into this world was effected by a series of divisions, one of which separated the male and female. (So Blake interpreted *Genesis* ii. 21-24.[3]) Salvation consists in re-uniting these divisions ; therefore the rôle of Milton, in Blake's book of that name, is the effecting of his union with the ' six-fold Emanation ' of his wives and daughters. We also have Crabb Robinson's record of Blake's belief that the eternal man is ' a union of sexes in man as in Ovid, an androgynous state.' [4]

But even though in Eternity there is no sex, yet here in this world sex has a very important function. It not only keeps man's senses open, his imagination stirred, and his Selfhood in abeyance ; [5] *it is actually a way*

[1] John Knowles, *Life and Writings of Henry Fuseli* (London, 1831), vol. i. ch. vii.

[2] Lines 178-186 of the *Visions of the Daughters of Albion* attack even chastity as foul and unnatural.

[3] Cf. *Gates of Paradise, Keys* (1) : ' My Eternal Man set in Repose, / The Female from his darkness rose.'

[4] H. C. R., Dec. 17, 1825.

[5] Cf. *Gates of Paradise, Keys* (6) : ' Lest the Sexual Garments sweet / Should grow a devouring Winding-sheet,' *i.e.* lest man's body should keep him ' dead ' in this world forever.

into Eternity, the only way left open to the man who has no creative power in poetry, painting, or music !

> Five windows light the cavern'd Man : thro one he breathes the air ;
> Thro one hears music of the spheres ; thro one the eternal vine
> Flourishes, that he may recieve the grapes ; thro one can look
> And see small portions of the eternal world that ever groweth ;
> *Thro one himself pass out what time he please*, but he will not ;
> For stolen joys are sweet, & bread eaten in secret pleasant.
> —*Europe*, Introductory lines 1-6.

Here Blake, as usual, identifies Sex and the sense of Touch. All the other senses in their normal, eternal condition should produce just as much ecstasy ; but in their temporal condition they are dead, sepulchred in the flesh.

Another passage, parallel to the one just quoted,[1] enumerates the five senses, Touch bringing out the complaint :

> Why a little curtain of flesh on the bed of our desire ?

Tiriel also teaches that Sex or Touch is the last means of leading the blindest back to the Vale of poetry. The death of the four senses and the cursing of the fifth is represented not only in *Tiriel*, but in the 6th Illustration to *Job*. But the clearest of all Blake's statements is that from the *Marriage of Heaven and Hell* which heads this chapter.

The meaning is simple. Blake's Eternity was the world of the Poetic Imagination (which he also called the Bosom of God). It is here that everything appears ' infinite & holy.' And from this I may hazard certain assumptions.

I believe that Blake was not emphasizing the sexual act entirely for its own sake. I think he found that it also induced the proper mental state in which to write poetry or imagine pictures. The ideal conditions for this are a perfectly relaxed body and a stimulated mind. The trouble with drugs and alcohol is that they generally deaden the mind with the body. So I believe that Blake, in the dreamy post-coitional state, found an unusual effervescence of ideas ; and this was what he meant by passing into the World of the Poetic Imagination by the Fifth Window.

This seems to be the only possible explanation of the 38th plate of *Milton*. This is a full-page illustration. On the rocky shore just above the Sea of Time and Space lie a man and woman. Her head is upon his bosom ; he gazes upward at the descending Eagle of Genius unseen by her.

The division of lover and beloved is made by the man himself when he casts out whatever seems inconsistent or unworthy of himself. (So Urizen cast out Ahania.) In judging himself, therefore, he divides himself, forgetting that in God's eyes all is good. And he must be united with this ' emanation ' before his salvation is perfect. The sexual act alone can stimulate and unite the highest and lowest functions of man.

Blake symbolized the same theory in another way. The realm of Eternity is surrounded on all sides by the realm of Beulah (love).[2] Thus, to reach Eternity, a soul must pass through this place of his rejected aspects, and so be made whole. But to the Eternals, Beulah is ' a mild & pleasant rest ' from ' the great Wars of Eternity, in fury of Poetic Inspiration.'[3] That is : what is to man on earth his highest ecstasy is to man in heaven a relaxation, so much more intense is Eternal life.

---

[1] *Thel*, lines 122-127. [2] *Milton*, 30 : 33. [3] *Ibid.*, 30 : 14, 19.

Of course, all this is directly against the traditions of the 'classic' occultists, who teach unconditional chastity. The carnal and the spiritual to them are inevitably opposed, and only by rejecting the one can we make progress in the other. But Blake rejects nothing, 'for everything that lives is holy'; and what is more, he even denies their premise that the body is distinct from the soul.

Man has no Body distinct from his Soul; for that call'd Body is a portion of Soul discern'd by the five Senses, the chief inlets of Soul in this age.[1]

In its eternal, or spiritual form,[2] with the five senses triumphant,[3] the glorified body is an essential part of the Eternal Man. (Tharmas always is one of the four Zoas; and in eternity he has the place of honour, to the right of Urthona.[4])

But though Blake breaks with all the ordinary occultists, there are a few who hint at the same theories.

Hermes Trismegistus, one of the great sources of all occultism, says:

[The Earth's] loins are under the region of heaven . . . the midst of her body is beneath the centre of heaven;[5]

and again:

If the mind can perceive any one truth more certainly and more clearly than another, it is the duty of procreation, which God of Universal Nature has imposed forever upon all beings, and to which He has attached the *supremest charity*, joy, delight, longing, and *divinest love*.[6]

It has been observed that Dante, in symbolizing Purgatory as a mountain pointing toward the Rose of Heaven, changed the traditional Purgatory from a cave; he did this in all probability with some phallic symbolism in mind. His substitution of Beatrice for the Eucharist in the Earthly Paradise, however, should leave no doubt.

Cornelius Agrippa (1486-1535) followed Hermes in placing the human centre 'in imo pectinis,' illustrating it by various designs of nudes placed in geometrical figures.[7] His fourth type of 'Phrensie' is inspired by Venus (III. xlix.).

Robert Fludd (1574-1637) also did the same:

Mundi circularis centrum est terra; humana vero rotunditas punctum centrale est secundum quosdam in umbilico; sed nos potius illud circum genitalia ponendum esse putamus, si quidem ut in mundo centro semina rerum reconduntur, sic etiam juxta hominis testiculos delitescit virtus eius seminalis.[8]

He followed Agrippa in illustrating this by numerous diagrams in the same work (pp. 67, 105, 112, 114, 241, 242, 245, 275), also on page 321 of the *Tractatus Secundus: De Naturae Simia*; and, best of all, on the magnificent title-page of his *Utriusque Cosmi: Microcosmi Historia*. Such

[1] *Marriage of Heaven and Hell, The Voice of the Devil.*
[2] 1 *Cor.* xv. 44, quoted by Blake in the margin of *To Tirzah.*
[3] As in plate 15 of *Milton.*
[4] *Milton*, 32. What is Urthona's right is our left, as we face the picture.
[5] *Virgin of the World*, Pt. II.
[6] *Treatise on Initiations* (*Asclepios*, Pt. VIII.)
[7] *De Occulta Philosophia*, lib. ii. cap. 27.
[8] *Historia, De Supernaturali*, Tract I., sec. 1, lib. iii. cap. i. p. 66; also 'Mundi minoris centrum est genitalium seu pudendorum,' *ibid.*, I. l. v. iii. p. 102; and again: 'Quadrati centrum est pudendorum,' *ibid.*, p. 113.

insistence cannot be due to a dry, unprofitable parallelism between Nature and Man ; it surely conceals what Fludd thought was a very valuable theory.

Perhaps these people were influenced by the pattern of the Sephiroth, the Kabalistic Tree of Life. For the central pillar, 'Mildness,' which is not only the very trunk of the Tree, but also the only direct path to the summit, Kether (the Crown), is sexual. Its lowest point is in Malkuth (the Bride) ; above her is Yesod (the Phallos) ; higher yet is Tiphereth (the Beauty of Union) ; thence it passes straight in one leap to Kether. Love thus begins lower and reaches higher than the two outside pillars, 'Justice' and 'Mercy.'

But closest to Blake, both in time and spirit, was the exquisite Thomas Vaughan ('Eugenius Philalethes,' 1621-1665), who was, like Blake, a mystic and a happily married man ; so it may not be surprising that he stated Blake's own mystical doctrines of sex, though still more obscurely. He wrote :

> Matrimony is no ordinary triviall busines, but in a moderate sense *Sacramentall*. It is a visible signe of our invisible *Vnion* to *Christ*, which S. *Paul* calls a *Great mystery*, and if the thing signified be so Reverend, the *signature* is no *ex tempore*, contemptible Agend.

> He that knows why the Tree of Life is sayd to be in the middest of the Garden and to grow out of the Ground, will more fully understand that which we have spoken.[1]

Even the Victorian Coventry Patmore (1823-1896), another happily married man, wrote :

> The Tree of Knowledge is become, to the chosen, the Tree of Life : 'Under the Tree where thy mother was debauched I have redeemed thee.'[2]

It is perhaps noteworthy that Blake had read Hermes, Dante, Paracelsus, Agrippa, the *Kabalah*, and Vaughan.

But if Blake finds few parallels among the Occidentals, he is very much in accord with the Orientals. Buddha, for example, rejected asceticism early in his life. Many of the Hindus and Persians make no distinction between sacred and profane love, between the love of God and the sexual life. What Europeans have used only as a symbol, the Easterners have applied literally. Their books may be read from either point of view.[3] Indeed, the *Song of Solomon* in our own Bible does exactly this ; and the writings of John of the Cross is another case we may recall.[4]

Blake, however, neither confused nor identified sacred and sexual love. The one is a road to the other, no more ; in eternity it will vanish.

His sexual theories, then, were to be applied both socially and mystically. Let us add that only a very pure man, or a very corrupt one, could have taught this immense freedom. Whether or not we accept his ideals, we must at least respect them ; for our own age is slowly coming to recognize the purity on which he insisted so strongly.

---

[1] Both these quotations are from his *Anthroposophia Theomagica*.

[2] *Rod, Root, and Flower : Aurea Dicta*, xxiii.

[3] See, for example, the poems of Vidyapati, exquisitely translated by A. Sen and Coomaraswamy, London, 1915.

[4] See also H. Stanley Redgrove's *Bygone Beliefs* for his chapter on *The Phallic Element in Alchemical Doctrine*.

CHAPTER XVI

BLAKE'S MAGDALEN

All vice arose from the ruin of healthful innocence.
—SHELLEY: Note to *Queen Mab.*

IN no one place did Blake give a complete expression of his theory of the sexes ; he preferred to drop hints here and there, so that incompetent seekers and blandiloquent puritans might not defame the holiness of the subject. This was not due to cowardice, as we shall see ; for in the *Visions of the Daughters of Albion* he expressed, as boldly as any, his views of the social side of the question.

The great problem of this book is that Free Love, which is so fine as an ideal, is not practical. Why ? Blake gives three answers : society persecutes the fallen, because it does not understand that the soul cannot be defiled ; the individual man allows jealousy to interfere between himself and his true love ; while the woman is not frank, but hypocritical. All are wrong, and in a more enlightened age these errors will be recognized and cast out. Till then, mankind will be punished with horrible burlesques of marriage or with the tortures of an unnatural chastity.

It was Blake's strength (or weakness, if you will) that he refused to accept this world as it is. He understood it quite well, but preferred his own ideal. Yet it must be confessed that his own nature was somewhat too sublimated, too pure, to grapple directly with reality. He placed his finger accurately enough upon the morbid spots in social life, but his cure is not expedient. We can agree with him and with Whitman that 'if anything is sacred, the human body is sacred,'[1] and we can preach the honesty of passion ; then, when we come to apply our theories, we find that prejudice and hypocrisy are over-powerful enemies, and we succumb. Thus we play our parts in the tragedy of 'The Easiest Way' ; admiring Blake for his courage, while condemning him as a fool.

But the book has another and deeper meaning. Since *The Book of Thel* had been written, Thomas Taylor had been publishing many more translations from Plato and his followers, besides some of his own compositions as well. In 1792 he reprinted three earlier books, besides two other books of his own ; in 1793, no less than five volumes appeared. But most interesting of all was his exposure of the Greek Mysteries.[2] Bishop Warburton, in the first half of the century, had already devoted a section of his famous *Divine Legation of Moses Demonstrated* to the same problem ; but Taylor, furious at the bishop's anti-heathenism, found much to say in their defence. These secret dramas of the descent and ascent of the soul were no legislative schemes to keep the people under, but revelations of the occult salvation by the inner light ! And this myth

---

[1] Walt Whitman, *I Sing the Body Electric.*
[2] *A Dissertation on the Eleusinian and Bacchic Mysteries* (n.p., n.d.). A fictitious reprint gives the place as Amsterdam. The year was probably 1790.

of Proserpine's rape by Pluto to Hell, and her escape from thence by the aid of Bacchus, were no idle tales, but symbols of the drama of every soul.

Blake, poring over Taylor's volumes, realized at last that his *Book of Thel* was in fact the first act of the mystic drama of Proserpine. So he set himself to finish the play.

The *Visions of the Daughters of Albion* thus appears as the second act: Proserpine in Hell—or, the soul in this world. The plot is simple. Oothoon, Blake's Magdalen of Eternity, is violated by Bromion, though Theotormon is her true mate. Custom forces her to marry Bromion, since Theotormon, for all his anguish, will have none of her. Most of the book is filled with Oothoon's lamentations, giving forth the wisdom which she has learned from suffering. Meanwhile the 'daughters of Albion,' representative of oppressed womanhood, echo her sighs. Their rôle in this book is less than that of the Greek chorus; in *Jerusalem*, however, as the spirits of the body, they are far more active, rising from their oppression and torturing man in turn.

In his defence of free love, Blake was not hiding behind his natural obscure mode of writing; on the contrary, he was speaking as clearly as he could without insulting his aesthetic conscience. And indeed, his thesis was a common one among the radicals. Tom Paine himself wrote a pretty allegory, *Cupid and Hymen*, in which the Swain is Theotormon; Gothic is Bromion; and Ruralinda, Oothoon. Mary Wollstonecraft tried putting the theories into practice, not with the happiest of results; while the unteachable Shelley later continued the tradition.[1]

But Oothoon is also Proserpine descended into Hell. She is Thel, who has now plucked the symbolic flower. She has forgotten her divine origin, yet still responds to the voice of God within her. As she fell by love, so she must rise by love; ·but while on this earth, she is still tormented between the two forces, Desire and Reason.[2]

Reason soon condemns Oothoon's free delights as Sin, thus separating her from her beloved. She repeats Thel's cry: 'Why a little curtain of flesh on the bed of our desire?' and begins to call for a better state of affairs, since through her suffering she has learned the wisdom still hidden from Theotormon and Bromion. She had been taught that she was shut from Eternity by the flesh, but now she has discovered the Divine Voice within her. All animals must obey this voice, since they act differently according to their instincts, though they have in common the five senses which should teach them the same lessons. Is man to be less than the beasts, by limiting himself to 'natural morality' and ignoring the Divine Voice within him, which they obey? And this Voice, these instincts, are pure; love cannot defile itself.

Theotormon answers her with a cry of complete bewilderment: how can joys be found and sorrows avoided? What is thought, and what terrible results may it have?

Bromion also begins to see that there may be other joys and sorrows

---

[1] Views exactly parallel to Blake's are to be found in Shelley's note, 'Even love is sold,' on *Queen Mab*, v. 189.

[2] In the epics, Theotormon, Bromion, Rintrah, and Palamabron (Desire, Reason, Wrath, and Pity) are the four sons of Los who remain ungenerated: they are the four forces which the Poet directs in his struggle for the protection of Liberty.

than those of riches and poverty ; yet he returns stubbornly to his old error, that all should live under one law, with one standard.

Oothoon soon discovers this error and curses Bromion's God, Jehovah-Urizen, Reason, the prohibitor, author of the Decalogue, and ruler by the Curse. Men are not the same ; therefore each should live under his own law. Religion is an evil imposition, which binds her ' who burns with youth ' to the man she loathes. The children of such unions can only be monstrosities, yielding to early corruption. All Nature protests against such ' Natural Morality.' True purity knows nothing of hypo-critical ' modesty,' which curses all else and is a conscious trap for man. By it, chastity is imposed on every one : chastity, the direct cause of secret, miserable vice. Oothoon will countenance none of this ; her love shall be free of restraint, of jealousy, of concealment. The sun, which kills all evil things, shall shine upon her loves.

But Theotormon cannot hear her exhortations ; he is lost in the world of dangerous shadows created by his own jealousy and repression. Here the poem ends.

In this, the last of his books of Experience, Blake helped himself abundantly to the classical symbols. The Sea of Generation now appears as the Sea of Time and Space ; the plucking of the Flower is dwelt on extensively ; the Cave of Plato and the Eagles of Prometheus are intro-duced ; while Urizen, Jehovah, and the Demiurgos are identified.

It is hardly necessary to point out that the critics have been much exercised over this book, since they have found in it only what Blake did not care to hide. Some, such as Swinburne, Symons, and Berger, have respected Blake's strength and sincerity, without taking his views of sex any more seriously than as a manifestation of the times. Others have been appalled, even shocked, as though Byron and Shelley had not also written. J. J. G. Wilkinson was impressed mainly by the spiritual evil of the book : ' He embodies no Byronisms—none of the sentimen-talities of civilized vice, but delights to draw evil things and evil beings in their naked and final state. The effect of these delineations is greatly heightened by the antiquity which is engraven on the faces of those who do and suffer in them. We have the impression that we are looking down into the hells of the ancient people, the Anakim, the Nephilim, and the Rephaim. Their human forms are gigantic petrifications, from which the fires of lust and intense selfish passion have long dissipated what was animal and vital ; leaving stony limbs and countenances expressive of despair and stupid cruelty ' (p. 18). This, however, is simply ' fine writing,' or at best, an over-personal reaction to Blake's book. Oswald Crawfurd refuses to believe that it deals with physical matters at all : ' The sense . . . has been especially misinterpreted. Oothoon repre-sents the human soul and Theotormon, her lover, who disdains her because of her levity, must be taken to symbolize the restraints of superstition, prejudice, and evil custom. Oothoon's indignation, her denunciation of Theotormon's timidity and coldness and indifference, her self-justification and assertion of her inherent purity, must be taken figuratively ; in every other sense the language is abominable. We trust that no intelligent reader . . . would fail to perceive that the myth of Oothoon and Theo-tormon is allegorical of the soul bound by superstition.' [1] Unfortunately,

---

[1] *New Quarterly Magazine*, 1874.

Blake's language is too specific for us to admit this type of allegorical interpretation. Mr. H. G. Hewlett is frankly overwhelmed: 'Regard for the reader's delicacy prevents us from extracting the passages wherein Blake has illustrated the practical working of his views. Though the language is put into the mouth of a woman, nothing can exceed their grossness' (p. 780). But the majority of critics, whatever they may think of Blake's theories, do *not* find his language so appalling. 'No writer has ever treated of emancipated passion with greater dignity and restraint. Even [here] . . . his joyous exaltation scarcely tempts him to the use of phraseology comparable to what Milton quaintly terms " the jolliest expressions " of the " over-frolic " Canticles.' [1]

[1] F. G. Stokes, pp. 39-40.

CHAPTER XVII

THE WESTERN BANNER AS NOAH'S RAINBOW

It is in Nature, as it is in Religion; we are still hammering of old elements, but seek not the America that lyes beyond them.
—THOMAS VAUGHAN : *Anthroposophia Theomagica.*

THE third act of the Eleusinian Mysteries was never written, for Blake had become interested in things nearer his own life. Perhaps he could not bring himself to write of a saviour other than the Christ ; certainly he was wearying already of the growing worship of things Greek. At any rate, he decided to redeem his old fiasco, *The French Revolution*, by a poem on the far more reputable Americans.

In *The French Revolution* Blake endeavoured to describe history as seen by the visionary ; in *America* he tried to describe eternity as it is symbolized by history. This book marks a new and final step in Blake's career as a symbolist. At last the primary emphasis is thrown on the spiritual events, not on the outward, physical ones. This difference is one of method, and not really one of psychology. *The Marriage of Heaven and Hell* began his own new spiritual epoch ; *America* is only the application of it to contemporary events.

This change of method, however, was actually marked by an occurrence in Blake's outward life. To him, who was so sensitive, the mere changing of his address was something so important, that he succeeded in making it important to the world. In 1793 he left Poland Street (where Shelley was later to live), and moved to 13 Hercules Building, a street in Lambeth. He was not far from the Archbishop's palace ; but this was not what made Lambeth so prominent in Blake's later works : it was the inspiration which Blake found there. For he had now a humble house of his own to which was appended a garden containing the famous grape vine which Blake characteristically never allowed to be pruned ; the result being much foliage, much tangle of long, leafless spirals, and the most insignificant grapes.

During the first three of the seven years of his residence, Blake enjoyed an immense overflow of creative energy, during which he produced *America*, the *Songs of Experience, Europe, Urizen, The Song of Los, The Book of Los, Ahania*, and the five hundred and thirty-seven illustrations to Young, besides less important work. He also began *The Four Zoas* here.

Ever since its discovery, America had been a land of dreams to mankind. It was not an easy thing to fit into the accepted universe, therefore it took its place in the clouds. But whether as the Lost Atlantis, a land of honey-rivers flowing over beds of jewels and pure gold, or whether as the primeval wilderness, where men still lived uncorrupted by civilization, it became vaguely a symbol of the highest European ideals.

Michael Maier's *Subtle Allegory Concerning the Secrets of Alchemy* [1]

---

[1] Lib. xii. (*Anonymi Sarmatae Symbolum*) of the *Symbola Aurea* (Frankfurt, 1617).

is divided into four portions, each dealing with a continent as symbolizing one of the four elements. Maier's symbols (Europe—Earth ; America—Water ; Asia—Air ; and Africa—Fire) are entirely Blake's, and his book yields something like a meaning (though perhaps not Maier's) to any one who is versed in Blake's symbols.

But this does not imply that Blake had read Maier. ' All men who are instructed in fundamental truths speak the same language, for they are inhabitants of the same country,' wrote ' the Unknown Philosopher,' Saint-Martin.[1] To Blake everything was a symbol, and the four continents fell in admirably with his four-fold division of man. Therefore he, too, planned four books dealing with the continents. *America*, though written the first, is really the third of the set, and *Europe*, which follows it, is the fourth. The first and second books, *Africa* and *Asia*, were bound together under one title, *The Song of Los*. They deal with history from the rise of civilization in Egypt to the Boston Tea Party ; while *America* and *Europe* continue the story to the outbreak of the French Revolution.

It is hardly necessary to explain what America meant to the radicals at the end of the eighteenth century. That a whole people should deliberately choose to throw off what had been considered the infrangible shackles of historic tyrannies ; that they should do so rationally and successfully ; and that only the finest of unselfish motives should move them (for Washington was the same symbol then as now) was the outward and visible sign of the Millennium, the first proof that mankind was, after all, indomitable. To Blake, as also to Shelley,[2] this Revolution was of the greatest cosmic significance. It was the hinge of all history, man's first movement upward since the days of Creation. The Fall was at last checked ; the steady increase of slaveries was deliberately rejected for freedom.

Therefore we must expect to see, through Blake's eyes, the West ' full of horses and chariots of fire ' ranged round Washington and his fellow patriots, as the King of Syria once saw them round Elisha. The real conflict was not a small political quarrel between Americans and British, but the eternal one between Oppression and Revolt, whose names are the Guardian Prince of Albion, and Orc. It becomes so extensive that finally Urizen himself is dislodged from his hiding-place in the zenith, and the flames of conflict consume the entire material world, leaving everything pure spirit.

Blake's careful symbolism leaves us in no doubt as to the exact nature of the conflict, which, he conceived, was taking place universally in Man, as well as spatially in the United States. The West always meant to him (in strict accordance with the old Christian iconography) the realm of the body. The body is always the first thing to revolt against oppression. Spiritual and mental tyrannies can be endured, even ignored ; but when the material man is touched, he speedily and violently reliberates himself.

The state of Experience is the enslavement of the body. It is the last act of the Fall, the nadir of existence. It is the ultimate effect of remote spiritual causes. In it man's senses are limited till he can no longer perceive the Infinite in everything (as he could when a child) ; and he is

---

[1] *Œuvres Posthumes*, i. 212.
[2] Cf. *The Revolt of Islam*, xi. 22-24 ; *Hellas*, 66-68 ; and the lines rejected from *Adonais*.

separated more and more into a hateful Selfhood, being gradually estranged from the early sympathetic communion with his friends.

Blake's own struggle with this state was described by him in various works which preceded this book. But finally his vision focussed to clarity, and he wrote *The Marriage of Heaven and Hell*. After finishing the last records of Experience, he then began the history of Eternity with *America*. Swedenborg had taught him that the 'historical' books in the *Old Testament* were 'sublime allegories' only; so he extended Swedenborg's teaching by practising on the theory that history itself was nothing more than symbol. Where Swedenborg saw not fact but emblem, Blake saw both united.

The first version of *America* has recently come to light. Blake, thinking his poem finished, actually engraved four plates before he decided to change things entirely. Three of the plates were carefully re-engraved for the final version. This is yet another proof of Blake's habit of intensive revision before he was satisfied with his work.

The cause of the change was obvious. Blake always believed in giving the devil his due : were Urizen to build a palace, it should be as glorious as possible ; did Rahab appear, she was veritably seductive. Otherwise, how could we explain their very real fascination for this world ?

And Blake discovered that his first version of *America* might well sound to the casual reader like a justification of England. The first and fourth plates were all right ; but what would ordinary people make of such lines as—

the vale was dark

With clouds of smoke from the Atlantic, that in volumes roll'd
Between the mountains. . . .
Then Albion's Angel rose resolv'd to the cove of armoury. . . .
His helm was brought by London's Guardian, & his thirsty spear
By the wise spirit of London's River ; silent stood the King breathing with flames
And on his shining limbs they clasp'd the armour of terrible gold.[1]

In vain Blake changed ' shining ' to ' aged ' ; in vain he substituted ' damp mists ' for ' Flames.' Of course, in England the King really did seem to stand on ' the vast stone whose name is Truth ' and to weep ' over a den in which his eldest son outstretch'd By rebel hands was slain ' ; yet Blake felt that in expressing this point of view, he might seem to be confirming it. And this would be judged as a hypocritical cowardice by his friends. Intolerable ! And moreover the poetry was a bit too Ossianic. Therefore he re-engraved the first plate, making a few changes in text and decoration ; he flung away the text of the second plate, but repeated the decoration in a larger form on what is now plate VI ; the third plate he abandoned altogether ; and the fourth plate he used unchanged as plate XV. There is also evidence of yet another plate wholly abandoned.

The plot of *America* in its final form is simple. Washington and his comrades are worn out by the English yoke, which is gradually becoming more ponderous. At their first words of protest, the wrath of England is displayed to terrify them into submission ; and immediately the spirit of Revolt is born. This spirit, Orc, prophesies the coming liberation of the soul of man, and calls upon the Thirteen Original States to arise.

[1] For the complete text, see Keynes, pp. 459-463.

England sounds to war at once, but America does not yet accept the challenge. The Thirteen States confer on the 'Atlantean Hills,' which are the place midway between Eternity and this world. Boston first refuses the old obedience, and the others follow his example. The thirteen governors, including the notorious Bernard, can do nothing ; the British soldiery themselves flee from the awful sight.

Now the events leave even this outline of history, and become purely symbolic. Albion's Angel summons forty millions of spirits armed with diseases ; but the Pestilence recoils upon Albion. In the confusion the poetry of England is corrupted ; nevertheless, regeneration begins, for the priests flee, leaving the doors of marriage open. Urizen himself, the God of the 'Age of Reason,' pours down his snows of repression, but nothing can quench the flames of Orc. Urizen's utmost power can only succeed in hiding the American success twelve years from Europe.

Then France 'receives the Demon's light.' Surely, Eternity is achieved at last ! Slowly Albion's Guardian and his hordes recoil, beaten back by the fires, which they fight vainly with mildews and diseases ; but the doors of perception are burned open, and in the general conflagration everything created is consumed, revealing Eternity.

Prefaced to *America* is an allegory of the liberation of Orc, which is continued in the *Preludium* of *Europe* ; and which is repeated, with some variations, in *The Four Zoas* (vii. 613-632) and *Milton* (extra pages 5, 8, 17). Comparing accounts, we learn that it describes the relations of the spiritual man with Nature. Without him, she is a mystery armed with disease ; but when he dominates her, she becomes passive and productive. Orc is the spiritual man, in his attitude of Revolt. He is at once the child and the prisoner of the poetic spirit (Urthona-Los). Nature is both his sister [1] and his destined bride. After fourteen years of bondage, Orc becomes potent, breaks the bondage imposed by Urthona (the soul), and dissolves the mystery surrounding Nature. She, who has been dumb till now, smiles her first smile, and acclaims him as her master, her God, who had descended to redeem her. So she yields herself completely to him.

[1] *Milton*, 5 : 40.

CHAPTER XVIII

THE UPWARD ARC

O immense Greatness! I *cannot* compare thee with any Thing, but *only* with the Resurrection from the Dead ; then will the Love-Fire rise up *again* in us, and embrace Man courteously and friendly, and rekindle again our astringent, bitter, and cold, dark and *dead* Quality, and embrace us most friendly.

—JAKOB BÖHME : *Aurora*, viii. 160.

EUROPE was chronologically the second of Blake's four books dealing with the continents. Like *America*, it used contemporary events as symbolic of an episode in the history of Man. The verse-form is freer, the myth obscurer. However, if we have followed Blake's method so far, little difficulty awaits us.

This book represents Blake's favourite theme of the passage from night to dawn, as exemplified in his own continent. It begins with the birth of Christ, the ' Secret Child,' in the human soul. All warfare ceases at once. But this harmony of Innocence is deceptive, as any hand-book on Mysticism warns one. For when Poetry arises, to overcome the old tyrant, Reason, with song, a false doctrine creeps in.

Before this can be explained, the important characters of Los and Enitharmon must be elucidated. Los is the ' temporal ' form of Urthona, the Spirit. He is the god of Poetry, of the Sun, and of Time. His partner, Enitharmon, represents Inspiration or spiritual beauty, the Moon, and Space. The two do not always agree : sometimes Enitharmon flees from Los, until he is nearly dead ; sometimes he misuses her, not understanding her true nature. Only after the ultimate Last Judgment are the two completely made one.

Just such a misunderstanding now arises. Enitharmon makes the mistake of imposing a female will (feminine ideals) upon Europe. ' In Eternity there is no such thing as a female will,' wrote Blake,[1] for he believed completely in the Miltonic ideal, that woman should submit to man, as man in his turn submits to God. Enitharmon, in short, is exerting her Selfhood, which is selfishness. She teaches that the love of woman is illicit, thereby extending a female dominion over the male.

> Enitharmon laugh'd in her sleep to see (O woman's triumph !)
> Every house a den, every man bound : the shadows are fill'd
> With spectres, and the windows wove over with curses of iron :
> Over the doors ' Thou shalt not,' and over the chimneys ' Fear ' is written :
> With bands of iron round their necks fasten'd into the walls
> The citizens ; in leaden gyves the inhabitants of the suburbs
> Walk heavy ; soft and bent are the bones of the villagers.

This binding of love is a shutting of the great door into Eternity.[2] It is

---

[1] *Last Judgment.*

[2] See the *Introduction*, lines 5-6 ; *To Tirzah (Songs of Experience)* ; and Chapter xv., *The Fifth Window*. The 99th illustration to Dante shows the dangers lying in Mariolatry.

a characteristic error of youth, which limits him to the flesh, so that he accepts the ' allegory ' of a future heaven, in place of its present actuality ; believing that he is only ' a worm of sixty winters.' Feminism is no healthy creed for a man.

The doctrine prevails (in history) for eighteen hundred years—until the eruption of the American Revolution. Then at last the true path of liberty is revealed ; and the perversion of European life becomes quite evident. As the body has been freed, so the mind simultaneously becomes liberated. The flames of Revolution begin to invade Europe. In self-defence, those in power reassert their false doctrines. Yet the truth spreads. Albion's Angel tries to define an ultimate judgment upon mankind by an appeal to the past. This is not accomplished until Newton, the arch-scientist, appears. His doctrine definitely places man as a material thing. Error is at last given a visible form ; it may now be recognized and cast out.

At once Enitharmon is roused from her sleep of custom. Again she calls upon the spirits of her mistaken doctrine ; but the morning comes and they flee.

And in the sunrays of the true light, Revolution awakes and enters France. Enitharmon is dismayed ; but her true Lord, Poetry, arises at last, and calls ' all his sons to the strife of blood.'

At this moment the book of *Europe* ends.

Those who believe that Blake accepted indiscriminately whatever Inspiration might offer will be surprised to find that here, as always, he insists that the poet be master of the thoughts which come to him. Enitharmon is always liable to error when she is not properly submitted to Los. The false doctrine of sex—that Free Love is sin—was not evolved by the cosmic villain, Urizen, but by the goddess of Spiritual Beauty herself.

The *Introduction*, though containing some of Blake's most delectable verses, appears in two copies only : the Linnell copy and the Hooper copy (owned by Mrs. Ward Thoron of Boston). Blake seems to have feared that the clue to one of his most sacred doctrines, which appears on this plate, was too definite a one. A century and a quarter has passed since he issued *Europe* ; yet I believe that till now no one has guessed its significance. Perhaps Blake gave the world more credit for brains than it deserved.

This *Introduction* represents Blake as inspired by the delights of nature, through which he learns to see the infinite behind all things. The five senses are really windows into Eternity ; the most important of which is the sense of touch (sex). The Fairy (who is a natural joy), when fed on love-thoughts, ' dictates ' *Europe* to the poet.

The *Preludium* which follows continues the *Preludium* of *America*. It is the wail of Nature at her own fruitfulness. In her weariness, she hides in the most material forms (clouds and water), yet still Light pours down fertility upon her. The stars in particular (Urizen) cause her to bring forth ' howling terrors ' ; Reason and Nature combined invariably create forms of terror.[1] ' Consumed and consuming ! . . . Devouring and devoured ' : such is the fate of Nature in the material world. In the *material* world, be it noted ; for Vala exists in Eternity with all things

[1] Cf. *The Four Zoas*, vii. 626 : ' She was Vala, now become Urizen's harlot.'

and this torment comes upon her only when Enitharmon (Space) stamps the spiritual fires with the signet of form, and Urizen ' binds the Infinite with an eternal band.'

Yet there is a promise of release from Creation.   The secret is told her ; Christ will descend into the flesh, to redeem even Nature to Eternity. Her lament ends at once.

It is quite clear that in *Europe* and also in *The Book of Ahania*, Blake was hinting at a doctrine which he did not care to state too clearly.   He intended to identify the spirit of Revolt with Jesus.   *The Everlasting Gospel* testifies to his conception of Jesus as a revolutionary character. The ' Secret Child ' of *Europe*, metred after Milton's *Hymn to the Nativity*, brings Jesus irresistibly to mind, though the Child is really Orc.   And later, the crucified Fuzon in *The Book of Ahania* strikes a parallel which is only too obvious.

But finally Blake decided that worldly warfare with its dubious results, and spiritual warfare which never killed a single person, were two different things, though of the same category.   Therefore in *Night the Eighth* of *The Four Zoas*, Orc and Jesus appear simultaneously against Urizen ; Orc being a fallen form of Luvah (the emotions), while Jesus descends ' In Luvah's robes of blood ' (the flesh).

CHAPTER XIX

THE COSMIC TRAGEDY

When he prepared the heavens I was there ; when he set a compass upon the face of the deep.—Proverbs viii. 27.

In the books from *The French Revolution* to *Europe*, also in *The Song of Los*, Blake dealt with historical themes, whose outward drama was played upon the boards of Time and Space. In *Urizen, The Book of Los*, and *Ahania*, Space has vanished, but Time remains. The three final epics eliminate, for the most part, even Time ; their action is set in Eternity and Infinity.

Urizen is the longest of the minor Prophetic Books, being one hundred and sixty-four lines longer than *Tiriel*. In its complete form, it contains one plate more than the combined *Marriage of Heaven and Hell* and *A Song of Liberty*. .

It deals with the problem of evil, which is the problem of Creation (or the Fall). It must be interpreted in two ways : first, as appearing in the creation of the world, about 4004 B.C.; and secondly, as recurring in the life of every man. The Macrocosm is repeated in the Microcosm. The Fall from Eternity into Matter is mirrored as the Fall from Innocence into Experience.

The central character of this book is Urizen, or Reason, the God of this world. His name in the Bible is Jehovah. Blake seems to have rediscovered, or perhaps adapted for himself, the early Gnostic heresy : ' The evil that is in the world must be due to the Creator of the world ; it must be inherent in the world from the beginning—the result of some weakness at least, or some ignorance, if not of some positive malignity in its first formation. . . . The Redeemer of the world must stand higher than the Creator ; for he is sent to remedy the imperfection of the Creator's work.' [1] Blake believed this thoroughly : ' Thinking as I do that the Creator of this world is a very cruel Being, and being a worshipper of Christ, I cannot help saying to the Son—Oh, how unlike the Father ! First God Almighty comes with a thump on the head, and then Jesus Christ comes with a balm to heal it.' [2] The theory was not limited to Blake : ' It is not a God, just and good, but a devil, under the name of God, that the Bible describes,' wrote Tom Paine from Paris, in a letter on his *Age of Reason*, May 12, 1797, three years after *Urizen* was engraved. Shelley, who evolved by himself many of Blake's ideas, recorded in the *Essay on Christianity* : ' According to Jesus Christ, and according to the indisputable facts of the case, some evil spirit has dominion in this imperfect world.'

Having called the God of this world evil, most of these theorizers are content if they also call him temporal merely. Blake, however, defined

---

[1] Mansel's *Gnostic Heresies*, Lect. II.   [2] *MS. Book.*

plainly the character of his Demiurge. Just as Shakspere's greatest villains are pure Intellects, so Blake's cosmic criminal is dominant Reason. Blake did not believe for a moment that Reason was either intentionally or essentially bad, which is a position taken by so many mystics ; on the contrary, he insisted that ' the fool shall not enter into heaven, let him be ever so holy.' [1] It is the *domination* of Reason : its usurpation of the throne which belongs to the Spirit ; its repression and measuring of natural joys ; its evolving of systems from emotional values ; its judging of all things by one standard—which make it a bad thing. Put in its place, under the domination of the Spirit (Urthona), Urizen works wholly for the happiness of man.

To Blake the mystic, this meant simply that Faith (Instinct) should dominate Dogma ; to Blake the poet and painter it meant that inspiration should dominate technique.

The plot is complicated. At the very opening of the book, Urizen's error has begun, and no explanation of that error is given us. Blake seems to have assumed that in Eternity all Contraries, joy and pain, truth and error, may be coincident.

Our first awareness of Urizen is our perception of his horrible shadow— his ' restrained desires,' ' self-clos'd, all-repelling.' Thus a Selfhood is already formed. Urizen is worshipping his own desires, and from this worship he derives his philosophy of Reason. The first act of the Creator, according to the *Kabalah*, was to mirror himself, that he might have something to act upon. To Blake, this doubling is a division, and therefore a fall from the original Unity. Other divisions are taking place, ' times on times . . . space by space,' but so remote are they from our corporeal understandings that they cannot be described. ' The forests of the night ' result ; strange shapes of elementals are born there ; and Urizen fights all these monsters, for whom he alone is responsible.

Creation is to Urizen still a Chaos, which he must order, for such is his nature. Therefore he collects all his forces to overcome the universe. His weapons are the storms of wrath and all the freezing powers of restriction.

Finally his position is so well formulated that he finds his voice : ' I have sought for a joy without pain,' he cries, not knowing that ' where there is capacity of enjoyment, there is the capacity of pain.' [2] ' I have sought for a solid without fluctuation '—though that solid be Satan. ' Why will you die, O Eternals ? '—for Urizen has yet to learn that the Mystic Death is Eternal Life. ' Why live in unquenchable burnings ? ' which are ' the fires of Hell . . . the enjoyments of Genius, which to Angels look like torment and insanity.' [3] He has overcome that fire in himself, and from the watery (materialistic) void he produced a solid— the firmament. There he wrote his metal books of wisdom, which are the tables of prohibitions. These he wishes to impose on all : the unjust ' one law for all,' which is Oppression.

> Let each chuse one habitation, . . .
> One command, one joy, one desire,
> One curse, one weight, one measure,
> One King, one God, one Law.

---

[1] *MS. Book.*   [2] H. C. R., Dec. 10, 1825.
[3] *Marriage of Heaven and Hell*, first *Memorable Fancy.*

The effect on Eternity is terrible. It is rent ; and the rejected Fires pour down on Urizen, for whatever is cast out becomes an enemy. In anguish, he finally piles up a shelter against them—a thick crust of materialism—in which he sleeps stonily, separated from Eternity. The wound he suffered in being rent from his original station was one that never healed.

Meanwhile a new actor has appeared : Los, the ' vehicular form ' of Urthona. He, too, has been dragged down and rent from Eternity in Urizen's fall, but his wound heals ; for Poetry can exist without Analysis (Reason) ; but Reason without Imagination (Poetry) is a sleep which is nearly death.

Los's function in the chaos is to snare all the horrors ; for as the God of Time, he can bind them into temporal limits, and so cut them off from Eternity. Therefore, with the aid of Poetry, this temporal Hell must end. As Blake says elsewhere : ' Time is the mercy of Eternity.'

Reason (Urizen), limited by Poetry (Los), becomes wrathful ; but this storm soon settles into the lake of the Indefinite, which in another book is named Udan-Adan. (It is to be noted that everything about Urizen tends to become watery—materialistic—or else opaque.) Forgetfulness of Eternity, dumbness of vision, necessity of law : these are his three characteristics ; and the more limited they become, the more definite their shape grows.

' Giving a body to Falshood, that it may be cast off for ever ' (*Jerusalem*, 12 : 13) ' is part of God's design ' (*MS. Book*) ; and this is the process that is now going on. An error, to be rooted out, must be recognized, made visible ; otherwise we cannot grapple with it. Los, therefore, in giving Urizen a body, is defining his ' states ' that they may be dealt with. In the seven ages of Creation, Urizen successively acquires, through the forging of Los, a skeleton, a heart, the gates of the senses, the digestive system, and his limbs. Jakob Böhme also described the Fall of Adam as the acquiring of a body.

Now when Adam was thus in the Garden of Eden, and the three Principles having produced such a strife in him, his Tincture was quite wearied, and the Virgin departed. For the Lust-Spirit in Adam had overcome, and therefore he sunk down into a Sleep. The same Hour his heavenly Body became Flesh and Blood, and his strong Virtue became Bones.[1]

Meanwhile Los at his task is dismayed to find that ' the Immortal endur'd his chains,' and he himself has fallen so far that ' his eternal life, like a dream, was obliterated.' His fires decay ; and pity over the misery of the situation is born. The appearance of Pity is a division of his own soul : the curse of Creation continues ; and soon the new emotion takes visible form—a heart, which grows into a woman. It is his Emanation, Enitharmon, once part of him, but now separate. Inspiration, divided from the Poet, becomes mere Pity, and not Love.

The Eternals, terrified, begin dividing the chaos from Eternity.

Los recognizes his mate, and the union of Poetry with Pity produces Revolt (Orc).

Then follows a curious passage. As Orc grows, Los becomes jealous of his love for Enitharmon.

---

[1] Böhme, *The Three Principles*, xiii. 2.

> But when fourteen summers & winters had revolved over
> Their solemn habitation, Los beheld the ruddy boy
> Embracing his bright mother, & beheld malignant fires
> In his young eyes, discerning plain that Orc plotted his death.[1]

In short, Revolt, in trying to impress himself upon Inspiration, would crush out the arts. Blake must have realized that social dogma in verse is not literature. There is hardly any good political poetry. The myth is probably a picture of Blake's own mental state when writing the *Songs*. Every writer is apt to pass through a period when he wants to use art for the effecting of certain reforms. But Blake, seeing how the political struggles of his own day were crushing out all European art and letters, took warning. So Los binds Orc with the Chain of Jealousy upon the Rock of the Decalogue, the 'Stone of Night.' Later the young God is to break loose, as we have already learned from the *Preludium* to *America*, when Blake's political beliefs, finally matured, did burst out—into superb poetry, too !

Meanwhile Urizen, stung to awakening by the life stirring about him, begins to explore the chaos once again. With dividers, scales, and weights, he formulates the Abyss, and there plants the Garden of Eden. Outside this Garden, the world is not so attractive ; Reason can build only a limited Paradise ; and vast enormities and fragments of existence everywhere mock Urizen with the bitter struggle for life. The four elements appear : first air, then water, earth, and fire ; and then sons and daughters which are not, like these, temporal, but eternal. All his children sicken Urizen.

> He curs'd
> Both sons & daughters, for he saw
> That no flesh or spirit could keep
> His iron laws one moment.

At this misery, of which he himself was sole cause, he wept, and ' he called it Pity ' ; yet it was not Pity, but Hypocrisy. And wherever he went, he trailed the slimy, unbreakable net of Religion—not the Everlasting Gospel, but the puritanic Religion of Restraint, empowered by the Curse.

Under it the giant inhabitants of earth shrink nearly to our present size. They cannot recognize the hypocrisy ; they only know that they are becoming flesh.

> Six days they shrunk up from existence,
> And on the seventh day they rested,
> And they bless'd the seventh day, in sick hope,
> And forgot their eternal life. . . .
> No more could they rise at will
> In the infinite void, but bound down
> To earth by their narrowing perceptions . . .
> And form'd laws of prudence and call'd them
> The eternal laws of God.

' So that now the poor Soul, which was from the first Principle, stood forth encompassed with this Beast wholly *naked* and bare,' is Jakob Böhme's phrasing of the Fall.[2]

---

[1] The reason for Los's action is not made plain in *Urizen*. This quotation is from *The Four Zoas*, v. 79-82.

[2] *Mysterium Magnum*, I. xxii. 15.

Thus civilization began in the thirty cities of Egypt, 'whose Gods are the Powers Of This World, Goddess Nature ; Who first spoil & then destroy Imaginative Art, For their Glory is War and Dominion.' [1] Egypt, it may be remembered, was later to enslave Jerusalem.

Those of Urizen's children who escaped the Curse called for a while to their brothers in vain ; then, led by the fire-elemental, Fuzon, who seems to be a form of Orc or Luvah, they left the world, which was now shrunken to a solid mass, and covered almost entirely by the dead Sea of Time and Space.

So *The Book of Urizen* ends.

It should be pointed out, that evil as Urizen is, he is quite unlike the conventional devil. He is seeking sincerely for what he considers ideal : the absence of pain, the repose and ordering of life, peace, love, unity, pity, compassion, and forgiveness. When he grieves over the sorrows about him, he does not know that his tears are self-deceptive. In fact, Urizen's only fault is his lack of Imagination. He has not enough intuitive insight to realize that ' One Law for the Lion & Ox is Oppression,' that the Eternals may prefer their various modes of life to his ; nor does he realize that the sufferings around him are really caused by himself alone.

The doctrines of *Urizen* were surely derived from Plato's *Timaeus*. Blake knew this very obscure work, as is evidenced by his many references to the Lost Atlantis, by the symbols in the eighteenth illustration to *Job*, and by several passages in *The Four Zoas*. Plato, of course, believed that the Creator and his work were as near perfection as possible ; Blake took the contrary standpoint. Otherwise we find that Plato told just the same story of the Creation, though under somewhat different symbols.

Plato's God was motivated precisely as was Urizen : ' He desired that all things should be as like himself as possible. This is the true beginning of creation. . . . God desired that all things should be good and nothing bad as far as this could be accomplished.'

He worked just as Urizen worked, by division and ordering ; for both are Reason. He brought order out of disorder and put intellect in the soul, and the soul in the body. Next he created the four elements and formed them into a globe which had no means of communication (sense-organs) with Eternity. ' He made one solitary and only heaven a circle moving in a circle,' where he placed the seven planets. Time was created with the heavens, in imitation of Eternity (or, as Blake put it, ' Los is the vehicular form of Urthona '). Then he made the lower gods, taking ' of the unchangeable and indivisible essence, and also of the divisible and corporeal, which is generated,' compressing these reluctant natures together. The lower gods (fire) then formed the other three races : the birds (air), the fish (water), and the animals (earth) ; had the Creator himself done this, his work would have been immortal as himself.

For the creation of Man, he sowed the immortal seeds in the moon, the stars, and the earth (which corresponds quite closely to Urizen's sowing of the Harvest of Eternity in *The Four Zoas*, IX.) ; then the lower gods wove bodies for them from the four elements. Thus divinity became enmeshed in mortality. Men were given four senses, and divided into Blake's three divisions of the head, heart, and loins. Their salvation was to live in accord with Reason, overcoming the passions sent to try

[1] Laocoon plate.

them. If they succeeded, they were to rise into a higher life among the stars ; but if they failed they were punished with diseases, and degraded to ' women and other animals ' in their ulterior lives.

Plato thus described the rule of Urizen to perfection ; but he gave no hint of any higher state. All is on the plane of Karma, of ' Experience.' That he made Man the lowest point in existence, and then gave him the chance of falling still lower, never troubled him at all. On account of such ideas as these, Blake hated Greek philosophy. It was correct as far as it went, but it was absolutely non-mystical, and had no promise of ultimate freedom, nor any chance of transcending the world and reaching a direct communion with God.

Blake knew Plato's doctrines, and adapted them to his own system ; but we have no reason for believing that he knew anything of Buddhism. Nevertheless, the Buddhist account of Creation is much nearer Blake's than was Plato's.

When in the cycle of forming universes the first tangible shapes of sun and earth and moon appeared, Truth moved in the cosmic dust and filled the whole world with blazing light. . . .

In the due course of evolution sentiency appeared and sense-perception arose. There was a new realm of soul-life, full of yearning, with powerful passions, and of unconquerable energy. And the world split in twain ; there were pleasures and pains, self and not-self, friends and foes, hatred and love. The truth vibrated through the world of sentiency, but in all its infinite potentialities no place could be found where the truth could abide in all its glory.

And reason came forth in the struggle for life. Reason began to guide the instinct of self, and reason took the sceptre of the creation and overcame the strength of the brutes and the power of the elements. Yet reason seemed to add new fuel to the flame of hatred, increasing the turmoil of conflicting passions ; and brothers slew their brothers for the sake of satisfying the lust of a fleeting moment. And the truth repaired to the domains of reason, but in all its recesses no place was found where the truth could abide in all its glory.

Now reason, as the helpmate of self, implicated all living beings more and more in the meshes of lust, hatred, and envy, and from lust, hatred, and envy the evils of sin originated. Men broke down under the burdens of life, until the saviour appeared, the great Buddha, the Holy Teacher of men and gods.[1]

Here we have something very like Blake's original heaven of Eternity ; the evolution of the Zoas ; the Fall by division ; the disastrous rule of Reason over this world ; and eventually the appearance of the Saviour. Reason is a lower faculty, of good intent, but the origin of evil in spite of itself. It is necessary for salvation, but is not self-sufficient, as another passage from the same sermon teaches us :

No truth is attainable without reason. Nevertheless, in mere rationality there is no room for truth, though it be the instrument that masters the things of the world.

It is curious how all the great thinkers seem to approach the same solution, though their paths be different !

[1] Paul Carus, *Gospel of Buddha*, p. 228.

CHAPTER XX

CREATION FROM THE OTHER SIDE

Thy pomp is brought down to the grave, and the noise of thy viols: the worm is spread under thee, and the worms cover thee.

How art thou fallen from heaven, O Lucifer, son of the morning! how art thou cut down to the ground, which didst weaken the nations!

—*Isaiah* xiv. 11-12.

THE Book of Los retells the story of *Urizen* from the standpoint of Los, the Poetic Spirit. It begins, as usual, after the trouble has started, with the fiery Fall described in *Urizen*, iii. 4. At that moment, Los first finds self-consciousness because, as Böhme says: ' No-Thing without Contrariety or Opposition CAN become Manifest *To it* self.' [1]

The opening five paragraphs are introductory, and are separated from the rest of the text by a decorative line, such as is found nowhere else in this book. This section is a lament of Eno (Enion), the Earth-Mother, over man's spiritual fall. Once, in the time of eternal plenty, man's meanest aspects were virtues from the very excess of their delights ; but now, spiritual poverty has narrowed them into Covet, Envy, Wrath, and Wantonness. This section explains in a completely rational manner Blake's strange remark to Crabb Robinson : ' What are called vices in the natural world are the highest sublimities in the spiritual world.' [2] Blake's idea was quite modern : that evil is only misdirected energy, starved into a bad aspect by the inadequacy of its legitimate expression. The whole problem of society is the ordering and satisfaction of such impulses.

The story of *The Book of Los* begins at paragraph 6. The revolt of the Eternals and the Fall (as described in *Urizen*, iii. 4) has just taken place, and Los wakes to consciousness, ' bound in a chain ' of Cause and Effect. He is ' compell'd to watch Urizen's shadow ' ; that is, he is submitted to the desires of Reason, the everlasting position of the Poet in this world. His gift (fire) is torture to him, and gradually the flames roll away from him, leaving him in a marmoreal blackness, which solidifies and limits ' his expanding clear senses.' Such is the mental state of the Poet in Experience.

He cannot endure it : and by an effort of will, he shatters the Rock, only to fall into the unbounded void of Error. ' Truth has bounds : Error none.' He falls in the customary upside-down position. At first he is angry, ' like the babe new born into our world ' , then he rears his head aloft again, ' and his downward borne fall chang'd oblique.'

> Incessant the falling Mind labour'd,
> Organizing itself : till the Vacuum
> Became element, pliant to rise,
> Or to fall, or to swim, or to fly,
> With ease searching the dire vacuity.

---

[1] *Theoscopia, The Highly pretious Gate*, 14. [2] H. C. R., Dec. 17, 1825.

122

To begin intercourse with this world, he must build himself some sort of a body. The first organ which acts upon the surrounding element is the lungs. But whatever he does to himself has its effect on the exterior world ; at once the Vacuum becomes a vast world of furious waters. He continues his self-development until he is ' an immense Fibrous form.' Now he smites the deep, separating the Solid, which sinks, and the Thin, which is Fire (or Light).

By this new light he beholds the backbone of Urizen. Astonished and terrified, Los gathers himself completely together, builds his furnaces (acquires a technique), and begins the binding of Urizen. In nine ages he forges a Sun—a centre for this system ; then to this he binds Urizen's spine. This sun is an illusion, being temporal, and Urizen quenches its light (truth) but not its heat (wrath). The torture causes Reason to form itself. The brain grows into a rock, and the heart is organized into the four rivers of Eden (the Four Zoas), obscuring the central Light (the Humanity) ;

> . . . till a Form
> Was completed, a Human Illusion
> In darkness and deep clouds involved.

Thus we reach Adam, the Natural Man, in his temporary Eden.

CHAPTER XXI

THE COSMIC TRAGEDY CONTINUED

The soul of man, like unextinguished fire,
Yet burns towards heaven with fierce reproach and doubt,
Hurling up insurrection . . .
              —SHELLEY : *Prometheus Unbound*, III. i. 5-7.

THE original title of *The Book of Ahania* was presumably *The Second Book of Urizen*; but for some reason Blake decided not to connect the two, though the story of *Ahania* continues that of *Urizen*. *Ahania* deals with a myth which Blake changed so much later, that he lost interest in this little book, of which one copy only is known to exist. Fuzon, one of the three characters, was abandoned entirely; in the later books, his struggle with Urizen is carried on under the name of Luvah.

The myth symbolizes the same revolt and defeat which Blake thought was concealed under the story of the release of the Israelites from the Egyptian rule, and their subsequent enslavement beneath the Decalogue; also in the story of the ministry and the crucifixion of Jesus. It is the eternal struggle of the liberating genius against convention.

Fuzon, a fire-elemental, the ' first begotten, last born ' son of Urizen, who escaped from his father's tyranny at the end of *The Book of Urizen*, now rises, in revolt against that false God of this world. Fuzon is Passion attacking Reason. His hurled wrath reaches its target, ' the cold loins of Urizen dividing.' Thus the Fall of Creation continues.

Reason, howling in his pain, decides to sacrifice his vulnerable part. Passion has interfered with his ' joy without pain '; therefore he must cast out Pleasure, in order to keep his dominion undisturbed.

Pleasure, whose name is Ahania, is thus separated from Reason (Urizen). He hides her and calls her ' Sin '; and she falls from him, a Shadow of suppressed desire.

> She fell down, a faint shadow wand'ring
> In chaos, and circling dark Urizen
> As the moon anguish'd circles the earth,
> Hopeless ! abhorr'd ! a death-shadow,
> Unseen, unbodied, unknown,
> The mother of Pestilence.[1]

Here Blake inserts a paragraph identifying Fuzon's flame with the pillar of fire which led the Israelites from Egypt, and which later was compacted into one person, the Christ.

Urizen is not content with casting out Pleasure; he must punish Passion as well. One of the unnatural productions of his ' dire Contemplations ' is the Serpent of Materialism. Urizen conquers this Serpent, forms from it the Black Bow of the Curse, loads it with the poisoned Rock of Moral Law, and aims it at Fuzon.

---

[1] Cf. ' He who desires but acts not, breeds pestilence.'—5th *Proverb of Hell*.

Meanwhile Fuzon thinks that he has slain Urizen, forgetting (the usual mistake of the gods) that an Eternal cannot be killed. Just at the moment of his triumph, when he is announcing himself as God, the eldest of things, the Rock smites him.

> But the rock fell upon the Earth,
> Mount Sinai in Arabia.

This Rock is the Decalogue. Just so the Israelites, escaping from the bondage of Egypt (Empire), entered into the worse bondage of the Decalogue (Moral Law). This, though Blake does not say so, was also the story of the Puritans who settled New England.

When Urizen had first shrunk away from the Eternals, in pity he began writing his Books of Law, as we have seen ; and then the Tree of Mystery (Religion) sprang up under his heel in such a profuse growth that with difficulty he himself escaped. Upon this Tree he now crucifies the helpless body of Fuzon. Conventional Religion is the instrument by which Reason tortures revolting Passion. The inevitable pestilences from the lake of Udan-Adan (the Indefinite) fly round ; and Los frantic-ally forges his iron nets to snare them. Meanwhile, for forty years (the time of the wanderings in the wilderness) 'they reptilize upon the Earth,' shrinking into the Worm of Mortality ; and Asia, the continent of the religions of oppression, 'sway'd by a Providence oppos'd to the Divine Lord Jesus,' [1] arises from the deep.

Meanwhile Ahania (Pleasure) wails over her separation from Urizen (Reason) round the Tree of crucified Passion. Her lament is one of Blake's fine passages of poetry which can never be forgotten.

[1] *Jerusalem*, 50 : 4.

CHAPTER XXII

HISTORY BEGINS

> Understand it thus: The Eternall *Abyssall* Will of the Life, had turned it self away from the divine *Ens*, and would domineer in Evill and Good: and therefore is the *Second* Principle, *viz.* the Kingdome of God, extinguished, to it; and in the stead thereof, is sprouted up, to it, the *Third* Principle in the own self Imaginability, *viz*: the Source or *Quality* of the Constellations and of the four Elements: Whence the Body is become *Grosse* and beastiall, and the Senses or *Thoughts* become *false* and *Earthly.*—Jakob Böhme: *Theoscopia*, ii. 9.

The Book of Los ended with the creation of Adam; *The Book of Urizen* ended with the first civilization rising in Egypt; *Ahania* ended with the rise of Asia.

The Song of Los continues the story of these three books, by showing the growth of Urizen's religion in its various forms, the spreading of statecraft, and the eventual Revolt of Man. Therefore this book is really the link between the later books and the earlier ones; *America* and *Europe* continue the world history where *The Song of Los* (which deals with *Africa* and *Asia*) breaks off. The *Prophecy* of *America* begins with the very line on which *Africa* ends. Blake tried to indicate this connection in his opening lines:

> I will sing you a song of Los, the Eternal Prophet:
> He sung it to four harps at the tables of Eternity.

Blake means that this is the song of Time, which now begins: Time, which is a prophecy of Eternity. The four harps at the feast of Eternity are the four books dealing with the four continents, two of which are here included under one title.

Africa opens while the two types of men behold Urizen's religion of death spreading over the earth. These types are symbolized by Adam, the 'Natural Man' or the 'Limit of Contraction'; and Noah, the Man of Imagination, who escaped the Deluge of Time and Space, and was the first to plant a vineyard.

> They saw Urizen give his Laws to the Nations
> By the hands of the children of Los.

That is, they see the arbitrary codes of ethics enforced by 'forms of worship from poetic tales'; the original symbol becoming literal dogma. This process was told at greater length on plate xi of *The Marriage of Heaven and Hell*. Thus man falls, and individual Eternals become supreme Gods in various parts of the world; for the narrowed mind of man can now perceive only one aspect of himself as ideal, forgetting that 'everything that lives is holy.'

So, in this book Moses sees 'forms of dark delusion' (Reason) [1] upon Mount Sinai; Rintrah (Wrath) gives an Abstract (inhuman) Philosophy to Brahma; Palamabron (Pity) gives another to Trismegistus and the Greeks; and Oothoon (the Magdalen) is heard by Jesus, who receives his

---

[1] Corresponding to Bromion, the fourth son of Los. The other three follow.

gospel 'from wretched Theotormon' (frustrate Desire). These four religions are the ethical, the logical, the aesthetic, and the imaginative, corresponding to the fourfold division of Man.

Orc (Revolt) by this time is already crucified. The human race begins to wither ; for the healthy build convents for themselves, 'secluded places, fearing the joys of Love ; and the diseased only propagated.' As a reaction, Antamon invokes Leutha (the false doctrine of sex), and gives Mahomet 'a loose Bible,' the Koran ; while in the North, Sotha (the glory of battle) presents Odin with 'a Code of War.'

Thus 'like a dream Eternity was obliterated and erased.' Poetry and Painting (Har and Heva) flee away, 'because their brethren and sisters liv'd in War & Lust' ; and in their flight they shrink to the Worm which man now is, and their vision of nature shrinks accordingly.

Finally Materialism, the 'Philosophy of Five Senses' is completed by Newton and Locke.

But this, the nadir of history, is the moment when man begins to return upward. Rousseau and Voltaire appear ; and 'the Guardian Prince of Albion burns in his nightly tent,' foreboding the American Revolution.

Here *Africa* ends.

Asia is the continent (or State) 'opposing the Divine Vision' (*Jerusalem*, 74 : 22). But the events of this book take place outwardly in Europe ; for Blake was describing the coming of Revolution.

The spider-like 'Kings of Asia,' terrified by the 'thought-creating fires' of Orc (Revolution), try to justify their power, which is sustained by Famine and Pestilence. Reason brings despair over the situation ; his books melt—lose their force in the great heat ; and he bellows aloud to see both types of man, Adam and Noah, shrunken and bleached into forms of death.

Then Orc breaks loose, trying men's souls in a Last Judgment, a casting-out of Error. For the first time, the Grave (this world, the Nameless Shadowy Female) has found her mate. To herself and her paramour Orc, War is an intoxicating orgy. Meanwhile Urizen weeps.

Some critics think that this book is an attack on Christianity, in favour of Mohammedanism. Mr. J. P. R. Wallis says : 'According to Blake's own statement . . . the asceticism of Jesus's gospel would have depopulated the earth, had not Mohammedanism, with its " loose Bible," that is, apparently, its laxer moral code, been set to counteract it ' (p. 194). Mr. Percy H. Osmond calls *The Song of Los* 'a eulogy of Mohammedanism at the expense of Christianity. There can be no reasonable doubt that by this time Blake's mind was becoming unhinged : a lengthy sojourn in the country was only just in time, if in time, to save his sanity.'[1]

This interpretation is preposterous. Blake distinctly says that Jesus forgave the Magdalen's sin ; but that the asceticism wrongly approved later by the Church had a bad effect on the human race by confining the best characters in convents. As a reaction from such mistakes of the Church, Mohammedanism was founded. All this is historic fact, and is no basis for a charge of madness. Blake was never known to reject the gospel of Jesus ; though he often protested against what he considered the Church's lapse from the Everlasting Gospel. Mohammedanism he neither rejects nor defends.

[1] *Mystical Poets of the English Church*, p. 281.

CHAPTER XXIII

LATER LYRICS

Poetry is the hunny of all flowers, the quintessence of all scyences, the marrowe of witte, and the very phrase of angels.
—Thomas Nash: *Pierce Penilesse His Supplication to the Deuill.*

After Blake finished the *Songs of Experience,* his main interest lay in the Prophetic Books. Nevertheless he did not wholly give up writing lyrics. Though he took little pains to preserve them, quite a few have been gathered together, mainly from the *MS. Book,* the *Pickering Manuscript,* and from his letters.

The *MS. Book,* also known as the ' Rossetti Manuscript,' is, after the manuscripts of *The Four Zoas* and of *Tiriel,* the most priceless of all the Blake relics. It is a notebook containing many sketches, over fifty poems, a number of epigrams, long passages of prose, and several personal notes. It was given by Blake's wife to Samuel Palmer, who on April 30, 1849, sold it to Dante Gabriel Rossetti for ten shillings. Eventually it reached its present owner, Mr. W. A. White of Brooklyn. In this book Blake had jotted down everything which seemed important during a period when paper was scarce. Two dates in it, 1793 and 1811, show how long he used it ; though these dates mark neither the beginning nor end of its service. As yet, only the poetry has been properly edited. The *Pickering Manuscript,* also in the possession of Mr. White, is a fair copy of ten poems, with a few corrections. These have been edited properly. Five more poems have been collected from letters written from 1800 to 1803. They are particularly important, as we know that they are autobiographical.

Considering these poems together, we find that Blake never lost his lyrical technique. His prosody became increasingly sensitive to the subtler variations of word-music ; while the thought was more and more fully expressed. Certain poems, indeed, are so brilliantly baffling that they deserve the most intensive analysis.

By far the most prominent is *The Everlasting Gospel,* which was Blake's record of what he believed had originally been the primal, universal religion.[1] It is also his analysis of the character of the historical Jesus. Assembled from its scattered and fragmentary form in the *MS. Book,* we can deduce the following doctrines : that Man is God (iii. 75-76) ; that Jesus was the ideal Man ; that he upset all the established laws (v. 15 *seq.* and vi. 11 *seq.*) ; and denied the accepted God as Satan (ii. 29-30) ; thought that the Creation was the Fall itself (iii. 89-96) ; and refused therefore to pray for the world (iii. 86). In ethics, Jesus was an out-and-out Revolutionist (v. 37-40), though Blake admitted elsewhere

---

[1] *Descriptive Catalogue,* No. v : ' All had originally one language and one religion ; this was the religion of Jesus, the Everlasting Gospel.'

that Jesus was wrong in his attacks on the government.[1] He did not believe in holiness (vi. 25-28) ; declared that hypocrisy was a sin (vi. 69-74) ; also chastity (vi. 1 *seq.*). In character Jesus was disobedient to his parents (ii. 11-12) ; wrathful (ii. 33-34) ; proud and authoritative (iii. 16, 65) ; anti-scientific (iii. 49-50) ; a violator of most of the Commandments ; and might even be called a murderer (v. 40).

Blake admits that his Jesus is not the accepted deity, since each man makes God in his own image (i. 1-4). His God is not the accepted friend of all mankind, which includes fools and hypocrites, but one who teaches divine truths almost in vain (i. 5-6). The opening section of the poem may be quoted, to illustrate Blake's epigrammatic brilliancy, which is shocking nearly to the point of blasphemy.

> The Vision of Christ that thou dost see
> Is my Vision's Greatest Enemy.
> Thine has a great hook nose like thine ;
> Mine has a snub nose like to mine.
> Thine is the Friend of All Mankind ;
> Mine speaks in Parables to the Blind.
> Thine loves the same world that mine hates ;
> Thy heaven doors are my Hell Gates.
> Socrates taught what Melitus
> Loath'd as a Nation's bitterest Curse,
> And Caiaphas was in his own Mind
> A benefactor to Mankind.
> Both read the Bible day & night,
> But thou read'st black where I read white.

But the spirit behind this is not blasphemy. It was the fierce bitterness of his attack on the false god worshipped under the divine name, and a confidence of familiarity with his own deity, that made Blake write as he did.

His similarity of doctrine with the Gnostics has already been amply treated ; in general it has been over-emphasized. His friendship with Tom Paine alone would account for his rejection of the God of this world. His belief that Man is higher than all the gods—that in himself is the only true God—is one of the oldest secret doctrines. Yet Blake may well have evolved it himself. His analysis of Jesus's character was undoubtedly a virile reaction from the ' Gentle Jesus, meek and mild,' of the sentimental pietists.

The Mental Traveller, however, has not been so easily explained. Blake developed the idea of the poem in symbols which are not used elsewhere. Certain lines had their effect upon two lines in *Milton* ; a couple of passages in *Jerusalem* may be derived distantly from this poem ; and we can also trace a certain vague resemblance to the blended myths of Orc and the Shadowy Female, of Tiriel, and of Los and Enitharmon. It is not to be wondered that each interpreter has had a different idea, and that none seems to be wholly successful. But let us recapitulate the story of the poem.

In a strange land of men and women, remote from this earth, the Babe who was begotten in woe is born in joy. If he is a Boy he is given to an

---

[1] H. C. R., Dec. 10, 1825 : ' He was wrong in suffering himself to be crucified. He should not have attacked the Government. He had no business with such matters.'

Old Woman who crucifies him upon a rock, feeding upon his sorrows, growing young as he grows old. When they reach the ages of Youth and Virgin, he breaks free ' and binds her down for his delight.' So far, this might well be the story of Orc and Vala, as told in the *Preludium* to *America*. He then fades quickly to an aged Shadow in an earthly cottage filled with the gems and gold which he had won by industry.

> And these are the gems of the Human Soul,
> The rubies & pearls of a love-sick eye,
> The countless gold of the akeing heart,
> The martyr's groan & the lover's sigh.

On these he feeds the outcast and the wanderer; until during their revelry a little Female Babe springs from the hearth-fire. She is ' all of solid fire and gems & gold '; so that none dare touch her, not even to swaddle her. But when she finds her lover, ' if young or old, or rich or poor,' they soon drive out the aged host, to wander as a beggar. Do we now touch upon the story of Tiriel? He wanders away in tears, blind and age-bent, until he wins a maiden. Once he is in her arms, the cottage and its garden fades, the guests are scattered, the senses roll together in fear, and the flat earth becomes a ball, ' for the Eye altering alters all.' Even the heavenly luminaries shrink away, leaving nothing but a boundless desert, without food or drink. But the two are self-sufficient and re-enact the early life of Los and Enitharmon. He feeds upon ' the honey of her Infant lips, the bread & wine of her sweet smile,' growing younger and younger every day, until they wander in terror through the desert. In love and hate he pursues her, while she flees afraid;

> Till he becomes a wayward Babe,
> And she a weeping Woman Old.
> Then many a Lover wanders here;
> The Sun & Stars are nearer roll'd;
>
> The trees bring forth sweet extasy
> To all who in the desart roam;
> Till many a City there is Built,
> And many a pleasant Shepherd's home.

But should any find the Babe which he has become, he flees away horrified; should any dare to touch him, his arm is withered. All the wild animals hide, howling, ' and every Tree does shed its fruit.'

> And none can touch that frowning form
> Except it be a Woman Old;
> She nails him down upon the Rock,
> And all is done as I have told.

So the story ends just where it began.

We need not wonder at the number of interpretations which have been applied to this poem. According to EY (ii. 34) it is ' at the same time a sun-myth and a story of the Incarnation. It is also a vision of Time and Space,, Love and Morality, Imagination and Materialism.' Berger (pp. 322-323) finds the symbols clear enough, ' but the meaning entirely eludes us. . . . And, indeed, it matters very little from a literary point of view whether *The Mental Traveller* . . . be the history of a thought passing from generation to generation, or that of a passion in the soul of man, or a Sun Myth, or a symbolical account of man's conception, generation and birth, or a vision of Time, or all these at once.' Swinburne conjectured it ' to record . . . the perversion of love ; which having annihilated all else, falls at last to feed upon itself. . . . The babe that is " born a boy " . . . I take to signify human genius or intellect, which none can touch and not be consumed except the " woman old," faith or fear.' W. M. Rossetti came fairly near the fundamental idea of the poem, which, he said, ' indicates an explorer of mental phaenomena. The mental phaenomena here symbolized seems [sic] to be the career of any great Idea or intellectual movement—as, for instance, Christianity, chivalry, art, etc.—represented as going through the stages of—(1) birth, (2) adversity and persecution, (3) triumph and maturity, (4) decadence through over-ripeness, (5) gradual transformation, under new conditions, into another renovated Idea, which again has to pass through the same stages. In other words, the poem represents the action and reaction of Ideas upon society, and society upon ideas.' [1]

But none of these interpretations have really disclosed the fundamental meaning. *The Mental Traveller* represents very definitely the life of the Mystic, in the identical five stages outlined in the opening chapter. These ' states,' as Blake called them, are always in existence.

> As the Pilgrim passes while the Country permanent remains,
> So Men pass on ; but States remain permanent forever.[2]

In *The Mental Traveller* they are represented as recurring in a vast cycle.

Blake begins, as was his custom, with the Fall, or ' Experience,' since the State of Innocence is not self-conscious. A child is born, Orc, the spirit of Revolt ; the child which is begot in pain, but brought forth with joy. As usual, before he can gather strength, he is repressed and tortured by the ' Woman Old,' who is the Shadowy Female, Vala, the goddess of Material Nature. His head (intellect) is circumscribed with the crown of thorns ; his heart (emotion) is extirpated ; and the whole crucifixion is re-enacted. Society feeds upon his agony, unconsciously growing younger as he grows more mature.

Then the next stage, the New Life, appears. Orc or Revolt breaks loose, organizes the world after his own youthful will, and establishes his own family, or system of things. From his previous suffering and his spiritual labours, he has amassed the gems and gold of ' treasures in heaven,' which are freely given to all comers. ' His grief is their eternal joy.'

But this cannot last. He is growing old ; and other errors are upon him. From his own hospitality (hearth—the liberality of his opinions), an established code of conduct springs up : a Church, outward religion. This is the ' Female Babe,' so sacred that none dare touch her. In Blake's later symbolism, she is named Rahab. She chooses her own paramour (ideal), and they drive the ' aged Host ' away ; they cast out the original impulse which was the beginning of their Church. And thus the Dark Night of the Soul is reached.

The Dark Night is spent in uniting the outcast with his Emanation.

[1] Quoted by D. G. Rossetti in Gilchrist, 1863, vol. ii. p. 98.
[2] *Jerusalem*, 73 : 42-43.

Orc is no longer Orc : he is rather Los seeking Enitharmon. In brief, the Man must be made whole. The search is bitter. He explores the world by means of science (stanzas 16 and 17), and all joy flees. But his Emanation (who might also be named Jerusalem) is nearby. She flees from him ; he pursues her. Gradually they become accustomed to each other ; in their ' various arts of love,' he is regenerated again, while she grows more mature.

Thus the ultimate stage of the Mystic Way is reached ; which Blake also identifies with the first stage, Innocence. Again the instinctive, pastoral existence appears in their Unitive life.

But it is not final, for nothing is final. Jerusalem becomes Vala ; spiritual freedom becomes aged into the outward form of Nature ; and again the Man takes on the form of Orc, the ' Frowning Babe,' ready again to revolt against any stagnation of the universe.

My Spectre around me night & day is much more easily explained. It was Blake's first use of a symbolism which otherwise does not appear until the epics. There it is elaborated far beyond this (comparatively) simple poem, so I feel that the lyric must have preceded the first epic, which was begun about 1797.[1] Quotations from it are found in *Milton*, 32*).

The Spectre is the dominant, logical part of Man ; the Emanation is the outcast imaginative part. Blake was very fond of repeating that Man in the state of Experience has rejected certain lovely aspects of life because they seem trivial, dangerous, or merely illogical. Man's salvation consists in overcoming this division, in synthesizing everything, in literally ' making himself whole.' When this harmony is attained, Man has transcended the world and is actually living in Eternity. Otherwise, he repeats the error of Urizen :

> Thro' Chaos seeking for delight ; & in spaces remote
> Seeking the Eternal, which is always present to the wise ;
> Seeking for pleasure, which unsought falls round the infant's path [2]

In modern psychology, the Spectre and Emanation are simply the Conscious and the Subconscious. Every artist intuitively tries to unite them, since all his creative moments are the suffusion of the former by the latter.

Blake's poem, then, represents the mental conflict of Fallen Man. His intellect has cast out pleasure and named her ' Sin.' Everywhere he tracks her remorselessly, in an effort to subjugate her completely. But any such domination of one mental faculty over the others is bound to bring misery.

' " Attempting to be more than Man We become less," said Luvah.' [3] The Emanation herself (who is then Inspiration) indicates this union as salvation.

The *Auguries of Innocence* is the only other long poem. It begins and ends with two of Blake's most exquisite quatrains, but the body of the poem itself is nothing but a series of ill-connected distiches, which Blake undoubtedly intended to rearrange. He surely would have omitted many whose literary value is questionable. Others, however, are remarkably

---

[1] Sampson (1913, p. 128) thinks that it was ' probably composed in October or November 1800, soon after Blake's removal to Felpham, when he resumed the use of his old sketch-book as a notebook for poetry.'

[2] *The Four Zoas*, ix. 169-171.   [3] *Ibid.*, ix. 706.

fine. It would not be fair to Blake to consider such a series of jottings as a completed poem, for it is obviously only the elaborate notes for the poem.

Blake's intended structure of the poem is clear enough. The opening quatrain, which is quoted in every 'Essay on Blake,' no matter how small, is a perfect description of the first act of Contemplation, which is the beginning of the Mystic Way. One can read nowhere in mystical literature without finding striking parallels, some of which are quoted in the Commentary.

' To see a World in a Grain of Sand ' is the beginning of Mysticism ; and unfortunately often the end. In such a case the Mystic becomes a Pantheist, finding God in Nature. Blake termed all such people (notably Wordsworth) ' Atheists,' for such people worship only the luminous veil. The *Auguries of Innocence* starts from this point, and was intended to move through various stages to the complete revelation of God, which is given in the last stanza :

> God appears, & God is light
> To those poor souls who dwell in Night ;
> But does a Human Form Display
> To those who Dwell in Realms of Day.

Just what these stages were, Blake did not make entirely clear. Evidently the first stage was the perceiving of Eternity in the mineral world (the Grain of Sand) ; then came the transcending of the vegetable world (the Wild Flower) ; then was to follow the animal world. But here Blake began to record various aphorisms against cruelty to animals, seeing in the outward fact an indication of spiritual evil. Such evil presages still greater ills in the material world, unless corrected.

> A dog starv'd at his Master's Gate
> Predicts the ruin of the State. . . .
> Each outcry of the hunted Hare
> A fibre from the Brain does tear.

Whatever we see in the outward world is really an externalization of ourselves.

> The Bat that flits at close of Eve
> Has left the Brain that won't Believe.
> The Owl that calls upon the Night
> Speaks the Unbeliever's fright.

This doctrine later was expanded into Enion's wonderful cry at the end of Night VIII. of *The Four Zoas* :

> So Man looks out in tree & herb & fish & bird & beast,
> Collecting up the scatter'd portions of his immortal body
> Into the Elemental forms of everything that grows . . .
> . . . . Wherever a grass grows
> Or a leaf buds, The Eternal Man is seen, is heard, is felt,
> And all his Sorrows, till he re-assumes his ancient bliss.

When Blake reached this point in the *Auguries,* he began to insert aphorisms against the scientific attitude of doubting everything until it is proved ; Blake's idea being that the perception itself is proof enough, and that doubt may even destroy the truth.

> If the Sun & Moon should Doubt,
> They'd immediately Go Out.

Instead of developing this doctrine, Blake indicated it by several scattered couplets, and then began to work on another doctrine : that in this world some are born to joy, while others are born to sorrow.   Yet

> Under every grief & pine
> Runs a joy with silken twine.

From our sorrows come the creative joys, the ability to understand and help others.   The idea is the same that we encountered in *The Mental Traveller*, where—

> His grief is their eternal joy ;

but the symbolism is different.

> Every Tear from Every Eye
> Becomes a Babe in Eternity
> This is caught by Females bright
> And return'd to its own delight.

That is : every sorrow is a spiritual birth.   The ' Female bright,' or the Muses (the ' daughters of Beulah '), take it in charge and make it a child of joy ; the grief has become understanding, which to the wise man is actual joy.

And here God appears : to those in the night of Error, he is the impersonal light of Truth ; but to those who have attained Truth, he is one of them, the Friend.

Naturally, since this series of notes is so uneven, the critics vary absurdly in their attempts to pass a definite judgment upon it as a complete poem.   Garnett says it is ' little remote from nonsense,' Chesterton finds its unevenness a sure sign of madness (p. 93), while W. M. Rossetti believes this poem to be ' among Blake's noblest performances.'   Many of the lines certainly seem absurd and insipid, when removed from their setting.

> Kill not the Moth nor Butterfly
> For the Last Judgment draweth nigh,

is not this like a bit of advice in some book intended to make children moral ?   But, on the other hand, there are long series of couplets whose powerful directness or whose imaginative penetration leave nothing to be desired.

> The Strongest Poison ever known
> Came from Caesar's Laurel Crown.
> Nought can Deform the Human Race
> Like to the Armour's iron brace.
> When Gold and Gems adorn the Plow
> To peaceful Arts shall Envy Bow. . . .
> The Whore & Gambler, by the State
> Licensed, build that Nation's Fate.
> The Harlot's cry from Street to Street
> Shall weave Old England's winding-Sheet.
> The Winner's shout, the Loser's Curse,
> Shall dance before dead England's Hearse.

About half of the remaining poems deal with love and its problems, in quite the spirit which we should expect of Blake.   Free Love is still held up as an ideal, which is confessedly impossible to attain (*Silent, Silent*

Night, and *Mary*) ; while lust is an intolerable bondage (*The Golden Net*), which pollutes and destroys love (*I laid me down*).

The rest of the poems vary from the Rabelaisian attack on Klopstock, to Blake's *Dedication* of his edition of Blair to the Queen. There are political poems ; such as *Lafayette*, which describes the good man with the wrong allegiance ; pacifistic poems, such as *I saw a Monk of Charlemaine* ; poems dealing with the two states of Innocence and Experience ; and several scattered subjects. All these are clear enough to need no explanation beyond a note or so in the Commentary.

Two of the poems in the letters to Butts are of great interest as poetic descriptions of Blake's own psychology. In the letter from Felpham, October 2, 1800, is a description of a mystical vision on the seashore. The sun was shining, when

> Over Sea, over Land,
> My Eyes did Expand . . .
> Into regions of fire
> Remote from Desire.

Here every particle became a jewel of light, which assumed the form of a man, leading Blake to his anthropomorphic doctrine that all the aspects of nature 'Are Men Seen Afar.' It is quite probable that here he was combining his Subjective Idealism with a theory of Reincarnation. After this revelation, he saw Felpham and the mystery of the soul's descent into the 'weak mortal birth.' Still the vision progressed, his eyes continued 'expanding' ; and finally all appeared as 'One Man,' who is Jesus (also Swedenborg's 'Grand Man,' the Hindu Maha-Pooroosh, and the Kabalistic 'Adam Kadmon'). Blake remained for a while in his sunny bosom, hearing a voice which called him 'O thou Ram horn'd with gold.'

> And the voice faded mild :
> I remain'd as a Child ;
> All I ever had known
> Before me bright Shone.

A second vision is described in a letter dated from Felpham, November 22, 1802. This vision had taken place a year before. At the time Blake was troubled by Hayley's attitude, and worried by the fear of poverty. In a pessimistic mood, he wandered out and was appalled by the adversity of nature, as symbolized by a thistle. Here Blake developed his famous theory of double vision.

> For double the vision my Eyes do see,
> And a double vision is always with me.
> With my inward Eye, 'tis an old Man grey,
> With my outward, a Thistle across my way.

This is obviously not the common power of visualization, seen by the 'eyen of his mynde, with which men seen after that they ben blynde' ; [1] but an entirely different faculty—that of perceiving by power of the imagination the humanity within external objects. The Thistle is the bitterness of adversity. Blake breaks it with his foot ; and suddenly the God of Poetry appears ; outwardly as the sun, inwardly as Los. Strengthened by the sight, he defies the world, where his happiness is not to be

---

[1] Chaucer, *Man of Lawe's Tale*, 454-455.

found, for 'Another Sun feeds our life's streams.' At once the whole universe reflects his intellectual warfare.

Lastly, the epigrams remain to be considered. These were never intended for publication ; therefore due allowances must be made for them. Blake was apt to compress the annoyance of a moment into a stinging couplet, jot it down, and then forget it. Some of these are excellent wit ; others are not so good.

It is generally agreed that Blake kept all these poisoned darts in concealment ; but D. G. Rossetti thought otherwise. In his copy of Gilchrist, he found the following epigram significant :

> The Fox, the Owl, the Beetle, and the Bat,
> By sweet reserve and modesty grow Fat.'

Rossetti underlined ' sweet reserve,' then annotated : On Stothard. This seems to show that Blake aired his MS. epigrams in confidence.' This is so far-fetched that it would hardly be worth noting, were it not that other evidence is to be found that Blake's epigrams were known in his day. A reviewer of Gilchrist in *The New Monthly Magazine* (vol. 130, London, 1864) wrote of them : ' The best specimen, in this way, was circulated (and attributed to Blake) in the first decade of the present century ; but it is not reprinted by Mr. Gilchrist.' The poem is then quoted.

> ' Tickle me,' said Mr. Hayley,
>   ' Tickle me, Miss Seward, do ;
> And be sure I will not fail ye,
>   But in my turn will tickle you.'
>
>   So to it they fell a-tickling.
>
> ' Britain's honour ! Britain's glory !
>   Mr. Hayley, that is you.'
> ' The nine Muses bow before ye !
>   Trust me, Lichfield's swan, they do.'
>
> Thus these feeble bardlings squand'ring
>   Each on each their lavish rhymes,
> Set the foolish reader wond'ring
>   At the genius of the times.

The poem is not Blake's ; it is a perversion of an epigram of Dr. Mansel's on the interchange of compliments between the Hermit of Felpham and the Swan of Lichfield.[1] All that this gossip proves is that Blake was known to write epigrams. But there is not the slightest evidence that they ever reached a victim.

Those epigrams which need the most explanation here are the ones dealing with his views of art. Blake as a painter was thoroughly out of sympathy with the contemporary tendencies and tastes. Naturally he did not spare those who differed from him ; so we find in the *MS. Book* puzzling attacks on famous names.

The secret is that painting was neither Blake's first nor second interest in life. He was primarily a mystic ; and to the exposition of his mystical ideas everything else was subordinated. His next interest was his poetry ;

---

[1] See E. V. Lucas, *A Swan and Her Friends*, ch. ix.

of which he made himself one of the great masters, anticipating the technical discoveries of the nineteenth century, and indicating the trend of the twentieth. It is only after these two interests that painting entered his life. He stood for the imaginative depiction of great ideas. Painting was mainly a means of expressing ideas : only by appreciating this can we understand what he meant when he told Crabb Robinson that the absurd diagrams in the Law edition of Jakob Böhme were equal to Michelangelo.[1] He simply meant that the conceptions behind them were as great as Michelangelo's conceptions.

This case is an extreme example of the perfectly defensible theory that the inspiration counts for more than the technique.   When Blake attacked Greek art, he was really attacking Greek philosophy. He considered Plato's *Timaeus* not sufficiently penetrating ; he found the poets turned out of the famous *Republic* ; inspiration was classified as a form of madness ; the whole theory of art was one of ' imitation,' which Blake took to mean Realism ; while the very Muses were called ' Daughters of Memory.' Obviously, such a people, who took Reason for the supreme ideal, who ignored Inspiration and called it Madness, and who tried to make art logical, could not be great artists.   And what had they produced? Blake was living in a day of Grecian cults : the day of Canova, Flaxman, David, Thorwaldsen, and the like.   Blake himself engraved a number of classic outlines for George Cumberland, over which he could not have been enthusiastic for more than a day.   Such was Greek art !   No wonder Blake protested ! What few statues he did know, he called ' justly admired.' [2]

Blake's admiration for the Italian primitives has been entirely justified. We need only pause to comment on the good taste of the man who could praise Michelangelo and Raphael in a day when Guido Reni and the Carracci were the fashion.   But when the Venetian painters, from Titian on, appeared, then Blake felt that the highest impulse of art had gone. The old reverence was replaced by palace decoration ; the Virgin had been ousted for ducal mistresses ; the flesh had overcome the spirit. Therefore Blake despised them.   This explains his attacks on the Venetians and on Rubens, both of whom were very much in favour in his day.   From the point of view of such a man, the soft sensualities of Correggio were surely the work of ' a soft and effeminate and consequently a most cruel demon.' [3]

Coming to Blake's contemporaries, we find that the tradition of the imaginative depicting of great ideas had absolutely vanished.   The Greeks, the Venetians, and the Flemish were the gods of the hour ; flesh was triumphant.   The portraitists Reynolds, Gainsborough, Romney, and Lawrence were mainly concerned with dresses, rouge, and pretty attitudes ; nowhere could one find a big idea or a superb emotion. Blake considered all their paintings as nothing but studies for paintings— experiments in technique, made in preparation for the vision, which never came.

Naturally he felt very bitterly against the popularity of the favourites ;

---

[1] H. C. R., Dec. 10, 1825.   [2] *Descriptive Catalogue*, No. II.
[3] *Descriptive Catalogue*, No. IX. Cf. Lavater's 485th *Aphorism*, ' The cruelty of the effeminate is more dreadful than that of the hardy.'

and he warned the future reader of his annotations on the lectures of Sir Joshua Reynolds in what spirit they were written :

Having spent the Vigour of my Youth & Genius under the Opression of Sr Joshua & his Gang of Cunning Hired Knaves, Without Employment & as much as could possibly be Without Bread, The Reader must Expect to Read in all my Remarks on these Books Nothing but Indignation & Resentment. While Sr Joshua was rolling in Riches, Barry was Poor & Unemploy'd except by his own Energy, Mortimer was call'd a Madman & only Portrait Painting applauded & rewarded by the Rich & Great. Reynolds & Gainsborough Blotted & Blurred one against the other & Divided all the English World between them. Fuseli Indignant almost hid himself. I am hid.

The painting of such a man, then, is most interesting from the standpoint of the philosophy behind it, the cosmos which it tries to represent, and the beauty of the conceptions ; rather than for triumphs of technique. ' Painting, as well as poetry and music, exists and exults in immortal thoughts.' Yet Blake is not to be sneered at because he insisted in painting ideas and poetry ; even as a painter pure and simple, his very blunders are of interest.

The most important feature of his technique was his recognition of the emotional value of line. It is now practically axiomatic that good drawing is the basis of good painting. ' The great and golden rule of art, as well as of life,' Blake wrote in the *Descriptive Catalogue*, ' is this : That the more distinct, sharp, and wiry the bounding line, the more perfect the work of art ; and the less keen and sharp, the greater is the evidence of weak imitation, plagiarism, and bungling. Great inventors, in all ages, knew this : Protogenes and Apelles knew each other by this line. Raphael and Michelangelo and Albert Dürer are known by this and this alone. The want of this determinate and bounding form evidences the want in the artist's mind, and the pretence of the plagiary in all its branches. How do we distinguish the oak from the beech, the horse from the ox, but by the bounding outline ? How do we distinguish one face or one countenance from another, but by the bounding line and its infinite inflexions and movements ? What is it that builds a house and plants a garden, but the definite and determinate ? What is it that distinguishes honesty from knavery, but the hard and wiry line of rectitude and certainty in the actions and intentions ? Leave out this line and you leave out life itself ; all is chaos again, and the line of the Almighty must be drawn out upon it before man or beast can exist. Talk no more then of Correggio or Rembrandt, or any other of those plagiaries of Venice or Flanders. They were but the lame imitators of lines drawn by their predecessors, and their works prove themselves contemptible disarranged imitations, and blundering misapplied copies.' The last word is to be understood in the Platonic sense.

From this it is clear that by ' line ' Blake meant form ; and the attempt to represent form by colour or chiaroscuro, which to him were exterior and ever-shifting accidents, was a fundamental mistake. The expressiveness of line is the great triumph of Blake's work. He rivals the best of the Orientals in his vigorous beauty and his inexhaustible fecundity of invention. On a few inches of paper he could surpass them and approach Michelangelo himself in majesty of design.

From Michelangelo he must have derived his own feeling for the

geometry of composition.   His best inventions often reduce themselves to
a circle, a cross, or a square.   The human figure itself is distorted for the
sake of added force or grace.   He omitted the right arm of the Creator
in the frontispiece to *Europe* ; he lengthened the legs of the Spirits of the
Blight (plate XI).

Yet here Blake's theory played him false.   His compositions become
nothing but designs in two dimensions.   He had, of course, a feeling for
tactual values, and his outlines are generally contours.   But line, not
form, triumphed at times.   The story that he ' kindled ' at the idea of
turning *The Morning Stars* from his *Job* into a stained-glass window
reveals significantly his plateresque tendency.   We cannot imagine one
of Botticelli's designs gaining in effectiveness as a window ; and Botticelli,
from the point of view of line, is the nearest Occidental to Blake.

Moreover it must be confessed that, from the purely artistic standpoint, Blake's designs often become monotonous.   The series for *Job* or
for *Paradise Lost* repeats too often the same pattern, the same simple
symmetries.

Though he despised colour as the prime means of gaining his effects,
Blake nevertheless was very proud of his command of it.   He ' defied
competition in colouring.'   And indeed, though he never used colour as a
means of expressing form (thereby approaching Puvis de Chavannes
instead of Cezanne), he used colour with a sensitiveness far beyond any
of his contemporaries.   Each copy of each book is based upon a different
chord of colour, whose triad contains effects quite parallel to ' altered
notes ' in music.   Each book is considered as a whole, even the effect of
one page after another being taken into account.

The Songs of Innocence was originally coloured with the tender
simplicity of a Fra Angelico, though with a distinct atmosphere of out-of-
doors.   Then, as other books appeared, the colours became richer and
richer, reaching a climax in *America*, whose brilliant and yet subtle pris-
matics leave nothing to be desired.   Meanwhile he was experimenting
in more subdued tones.   The copy of the *Songs* which he made for
Flaxman seems very pallid beside other copies ; but the same austerity
reappears in both the water-colour series for *Job*.   We find a new tendency
in the poisonous colours for *Europe* and *Urizen* : dark, powerful, but
never muddied.   Indeed, through all Blake's works, the perfection of
surface is such that any portion whatsoever, however large or small,
seems as jewelled and complete as a butterfly's or moth's wing.

Blake's limitations, then, are clear ; but it must be acknowledged
that they were such as grew out of the very nature of his books.   But
even without these limitations, it is difficult to find, throughout the whole
range of English art, another with either the power or the variety of the
poet-mystic.

CHAPTER XXIV

COSMOGRAPHY

As I ponder'd in silence,
Returning upon my poems, considering, lingering long.
A Phantom arose before me, with distrustful aspect,
Terrible in beauty, age, and power,
The genius of poets of old lands,
As to me directing like flame its eyes,
With finger pointing to many immortal songs,
And menacing voice, *What singest thou?* it said ;
Know'st thou not, there is but one theme for ever-during bards ?
And that is the theme of War, the fortune of battles,
The making of perfect soldiers ?
Be it so, then I answered,
I too, haughty shade, also sing war—and a longer and greater one than any,
Waged in my book with varying fortune—with flight, advance, and retreat—Victory
    deferred and wavering.
(Yet, methinks, certain, or as good as certain, at the last),—The field the world ;
For life and death—for the body and for the eternal Soul,
Lo ! I too am come, chanting the chant of battles,
I, above all, promote brave soldiers.
                         —WALT WHITMAN.

IN the beginning—but Blake's system has no 'Berashith.' There never was a beginning, and there never will be an end, for Time is only an illusion of our senses. 'Many suppose that before the Creation all was solitude and chaos. This is the most pernicious idea that can enter the mind, as it takes away all sublimity from the Bible, and limits all existence to creation and chaos—to the time and space fixed by the corporeal vegetative eye, and leaves the man who entertains such an idea the habitation of unbelieving demons. Eternity exists, and all things in eternity, independent of Creation, which was an act of Mercy.'[1]

Eternity is the only real existence. 'The world of Imagination is the world of Eternity. It is the Divine Bosom into which we shall all go after the death of the vegetated body. This world of Imagination is infinite and eternal, whereas the world of Generation, or Vegetation, is finite and temporal. There exist in the eternal world the realities of everything which we see reflected in this vegetable glass of nature.'

'Eternity' is not synonymous with 'everlasting.' It does not mean an endless succession of Time ; but something quite different from Time, in which all Time is included as a mere parenthesis of six thousand years. The 257th design for Young's *Night Thoughts* represents the Everlasting of Nature as a serpent coiled upon itself, endlessly revolving ; while above it stands Man, a straight line poised upon the circle.

The sun-like World of Eternity, then, is all that really exists, for Creation was a Fall away from Reality into Illusion. There is no Purgatory, much less a Hell, in Blake's scheme. The Earth itself is the nadir of the universe, a limit fixed to the Fall by the mercy of the Saviour. When

---

[1] *Vision of the Last Judgment.*

Blake represented a Hell in his Last Judgments, the flames symbolize instant annihilation, not torment ; and everything which falls there is but error and illusion.[1]   Nothing else can be destroyed.   ' Hell ' is simply Non-Existence.

In Eternity are all individuals dead or unborn ; only those now on this earth are outside it.   Blake anticipated Walt Whitman's theory : ' I believe of all those billions of men and women that filled the unnamed lands, every one exists this hour, here or elsewhere, invisible to us, in exact proportion to what he or she did, felt, became, loved, sinn'd in life.' [2] But Blake goes farther : the Eternals may never have descended into this world ; or they may have come as spiritual forces ; or, with or without some divine mission, they may actually have taken on the mortality of this body.   Incarnation is likely ; reincarnation is possible.   ' Man Brings All that he has or Can have Into the World with him.   Man is Born Like a Garden ready Planted & Sown.   This world is too poor to produce one Seed.' [3]   But incarnation is a terrible thing ; to the Immortals it seems like Death—indeed, it is the nearest to Annihilation that any can approach.   Blake therefore names it boldly ' Eternal Death.'

Meanwhile the Eternals, who are the Divine Family, live a tremendous life of ' War & Hunting, the Two Fountains of the River of Life ' : [4] the warfare of the intellect and the hunting of ideas.   In this world, war and hunting pursue and kill bodies ; but in Eternity they give life, not death. When they are not hunting and warring, or engaged in the furies of poetic composition, they gather about the tables in the Halls of Los, drinking the Wine of Brotherhood and eating the Bread of Thought.   Sometimes they sing of spiritual events upon the harp ; sometimes they discuss what is taking place below them.   They laugh heartily among themselves at the monstrous folly of men upon earth, or they pity and send guardians to follow them and save them.   Among them are Chaucer, Shakspere, and Milton ; and Bacon, Newton, and Locke.[5]   Here are the iridescent meadows where Thel guards her sheep.   Their life is so intense that our highest joys seem only a dream and a repose to them.

Eternity remains, now as ever, perfect.   It includes all things.   ' Not one smile nor sigh nor tear, One hair nor particle of dust ; not one can pass away.' [6]   Even the errors and illusions which have made this world what it is exist there in Memory and Possibility.

> When all their Crimes, their Punishments, their Accusations of Sin,
> All their Jealousies, Revenges, Murders, hidings of Cruelty in Deceit
> Appear only in the Outward Spheres of Visionary Space and Time,
> In the shadows of Possibility by Mutual Forgiveness for evermore,
> And in the Vision & in the Prophecy, that we may Foresee & Avoid
> The terrors of Creation & Redemption & Judgment.[7]

Eternity is not all bliss.   ' There is suffering in heaven, for where there is capacity of enjoyment, there is the capacity of pain.' [8]   ' Heaven & Hell are born together.'   Thus Thel was forced to leave her Eden and become incarnated, so that she might pass through the stage of Experience,

[1] The ' Hell ' in *The Marriage of Heaven and Hell* was only a paradox, which Blake did not sustain in his later books.

[2] *Unnamed Lands.*
[4] *Milton*, 35 : 2.   [5] *Jerusalem*, 98 : 9.
[7] *Ibid.*, 92 : 15-20.

[3] Reynolds marginalia.
[6] *Ibid.*, 13 : 66 14 : 1.
[8] H. C. R., Dec. 10, 1825.

in order to rise to a broader life. To be an Error and to be cast out is part of God's design.'[1] Thel is almost the only woman we hear of in the Heaven of Eternity. Blake later came to believe that a woman exists in a separate form from her husband only through the error of Creation ; in Eternity the two are made one, and her sex disappears.[2] Milton, for example, had not achieved this union on earth, therefore he had to redescend and work out his unsolved problem.

Thus the great emotion in Eternity is that of Brotherhood. To love is impossible on the highest plane, because it necessitates a separation of lover and beloved, which is a descent.

> No one can consummate Female bliss in Los's World without
> Becoming a Generated Mortal, a Vegetating Death.[3]

However, love on this earth is, of course, a reuniting, and therefore an ascent.

Eternity can only be attained when all reconciliations are made and all errors cast out. Then it will take the form of One Man, Jesus. Visions of this ultimate union constantly haunt the dreams of the inspired. But this union is not a losing of the individuality, as a drop of water is lost in the sea ; nor is it the attainment of a desireless Nibbana. On the contrary, 'each identity is eternal.'[4] Everything is to be exalted ; the least event glorified ; and the whole will be organized into one harmonious life. In this all-inclusive union, even Nature is to participate : 'All Human Forms identified, even Tree, Metal, Earth, and Stone.'[5] 'Everything has as much right to Eternal Life as God who is the breast of Man.'[6]

In the symbol of the visible universe (for to Blake the Visible is nothing but a 'vegetable reflection' or symbol of the Invisible), the world of Eternity, of the Imagination, is represented by the Sun, which gives both light and heat.[7] Between this and the Earth there are two other planes of existence.

The Moon is the symbol of the state known as 'Beulah.' It represents the night of Love. As the Moon reflects the light of the Sun, making it endurable, so the joys of Eternity pass through Beulah to the Earth. The 'Daughters of Beulah' are Blake's muses. He chose the name 'Beulah' (married) since Man becomes aware of Eternity (or becomes inspired) just insomuch as he becomes united with his Emanation, which upon the Earth is known as his wife.[8] What is the highest inspiration for the Man upon earth is for the dwellers of Eternity merely a place of repose.

> . . . But to
> The Sons of Eden, the moony habitations of Beulah
> Are from Great Eternity a mild & pleasant Rest.

---

[1] *Vision of the Last Judgment.*
[2] 'In Eternity, woman is the emanation of man ; she has no will of her own ; there is no such thing in Eternity as a female will' (*Vision of the Last Judgment*).
[3] *Jerusalem*, 69 : 30-31.
[4] *Vision of the Last Judgment.*
[5] *Jerusalem*, 99 : 1.   [6] Thornton marginalia.
[7] Both this theory of the Fall and its symbolizing were adapted from Jakob Böhme. In the 14th illustration to *Job*, Blake shifted these symbols of the sun, moon, and stars in accordance with a later arrangement of the universe. This did not obtain until the *Job*, and will be discussed there.
[8] For a more detailed discussion of the relations between love and poetic inspiration, see Chapter xv., *The Fifth Window.*

And it is thus Created. Lo, the Eternal Great Humanity
To whom be Glory & Dominion Evermore, Amen,
Walks among all his awful Family seen in every face :
As the breath of the Almighty such are the words of man to man
In the great Wars of Eternity, in fury of Poetic Inspiration,
To build the Universe stupendous : Mental forms Creating.

But the Emanations trembled exceedingly, nor could they
Live, because the Life of Man was too exceeding unbounded.
His joy became terrible to them, they trembled & wept,
Crying with one voice : ' Give us a habitation & a place
In which we may be hidden under the shadow of wings :
For if we, who are but for a time & who pass away in winter,
Behold these wonders of Eternity, we shall consume :
But you, O our Fathers & Brothers, remain in Eternity,
But grant us a Temporal Habitation, do you speak
To us ; we will obey your words as you obey Jesus,
The Eternal, who is blessed for ever & ever. Amen.'

So spake the lovely Emanations : & there appeared a pleasant
Mild Shadow above, beneath, & on all sides round.

Into this pleasant Shadow all the weak & weary
Like Women & Children were taken away as on wings
Of dovelike softness, & shadowy habitations prepared for them
But every man return'd & went, still going forward thro'
The Bosom of the Father in Eternity on Eternity,
Neither did any lack or fall into Error without
A Shadow to repose in all the Days of happy Eternity.[1]

Beulah, then, is the place of the Emanations, who are those tender
and gentle joys of man which cannot endure the full glory of Eternity.
It entirely surrounds Eternity, so that travellers to and from Space must
pass through it. It is the Female of the masculine Sun.

But here Illusion begins. The Immortal who enters Beulah sleeps
upon a couch of gold, while his outward aspects tend to sink downward
into a lower state. In Beulah is woven the Shadow, which is the vehicle
of the Immortal through the lower worlds. On earth it becomes his
physical body.

Below the Moon of Beulah appear the Stars. Here Urizen is king,
since their scattered and ineffectual sparks of light which reveal nothing,
and the inevitable mechanism of their motion, are doubly symbolic of the
realm of Reason.[2] This is the mechanical world of Science, of ethical
laws, of Fate.

Lowest of all is the Earth, the shrunken form of Man, whose name is
Albion. Once his limbs contained the Sun, Moon, and Stars, but in his
Fall they were rent from him.[3] Not patriotism alone caused Blake to
choose the name of the ancient Giant as the name of the Eternal Man, for
both geography and the traditional history of Albion, or England, were

---

[1] *Milton*, 30 : 12-31 : 7.
[2] Cf. the opening lines of Dryden's *Religio Laici*.
[3] Cf. Jakob Böhme's *Three Principles*, xiv. 2 : ' For when Man departed from Paradise
into another Birth (viz. into the Spirit of this World, into the Quality of the Sun, Stars,
and Elements) then the Paradisical [Vision or] Seeing ceased, where Man sees from the
divine Virtue without the Sun and Stars.'

unusually felicitous as symbols. Man, like England, is a little island entirely surrounded by the Sea of Time and Space. It was originally inhabited by Giants (natural forces), which were subdued by a noble, the Trojan Brutus, who was exiled from a finer land (symbolically from Eternity). But Albion's ocean wall did not prove a definite barrier : it sent its ships across the Sea of Time and Space, just as the Poet is the Explorer of Eternity.[1]

This world is ruled by the Stars of Reason, to the exclusion of the Moon of Love and the Sun of Imagination. Being the lowest point of Creation, it is the farthest from the Truth. Everything we approach is veiled from us by illusion ; for Error has covered everything with ' An outside Shadowy Surface superadded to the real Surface.' [2] Sometimes this is called the Mundane Shell, by which Man is protected till he is ready to fly forth, as a Bird of Eternity. Error is caused by the wrong way of seeing ; and it is perfectly real to those who see it, having both cause and effect.

> . . . . What seems to Be, Is, To those to whom
> It seems to Be, & is productive of the most dreadful
> Consequences to those to whom it seems to Be ; even of
> Torments, Despair, Eternal Death ; but the Divine Mercy
> Steps beyond and Redeems Man in the Body of Jesus. Amen.[3]

Such wrong way of seeing is caused by the limitation of the sense-organs on this plane. Originally, Man was like the spirits which Milton describes :

> All Heart they live, all Head, all Eye, all Eare,
> All Intellect, all Sense ;

but now, at least four of his senses are dulled and localized :

> The Eye of Man, a little narrow orb, clos'd up & dark,
> Scarcely beholding the Great Light, conversing with the ground :
> The Ear, a little shell, in small volutions shutting out
> True Harmonies, & comprehending great as very small :
> The Nostrils, bent down to the earth & clos'd with senseless flesh
> That odours cannot them expand, nor joy on them exult :
> The Tongue, a little moisture fills, a little food it cloys,
> A little sound it utters, & its cries are faintly heard.[4]

Below the Earth is nothing. This Nothing Blake called the Void of Non-Entity. Its existence is purely theoretical. Immortals are often forced to its borders ; but the only things which can enter non-existence are Illusions, Negations, Prohibitions, and other Unrealities.

Man originally was, and shall be eventually, the whole ; and even in his fallen state he has not lost the rudiments of anything. Therefore the analysis of the Universe is nothing but an analysis of himself.[5] The Sun, Moon, Stars, and Earth are his fourfold division, which is the basis of all Blake's epical symbolism. Blake used other names to designate them when he was writing of Man, and not of the universe at large. These names he invented himself.

Around the Divine Throne, which is Man's central point, stand the

---

[1] The first use of this symbol occurs as early as the Song of the Minstrel in the last scene of *King Edward the Third* (*Poetical Sketches*).
[2] *Jerusalem*, 83 : 47.   [3] *Ibid.*, 36 : 50-54.   [4] *Ibid.*, 49 : 34-41.
[5] Albion is the Kabalistic Adam Kadmon and Swedenborg's Grand Man.

Four Zoas, or ' Living Creatures.' [1]   They are the Spirit, the Emotions, the Reason, and the Body with its Senses ; they are named respectively Urthona (Sun), Luvah (Moon), Urizen (Stars), and Tharmas (Earth).[2] None can exist without the others. ' A perfect Unity cannot exist but from the Universal Brotherhood of Eden, the Universal Man.' [3]   Whenever one of these Zoas tries to usurp the place of another, a Fall results, and all Eternity is rent apart. Blake's books are mainly accounts of these usurpations, divisions, and conflicts. In pursuance of his geographical symbolism, Blake assigned a point of the compass to each : the North, now frozen solid, is Man's spiritual realm (Urthona) ; the East, now void, belongs to the Emotions (Luvah) ; the South, a blazing desert, is the intellectual domain (Urizen) ; while the West, overwhelmed by the Sea of Time and Space, stands for the Body (Tharmas). At the Fall, the Four shrunk together into their present condition ; yet even now, in the midst of them, the world of Poetry, ' the sublime Universe of Los & Enitharmon,' is built eternally. For in the centre of Man is God.

But before we can consider Deity, we must recall another division of Man ; that into Spectre and Emanation. These two are Reason and Inspiration ; and they exist separately only when the Humanity (Man's essential individuality) has sunk into the sleep of the subconscious. Then Reason dominates Man and casts out all Inspiration. Occasionally a fourth aspect is recognized : the Shadow, who is both suppressed desire and the material body.

The four Zoas, in their fall, assume these same four positions. Urthona, the Spirit, sinks sleeping into the depths. Urizen and Luvah, Reason and Emotion, fight as Spectre and Emanation. Tharmas, the Body, takes on the illusory aspect of matter, and becomes the Shadow.

To complicate affairs, each Zoa may split into Spectre and Emanation. Urthona, to be sure, never appears divided ; but in a lower form, as Los (poetry), he has for emanation Enitharmon (spiritual beauty). Luvah (the emotions) has for emanation Vala (natural beauty). Urizen (reason) has Ahania (pleasure). Tharmas (the body) has Enion (the generative instinct). In Eternity, these emanations are absorbed into the bosoms of their respective Zoas ; who, in their turn, live interlacing forever in perpetual harmony.

This, in brief, is Blake's analysis of Man. It appears at first to be quite original, and perhaps rather arbitrary ; but this is only on account of the names which he invented. In fact, the four Zoas correspond quite closely to the traditional analysis of the philosophers : Ethics being Urthona ; Logic, Urizen ; and Aesthetics, Luvah ; with the addition of the Body and its sensations (Tharmas), as an equally essential part of Man. Blake is even in accord with Eastern mysticism : Urthona is Dharma ; Urizen, Karma ; while both Tharmas and Luvah are included in Maya. When ten or so of Blake's names are memorized, even the longest of the Prophetic Books becomes comparatively simple. And how much may be discovered without this key was demonstrated by Swinburne, who never once mentioned the Zoas as such.

[1] The word *Zoa* occurs in *Revelation*, and is translated ' Living Creature.' It evidently refers to the ' Beasts ' in Ezekiel's vision.

[2] A diagram of the Four Zoas as four interlacing circles is to be found in *Milton*, 32. Another, with interesting variations, is the celebrated 14th illustration to *Job*.

[3] *The Four Zoas*, i. 4-6.

Man is more than the central figure in Blake's cosmography; he is the whole of it. Even Deity himself is only of parallel importance. Blake practically says that God is Man's highest powers, which was a heresy characteristic at once of Blake and of his century. 'On my asking in what light he viewed the great question concerning the Divinity of Jesus Christ,' noted Crabb Robinson,[1] 'he said—"*He is the only God.*" But then he added—"And so am I and so are you."' God, then, is Jesus, who exists only in his immanence in Man. The two are inseparable. 'God is Man & exists in us & we in him.'[2] 'When separated from man or humanity, who is Jesus the Saviour?'[3] 'God only Acts and Is, in existing beings or Men.'[4] 'Thou art a Man: God is no more [than Man]; Thine own Humanity learn to adore.'[5]

This Jesus is the Divine Imagination, Faith, the Poetic Genius, and the Forgiver of Sins. He is not omnipotent: 'the language of the Bible on that subject is only poetic or allegorical,'[6] being statements intended to induce 'a firm persuasion' (and hence the actuality) of that desirable state. Jesus resides in the inmost part of Man. He is the power by which one can enter into and control any one of the four great divisions, or Zoas. Man in turn is the breast of God.[7] Mutual Immanence is the true Paradise of Eternity.

But though Jesus is the only true God, the other powers of the soul endeavour to become gods at times. 'These Gods are visions of the eternal attributes, or divine names, which, when erected into gods, become destructive to humanity. They ought to be the servants, and not the masters, of man or of society. They ought to be made to sacrifice to Man, and not Man compelled to sacrifice to them.'[8]

The Zoas themselves are the most important of these gods. Their histories are much interwoven, for they can be born of each other; they can fall, though still existing unfallen; they can die and live again; they can appear in several aspects at once. Yet, fundamentally, the course of their evolutions is not complicated.

Briefly, each one falls, divides, and is reborn in some lower form. Each is separated from his emanation; each wars with the other Zoas; each thinks himself triumphant, announcing himself to be God; and each is eventually humbled.

This warfare of the Zoas is traditional. Thus in the *Apocalypse of Abraham* we read: 'And I heard a voice like the roaring of the sea; nor did it cease on account of the rich abundance of the fire. And as the fire raised itself up, ascending into the height, I saw under the fire a throne of fire, and round about it four all-seeing ones, reciting the song, and under the throne four fiery living creatures singing, and their appearance was one, each one of them with four faces. . . . And when they had ended the singing, they looked at one another and threatened one another. And it came to pass when the angel who was with me saw that they were threatening each other, he left me and went running to them and turned the countenance of each living creature from the countenance immediately

---

[1] H. C. R., Dec. 10, 1825. Swedenborg also taught that Jesus was the only god. For Blake's corollary, see *John* x. 34.

[2] Marginalia to *Siris.*   [3] *Descriptive Catalogue.*
[4] *The Marriage of Heaven and Hell.*   [5] *The Everlasting Gospel.*
[6] H. C. R., Dec. 17, 1825.
[7] Thornton marginalia.   [8] *Descriptive Catalogue.*

confronting him, in order that they might not see their countenances threatening each other.'

Urthona, the Spirit, is the deepest and most obscure of the Zoas. He alone is not given an emanation ; for he must suffer a fall before he can be divided. In his fallen form he divides into Los and Enitharmon. Los, Poetry, is the ' temporal ' form of the Spirit ; he can fall still lower and become Religion. Enitharmon represents Spiritual Beauty, which is also Inspiration. When the two fall, Inspiration becomes divided from the Poet, causing him great anguish by her capriciousness. From them all philosophies and religions are born.[1] Their most prominent child is Orc, the Fire of Youth, or Revolution ; but he will be discussed later since he is a form of Luvah. Los, as the Poet, creates the Visible Universe ; for the Imagination is one of the Creators : ' Everything that Seems, Is.' He alone never lost the Divine Vision in time of trouble. He is the great friend of Man, and his form is that of the Divine Appearance itself. Enitharmon is also a Creator ; she weaves the bodies for the unbodied, in mercy for their blind and helpless wanderings.

Luvah, the passions and the emotions, has for emanation Vala, who is natural beauty, or Nature herself. One of the most important moments of the Fall took place when Luvah made himself charioteer of the car of Intellect. He smites Man, attempting to dominate him ; and when Man tries to cast him out in return, Luvah curses Man with spiritual disease. Man at last succeeds in binding him ; then Vala tortures Luvah, not knowing he is her proper consort. The two fall still lower, and are born of Los and Enitharmon as Orc (Revolution) and the Shadowy Female (Materialized Nature). The union of these two is the outbreak of war upon earth, which continues until it is absolutely unhindered, and then it burns itself out. As War exhausts itself, Matter is consumed, and the two reappear in their original forms as Luvah and Vala. Luvah has yet another avatar : that of Jesus, who descends to this earth in ' Luvah's robes of blood ' (the flesh). One of the great moments in *The Four Zoas* represents Urizen aghast to behold both Jesus and Orc, forms of his old enemy Luvah, arrayed against him. He cannot understand how the Prince of Peace and the God of War can both be manifestations of Passion.

Urizen (Reason) is the original causer of the Fall. He begins it by trying to usurp the throne of Urthona (the Spirit). He also tries to conspire with the other Zoas to dominate Man. His emanation is Ahania (Pleasure). When he discovers that she is separated from him, that Intellect and Pleasure have become two different things, he casts her out and names her Sin. The rest of her existence is spent wandering on the verge of Non Entity, until the Last Judgment, when she resumes her ancient throne. Meanwhile Urizen, in a mistaken attempt to be more and more purely himself, sinks lower and lower. He becomes the Architect of the Visible Universe. He supports the Religion of Moral Virtue, which finally snares even himself. He tries to reign by power of the curse, and blights everything with which he meddles. Blake often identifies him with the Jehovah of the Pentateuch, and with Satan ; for Reason is the god worshipped in this world. Finally he sinks so low that he loses all semblance of humanity, and is nothing but a ravening dragon. But as soon as he gives up his dreams of universal dominion,

---

[1] *All Religions are One.*

he is restored to his ancient glory. He has many children, the most important of whom are the four elements (his sons) and the threefold division of Man (his daughters).

The fourth Zoa is Tharmas, the Body and the Senses. In Eternity he is the spiritual body; in the Fall he acquires the outward illusion of the physical body. His emanation is Enion, the Generative Instinct, and consequently the Earth Mother. Tharmas is long-suffering. He pities Man; and even when he thinks himself Man's god, he regrets it. He seconds Urthona, the Spirit, when the latter is attacked. He never rejects his emanation; but none the less she is cruelly separated from him, to wander in the Void, sometimes reduced to a mere voice. Though these two seem the lowest of the Zoas, they play very important parts. In the realm of Tharmas the reversal of the Fall begins. He is always the friend of Urthona-Los. Of him and Enion are reborn the fallen Los and Enitharmon. Enion in her own way is a prophetess. Under the name of Eno (an anagram of ' Eon ' or ' emanation ') she performs the mystical task of extending a moment till it covers all history, and unfolding a grain of sand till it includes the universe. By her aid, therefore, we see a World in a Grain of Sand; through her the Moment reveals Eternity.

Besides the four Zoas, there is a fifth god who works mighty damage. He is Satan, the spirit most directly opposed to Jesus. He is the Selfhood (or selfishness), the Accuser, and false doctrine in general. He is, however, unique in having no real existence; he is Illusion. ' His Judgment shall be Forgiveness that he may be consumed on his own Throne.' [1]

No other Immortal can be destroyed; they all live, and therefore they are all holy. Blake never gives us a complete list of them, for they are innumerous, being various aspects of the human soul. They love, hate, seek dominion; but at the Last Judgment they will realize and give over the inevitable suffering which must ensue when ' Gods combine against Man, setting their dominion above the Human form Divine.' [2]

Thus Blake has symbolized the Fall as the lack of harmony and the consequent division within the soul of Man. Simultaneously with this symbol he developed another, which represents the Fall as a literal descent. The first symbol deals with the forces within Man; the second describes the Individual in relation to the Universe. It contains Blake's complete theory of incarnation.

The causes of the Individual's leaving Eternity have already been detailed: a lack of balance among his Zoas; a desire for the consummation of love; a search for some missing portion of himself; or the duty of correcting some error. But this only applies to the great souls. The little ones were scattered through the Void during the first great Fall from Eternity.

The Individual first descends into Beulah, where his Humanity (his real existence) falls into a sleep upon a golden couch. Here his Shadow is woven, which he enters, forgetting both Eternity and Beulah. There is nothing now to stop his falling any distance. He might even enter the Void of Non Entity, did not the Divine Mercy set limits within his bosom. He sinks down into the World of Generation, and often even into the deadly state of Ulro (pure matter). Here he beholds spirits petrified into rocks, stones, and metals; for everything is a part of the original Man,

---

[1] Thornton marginalia. [2] *The Four Zoas*, ix. 364.

divided from him by the illusion of Time and Space. The 'Spectres,' as yet unsnared in matter, wander disembodied and aimless, being 'piteous Passions & Desires With neither lineament nor form . . . meer passion & appetite.'[1] They might wander so forever, were not Los and Enitharmon inspired by the Divine Mercy to weave forms for them. The Spectres are terrified at the thought of entering physical forms, but Los and his sons snare them, while Enitharmon and her daughters weave them beautiful bodies on the Looms of Cathedron.

> They labour incessant, with many tears & afflictions,
> Creating the beautiful House for the piteous sufferer.
>
> Others, Cabinets richly fabricate of gold & ivory,
> For Doubts & fears unform'd & wretched & melancholy.
> The little weeping Spectre stands on the threshold of Death
> Eternal : and sometimes two Spectres like lamps quivering
> And often malignant they combat (heart-breaking. sorrowful & piteous).
> Antamon takes them into his beautiful flexible hands,
> As the Sower takes the seed or as the Artist his clay
> Or fine wax, to mould artful a model for golden ornaments.
> The soft hands of Antamon draw the indelible Line :
> Form immortal with golden pen ; such as the Spectre admiring
> Puts on the sweet form ; then smiles Antamon bright thro' his windows.
> The Daughters of beauty look up from their Loom & prepare
> The integument soft for its clothing with joy & delight.
>
> But Theotormon & Sotha stand in the Gate of Luban anxious . . .
> They contend with the weak Spectres, they fabricate soothing forms.
> The Spectre refuses : he seeks cruelty. . . .
> Terrified the Spectre screams & rushes in fear into their Net
> Of kindness & compassion & is born a weeping terror. . . .
> Howling the Spectres flee : they take refuge in Human lineaments.[2]

Each is given the clothing most appropriate, which will help him rise the soonest. Some become plants,[3] others animals,[4] and the best become men. But progress is not certain : it depends on the will-power and the intelligence of the Spectre. If given the form of man, he can yet become a beast.[5] In Blake's technical phraseology, such 'burst the bottoms of their tombs.'

The state of the average man in this world is thus described :

> They wander moping, in their heart a sun a dreary moon
> A Universe of fiery constellations in their brain
> An Earth of wintry woe beneath their feet, & round their loins
> Waters or winds or clouds, or brooding lightnings & pestilential plagues
> Beyond the bounds of their own self their senses cannot penetrate
> As the tree knows not what is outside of its leaves & bark
> And yet it drinks the summer joy & fears the winter sorrow.[6]

By self-expansion ; by hearkening to those Daughters of Beulah (Blake's Muses) who come willingly to us with messages from above ; by casting off the illusions which seem to limit us (the deadly Selfhood) ; by transcending mechanic laws through the development of our imagination ; we can rise again until our physical body fades into invisibility,

---

[1] *Milton*, 26 : 26-29.   [2] *Ibid.*, 27 : 6-28.   [3] *The Four Zoas*, ii. 164.
[1] *Jerusalem*, 59 : 45.   [5] *The Four Zoas*, viii. 116.   [6] *Ibid.*, vi. 90-97.

and so reachieve Eternity. Perhaps most important of all, however, is the *rightful* exercising of our intellects. ' Men are admitted into heaven . . . because they have cultivated their understandings. . . . The fool shall not enter into heaven, let him be ever so holy.' [1]

This symbol of the Fall applies both to the Individual and to Man as a race. The double limit fixed by Divine Mercy to the Fall was the creation of Adam and Satan. Man could fall no lower than Rousseau's ideal, the ' Natural Man ' ; Error could extend no farther than Illusion.

Adam was therefore created heir to all the ills begun in Eternity. At first he was happy in the state of Innocence ; but the ' Creation ' continued. Eve was separated from him in his sleep ; Good and Evil were divided ; ' coats of skin ' (the mortal flesh) were imposed ; and finally the two were driven from the Garden into the thorny state of Experience.

With Adam began the cruel religion which Blake called ' Druid.' Adam was a Druid, and Noah ; also Abraham was called to succeed the Druidical age, which began to turn allegoric and mental signification into corporeal command, whereby human sacrifice would have depopulated the earth.' [2] The Druidic religion worships Reason, cultivates the Selfhood, and sacrifices others to it. It began when Adam accepted the false standards of Good and Evil ; and its result was the Deluge of the Sea of Time and Space : that overwhelming of the world with the Spatial and the Temporal, from which only the man of imagination, Noah (the first one, it will be remembered, to plant a vineyard) could survive. With him remained Poetry, Painting, and Music, ' the three powers in man of conversing with Paradise, which the Flood did not sweep away.' [3]

But in spite of Noah and the poets (or Prophets) who followed him, Materialism triumphed. Jesus the man appeared, with his revolutionary ethics ; but he fought the progress of Materialism seemingly in vain. He was the greatest incarnation of Deity. His descent was deliberate, and was the greatest self-sacrifice that ever was or ever will be made. His life for the most part was purely instinctive ; and his recognition of this instinct enabled him to break in some degree or other most of the Ten Deadly Prohibitions which Moses had formulated. [4] But Jesus was not wholly perfect. He erred in praying for the world, [5] and he erred in entering public life and attacking the government. [6] Thus Error triumphed over him ; and he was sacrificed to Satan upon Calvary. [7]

' Jesus and his Apostles and Disciples were all Artists. Their Works were destroy'd by the Seven Angels of the Seven Churches in Asia, Antichrist, Science.' [8] The very attempt to formulate the instinctive life of Jesus into a religion was its deathblow. The Seven Churches were as much given to arguings and analytics as their predecessors ; and the Everlasting Gospel seemed dead. As a matter of fact, it *was* dead, entombed in the dogmas of the Churches ; but the time will come when it will rise from this sepulchre, casting off the dogmas which preserved it. Meanwhile, Materialism and the worship of Reason continued. Man became bound ' more and more to Earth, closed and restrained ; till a

---

[1] *Vision of the Last Judgment.*
[2] *Descriptive Catalogue.*   [3] *Vision of the Last Judgment.*
[4] *The Everlasting Gospel,* 5, and the last *Memorable Fancy* in *The Marriage of Heaven and Hell.*
[5] *The Everlasting Gospel,* 3.   [6] H. C. R., Dec. 10, 1825.
[7] *The Ghost of Abel,* 47.   [8] Laocoon plate.

Philosophy of Five Senses was complete : Urizen wept and gave it into the hands of Newton and Locke.' [1]

However, Blake saw Regeneration close at hand. Already Rousseau and Voltaire had appeared : the former giving Error a definite form to be cast off ; the latter exposing the superstitions of religion. These were, to be sure, negative teachers ; the positive were such people as the Methodists, Swedenborg, and Irving. None of these were complete initiates, and Blake considered himself, with some justice, the greatest of them all. The world of Eternity was stirred throughout. Revolutions in America and France revealed the inner regeneration. The six thousand years allotted to the created world were nearly finished : ' the end approaches fast.' [2]

The effecting of this great hope is a simple matter. Since the Fall was a process of division, Man's salvation must consist in seeking the original Unity of Eternity. This he does in two ways : (1) by ' entering the bosoms' of others, by sympathizing with them so strongly that they become part of himself ; (2) and by knowing himself, for such knowledge is the key to the knowledge of others. The first is the outward path to Unity ; the second, the inward path. Eternity and Infinity lie behind every manifestation of Time and Space whatsoever.

> The Vegetative Universe opens like a flower from the Earth's center
> In which is Eternity. It expands in Stars to the Mundane Shell,
> And there it meets Eternity again, both within and without. [3]

Everything that *lives* is holy ; man must reject nothing real, lest it become his enemy. Thus will be brought about the great Brotherhood of Eden. The motive force in this is Imagination (or God), by which one can understand all things. Understanding is forgiveness ; forgiveness judges nothing, but accepts. Therefore accusation, judgments, and punishments are to be replaced by understanding, sympathy, and toleration. When every one understands every one else completely, the original harmony will be restored.

There is a negative work in the process of salvation which is hardly less important. To acquire Truth, one must cast out Error. Error consists of all Illusions, Prohibitions, and Negations, which of their very nature have no real existence. A Contrary, as Blake warns us, is not a Negation, but a positive thing. Contraries must be reconciled ; for if one Contrary is rejected, the domination of its fellow ensues, and Truth is divided. Negations, however, are illusions. All such Errors are Devils. The greatest Error is Satan, the Accuser. He springs from the Selfhood— or rather, ' selfishness,' for Blake never denied the Individual. Self-assertion at the expense of another is Satanic ; selfishness is a contraction, a rejection, therefore a negation and an error. Its positive is the old Christian paradox that to give one's life is to find it. The Mystical Death is Eternal Life itself.

> Jesus said : ' Wouldest thou love one who never died
> For thee ? or never die for one who had not died for thee ?
> And if God dieth not for Man & giveth not himself
> Eternally for Man, Man could not exist ; for Man is Love
> As God is Love ; every kindness to another is a little Death
> In the Divine Image, nor can Man exist but by Brotherhood.' [4]

---

[1] *Song of Los : Africa*, 45-48.   [2] *Milton*, 22 : 55.
[3] *Jerusalem*, 13 : 34-36.   [4] *Ibid.*, 96 : 23-28.

The negative work, the casting off of errors, was symbolized by Blake as a Last Judgment. 'Whenever any individual rejects error and embraces truth, a Last Judgment passes upon that individual. . . . Error is created, truth is eternal. Error, or creation, will be burned up, and then, and not till then, truth or eternity will appear.'[1]

Of course there must be innumerable such Last Judgments, which will not end until the ultimate day terminating this continuous eschatology. No Last Judgment will be final until the six thousand years are completed. 'Many persons, such as Paine and Voltaire, with some of the ancient Greeks, say : " We will not converse concerning Good and Evil ; we will live in Paradise and Liberty." You may do so in spirit, but not in the mortal body, as you pretend, till after a Last Judgment. For in Paradise they have no corporeal and mortal body :[2] *that* originated with the Fall and was called Death, and cannot be removed but by a Last Judgment. While we are in the world of mortality, we must suffer— the whole Creation groans to be delivered.'[1]

It may seem puzzling that Blake should have allowed an ultimate Last Judgment, as well as any number of them in everybody's life. This was due to his acceptance of the old doctrine of the Macrocosm and the Microcosm : that everything enacted in Eternity is repeated in the life of each individual. The famous *Smaragdine Tables* of Hermes Trismegistus, which are the basis of all magic, begin : 'It is the truest and most certain thing of all things ; that which is above is as that which is below, and that which is below is as that which is above, to accomplish the one thing of all things most wonderful.' According to *Genesis*, Man is made in the image of God. In Blake's day the Methodists had recently discovered that in the soul of man the life of Christ was re-enacted. And to-day the scientists claim that man reflects in his body his complete biological history.[3]

So Blake was on firm ground when he believed that each man repeats in miniature the whole of spiritual history, past and to come. The Fall appears in the very act of birth, which is a division. Then for a while Man lives in the Earthly Paradise as a child ; but the seeds of Error are in him : 'Man is born a Spectre or Satan ' ;[4] and sooner or later he falls from Innocence into Experience, which is Death from Eternity. From this he is rescued by a Last Judgment—whether in a vision of mere Hope and Fear (as in *The Gates of Paradise*), or in a mystical revelation (as in the *Inventions to Job*), or not until death, depends upon the man himself.

Mystical revelation is the highest moment possible to the flesh. Blake often describes it, but says little more about it : such as how necessary it is, or how it may be induced. He must have realized what a rare thing it is. However, he felt that the same thing was mildly repeated in prayer

---

[1] *Vision of the Last Judgment.*   [2] Cf. 1 *Cor.* xv. 44.

[3] The theory of Correspondence was made famous by Swedenborg, though it had already existed for centuries. The argument by analogy was always a good one among the alchemists and their kin. See, for example, Agrippa's *Occult Philosophy* I. xv. : 'How we must find out, and examine the Vertues of things by way of Similitude.'

Blake's idea of Last Judgments was thoroughly Swedenborg's. 'The last judgment with every one is the coming of the Lord, both in a general and in a particular sense ; thus the Lord's advent into the world was the last judgment ; it will be the last judgment when he shall come again to glory ; it is the last judgment when he comes to each man individually ; and it is so also with every one when he dies' (*A.C.* 900).

[4] *Jerusalem*, 52.

and in art. The three modes of conversing with Paradise are Poetry, Painting, and Music ; during the moment of inspiration, the artist is actually in Eden. Thus Eternity obtains in the flesh. ' What is Immortality but the things relating to the Spirit, which Lives Eternally ? What is the Joy of Heaven but Improvement in things of the Spirit ? ' [1] ' A Poet, a Painter, a Musician, an Architect ; the man or woman who is not one of these is not a Christian.' [2] ' I know of no other Christianity and of no other Gospel than the liberty of body & mind to exercise the Divine Arts of the Imagination : Imagination, the real & eternal World of which this Vegetable Universe is but a faint shadow, & in which we shall live in our Eternal or Imaginative Bodies, when these Vegetable Mortal bodies are no more. The Apostles knew of no other Gospel.' [3] Note that last sentence ; for it gives us the interpretation of Blake's phrase, ' the Practice of Art.' Art is Imagination and Instinct in their widest application ; therefore Blake could say that ' Jesus and his Apostles and Disciples were all Artists,' though Jesus, at least, never wrote a poem, painted a picture, composed a song, or designed a building. He *lived* intuitively. Material works are the mere ' excess of delights.' [4]

Two other sentences will complete Blake's conception of the life of salvation. ' All life consists of these two : throwing off error and knaves from our company continually, and receiving truth and wise men into our company continually.' [5] ' The worship of God is : Honouring his gifts in other men, each according to his genius, and loving the greatest men best : those who envy or calumniate great men hate God ; for there is no other God.' [4]

God himself cannot hold aloof from the man who leads such a life. Between the two there is a constant flux and reflux. ' God becomes as we are, that we may be as he is.' [6] Such is the highest Mystery, the never-ending crucifixion of God ; for all descent is a sacrifice of himself, to bring about the resurrection of Man.

[1] *Jerusalem*, 77.
[3] *Jerusalem*, 77.
[5] *Vision of the Last Judgment.*
[2] Laocoon plate.
[4] *The Marriage of Heaven and Hell.*
[6] *There is No Natural Religion.*

CHAPTER XXV

THE COMPLETED SYMBOL

He answered and said, Lo, I see four men loose, walking in the midst of the fire, and they have no hurt : and the form of the fourth is like the Son of God.

—*Daniel* iii. 25.

In the years that followed the Lambeth booklets, Blake learned a bitter truth : no one cared anything about his visions. As an engraver, he had won a modest place in the world ; as a human being, he could find a few friends of a fairly sympathetic sort ; as an artist, he could command consideration upon occasion ; as a poet, he heard some of his early lyrics still repeated ; but as a visionary, as a revealer of fundamental truths, he was adjudged at best eccentric, and at worst crazy. His closest companions undoubtedly read his books only out of politeness, and could make nothing of them. Hayley, who had promised so well, was the stupidest of them all. The world at large, moreover, seemed to be going to pieces mentally and morally, so nothing could be expected there. But a New Age *must* come, an age when his books would be invaluable as wells of truth. To this New Age, therefore, Blake addressed himself. His life-work was henceforth to be for the Future. To preserve his work, he had to veil it with a brilliant covering of mystery. Only the intelligent should be his audience ; for them Blake elaborated his symbols, planned his finest designs, and composed his most wonderful poetry. ' That which can be made explicit to the idiot is not worth my care,' he wrote to the Rev. Dr. Trusler (Aug. 23, 1799) ; and he explained his purpose better to Thomas Butts (July 6, 1803) : it was ' to speak to future generations by a sublime allegory.'

Just such an ' allegory ' was *The Four Zoas*, in which he intended to combine all that was best in the minor Prophetic Books, to expand their various myths, and to add all the links between them which he had previously omitted. It was to be the complete account of the Fall and the Resurrection, and was to be read with a double meaning : as the history of the cosmos, and as the psychology of every individual. A third meaning, very obscure, and possibly not intended, is that of Blake's own life.

The elaborate erasures and the many rewritings in the manuscript evince the great care which he put into his epic. This is yet another refutation of the theory, first advanced by those who wished to excuse their own tamperings with his texts, that Blake was incapable of revising his work. How early he began *The Four Zoas* we cannot say ; but it was surely after *Ahania*, since his fundamental conceptions had become much deepened. Between 1795, then, and 1797, he began it ; and in the latter year he thought it completed sufficiently to begin a fair copy. A few fragments of the earlier copy with some notes for it remain. But the new copy was unsatisfactory : what had been *Night the First* became *Night the Second* ; and even his second *Night the First* was revised and compressed. Then he finished it, through *Night the Seventh*, and probably laid it aside, until the Felpham days. There he wrote another *Night the Seventh*, and some time later finished the whole poem, probably at London, for he included references to his quarrel with Hayley. Then he got the idea that British names were as sacred and full of meaning as the Hebrew names which he had been using; so he gave 'The Man' the name of 'Albion,' and changed some of the names of places in Palestine to places in England. He inserted in the margins new passages containing references to Albion's family and to the Seven Eyes of God—symbols which really belong to the period of *Milton* and *Jerusalem*. Finally, when he had begun work on these two last books of his, he abandoned *The Four Zoas*, which he had never intended for the public, leaving it without that final revision which would have made it a finished work.

His fundamental conceptions of the universe had developed enormously as we have already seen. The greatest conception is, of course, that of the Four Zoas themselves. Hitherto they had been independent gods, with no sense of interrelationship. Tharmas had not appeared at all; Luvah was hardly more than a name; Urthona was a vague huge figure in the background of all the conflicts. Urizen alone had been clearly defined. It is just possible to trace some hints of the Four in the earlier works. For instance, the two rivers of Paradise mentioned in *The French Revolution* (line 184) certainly imply the existence of the other two rivers; in one of the plates rejected from *America*, and in *Europe* (lines 12-15) the whole theory is latent; also in *Africa* (lines 10-24). But never till now had it been actually expressed.

The theory of Spectre and Emanation was also new; though it had been described much simplified in the lyric *My Spectre Around Me*. Enitharmon and Ahania were already familiar; but hitherto Vala had only appeared in her fallen form as 'The Shadowy Female,' while Enion had been barely indicated under the name Eno.

The idea of a fundamental, sleeping individuality, now named 'Albion,' was also new.

With these theories Blake had at last ordered his cosmos. His epic was to be a complete chronicle of Eternity and Time. He begins, as usual, *in medias res* with the State of Experience; describes the various conflicts of the Zoas, during which each successively announces himself as God; passes through the eating of the fruit in the Garden of Eden, the birth, crucifixion, and resurrection of Jesus. The poem comes to a climax with the Last Judgment and the ultimate salvation, by reducing all gods to their proper servitude to man.

This simple outline is divided into nine *Nights*. *Night the First* deals with the first confusion of the Fall; the separation of the Senses from the Earth Mother, and the birth and early life of the Poet and Inspiration. *Night the Second* describes the triumph of Reason. *Night the Third* narrates the casting out of Pleasure and the further fall of the Body. *Night the Fourth*, however, allows the fallen Body to triumph. *Night the Fifth* follows with the inevitable birth of Revolt. *Night the Sixth* describes Reason's vain attempt to invade the realm of the Spirit. *Night the Seventh*, 'the psychological seventh,' begins the return toward Truth with the outbreak of Revolution and the Poet's first perceptions of divine reality. *Night the Eighth* is concerned with the triumph of all errors in the

Crucifixion (the necessary preliminary for the Millennium). *Night the Ninth* ends the whole with the triumphant destruction of Error, the welcoming of Man to his place in Eternity, the salvation of all the characters (except Satan, who is destroyed), the making of the Bread and Wine of Eternity, and the dawn of the ultimate Sabbath.

Such is the skeleton of the poem, showing the simple unity of its essential structure. Blake's abundant imagination has so developed and enriched his scheme that many critics have been too puzzled to perceive its underlying order.

The opening lines of *Night the First* state the theme of the epic, identifying Los (the Poet) with Man, since Los is the highest part of Man, Blake calls upon his Muses to sing of

> His fall into Division & his Resurrection into Unity.
> His fall into the Generation of Decay & Death & his
> Regeneration in the Resurrection from the dead.

Then the plot begins with the first signs of the Fall into Experience : the Body is losing its exultation in life, and is out of communication with the Earth Mother (Enion). Already the sense of Sin, of self-analysis, has crept in ; and Tharmas (the Body) is divided by the sophistication of Ethics and becomes a Spectre, or Reasoning Force. Enion, who also represents the Generative Instinct, tries to kill herself as a sacrifice to her lord, the Body ; and the result is a further Fall. Tharmas sinks into the Sea of Time and Space, and his Spectre alone remains to accuse and torture Enion. In the struggle of the Generative Instinct with the Bodily Reason, two children are born—the Poet and his Inspiration. They scorn their mother (Enion, the Generative Instinct), though they still draw their life from her.

Meanwhile in Eternity, the Good Shepherd watches over these new developments, through the mediation of the Muses (Daughters of Beulah).

Los and Enitharmon wander in the State of Innocence, but elements of mutual jealousy arise. She sings ' a song of death ' : how Passion and Nature rose to the Brain of Man, and how Passion guided the horses of Instruction. Los will not recognize her song as one of true Inspiration ; he smites her and blames her for trying to debase—even kill—himself, with her visions of a Fall. Man, he admits, has fallen :

> But we immortal in our own strength survive by stern debate
> Till we have drawn the Lamb of God into a mortal form
> And that he must be born is certain for One must be All
> And comprehend within himself all things both small and great
> We therefore for whose sake all things aspire to be & live
> Will so receive the Divine Image that among the Reprobate
> He may be devoted to Destruction from his mother's womb

(Such is Blake's usual punctuation !) In spite of this hope the young Los is a thorough materialist :

> Tho' in the Brain of Man we live, & in his circling Nerves.
> Tho' this bright world of all our joy is in the Human Brain
> Where Urizen & all his Hosts hang their immortal lamps,
> Thou ne'er shalt leave this cold expanse where wat'ry Tharmas mourns.

Inspiration is shocked at her Poet's attitude, and she invokes Urizen (Reason) to contradict him. Urizen promptly descends and announces himself as God, but thinks it best to attempt an alliance with Los to over-come Luvah (Passion). Los recognizes that only one can be master, and spurns Urizen's dissimulation; he even repents of his affront to Enitharmon. They are reconciled, and their marriage song is the song of human warfare and revolution. Meanwhile Luvah and Vala remain forsaken, not seeing the Divine Vision who watches over them; and Enion laments the cruelty of the Struggle for Life throughout all Nature. By this Blake means that the growing Man is puzzled to place his Emotions in his universe. Reason tries to dominate them; but a higher instinct protests.

Then Man (Albion) sinks into the sleep from which he is never to be wholly wakened until the Last Judgment, and the Council of God appoints successively seven Deities to watch over him; but only the last of these, Jesus, accomplishes his task. The Daughters of Beulah bring fresh news of disaster. During Albion's sleep Urizen has tried another alliance, this time with Luvah (Passion). Again he was scornfully repulsed. The warfare of Reason and Passion over the body of the Sleeping Man follows, resulting in the sudden fall of the whole theogony. Even the Spirit (Urthona), unconcerned with all this strife and working at his anvil, is suddenly divided and sinks downward. He splits, of course, into Los and Enitharmon; who sink into the bodies of Tharmas and Enion, of whom they are born. This birth has already been described; the Daughters of Beulah are reporting news which the reader knows already.

Night the Second finds Albion upon his Couch of Death, struggling against the deadly sleep which is mastering him. In his weakness he calls Urizen and gives him dominion, at the same time exhorting him to mercy. 'Mighty was the draught of Voidness to draw Existence in,' and Urizen, terrified, calls his bands to build the Material World as a barrier against Non-Existence. Eternity is further divided and Albion groans, while Urizen's forces joy in their task, 'petrifying all the Human Imagination into rock and sand.'

Luvah (Passion) is cast into the furnaces of Affliction, while Vala (Nature) feeds the fires round him, forgetting that she is his true consort. At last he is entirely molten, and the fluid is cast into the Void, where it hardens into Matter. Nets are hung everywhere, and many spirits are snared, becoming plants and animals. The palace of Reason is built; and though Urizen makes a place in it for his Emanation, Pleasure (Ahania), he is distressed to find that already she has become a separate form. Los and Enitharmon unsympathetically rejoice over these immense labours, and plot to divide Urizen and Ahania wholly. They even rejoice over the sorrows of Luvah and Vala, now quite separate. Meanwhile 'the visible flows from the invisible' by Divine permission, lest Man should fall into Eternal Death.

Los and Enitharmon, it should be noted, are still in the State of Innocence :

> For Los & Enitharmon walk'd forth on the dewy Earth,
> Contracting or expanding their all flexible senses
> At will to murmur in the flowers small as the honey-bee,
> At will to stretch across the heavens & step from star to star
> Or standing on the Earth erect, or on the stormy waves
> Driving the storms before them or delighting in sunny beams
> While round their heads the Elemental Gods kept harmony.

Nevertheless trouble is near ; Inspiration is not so enamoured of the Poet as he is of her. She accuses him of embracing Pleasure (Ahania) in mistake .for herself, and selfishly flies away. Literally, Los cannot live without her, and dies ; yet at will she can revive him with a splendid chant. He has profited by this experience, for he tries to drive the Generative Instinct (Enion) into Non-Entity, that Pleasure (Ahania) may follow her. A lament of Enion's over the bitterness of the State of Experience reaches Ahania's ears, who thenceforth never can rest.

In *Night the Third*, Ahania carries her woes to Urizen. All the universe is obedient to him ; why should he then ' look upon Futurity, darkening present Joy ? ' Urizen foresees trouble : a Boy is born of the Dark Ocean—Orc (the Revolt of Youth) is rising from the Sea of Time and Space—and this Boy some day will rule Urizen. Ahania tries to comfort Urizen by recommending trust in the Eternal One, and relates a vision : how Man came to worship the Shadow of his own desires, and how Passion (Luvah) descended and smote Man with disease ; then how Luvah and Vala invaded the Paradise of the human heart, shrinking into material forms as they did so. Urizen is horrified at this victory of Passion over Man ; he blames Pleasure for it ; and casts her from his palace. The resulting confusion throughout the entire Universe is terrible, and from the tumult emerges the Human Form—Tharmas (the Body) materialized at last. The Generative Instinct (Enion) meanwhile has become only a voice, pleading piteously for even so much existence. Pleasure has followed Enion : Ahania also wanders in the Void, nearly falling into the Abyss of eternal sleep, which is death.

Night the Fourth, however, proves that the definite form which Tharmas has assumed brings with it a certain power. He flings ' the all-powerful Curse of an honest man ' against Urizen and Luvah (a curse which has at least no immediate effect), and asks his son, Los, to rebuild a better Universe. Los indignantly refuses the command, saying that Urizen is the only god, while he himself has risen superior to the Spirit (Urthona) from which he fell. The Body, so treated, is at first wrathful, but then pitying ; and as a lesson to Los, he suddenly removes his Inspiration (Enitharmon). Never before have they been so completely separated ; and the usual effect of all such divisions results : Los remains a Spectre. Without Inspiration, nothing but Poetic Logic remains ; nevertheless the separation brings also the wisdom of Experience. The Spectre remembers his fall from his original form, Urthona ; while the Body remembers that the Spirit was once his protector. Tharmas therefore returns Enitharmon to Los, and announces himself as the God of fallen Man, though he would rather be human. Being God, however, he commands Los to rebuild the universe as Poetry. Los's work is to limit Urizen to Time and Space by giving him a materialized form. The description of this building of Urizen's body is repeated from *The Book of Urizen*. This task has its effect on Los : he too becomes bounded.

Urizen's forecast was correct ; and *Night the Fifth* describes the birth of Revolt (Orc). His parents are Los and Enitharmon. The Poet sees Eternal Death in this state, but Inspiration has full faith in her child. The girdle of Jealousy grows to the Chain of Jealousy ; and the Poet, fearful lest mere Revolt should beget children on Inspiration, binds him with the chain. But though Orc is suppressed, his unseen influence flies abroad through the whole universe. Repentance overtakes the parents ; but too late ; for the Chain has become not only part of Orc, but reaches into the foundation of the world itself. In the midst of their grief, Enitharmon (this time as Space) conceives another child—Vala, who is to be reborn as physical nature (the Shadowy Female). The *Night* ends with a lament of Urizen over his imprisonment. Yet he has hopes ; he foresees release in the birth of Orc ;

> When thought is clos'd in caves, then love shall shew its roots in Deepest Hell.

In *Night the Sixth*, Urizen rises from his lamentations with a resolve to explore the material universe. At first he meets his three daughters (who represent the logical division of Man into Head, Heart, and Loins) ; they recognize him immediately and shrink into rocky forms. He curses them, and Tharmas comes at the curse ; but finds his once powerful waters 'froze to solid,' and over them Urizen moves undaunted. Onward he moves, seeing everywhere ' the Ruin'd Spirits once his Children & the Children of Luvah.' There are vistas of torture ; there are armies of rampant Female Wills ; there are men sunk below the human form into the forms of Tygers, Lions, Serpents, Worms, and nameless monsters. None can answer his questions, for to them his voice is only inarticulate and threatening thunder.

> Then he had time enough to repent of his rashly threaten'd curse.
> He saw them curs'd beyond his Curse. His soul melted with fear.
> He could not take their fetters off, for they grew from the soul.

Having passed the terrors of the South (his own realm), he comes to the East, which since the fall of Luvah (Passion) has remained a Void. Into this he throws himself ; but Reason cannot chart the passions, and he would have fallen eternally had not the Ever-pitying One created a bosom of Clay. Here Urizen rests, and is reborn in the same form. Meanwhile he has brought his Books of Laws with him, which he constantly regulates. Yet nowhere can he find a place to stand : everything vanishes beneath his touch ; and even the directions in which he moves reverse themselves. He decides, however, to organize that which he has already explored ; the result is the slimy web of Natural Religion, beneath which creation shrinks yet more.

Urizen now begins falling into the West, the realm of the Body ; yet soon we find him approaching the Northern realm, and at the same time hearing ' distincter & distincter ' the howls of Orc, who is chained in the South. This is a characteristic and intentional confusion of Blake's, who always feared that his symbols would be charted into dead maps. Urizen falls into the West, because his whole progress is a Fall into Matter ; he approaches the North, because his aim is to invade the realm of the Spirit ; he hears Orc nearer and nearer, because Revolt is the nearest point to the Spirit which he can reach.

Soon he sees Urthona, now only a Spectre ; and Tharmas also, who has taken refuge here. The armies of Time and Matter, however, oppose Urizen's invasion of Eternity and Infinity, and Reason is forced to fall back to his Web of Religion.

There are two versions of *Night the Seventh*. Both continue the story of *Night the Sixth*, and could lead directly into *Night the Eight* ; but each

lacks some essential episode which is found in the other. Blake undoubtedly intended to blend the two, but he did not ; so we must be
satisfied with reading one after the other.

The first version begins with Urizen's returning, strengthened by his
Religion, to the attack on the realms of the Spirit. Now nothing can
withstand him. He descends to observe the strange sight of Orc, the
Youth, crucified in his cavern ; and watching him, he composes the Book
of War. As he writes, the Tree of Mystery (symbolic of the Outward,
Worldly Church) springs up so densely that Reason himself is nearly
snared in its tangles. He escapes, but is obliged to leave the Book of War
in its keeping. Again he observes Orc ; and now that his code of War
is complete, he ventures to address the tortured demon, demanding what
he is.

Orc answer'd : Curse thy hoary brows ! What dost thou in this deep ?
Thy Pity I condemn. Scatter thy snows elsewhere.
I rage in the deep, for Lo, my feet & hands are nail'd to the burning rock ;
Yet my fierce fires are better than thy snows. Shudd'ring thou sittest ;
Thou art not chain'd. Why shouldst thou sit, cold, grovelling demon of woe,
In tortures of dire coldness ? now a Lake of waters deep
Sweeps over thee, freezing to solid ; still thou sitst clos'd up
In that transparent rock, as if in joy of thy bright prison,
Till overburden'd with its own weight, drawn out thro' immensity,
With a crash breaking across, the horrible mass comes down.
Thundering & hail & frozen iron, hail'd from the Element,
Rends thy white hair. Yet thou dost, fix'd, obdurate, brooding, sit
Writing thy books. Anon a cloud fill'd with a waste of snows
Covers thee ; still obdurate, still resolv'd, & writing still,
Though rocks roll o'er thee, tho' floods pour, tho' winds black as the Sea
Cut thee in gashes, tho' the blood pours down around thy ankles
Freezing thy feet to the hard rock ; Still thy pen obdurate
Traces the wonders of Futurity in horrible fear of the future.
I rage furious in the deep ; for lo, my feet & hands are nail'd
To the hard rock, or thou shouldst feel my enmity & hate
In all the diseases of man falling upon thy grey accursed Front.

Urizen replies that all, even warfare, is to be learned of himself ; and
he summons his three daughters to feed Orc with the bread of Materialistic
Thought. Then Urizen reads from his Book of Brass a passage on his
false charity, the hypocrisy of which maddens Orc. At last Urizen is
terrified ; he recognizes in Orc his old enemy Passion (Luvah). His
triumph has a strange and horrible result : Orc himself begins to turn
into the serpent of Hypocrisy ; he is furious at the dictates of Reason,
yet, being unable to break from his bonds, he cannot act otherwise.

Meanwhile Los laments over Enitharmon, who has become a Shadow
(suppressed spiritual desire) while he is only a Spectre (poetic logic without intuition). They hardly know each other now, as they gather
about the Tree to re-enact the Fall told in *Genesis*. They think that this
Tree (outward Religion) will protect them forever from the storms of
Eternity. Enitharmon relates a vision : how Albion in Beulah loved
Vala (Nature) ; how their child was Urizen, ' First-born of Generation ' ;
and how Vala was divided into an Enormity which was Luvah and Vala ;
and how thenceforth Man could never find his way back to Beulah, though
Urizen flourished there. Then further she relates the wars of Luvah and

Urizen which caused the universal Fall; and ends with a demand that the Poet punish Vala and subject her to Orc. Los tells her the part of the story that she has forgotten: how Urthona was divided into their two forms, which were born of Enion; and he promises to subject Vala to Orc.

So they confer in the intoxicating fumes of the Tree of Mystery, till at last Vala (Nature) is born of Enitharmon (Space) as the Shadowy Female. This birth bursts open forever the gates of Enitharmon's heart, which have been wilfully closed since *Night the First*, but which can never be closed again. Meanwhile the Spectre tries to overcome Los by false teachings, saying that Los can never possess Enitharmon again; but Los has already felt the interior world opening; and instead of rejecting the Spectre, he wishes to take both him and Enitharmon in his arms. This would have been an ideal reversal of the previous Division, had not Enitharmon fled away to the Tree of Mystery. Still the united Los and his Spectre 'wondering, beheld the Centre open'd'; and at last they begin building the City of Art, which is the re-creation of the Universe in its ideal form.

At this moment Enitharmon returns from the Tree, saying that she has eaten of its fruit, and that her eyes have been opened to her sins. She knows she is damned by them; but she has more faith in Los: if he will also eat of the fruit, and gain thereby knowledge of Good and Evil, he may be able to show her some hope of Eternity, and rescue her from her fate. Los also eats, and is given over to eternal despair, for this is the inevitable result of accepting the false doctrine of the division of Life into Good and Evil.

The Spectre weeps and blames himself; but he finds salvation for such as he in the obtaining of ideals ('counterparts'):

> But I have thee, my counterpart miraculous.
> These Spectres have no counterparts, therefore they ravin
> Without the food of life. Let us create them coun[terparts],
> For without a created body the Spectre is Eternal Death.

Then within the broken heart of Enitharmon, Los beholds the descent of the Lamb of God. Repentant and forgiving, Los tries to allay her terror. He begs for a little sympathy. Enitharmon sees the Lamb indeed, but is too morbidly convinced of the reality of her sins to believe that she can be forgiven. Undiscouraged, Los has found a scheme whereby they can make some measure of atonement: this is the creation of Art. He describes such works as—

> . . . Embodied Semblances in which the Dead
> May live in our palaces & in our gardens of labour.

Enitharmon readily agrees to give him all possible Inspiration, those 'piteous forms that vanish again' in her bosom; Los is to perpetuate these as ransoms for their souls. Thus is the work of Art begun. It develops; and all the enemies of Los break their ranks, to come as children into his power.

> Startled was Los. He found his enemy Urizen now
> In his hands. He wonder'd that he felt love & not hate.
> His whole soul loved him. He beheld him an infant
> Lovely, breath'd from Enitharmon. He trembled within himself.

So the first version of *Night the Seventh* ends. The second version, far from continuing the first, returns to the triumph of Urizen through his Religion. He institutes the cruelties of organized civilization, and builds the temple of Chastity where the phallos is worshipped. Los and Tharmas, Poet and Body, war against him. Enitharmon in terror cries for light.

Then Orc, the long-threatened Revolt of Youth, breaks loose at last. His destined bride stands before him, the Shadowy Female, who is Nature in her form of Matter ; Orc rends his fetters and embraces her—War enters the Material World. The battle is terrible : all the forces of Reason leave the works of peace for the works of war. Tharmas and Vala meet, bewailing their state ; and the Body blames Nature for the calamities. Redemption through faith is promised ; though meanwhile the climax of the Fall comes—Satan himself appears.

Night the Eighth is the culmination of all the errors which have been gathering force in the preceding books. This culmination is essential in the scheme of salvation ; the errors must be completely embodied before they can be recognized and dealt with. Not until then can Man be saved, and return to his original condition in Eternity. But when Los and Enitharmon began to see clearly in *Night the Seventh*, the nadir was already passed.

Now Man begins to awake at last, while Los and Enitharmon find their Saviour in their hearts. Now they see the plight of the Spectres who wander bodiless and despairing through the Universe. Enitharmon weaves for them human bodies, for they have fallen so low that the acquiring of the mortal form is an ascent, a transition towards immortality.

In the preceding *Night* (vii. 413) Jesus descended into the world. He now stands before Urizen, who is terrified to see Passion in two forms— as Jesus and Orc (Peace and War). He gives the signal for battle ; and again is terrified when the Hermaphrodite of Contradiction, which is Doubt, appears in the tumult. The voice of Matter (the Shadowy Female) rises in protest ; and suddenly Reason beholds that the whole basis of his philosophy is Matter. And the entire fabric of his Religion falls, snaring him in its folds.

Meanwhile Enitharmon has woven an ideal woman—Jerusalem, or Liberty. Again the Nativity takes place (from which we may assume that the preceding account was to have been deleted) ; the Forgiveness of Sins is born of Freedom. The sons of Eden sing a triumphant chant describing the Incarnation and Satan's attempt to convict the Flesh of sin.

In spite of this, the warfare in the realms below continues to rage ; and from the Hermaphrodite of Doubt is born Satan, who is Error and Accusation. (The birth of Satan is still another event already described in *Night the Seventh*.) The Lamb confronts his enemy ; is taken ; and is judged by the Sons of Albion. In the court appears against him Rahab, the perfected form of the Worldly Religion. Jesus is condemned and crucified on the Tree of Mystery ; Jerusalem flees, appealing in vain to Reason ; and Los preserves the dead body, laying it in a speulchre.

Yet death is the triumph of the Lamb. When his earthly part is removed, his Divinity is disclosed. Within his revealed Heart all his enemies are discovered. Even Rahab is there.

Inspired by this revelation, Los tries to convert Rahab. He recites the list of his progeny, tells of the quarrel between Pity (Palamabron) and

Error (Satan), and describes the successive deities worshipped by Man. On these grounds he condemns Rahab ; and she indignantly turns to Reason.

But Urizen has already been caught in his Net of the Outward Religion. At Rahab's arrival he sinks below even a semblance of humanity, and in spite of all his regret becomes a ravening dragon. Orc triumphs in the downfall of his enemy ; while the other two Zoas, Tharmas and Urthona, vegetate and stonify in a farther Fall. Yet they lend all their diminished strength to the Poet, in fear of Orc and Urizen.

The *Night* ends with two chants : the first a lament of Pleasure (Ahania) at the condition of Fallen Man ; the second the response of Enion, who has seen the descended Lamb, and now knows that Man is all.

Night the Ninth has for sub-title *The Last Judgment.* Jesus appears to Los and Enitharmon, separating their spirit from the body. This is Death, which they interpret as Annihilation. In his agony Los destroys the material sun and moon. At once the fires of Eternity descend to consume the world of Matter, and a trumpet summons all to Judgment.

The souls start forth in terrible confusion. The oppressed on earth now smite their oppressors, until all earthly tyrannies are destroyed. Albion laments over the universal misery, and calls upon Urizen to restore order. But Urizen in his bestial form cannot answer Albion, who in wrath threatens to cast him out forever. Urizen weeps, and at last renounces his control over the other Zoas and the Future. Immediately he springs upward into Eternity, in his original form as a glorious youth. Ahania follows him, but she cannot exist as yet—this is not the time for Pleasure. Urizen confesses his errors of the past.

Now the Universe explodes, its shell of Matter being unable any longer to restrain the expansion of Eternity, which has always lain dormant in its Centre. All souls are exposed to each other. Those who died unavenged now take their vengeance ; those who were cruel on earth see in each of their victims the crucified Saviour. The Throne appears in heaven, surrounded by the Four and Twenty Elders and by the Four Zoas. Man and Urizen arise together to meet the Lord, but the flames repulse them ; there is work yet to be done.

In six days heaven and earth had been created, according to *Genesis*, and on the seventh day the Lord rested. In six days, therefore, that work is to be reversed, before the Sabbath of the Millennium can arise. These six days are spent in a final Harvest and Vintage of the world, to make the Bread and Wine of Eternity. Urizen threshes the corn which Urthona bakes into the Bread of Philosophy, while Luvah presses the grapes into the Wine of Ecstasy ; and all the chaff and refuse is cast into Non-Entity. This lovely festival in the spiritual world is the reality of what on earth seems to be the final catastrophes of the Apocalypse. During this time Orc burns himself out ; Ahania and Enion rise to their former glory ; Luvah and Vala regain their original State of Innocence ; while Los takes on his original form, Urthona. The terrific vision ends in a splendid peace :

> How is it we have walk'd thro' Fire & yet are not consum'd ?
> How is it that all things are chang'd even as in ancient time ?
> The Sun arises from his dewy bed & the fresh airs
> Play in his smiling beams, giving the seeds of life to grow.
> And the fresh Earth beams forth ten thousand thousand springs of life.

Urthona is arisen in his strength, no longer now
Divided from Enitharmon, no longer the Spectre Los.
Where is the Spectre of Prophecy ? Where is the delusive phantom ?
Departed, & Urthona issues from the ruinous Walls
In all his ancient strength to form the golden armour of science
For intellectual War—the War of swords departed now—
The Dark Religions are departed—& sweet science reigns.

One is tempted to apologize for the faults of *The Four Zoas*, but it is hardly necessary, and even a little absurd. Obvious as they are, its merits are more obvious. The epic of course is not finished : Blake never gave it the final rereading during which a mere stroke of the pen here and there would have prevented many repetitions.[1] But none the less, *The Four Zoas* has one of the greatest plans in all literature, and Blake bid fair to fulfil his plan. His execution followed hard after his conception. In spite of obscure transition passages, page after page of glorious rhapsody and dramatic opposition thrills us. Flame-bound Orc's defiance of the complacent Urizen not only carries the Promethean overtones, but awakes a strong sympathy for all the oppressed. As symbolizing the struggles of the Poet with his Ideal, Los's struggles with Enitharmon are interesting ; as the human description of a young married couple, they are stirring.

But most stirring of all are the great choruses : sustained lamentations, bitter with all the knowledge of experience ; flaming ecstasies, now including the tenderness and simplicity of the *Songs of Innocence* and *Thel*, now rising with a spiritual fierceness into the supersensual itself. Such are the Marriage Song of Los and Enitharmon, and the lament of Enion from *Night the First* ; Enitharmon's chant over the dead Los, and Enion's description of Experience from *Night the Second* ; the ecstasy of Orc, and the woes of Urizen from *Night the Fifth* ; such are Orc's answer to Urizen, the selection from the Book of Brass, Los's lament over Enitharmon, the battle round Vala, and her wanderings from *Night the Seventh* ; Enion's revelation from *Night the Eighth* ; while practically all of *Night the Ninth* challenges comparison with anything else of its kind.

But of course *The Four Zoas* is in part ' obscure.' All critics, with some justice, have lamented the incoherence of the plot and the confusion among the characters themselves. Nevertheless, these difficulties were at least partly deliberate, being due to Blake's fear of producing nothing but a formal ' Allegory.' And Allegory is very different indeed from Vision. His prose on *The Last Judgment* begins with just such a warning : ' The Last Judgment is not Fable, or Allegory, but Vision. Fable, or Allegory, are [*sic*] a totally distinct & inferior kind of Poetry. Vision, or imagination, is a Representation of what Eternally Exists, Really and Unchangeably. Fable, or Allegory, is Formed by the Daughters of Memory. Imagination is Surrounded by the daughters of Inspiration, who, in the aggregate, are called Jerusalem. . . . Allegories are things that relate to

[1] For example, the tale of Urthona's fall into Los and Enitharmon, who are then born of Tharmas and Enion, is told twice (i. 491 *seq.*, and vii. 282 *seq.*) ; Golgonooza is twice built (v. ,76 and vii. 375) ; Satan is twice revealed (vii. 789 and viii. 247) ; Los and Enitharmon twice find the Saviour in their hearts (vii. 411 and viii. 20). Urizen sees the Saviour (viii. 58) ; yet the Nativity does not take place until later (viii. 256) ; after which Jesus again confronts Urizen-Satan (viii. 263). And twice Los lays the dead Christ in the sepulchre (viii. 332 and 579). The majority of these repetitions occur in the *Seventh* and *Eighth Nights*, which are the least revised.

the Moral Virtues.   Moral Virtues do not Exist : they are Allegories and Dissimulations.'

Let those who still cannot accept Blake's theory compare his work with the work of others who have tried to do the same thing.   Let them compare his tumultuous cosmos with the courtly pageant of *The Faerie Queene* ; Blake's energetic, if inhuman, characters with Spenser's stilted, though beautifully clad, personifications.   Spenser may often be more charming, but is his picture of life truer ?   Or, for a still closer parallel, let them turn to the ancient Hindu drama, the *Prabodha Chandrodaya*, which was not translated until 1811.   As can be seen from the following quotation, the theme is the same : the Fall and Resurrection of Man. 'Thus the Lord, having fallen into the sleep of Maya, forgot his own nature, pursued the operations of mind, and beheld many kinds of dreams ; such as, I am born, this is my father, my mother, my family, wife, tribe ; these are my children, friends, enemies, goods, strength, science, relations, and brothers.'   The solution is also somewhat the same : ' Intellect will rise when the goddess Revelation, who is offended and jealous on account of our long separation, is united to me, explains Reason.   Even most of the action is the same : one Act describes the struggle of Passion with Reason ; another describes the union of Passion and Delusion (Vala) ; and the last tells of the triumph of Man, who is identified with the Eternal God.   And yet how stiff, how limited the whole drama is, when compared with Blake's !   How uninteresting these walking names !

The literary influences upon *The Four Zoas* are few and obvious. The Bible, of course, has always been a common source-book for inspiration, and Blake helped himself largely to its symbols, its ideas, and at times to its poetry.   Such is the usage of all mystics, who intend their Biblical phrases to be cross-references and even interpretations of the sacred text.   In *The Four Zoas* some passages, notably the great lament upon Experience, are almost in the Biblical style.   *Night the Ninth*, being an Apocalypse, could not have been written without some references to *Revelation* ; and we find several of St. John's paragraphs expanded into magnificent pages.   But Blake was not dominated by St. John ; indeed, he only accepted those portions which he could make wholly his own, and the balance between orthodoxy and originality is admirably sustained.

The second influence, as might be expected, was that of Milton. Nowhere does Blake show more indebtedness to his ideal poet.   Indeed, he used *Paradise Lost* almost as freely, and in quite the same way, as he had used the Bible, and while we find practically no cross-references, we can easily trace Miltonic incidents in their Blakean dress.   The struggle of Satan towards Heaven suggested Urizen's journey to the realms of Urthona ; the diabolic artillery reappears ; and other less obvious parallels can be discovered.[1]

Plato had long since been thoroughly assimilated into Blake's symbolic system.   *The Book of Urizen* is steeped in the *Timaeus*, as we have seen ; and naturally *The Four Zoas* did not escape.   A few new figures and philosophic conceptions, such as the sowing of the human seed, the chains of stars, and the Chariot of Day, are Platonic in origin.   But for

---

[1] See Denis Saurat's *Blake and Milton* (Bordeaux, 1920) and R. D. Havens's *The Influence of Milton on English Poetry* (Cambridge, 1922, pp. 217-228).

the most part, Plato, with Böhme and Swedenborg, affected Blake's theories, rather than his poetical style.

The influence of Plato, however, was very deep; less fundamental, but more direct, was the influence of Paracelsus. Indeed, his *Philosophy Addressed to the Athenians* may have helped the solution of Blake's system of the Zoas. This work is so curious and so Blakean, that a brief analysis will not be out of place here.

Paracelsus is concerned with Creation and Redemption. 'The principle, mother, and begetter of all generation was Separation' (i. 8).[1] The first thing separated from God was the Mysterium Magnum (the First Matter), which was unlike everything, and which contained everything in a latent form. The emanation from the Mysterium Magnum was four-fold: that of the Elements, which Paracelsus carefully distinguishes from their offspring, the physical, visible elements (i. 11, 17, etc.). The four occult Elements are simply Blake's Zoas, with slight differences in the symbols. Blake himself identifies the fallen Zoas with the physical elements later (*Jerusalem*, 36: 31-32).

From the physical elements, their inhabitants are created; these in turn propagate and overspread the world. But at the Last Judgment, 'all things are reduced to their supreme principle, and that only remains which existed before the Mysterium Magnum, and is eternal' (i. 21). Creation will vanish to nothing: illusion is to be destroyed, leaving Truth, as a fire burns itself away, leaving a jewel. This is desirable, as it is the triumph of the eternal. The Mysterium Magnum itself, which is, as it were, a smoke produced by a certain torment (iii. 3), will disappear, leaving all pure spirit. Such eternity exists in everything, no matter how 'frail or fading.' 'That philosophy, then, is foolish and vain which leads us to assign all happiness and eternity to our element alone, that is, the earth. And that is a fool's maxim which boasts that we are the noblest of creatures. There are many worlds: and we are not the only beings in our own world. . . . We are not the only beings made: there are many more whom we do not know. We ought to conclude, then, that not one simple single body but many bodies were included in the Mysterium Magnum, though there existed in general only the eternal and the mortal. But in how many forms and species the elements produced all things cannot fully be told. But let all doubt be removed that eternity belongs to all these. . . . It is opposed to all true philosophy to say that flowers lack their own eternity. They may perish and die here; but they will reappear in the restitution of all things. Nothing has been created out of the Mysterium Magnum which will not inhabit a form beyond the aether.'

Thus perfection is to be reattained in precisely the Blakean manner. Will another Creation then take place? Paracelsus, with Blake, admits the possibility: 'After the passing away of the present creation, a new Mysterium Magnum may supervene' (ii. 12).

Paracelsus then discusses the nature of Deity. There is, of course, only one Supreme God; but Creation itself, which is a futile and often evil illusion, is the proof that 'there is some difference of gods.' 'Since created things are divided into eternal and mortal, the reason of this is that there existed another creator of mysteries, who was not the supreme

---

[1] The quotations are taken from A. E. Waite's translation of Paracelsus (London, 1894).

of the most powerful ' (ii. 1). This is evidently Urizen. But there are others as well, such as the stars, fate, and evil impulses, over whom both God and Man should rank. ' We are creatures who do not receive what is good and perfect from our masters, but we are chiefly built up by the mortal gods, who in the Mysterium Magnum had indeed some power, but nevertheless were placed by the Eternal for judgment, both to themselves and to us.' What these gods are, Paracelsus does not say ; but his immediate passing to a discussion of the four ' Elements,' which rule the fourfold universe, and which are ' really neither more nor less than souls,' is significant.

In the *Philosophy Addressed to the Athenians* may also be found the image of the Last Judgment as a final harvest (i. 10) ; the theory of Air as the ' Astral Plane ' ; besides such Blakean sentences as : ' Nothing exists without friendship and enmity.' [1]

In *The Interpretation of the Stars* by Paracelsus, we even find an astrological passage which must have been the origin of Blake's doctrine of the Seven Eyes of God. With Blake, ' stars ' and ' eyes ' were parallel symbols.

Another book which Blake read with delight about this time was the *Bhagvat-Geeta*, translated by Wilkins in 1785. Blake not only painted a picture of Wilkins in the act of translation, but took one of the names in the book for his fourth Zoa, Tharmas, who till then had been nameless.

The use of several phrases from Henry More's *Divine Dialogues* (London, 1668) indicates where Blake had been browsing. Perhaps Dr. More's discussion of the symbolism of the four ' Living Creatures ' in his *Fifth Dialogue* stimulated the production of Blake's epic. If Blake turned to Dr. More's *Philosophic Poems*, he found plenty of sympathetic material there : descending souls, ' centres,' pre-existence, veils, caves, ideas and mirrors, spiritual causes, and all the rest of the Platonic paraphernalia ; but while it is possible to trace several parallels in thought and symbol, there seem to be no passages that prove definitely that Blake ever really read these dreary stretches of spenserians.

Such literary influences have been emphasized in this chapter, not because Blake borrowed much, but because he assimilated everything so well that it became entirely his own. *The Four Zoas* is a completely original work. Unrevised though it be, it is the first and greatest complete expression of his vision of the universe.

[1] i. 10 ; cf. the extra-textual sentence in *The Four Zoas*, p. 43*b*, quoted in the description of the Illustrations.

CHAPTER XXVI

THE MOMENT *VERSUS* PURITANISM

And if, as we have elsewhere declared, any have been so happy as personally to understand Christian Annihilation, Extasy, Exolution, Transformation, the Kiss of the Spouse, and Ingression into the Divine Shadow, according to Mystical Theology, they have already had an handsome Anticipation of Heaven ; the World is in a manner over, and the Earth in Ashes unto them.

—Sir Thomas Browne: *Christian Morals.*

With *The Four Zoas* Blake had completed simultaneously the huge outlines of his philosophy and his symbolic system. Now he was able to play variations upon them, and concentrate on this or that particular phase of Eternity.

While working over the last *Nights* of his epic, he was passing through a series of disagreeable events, outwardly trivial enough, yet which were to be the starting-point of his next epic, *Milton.* Through Flaxman he had found at last a patron who promised to be ideal : generous, influential, and intelligent. This patron was William Hayley, then one of the well-known poets of the day, popular enough to have been offered the Laureateship, and correct enough to have refused it ; now forgotten almost entirely, except for this coming quarrel.

Hayley had been the friend of Gibbon, Cowper, and Romney ; and had written important *Memoirs* on the last two. He had won (as it seemed) a permanent place in English literature with his *Triumphs of Temper,* which was going through an unbelievable number of editions. We must not fall into the common error of judging him by his effect on Blake. We must see him as he appeared to his contemporaries : talented, good-hearted, easy-going, and able to carry off the few eccentricities allowable to every Great Man. He dominated the Blue-Stocking coterie of Miss Seward, ' the Swan of Lichfield.' He was cultivated by the neighbouring nobility. He was fond of books, dabbled in all arts and languages, turned out verses on all occasions, and every day rode a dangerous cavalry horse. He was broad-minded enough to absent himself from church (he admired Voltaire and Rousseau !) ; but nevertheless saved his reputation by having in his own home the customary services, for which he wrote the hymns.

But there was something unbalanced about the man that withholds our final sympathy from him. He never could get closely at grips with life. His verses are pitifully inhuman ; they reflect only too clearly his substitution of sentimentality for reality. His most sincere feelings are hopelessly lost in this mental fog. Even his verses on his dead son are pathetic because they are not pathetic at all. He wanted to be kind to everybody ; but his preconceived notions of sympathy, and an amazing intellectual blindness, turned his emotion into a warm gush of nothing. He was a strange man indeed to be associated with Blake.

Hayley's generosity is as appropriate an expression of the man as we

168

can find. He had been so generous in his early life that his ill-judged
charities (aggravated by lavish expenditures of other sorts) had materially
reduced his circumstances. To economize, he gave up his old home at
Eartham and moved to his marine villa with the Gothic turret at Felpham.
His wife had died in 1797, after nearly thirty years of married life ; and
in 1800 his only son, the talented and illegitimate Thomas Alphonso, also
died. Blake sent the lonely father a letter of condolence, with a pencil-
sketch of the boy. For several months 'the Hermit' lived alone at
Felpham, indulging his sorrow with midnight epitaphs and morning
sonnets ; then Blake's situation moved him, and he sent for the poet.

This was Hayley's most pertinent generosity ; none has proved more
disastrous to him ! He did his best for Blake ; and it has been turned to
a weapon against him. He meant so well, yet succeeded so ill, that life
at Felpham was an inferno for his friend. We should not wonder that
Blake renamed him 'Satan' for Eternity.

It all began with Flaxman's enthusiasm, which aroused Hayley's ever-
ready compassion for unrewarded merit. He proposed that Blake join
him at Felpham, where plenty of employment was to be found, not only in
engraving the plates for Hayley's works, but in commissions from the
neighbouring nobility as well. Blake accepted with delight a scheme
which would take him from London to the sea, which would relieve him
from the constant danger of poverty, and which would give him a poet for
friend. On September 16, 1800, he wrote Hayley : 'My wife is like a
flame of many colours of precious jewels whenever she hears it named—
My fingers emit sparks of fire with Expectation of my future Labour.'[1]
A day or two later he and his wife travelled all day, shifting their 'sixteen
heavy boxes and portfolios full of prints' in and out of seven different
chaises ; till late at night they reached the tiny cottage which Blake had
already hired for twenty pounds a year. It had a garden, in which he
was to see the Fairy Funeral, and into which the virgin Ololon was to
descend. There were cornfields all about, through which Blake and
Hayley were to ride,[2] and beyond lay the sea, whose ever-shifting colours
proved strangely fascinating to the man from town. Everything seemed
ideal for the production of the most splendid works. The Sussex air was
heavy with beauty ; and the ecstasies, both artistic and mystical, which
Blake experienced at once, are famous from his letters to Flaxman and
Butts.

Hayley certainly acted well towards the artist and his wife. He gave
his new friend Thomas Alphonso's own copy of the famous *Triumphs of
Temper*, and wrote in it a dedicatory poem to his 'gentle, visionary Blake,
whose thoughts are fanciful and kindly mild.' He took Blake to call on
Lord Egremont of Petworth, Lord Bathurst of Lavant, and the wholly
sympathetic Mrs. Poole. He taught Blake Greek, through the medium
of Cowper's Homer. He gave Blake a place to work in his own library.
When Hayley's eyes grew tired, as they often did, Blake was the
amanuensis.[3] We find them acting together in joint charities : writing

[1] Keynes, p. 58.
[2]   'And Felpham Billy rode out every morn
         Horseback with Death [Blake] over the fields of corn.'—*MS. Book*.
[3] This surely accounts for the mysterious manuscript of *Genesis, The Seven Days of
the Created World*, which is written, with corrections, in Blake's handwriting, but in nothing
which remotely resembles his style.

and decorating a broad-sheet ballad, *Little Tom*, for the Widow Spicer of Folkestone; or attending the death-bed of a villager, whose epitaph Hayley took occasion to improvise.

But Hayley had a scheme in his head, which soon became quite obvious. His gentle Blake was known to be given to neglecting all work for the sake of amusing himself with impossible poems and unmarketable pictures of his own. This was unfair to himself, and extremely hard on his wife. All his friends admitted it; Fuseli and Johnson, among others, had warned Blake many a time, and were rewarded with Blake's fullest resentment. Hayley's scheme was a practical one: it was simply to give Blake so much lucrative work to do that, willy nilly, he would soon find himself comfortably off.

So Blake's labours began with the engraving of two plates for Hayley's *Essay on Sculpture*; then he was commissioned to paint a frieze of poets' heads from Homer to Hayley himself 'encircled with cooing doves' for the 'Turret' library; next he was obliged to learn miniature painting under Hayley's guidance that he might be able to accept commissions from the neighbourhood. The Countess of Egremont kindly ordered a *Last Judgment*, which she received, accompanied by some pathetically thankful verses; but Lady Bathurst (or another) ordered a set of fire-screens—which she never got.

Hayley was amazed at his success with Blake; on October 1, 1801, he wrote the Rev. Dr. Johnson (of whom Blake did a miniature): 'Warm-hearted, indefatigable Blake works daily by my side on the intended decorations of our biography [the memoir of Cowper]. Engraving, of all human works, appears to require the largest portion of patience; and he happily possesses more of that inestimable virtue than I ever saw united before to an imagination so lively and prolific.' So he continued to give his patient Blake profitable work: besides the engravings for the *Life of Cowper*, there were engravings for the new illustrations in the twelfth edition of *The Triumphs of Temper*, and when those were finished Hayley wrote a *Series of Ballads* on moral animals 'for the emolument of Mr. Blake, the artist.'[1] When Blake was tired of engraving, there were always miniatures, or teaching at some house or other.

Unfortunate visionary! He found himself overwhelmed with obligations to Hayley; therefore he could not turn away the well-meant generosity. He accepted patiently this great mass of work, which entirely prevented his own inspiration. When he wanted to be painting huge frescoes of the world of his imagination, he was forced to what seemed the most detestable of all forms of Art: 'copying Nature,' and that in the smallest possible form. When he wanted to concentrate on his own epics, Hayley would translate Klopstock to him. For a whole year Blake endured this; then we find his first murmur, a sort of whimsical self-condemnation, in a letter to his old friend, Thomas Butts. 'I labour incessantly. I accomplish not one half of what I intend, because my abstract folly hurries me often away while I am at work, carrying me over mountains and valleys, which are not real, into a land of abstraction where spectres of the dead wander. This I endeavour to prevent; I, with my whole might, chain my feet to the world of duty and reality.

[1] *Memoirs of the Life and Writings of Wm. Hayley, Esq.*, edited by John Johnson, LL.D. (London, 1823), vol. ii. p. 37.

But in vain ! the faster I bind, the better is the ballast ; for I, so far from being bound down, take the world with me in my flights, and often it seems lighter than a ball of wool rolled by the wind.' He admits that Hayley's library is as yet unfinished, and that Mr. Butts's own commissions are neglected ; for he is now engraving plates for the *Life of Cowper*, which is, he confesses, ' a work of magnitude.'

The progress of his disillusionment under the dreary round of the dreary work can be traced easily enough in his letters. For three long years he endured, overcome by arguments which urged his wife's welfare and his own ingratitude. Hayley seems to have noticed nothing ; in the printed portions of his *Diary* we find no trace of suspicion. He met any impatience with a slightly increased air of patronage, which strained Blake's outward courtesy to the utmost. Only when alone could Blake vent his indignation and despair in bitter jottings which took the form of now famous epigrams.

He was the wise man under the fool's rod ; worse, he was the artist in the very real agony of restraint from production ; and worst of all, he was committing spiritual suicide, which was treachery to his God. ' I too well remember the threats I heard !—" If you, who are organized by Divine Providence for spiritual communion, refuse, and bury your talent in the earth, even though you should want natural bread, sorrow and desperation pursue you through life, and after death shame and confusion of face to eternity. Every one in eternity will leave you, aghast at the man who was crowned with glory and honour by his brethren, and betrayed their cause to their enemies. You will be called the base Judas who betrayed his friend ! " '

At last, any restraint of any sort became intolerable to his chafed nerves. Letters to Butts and epigrams were not a sufficient relief. He finally astonished Hayley with accusations ; Hayley wept and refused to believe that his good intentions were responsible ; Blake became furious ; Hayley blamed Blake's temper, mentioned ingratitude and malice, and finally lost his own temper. An awful silence fell upon the two, and Mrs. Blake took advantage of it to intervene. Blake could not be angry long ; Hayley was not the man to nurse resentment against the temperament of an ' enthusiast ' ; so the two parted, it being agreed that, though Blake returned to London, they should remain friends.

Such is Blake's own account of the quarrel, as it is to be deciphered in *Milton*. Furious as he was, he seems to have understood the exact situation, nor did he think his case so weak as to need colouring in his own favour. Just when this quarrel occurred we do not know, but it could not have been long before his triumphant letter to Butts dated April 25, 1803.

' And now, my dear sir,' he wrote, ' congratulate me on my return to London, with the full approbation of Mr. Hayley and with promise. But, alas ! now I may say to you—what perhaps I should not dare to say to any one else : that I can alone carry on my visionary studies in London unannoyed, and that I may converse with my friends in eternity, see visions, dream dreams, and prophesy and speak parables unobserved and at liberty from the doubts of other mortals. . . . If a man is the enemy of my spiritual life while he pretends to be the friend of my corporeal, he is a real enemy ; but the man may be the friend of my spiritual life while he seems the enemy of my corporeal,[1] though not vice versa.' Then follows the first record we have of the *Milton*.

Blake had been pondering the whole situation, which some time before had begun to resolve its problems into a new poem. Hayley was not an accident : he was typical. It was just such poetasters as he who got the applause of the world and prevented the real artists from winning their due ; and thus kept the world immersed in bad taste. But what was the cause of the Hayleys ? Had they always been in power ? No : there had been the days of Elizabeth, a time which would be the glory of England forever, a time of peace, of wealth spiritual and material, a time of great poets. What had happened since then ? Blake saw the black cloud of Puritanism spreading over Europe, ruining the cathedrals and abbeys, closing the theatres, preaching the deadly duties of warring upon our neighbours. It had blotted out the glories of the Renaissance, it had scorned and suppressed all beauty, had reduced religion to a system of ethics enforced by law, had turned all but a very few into fools or hypocrites, and had dealt the old spirit of ' merry England ' a blow from which it had never recovered. Outwardly, Puritanism had involved England in a series of wars such as would have been impossible under the pacifistic policy of Elizabeth ; internally, it had brutalized the people with a cruel system of impossible ideals. Chief among these were the conceptions of absolute chastity for the unmarried, and perfect fidelity for the married. And who was responsible for Puritanism ? The answer must have been unexpected even to Blake : it was his beloved Milton !

For though Milton ' was a true Poet, and of the Devil's party,' he was led astray by the mad logic of his times. He had supported Cromwell's schemes for making England moral by force of armed law ; he had celebrated Virtue and taught that Lust was Sin ; and he had reduced his Deities to Abstractions. Being the greatest man of his time, he was therefore its greatest sinner ; all the more so, since his pernicious errors still were spreading.

These thoughts must have been arranging themselves into epical form when Blake wrote Butts (Nov. 22, 1802) : ' I have conquered and shall go on conquering. Nothing can withstand the fury of my course among the stars of God and in the abysses of the Accuser.' The simple fact that he had seen the error of Puritanism clearly was in itself the divine commission to expose it. By April of the next year the first draft must have been finished : ' But none can know the spiritual acts of my three years' slumber on the banks of ocean unless he has seen them in the spirit, or unless he should read my long poem descriptive of those acts ; for I have in these years composed an immense number of verses on one grand theme, similar to Homer's *Iliad* or Milton's *Paradise Lost* : the persons and machinery entirely new to the inhabitants of earth (some of the persons excepted). I have written this poem from immediate dictation, twelve or sometimes twenty or thirty lines at a time, without premeditation, and even against my will. The time it has taken in writing was thus rendered non-existent, and an immense poem exists which seems to be the labour of a long life, all produced without labour or study. I mention this to show you the grand reason of my being brought down

---

[1] Cf. ' Opposition is True Friendship ' (*Marriage of Heaven and Hell*). This proverb is often deleted.

here.'   In June what seemed a final version was completed, according to a letter to Hayley : ' Thus I hope that all our three years' trouble ends in good luck at last, and shall be forgot by my affections, and only remembered by my understanding ; to be a memento in time to come, and to speak to future generations by a sublime allegory, which is now perfectly completed into a grand poem.[1] I may praise it, since I dare not pretend to be any other than the secretary ; the authors are in eternity. I consider it as the grandest poem that this world contains. Allegory addressed to the intellectual powers, while it is altogether hidden from the corporeal understanding, is my definition of the most sublime poetry. It is also somewhat in the same manner defined by Plato. This poem shall, by Divine assistance, be progressively printed and ornamented with prints, and given to the Public.'

' Secret Calumny & open Professions of Friendship are common enough all the world over, but have never been so good an occasion of Poetic Imagery. When a Base Man means to be your Enemy, he always begins with being your Friend,' Blake jotted in the *MS. Book*. It may fairly be asked : ' Does this not apply more closely to Blake, who was calling Hayley " Satan " in a work about to be published, and who, at the same time, was writing affectionate letters to that same Satan ? ' The answer is simple : the person Hayley had long since passed from Blake's mind as a character in his *Milton* : the individual and his acts had grown into a symbol. Blake was quite sincere. He even took pains to show his epic to Hayley, who understood not one word of the part he read ' at his own desire ' and ' looked with sufficient contempt to enhance my opinion of it.' Besides, why should the world ever connect ' Satan ' with the respectable Hayley ; how could it trace a tragedy in Eternity to some hot words of which it could not possibly know, long since passed at Felpham and forgotten ? ' Burn what I have peevishly written about any friend,' he directed Butts. The disguise seemed perfect, the epic justified.

Unfortunately, Butts did not burn the letter ; and far from keeping quiet about it, he warned James Blake of his brother's latest quarrel. James, probably worried about William's finances, wrote to find out just what had happened ; on January 30, 1803, William wrote back that it was all right : he had plenty of money and work, and that he now could bring out ' many very formidable works, which I have finish'd and ready.' As for the quarrel, ' H. is Jealous as Stothard was & will be no further My friend than he is compell'd by circumstances. The truth is As a Poet he is frightened at me & as a Painter his views & mine are opposite ; he thinks to turn me into a Portrait Painter as he did Poor Romney, but this he nor all the devils in hell will never do. I must own that seeing H. like S. envious (& that he is I am now certain) made me very uneasy, but it is over & I now defy the worst & fear not while I am true to myself which I will be. This is the uneasiness I spoke of to Mr. Butts but I did not tell him so plain & wish you to keep it a secret & to burn this letter because it speaks so plain.' [2]

[1] *Milton* was not as yet ' perfectly completed.' Blake always revised, deleted, and added a great deal to first drafts. The five ' extra pages ' were added between 1808 and 1818, while page 17 contains a reference to Scofield, the soldier, who as yet had not attacked him.

[2] Keynes, p. 449.

But James Blake was as chary of burning letters as Butts. And there are plenty of other records of this part of the poet's life. We have his letters, we have his *MS. Book*, and we have Hayley's *Diary*. The personal note crops out once too often in the poem and the identification has been made. Therefore the warning must be repeated : ' Satan ' is not primarily Hayley ; ' Satan ' is rather Hayley's attitude, his type, his philosophy.

As soon as he was settled at his new lodgings in South Moulton Street, London, Blake began the engraving of his new book, dating the title-page 1804. He continued to arrange, to add, and to decorate, until the work was finally ready for the public in 1808. The *Public Address* of that year contains the following passage : ' The manner in which my Character both as an artist & a Man may be seen particularly in a Sunday Paper cal'd the Examiner Publish'd in Beaufort Buildings. We all know that Editors of Newspapers trouble their heads very little about art & science & that they are always paid for wh[at] they put in on these un-gracious subjects, & the manner in which I have rooted out this nest of villains will be seen in a Poem concerning my Three years' Herculean Labours at Felpham which I will soon Publish.' [1] Soon after, he issued three copies of *Milton* (watermarked 1808), two of them practically identical, and the third with some changes : the addition of five pages the omission of one, a few rearrangements, and also one slight deletion. These three copies are the only ones known to exist. In 1818 he men-tioned another copy, of fifty pages, price 10 guineas, in the list of books sent Dawson Turner ; but this seems to have vanished. *Urania, or the Astrologer's Chronicle* (1825) refers to yet another copy on which Blake was working : ' He has now by him a long poem nearly finished, which he affirms was recited to him by the spirit of Milton.' This can only have been a copy of the book, since the poem itself had been completed many years before.

We now have seen how the *Milton* came into being, and with what problems it dealt. Blake was again asking : ' What is wrong with the world ? ' but answering this time with ideas drawn from personal experi-ence. The mystical element is stressed : so much so that at times it is puzzling to distinguish between the literal record of psychological fact and the poetic transmutation of mental struggles into a warfare of personified forces.

Book the First begins with a description of the dead Milton, ' unhappy tho' in heav'n.' As Blake conceived him, Milton had been a man originally gifted with the Divine Imagination, but who became ' an Atheist, a mere politician busied about this world . . . till in his old age he returned back to God whom he had had in his childhood.' [2] His errors were the errors of all Puritanism. He had worshipped Urizen-Jehovah, and not the Christ. ' In Milton, the Father is Destiny, the Son a Ratio of the five Senses, and the Holy Ghost a Vacuum ! ' [3] He opposed Reason and

[1] *MS. Book*, p. 52. It is evident that Blake attacked the editors of the *Examiner* simply as of the spiritual tribe of Hayley, although on Aug. 7, 1808, it had published an outrageous review of Blake's edition of Blair's *Grave*. In the *Milton* there is no specific reference to the *Examiner*, but plate 43 contains some lines which apply very generally —lines 8-9, ' That it no longer shall dare to mock with the aspersion of Madness Cast on the Inspired by the tame high finisher of paltry Blots,' refer to some artist or group of artists, and not to the *Examiner's* accusation, which only appeared in the following year, Sept. 17.

[2] H. C. R., Jan. 6, 1826.   [3] *Marriage of Heaven and Hell*.

Restraint to Impulse and Indulgence. *Comus* resolves itself into the most passionate praise of Virtue. His troubles with his wives and daughters, however, were the most serious; they proved that he had not understood, and therefore had cast out, the finer aspects of himself. He had tried to differentiate between Love and Lust in *Paradise Lost*; making Lust the result of the Fall. This is the explanation of Blake's remark to Crabb Robinson (Dec. 17, 1825) : ' I saw Milton *in imagination*, and he told me to beware of being misled by *Paradise Lost*. In particular he wished me to show the falsehood of his doctrine that the pleasures of sex arose from the fall.[1] The fall could not produce any pleasure.' Crabb Robinson continues : ' I answered, the fall produced a state of evil in which there was a mixture of good or pleasure. And in that sense the fall may be said to produce the pleasure. But he replied that the fall produced only generation and death. And then he went off upon a rambling state of a union of sexes in man as in Ovid, an androgynous state, in which I could not follow him. As he spoke of Milton's appearing to him, I asked whether he resembled the prints of him. He answered, " All." Of what age did he appear to be ? " Various ages—sometimes a very old man." '

Therefore Milton in Eternity could see that he had not attained to Truth. He had not ' made himself whole ' by becoming at one with his wives and daughters. These six, as his ' Sixfold Emanation,' personify his errors, which are still wandering in the void. To redeem them, Milton must sacrifice his ' Selfhood ' (those personal prejudices which still surround the true Individuality or Humanity as the shell of the egg surrounds the bird), thus enabling himself to expand until he absorb them into himself. In order to accomplish this, he must leave heaven and descend again into ' Eternal Death ' where his Emanation is lost.

He is finally moved to action by the song of a Bard at the tables of Eternity. This song pictures the bondage of the great under the rule of Puritanism. It begins briefly with the familiar story of the Fall of Albion and the Binding of Urizen, then passes to the struggle of Satan and Palamabron.

This struggle is Blake's version of the quarrel with Hayley. Satan is the respectable dilettante who wishes to usurp the place of the true artist. He is the mild man who requires absolute obedience. He is the would-be patron of Art, who perverts all Art that comes within his reach. He believes himself to be a friend, but lacks the necessary understanding. In short, he is every error, masquerading in the most dangerous form as its opposing truth, and thereby rules the world. Under him is Palamabron, who may be taken to represent Blake, but who is, specifically, Pity as the artist. His father Los enters the combat ; and Rintrah (Wrath) inflames now one side, now another. At last Palamabron calls all to judgment upon the case ; Satan wins the verdict ; announces himself as God ; and Puritanism is triumphant.

This verdict is justified in Eternity, because ' if the Guilty should be condemn'd he must be an Eternal Death.' But the question is not allowed to rest there ; the nature of the various inspirations of the two

---

[1] In recopying this passage (Feb. 26, 1852) Crabb Robinson made a very serious error. He omitted ' the pleasures ' and simply wrote : ' sexual intercourse arose out of the Fall '—a doctrine expressly denied in *Paradise Lost*.

men comes up. Is Satan to be blamed because his Inspiration is false ?
She appears in court, taking the blame on herself. She is Leutha, who
has already appeared in other books as the false (Puritanic) doctrine of
love. She confesses her error, and her opponent, Elynittria (Blake's
own doctrine of love), takes her in and tries to convert her.

Here the song of the Bard ends.

> Then there was great murmuring in the Heavens of Albion
> Concerning Generation & the Vegetative Power & concerning
> The Lamb the Saviour.

And Milton sees clearly that ' this terrible Song ' is the result of his own
unredeemed errors.

> ' What do I here before the Judgment ? without my Emanation ?
> With the daughters of memory & not with the daughters of inspiration ?
> I in my Selfhood am that Satan. I am that Evil One !
> He is my Spectre ! in my obedience to loose him from my Hells,
> To claim the Hells, my Furnaces, I go to Eternal Death.'

The descent of Milton to the earth is described with a great imaginative
force. As he passes downward, his ' real and immortal Self,' guarded by
the Seven Eyes of God, sinks upon a couch of gold in Beulah, to sleep
during his absence ; ' but to himself he seem'd a wanderer lost in dreary
night.' He has now entered his Shadow, that illusory vehicle which in its
lowest form becomes the physical body ; and as it passes among the
Spectres he sees, one by one, the truths of the realms below. He sees Man
himself sunk into the sleep which only Judgment can break ; he sees all
the cruelties of the world of Matter ; and he sees that his own sojourn there
was

> To Annihilate the Self-hood of Deceit & False Forgiveness
> In those three females whom his wives & those three whom his daughters
> Had represented and contain'd, that they might be resum'd
> By giving up of Selfhood.

The various Zoas behold the descent in terror, fearing all the energies
and errors that may be unloosed by it : for Milton is at heart a Revolutionist. Los and Urizen oppose his passage ; while Orc (the revolt of
Youth) strains hard to free himself. Milton struggles long with Reason
(Urizen) moulding him into a suitable philosophy, and Albion begins to
awake. Los is in complete despair until he recalls an old prophecy in
Eden that Milton should reascend from the Vale of Felpham. And, in
fact, Milton has at last fallen until he has entered the body of Blake.

For a long time Blake had taught that the world of the Imagination was
the only real world ; and it easily follows that the thought of a dead
person is communication with him in Reality. ' Thirteen years ago I lost
a brother,' Blake once wrote in a letter of condolence, ' and with his spirit
I converse daily and hourly in the spirit, and see him in my remembrance,
in the regions of my imagination. I hear his advice, and even now write
from his dictate.' Blake's communion with Milton in this manner had
been so prolonged and so intense that Milton could easily be said to have
entered into Blake. ' Milton lov'd me in childhood and shew'd me his
face ' was simply Blake's way of saying that he loved Milton. Throughout Blake's works, from the very first poem in the *Poetical Sketches*
through *The Four Zoas*, we have found imagery, phraseology, revolutionary

fervour, metrical experiments, and even quotations, that were obviously derived from Blake's great predecessor.   And now that Blake had come to the point of dealing directly with Milton's errors in order to correct them, it was quite characteristic of him to say that Milton himself, in an attempt to revise his doctrines, had entered Blake.   This statement was simply a symbol, not to be literally interpreted, of Milton's influence upon Blake.

> But Milton entering my Foot, I saw in the nether
> Regions of the Imagination : also all men on Earth,
> And all in Heaven, saw in the nether regions of the Imagination,
> In Ulro beneath Beulah, the vast breach of Milton's descent.
> But I knew not that it was Milton, for man cannot know
> What passes in his members till periods of Space & Time
> Reveal the secrets of Eternity : for more extensive
> Than any other earthly things, are Man's earthly lineaments.
> And all this Vegetable World appeared on my left Foot
> As a bright sandal form'd immortal of precious stones & gold :
> I stooped down & bound it on to walk forward thro' Eternity.

The Zoas now realize ' that it was Milton the Awakener ' who had descended, and Los repents so far as to enter into Blake also.   This entry of the Poet into Blake symbolizes his Lambeth period of inspiration.

> . . . What time I bound my sandals
> On, to walk forward thro' Eternity, Los descended to me :
> And Los behind me stood : a terrible flaming Sun : just close
> Behind my back : I turned round in terror, and behold,
> Los stood in that fierce glowing fire : & he also stoop'd down
> And bound my sandals on in Udan-Adan : trembling I stood
> Exceedingly with fear & terror, standing in the Vale
> Of Lambeth : but he kissed me and wish'd me health.
> And I became One Man with him arising in my strength :
> 'Twas too late now to recede. Los had enter'd into my soul :
> His terrors now possess'd me whole ! I arose in fury & strength.

Los and Blake go together to the City of Art ; but they are met at the gate by two of Los's sons, Wrath and Pity (Rintrah and Palamabron), who fear to admit Blake.   Seeing the triumph of misery upon the earth, they cannot conceive that good shall arise from the presence of such a one in the sacred city, especially since he contains the dangerous spirit of Milton. ' Milton's Religion is the cause,' they cry ; and reveal the development of Materialism from his day, through Voltaire and Rousseau, through Swedenborg, even through Whitefield and Wesley, whose Methodism was reawaking faith in the inward God, up to the horrors of the two Revolutions.

Los is angry for a moment ; then he begs them to be patient.   The period of six thousand years allotted to creation has nearly passed away ; the justification for all errors is about to be revealed. Now that Milton is reunited with Los in the brain of Blake, Milton can redeem himself and correct his doctrines, as has been foretold :

> I have embrac'd the falling Death, he is become one with me. . . .
> I recollect an old Prophecy in Eden recorded in gold ; and oft
> Sung to the harp : That Milton of the land of Albion
> Should up ascend forward from Felpham's Vale & break the Chain

Of Jealousy from all its roots ; be patient therefore, O my Sons . . .
But as to this Elected Form who is return'd again,
He is the Signal that the Last Vintage now approaches,
Nor Vegetation may go on till all the Earth is reap'd.

In Blake's case, mystical vision was always followed by the revelation of some Truth. His entry into Golgonooza is indicated by a sudden perception of all creation, which continues to the end of *Book the First.* This is Poetic perception, of course, as opposed to Scientific analysis. *Sub specie aeternitatis,* the Body ' in its inward form is a garden of delight & a building of magnificence '; its functioning is the harmony of a great orchestra ; its warfare is the pressing of wine. Blake beholds the descent of souls, and their merciful ensnarement in material forms, which gives them a purpose, a chance to ascend again. The mysteries of Time and Space are fully disclosed. He sees the Humanity behind all nature ; he sees the windows opened in the body ; the redemption through Poetry.

In fact, a Last Judgment has arrived. Mankind is to be finally classified. Los gives his directions :

. . . Under pretence to benevolence the Elect Subdu'd All
From the Foundation of the World. The Elect is one Class : You
Shall bind them separate : they cannot Believe in Eternal Life
Except by Miracle & a New Birth. The other two Classes :
The Reprobate who never cease to Believe, and the Redeem'd
Who live in doubts & fears perpetually tormented by the Elect,
These you shall bind in a twin-bundle for the Consummation :
But the Elect must be saved from fires of Eternal Death,
To be formed into the Churches of Beulah that they destroy not the Earth.
For in every Nation & every Family the Three Classes are born.

Before this vision was revealed, events were unfolding in Eternity. Ololon, who is at once one and many, who is simultaneously ' a sweet River of milk & liquid pearl ' and ' a Virgin of twelve years,' is especially smitten at the loss of Milton. Though she does not know it, she is the Truth which he rejected : she is the immortal counterpart of the erroneous (and hence mortal) ' Sixfold Emanation.' Drawn by an uncomprehended impulse, she is moved to follow him :

And Ololon said : ' Let us descend also, and let us give
Ourselves to death in Ulro among the Transgressors.[1]
Is Virtue a Punisher ? O no ! how is this wondrous thing ?
This World beneath, unseen before ; this refuge from the wars
Of Great Eternity ! unnatural refuge ! unknown by us till now.
Or are these the pangs of repentance ? let us enter into them.'

The voice of Jesus answers her :

' Six Thousand Years are now
Accomplish'd in this World of Sorrow ; Milton's Angel knew
The Universal Dictate : and you also feel this Dictate.
And now you know this World of Sorrow, and feel Pity. Obey
The Dictate ! Watch over this World, and with your brooding wings
Renew it to Eternal Life : Lo ! I am with you alway :
But you cannot renew Milton : he goes to Eternal Death.'

So she descends, and all Beulah laments over her. *Book the Second* opens with Blake's clearest description of the state of Beulah ; and continues

[1] Or, the reprobate.

with the celebrated lamentation, which on earth is perceived as the dawn-song of the lark and the early perfume of the flowers, particularly of the wild thyme.

Here we come to a very curious thing.   Practically all the action of the epic passes in one moment.   Throughout the whole poem Blake has been dropping hints to this effect :

> When Luvah's bulls each morning drag the sulphur Sun out of the Deep
> Harness'd with starry harness, black & shining, kept by black slaves
> That work all night at the starry harness : Strong and vigorous
> They drag the unwilling Orb : at this time all the Family
> Of Eden heard the lamentation, and Providence began . . .
>
> Every Time less than a pulsation of the artery
> Is equal in its period & value to Six Thousand Years,
> For in this Period the Poet's Work is Done ; and all the Great
> Events of Time start forth & are conceiv'd in such a Period,
> Within a Moment, a Pulsation of the Artery. . . .
>
> There is a Moment in each Day that Satan cannot find,
> Nor can his Watch Fiends find it, but the Industrious find
> This Moment & it multiply, & when it once is found
> It renovates every Moment of the Day if rightly placed :
> In this Moment Ololon descended. . . .

During just such a moment, while Blake was walking at sunrise in his garden, he was caught up into Golgonooza.   In one flash he beheld all the errors of Milton's philosophy, with their solution ; symbolized as the meeting of that poet with Ololon.   We have seen elsewhere how the sight of agricultural implements filled Blake with creative fervour ; so now the song of a lark and the scent of the wild thyme in that still hour became charged with the secrets of the universe.   At such a moment, vision and truth, Imagination and Logic, vibrate in swift alternation. The contents of that moment required an epic as an adequate vehicle.

The rest of this poem is simply the counterbalancing of vision and truth.   The first vision was that of the descent of Los, followed by the poetic revelation of the world.   Then came the resolve of Ololon, followed by her questioning of this world :

> '. . . How are the Wars of man, which in Great Eternity
> Appear around in the External Spheres of Visionary life,
> Here render'd deadly within the Life & Interior Vision ?
> How are the Beasts & Birds & Fishes & Plants & Minerals
> Here fix'd into a frozen bulk subject to decay & death ?
> Those Visions of Human Life & Shadows of Wisdom & Knowledge
> Are here frozen to unexpansive deadly destroying terrors.
> And War & Hunting, the Two Fountains of the River of Life,
> Are become Fountains of bitter Death & of Corroding Hell :
> Till Brotherhood is chang'd into a Curse & a Flattery,
> By Differences between Ideas, that Ideas themselves (which are
> The Divine Members) may be slain in offerings for sin.'

Soon she finds Milton's couch in Beulah, where his Immortal Self lies sleeping, guarded by the Seven Eyes of God.   At once she falls on her knees, repentant and confessing ; and at once it is seen that her descent has opened a breach into Eternity.   But to Blake on earth this vision appeared otherwise.

> And as One Female, Ololon and all its mighty Hosts
> Appear'd : a Virgin of twelve years : nor time nor space was
> To the perception of the Virgin Ololon, but as the
> Flash of lightning, but more quick, the Virgin in my Garden
> Before my Cottage stood, for the Satanic Space is delusion . . .
> Walking in my Cottage Garden, sudden I beheld
> The Virgin Ololon & address'd her as a Daughter of Beulah.
>
> ' Virgin of Providence, fear not to enter into my Cottage.
> What is thy message to thy friend : What am I now to do ?
> Is it again to plunge into deeper affliction ? behold me
> Ready to obey, but pity thou my Shadow of Delight : [1]
> Enter my Cottage, comfort her, for she is sick with fatigue.'
>
> The Virgin answer'd : ' Knowest thou of Milton who descended,
> Driven from Eternity ? him I seek, terrified at my Act
> In Great Eternity, which thou knowest : I come him to seek.'
>
> So Ololon utter'd in words distinct the anxious thought :
> Mild was the voice, but more distinct than any earthly.

The utterance of her wish is its execution.   At the sound of her voice Milton appears, with all his errors manifest to Blake's eyes.   Yet he stands ready to confront his Satan, the enemy hidden in his bosom :

> ' Such are the Laws of Eternity, that each shall mutually
> Annihilate himself for others' good, as I for thee.
> Thy purpose & the purpose of thy Priests & of thy Churches
> Is to impress on men the fear of death ; to teach
> Trembling & fear, terror, constriction : abject selfishness.
> Mine is to teach Men to despise death & to go on
> In fearless majesty annihilating Self, laughing to scorn
> Thy Laws & terrors, shaking down thy Synagogues, as webs.
> I come to discover before Heav'n & Hell the Self righteousness
> In all its Hypocritic turpitude, opening to every eye
> These wonders of Satan's holiness, shewing to the Earth
> The Idol Virtues of the Natural Heart, & Satan's Seat,
> Explore in all its Selfish Natural Virtue, & put off
> In Self annihilation all that is not of God alone :
> To put off Self & all I have, ever & ever.   Amen.'

Satan tries to meet this by the old claim that he is God ; but

> Suddenly around Milton on my Path, the Starry Seven
> Burn'd terrible : my Path became a solid fire, as bright
> As the clear Sun, & Milton silent came down on my Path.
> And there went forth from the Starry limbs of the Seven, Forms
> Human, with Trumpets innumerable, sounding articulate
> As the Seven spake ; and they stood in a mighty Column of Fire
> Surrounding Felpham's Vale.

In vain Satan invokes a parallel pageant for himself : Albion begins to awake ; and Milton himself sees Ololon, perceiving at last ' the Eternal Form of that mild Vision.'   Again she confesses her faults, blaming her-

[1] Blake's wife.

self for all the cruelty of the world ; and at her words Rahab is revealed by Satan's side—Rahab, the perfected form of the mundane religion, Moral Virtue.

Milton answers with the splendid pronouncement of his ideals, which begins :

> To bathe in the waters of Life : to wash off the Not Human,
> I come in Self-annihilation & the grandeur of Inspiration.

Ololon trembles, yet is ready for the great sacrifice.   Inspiration must be dominated by the poet, Truth by the will.   She divides ; and the errors, as the Sixfold Emanation, are cast out with Milton's Shadow. Milton, now made whole, unites with the Seven Eyes of God, and becomes Jesus himself, clothed in Ololon as in a garment.

But even this is not the final union.

> . . . Jesus wept, & walked forth
> From Felpham's Vale clothed in Clouds of blood, to enter into
> Albion's Bosom, the bosom of death, & the Four surrounded him
> In the Column of Fire in Felpham's Vale : then to their mouths the Four
> Applied their Four Trumpets, & then sounded to the Four winds.

Mortal consciousness is not able to endure this ultimate vision of the union of God with Man.

> Terror-struck in the Vale I stood, at that immortal sound :
> My bones trembled, I fell outstretch'd upon the path
> A moment, & my Soul returned into its mortal state,
> To Resurrection & Judgment in the Vegetable Body :
> And my sweet Shadow of delight stood trembling by my side.

Immediately the lark sings, the wild thyme sheds its perfume, their ecstasy reminding Blake that all this vision was but the work of a moment, and he sees that mankind is at last prepared for ' the Great Harvest & Vintage of the Nations,' which is the Last Judgment.

In the *Milton* we find little development of the system of *The Four Zoas*, but some amplification.   The distinction between the illusory Selfhood and the real Humanity is new ; so is the addition of a man's own ' Angel ' to his guardian Seven Eyes of God ; so is the threefold classification of mankind into the Elect, the Redeemed, and the Reprobate (or Transgressor).   The four sons of Los (Rintrah, Palamabron, Theotormon, and Bromion) have been gathered from earlier books and made the reflections of the Four Zoas in this world : as Wrath, Pity, Desire, and Reason.   New also are the Twenty-seven Heavens and Hells of the twenty-seven fundamental religions (named by Blake with great care), which shut us out from Eternity, and which must be passed through to reach Eternity.   But most interesting of all are the regions of Bowlahoola and Allamanda : the physical processes of assimilation and perception— the digestive and nervous systems—whose place in Blake's philosophy is at last unfolded.   References to them were inserted in *The Four Zoas*, probably while *Milton* was being contemplated, or even written ; but not till now did Blake develop their theory.

As literature, *Milton* has the simplest plan of all Blake's long works. It deals with one event only, and distinguishes carefully the manifold factors involved in that event.   To be sure, there are numerous references to other portions of his mythology, which are certainly perplexing to the unprepared reader ; but there is only one indication of a sub-plot, and that is not important. This is the familiar story of the bondage and freeing of Orc. We first see him striving against his bondage, in agony over his consort, the Shadowy Female, who is about to take on material form (17*) ; then it is prophesied that Milton is to release him (18 : 61) ; and early in the story he is released, rising in blood and fire over America (22 : 6).

Such references may be confusing, but only momentarily. The reader who is alert for the splendid orchestration of profound thought and mystical psychology will find that the *Milton*, far from being a morass with a few green and flowery islands, unfolds surely, however slowly, into a magnificent unit. While it contains fewer lyrical moments than *The Four Zoas*, it compensates for them by many passages of rhapsodic philosophy, any one of which is sufficient to make the whole work memorable. For *Milton* is the most personal document which Blake has left us.

CHAPTER XXVII

THE ULTIMATE CITY

> Not fables of Gods, not thunderbolts nor heaven with ominous menace, could intimidate him ; they but roused the more his eager spiritual courage, stirring him with the want to be the first to shatter the fast bars of Nature's gates. Therefore the living strength of his soul conquered. On he passed, far beyond the flaming walls of this world, and pastured both mind and spirit upon the immeasurable Void. Thence he returns, a conqueror, to tell us what can, what cannot, be created ; briefly, on which principle each Thing has its power defined, where its ultimate boundary lies. Therefore Religion is thrown before our feet, is trampled upon ; his victory brings us level with heaven.—LUCRETIUS : *De Rerum Natura*, I.

BEFORE Blake got away from Felpham, a certain event brought him into the greatest danger he had ever known, and incidentally started a train of thought which led to his last epic, *Jerusalem*.

In May 1803, England declared war upon Napoleon, and the whole country promptly suffered a bad attack of the spy-and-traitor fever. In August, during its height, Blake saw a drunken soldier in the sacred garden where Milton and Ololon had appeared. Not knowing that this was another immortal, he asked the soldier ' as politely as possible ' to leave. But the soldier, a demoted sergeant named John Scofield, had the gardener's invitation to be there—a fact which he held in reserve. Finally Blake lost his temper at Scofield's impertinent refusals, took him by the elbows and ran him out the gate. Once out, the released soldier ' put himself in a posture of defiance, threatening and swearing ' at Blake ; till the latter emerged from the garden, took the soldier again by the elbows, ' putting aside his blows,' and indignantly ran him back to his quarters.

To avenge his honour, Scofield and a friend, Trooper Cock, swore before the nearest justice that Blake had uttered an amazing amount of sedition during the run down the road. Blake found himself due to be tried for High Treason at Chichester the following January.

His danger was very great. In those times of peril a soldier's word was believed before a mere citizen's, especially when that citizen was known once to have been a wearer of the Red Cap. The public was taking no chances. Blake might well have been executed or transported for life.

But he was saved after all. Such charges of sedition made by soldiers after their quarrels were getting just a trifle too common ; the Felpham villagers to a man testified in defence of Blake ; and as a climax, the Great Hayley graciously appeared in court, though his horse, shying at the famous umbrella with which Hayley always shaded himself while riding, had given him a very bad fall. Blake was acquitted amid loud rejoicings.

What he suffered through his supersensitive imagination can only be deduced from *Jerusalem*. He had seen the whole world as a diabolic Court of Justice, in which the Satanic Trinity, the Accuser, Judge, and

183

Executioner, were openly arrayed against the Individual. How was it that a man like himself, who had abstained so long from any participation in such worldly things, could be placed in such a situation ? Was the laborious and triumphant ordering of his soul of no use ?

This ordering of the soul had been the subject of *The Four Zoas*. Now Blake saw that the greatest source of evil was not so much the conflict within the individual as the Cruelty of Man to Man. Therefore, instead of revising and engraving his Chronicle of Eternity, he began a new epic, *Jerusalem*, the History of Man. The four Zoas are only incidental characters, while Albion has risen to his proper place as the protagonist.

1804, the date on the title-page, shows that Blake began engraving it at the same time that he began engraving *Milton* ; but it was not finished until Blake's very last months on earth. In the *Descriptive Catalogue* (1809) he describes it, as though hoping that some one might be curious enough to order a copy : 'Mr. B. has in his hands poems of the highest antiquity. . . . All these things are written in Eden. The Artist is an inhabitant of that happy country ; and if everything goes on as it has begun, the world of vegetation and generation may expect to be opened again to Heaven, through Eden, as it was in the beginning.' Then, having spoken of the Human Sublime, Pathetic, and Ugly (the Head, Heart, and Loins), he continues : 'They were originally one man, who was fourfold ; he was self-divided, and the form of the fourth was like the Son of God. How he became divided is a subject of great sublimity and pathos. The Artist has written it under inspiration, and will, if God please, publish it ; it is voluminous, and contains the ancient history of Britain and the world of Satan and of Adam.'

This seems to have brought no encouragement ; nevertheless, eleven years later, *Jerusalem* was on the road to completion, for a friend of Blake's, the aesthete and poisoner, Thomas Griffiths Wainwright, inserted a paragraph on it in *The London Magazine* for September 1820. It is brief enough to be quoted here : 'Mr. Janus Weathercock's Private Correspondence. . . . Talking of articles, my learned friend Dr. Tobias Ruddicombe, M.D., is, at my earnest entreaty, casting a tremendous piece of ordnance, *an eighty-eight pounder*! which he proposeth to fire off in your next. It is an account of an ancient, newly discovered illuminated manuscript, which has to name "JERUSALEM THE EMANATION OF THE GIANT ALBION"!!! It contains a good deal anent one "*Los*," who, it appears, is now, and hath been from the Creation, the *sole* and four-fold dominator of the celebrated city of *Golgonooza*! The doctor assures me that the redemption of mankind hangs on the universal diffusion of the doctrines broached in this MS. But, however, that isn't the subject of this *scrinium*, scroll, or scrawl, or whatever you may call it.'

There was not enough interest, even after this, to warrant Wainwright's article on Blake, which never appeared.

We have no record of a finished copy of *Jerusalem* till April 1827, only four months before Blake's death, when in a letter to George Cumberland, he wrote : 'The last work I produced is a poem entitled *Jerusalem, the Emanation of the Giant Albion*, but find that to print it will cost my time the amount of twenty guineas. One I have finished, but it is not likely

I shall find a customer for it.' He did not sell it, and it passed after Mrs. Blake's death into the hands of Frederick Tatham. It is the only coloured copy now existing. A second coloured copy was apparently cut up by Ruskin.[1] A few others were finished in black and white. Several more were printed after Blake's death.

The plot of the *Jerusalem* is at once broad and vague. It is simply that of the Fall and its delusions, ending with the awakening of Man from Error, and his final entrance into Eternity. Blake himself states it clearly at the head of his first chapter : ' Of the Sleep of Ulro ! And of the Passage through Eternal Death ! And of the Awaking to Eternal Life ! ' Albion, the ancient British giant, is the symbol of Man, and around him revolve such familiar characters as Jesus, Jerusalem, Vala, Los, Enitharmon, and Rahab. There is nothing remotely resembling what could be called a sub-plot.

But though the plot is so simple, *Jerusalem* is the obscurest of the three epics. Almost all the characters which Blake ever invented live in the subliminal consciousness of this poem. Time and again the depths are stirred and a gush of half-forgotten names emerges for the moment, to be lost immediately in the impenetrable black. All Blake's technical terms are used to their fullest possible extent, as a sort of convenient shorthand to note an idea rapidly before it vanishes.

To add to the difficulty, biblical characters appear and disappear momentarily with the most unfamiliar gestures. Vainly we try to discover some sequence, some reason, in their actions ; and not until we guess their significance as symbols do their apparitions take on any meaning.

The most annoying of them is Reuben, who represents the ' vegetated ' man, living only in the flesh. At first he sleeps on London Stone, existing ' in the shadows of Possibility ' ; but when Woman separates the intellectual, sentimental, and physical passions, Los (the Poet) creates Man in his physical form (Reuben), as a limit to these errors. First Reuben's emotions are bounded (34 : 47), then his intellect (34 : 53), his senses next (36 : 6), and finally his spirit (36 : 13). He is sent forth, and all the nations become as he when they behold him, and materialize. The rest of Reuben's story is simply a vague wandering over the globe (sometimes twelvefold, as the tribes) ; or, in another symbol, falling head downward. His usual symbol, however, is ' enrooting,' since he is the ' vegetating man ' ; and this enrooting, this taking of substance from the earth, is Blake's interpretation of the guilty love which the biblical Reuben bore his mother. His divisions are the dividing of the Nations. Woman is seduced when he appears (74 : 33), mistaking outward beauty for inward soul. Finally Los leads him to Canaan, which is an Enitharmic ' moony space ' of real love, and limits his stay there to six thousand years (85 : 4). After that, Reuben presumably sinks again into his eternal sleep ' in the shadows of Possibility,' though we are not told of it.

Another such character, without even this much story, is Joseph, the man of genius sacrificed to family hate. Woman's cruelty subjects him to her beloved ; time and again the baulked harlot exposes the shame of him who despises her (strips off his coat of many colours), or she makes him a slave under Reason (Egypt).

[1] Keynes, p. 168.

But of all the difficulties, by far the greatest are those caused by Blake's geographical symbols, which are sprinkled profusely on almost every page. For the most part Blake abandoned the names taken from the Holy Lands, in preference to those from the British Isles. And the more we study these, the more we discover that Blake chose them for personal associations rather than for their relation to the points of the compass.

Of course Blake knew that future commentators would have their troubles over such names, so he tried to clarify matters by arranging them in systems of his own. Therefore we find elaborate groupings of cities and counties and continents under their protecting deities and demigods; groupings which probably were never intended to be read as poetry, but to be used for reference only.

Perhaps the most prominent of all these groups is that of the Twenty-eight Cathedral Cities, which is worth unravelling as far as possible in order to show how Blake's mind was working, rather than to explain *Jerusalem*. The first part of the list is given on plate XL, the second half on plate XLVI —a characteristic division. Of the twenty-eight names, the first seven and the last four are stressed as important. The first seven are Selsey (Chichester), Winchester, Gloucester, Exeter, Salisbury (vicinity of Stonehenge), Bristol (Chatterton's City), and Bath. Since Blake was tried at Chichester, we may assume that it represents the place of the Accuser; an assumption borne out by its parallelism with ' Adam ' in the list of the Twenty-seven Religions. Bath is very definitely identified with the Body, and Salisbury with Reason; so we may assume that Bristol represents the Spirit, and Exeter the Emotions. The last four cities in the list, Edinburgh, London, Verulam, and York, represent the Four Zoas (74 : 3). The remaining seventeen cities are included in Bath (45 : 37); beyond this we have almost no clue to their meanings.

And having solved this problem thus far, we turn to the rest of the epic, and find that the solution is of practically no value. There are not enough references to these cities to make their symbolism of any importance.

So the reader may pass over all geographical symbols which are not immediately self-explanatory. Almost invariably a paragraph of the obscurest names can be covered by one sentence, such as : ' The whole earth shook,' or ' The nations overspread the world.' Even a passage like the Homeric Catalogue of Counties (16:28-60, 72:17-27) reduces to a simple truth, whose details are quite unimportant.

These references sully sadly the poetic dignity of *Jerusalem*; but ignored, they do not much hinder our understanding of the epic.

One set of symbols alone needs explanation before *Jerusalem* can be properly understood. These are the Sons and the Daughters of Albion. The former represent the Cruelty of Man to Man; the latter the Cruelty of Woman to Man. For the first time in Blake's writings they emerge as individuals.

The twelve Sons are divided into three groups: the fourfold Executioner, the fourfold Judge, and the fourfold Accuser. This is clear enough as soon as we recognize in their names Blakean misspellings of the people arrayed against him in his trial at Chichester. Since they represent Man in this world, Blake inverts their eternal order, putting the lowest specimens first. (This is the Crucifixion Upside Down.) Hand, who heads the list, is the most prominent of them. He is the Rational Man, the finished product of the Church of Moral Virtue. Hyle (Hayley) is the Bad Artist. The only other of the twelve needing explanation is Scofield, Blake's accuser, who is identified with the Natural Man, Adam. Each of these Sons has an emanation (or sister), of whom only the emanations of Hand and Hyle are important. They are Gwendolen (Selfish Pleasure) and Cambel (False Inspiration). All but one of these Daughters are named after characters in Geoffrey of Monmouth's mythological *British History*.

We are now ready for an analysis of the action of *Jerusalem*.

The first chapter pictures Man already below Eternity, falling into Beulah. The second chapter continues the Fall, bringing him into Generation. The third chapter contains the triumph of Error, the Conception of Christ, the Nativity, and the Crucifixion. The fourth chapter describes the first perceptions of Truth, the appearance of the Antichrist, and the ultimate Resurrection of Man.

Chapter I. opens with a short passage in which Jesus calls to Man, who has lost all faith; and Blake accepts the task of redeeming him, though Albion's Sons and Daughters are already raging against the City of Art (Golgonooza): ' Abstract Philosophy warring in enmity against Imagination.'

The Poet, Los, working at his anvil, is already divided. His Spectre (Reason) hangs over him, trying to dissuade him from his work. It is the temptation in the Wilderness. In vain the Spectre describes Man's spiritual desolation; in vain he insists on Man's unworthiness of being saved. Los is but the more stubborn in pursuing his labours. He even forces the Spectre himself to labour with him, when he analyses the Spectre's place in Man.

> And this is the manner of the Sons of Albion in their strength:
> They take the two Contraries which are call'd Qualities, with which
> Every Substance is clothed; they name them Good & Evil.
> From them they make an Abstract, which is a Negation
> Not only of the Substance from which it is derived,
> A murderer of its own Body; but also a murderer
> Of every Divine Member. It is the Reasoning Power,
> An Abstract objecting power, that Negatives every thing.
> This is the Spectre of Man: the Holy Reasoning Power,
> And in its Holiness is closed the abomination of Desolation.

Against this Rational Philosophy, which kills everything it touches, Los heats his furnaces. His labours are rewarded; his works (Sons and Daughters) issue in ecstasy from the furnaces; and together they build Golgonooza, the City of Art.

The City is described at great length, as well as the desolate stretches outside, which are the world as seen by Science, with all the ' Self-righteousnesses conglomerating against the Divine Vision.' Los is tempted to yield wholly to his inspirations; but he exhibits his Spectre (Reason), and thus escapes being seduced by his own works. Yet the effect is not wholly good; for he divides still farther; and Enitharmon (his great Inspiration) is separated from him.

Then after a short transitory passage, in which the Sons of Albion in their worship of Nature (Vala) cry out against Freedom (Jerusalem), the story changes to that of Albion, Jerusalem, and Vala.

Man is smitten. Over him Freedom and Nature (Jerusalem and Vala) sorrow, Freedom complaining of Nature's dominion over Man. He in turn accuses them both of polluting Love. In vain Freedom protests, crying :

'Why should Punishment Weave the Veil with Iron Wheels of War,
When Forgiveness might it Weave with Wings of Cherubim ? '

But Man mistakes Pity for Love ; he tries to tear away the Veil of Moral Virtue (Vala's Veil) ; and sinks into the sleep of Beulah, after a last soliloquy of doubt and despair over his miserable shame. The chapter ends with a wailing protest from Beulah over the Cruelty of Man to Man.

Chapter II. opens with the illusions of Man in his deathly sleep.[1]

Every ornament of perfection, and every labour of love,
In all the Garden of Eden, & in all the golden mountains,
Was become an envied horror, and a remembrance of jealousy ;
And every Act a Crime, and Albion the punisher & judge.

He freezes the Invisible into a visible rock, as a firm foundation ; and this appearance of Matter separates man from man. Once Matter is produced, the Tree of Mystery, which is the growth of Moral Virtue, springs up, and the Druidic Religion is founded.

The Chaos (produced by Memory, not by Inspiration) appears when Albion turns his back on the Divine Vision ; and the Chaos, to which Reason reduces Infinity, preaches Materialism :

'I am your Rational Power, O Albion, & that Human Form
You call Divine, is but a Worm seventy inches long
That creeps forth in a night & is dried in the morning sun,
In fortuitous concourse of memorys accumulated & lost.
It plows the Earth in its own conceit, it ovewhelms the Hills
Beneath its winding labyrinths, till a stone of the brook
Stops it in midst of its pride among its hills & rivers. . . .
The ancient Cities of the Earth remove as a traveller,
And shall Albion's cities remain when I pass over them,
With my deluge of forgotten remembrances over the tablet ? '

Then Nature herself appears, materialized in the Chaos, and she mourns that Albion knows her no longer.

He is still whole, though he is falling rapidly into Error (Ulro) ; and Los protests in vain against the triumph of Nature's ' Female Will ' over Albion, for Nature should be the slave, not the master, of Man.

' If Perceptive Organs vary, Objects of Perceptions seem to vary.
If the Perceptive Organs close, their Objects seem to close also
Consider this, O mortal Man, O worm of sixty winters,' said Los,
' Consider Sexual Organization & hide thee in the dust.'

Then the Divine Vision fixes the twin limits of the Fall—the limits of Opacity and Contraction—so that Man can fall no farther. He announces

---

[1] In the original arrangement of this *Chapter* certain contradictions appear, which Blake endeavoured to correct by a new order of pages. I have followed the new order in this summary, though in the Commentary I felt it better to follow the old order, which has been accepted as the standard. The second order, which appears in several copies, is as follows : 28, 33-41, 43-46, 42, 29-32, 47-50. None of the other chapters is rearranged in any copy.

that Man has entered the State of Error (Satan) ; and that by limiting
States the Individual can be redeemed from them. The vegetated man,
Reuben, appears at once ; for he himself is the Limit of Contraction ; and
all the Nations separate and flee before him. Division follows division.
The Zoas themselves rage, and become materialized as the four elements.

> And many of the Eternal Ones laughed after their manner :
> ' Have you known the Judgment that is arisen among the
> Zoas of Albion ; where a Man dare hardly to embrace
> His own Wife, for the terrors of Chastity that they call
> By the name of Morality ? their Daughters govern all
> In hidden deceit ! they are Vegetable, only fit for burning.
> Art & Science cannot exist but by Naked Beauty display'd.'

> Then those in Great Eternity who contemplate on Death
> Said thus : ' What seems to Be, Is, To those to whom
> It seems to Be ; & is productive of the most dreadful
> Consequences to those to whom it seems to Be ; even of
> Torments, Despair, Eternal Death ; but the Divine Mercy
> Steps beyond and Redeems Man in the Body of Jesus. Amen.'

The Poet calls on Man to rise from his sleep against the Spectre ;
but Albion only flees the more indignantly, though the Saviour follows him,
describing the life in Eternity. Albion flees until he comes to the Gate
of Los, which opens between Beulah and the world of Generation ; and
here Los stops him for a moment of despairing conversation. The
Twenty-eight Cathedral Cities of Albion crowd to him in his distress ; they
swear fidelity to him, though the Zoas turn against them and Albion
himself seek to destroy their emanations. The Poet rages against the
futility of it all :

> ' Why stand we here trembling around
> Calling on God for help, and not ourselves in whom God dwells,
> Stretching a hand to save the falling Man ? '

And finally he persuades them ; the Cities rise and try to bear Albion
back to Eternity ; but they cannot do it against his will. ' Strucken with
Albion's disease, they become what they behold,' and also suffer the
divisions and the descent into Matter. Yet still they can protest ; Bath
(the Body) cries out to the Christ, and the other cities second his appeal,
but in vain.

Los still tries to make Man aware of his condition.

> But when Los open'd the Furnaces before him
> He saw that the accursed things were his own affections,
> And his own beloveds : then he turn'd sick : his soul died within him.

For this Man attacks the Poet, accusing him of selfishness and immorality;
but Los is ready with his answer :

> ' Thou wast the Image of God surrounded by the Four Zoas.
> Three thou hast slain ; I am the Fourth, thou canst not destroy me.
> Thou art in Error ; trouble me not with thy righteousness.
> I have innocence to defend and ignorance to instruct ;
> I have no time for seeming, and little arts of compliment,
> In morality and virtue, in self-glorying and pride.'

He tells Man of the two limits ; he also tells him how the Saviour forms
Woman from the Limit of Contraction, ' that Himself may in process of

time be born, Man to redeem.   But there is no limit of Expansion, there is no Limit of Translucence, in the bosom of Man.' Albion is only incensed ; he sends Hand and Hyle, the Rational Man and the Bad Artist, to seize Los, but they cannot reach him.   And while Albion builds his altars to the false gods, Los puts a limit to his errors by circumscribing them with the Mundane Shell.

Again the Divine Vision appears lamenting over the Fall.   He announces that Satan (the Reactor) cannot be revealed until the results of his works are seen.   The Fall continues ; for Los's Spectre and Emanation desert Man, fleeing from his brain.   They report a new phase of the tragedy : Man's struggle with Luvah.

For Man has come to worship the Shadow of his own suppressed desires, and out of this Shadow, Luvah (his Passions) descends and smites him with spiritual disease.   In his agony, Man thinks to gain relief by rejecting his Passions.   But instead of killing them, this only makes an enemy of them.

Los welcomes his Spectre and Emanation, who had fled from him in the previous *Chapter* ; and he prays to the Saviour for Albion, now descended into the world of Generation, from which he can only escape by a Last Judgment—a casting off of Error.   Then Los searches in vain through Man's inner life for Satan, who lies concealed behind everything. Los sees only all the ' Minute Particulars,' which are Man's jewels, degraded and despised in the worship of Abstract Laws.   He tries to continue his old work ; but all of Albion's sons arise and bear him, helpless, to the Death-couch of Beulah.

Meanwhile Man's battle with the Passions continues.   Nature definitely triumphs over Man during the conflict ; and the Passions break loose from Albion's loins to overspread the earth, inspiring all the Druidic idols and false gods with cruelty.

At this Albion sinks for the last time, crying ' Hope is banish'd from me ' ; the Saviour receives his falling body ; and reposes it on the Couch of the inspired Scriptures.

The scene then shifts back to Beulah (Love) where Jerusalem is awakened ; she descends after Man, to save him if possible by self-sacrifice.   Erin (the Body) laments as the Starry Heavens flee from Albion's limbs ; but she is roused to tremendous enthusiasm at the vision of the God who supports him.   All the Daughters of Beulah echo her cry of hope with a prayer that the Saviour descend and destroy the idea of Sin.

Chapter III. describes the triumph of Error.   It opens with a re-statement of the Fall.   Moral Virtue begins to enter even the Poet, when the Spectre announces himself as God.   The Eternals wonder at the confusion, especially since Man's Humanity (the essence of his individuality) still sleeps with all his strength in Beulah ; and they call on ' him who only Is ' for a decision.   As a result, the Seven Eyes of God are appointed to watch over Man.   Los raises a mighty song, to which the Daughters of Albion respond in chorus, chanting Man as the babe of Eternity sleeping in the cradle of the world.

But still Man flees from the Divine Vision ; and in the eternal work of the Zoas he is caught and plowed under with the Dead.   Woman triumphs, torturing her victims on the altars of Moral Virtue, while Los creates the world of Generation from this world of Death.   Reason himself directs the building, and the Veil of Vala, which Man had once cast into the Sea of Time and Space, becomes the Mundane Shell, in whose centre the Looms of Cathedron weave material forms with tears.

Then the Lamb is heard lamenting over Freedom (Jerusalem), now half mad among the Satanic Mills. Yet she answers with faith ; and as a consolation, he reveals to her the Conception of Christ, which is the triumph of Free Love. Jerusalem continues to wail because she is still called a harlot ; but she is comforted. The Nativity takes place.

Meanwhile, in spite of Los's protests, there is an orgiastic triumph of error. Blake searches warfare and the Industrial Revolution for illustrations. The Crucifixion is enacted, during the battle round Vala (Nature) ; and amid Druidic revels of cruelty the temple of Puritanism is built, where the Mocking and the Sacrifice are repeated. The Twelve Daughters of Albion become Rahab (sexual licence) and Tirzah (sexual repression), glorying in their heartlessness. The Twelve Sons become Warriors ; as one they torment Jerusalem. Their consort is Vala-Rahab, the goddess of Moral Virtue and Natural Religion. All the nations separate, and the world is divided among them. Los's work continues ; he labours in Golgonooza offsetting every move of his enemies, while the Looms of Cathedron weave the forms which are the path to salvation. Thus when Rahab and Tirzah create the kings, Los creates the prophets. The chapter ends with a cry from Blake for inspiration, while he recapitulates the Fall.

Chapter IV. concludes the drama. It begins with Error so completely triumphant that the Twelve Sons are attacking the very essence of Man's individuality, his ' Sleeping Humanity,' which the Poet guards. Freedom (Jerusalem) is ruined and sold. She laments her former blissful state, contrasting it with the present degeneracy. She ends in complete despair ; Error has at last overcome her.

> ' I walk in affliction : I am a worm, and no living soul !
> A worm going to eternal torment : rais'd up in a night
> To an eternal night of pain, lost ! lost ! lost ! for ever ! '

Nature also laments, for she is tortured in the battle between Man and the Passions. But suffering has brought wisdom ; she has learned that Jesus alone can solve the problem.

And now the lowest episode of the Fall takes place : the ruin of the Rational Man (Hand) and the Bad Artist (Hyle). The latter is dominated by the ideal (emanation) which properly belongs to the former. He turns to Gwendolen (Pleasure) and not to Cambel, his normal inspiration. Gwendolen has been lamenting over the seduction of the earthbound Imagination (Merlin), for she sees her own cruelty, and fears that the future will degrade her as Jerusalem has been degraded. To escape, she tells a falsehood : how Forgiveness, practised on earth, would be ruin. She even blames the Poet and his Inspiration for the harshness of the moral virtues. In justification for this, she claims that Hyle under her control is a babe in the State of Innocence ; but when she reveals him, he has sunk to the lowest possible form : the Worm, which has neither Head, Heart, nor Loins, and is only a devouring Stomach. Cambel produces the same result in Hand ; for the Rational Man, dominated by False Inspiration (we might say Sentimentality), is also nothing but a Worm.

The error is manifest ; Gwendolen repents, and strives to mend her mistake by moulding the Worm into ' a form of love.'

At this, the Poet is comforted, though still tormented by a fear that he will forget Eternity during his labours in Generation (the Loins). Under the reign of moral terror, he sees ' sins ' hiding from exposure, and he approves their ' hypocrisy.' He descends from Golgonooza to his watch on earth, and from his mountains he can hear the lament of the Daughters of Albion, calling to him.

Yet they are still in the State of Rahab (the Church of Moral Virtue) ; terrified at the philosophy of the Warriors (the Sons of Albion), they build Gwendolen's falsehood into an allegory about the Worm ; from her false premise they elaborate the errors which always follow the Female Will.

Meanwhile Los sings his Watch-Song, and sees a vision of Jerusalem in her eternal aspect, which inspires him with a great fury of inspiration among the Furnaces. Then again Enitharmon is separated from him ; they fall and are reborn of Tharmas and Enion as two children. Los woos her fervently, but she is fickle, and wishes to dominate him. (This episode is repeated from *The Four Zoas, Night I*.)

The Spectre, knowing he has caused their division, smiles and rejoices. It is the completion of his domination ; and he is revealed as the Antichrist, the Covering Cherub. The drama of the Last Judgment has begun at last.

Los arises, announcing doctrine after doctrine, though he terrifies now the Daughters, now the Sons. In spite of the creations of the Spectre, he continues, until the Spectre sees himself as a mere fly in Infinity. But though Los himself is despairing, he beholds the Nations amalgamating once more, and re-entering Albion's loins. The great act of Union is inaugurated.

Enitharmon is in terrible fear ; for if Albion be raised into Eternity, her labours at the loom must cease, and she herself will lose her separate existence, which she thinks will be annihilation. But Los assures her that she will not be non-existent ; she will live as one with him, since in Eternity all are one.

Time is finished : the six thousand years of the earth's existence are over. Albion's emanation (' Brittannia,' or England) is the first to awake ; and she wails that she has slain her lord during her cruel dreams. Her penitent voice rouses him ; he rises and strides into Eternity once again. Britannia meanwhile enters his bosom.

So Man is made One ; but as yet he is separate from Jesus ; and the Covering Cherub threatens them as they converse. Albion fears that the Cherub, whom he now recognizes as his own selfishness (Selfhood), will slay Jesus.

> Albion said : ' O Lord, what can I do ? my Selfhood cruel
> Marches against thee, deceitful, from Sinai & from Edom
> Into the Wilderness of Judah to meet thee in his pride.
> I behold the Visions of my deadly Sleep of Six Thousand Years,
> Dazling around thy skirts like a Serpent of precious stones & gold.
> I know it is my Self, O my Divine Creator & Redeemer.'
>
> Jesus replied : ' Fear not, Albion : unless I die thou canst not live ;
> But if I die, I shall arise again & thou with me.
> This is Friendship & Brotherhood : without it Man Is Not.'

> So Jesus spoke : the Covering Cherub coming on in darkness
> Overshadow'd them & Jesus said : ' Thus do Men in Eternity,
> One for another to put off, by forgiveness, every sin.'

> Albion reply'd : ' Cannot Man exist without Mysterious
> Offering of Self for Another : is this Friendship & Brotherhood ?
> I see thee in the likeness & similitude of Los my Friend.'

> Jesus said : ' Wouldest thou love one who never died
> For thee, or ever die for one who had not died for thee ?
> And if God dieth not for Man & giveth not himself
> Eternally for Man, Man could not exist, for Man is Love
> As God is Love : every kindness to another is a little Death
> In the Divine Image ; nor can Man exist but by Brotherhood.'

Then the Selfhood separates them ; and Albion practises what he has just learned. He flings himself into the Furnaces of Affliction ; but at once they become the Fountains of Living Water ! His sons and daughters awake ; the Zoas re-enter his bosom ; he calls upon Jerusalem, and seizes his Bow of spiritual warfare. One shot of the fourfold arrow slays the Covering Cherub forever. And all appear in heaven, harmonized into Unity. True Art and Science are revealed. A great cry arises from all the regions in wonder at the disappearance of the old illusions.

> All Human Forms identified, even Tree, Metal, Earth, & Stone ; all
> Human Forms identified, living, going forth, & returning wearied
> Into the Planetary lives of years, Months, Days & Hours, reposing
> And then Awaking into his Bosom in the Life of Immortality.

> And I heard the Name of their Emanations : they are named Jerusalem.

It is perfectly evident from this synopsis that Blake had not developed his narrative powers. There are many incoherences, and even some contradictions. For example, Albion utters twice his last words in Eternity (23 : 26 and 47 : 17). The surmise is that Blake did not conceive the Fall as one steady act, but as a spiral alternating upward and downward ; sometimes gleaming with the old light, sometimes passing a point already passed before. We cannot accuse Blake of carelessness, knowing his habit of elaborate revision ; especially when we remember the many years he spent on *Jerusalem*. He undoubtedly preferred accurate psychology to an over-simplified map of the Mystic Way.

Some of the incoherence may also be due to his ' inspirational ' method of writing. He wrote twelve to thirty lines at a time, just as they came to him. He would rephrase an old thought more epigrammatically ; he would explain one symbol by another ; or repeat an essential part of the story ; or insert invocations and choral passages, jotting them down as they came to him within the broad outline of each chapter.

We know that Blake could write directly when he chose. The four prose bits which head each chapter are startlingly clear in contrast to the epic itself. They are as definitely perfect in their way as the *Job* engravings. The man who was engaged on the *Job* and this prose simultaneously with the epic cannot be accused of any loss of power. Blake's purpose is evident. The prose is the propaganda which is to lead readers into the labyrinth. It is one end of the Golden String.

Jerusalem contains all the old doctrines and at least two new ones.

The first of the latter is the identification of the Father and the Son, of the Creator and the Redeemer. At last Blake synthesizes the two Testaments. He had always insisted that Reason has its place in the Universe; but never before had he insisted so definitely on the Goodness of Creation. To explain this, Urizen now plays only a small part in Creation, most of it being done by Los, as a defining of Error; while the Divine Mercy himself creates at least two things: the various States and Woman. Blake had originally considered Creation as the lowest point of the Fall; now he insists that it is the first step upward from the nadir. The Fall scattered many forces which, once given a body in which to work, can find again some purpose and eventually return to the zenith. The State of Error is the exploration of Possibility, which must end in the confirming of Eternal Reality. For the path of Possibility, being rigidly limited by Cause and Effect, always returns to Paradise.

The second new doctrine is that of the State and the Individual. The error, and not he who errs, is to be blamed; and by defining the error, it can be recognized and escaped, or put off. This is Blake's rephrasing of the Christian command, to ' hate the sin, but love the sinner.'

A third doctrine, though not new, is strongly emphasized throughout *Jerusalem*. Eternity is Friendship; Beulah is Love. The perfect man is androgynous—contains both sexes; therefore love, in the mundane sense of the word, is impossible to him, unless he descends from his high state in Eternity to a lower one. Any love which is consummated is actually a fall from Eternity into the sleep of Beulah, which entails in turn a descent into the world of Generation.

> But no one can consummate Female bliss in Los's World without
> Becoming a Generated Mortal, a Vegetating Death;

and again—

> Nor can any consummate bliss without being Generated
> On Earth.

For such love, a union though it seems, presupposes a division, which it overcomes only partially. In Eternity the Lover and his Beloved are to be literally one. But in this world Man need fear no fall through Love; for Beulah is above, not below him.

At first sight, *Jerusalem* contains less poetry than any of Blake's other works. There are stretches of splendid lamentation; there are impressive philosophical choruses; but there is nothing resembling the lyrical quality found so often in *The Four Zoas* and at times in *Milton*. *Jerusalem* is pitched in a key at once darker and more sublime. The dignity of its profound thought and the spiritual fervour set the tone. The reader's imagination, however ignorant of the meaning behind the words, is stirred continually by such lines as—

> Then the Spectre drew Vala into his bosom, magnificent, terrific,
> Glittering with precious stones & gold, with Garments of blood & fire.
> He wept in deadly wrath of the Spectre, in self-contradicting agony,
> Crimson with Wrath & green with Jealousy, dazling with Love
> And Jealousy immingled, & the purple of the violet darken'd deep
> Over the Plow of Nations thund'ring in the hand of Albion's Spectre.

Between such passages and the elaborate choruses stand a great many epigrams, which in number and force surpass even those of *The Marriage of Heaven and Hell.* Obscure as Blake's plot may be, his teachings are never in doubt. Cloudy as his Eternity may seem, his ' spiritual arrows ' are sharp and well aimed. Had Blake never written more than this one epic, it would be preserved (though only by the curious, I am afraid) for the abundance of such thoughts as :

> I have tried to make friends by corporeal gifts, but have only
> Made enemies : I never made friends but by spiritual gifts,
> By severe contentions of friendship & the burning fire of thought.
>
> What is a Wife & what is a Harlot ? What is a Church ? & What
> Is a Theatre ? are they Two & not One ? can they exist Separate ?
> Are not Religion & Politics the same Thing ? Brotherhood is Religion.
>
> He who would do good to another must do it in Minute Particulars.
> General Good is the plea of the scoundrel, hypocrite, & flatterer.
>
> It is better to prevent misery, than to release from misery ;
> It is better to prevent error than to forgive the criminal.

And yet, on a second consideration of this ' choral tempest ' as pure poetry, the effect is whole and mighty. There is a completeness to the apparent chaos which can neither be escaped nor defined. One feels as though a new, great symphony had just been heard : there are definite statements of themes, there is the struggle of interweaving voices one cannot quite follow, there are involved development-passages of huge emotional sweep and change, which finally burst forth into the triumphant apotheosis. There is a new, dark splendour, a vast breadth, a sense of towering structure. The dimensions are threefold, solid, no longer mere frescoings. Such is the literary effect ; the ideas are another matter.

Jerusalem, then, is the last and obscurest of Blake's epics. It should not be read until the reader has a considerable familiarity with Blake's technical vocabulary. Otherwise, all the subtler embroidery on his great themes will pass unnoticed, and *Jerusalem* will appear merely as an amazing chaos. But when the casual references to the mythology are immediately recognized, *Jerusalem* will be revealed as Blake's biggest storehouse (we dare not say ' vehicle ') of thought, decorated with splendid passages of poetry, austere, profound, and proudly beautiful.

CHAPTER XXVIII

'SPIRITS' AND THEIR 'DICTATION'

'In a dream, in a vision of the night, when deep sleep falleth upon men, in slumberings upon the bed;
Then he openeth the ears of men, and sealeth their instruction.'
—*Job* xxxiii. 15-16.

JOHN VARLEY, 'Father of the English School of Water-colour Painters' and enthusiastic astrologer, was convinced that Blake was a Spiritist medium. Blake denied this, but wickedly encouraged Varley's belief by drawing for him the 'Visionary Heads.' Blake's first editor, the American Swedenborgian, J. J. Garth Wilkinson, stated that Blake was a medium whose literary work was ruined by his indiscriminate submission to supermundane 'controls.' Others, including G. K. Chesterton, have revived this theory; and since these questions are receiving so much attention just now, it will not be uninteresting to trace Blake's tangency upon them, the more so as the question involves the whole psychology of poetic composition.

Blake's connection with Spiritism must be reduced to three phases only: telepathy, visions, and automatic writing. There were no mysterious raps, crystal-gazing, dancing tables, hauntings, poltergeists, materializations, or physical manifestations of any sort.

Of Blake's telepathy, we have only a single anecdote, though it is quoted as characteristic. Blake and various friends were at Hampstead, and one of them, Samuel Palmer, left for London. 'Presently Blake, putting his hand to his forehead, said quietly: "Palmer is coming; he is walking up the road." "Oh, Mr. Blake, he's gone to London; we saw him off in the coach." Then, after a while, "He is coming through the wicket—there!"—pointing to the closed door. And surely, in another minute, Samuel Palmer raised the latch and came in amongst them.' [1]

Allied to this sort of incident are two cases of what might be called prophetic intuition. Once, when a boy of fourteen, he stoutly refused to be apprenticed to the celebrated engraver Ryland, saying: 'Father, I do not like the man's face: it looks as if he will live to be hanged.' So young William was apprenticed to the less fashionable Basire instead; and twelve years later Ryland won his place in history as the last man to be hanged at Tyburn. Of course, in those days 'will live to be hanged' meant nothing but 'will come to a bad end'; nevertheless, the story is curious. We must also remember the time when Blake saved Tom Paine's life, by bundling him off to France after a violent speech, without letting him even return to his lodgings for his effects, where the officers of the law were actually waiting. And since we are searching for incidents of this sort, we should mention the events which led to Blake's marriage. Blake, aged twenty-four, had been scorned by a certain lively girl, until he became really ill. One evening at a friend's house he was bemoaning in a corner his love-crosses. His listener, a dark-eyed, generous-hearted girl, frankly declared 'She pitied him from her heart.' '*Do* you pity

---

[1] *Memoir of Edward Calvert*, p. 36.

me ? ' ' *Yes!* I do, most sincerely.' ' Then I love you for that ! ' [1] And so they were married. Yet Mrs. Blake's place in history is that of one of the most perfect wives ever won by a genius. This story is made a little more impressive by Mrs. Blake's tale (which she was so fond of repeating after William's death !) that when she first saw her husband-to-be, she came so near fainting that she had to leave the room at once.

The last two of these incidents, at least, are wholly within the realm of the normal. But all four cases seem to be related. They are varying degrees of the same thing. The first is certainly supernormal ; the second nearly so ; the third might have been nothing but quick wits ; while the fourth may be dismissed (but not explained) as a characteristic sexual phenomenon. All of them demonstrate Blake's sensibility to impression. It is impossible to draw a logical line between telepathy and common-sense.

This clears the ground for the discussion of what are usually known as Blake's ' visions ' and his ' automatic writing.'

Blake's first vision came at the age of four, when God put his forehead down to the window and set William screaming.[2] Later his mother beat him for saying he saw Ezekiel under a tree.[3] About the age of eight he saw ' a tree filled with angels, bright angelic wings bespangling every bough like stars.' [4] This time his mother thought better, and prevented the father from beating him. Perhaps she did this less in sympathy with her son's imagination than in fear of the consequences of a flogging ; for William resented blows so strongly that he was never sent to school. During his apprenticeship (from fourteen to twenty-one) he used to draw for hours in Westminster Abbey, which was a wonderful place for visions. Once he saw Christ and the Apostles ; [5] another time ' the aisles and galleries of the old cathedral suddenly filled with a great procession of monks and priests, choristers and censer-bearers, and his entranced ear heard the chant of plain-song and chorale, while the vaulted roof trembled to the sound of organ music.' [6] The Abbey, however, was not entirely ideal. The Westminster schoolboys used to play there, and very naturally they selected Blake—a boy of their own age, but not of their crowd—as a butt for practical jokes. Finally one of them climbed upon a pinnacle to reach Blake's own exalted position ; whereupon Blake flung him to the ground and protested the matter to the Dean. Since then the boys have never been allowed to use the Abbey as a playground.

Such ' visions ' during childhood or even puberty are nothing abnormal in any imaginative person. But Blake never lost them. About 1788 his dead brother Robert appeared to him and revealed the process for producing the *Songs of Innocence.* In 1794 he engraved the *Ancient of Days,* the famous frontispiece of *Europe,* from a vision which hovered over him at the top of his staircase.[7] ' I have been commanded from Hell not to print this as it is what our Enemies wish,' he added to his revolutionary annotations of 1798 on the margins of Bishop Watson's *Apology for the Bible.* In the early part of 1803 occurred the visions recorded in *Milton*

[1] Gilchrist, ch. v. The same story is repeated even more abruptly in Tatham's *Life of Blake* and in J. T. Smith's *Biographical Sketch.*
[2] H. C. R., Feb. 25, 1852. [3] Tatham.
[4] Gilchrist, ch. ii. [5] *Ibid.,* ch. iii.
[6] Quoted from Oswald Crawfurd's *William Blake : Artist, Poet, and Painter* (*The New Quarterly Magazine,* vol. ii., 1874). Mr. Crawfurd's source is one of Blake's unprinted letters, apparently to Butts, which contains several of Blake's early visions.
[7] J. T. Smith, *Biographical Sketch.*

and *Jerusalem*. In 1819 and 1820 Blake drew for the occultist Varley various heads of historical and imaginary characters, including the celebrated *Ghost of a Flea* and a portrait of himself. He would draw these apparently from models visible only to himself, complaining that they moved, vanished, or interfered with each other. Five years later Crabb Robinson heard Blake still discoursing freely of his visions. Even on his death-bed, ' in a most glorious manner . . . he burst out into singing of the things he saw in heaven.'

These are brief and bald accounts of what has been called his ' clairvoyance.' Blake's own poems and letters often corroborate the tales and testimony of his friends.

There seems at first little reason to think that Blake did not mean that he saw these things literally. Yet a careful examination of all the evidence shows that *not once* did he allow these visions any objective, or external, existence. We should be warned by his reiterated insistence that Imagination is Truth, and we should be in his secret when we read that he sees not *with* but *through* his eyes.

Yet here a distinction must be made. Blake had *two* kinds of mental ' sight.' The first was the *Oculis Imaginationis* of the Scholastics, Wordsworth's ' inward eye which is the bliss of solitude,' or in modern terms, the Visualizing Power. The second method visualized not the literal forms but the ' spiritual forms.' Then Blake transmuted everything—even the entire Universe—into a human figure.[1] Sometimes he divided this power into four parts, one for each Zoa : Single-Vision being pure sensation, Double Vision adding an intellectual appreciation, Threefold Vision infusing the emotional values, and Fourfold Vision crowning the whole with spiritual interpretation ; as in the Letter to Butts, November 22, 1802 :

> Now I a fourfold vision see,
> And a fourfold vision is given to me ;
> 'Tis fourfold in my supreme delight,
> And threefold in soft Beulah's night,
> And twofold always. May God us keep
> From single vision, and Newton's sleep.

Once comprehending his attitude, we can understand a certain method of self-defence which he cultivated against the world. Whenever he met any unsympathetic person, he deliberately puzzled him with ambiguous speeches, for he liked fun, and what is more fun than amazing the bourgeois ? ' In society,' Gilchrist wrote, ' people would disbelieve and exasperate him, would set upon the gentle fiery-hearted mystic, and stir him up into being extravagant, out of a mere spirit of opposition. Then he would say things on purpose to startle, and make people stare. In the excitement of conversation he would exaggerate his peculiarities of opinion and doctrine, would express a floating vision or fancy in an extreme way, without the explanation or qualification he was, in reality, well aware it needed ; taking a secret pleasure in the surprise and opposition such views aroused.' [2]

Crabb Robinson's visit to him on June 13, 1826, was a typical case. Blake evidently set out to shock and puzzle his earnest Boswell ; so, after

---

[1] Cf. Letter to Butts, Oct. 2, 1800.

[2] Gilchrist, ch. xxxv. Every one of Blake's friends confirms this. See, for example, Tatham's *Life* (pp. 38-39) ; Linnell's letter to Bernard Barton (*Letters of William Blake*, p. 229) ; and Palmer's letter quoted by Gilchrist, ch. xxxiii.

approving a community of wives on the authority of the Bible, he ' asserted that he had committed many murders, that reason is the only evil or sin, and that careless, gay people are better than those who think, etc., etc., etc.' [1]   We hardly need the explanation which Crabb Robinson lacked. A murderer is one who hates another to the point of wishing his death, since ' thought is act.'   Reason (Urizen) is the primal cause of disturbance in Blake's cosmos.   The ' gay, careless people ' are those who live instinctively, rather than reasonably.

In fact, Blake was simply extending his symbolism to his conversation. ' I have conversed with the Spiritual Sun—I saw him on Primrose Hill. He said, " Do you take me for the Greek Apollo ? " " No," I said. " That " (and Blake pointed to the sky)—" that is the Greek Apollo. He is Satan." ' [2] Crabb Robinson could not explain such nonsense, but we can.   Blake is referring to some poetic moment of inspiration (the Spiritual Sun) on Primrose Hill.   This moment showed him the difference between Poetry and Intellect (the Greek Apollo [3]).   Pure Intellect brings us to Materialism—a belief in the reality of Space and Time.   This is a false religion, or Satan.[4]

Simpler, but of the same sort, was the vision related at Mr. Aders's party.   ' " The other evening," said Blake in his usual quiet way, " taking a walk, I came to a meadow, and at the farther corner of it I saw a fold of lambs. Coming nearer, the ground blushed with flowers ; and the wattled cote and its woolly tenants were of an exquisite pastoral beauty. But I looked again, and it proved to be no living flock, but beautiful sculpture." '   What Blake meant was that the loveliness of the scene suddenly became fixed imperishably as a thing of beauty.[5]

[1] H. C. R., June 13, 1826.   [2] *Ibid.*, Dec. 10, 1825.
[3] Apollo was the God of Light and Poetry to the Greeks.   Blake considered that their Guiding Light was really the Intellect, and that their Muses were processes of Memory. Therefore their Apollo stood for Reason and Memory, not for Inspiration.   (See the 14th Illustration to *Job*.)
[4] ' Devils are False Religions.'—*Jerusalem*, 77.
[5] Two curious and opposing sensations have played a surprisingly large part in all philosophy.   The first, the Evanescence of Things, resolves the world into a fleeting mist. Its contrary, the Eternity of Things, suddenly transmutes various details of the fleeting world into Everlasting Forms.   These forms were called by Blake the Bright Sculptures of Los's Halls.   Keats's *Grecian Urn* was inspired by this feeling.   The two following poems are examples of this same sensation as treated by two modern poets :

OMBRE CHINOISE

RED foxgloves against a yellow wall streaked with plum-coloured shadows ;
A lady with a blue and red sunshade ;
The slow dash of waves upon a parapet.
That is all.
Non-existent—immortal—
As solid as the centre of a ring of fine gold.
                              —AMY LOWELL : *Pictures of the Floating World.*

THE GARDEN

You are clear,
O Rose, cut in rock,
Hard as the descent of hail.

I could scrape the colour
From the petals,
Like spilt dye from a rock.

If I could break you
I could break a tree.

If I could stir
I could break a tree,
I could break you.
                              —H. D. : *Some Imagist Poets* (1915).

Of the same sort of apparition, though for once without symbolism, was the 'Fairy's Funeral.' To appreciate the amusing side of the story we must picture Blake ' in company ' sitting beside some lady of whom he knew little. Conversation lagged ; his mind wandered. Then, realizing that he must say something to the lady, he swiftly decided to tell her about a vision of the previous evening, which was too exquisite to be lost. So in all solemnity he asked : ' Did you ever see a fairy's funeral, madam ? . . . I have, but not before last night. I was walking alone in my garden, there was great stillness among the branches and flowers and more than common sweetness in the air ; I heard a low and pleasant sound, and I knew not whence it came. At last I saw the broad leaf of a flower move, and underneath I saw a procession of creatures of the size and colour of green and gray grasshoppers, bearing a body laid out on a rose leaf, which they buried with songs, and then disappeared. It was a fairy funeral.' [1]

This is the stuff of poetry, not fact. Every real poet is continually working out such conceits in his mind. That such a thing entered Blake's head was enough for him to say that it was true.[2] Things exist as they are perceived. Blake saw the world looked flat ; said it *was* so to Crabb Robinson ; and wrote the same theory into his *Milton*.[3]

It should now be perfectly obvious that his ' spirits, who taught, rebuked, argued, and advised with all the familiarity of personal inter-course ' [4] existed only in his imagination ; and what is more, he knew it. Not once did he ever admit their objective existence. ' I beg pardon, Mr. Blake, but *may* I ask *where* you saw this ? ' said the lady who had been told of the sculptured sheep. ' *Here*, madam,' answered Blake, touching his forehead, and bewildering the lady more than ever.[5] Gilchrist continues : ' He would candidly confess they were not literal matters of fact ; but phenomena seen by his imagination ; *realities* none the less for that, but transacted within the realm of mind.'

Visions and spirits, being simply the functioning of his imagination, were deeply involved with his painting. Every artist without exception has a developed power of visualizing—of seeing anything he wishes. Tatham, not realizing this, carefully recorded of Blake : ' He always asserted that he had the power of bringing his imagination before his mind's eye, so completely organized, and so perfectly formed and evident, that he persisted that while he copied the vision (as he called it) upon his plate or canvas, he could not err, and that error and defect could only arise from the departure or inaccurate delineation of this unsubstantial scene.' [6] This explains at once the too-famous ' Visionary Heads,' already mentioned, which Blake drew from invisible sitters for the thrilled and baffled Varley. Nor are we surprised that both Milton and Shak-spere so invoked, resembled the old prints of them,[7] for there was more of memory in these feats than Blake admitted. Such powers are, of course, entirely normal, and Blake realized it. He knew that ' all men partake of it, but it is lost by not being cultivated.' [8]

---

[1] Allan Cunningham, *Life of Blake.*
[2] Cf. ' Everything possible to be believ'd is an image of truth.'—38th *Proverb of Hell.*
[3] H.C. R., Dec. 10, 1825 : ' Thus is the earth one infinite plane ' (*Milton*, 14 : 32 ; see also 28 : 5-18).
[4] Tatham, p. 19.   [5] Gilchrist, ch. xxxv.   [6] Tatham, p. 18.
[7] H. C. R., Dec. 17, 1825 ; and *Ibid.*, Feb. 18, 1826.
[8] *Ibid.*, Dec. 17, 1825.

Naturally he cultivated it to the best of his abilities. He and his wife often gazed into the fire until they saw forms there,[1] and Blake himself once remarked that he could look at a knot of wood until he was frightened at it.[2] And when inspiration failed, he and his wife knelt in prayer,[3] just as Fra Angelico had done five centuries before. In fact, Blake once defined such powers as 'Imagination heightened to the point of Vision.'

These visions must have been at times a strain upon his physique. In *Milton* he described himself as swept by huge emotions during the Felpham visions, until he collapsed trembling upon the garden-path, recovering when his wife came to his assistance. Yet even after such a moment, instead of being in a state of nervous exhaustion, he found his senses made more keen and vigorous towards the beauties of the world.

There is even one case on record, apparently a unique episode in Blake's life, when a vision came uncontrolled, attended by a morbid fear. What apparently happened was this. Blake's imagination, being powerful, had a subliminal life of its own. When not fed with thoughts and feelings of a beautiful kind (as happens now and then when the poet's stock is temporarily exhausted), it seized arbitrarily upon some casual grotesque, swiftly built it into a presentable figure, and offered it to Blake's startled consciousness. Being instantly rejected, the ghost vanished for good. Gilchrist tells the tale as follows : 'When talking on the subject of ghosts, he was wont to say they did not appear much to imaginative men, but only to common minds, who did not see the finer spirits. A ghost was a thing seen by the gross bodily eye, a vision, by the mental. "Did you ever see a ghost ? " asked a friend. "Never but once," was the reply. And it befell thus. Standing one evening at his garden-door in Lambeth, and chancing to look up, he saw a horrible grim figure, " scaly, speckled, very awful," stalking downstairs towards him. More frightened than ever before or after, he took to his heels, and ran out of the house.' [4]

This episode alone should distinguish Blake from the Spiritist medium. Blake even went to the extent of believing that the visions of the prophets and saints were merely poetic. 'The Prophets Isaiah and Ezekiel dined with me,' he boldly wrote,[5] startling even those who recognize in this casual statement a satire on Swedenborg. But at once he put an oblique explanation on this strange meal into the mouths of his imaginary guests. 'I asked them how they dared so roundly to assert, that God spake to them ; and whether they did not think at the time, that they would be misunderstood. . . . Isaiah answer'd : " I saw no God, nor heard any, in a finite organical perception ; but . . . as I was then perswaded, & remain confirm'd, that the voice of honest indignation is the voice of God, I cared not for consequences, but wrote." '

If this disappoints lovers of the marvellous, they may find consolation in the fact that St. Thomas Aquinas agreed with Blake in believing that

---

[1] In his *Genesis* we catch Blake working from pattern towards concrete forms.

[2] This was undoubtedly self-hypnosis. In the same way Kant found he could think better when gazing steadily at a neighbouring church-steeple, Böhme had a vision from a reflecting pewter dish, and St. Ignatius Loyola had an 'intellectual perception' by staring into a stream.

[3] Symons, p. 233.   [4] Gilchrist, ch. xiv.   [5] *Marriage*, plate 12.

such visions as Isaiah's, John the Divine's, St. Stephen's and St. Peter's were beheld by the power of the imagination.[1]

Naturally Blake talked the same jargon about his method of writing. Perhaps no question is oftener asked of poets than ' How do you ever think of such things ? ' and few questions are harder to answer.   Blake casually cited ' some Spirit ' as his authority, for in his day the miraculous element of composition was being stressed.   But nowadays poets try to behave like other men, and refer to their ' stuff ' in a deprecatory way.   The advantage of the picturesqueness, at least, lies with Blake.   Let us see how he told the wide-eyed Crabb Robinson that he wrote :

' " I write," he says, " when commanded by the spirits, and the moment I have written I see the words fly about the room in all directions.   It is then published, and the spirits can read.   My MSS. are of no further use.   I have been tempted to burn my MSS., but my wife won't let me." " She is right," said I—" and you have written these, not from yourself, but by a higher order.   The MSS. are theirs and your property.   You cannot tell what purpose they may answer—unforeseen to you."   He liked this, and said he would not destroy them.' [2]

Blake himself told Butts that he had written *Milton* ' from immediate dictation, twelve or sometimes twenty or thirty lines at a time, without premeditation, and even against my will.   The time it has taken in writing was thus rendered non-existent, and an immense poem exists which seems to be the labour of a long life, all produced without labour or study,' [3] and later he added : ' I may praise it, since I dare not pretend to be other than the secretary ; the authors are in eternity.' [4]

This writing seems to have been unusually active at night.[5]   Tatham speaks of it with his usual awe.   ' He was very much accustomed to get out of his bed in the night to write for hours, and return to bed for the rest of the night after having committed to paper pages and pages of his mysterious fantasies.   He wrote much and often, and he sometimes thought that if he wrote less he must necessarily do more graving and painting, and he has debarred himself of his pen for a month or more ; but upon comparison has found by no means so much work accomplished, and the little that was done by no means so vigorous.' [6]

No wonder that Blake wrote : ' The Daughters of Beulah follow sleepers in all their dreams ' (*The Four Zoas*, i. 208).

Gilchrist tells of Mrs. Blake's heroic part in these periods : ' She would get up in the night, when he was under his very fierce inspirations, which were as if they would tear him asunder, while he was yielding himself to the Muse, or whatever else it could be called, sketching and writing.   And so terrible a task did this seem to be, that she had to sit motionless and

[1] *Summa Theol.*, Secundae Partis, Quaest. 175.   Robinson Crusoe, being ' far from enthusiastic,' came to the same decision.   In his *Vision of the Angelic World* (Defoe, *Works, ed.* Aitken, iii. 258 *seq.*), he described an imaginative vision of his own, which he humbly compared to those of ' the famed Mr. Milton,' and suggested that through them we might actually get in touch with the workings of futurity.   ' Let men pretend to what visions they please, it is all romance ; all beyond what I have talked of above is fabulous and absurd ' (p. 277).

[2] H. C. R., Feb. 18, 1826.   Robinson doubtless thought he really had prevented a holocaust of some very curious things.

[3] Letter to Butts, April 25, 1803.   [4] *Ibid.*, July 6, 1803.

[5] ' The most propitious time ' for the Visionary Head was also ' from nine at night to five in the morning,' according to Cunningham.

[6] Tatham.

silent; only to stay him mentally, without moving hand or foot: this for hours, and night after night.'[1]

After such information as this, it really would seem as though our first question should be what species of Ouija or Planchette board he used, or just how he held the pencil, and whether he kept the lights on or not. For no Automatic Writer before or since has produced anything like as good literature. But, as usual, no sooner do we turn from these extreme utterances to others less enthusiastic, than we find that Blake's spirits were exactly those invoked by every writer.

There is a certain amount of automatism in all authors. Lines 'come' in a complete and final form; characters 'get away' from the author's guidance; whole scenes 'suddenly appear'; a perfect ending, quite different from the original plan, 'insists on itself.' The subliminal mind has outstripped the rational processes of consciousness, leaping to the final form rather than calculating it. The very pen becomes a hypnotic agent; no sooner is it picked up than the ideas begin to flow; and many authors must have something in their fingers when they compose, even if they do no actual writing.[2] A good deal of physical excitement accompanies the process. They generally pace up and down in a mood which might be described as a cold fury, perhaps stamping and tossing their heads to drag out some reluctant word. They may not fall trembling upon garden paths, but their restlessness is certainly akin to Blake's.

There are times, however, when the body does not interpose itself between the conscious and the subconscious mind. Under the influences of certain drugs and even alcohol, the body may become perfectly passive, while the mind is released and can exert its greatest powers. Poe, undoubtedly under some abnormal influence, wrote in *Eleonora*: 'They who dream by day are cognizant of many things which escape those who dream only by night. In their gray visions they obtain glimpses of eternity, and thrill, in waking, to find that they have been upon the verge of the great secret. In snatches they learn something of the wisdom which is of good, and more of the mere knowledge, which is of evil. They penetrate, however rudderless or compassless, into the vast ocean of the light ineffable and again, like the adventurers of the Nubian geographers, *aggressi sunt mare tenebrarum, quid in eo esset exploraturi*.' In such a condition one of the greatest poems of the world, *Kubla Khan*, was written. The habitués of opium and hasheesh, however, have uttered warnings which need no repetition. And putting aside the dangers of all such drugs, the likelihood remains that the mind will be stupefied with the body, for only under exceptional circumstances does the mind escape poisoning.

But there is a normal state in which the same results may be produced. This is the condition of semi-sleep. Inquiry has shown that very many writers do their best work when falling asleep or waking up. A 'hypnoidal' state is readily induced by the limitation of sense-impressions, the cessation of voluntary movements, and the monotonous stimulus of breathing.[3] In deep sleep the critical faculty vanishes entirely; but in

[1] Gilchrist, ch. xxxiv.
[2] 'Dear Sir, excuse my enthusiasm or rather madness, for I am really drunk with intellectual vision whenever I take a pencil or graver into my hand, even as I used to be in my youth' (Letter to Hayley, Oct. 23, 1804).
[3] The importance of the breath in Oriental methods of meditation at once suggests itself.

the lighter forms of slumber, it is still powerful enough to keep the insistent logic of the mind from pushing itself to absurd extremes. At such moments, then, the consciousness is at once Actor and Author, actually putting its adventures into words as they occur, and even controlling by this discipline of phrase-making those emotions that threaten an awakening. A whole pageant of brilliant visions is enacted, which the blissful dreamer struggles to make permanent in some verbal incarnation.

This is too common for us to wonder at it. In fact, our literature begins in a dream : for Caedmon (the first poet we can name and date) thus found himself first able to sing. Chaucer was curiously interested in the subject. And skipping to our own times, Stevenson's ' Brownies,' who presented him with *Dr. Jekyll and Mr. Hyde,* and who worked out so many of his other stories,[1] at once identify themselves with Blake's ' Spirits.' Blake did not consider his case unique. In writing to Dr. Trusler of certain pictures, he said : ' Though I call them mine, I know that they are not mine, being of the same opinion with Milton when he says that the Muse visits his slumbers and awakes and governs his song when morn purples the east,[2] and being also in the predicament of that prophet [3] who says : " I cannot go beyond the command of the Lord, to speak good or bad." ' [4]

With the same meaning he wrote at the end of Lavater's *Aphorisms* : ' I say this Book is written by consultation with Good Spirits, because it is Good.'

He was thoroughly conscious of the richness of his subliminal mind.

In my brain are studies and chambers filled with books and pictures of old, which I wrote and painted in ages of eternity before this mortal life ; and those works are the delight and study of archangels.' [5]

' In my brain '—note that phrase. Blake understood perfectly where his inspirations came from. ' Muses who inspire the Poet's Song,' he cried, ' Come into my hand By your mild power ; descending down the Nerves of my right arm From out the Portals of my brain.' [6]

In his *Descriptive Catalogue of Pictures* (1809) Blake went into considerable detail about the subliminal world, though veiling his description with a characteristic ambiguity :

The two pictures of Nelson and Pitt are compositions of a mythological cast, similar to those Apotheoses of Persian, Hindoo, and Egyptian Antiquity which are still preserved on rude monuments, being copies from some stupendous originals now lost, or perhaps buried till some happier age. The artist having been taken in vision into the ancient republics, monarchies, and patriarchates of Asia has seen

---

[1] *Across the Plains : A Chapter on Dreams.*

[2] Dante's hour 'che la mente . . . men da' pensier presa, Alle sue vision quasi è divina ' (*Purgatorio,* ix. 16-18). Cf. also Sir Thomas Browne's *Letter to a Friend* : ' The Thoughts of Sleep, when the Soul was conceived nearest unto Divinity.' Ennemoser (*History of Magic,* Bohn's ed., vol. i. pp. 60, 128) quotes Xenophon (*Cyrop.,* viii. 7, 21), Josephus (B. J., vii. 8, 7), Arrianus (*De exped. Alex.,* vii.), Aretaeus (*De Causis et signis morb. acut.*), Hippocrates (*De Insomnis* and *De Vita*), Scaliger, Galen, and Cicero to the same effect. Blake's reference is to *Paradise Lost,* vii. 29-30, the invocation to Urania, who ' Visit'st my slumbers Nightly, or when Morn Purples the East.' Milton, being blind, laid special stress on his inward sight ; and he used to dictate his poetry to his daughters before he had risen in the morning. In another place (*Paradise Lost,* ix. 21-24), he is even more definite about his ' Celestial Patroness, who deignes Her nightly visitation unimplor'd, *And dictates to me slumb'ring,* or inspires Easie my unpremeditated Verse.' (See also Design 166 for Young's *Night Thoughts.*)

[3] *Num.* xxiv. 13.   [4] Letter to Trusler, Aug. 16, 1799.
[5] Letter to Flaxman, Sept. 21, 1800.   [6] *Milton,* 3 : 1-7.

these wonderful originals, called in the sacred scriptures the Cherubim, which were sculptured and painted on walls of Temples, Towers, Cities, Palaces, and erected in the highly cultivated states of Egypt, Moab, Edom, Aram, among the Rivers of Paradise—being the originals from which the Greeks and Hetruvians copied Hercules Farnese, Venus of Medicis, Apollo Belvedere, and all the grand works of ancient art. They were executed in a very superior style to those justly admired copies, being, with their accompaniments, terrific and grand in the highest degree. . . . Those wonderful originals seen in my visions, were, some of them, one hundred feet in height : some were painted as pictures, and some carved as basso-relievos and some as groups of statues, all containing mythological and recondite meaning, when more is meant than meets the eye.

Here, in this amazing brain, were the originals of his pictures ; and here, too, the spirits 'dictated' his poems. But he did not accept the 'dictation' of these spirits just as it came. No poet does. Every fragment of inspiration is subjected to the sternest tests of the intellect. It is this very struggle between the Conscious and the Subconscious that raises poetry to its heights.[1] After announcing, 'We who dwell on Earth can do nothing of ourselves, everything is conducted by Spirits, no less than Digestion or Sleep,' Blake casually remarks : 'When this Verse was first dictated to me ' ; and at once the careless reader assumes that all *Jerusalem* was produced entirely automatically. But Blake continues to tell how he considered this or that metre, finally selecting an irregular line as the most expressive. Now it is obvious that one cannot take from dictation and at the same time figure out how to choose and arrange one's words. The essential feature of Automatic Writing proper is that the transcriber shall never interfere in any way with the message as it comes. And to demolish forever the idea that Blake put down blindly and automatically whatever came to him, we need only point out that all his manuscripts are overloaded with correction upon correction, made *during* the first draft, as well as after it was completed.[2]

It should now be entirely plain what separates Blake—and all poets— from the Spiritist Automatic Writers. The former guide and correct their poetic impulses, and produce great poems ; while the latter let the same impulses flow unregulated, and produce drivel. Moreover, the Automatic tends towards a definite schizophrenia ; Blake, on the contrary, struggled his whole life through to join the Conscious and Subconscious.

Blake, then, clearly wrote just as others do, and understood better than many of them what happened. The whole difficulty has been that in reading Blake's accounts of his 'spirits' we feel that he means something real, while, when we read of Milton's Urania or Stevenson's Brownies, we pass off such remarks as nothing but pleasant fancies. Yet even in Blake's case, when he wrote :

> This theme calls me in sleep night after night & ev'ry morn
> Awakes me at sun-rise, then I see the Saviour over me
> Spreading his beams of love, & dictating the words of this mild song,

the 'sanest' critics have not imagined that Blake meant that Christ was

[1] Or, to use Blake's symbol, Los and his Spectre strike alternate blows upon the anvil.
[2] With the exception of the 'Pickering MS.,' which was evidently a fair copy. Yet even here Blake made a few corrections. Of course letters and the like are not included in this discussion. Those who are curious about the matter should read *The Tyger*, which seems to have been poured out perfect, at white heat, and then examine the corrections made on the manuscript, as reprinted by Sampson.

the actual author of *Jerusalem*. They understood—as Blake understood—that it was inspired (dictated) by the spirit of love (Jesus).

One or two more examples of 'dictation' by other writers should clinch the matter ; and there are so many to choose from that we will limit ourselves to the very authors whom Blake had read.

King David, it seems, wrote automatically : 'All this, said David, the Lord made me understand in writing by his hand upon me' (1 *Chron.* xxviii. 19). Jakob Böhme said : 'Art has not wrote here, neither was there any time to set it punctually down. . . . The Reason was this, that the burning Fire often forced forward with Speed, and the Hand and Pen must hasten directly after it ; for it comes and goes as a sudden Shower.'[1] Blake's favourite poet, Milton, has already been discussed. St. Teresa 'declared that in writing her books she was powerless to set down anything but that which her master put into her mind.'[2] Madame Guyon was even more automatic : 'In copying a passage [from the Scriptures] I had not the least idea of its meaning ; and as soon as it was copied, I was given the power of explaining it, writing with an inconceivable speed. . . . I began to reflect ; I was punished for it ; my power of writing dried up immediately, and I waited like an idiot for the next illumination.'[3] It was natural that this irresistible impulse to write should be considered as a Command. Blake spoke of a Command from Hell (Watson marginalia) ; Swedenborg noted twice in his *Diary* that he was commanded to write : 'Jussus sum. Ita videar jussus.'[4] Thomas Vaughan ('Eugenius Philalethes') said the same thing, though with his characteristic ambiguity. 'This is all I think fit to communicate at this time, neither had this fallen from me but that it was a command imposed by my superiors, etc.'[5] But immediately he added a Postscript : 'This small discourse was no sooner finished—though by command—but the same authorities recalled their commission ; and now being somewhat transformed, I must as some mysteriously have done—live a tree.'[6] We must look in vain on this earth for these Superiors, since (according to his editor) Vaughan was not a Rosicrucian, nor was he initiated into any school. There is a vague possibility that Vaughan was submitted to some totally unknown society ; but it seems far more likely that these capricious 'superiors' were nothing but the same spirits that dictated to Blake. Of Shakspere's method of writing we can guess but little. Yet we hazard the suggestion that these 'spirits' of Blake's were the very ones to which Shakspere referred in that famously obscure sonnet, the 86th. In the 43rd Sonnet, Shakspere had already emphasized the importance of dreams to the poet. In the 86th he is bewailing the fact that the Rival Poet can praise Mr. W. H. successfully, while Shakspere cannot.

> Was it his spirit, by spirits taught to write
> Aboue a mortal pitch, that struck me dead ?
> No, neither he, nor his compiers by night
> Giuing him ayde, my verse astonished.

---

[1] Quoted by William Law in the *Prefatory Life* to Behmen's Works.
[2] G. Cunningham Graham, *Santa Teresa*, vol. i. p. 202.
[3] *Vie de Madame J. M. B. de la Mothe-Guyon, écrite par Elle-même.* Tome II, IIᵉ Partie, ch. xxi.
[4] J. J. G. Wilkinson, *Emanuel Swedenborg, A Biography.*   [5] *Aula Lucis.*
[6] 'Live automatically,' or (in Blake's phrase) 'vegetate' ? Mr. A. E. Waite explains : 'the writer must submit to live like a spirit shut up in a tree.'

He, nor that affable familiar ghost
Which nightly gulls him with intelligence,
As victors of my silence cannot boast. . . .

Surely these spirits were the same as Blake's ! We need not believe, as so many commentators have done, that Shakspere was referring to an actual practice of the Black Arts. And my theory becomes quite plausible when we learn that Chapman (whom many have considered to have been the Rival Poet himself) boasted of a vision of Homer, who promised inspiration (*Euthymiae Raptus*).

As a coda to this chapter (for it does not deserve a chapter to itself), we may consider the senile question of Blake's madness, since it rests entirely upon these Visions and their Dictation. Apart from these, Blake lived an entirely normal, quiet life. It is only fair to admit that there were two curious anecdotes about him ; but these are universally rejected as scandal—the only wonder being that there were not more and worse stories. The first was the tale of his attempt to introduce a concubine into his household ; this story has already been dismissed in Chapter xiv. The other tells how Mr. Butts came upon William and Catherine naked in their back garden, where they were reading *Paradise Lost*. 'Come in !' cried Blake ; 'it 's only Adam and Eve, you know.'[1] This story has been made too much of. John Linnell denied it vigorously, as being thoroughly uncharacteristic. However, we must remember that (thanks to Rousseau, I believe), air baths were quite the fashion. Benjamin Franklin, under similar circumstances, rushed out to get the mail ; yet he did not suffer from the imputation of madness. I think the story may be accepted, especially since Butts, a close friend of the Blakes, was the authority for it. Even Blake's courteous remark at that startling moment was characteristic both of himself as a philosopher and artist : 'It 's only Adam and Eve you know,' meaning 'It 's perfectly innocent.'

What is madness ? To the eighteenth century it was little more than 'Enthusiasm.' All poets were at least a little mad, they firmly believed ; and to corroborate them, Collins, Cowper, Savage, Kit Smart, besides several others whose names lived but little longer than their wits, perished in madhouses. John Clare, climbing from the theatre-box to attack Shylock, was thought to be suffering merely from a spasm of temperament. The attitude of the century alone is sufficient to account for the *Examiner's* venomous attack on Blake, when it called him 'an unfortunate lunatic, whose personal inoffensiveness secures him from confinement.'[2] Personal invective was still allowed as criticism. And this or another similar attack in turn caused Blake's lines on 'the aspersion of Madness, / Cast on the Inspired by the tame high finisher of paltry Blots' (*Milton*, 43 : 8-9).

Against this one open accusation and the casual remarks of a few who once or twice had heard Blake talking his wildest, we have the unanimous testimony of all his personal friends and the judgment of all his sympathetic critics. It is useless to marshal yet again before the public all their testimony ;[3] and it would be cruel to print even the names of those hearty critics who have frankly pronounced Blake mad because they could

[1] Gilchrist, ch. xii.   [2] Sept. 17, 1809.
[3] See Gilchrist, ch. xxxv. ; also *Fictions Concerning William Blake* in the *Athenæum*, Sept. 11, 1875 ; and Seymour Kirkup's letter in T. Wemyss Reid's *Life of Richard Monckton Milnes* (vol. ii. p. 222).

not understand him.   Blake's case has become analogous to Hamlet's : the question will probably be raised time after time, though all the evidence points one way.

For the charge of madness is always hard to beat off ; people are never quite easy—it would almost be a reflexion on their own sanity if they were ' taken in ' by some ' case ' ; so they keep on the safe side by professing a little suspicion. ' There must be some fire to all this smoke.' Curiously enough, perhaps there *was* a fire, a pathetic little blaze, whose smoke managed to tarnish Blake's reputation.   There actually may have been a Blake who was mad, who spent thirty years in an asylum, and who has been frequently confused with the poet.   This confusion is traceable to an unsigned article in the *Revue Britannique*, July 1833, which A. Brierre de Boismont perpetuated by quoting it as the thirty-fifth case in his *Des Hallucinations*.   The article is remarkable enough to be quoted in full.[1]

The two most celebrated tenants of Bethlem Hospital are the incendiary Martin, elder brother of Martin the painter, and Blake, nicknamed the *Seer*.   When I had passed in review and submitted to my examination all this criminal and mad population, I had myself taken to Blake's cell.   He was a big and pale man, a good speaker and truly eloquent ; in all the annals of demonology nothing is more extraordinary than the visions of Blake.

He was not the victim of a simple hallucination, he believed firmly and earnestly in the reality of his visions : he conversed with Michael Angelo, chatted with Moses and Semiramis ; there was nothing of the impostor about him, he was sincere.   The past opened its gloomy portals ; the world of shadows sped to him ; all that had been great, astonishing, and famous, came and posed before Blake.

This man had constituted himself the painter of ghosts (*spectres*) ; before him on the table, pencils and brushes were always in readiness for him to reproduce the faces and attitudes of his heroes, who, he said, he never evoked, but who came of themselves to ask him to paint their portraits.   I have looked through heavy volumes filled with these effigies, among which I have noticed the portrait of the Devil and that of his mother.   When I entered his cell he was drawing a flea, whose ghost, he made out, had just appeared to him.

Edward III. was one of his most constant visitors ; in recognition of this monarch's condescension he had painted his portrait in oils in three sittings.

I addressed him questions to perplex him, but he answered them quite simply and without hesitation.

' Do these gentlemen have themselves announced ? ' I asked him, ' Are they careful to send you in their cards ? '

' No, but I recognize them as soon as they appear.   I did not expect to see Mark Antony yesterday evening, but I recognized the Roman as soon as he set foot in my room.'

' At what hour do your illustrious dead visit you ? '

' At one o'clock ; sometimes their visits are long, sometimes short.   I saw poor Job the day before yesterday ; he would only stay two minutes ; I had hardly time to make a rough sketch of him which I afterwards copied in etching—but hush !— here is Richard III. ! '

' Where do you see him ? '

' Facing you, on the other side of the table ; it is his first visit.'

' How do you know his name ? '

' My spirit recognizes his, but I do not know how.'

' What is he like ? '

[1] Quoted from William T. Horton : *Was Blake ever in Bedlam ?* (*The Occult Review*, November 1912).

' A rugged face but beautiful : I only see his profile as yet. Here he is at three-quarters. Ah ! now he turns towards me ; he is terrible to behold ! '

' Can you question him ? '

' Certainly, what do you wish me to ask him ? '

' If he pretends to justify the murders he committed during his life-time ? '

' Your demand has already reached him. We converse soul to soul by intuition and by magnetism. We have no need for words.'

' What is His Majesty's answer ? '

' Here it is, a little longer than he gave it me ; you would not understand the language of Spirits. He tells you that what you call murder and carnage is nothing ; that in slaughtering fifteen or twenty thousand men one does them no harm ; that the mortal part of their being is not only preserved but passes into a better world, and that the murdered man who would address words of reproach to his murderer would render himself guilty of ingratitude, as the latter has only enabled him to procure a more commodious lodging and a more perfect existence. But leave me. He poses very well now, and if you say a word he will go.'

I left this man against whom none could bring any reproach, and who was not without talent as an engraver and draughtsman.

What are we to make of this extraordinary case ? Is this a reference to the poet and painter, or to some insane double ? The Ghost of the Flea, the etchings of *Job*, the familiarity with Edward III. (whom Blake had tried to put into a historical drama) and with Michaelangelo, all point very definitely to the man we know. On the other hand, can we imagine Blake approving the murders of Richard III. ?

My own opinion is that some casual visitor had seen Blake drawing the Visionary Heads, that he asked foolish questions, and was answered in kind by the annoyed painter, who eventually silenced and dismissed him with an ambiguous courtesy. Then some years later, the writer, hearing that Blake had lived some time at Lambeth (where Bethlem was situated), and believing thoroughly that Blake had become mad, wrote this article to satisfy some desire to appear in print. He undoubtedly thought that a few misstatements (such as laying the scene in Bethlem itself) would not hurt a man already dead and forgotten. Fortunately we know that Blake drew the Ghost of the Flea, as well as a picture of Edward III., at his residence at 17 South Moulton Street, London, W., some years after the residence in Lambeth ; while the *Job* drawings were not begun till 1823. Mr. Horton, who wrote the article for *The Occult Review*, searched the records at Bethlem from 1815 to 1835, and found no mention of any Blake whatsoever.

This tale later became combined with another story of Blake's insanity, which is even more easily disproved. Dr. Richardson, in an essay on hallucinations (*Chambers's Journal*, 1872), repeats the account of the drawing of the Visionary Heads, ending with the statement that Blake ' became actually insane, and remained in an asylum for thirty years. Then his mind was restored to him, and he resumed the use of the pencil ; but the old evil threatened to return, and he once more forsook his art, soon afterwards to die.' Other accounts assert that Blake actually died in a madhouse.

I have not been able to trace these irresponsible tales to the original sources ; but that would be unnecessary. We have full accounts of Blake's death ; we know that towards the end of his life he not only had not deserted his art, but was producing his biggest works as a symbolic painter, the *Job* and the *Dante* ; and we know that there is nothing like a period of thirty years to be accounted for in his life. Through letters, dated works, and other means, we can account for every year of his life, except for the period between 1811 and 1817. These were the years after the failure of his exhibition, when he was breaking with his old friends and had not yet found his new friends. However, there is enough evidence to show that the ' thirty years of Bedlam ' cannot be explained by this period, since Blake continued to work, though not very steadily ; for his own inspiration seems to have been in abeyance, and the publishers were neglecting him. The following list of works covers the period fairly well.

? 1811. Engraving of the Right Honorable Earl Spenser (after Phillips).

1812. Reprint of *The Prologue and Characters of Chaucer's Pilgrims.*

1813. The engraving of *The Chaining of Orc* ; also possibly *Mirth and her Companions* (Nos. 26 and 27 in A. G. B. Russell's *Engravings of William Blake*).

1813. Two copies of *America* and two of *Europe* are water-marked for this year.

Oct. 1814-Dec. 1816. Thirty-seven plates engraved after Flaxman for the *Compositions from Hesiod* (published January 1, 1817). To this year also probably belong Blake's eighteen engravings for Wedgwood's *Book of Designs.*

1815-1818. Seven engravings for Rees's *Cyclopaedia*, published at dates ranging from October 1, 1815 to 1819.

Moreover, Mr. Horton's searching of the Bethlem records went back as far as 1815 ; so we may be certain that, if Blake ever were confined there, it was in the latter part of 1813 or 1814.

Thus it appears that there is not a grain of positive evidence in proof of the posthumous theory of Blake's residence in Bethlem ; and, what is more, by means of negative evidence, we can reduce the charge to an absurdity. Does it not seem far more likely that Blake's picturesque eccentricities were responsible for the report ? And that the report was probably ' confirmed ' by some joking reference to Blake's house in Lambeth, a district notorious for its madhouse ? Add to this the possibility that there may have been some other Blake confined as an inmate (a supposition which is really not necessary at all), and the whole story is explained.

But putting aside all this talk as unproven on the one hand, and all the contrary testimony of Blake's friends as prejudiced on the other, what are we to make of Blake's sanity from the evidence which remains to us— his life, as we know it, and his works ? To answer that, we need a definite statement what madness is ; and there is no such statement. By the Law's rule-of-thumb definition, Blake was legally sane, since he always was entirely conscious of the nature and significance of his acts. As for the psychologists, they can point out certain tendencies which are of more significance to them than to us. The very fact that Blake liked to talk queerly and puzzle people is suspicious. His exalted moments have a morbid flavour to them. He was obstinate. Then, when all the evidence is laid before them, they hedge, and refuse the flat term ' mad,' substituting some more ambiguous word like ' psychopathic.'

Yet this settles the question for us, since all poets and mystics are ' psychopaths.' The whole question ceases to have any meaning. Everything Blake painted, wrote, and even said (as far as we have any records) sprang entirely logically from premises that are essentially sane. We not only can accept his logic ; we must also respect his ideas, whether we agree with them or not.   This has already been so clearly discerned by all the penetrating critics, that we continually meet with such extreme statements as that of Arthur Symons's : ' It is true that Blake was abnormal ; but what was abnormal about him was his sanity.'

Let us call him mad, if we must ; but in doing so, we call all mystics and all poets mad.   And at the end we will find that, having merely changed the fundamental meaning of the word, we are already mocked by Blake himself ; for, anticipating this, he recorded in *The Marriage of Heaven and Hell* (plate 6) that ' the enjoyments of Genius ' invariably seem to ourselves, the Angels, ' like torment and insanity.'

CHAPTER XXIX

ILLUSTRATIONS TO OTHERS

I must Create a System, or be enslaved by another Man's.
I will not Reason & Compare : my business is to Create.
—*Jerusalem* 10 : 20-21.

BESIDES decorating his own works, Blake made several sets of illustrations for works which pleased or paid him.

His method of illustrating, like everything else he did, was quite his own. He often did not follow the text, but made pictorial commentaries upon it. The book became merely a sort of spring-board, from which he leapt into his own heaven, leaving the author far behind.

Even his first set of illustrations—those to Mary Wollstonecraft's *Original Stories From Real Life* (London, 1791)—wanders from the text at least once. When Mrs. Mason, that early and terrible example of the British matron, comes upon an old Welsh harper by night, Blake could not be literal. Something in the stilted prose stirred his poetic sense ; so he changed the solid Mrs. Mason to a slender, ethereal girl wandering in a starlit garden, while the old man appeared as a radiant angel harping among Gothic ruins. Doubtless Blake would have defended this picture by claiming that such were the 'spiritual' forms ; the outward, visible forms needing no reproduction. In the same way he presented John the Divine at Patmos as a beautiful youth, not as the last of the apostles left on earth.[1]

If the text were sufficiently inspired in itself, Blake was not so apt to wander from it. Bürger's *Leonora* (1796) afforded him a wonderful chance for a supernatural frontispiece. His illustrations to Milton's poems are a more extended example. The six water-colours to the *Hymn on the Morning of Christ's Nativity*, among which are some of Blake's most exquisite conceptions, are quite literal. The *Comus* is equally so, except for one plate, *The Brothers and the Attendant Spirit*. Above the three figures we see the Moon-goddess in her serpent-drawn chariot ; and if we have already noted the same figure in the famous *Morning-Stars* of *Job*, we realize that Blake was picturing what Milton intended : that the Chaste Goddess was ruling the hour. In *Paradise Lost*, however, we find certain extensions of Milton's ideas. Sin and Death become almost leading characters,[2] pouring down arrows and vials of disease in *So Judged He Man*, and finally lying lifeless at the foot of the Cross. In the *Creation of Eve*, Blake represents her hovering between the sleeping Adam's heart and the moon. There can be no doubt that here he was utilizing the symbols of Jakob Böhme. Not by accident did Blake

---

[1] *The Angel of the Revelation*, a water-colour drawing at the Metropolitan Museum, New York City.

[2] In the set owned by Mr. Henry Huntington. In the Boston Art Museum set, Sin and Death appear only once, at the foot of the Cross.

represent Eve's creation during Adam's sleep, and Adam's vision of the Saviour during her sleep ; for in Adam's temporary self-loss, Eve was separated into a distinct Personality, and only by her return to her pre-natal sleep in Adam's bosom can he be made whole and find his salvation.[1] Whether or not these were Milton's ideas is a question open to conjecture. At any rate, the text indicates the sleep.   In *Man Shall Find Grace*, the Saviour about to descend into the material world hovers in the attitude of the Cross ; the true Crucifixion being his voluntary fall into flesh, not his enforced release from it.

The twelve illustrations to *L'Allegro and Il Penseroso* are less philo-sophic but more poetic.   Blake's imagination now bubbled over with the most delightful conceits.   Realizing that the pictures might seem obscure, he wisely appended brief notes.   The lark becomes ' an Angel on the Wing.'   His conception of the ' Sunshine Holiday ' is as follows :

Mountains Clouds Rivers Trees appear Humanized on the Sunshine Holiday.[2] The Church Steeple with its merry bells.   The Clouds arise from the bosoms of Mountains While Two Angels Sound their Trumpets in the Heavens to announce the Sunshine Holiday.

In a similar spirit are the recently recovered illustrations to Gray's poems.[3]   Blake explains his purpose in the couplet :

> Around the springs of Gray my wild root weaves,
> Travellers repose and dream among my leaves.

The important thing to notice is that he distinguishes between his work and Gray's.   The ' Travellers ' are, of course, the travellers through this mundane life.   Blake describes his third illustration of the *Ode on the Spring* :

The purple year awaking from the roots of nature and the hours suckling their flowery infants.

Only a few times do Blake's own peculiar symbols occur ; one of these is ' Grief among the Roots of Trees,' illustrating the *Hymn to Adversity*.[4] Of course Selima, Walpole's cat who was drowned in the aquarium, inspired some delightful illustrations.   Blake, with exquisite humour, represents her in her ' spiritual form,' clad in stays and kerchief.   As for the goldfish, did not Gray himself describe them as ' two angel forms ' ? Painting need not lag behind poetry ; Blake, here as elsewhere, interpreted the symbol literally ; and the goldfish are angels.   Selima herself becomes wholly human in her death-agony.[5]

Before considering Blake's more complicated illustrations, we may mention, regardless of chronology, all the rest which have little or no hidden meaning.   Hayley's *Ballads* (1802) gave Blake no inspiration whatsoever, although there is a certain element of terror in the picture of

---

[1] Cf. Ololon's self-judgment and self-annihilation in *Milton*, 44 : 3-6.   Defoe, for one, suspected some sort of symbolism in Milton when he wrote : ' Strange Fate of sleeping in *Paradise* ! that whereas we have Notice but of two Sleeps there, that in one a *Woman* should go out of him, and in the other the *Devil* should come into her ' (*Political History of the Devil*, ch. viii.).

[2] Cf. the spiritual forms in *Thel* and the letter to Butts, Nov. 22, 1802.

[3] The printed text is dated 1790, therefore Blake's marginal illustrations must have been made later.

[4] See the Commentary on *Thel*, 110-111.

[5] From Selima to the Ghost of the Flea is but a short step.

the bather saved from the crocodile by his dog. Malkin's *Father's Memoirs of his Child* (1806) has for frontispiece a portrait surrounded by Blake's design of an angel leading the boy from his mother towards realms of light. Most notable of all are the woodcuts in Dr. Thornton's school edition of Virgil (1820). Blake was not used to this medium, and his cutting of the blocks was so unsophisticated that the publishers objected. Fortunately certain artists had seen them and discussed them with such enthusiasm that Dr. Thornton decided to use them after all, though he appended a cautionary note :

> The Illustrations of this English Pastoral are by the famous Blake, the illustrator of Young's *Night Thoughts*, and Blair's *Grave* ; who designed and engraved them himself. This is mentioned, as they display less of art than of genius, and are much admired by some eminent painters.[1]

If it be Art to express what you wish to say, then these woodcuts are very high in the artistic order ; but if Art be the acquiring of technique, then these cuts are not of much value. The intensity of Blake's inspiration more than overcame his technical ignorance ; and these very cuts, admitted after so much doubt, place an unbelievable value on a volume that otherwise would be entirely worthless to us.[2]

Blake never again tried to make woodcuts.

In 1796 Blake was commissioned to illustrate Young's *Night Thoughts*. He sat down to work with one of his usual bursts of inspiration and completed five hundred and thirty-seven marginal designs in water-colours. The publisher had him engrave forty-three of them, selected from the first four *Nights* ; then, discouraged by the public's indifference, he ordered no more. The public, as usual, was wrong. The *Night Thoughts* contain many of Blake's loveliest designs. His invention never flags ; on the contrary, as he works into the poem, the pictures become richer, more poetic ; and the last *Nights* are a continuous crescendo of glory.

Any one who has read Young must be amazed that Blake found any inspiration in this soporific philosophy. It begins well enough to gain it a place among the minor classics of English blank verse, then only too soon it sinks into a dull succession of didacticisms.

But Blake, through his painting, turned it into poetry. Phrase after phrase, which was to Young merely a conventional and automatic way of saying something, Blake took literally, visualized it, and produced a rare bit of imagination, which Young was entirely innocent of. ' Woes cluster ; rare are solitary woes,' Young wrote, meaning that troubles never come singly ; then Blake seized upon the banality and transmuted it into a weird night sky where the Woes, personified, are knotted together into

---

[1] Perhaps this note, with the episodes leading to it, was the cause of Blake's lack of sympathy for Dr. Thornton. Blake disliked Virgil, as he exalted Empire above Art (' Empire against Art—see Virgil's *Æneid*, Lib. VI. 5. 848 '—Laocoon' plate) ; and Blake had a particular dislike against the *First Eclogue*, which Thornton gave him to illustrate (' . . . Caesar, Virgil's Only God, see Eclogue 1 '—Thornton marginalia). Seven years later Dr. Thornton published a new translation of the Lord's Prayer ; and Blake's indignant annotations have preserved it ! I feel, however, that most of Blake's dislike for Dr. Thornton must have come after the Virgil cuts were finished ; for it is inconceivable that such exquisite work could have sprung from such a fundamental distaste.

[2] The *Athenæum*, as late as Jan. 21, 1843, reproduced one of them side by side with the same plate recut by one who knew the trade, and then points the obvious moral. This is one of the few appreciative remarks on Blake to be found between the date of his death and the publication of Gilchrist's *Pictor Ignotus*.

wailing groups. 'Each moment plays His little weapon . . . and cuts down The fairest bloom of sublunary bliss' (i. 205-208) shows them armed with tiny sickles and swarming all over a huge wheat-stalk (design 19). Such translations of Young occur in design after design.

But furthermore Blake introduced freely his own peculiar symbolism. Many of the figures are to be seen ' vegetating ' (turning into trees), as in designs 70, 215, 258, and 495. The Mundane Shell appears several times, notably in designs 13, 101, and 142. To recognize such symbols as these and others adds to our pleasure in looking over the two volumes, but there is no real need to understand them : it is merely an added pleasure, a private intimacy.

From now on, Blake decided that his illustrations were more important than the text, and that another man's poem should not hinder his own deep purposes. As in his own works Blake had disregarded his text and made the pictures a series complete in itself, so now he decided to treat the poems of others in the same way.

The illustrations to Blair's *Grave* (1805, published 1808) retell practically the same story that is found in the plates of *The Gates of Paradise*, *America*, and *Job*. Of course Blake did not divulge his purpose. That was left for kindred souls to discover. The binder was not a kindred soul, and rearranged the plates to suit himself ; but at the end of the volume we have the list of titles in the correct order, with the significant note :

By the arrangement here made, the regular progression of Man, from his first descent into the Vale of Death, to his last admission into Life eternal, is exhibited. These Designs, detached from the Work they embellish, form of themselves a most interesting Poem.

Such was Blake's ' word to the wise,' whose meaning no one seems to have noticed till now. It declares his independence of the rather stupid poem, and asserts a system—an idea—in the plates. In fact, the illustrations are a complete contradiction to the text, preaching hope instead of despair. But what Blake's declaration did not state is just what Blake meant by ' the Vale of Death.' My readers should know by now that Blake meant *this world*, which is man's nearest approach to ' death,' being the farthest point from the Life Eternal. Blake is telling us, then, the old story of the Fall and Resurrection—nothing less !

His ignoring of Blair's poem is so obvious that we need not trouble ourselves with the text any more than he did. And this independence, being dimly felt, has given a curious history to the plates. After doing their duty by Blair, they were used for Janquin de Mora's *Meditaciones Poeticas* (Londres, 1826), and then came to America, where they 'illustrated' Martin Tupper's once-famous *Proverbial Philosophy* ! [1]

I. The series begins at the descent of Christ with the keys of liberation into the ' grave,' for it was Blake's most catholic doctrine that ' God becomes as we are, that we may be as he is.' His Mercy thus changed our ' death ' into sleep ; by his descent (the incarnation in every man) we remember our divine origin and strive to return.

II. The second plate represents the descent of man into the Vale of Death. This is a characteristic ' story-picture,' all the types of humanity

---

[1] Gilchrist, ch. xxiv. I have not seen this edition of Tupper. It is omitted from the Keynes bibliography.

being shown in their Fall, some rushing blindly downward, while others hesitate in fear.

III. Next follows the celebrated *Death's Door*, a design of which Blake was very fond.[1] It represents an old man tempest-blown into his rocky tomb, while above is seen his ' spiritual form,' a youth gazing upward in a glory. Blake already had used this picture in *America* to symbolize the entrance into the state of Experience, which is the death of the senses ; and that is the meaning here.

IV-VI. In these plates Blake shows how the ' Strong Wicked Man,' the ' Good Old Man,' and the Youth endure this death. The usual order is twisted. We naturally expect to begin with the Youth and end with the Old Man ; but Blake had a reason for this transposition. The Wicked Man is the farthest from Truth ; the Good Man comes next, while the Youth, being still under the free impulse of inspiration, is the climax of verity in his visions.[2]

The two men see only their outward selves in their dreams. The Strong Man, solitary in a flame of desire, imagines nothing but unreal (invisible) terrors, for he is still in the turbulent state of Experience. The Old Man, who has found a guide in the *New Testament*, is uplifted by angels.

The Youth, however, in his dreams sees—not himself—but a feminine form ! Who is she ? The Beloved ? That seems trivial and inconsequential. Or, as the title itself says, is she his soul ? Curiously enough, many mystics have represented the soul as feminine : for example, the author of the *Song of Solomon* and Coventry Patmore. Yet this cannot be Blake's meaning, for he had said clearly that ' man has no body distinct from the soul ' ;[3] and he would not now have departed from one of his fundamental beliefs, especially when he was deliberately expressing himself, at Blair's expense. No, the feminine form is unmistakably the ' Emanation,' or Inspiration, or Daughter of Beulah ; or, in modern terms, the Subliminal Self. In sleep the Emanation is released from her prison in the subconscious mind ; then man is nearest complete self-expression. It was in his sleep that Blake wrote much of his poetry, finding his inspiration unhampered.[4]

All three plates represent, for once, literal sleep, since men (as our contemporary psychologists have just discovered) are at their most characteristic in their dreams. The suggestion of dawn in the three plates is also significant ; it is then that dreams become most orderly and nearest consciousness. In all probability Blake was thinking of a passage in Dante's *Purgatorio* :

> Nell' ora, che comincia i tristi lai
> La rondinella presso alla mattina,
> Forse a memoria de' suoi primi guai,

---

[1] There is a water-colour of this in the Widener Collection at Harvard University, and Mr. A. Edward Newton of Philadelphia has an elaborate drawing of it intended for a mortuary monument. The lower half (the old man) appears at the end of the *Gates of Paradise* and on the 14th plate of *America*. The upper half (the young man) is to be found in several places, notably plate 21 of *The Marriage* and plate 8 of *America*.

[2] Cf. the rôle of Elihu in the 12th Illustration of *Job*.

[3] *The Marriage of Heaven and Hell*, plate 4.

[4] For a more extended discussion of this point, see Chapter xxviii., ' *Spirits* ' *and their* ' *Dictation*.'

E che la mente nostra pellegrina
Più dalla carne, e men da' pensier presa,
Alle sue vision quasi è divina.[1]

VII. During sleep the Emanation makes strange journeys. Now it explores the recesses of the grave, while the true light is absent, seeking for consolation in this world, and finding none.

VIII. For in this grave, all—Counsellor, King, Warrior, Mother and Child—are sleeping side by side, ignorant of their diverse functions, their different individualities.[2]

IX. But this shall not be so always. Man is not doomed to the material plane forever. An angel, messenger of the Lord, will descend and reawaken the skeleton to which man has shrunk.[3]

X. Then man's divided self (' Spectre and Emanation,' to use Blake's technical vocabulary) will be made one ; the illusion of matter will blaze away to nothing ; and the eternal Unity will be accomplished.

XI. But no Self exists alone by itself. A man's family is, in a lesser degree, part of himself. So the process of reunion continues ; after the Self has become One, the Family follows suit.

XII. And at the very end is the casting out of Error into extinction and the raising of Truth into the Eternal Ecstasy, which is the Last Judgment, the second coming of Christ.

Such was Blake's new series of pictures representing Man's Fall from Life and his Return.[4] It was a subject which had concerned him throughout his career, and the final expression of it was yet to appear in his ' Inventions ' to the *Book of Job*.

The story how Cromek, exploiter of unrecognized geniuses, cheated Blake over Blair's *Grave* is an old tale. He gave Blake—verbally—an order for twenty pictures with a promise of the very profitable job of engraving them. But as soon as Cromek got the designs, he had them engraved by the popular Schiavonetti—and only twelve at that. I bring this matter up as there have been some who have defended Cromek against erratic Blake. Was not Blake assuming too much, they say, when he thought he was to engrave his own pictures ? The answer is to be found in the following letter to Hayley (Nov. 27, 1805) : [5]

Mr. Cromek the Engraver came to me desiring to have some of my designs. he namd his price & wishd me to Produce him Illustrations of the Grave a Poem by Robert Blair. in consequence of this I produced about twenty Designs which pleasd so well that he with the same liberality with which he set me about the Draw-

---

[1] *Purgatory*, ix. 13-18, the prelude to Dante's first dream : ' In the hour when the swallow begins her sad lays, near to the morning, in memory of her former woes, and when our mind, pilgrim rather from the flesh and less bound by its thought, is in its visions as it were divine ' (translated A. J. Butler). We know that Blake did not grow enthusiastic over Dante until his last years ; nevertheless the reference in *The Marriage of Heaven and Hell* (plate 22) proves that even then Blake ranked Dante with Shakspere.

[2] In the early sketch for this plate (reproduced by Keynes, p. 220), the black mist (line 17) hangs over the dead, and some variety is introduced into their postures.

[3] This plate is repeated on p. 19 of the engravings to Young's *Night Thoughts*.

[4] Mr. Gabriel Wells owns a handsome ink sketch of the *Death of the Voluptuary*, which was never engraved for this series. The youth, naked and crowned with vines, lies on the ground ; above him his Emanation hovers with uplifted hands. On the back of the sheet is a pencil-sketch, also marked ' Blair's Grave ' : it represents Jesus intervening between Achilles and Agamemnon, before a crowd of warriors (Christian Forbearance quelling Pagan Pride).

[5] Printed by the kind permission of Miss Amy Lowell.

ing has now set me to Engrave them. He means to Publish them by Subscription with the Poem as you will see in the Prospectus which he sends you in the Pacquet with the Letter. You will I know feel as you always do on such occasions, not only warm wishes to promote the Spirited Exertions of my friend Cromek. You will be pleased to see that the Royal Academy have sanctioned the Style of work.

Certainly this proves beyond question a distinct, second contract, subsequent to Cromek's approval of the designs. Our further knowledge of Cromek's unscrupulousness towards others makes all future argument on the subject absurd.

For his next encounter with Blake was equally crooked. He commissioned Blake (again verbally) to make a painting of Chaucer's *Canterbury Pilgrims*; and again he went back on his word. Having learned Blake's ideas—picked his brain, as it were—he suddenly gave both commission and ideas to Stothard. This time his trickery caused a permanent break between the two old friends.

The inside story of Cromek's double-dealing seems little known. Richter, the worker in scagliola, was a neighbour of both Cromek and Stothard in Newman Street, Oxford Street. He wanted to get his son Henry into Stothard's studio as a pupil; and in order to lay the painter under an obligation, induced Cromek to swing the commission as he did. But Richter's politics were useless: Stothard, disgusted (we should like to think) at such methods, refused to teach the young Henry after all, on the excuse that he never took pupils.

Yet Stothard was not disgusted enough to throw up the commission in favour of Blake, who may well have said outrageous things in the heat of the moment. And though Stothard's picture was a great success, he received little of the profit. For the astute Cromek gave him a mere sixty guineas for the picture; promising, however, to make it one hundred if he would spend a month more on it. This Stothard did; but Cromek, though he sold the picture for three hundred guineas (some say five hundred), conveniently forgot the extra forty.[1]

Blake's picture, which he engraved in spite of Stothard's success, is not exactly an illustration, but its symbolism may be discussed here. The pilgrims are starting in the dawn (of English poetry) before the sun (Shakspere, one presumes) has risen, and the full blaze of a day (the Elizabethan movement) has arrived. In the sky is the lonely morning-star, who represents Chaucer himself.

The last years of Blake's life were entirely given up to three big series of illustrations: *Job*, *The Divine Comedy*, and the *Bible*. Of the Bible he completed only a few pages of *Genesis*;[2] for the *Divine Comedy* he made one hundred and two water-colours, seven of which he partially engraved; but *Job*, which is the climax of his work as a symbolic artist, was completed. I have reserved this for the separate chapter it deserves.

The illustrations to Dante, if Blake had lived to finish them, might have equalled the *Job* series; but as they now remain (102 water-colours, of which only seven were engraved), they lack the well-defined system which is found even in the first water-colour series for *Job*. Nevertheless, in the Dante the symbols are plentiful.

[1] John Sartain, *The Reminiscences of a Very Old Man* (N.Y., 1898), p. 112. Sartain got his information in 1827 direct from Henry Richter.
[2] The first version of the title-page is water-marked 1826.

In the very first picture the sun sets ; in the first of the scenes in Purgatory (plate 70) it rises again, but is soon clouded over ; in Paradise it was presumably to be cleared.

In the third plate, we see Blake's conception of the great journey : Dante flees inward from the beasts through the Gates of Hell ; Virgil (his inspiration, such as Milton was to Blake himself) appears to him, while above them three exquisite Daughters of Beulah float upward, indicating his great theme : 'The Angry God of this World,' his hands outcasting flames, his left foot cloven, while before him Empire kneels, swinging a censer. On the extreme left, unperceived by these two, is a little vine-framed space in which sits Beatrice before a spinning-wheel. (This is, presumably, Enitharmon's 'moony space' : the refuge of love in this world.)

Plate 7 ('Homer and his companions') is a map of the classical conception of the universe. It is the Ptolemaic system of the seven spheres, the outer one being divided in turn into eleven spheres. This is marked the 'Limbo of Weak Shadows' : at the centre is Purgatory ; then comes the Terrestrial Paradise as 'an Island in Limbo' ; then the Moon, Mercury, Venus, Sun, Mars, Jupiter, Saturn, the Starry Heavens, and Vacuum. This plate contains a long inscription, the decipherable parts of which read : 'Every thing in Dante's Comedia shews that for Tyrannical Purposes he has made This World the Foundation of All. The Goddess Nature is [? a Mirrour and] not [Purgatory] the Holy Ghost is her Inspirer.[1] As Poet Shakspere [2] said, Nature thou art my Goddess. [? Round] Purgatory is Paradise & [? round] Paradise is Vacuum or Limbo, so that Homer is the Centre of All. I mean The Poetry of the Heathen Stolen & Perverted from the Bible not by Chance but by Design by the Kings of [? Asia] [3] & their Generals The Greek Heroes & lastly by The Romans. Swedenborg does the same in saying that in this World is the Ultimate of Heaven. This is the most damnable Falshood of Satan & his Antichrist.' [4]

In the plates that follow, there are many symbols which should be recognized by any one familiar with Blake's writings. The Giants of the *Inferno* (plate 60) are five in number—the Five Senses, half buried in the storm of Materialism. The ice-circle of plate 65 corresponds to the ice in *Jerusalem*, when Albion begins to freeze ; while on the right of the picture we see the 'Crucifixion Upside Down' ; or Man with his lowest instincts dominating both heart and brain. In the *Purgatory*, the angel-boat (plate 72) is the Moon-Ark of *Jerusalem* 44. The poets (plate 73) tend the same flame which Job tends. We also see the Ark (plate 80) guarded by the Cherubim, from between whose wings darts an electric flame smiting a follower, so that he falls backward in the same ecstasy as William and Robert in *Milton*. Plate 90 shows Dante adoring Christ ; this is the ecstatic counterpart of the tragic crucifixion in *Jerusalem*. Plate 99, the Rose of Heaven, is the most paradoxical of

---

[1] This originally read 'The Goddess Nature is not the Holy Ghost' ; then Blake added some words almost wholly obliterated.

[2] Apparently a reference to Edmund's speech, *King Lear*, I. ii. : 'Thou, nature, art my goddess.' 'Poet Shakspere' is very much blurred : the words might be read 'Poor Machiavelli.'

[3] Other suggestions are 'Africa,' 'Persia,' and 'Sirrea.'

[4] Mr. Grenville Lindall Winthrop, the owner, has been kind enough to compare my reading of this passage from the reproduction with the original.

all the designs, for it clearly represents the evil dominion of the Female Will. At the top sits Mary, naked, holding a sceptre and looking-glass (evidently the symbols of sex). Below her, to left and right, crouch the two sphinxes of 'Laws' and 'Dominion' upon the two Testaments, 'chain'd round,' while Aristotle and Homer are wide open. Lower yet are the petals of the Rose, each of which contains embracing figures, or others playing upon lyres. We must presume this picture to symbolize Blake's conception of the evil effects of the dogmas of the Immaculate Conception and the Virgin Birth.

In fact, there were many things in Dante (who always returned to the region of stars) which Blake did not approve of. Plate 101, the diagram of the circles of Hell, contains a long inscription, mainly illegible, which begins : 'Reason is Adam's Supreme Good' and ends 'he gives his son to the Evil & the Good, & his Sun to the Just & the Unjust. He could never have built Dante's Hell nor the Hell of the Bible neither, in the way our Present system is. It must have been formed by the Devil himself. So I understand it to have been.'

Dante and Virgil throughout appear in their 'spiritual forms '—as youths ; the devils themselves are sprightly youths ; and the centaurs rival Botticelli's for their supple virility. Perhaps most interesting to the artist is Blake's discovery of the emotional value of solid form : the perspectives of rocky bridges, the stony postures of the characters, and the rows of spiky flames are often remarkably effective.

Although the *Genesis* was left as a few sketched pages, it has a great deal of interest in its audacious interpretations. Blake for a long time had been planning a *Bible of Hell*, and this was his final attempt. He used the King James text, but added his own chapter-headings and illustrations, thereby inverting the meaning when he so pleased. The most interesting feature of these illustrations is his acceptance of the Trinity. Previously he had identified the Second and Third Persons,[1] and rejected God the Father entirely, as the Evil Creator. In *Jerusalem* and *Job*, as we shall see, he accepted the Father. Now he interprets ' the Elohim ' of *Genesis* as the Trinity itself, and shows them working side by side. The most radical feature, however, is his treatment of the story of Cain. According to accepted interpretations, Cain was branded upon the forehead that no man might interfere with Divine Vengeance. But Blake, who had been preaching against such Justice all his life, adroitly inverted the episode into the opposing doctrine, the Forgiveness of Sins ! He interprets the Mark as the Kiss of the Forgiveness of Sins, for ' If I should dare to lay my finger on a grain of sand / In way of vengeance, I punish the already punish'd ; O whom / Should I pity if I pity not the sinner who is gone astray ? '[2]

The first page shows the Trinity grouped about the title *Genesis*. The Father and Son are represented according to tradition, but the Holy Ghost is a nude, beardless youth.[3] Above them is the Angel of Revelation. Below them, between the two Trees of Eden, are the four Evangelists, represented (with a curious reversion to the ideas of *The Marriage of*

---

[1] ' Jesus ours, to thee who art in thy Heavens call'd by thy Name the Holy Ghost ' (Thornton marginalia).

[2] *Jerusalem*, 31 : 33-35.

[3] It is quite possible that the letter I of the title, which partially covers the body of the Holy Ghost, is intended to have some phallic significance.

Heaven and Hell) as four demons. But Blake preserves their traditional aspect somewhat by giving three of them the conventional heads of lion, ox, and eagle. The fourth is unmistakably a demon ; and all four are scaled and crowned.

Blake was not satisfied with this title-page, so he left it unfinished and began another. The Holy Ghost is given more prominence ; Christ emerges from a sphere and points to the Father ; and he, in his turn, uplifts the Bow of Spiritual Warfare. All three figures show much more energy, and give a sense of the inner life of the Trinity. The Trees and the Evangelists are replaced by the twelve Apostles, who are not represented as demons, but who float in ecstasy crested with the Pentecostal flames.

Page 1. Chapter I. 'The Creation of the Natural Man.'[1] The Father, supported by two angels, reaches down with his left hand, and blesses his work with his right hand. The text (verses 1-18) is in green ink.

Page 2. Verses 19-24. Below Verse 19, three angels move among the heavenly luminaries. Below Verse 21, two figures hover over waters and a dolphin. Below Verse 24 are some vague lines as yet unworked into definite figures.

Page 3. Verses 25-31. Below, Adam stands in amazement and praise before the Trinity, who extend their right hands.

Page 4. Chapter II. 'The Natural Man divided into Male and Female and of the Tree of Life and of the Tree of Good and Evil.' Above this heading are the Trinity, Man, and the two Trees. Below are Verses 1-12. The first five Verses are in green ink, but from Verse 6 all the rest of the text is only sketched in with pencil.

Page 5. Verses 13-25. Below the text, Man sleeps with a girdle about his chest.[2] Above him, Eve hovers horizontally beneath the Trinity. The Father is nearest her.

Page 6. Chapter III. 'Of the Sexual Nature and the Fall into Generation and Death.' Verses 1-14. Above the heading, Adam and Eve kneel by the Tree and its Serpent. Eve repeats the gesture of the Medicean Venus.

Page 7 exists as two sketches. The first contains the text of Verses 15-24, with a vague scroll-like pattern of lines below.[3] The second contains Verse 15, with lines ruled for the rest of the text, below which the Son kisses kneeling Cain upon the forehead.

Page 8. Chapter IV. 'How Generation and Death took Possession of the Natural Man and of the Forgiveness of Sins written upon the Murderer's Forehead.' Above the lines ruled for the text, Adam supports Eve on the left, over Abel's body, whose ghost floats in mid air. Cain flees away to the right.

Here Blake's transcription of the *Bible* ends.

Interminable accounts might be written of the separate paintings which Blake made to illustrate the *Bible* and Shakspere. It is no accident, for example, that the 'ladder' in *Jacob's Dream* and the apparitions over the *Death-Bed of Queen Catherine* are in spirals. Blake was

---

[1] The Natural Man is Adam, the Limit of Contraction (see *Milton*, 11 : 20).

[2] Cf. Los's Chain of Jealousy.

[3] It is interesting to learn from these that Blake worked from pattern to forms, not *vice versa*.

representing the dizzy sensation which accompanies such visions.   Again in the *Michael and Satan* (Fogg Art Museum of Harvard University) the design obviously reduces to the oriental Tomoë, whose function is to wheel endlessly.   Blake believed that Good and Evil are co-existent illusions ; as long as one lasts, the other lasts.   Therefore, by the geometry of his design he showed, not the ultimate triumph of Good, but the revolution of both until both are destroyed.

It is almost a rule that when Blake seems to picture something which violated his own conviction, he concealed in it his own opinion.   By remembering this always, we find that what seem to be curious and wilful eccentricities are, after all, worthy of our most serious consideration.

CHAPTER XXX

THE INVENTION OF JOB

O Human Imagination, O Divine Body I have Crucified,
I have turned my back upon thee into the Wastes of Moral Law.
—*Jerusalem* 24 : 23-24.

THE series of *Illustrations to the Book of Job* was the last complete work of William Blake, and it is the climax of his career as a symbolic artist. These ' Inventions ' are both the clearest and the profoundest of all his pictorial diagrams charting the spiritual life of man ; for this book, like so many others of his, is not primarily a set of illustrations to a given text, but a map of the mystic Way.

Job had always been favourite reading of Blake's. In *The Ghost of Abel* (1788) he had quoted from it ; and there are many subsequent quotations and pictures. About 1821, then aged sixty-four, he made a set of water-colours for his friend Thomas Butts.[1] Two years later he painted another set for John Linnell,[2] who then commissioned him to engrave them. These engravings were finished in two more years, and published March 1826. The next year Blake died.

These engravings have been reproduced many times, the first reproduction having been made by Professor Charles Eliot Norton of Harvard University in 1875. Originals are not uncommon. Yet the method of reading them was not discovered until 1910, when Mr. Joseph H. Wicksteed published *Blake's Vision of the Book of Job.*[3]

This meaning is simply the inner meaning of the life of every mystic. Blake for the last time was trying to reconcile all the great contradictions of the universe and ' justify the ways of God to men.'

The story was one which allowed him great philosophic freedom, and of which he characteristically took full advantage. The Job of the Bible is the innocent and just man suddenly struck down by overwhelming misfortunes. The author was endeavouring to refute the idea that catastrophe is the punishment of sin. Job is upright, yet he is ruined in a moment. But he is saved by faith ; for God descends in a whirlwind, talks with him, and at the end leaves Job more prosperous than ever. The problem of evil, nevertheless, is left unsolved : the Deity says that Job cannot understand the Divine Way, and is presumptuous in questioning it. Faith, and not knowledge, is the secret of salvation.

Blake was not satisfied with such an evasion of the great world problem. He himself was not of the ordinary type of mystic who feels a truth in vision, but can never express it. Blake had grasped a solution

---

[1] Now owned by Mr. J. P. Morgan.
[2] Now dispersed. Mr. Grenville Lindall Winthrop of New York City owns seventeen of the twenty-one.
[3] This chapter inevitably follows many points of Mr. Wicksteed's interpretation. At present he is engaged in completely rewriting his book.

which satisfied him ; so he deliberately outdid the author of the *Book of Job* by giving the answer which had been withheld.

His answer was this : that Job, living in accordance with laws written by others, rather than by the instincts of his own heart, had left himself open to the inroads of Satan. He had relied upon a moral code for his happiness, not realizing that the invulnerable happiness comes only from a sacrifice of self. This knowledge is revealed during the inevitable passage through the state of 'Experience.' The catastrophes poured upon him by Satan really spring from his own false notions of virtue ; and as long as Job is self-satisfied, he will be afflicted by these unexpected turns of 'fate,' a fate which he himself invoked upon others, and which recoil upon himself eventually. But his troubles drive him to look inward, into his own soul. As soon as he does this, he not only recognizes and casts out the error of his life ; he sees Divinity itself ; and after such a vision, nothing more can trouble him.

Such is the philosophy of Blake's *Job* ; but its story is that of the descent of God and the ascent of Man.

Blake departs from the Bible not only in his philosophy but in many other ways. He follows the story fairly accurately up to the Whirlwind ; then he gives a succession of mystical visions explaining the Universe which are not found in the Bible. Most of the characters are changed. Blake's God does not consider Job presumptuous for challenging the divine wisdom. Job is fearless, not humble, and entirely capable of understanding the occult mysteries. Job's wife is not the woman who advised her husband to curse God and die ; on the contrary, she has the fullest love and confidence in him. The minor characters are also modified to a certain extent.

The plates seem so simple at a first viewing that many commentators have imagined that Blake abandoned all his symbolism. As a matter of fact, every plate is crowded with it. He has, however, excluded all the visionary characters with inexplicable names.

The first thing to be understood is that Blake saw in Job's fall and reascent the usual set of 'States' which he had formulated as the 'Seven Eyes of God.' These seven States were divinely instituted so that man should mechanically be brought back to communion with God. In the epics, Blake's technical names for the Seven are Lucifer, Molech, Elohim, Shaddai, Pahad, Jehovah, and Jesus. They represent respectively Pride in the Selfhood ; the Executioner ; the Judge ; the Accuser ; Horror at the results ; the Perception of Evil ; and finally the Revelation of the Good. This is Man's customary course through Experience. Blake devotes two plates to each in turn ; then, the climax having been reached, the order is reversed, the final plate ending where the first began. These last seven plates show, as might be expected, the same impulse, or 'Eye,' in its redeemed aspect.

Blake's choice of names for the seven States is not so arbitrary as might appear at first glance. Lucifer, who was the first to fall from Heaven, fell through Pride. A person in the state of Lucifer naturally thinks himself perfect (as does Job), so he has to look abroad for sins to condemn. This is the second stage, which is named after Molech, because to Molech were sacrificed others—never the Self. (Molech was particularly fond of the holocausts of children ; Job sacrifices his in the flames of wrath.) Elohim means Judges in Hebrew. Shaddai, the 'all powerful,' is the Accuser. Pahad has always been the God of Terror. Jehovah, dictator of the Decalogue, rules the State in which the Decalogue (symbolic of all Law by which we think to make ourselves perfect) must reveal its evil possibilities. And finally, once this error is cleared away, with Jesus comes the saving revelation of the sacrifice of the Selfhood and the forgiveness of sins.

This outlines briefly, if vaguely, the course of spiritual events through which Job passes, and gives some indication that Job himself is to blame for his misfortunes. For it is his God and his Devil, which he has made in his own likeness, that work all the mischief. At first the two seem separate ; but at the climax, they are beheld as one.

In order to get the fullest expressiveness for these ideas in his designs, Blake developed to its extreme possibilities the traditional significance of ' right ' and ' left.' From the earliest Christian times until to-day [1] the right has been auspicious and the left (as the word itself signifies) sinister. The right hand is the place of honour. Therefore in all Last Judgments we see the blessed ascending on the right hand of the Lord, and the damned falling upon his left. Blake accepted this, interpreting the right of the characters (the ' stage-right,' but *our left* as we face the picture) as the spiritual half of the plate, and the left (our right) as the material. The use of the right or left hand, the exposure of this or that foot, shows clearly the spiritual attitude of any character. The symbolism of upward and downward is too obvious to need explanation. Any inward action (such as Job's prayer) is shown by the character's turning his back to the spectator and facing the interior of the picture.

A still more daring symbolism is the anachronistic use of Gothic architecture to denote the true Church, and of Druid architecture for its opponent, Moral Law. Blake had always held that ' Gothic is Living Form ' (*On Virgil*) ; while the Druid signified to him the primal ' Natural Religion ' which sacrifices others but not the Self. It is worth noting that in both the water-colour series Blake had used classical instead of Druid architecture. The symbol of the Cross—another anachronism— is also used during Job's period of trial. Other symbols will be dealt with as they appear.

It might be added that the differences shown by a comparison of the two sets of water-colours and the engravings show no change in the fundamental conception, though there are many improvements in the symbols. The colouring of the paintings is very subdued, even pale, but imaginative. The margins appear only in the engravings.

TITLE-PAGE. The first symbol appears in the flight of the angels. They are the Seven Eyes of God, the Seven of the Apocalypse. They descend on the material side of the plate and ascend on the spiritual ; this is a summary of the entire book, a representation of the greatest Christian mystery, a statement of the secret which every mystic tries to tell.

ILLUSTRATION I. ' There was a Man in the Land of Uz, whose Name

---

[1] As, for example, in *Matt.* xxv. 33 : ' And he shall set the sheep on his right hand, but the goats on the left.' This symbolism can be traced back to ancient Zoroastrianism. The Gnostics laid great stress on it ; from them it passed into the Kabalah.

was Job, & that Man was perfect & upright, & one that feared God & eschewed Evil ; & there was born unto him Seven Sons & Three Daughters.' [1]

Job and his family are still in the age of Innocence, but the sun is setting.[2] They sit beneath the ' Oak of Albion ' (now symbolic merely of this world) at their evening prayers. These prayers are being read from the books written by others ; the musical instruments of spontaneous praise hang silent upon the tree. This is Job's error : that he relies upon ' the Letter that killeth,' not upon his own inward promptings. On Job's right we see his spiritual wealth, the true Church or the Gothic cathedral (for, after all, Job is living his life in the way he thinks best, and such are always blessed, though not—as the Bible said—' perfect ') ; and on his left is his material wealth, the flocks and barns.

Across the face of the sun (in the water-colours) are written the opening words of the Lord's Prayer.[3]

ILLUSTRATION II. ' There was a day when the Sons of God came to present themselves before the Lord, & Satan came also among them.'

Job's inward life is now opened for us. His God (whose face and form is therefore Job's) reigns supreme with the book of Law in his lap. But Law implies Judgment ; and Satan the Accuser at once appears before the Lord.[4] In other words, Job is judging himself (since all this is taking place in his own brain, as is indicated by Blake's familiar cloud-boundaries) and cannot but find himself perfect. The angels cast before the throne all the books of Laws that Job has kept ; and below they minister to him and his family, all of whom are furnished with more books. Job surely has ' eschewed evil ' ; but the highest virtue is positive, not negative. Although angels minister to him, yet the sense of his own perfection is itself a contempt of others. The Accuser is in his heaven.

The two dim faces beneath the arms of Satan are the shadowy error of Job and his wife. Until that error is given definite form, it cannot be recognized and cast out. This process is the state of ' Experience.'

Why is Job's wife included ? Because of Blake's belief that a man and his mate are literally one spirit, divided into two bodies during Adam's sleep in the Garden of Eden. Job, spiritually, is still in Eden ; and the spiritual division of his wife from him does not take place until the 6th Illustration. In Eternity, as we have seen, they will be united again into one spiritual body, for in Eternity there is no marrying nor giving in marriage. In the same way, but in a lesser degree, a man's children and even his friends are part of him.

The symbolism of left and right is used to show the temporary harmony. God in his heaven reveals his right foot ; Job on earth exposes his left foot. Satan also extends the right foot, for the evil he represents is a spiritual evil, not yet apparent in the material world.

The margin repeats the idea of the plate. Below we see the pastoral, or ' innocent ' state of Job and his wife. Among the living Gothic

---

[1] Blake seems to have quoted these texts (copied here from the engravings) from memory, as they show unimportant textual variations.

[2] So, too, the frontispiece of the *Songs of Experience* shows the youthful shepherd striding forward in a sunset.

[3] Butts illustrations : ' Our Father which art in Heaven / Hallowed be thy Name / Thy Will be.' Linnell illustrations : ' Our Father which art in h.'

[4] Cf. ' Prisons are built with stones of law ' (21st *Proverb of Hell*).

decorations nest the gorgeous birds, which already have figured in the *Songs of Innocence*.[1] But the pillars of cloud and flame are prominent which led the Israelites to Mount Sinai, where the Law was given; hovering over them are weeping angels.[2]

ILLUSTRATION III. ' Thy Sons & thy Daughters were eating & drinking Wine in their eldest Brother's house, & behold there came a great wind from the Wilderness, & smote the four faces of the house, & it fell upon the young Men, & they are Dead.'

But all things which we cast out become our enemies. The very sins that Job hates most, his children (by the customary swing of the pendulum) revel in; and on them his wrath lights. The seven sons and their concubines [3] rejoice with music and wine; then suddenly the entire structure of their (classical) palace of delights topples about them. The black flames of anger shoot from heaven and meet others springing from the earth. And being the children of Job, they are quite unprepared for catastrophe. The eldest son tries to rise—by the left foot—but all material means fail him at the supreme moment. Even the innocent baby—a bastard—is smitten (for such curses are ' unto the third and fourth generations '). Two other sons fall in the attitude of the ' Crucifixion Upside Down '—which means that the lowest desires rule both heart and brain.[4]

What is the cause of their ruin? Visibly, it is the Executioner, under whose weight the whole building falls apart. Yet he is only the creation of the brain of Job: it is Job himself who is invisibly ruining his children with the Curse of his ideas of moral conduct. But *he* sees it, of course, as the wrath of God.

In the margin are repeated the flames of destruction and the vermin of corruption. The folds of the great serpent, Materialism, are becoming evident through the clouds.

ILLUSTRATION IV. ' And there came a Messenger unto Job & said, The Oxen were plowing & the Sabeans came down, & they have slain the Young Men with the Sword. While he was yet speaking there came also another & said, The fire of God is fallen from heaven & hath burned up the flocks & the Young Men, & consumed them, & I only am escaped alone to tell thee.'

With the news of the disaster, Satan enters even deeper into Job's soul. The sword in his left (material) hand, he surmounts the globe and moves inward. The messengers arrive left foot first, except the third (omitted in both sets of water-colours), who comes right foot first, presaging the spiritual disaster already upon the horizon. Job is horrified, but still he has faith in his false God, for he does not yet understand the true cause of the disaster—himself. The Gothic church appears for the

---

[1] Cf. also ' The pride of the peacock is the glory of God ' (23rd *Proverb of Hell*).

[2] Cf. ' Tho' Vala's cloud hide thee & Luvah's fires follow thee ' (*Jerusalem*, 62 : 28). Thus it is Nature and Passion that lead Man to fatal Sinai.

[3] As there are seven of them, and not three, they cannot be Job's daughters, who disappear until the 20th Illustration. These daughters represent ' Man's three modes of conversing with Paradise ' (*Last Judgment*). Blake's meaning is that an artist's gifts are never wholly destroyed, but they vanish in periods of spiritual affliction. Job's deliberately unsympathetic attitude explains why this happens to him.

[4] This attitude is also to be found in *America*, plate 5; *Urizen*, plate 7; and in the last engraved plate of Dante's *Inferno*.

last time. Over Job's head is a heavy bit of masonry suggesting the Cross. This will be broken in the 19th Illustration.

In the margin are the flames of affliction and the lightning bolt of disaster. On the upper corners of the picture are the dead forms of angels—the innocent joys, or the spiritual blessings—which later will revive.

ILLUSTRATION V. 'Then went Satan forth from the presence of the Lord.'

This scene is not in the Bible, but it is one of the finest in Blake's system. Job is sharing his last meal with a beggar. He does this for the same reason that he has done everything—because it is the correct thing to do, not because he naturally wishes to do it, as a man would share his last meal with a starving friend. Such charity as Job's can only be given —and taken—with the left hand; for the true sympathy is absent. He can make the gesture of charity to a beggar whose sins he cares nothing about, although he could treat his own children so harshly. Yet this charity is a spiritual act (the right foot) after all, since Job wants to do the best thing, even if he cannot do it in the proper spirit. Therefore angels still minister to him.

Therefore also God still keeps his seat by clinging to the book of Law; though, with a dimmed and sinking halo, he is dragged down on the material side. It is through Job's very virtues that he sins; the flames that robe the angels are the same flames flowing into Satan's hand, though they appear to be separate.

The Gothic cathedral has disappeared, for Job is now in error. The 'Druid' architecture has replaced it: symbolic of the primal, brutal religion of Moral Law which sacrifices others, but not the Self.

The sympathy of Job's wife is in direct contradiction to the Bible. There she encouraged her husband to curse God and die; here we see her supporting her husband with perfect confidence and love.

The margin is filled with flames and thorns, and below is the serpent, at last fully revealed, though not to Job.

ILLUSTRATION VI. 'And smote Job with sore Boils from the sole of his foot to the crown of his head.'

Now Job's errors manifest themselves in a physical form. Taken literally, the cursing with boils is an anticlimax after the loss of all Job's family; but the inner meaning makes it a true climax. Previously, Job lost all he stood for in the world; now his deepest self is corrupted. Previously, he had been in the state of Innocence, when his senses perceived the Infinite in everything; but now he has entered the bitter state of Experience (symbolized by the broken shepherd's crook in the lower margin). The characteristic of the state of Experience is the limiting of the senses. The death of four of them (sight, hearing, taste, and smell) is indicated by the four arrows descending from Satan's right hand. The fifth sense, touch (which communed with the infinite through sex) [1] is smitten with sickness. The traditional explanation of Job's boils has always been that of a sexual disease. [2] As Satan is standing on Job's right

---

[1] For the death of the four senses see *Tiriel*, v. 248 and *Urizen*, iv a, par. 8-11. For the cursing of the fifth with disease see *Tiriel*, vi., vii., and *Europe, Introduction*, 5.

[2] Cf. *Jerusalem*, 29 : 64 : 'Cover'd with boils from head to foot, the terrible smitings of Luvah' (the passions).

leg, we may assume that this disease is spiritual, not a physical one. Job's wife is separated from her husband at last by this closing of his senses ; nevertheless she still ministers to his lowest needs. Job does not see the sun again until the last plate. In the margin are the spirits of corruption, the broken shepherd's crook, and the broken potsherd.

ILLUSTRATION VII. ' And when they lifted up their eyes afar off, & knew him not, they lifted up their voice & wept : & they rent every Man his mantle, & sprinkled dust upon their heads toward heaven.'

There are no new points of symbolism in this plate. The three friends arrive left foot first. The sun has set. The suggestion of the cross over Job's head is still more marked. In the margin are the Shepherd and Shepherdess of Innocence mourning over their new state.

ILLUSTRATION VIII. ' Let the Day perish wherein I was Born.'

Job's despair at last finds an outlet. He will curse everything—except his God. This attitude of Job's, usually considered praiseworthy, is to Blake the sure sign that Job is still in error. It is interesting to notice how Job's gesture is repeated in the column of cloud. There are raining clouds (the storm of materialism), thorns, and toadstools in the margin.

ILLUSTRATION IX. ' Then a Spirit passed before my face : the hair of my flesh stood up. . . . Shall mortal Man be more Just than God ? '

Into this illustration is condensed all the long argument of Job's friends. ' God is just,' they say, ' therefore Job must have sinned.' Eliphaz is describing his dream of God ; so the vision resembles, not Job (for once), but the speaker. It is the terrible God of Justice, whose arms are bound : he *must* reward or punish, according to the deserts of mankind.

In the margin is a symbol much older than Blake. It is the ' forest of the night,' the sterile growth of error, where false theories block the path and hide the sky.

ILLUSTRATION X. ' The Just Upright Man is laughed to scorn. . . . Have pity upon me : Have pity upon me ! O ye my friends, for the hand of God hath touched me.'

Job's first sin was the admission of Satan, the Accuser, into his mind. Now that sin is reflected in the material world : his friends repeat the judgment. As Job judged his children, so the friends judge him. They separate themselves from him, when they should ' enter his bosom ' ; for they think to make themselves more holy by treading him down.

But this very trial benefits Job. Accused by the friends, he turns to his God for comfort and justification. The result, as the next plate demonstrates, is a terrible revelation.

The figures of Job and his wife are copied from an engraving of Blake's made thirty-two years before. This shows how long the subject had interested him.

In the margin are the scrolls of judgment, the raven of night, and the owl of unbelief.

ILLUSTRATION XI. ' With Dreams upon my bed thou scarest me & affrightest me with Visions.'

Yet Job's God is identical with the God of Eliphaz. It is the same God of Justice, since he points to the stone tables of the Law, from which start the lightnings of judgment. He is entwined with the serpent of Materialism. But now Job sees for the first time the cloven hoof of the left foot ; [1] for the God of Justice is only Satan, masquerading as an angel of light. He is the Accuser, who knows that no man is so pure as to be perfect ; and therefore, every man, judged by this god—the god of this world only—is condemned to the ' black flames ' of Hell.

This is Blake's most insistent doctrine. The true God is not this evil and temporary god of Justice, but Jesus, who forgives all sins and requires no penalty. The sinner is already punished in the very act of his sin ; what profit, then, to inflict mechanically some preordained chastisement ? Understanding which is forgiveness is the true Saviour.

This is the nadir of Job's life. Here only, by bitter Experience, literally ' bought with the price of all that a man hath,' he has seen and recognized that his God was also his Devil.

Mr. Wicksteed points out certain significant changes in the Biblical texts of the margin. ' The longer text beneath is nearly the same as *Job* xix. 22-27, until we come to the last sentence, where Blake alters " though my reins be consumed within me " of the Bible to (presumably his own) " Tho consumed be my wrought Image." This suggests that Job is now learning the insignificance of his personal life as being merely the " wrought image " of his own eternal being. Another significant alteration is the change of " *worms destroy this body* " into " destroy *thou* this body." The *thou* refers, no doubt, to Nature as the Satanic power, which is sometimes symbolized by the serpent and sometimes (especially man's mortal nature) by a worm ' (p. 89).

ILLUSTRATION XII. ' I am Young & ye are very Old ; wherefore I was afraid.'

Elihu, the young newcomer, is angry with Job. He does not pretend to be a friend, therefore he is no hypocrite. Blake says elsewhere : ' A man may be the friend of my spiritual life while he seems the enemy of my corporeal, though not *vice versa*.' In such cases, ' opposition is true friendship.' But Elihu is Job himself at the beginning of the Path of Experience—his inexperience is sure what is right and what is wrong.

To him, then, the stars represent the glorious mechanism of the universe, the ordered Reason which rules all things : therefore he considers Job wrong in ' fighting against the stars.' [2] But this positive statement of Job's former error merely confirms Job's perception of the cruelty of the stars' dominion—the falsity of the material order. He now sees only too clearly that man is crucified upside down. This world is not the fulfilment which makes Elihu rejoice, but the promise of something much greater. Thus to Job the stars are light which penetrate even the darkest night, showing by dim reflexion the glories which must lie beyond. The enthusiasm of the youth stirs him perhaps to memories of his own early days, when the world seemed beautiful. Now his faith is shifted from the Temporal to the Eternal.

Job's wife, meanwhile, still grieves, but she has learned resignation,

---

[1] A similar figure, with the same cloven hoof, is labelled ' The Angry God of This World ' in the Dante illustrations (plate 5).

[2] This is pure astrological fatalism. Blake knew at least one astrologer well, Varley, and from his letter protesting at the arrest of another, we know he sympathized with them. Urizen is commonly called ' starry king.'

and is no longer dominated by the frantic despair which she showed during the Curse.

The margin represents Man sleeping, while his dreams aspire upward.

ILLUSTRATION XIII. 'Then the Lord answered Job out of the whirlwind.'

The great moment, the climax of all mysticism, has come. God descends in the mystical tempest to this world, actually passing below the line of clouds which separates the spheres. For God, this is the eternal crucifixion : it is God becoming ' as we are,' descending into the world of matter for the salvation of man.[1] It is the true God, for he shows his right foot.[2]

The friends are overcome, but Job and his wife together face the Deity fearlessly. The blast of the great moment stirs even the most outward parts of their physical bodies.[3]

In the margin, the whirlwind blows flat the forest of error.[4] The six figures above are the rest of the round of the ' Seven Eyes of God.' The beginning of another figure can just be discerned in the left-hand margin : he is the ' Shadowy Eighth ' whom Blake added in *Milton* and *Jerusalem*.

ILLUSTRATION XIV. 'When the morning Stars sang together, & all the Sons of God shouted for joy.'

The moment of mystical vision is followed immediately by an ecstatic perception of the Truth lying hid in the Universe.

This picture, with the poem of *The Tyger*, kept Blake's name alive in the years of obscurity which followed his death. Every one has felt the splendour and passion of it, though few have really understood the meaning from which all this glory sprang.

It is not merely a wonderful design. It is a map of the four-fold soul of man—or of the Universe, if we will. Below, shut in by clouds, is the world of flesh and its sensations ; above, to the left, is the realm of the intellect ; to the right is the realm of the emotions ; and at the top, connected only by the head of the middle figure, is the world of pure spirit. Binding all together, in the centre is God, the Divine Imagination, by whom man can pass into any realm at will.

The intellect, on the left, is represented by the Greek God, Apollo. Blake in these later years was trying to reconcile all his hatreds ; and for some time he had detested anything Greek, partly because it was built on the flesh, but mainly because it exalted Intellect above everything else. Here he puts the Greeks in their proper place, by making their Sun God the highest type of the intellect.[5] He is pushing against the walls of his world, trying to enlarge it. This was the primal cause of the Fall. Opposite is Diana, the goddess of purity, guiding the serpents of Nature

[1] Cf. the crucified attitude of the descending Christ in the illustrations to *Paradise Lost*.

[2] It is interesting to note that in the Butts illustrations the Deity is represented without feet, to imply that he has no lower nature. But Blake changed this for the sake of contrast to the revealed Satan of the 11th Illustration.

[3] In the movement of Job's hair, which appears only in the engraving. Such visions are apt to affect man's entire physique. Cf. the end of *Milton*.

[4] Cf. the lower margin of the 6th plate of *America*.

[5] This partly explains that curious bit of conversation recorded by Crabb Robinson : ' I have conversed with the Spiritual Sun [Los]—I saw him on Primrose Hill. He said, " Do you take me for the Greek Apollo ? " " No," I said, " that " (and Blake pointed to the sky)—" that is the Greek Apollo. He is Satan " ' (H. C. R., Dec. 10, 1825).

in the night of the passions.[1] Just above them are blank spaces, suggesting other realms in the human soul as yet unknown. It is worth noting that the Intellect and the Emotions are closely bound to the realm of the body ; while the realm of pure spirit is definitely separated from them by a line of space, although the barrier clouds are much thinner than those which bound the other worlds.

This picture is a revision of the geometrical diagram on the 32nd plate of *Milton*. There we see the four circles complete, while here they extend beyond the margin. In fact, the margin here takes the place of the egg-shaped figure superimposed upon the circles, which represents the normal consciousness, whose circumference is Reason.[2] The four circles in *Milton* (as here also) represent the Four Zoas ; but there is an important rearrangement. In the *Milton*, Intellect was given the lowest place ; now it stands in the place of honour, on the right hand of God. As the four Zoas are arranged in the *Job*, then, they are : Tharmas below, Urizen and Luvah as Apollo and Diana, and at the top Urthona.

In the margin are the six days of creation, which are but a framework to this, the seventh and last creation, the spiritual rebirth of Man. The lower part of the margin continues the realm of the body, and includes the worm of the material body, the Leviathan of Nature in the Sea of Time and Space, and the flames of annihilation which already are consuming them.

In both the water-colour versions of this plate there are only four seraphim. The arms to right and left which extend their ranks through Infinity were an inspired afterthought, although these unseen seraphim are really standing on nothing.

Job is showing his left, or material foot, for he sees that at present his place is in this world. God shows his right foot, since he is re-established in his heaven. Again the true harmony is brought about. The position of God's arms repeat the gesture of the Crucifixion, since Man sees God eternally giving himself.

ILLUSTRATION XV. ' Behold now Behemoth which I made with thee.'

The Creator explains why he created this material world, this ' War by Sea enormous & the War / By Land astounding : erecting pillars in the deepest Hell, To reach the heavenly arches.' [3] The Creator—no longer the evil Demiurge, Urizen, but God himself—works (like all of Blake's Creators) with his left hand. He points out to Job the globe suspended in space, and its natural forces, while the bulrushes suggest Egypt, where civilization first rose.

The forces of Nature are symbolized by Behemoth and Leviathan, whom modern research has identified with the hippopotamus and the crocodile. Blake, not knowing this, gives them visionary forms ; Leviathan (which means ' wreathed ' or ' coiled ') being represented in a huge spiral—the round of Nature. The two political pictures of Pitt and Nelson used these same symbols ; and the Leviathan, in the same coil, appears on the 20th plate of *The Marriage of Heaven and Hell*. These monsters are part of the world in which Job is living, as is shown by the

---

[1] Blake was fond of this idea. Cf. the last plate of *Thel*, the 13th plate of *America*, the *Comus*, and the many descriptions of Beulah.

[2] Cf. ' Reason is the bound or outward circumference of Energy ' (*The Marriage of Heaven and Hell*, plate 4).

[3] *Jerusalem*, 91 : 39-41.   [4] As in the frontispiece to *Europe*, and page 1 of *Genesis*.

extension of the boundary clouds to include them ; but none the less, Job and his friends are definitely above the globe.

For once Blake's illustration seems almost as obscure as the Bible itself. There the Deity defies Job to understand ; but here he is giving a most amicable explanation. Yet though we cannot hear his words, it is not necessary, for this whole series is the answer—the explanation of Creation.

Behemoth and Leviathan, like the shells in the margin, are the empty forms produced by the Sea of Time and Space. The inverted eagles also suggest that they are the workings of the Divine Genius in the Abyss.[1] But *why* were they created ? The quotation in the left margin : ' Also by watering he wearieth the thick cloud ; He scattereth the bright cloud, also it is turned about by his counsels ' (*Job* xxxvii. 11-12), seems to suggest Thel's answer : that in Change and Death is the secret of Eternal Life. But this was an early solution of Blake's, and was later considerably modified. The quotation in the right margin : ' Of Behemoth he saith, He is the chief of the ways of God ; Of Leviathan he saith, He is King over all the Children of Pride ' (*Job* xl. 19 ; xli. 34) seems to suggest that Creation is the glory of God.[2] On the whole, however, Blake's own books say over and over again that Creation is ' Ulro,' or illusion, that it is an Error in the Universe which in mercy had to be given material form, and limited to Time and Space, so that it may be cast out and destroyed, which is the course of all error. Meanwhile, marginal spirits record the laws of creation. Blake places the blame for this error usually on Urizen. But perhaps Blake meant the whole question to be left as unanswerable, as the quotation above seems to indicate : ' Can any understand the spreadings of the Clouds, the noise of his Tabernacle ' (*Job* xxxvi. 29).[3]

ILLUSTRATION XVI. ' Thou hast fulfilled the Judgment of the Wicked.'

Whenever an Error is recognized—given bodily form—and rejected forever, a ' Last Judgment ' takes place, according to Blake. This is the most dramatic moment of the scheme of salvation, and was a favourite subject of his. Satan, the Accuser, is cast out, and with him falls the evil that had arisen in Job and his wife, which were seen as the dim faces under Satan's arms at his first appearance. They fall into the flames of annihilation (not of eternal torment, for such a hell found no place in Blake's cosmography), since Error recognized must be Error destroyed. God's halo is again bright ; and in it have appeared the spirits of pity and forgiveness. This Last Judgment does two things. It pierces the clouds that separate the worlds, and it opens a gulf—or shows the difference— between Job and his friends.

ILLUSTRATION XVII. ' I have heard thee with the hearing of the Ear, but now my Eye seeth thee.'

In the whirlwind God descended below the clouds, and ' became as we

---

[1] Cf. *The Four Zoas*, ii. 150-153 : ' While far into the vast unknown the strong-wing'd Eagles bend / Their venturous flight in Human forms distinct ; thro darkness deep / They bear the woven draperies ; on golden hooks they hang abroad / The universal curtains.'

[2] Cf. ' The pride of the peacock is the glory of God. The lust of the goat is the bounty of God. The wrath of the lion is the wisdom of God. The nakedness of woman is the work of God ' (22nd-25th *Proverbs of Hell*).

[3] Cf. ' The roaring of lions, the howlings of wolves, the raging of the stormy sea, and the destructive sword are portions of eternity too great for the eye of man ' (27th *Proverb of Hell*).

are ' ; now he has returned to heaven, and brought man with him. This is clearly indicated by the clouds on which the Deity stands.

Four lines from the *Auguries of Innocence* explain this plate.

> God appears, and God is light
> To those poor souls who dwell in Night,
> But does a human form display
> To those who dwell in realms of Day.

The friends are still in the night, and the light to them is intolerable ; but Job and his wife face God and know him for a comrade, in whose image they were made.

The margin contains texts identifying the Father and the Son.

ILLUSTRATION XVIII. ' And my Servant Job shall pray for you.'

Though the mystical ecstasy is temporary, it affects the entire after-life of man. God has now withdrawn from his complete manifestation as Man to the likeness of a great sun in the heavens. Meanwhile Job finds that in prayer the great mystical descent (typified by the angels in the margin) is mildly repeated. He cannot hate his friends now ; he merely pities them for not having seen what he has seen, since without the vision they must remain what they are. So he admits them to his prayers. This is self-sacrifice (represented by his cruciform attitude), an inward act (since he faces inward). And the flame of his sacrifice [1] pierces the clouds which separate the worlds and reaches to the heart of God. The wheat in the margin signifies that Prayer is the Daily Bread of the soul. The Wine, the other aspect of the Eucharist, the Wine he cursed his sons for enjoying, appears two plates later.

What makes this plate particularly interesting from the symbolic standpoint is that Blake, having accepted the Greeks in the 14th Illustration, now makes use of certain symbols from Plato's *Timaeus*, that great source of so much medieval metaphysics. There we read : ' To earth, then, let us assign the cubical form. . . . The solid form of the pyramid is the original element and seed of fire.' Therefore Blake means that our body, the cubical form of earth, is the altar whereon blazes the spiritual pyramid of flame. As early as *Tiriel* (line 29) he had used fire as a symbol of soul. The same symbols from Plato, moreover, had been used already by Agrippa in his *Occult Philosophy*, II. xxiii. and Thomas Vaughan in *Lumen de Lumine*, section 1.

The Ascending Triangle as a symbol of the soul of Man was also widely adopted by the Kabalists. On every synagogue we see to this day the combination of ascending and descending triangles, the union of God and Man. Blake, however, could not use the six-pointed star here, as God had descended earlier, in the 13th Illustration.

These Platonic and Kabalistic symbols are not to be found in the two sets of water-colours, nor in the *Prayer of Noah*, a similar painting owned by Mr. W. A. White. In this picture, the flame is three-pointed, and reaches to the centre of the rainbow. In the *Job* water-colours, the top of the flame, which is irregular, is cut off by the top of the picture, and Job faces outward.

Blake was particularly fond of the engraving. In the margin he has

---

[1] As this is sacrifice of the Self (the mystical death) Blake has omitted the burnt offerings of seven bullocks and seven rams which the Bible mentions.

placed the scrolls of his poems, his palette, and his graver, to show that they, too, are modes of prayer.

ILLUSTRATION XIX. 'Every one also gave him a piece of Money.'

As Job lost virtue by giving to a beggar, so now he gains it by receiving from his friends. This is the true charity springing from personal sympathy, which was missing in the 5th Illustration. Such humility as Job's was very difficult for Blake ; to receive when one used to give would try us all. As Mr. Wicksteed points out, this is a ' tender and delicate acknowledgement ' of Blake's obligations to the Linnells.

At last the heavy cross over Job's head is broken. Prosperity is shown in the fig-tree of fertility and the standing wheat. Angels crowd round the corners of the design with the palms of victory ; and below we see the roses and lilies of material and spiritual beauty.[1]

An early sketch for this plate is reproduced as No. 93 of Laurence Binyon's *Drawings and Engravings of William Blake* (London, 1922), but it is mistitled ' Job and His Daughters.' The neighbours enter from right and left to Job and his wife, who sit beneath the customary tree in the centre. Later Blake realized that this central position did not accord too well with Job's new humility, so in the water-colours and the engraving he moved the pair to the right. In the sketch, above the tree there is a whirl of descending angels, among whom sits the Lord, his left hand upraised, his right apparently on a book.

ILLUSTRATION XX. 'There were not found Women fair as the Daughters of Job in all the Land, & their Father gave them Inheritance among their Brethren.'

Job is recounting his experiences. It is not enough to be saved ; the redeemed must show the way to others. This Blake had been trying to do all his life ; this is what he meant to do by this very series of pictures.

He is recounting his experiences to the three daughters, Poetry, Painting, and Music, who had vanished during the period of Job's trial. They represent the artistic mediums ; and they are enriched (by their inheritance of Job's experience) for their spiritual brethren.

The production of Art is the giving of oneself ; it is the human equivalent of the Divine Sacrifice ; therefore Job is in the cruciform position. Indeed, the parallelism of God and Job in this picture is as marked as possible. On his right we see the spiritual disaster of the destruction of his children ; on his left the material disaster of the loss of his harvest ; and above him is the central feature of the story—the descent of God in the whirlwind. Below these designs are the forms of Job and his wife (she being placed, as usual, on the spiritual side) oppressed by the lightnings of the state of Experience.

In the water-colours made for Butts, this whole scene takes place out of doors among the flocks, and the daughters are actually writing Job's words into books—Prophetic Books, we may be sure. In the Linnell water-colours the flocks are still there, so we may assume that the scene is still laid in the open ; but the visions, instead of being in the sky, have taken their places as though upon the walls, the outlines of which are dimly traceable. In the engraving, however, the scene is indoors—in

---

[1] A similar design appears on the 18th plate of *Jerusalem*, where the two figures represent Vala and Jerusalem.

Los's Halls, probably. The flocks are omitted as meaningless, and a floor with a curious design is added. This floor consists of a great circle tessellated with many smaller interlacing circles. No doubt this represents the communion of the heaven of art ; the small circles representing the individuals entering each other's bosoms (the inscribed portions being significantly four-sided), all of them being contained in one great circle, who is the One Man, Jesus himself.

In the margin we see further symbols of the ecstasy of art : vines with their grapes, and instruments of music. The little angels who embrace on the corners repeat this communing of delight.

ILLUSTRATION XXI. ' So the Lord blessed the latter end of Job more than the beginning.'

And here the story of Job ends. The books of Law are replaced by scrolls of song. The musical instruments are no longer hung silent upon the tree. The long night is over, and the sun rises.

In the two sets of water-colours Blake wrote across the face of the sun the text from *Revelation* xv. 3, which later was engraved in the upper margin.[1] It is ' the song of Moses the servant of God and the song of the Lamb ' : the song of both Testaments reconciled. At last Blake felt that he had synthesized the teachings of the two books. The circle is complete.

Having gone through Job's story, we can see clearly the exact division of his experience into the Seven Eyes. As has been said before, the first fourteen plates are arranged in pairs, one for each Eye. Illustrations I. and II. are dominated by Lucifer, who from pride first fell from Heaven : Job is just falling from his Heaven, which is already divided into the Judge and the Accuser. The second two plates correspond to Molech, the Executioner : under his influence, Job sacrifices his children, and so lays himself open to judgment. The third pair of plates represents Elohim (the Judges), where Job's purely ceremonial charity and the corruption of his inner self mark how his ethics affect him. Under Shaddai (the Accuser), the judgment Job has pronounced is turned back upon himself. Under Pahad, the God of Fear, he sees the horror of his God, and experiences the mocking. Under Jehovah-Urizen, he perceives the evils of the Stone Tables and learns to read the true meaning of the stars. Then at last, under Jesus, he experiences the mystical ecstasy and beholds the universe as Imagination in the vision of the morning stars. So much for the first fourteen plates. There are seven left, each of which represents an interpretation of an Eye from the eternal point of view—for having found the true God, Job can never abandon him. Thus the Creation by Jehovah (plate 15) is now good ; the Judgment by Jesus (plate 16) is merciful ; the meeting God face to face (Pahad) is no longer terrible ; the false friends and the cursing under Shaddai become the prayer for his friends ; the false charity of the Elohim has become true charity ; the destruction of his children under Molech is now their cultivation ; and finally we end with the sun's rising on the scene in which Lucifer appeared. Thus the last seven Illustrations reverse the order of the Seven Eyes, except for Jehovah and Jesus in plates 15 and 16.

---

[1] Butts water-colour : ' Great & Marvellous are thy / Works Lord God Almi[ghty] / Just & true.' Linnell water-colours : ' Great & Marvellous are thy Works Lord.' The engraving repeats the text substantially as it appears in the Bible.

The correspondence of the Job engravings to the Tarot cards is too striking to be ignored. Court de Gebelin in 1781 (*Monde Primitif*, VIII.) had announced that these cards, introduced into Europe centuries before by the gypsies, and used everywhere for games and fortune-telling, were really a book written by the ancient Egyptians to explain through symbols ' the entire universe and the various states to which the life of man is subject' (p. 367). This book, he asserted, was highly systematized, being based on the sacred number 7. But Gebelin's explanations of the individual cards were superficial, and his system involved considerable rearrangement ; Etteilla, a later student of the cards in the eighteenth century, also missed the system in the normal order. Since their day, and Blake's, a vast literature has grown up round the Tarot, a thorough knowledge of which is considered essential to any understanding of Kabalistic philosophy. Its origin is no longer thought to be Egyptian but Hebraic, for its relations to the Hebrew alphabet and the *Sepher Yetzirah* are obvious.

In these few pages it would be impossible to explain the system of the Tarot, a subject which' already has filled volumes. We can only give Blake's interpretation of the cards, trusting Tarot students to see for themselves where Blake has penetrated the traditional meanings, and where he has abandoned it in favour of his own system. His order, however, is the normal order. For the general reader it should be suffi- cient to state that, as usual, Blake accepted only as much as he saw fit, and often inverted meanings in his paradoxical way, calling some things bad which seem good, and *vice versa*.

0. *The Fool*, in both systems, represents the descent of the Uncreated.

1. *The Magician* is the hero at the beginning of the great story.

2. *The High Priestess* (' la Papesse '), holding the book of the Torah (law), represents to Blake the evil of moral law in the spiritual world. The prominence of the books in Job's heaven are the key to this plate.

3. *The Empress* signifies the descent of moral law from the spiritual to the material plane ; Blake shows us the result of this in the destruc- tion of Job's children.

4. *The Emperor* symbolizes Job, the tyrant on the material plane.

5. *The Hierophant* (' le Pape ') symbolizes Job's God, the tyrant on the spiritual plane.

6. *The Lovers* is almost unchanged in Blake's plate, except that he substitutes Satan with his arrows for the armed Cupid. (An archangel replaces Cupid in Mr. Waite's modernized version of the Tarot.)

7. *The Chariot* drawn by the sphinxes of Good and Evil is represented by the arrival of Job's friends.

8. *Strength* (in the old cards) is symbolized by a woman who opens a lion's mouth. ' After this opened Job his mouth and cursed his day.'

9. *The Hermit* wandering at night in the snow is paralleled by Eliphaz in the Forest of Error.

10. *The Wheel of Fortune* is demonstrated by the mockery of Job's friends.

11. *Justice* : Job beholds the God of Justice.

12. *The Hanged Man* (the ' Crucifixion Upside Down ') is surely what Job sees, as his eyes are now being opened.

13. *Death* is represented by Blake as the mystical whirlwind, which is the Death of the Selfhood. The thirteenth plate of *The Gates of Paradise* is also a mystical vision connected with Death.

14. *Temperance* in the Tarot appears as an angel transferring the contents of a cup in the left hand to a cup in the right hand : the symbolic significance is Transmutation. Blake interprets it as the New Birth in the vision of the Morning Stars.

15. *The Devil*, according to Tarot doctrine, is the apparent evil of generation. Blake's plate represents the Creator explaining the material world.

16. *The Tower* is almost exactly Blake's Last Judgment—the casting out of error.

17. *The Star* pours out its influences : Job sits in mystical contemplation.

18. *The Moon* draws lower animals upward ; so Job is drawn upward by prayer.

19. *The Sun* is apparently not paralleled at all, unless we say that Job is now basking in the rays of his neighbours' love.

20. *Judgment* (really the Resurrection) is according to Blake a contrast with 16, which was a casting out of Error : this is a second Judgment, being the appraisal of the True by means of art. Job's three daughters are revived ; the Tarot trump (in the old cards) shows the resurrection of three people.

21. *The World* (or rather, the Universe) represents in both series the final, complete attainment.

Thus it was that Blake revised according to his own doctrines the ' Book of Thoth,' in his day considered the oldest book in existence. His ingenuity in following the Tarot, card by card, yet not swerving from his own system of the Seven Eyes of God, is astonishing. The Tarot has been called a mirror for each mind ; we may wait long before another interpretation equally admirable is given to the world.[1]

---

[1] While this was passing through the press, I discovered that Blake was not the first to behold the ' Vision of the Morning Star,' which he depicted so triumphantly in Illustration XIV. Many centuries before, one Timarchus had seen precisely the same vision in the Cave of Trophonius, according to Plutarch (*Concerning Socrates's Daemon*).

CHAPTER XXXI

THE CURTAIN FALLS

If the red slayer think he slays,
Or if the slain think he is slain,
They know not well the subtle ways
I keep, and pass, and turn again.
—EMERSON : *Brahma.*

THE last of Blake's writings which he himself published was one of the first he ever wrote. In all the development of his philosophy, he had never contradicted a single fundamental principle. *The Ghost of Abel*, a drama small enough to be engraved on two small plates, was dated 1822, with a note that ' W. Blake's Original Stereotype was 1788.' This ' Revelation in the Visions of Jehovah seen by William Blake ' in 1788 must have lain forgotten among his manuscripts until 1821, when Byron made a stir with his *Cain, A Mystery*. Then Blake locked up his own play on the subject, revised it perhaps, and re-engraved it, adding the dedication : ' To Lord Byron in the Wilderness.'

Byron had long since fled as a social outcast to Italy. In the bitterness of his sufferings, the problem of Good and Evil had been forced upon his mind ; and *The Mystery of Cain* was the expression of his hopelessness at any solution. Byron was frankly ' of the Devil's party,' siding with Lucifer and Cain against the Evil Creator. But Byron's analysis of the situation hardly went farther. He unconsciously identified Good and Evil with Happiness and Misery ; but only unconsciously—and this key fell from his hands. Most of his arguments are directed against the contemporary doctrines of the Church of England and not against the essential problems.

In short, Byron was only in the kindergarten of the School of Experience, where Blake had become a master. The older poet must have sympathized thoroughly with the young Romanticist for his reckless revolutionary tendencies, his frank free-thinking, his outspoken sensuality, and his scourging of hypocrisy. Blake knew the long, bitter path where such ideas were gathered, and he saw that as yet the young lord was still in the Forests of the Night. Therefore he dedicated his *Ghost of Abel* ' to Lord Byron in the Wilderness,' hoping that the younger man, and perhaps even the public, might find in the two pages of Blake's play an answer to the questions posed so vainly in the three acts of Byron's.

' What dost thou here, Elijah ? ' cries Blake, as the vision rolls upon him. Then, after a brief affirmation upholding Imagination as eternal reality, in contrast to Nature, which ' has no Supernatural and dissolves,' the scene opens upon the first great dissolution of Nature, the first death in this world, the grave of Abel.

Overwhelmed by the irremediable tragedy, Adam refuses to listen more to the ' Spiritual Voice ' of Jehovah. The consequences are immediate.

A cry is heard coming on ; and the Ghost of Abel rushes in, shrieking for vengeance.

During the Last Judgment in *The Four Zoas*, all the murdered rise up, clamouring automatically for vengeance ; even the Massacred Innocents indulge the passion for revenge which death only interrupted. So now the gentle Abel is transformed into a cry demanding the sacrifice of his murderer. Eve, the woman, knows at once that he is not ' the real Abel,' but merely the Voice of Blood, an impulse cast off from the freed spirit.

A whole essay might be written on the curious effect of the effluvium of blood. From the earliest ages, spilled blood was offered to gods and spirits. Many people are peculiarly susceptible to the mere sight of blood, even when they have no idea what it is. The same effect may be observed among certain of the higher animals. Two of the most poignant moments in all literature centre about this subtle fume : the cry of Cassandra before the palace of Agamemnon, and the somnambulism of Lady Macbeth. Blake was guided rightly by his intuition when he gave the Voice of Blood its part to play.

Abel's Ghost, however, interests us not so much for what thing he is, as for the thing he becomes. He is actually the occult power from which Satan, and all the worldly religion, is to arise. Again he calls upon Jehovah for vengeance: ' Life for Life ' ; but his prayer cannot be granted.

Adam cries out to Eve to come away and leave these vain delusions. But the recognition of the unreality of the Ghost brings out the reality of Jehovah. At once the ' Form Divine, Father of Mercies ' appears to the afflicted couple (in their ' Mind's Eye,' as Blake carefully explains). Eve immediately knows that it is better ' to believe Vision,' where Abel still lives, than to believe in the material world where he is dead ; and the two kneel before the Revelation.

But the Ghost, into whom the Accuser has entered, cannot rest. Even when he sinks out of the sight of memory into his grave the form of Satan arises from it at once, pronouncing that he, Vengeance (and therefore but another form of the Ghost), is the God of Men ; that Jehovah is human also ; and hence ' Thou shalt Thyself be sacrificed to Me, thy God ! on Calvary ! ' But in thunder Jehovah reveals the ultimate mystery : that Satan himself shall enter Self-Annihilation, till even he is saved.

A chorus of Angels ends the play, singing how ' the Elohim of the Heathen swore Vengeance for Sin ' ; until ' Elohim Jehovah ' stood revealed in their midst, preaching the Forgiveness of Sins. Then the Elohim saw their Oath was the eternal fire of Hell itself ; and, conquered, ' They roll'd apart, trembling, over the Mercy-seat, each in his station fixt in the firmament by Peace, Brotherhood, and Love.'

And with this statement of the triumph of Jesus as the regulating force of the universe, ' the Curtain falls ' on Blake's literary works.

Peculiar to *The Ghost of Abel* is the use of the name ' Jehovah ' in place of Blake's customary ' Jesus,' which would have been an anachronism. Towards the end of his life, Blake had reconciled the Father and the Son, the Old and the New Testaments, as we have seen in his Illustrations to *Job*. ' Jehovah ' is no longer Urizen ; he is the Intellectual Fountain of Vision. Opposed to him are ' the Elohim ' (Judges) ' of the Heathen,' who are summed up in Satan. But Jehovah himself is also Elohim, though in spiritual, not material things; and finally to him all powers are subjugated and fixed in their places.

The redemption of Satan is also a new point. Satan, as Error, can be annihilated; Satan, as the Accuser, is a vital force which cannot be destroyed, but which is to be turned to the rightful direction. Divested of ' Selfhood ' (Selfishness), the Accuser becomes the Friend.

Cain, the Criminal, does not appear in the play. But we know that Blake's sympathy, with Byron's, lay with the sinner rather than the others, whose sufferings were less. What was the mark, Blake asked, which was fixed upon the murderer's forehead to prevent the Vengeance of ' Life for Life ' ? The answer was clear : Cain's crime was pardoned ; the mark was the Kiss of the Forgiveness of Sins.

CHAPTER XXXII

EPILOGUE IN CRESCENDO

Would God that all the Lord's people were prophets !
—*Numbers* xi 29.

IT is a curious puzzle to explain why Blake was not better known in his own day. He seems to have come into contact with many of the famous and influential ; he always won some recognition of his genius from them ; and he was always forgotten almost at once.

At the house of Mrs. Aders in Euston Square, Blake probably met Coleridge, Lamb, and Henry Crabb Robinson ; and we may be sure that Flaxman and Linnell, who also had entry to that circle, were not backward in praising their friend. Robinson recited *The Tyger* with such success that Lamb remembered it as ' glorious,' while Linnell, for long after, tried to copy Robinson's elocution. Lamb's enthusiasm was so well aroused that he called on Blake, wrote to Bernard Barton, the Quaker poet,[1] that he considered Blake ' one of the most extraordinary persons of the age ' ; sent the first *Chimney-Sweeper* to Montgomery's propagandic *Chimney-Sweeper's Friend*, (1824) to which Cruikshank contributed the customary illustrations ; and proclaimed that the *Descriptive Catalogue* contained ' the finest criticism he had ever read of Chaucer's poem.' Coleridge seems to have visited Blake several times, having earlier passed a favourable judgment upon the *Songs*.[2] H. Crabb Robinson called upon Blake several times, carefully noting in his diary all of his wildest sayings. Blake was getting old, and evidently saved his most startling epigrams and pet heresies for just such visitors. Robinson noted that he repeated himself often after the first call ; and practically every one of Blake's remarks which he recorded find their explanation in important passages of the Prophetic Books. Samuel Rogers, ' the banker poet,' ordered a fine copy of the *Songs*. Wordsworth was not interested enough to meet his great admirer, yet was completely captivated on picking up by chance a copy of the *Songs*.[3] Landor jotted in a notebook : ' Blake : Never did a braver or a better man carry the sword of justice.'[4] A *Songs of Innocence* may have reached Keats through his friend Charles Wentworth Dilke, an early Blake collector, since the *Daisy's Song* has a Blakean flavour ; but Keats in all his works makes no reference to Blake. Neither does Shelley ; though here there must have been some influence, however indirect, through Godwin. Among the artists, Sir Thomas Lawrence kept Blake's *Wise and Foolish Virgins* on his table ; while the poisoner-painter Wainwright

---

[1] May 15, 1824. Bernard Barton never met Blake, but became sufficiently enthusiastic over the *Job* engravings to write a sonnet on Blake, which is preserved in A. T. Story's *Life of John Linnell*, vol. i. p. 194.

[2] Letter to C. A. Tulk, 1818.

[3] *Life and Letters of Samuel Palmer*, p. 248.

[4] Keynes, p. 335.

242

not only bought a *Songs of Innocence*, but inserted a paragraph on the *Jerusalem* in *The London Magazine* for September 1820. Dibdin gives a romantic account of a Blake collector in 1824 : ' My friend, Mr. [Isaac] D'Israeli, possesses the largest collection of any individual of the very extraordinary drawings of Mr. Blake ; and he loves his classical friends to disport with them, beneath the lighted Argand lamp of his drawing room, while soft music is heard upon the several corridores and recesses of his enchanted stair-case.   Meanwhile the visitor turns over the contents of the Blakean portefeuille. Angels, Devils, Giants, Dwarfs, Saints, Sinners, Senators, and Chimney Sweeps, cut equally conspicuous figures : and the *Concettos* at times border upon the burlesque, of the pathetic or the mysterious.   Inconceivably blest is the artist, in his visions of intellectual bliss.   A sort of golden halo envelopes every object impressed upon the retina of his imagination ; and (as I learn) he is at times shaking hands with Homer, or playing the pastoral pipe with Virgil.   Meanwhile, shadowy beings of an unearthly form hang over his couch, and disclose to him scenes . . . such as no other Mortal hath yet conceived !   Mr. Blake is himself no ordinary poet.' [1]

What became of the enthusiasm of all these people ?   Blake made no effort to utilize it.   And they in their turn usually looked upon the fascination of this or that work of Blake's as merely a curiosity which happened to be personally appealing.   And so Blake was passed by as something extraordinary ; but eccentric, and not of ultimate importance.

Still, Blake was too big a personality, at the very least, not to have left some direct influence.   This influence was not to be through his mysticism, his metaphysics, nor his poetry, but through his painting, which was perhaps the least masterful of his accomplishments.   In his old age, Blake found a group of young artists gathering about him, bound by a mutual admiration for the sage, to walk with whom was like ' walking with the Prophet Isaiah.'   Far from observing any startling eccentricities in him, they referred to him and Michelangelo or Dante in the same breath. The way his doctrines saturated their souls and hearts is revealed, not only in their paintings, but even in their letters, where phrase after phrase has been written down almost as Blake himself had written it previously. His rooms were ' the House of the Interpreter,' the disciples were ' the Ancients.'

These young ' Ancients ' were John Linnell, Edward Calvert, Samuel Palmer, George Richmond, Frederick Tatham, Oliver Finch, Henry Walter, and W. Sherman.   They adored landscape, above all things, which they painted and engraved to the end of their lives, in an attempt to catch its ' spiritual significance,' while avoiding mere topography. Linnell was the oldest and the staunchest of them ; Calvert the most spiritual ; Finch the most inclined to believe in Blake's revelations ; Palmer the most susceptible to what artistic doctrines he understood ; while Walter was perhaps the least influenced in any way.

Blake accepted these disciples heartily, opening his rooms to their monthly meetings.   He took great pains to save their artistic souls by preaching the spiritual basis of Nature, without an understanding of which Nature becomes the worst of errors.   They were to work ' in fear and trembling.'   And far from turning ' Atheist,' they understood and

---

[1] T. F. Dibdin, *The Library Companion*, p. 734.

accepted his doctrine of vision, till their descendants looked with stern disapproval on their sickly susceptibility to the supernatural. A. H. Palmer quotes one of his father's written prayers for inspiration, then adds : ' The remarkable rhapsody from which I have quoted is laboriously and crabbedly written, and shows no signs of being otherwise than honest. It is needless to point out how strongly it savours of Blake ; and assuming that it is the honest expression of mental action, it must create no little wonder that even Blake could have infected any healthy mind to such a great degree with his own nebulous way of regarding simple things. I must not be understood as making any reflection upon the unmistakable tone of piety which runs through the whole, but merely as deprecating a certain morbid and effeminate tendency of thoughts, and the strange hallucination that difficulties arising from want of knowledge or want of physical energy arose from want of direct inspiration from on high.' [1]

The watchword of the ' Ancients ' was ' Poetry and Sentiment.' They loved to go on sketching tramps, startling the villagers with their strange costumes and their camp-stools (then a new invention). They affected amazing cloaks, went unshorn, and turned day and night topsy-turvy. They recited Virgil under trees ; improvised tragedies in the haunted Black Lane ; and were given to singing Locke's *Macbeth* music at night ' in hollow clefts and deserted chalk-pits.' They sat up for sunrises, they rushed out into the worst thunderstorms. They made friends with the village idiots and ostlers. They experimented in new techniques ; and a forgotten bottle of egg-mixture once exploded horribly in a pocket during a visit to London. Hard-working now and then, they seem (Linnell excepted) generally to have been rather fond of lingering over the day-dream, of inhaling ' perfumed and enchanted midsummer twilights,' while waiting for inspiration. Their philosophy evaporated in such dicta as Calvert's ' Light is Orange.' They courted ridicule and affronted fashion, since they despised worldly success as much as worldly scorn. Yet lazily and intermittently as they laboured, their pictures became intense with a peculiar beauty of their own.[2] Calvert's *Ten Spiritual Designs* are perhaps the height of the school's achievement.

But they were not the men to understand Blake. His parables and paradoxes became in their mouths the affectation of eccentric speech. His hatred of science and reason reappeared as railings against women's bonnets and gas-lighting. His doctrines of inspiration degenerated into something very near the superstition of Spiritism. His honest elevations of soul were transmuted into mere aestheticism. To these disciples, Blake's most beloved work was the Virgil woodcuts. Such work they admired ; but they absorbed only a little of Blake's mysticism, and that irrationally ; paid no attention to his poetry ; and looked askance at his philosophy.

Then followed the betrayal by the disciples. Fearing (as Blake himself never feared) the world's misunderstanding of their master, they tried to sweeten his memory by suppressing his thought. They were afraid of that misinterpretation which Blake challenged during his life.

[1] *Life and Letters of Samuel Palmer*, p. 34.
[2] ' Mr. Wright, having heard from his boyhood all about " The Ancients," wrote a parody of their strange doings and opinions, in which he made " Cobweb Castle " their headquarters. The title was, I think, *Noctes* ' (*Life and Letters of Samuel Palmer*, p. 373). I have been unable to trace this volume.

So John Linnell from sheer prudery defaced many of the illustrations to *The Four Zoas*, and in 1855 recorded for posterity : ' With all the admiration (possible) for Blake, it must be confessed that he said many things tending to the corruption of Christian morals, even when unprovoked by controversy ; and when opposed by the superstitious, the crafty, or the proud, he outraged all common-sense and rationality by the opinions he advanced, occasionally even indulging in the support of the most lax interpretations of the precepts of the Scriptures.' [1]

Samuel Palmer sold the *MS. Book* for ten shillings (fortunately to a worthy buyer) ; militated against Blake's ' Manicheism,' which he believed was inspired by evil spirits ; [2] and advised Mrs. Gilchrist to expurgate *The Marriage of Heaven and Hell* : ' Life is uncertain, and lest I die before I have time to say it, I will say *at once* that I think the whole page at the top of which I have made a cross in red chalk would at once exclude the work from every drawing-room table in England.' And in order that *The Marriage* be a fit drawing-room ornament, Palmer gives more specific directions : ' I should let no passage appear in which the word Bible, or those of the persons of the blessed Trinity, or the Messiah were irreverently connected. . . . I should simply put ***s ; and in case of omitting a page or chapter, simply say " The ——th Chapter is omitted." This sometimes gives a zest—a twinge of pleasant curiosity to the reader, the more attentive through not having the whole.' And Mrs. Gilchrist followed his advice.

But the Judas seems to have been Tatham. Mrs. Blake, whom he had charitably taken in as a housekeeper, left him all of Blake's unsold works, ' being writings, paintings, and a very great number of copper plates,' according to Tatham's own statement. What became of them ? The story goes that Tatham entered the Irvingite Church, accepted Palmer's belief as to the evil origin of Blake's inspiration ; and in spite of Edward Calvert's protests, destroyed at least the greater part of the relics. When this deed finally became public during the search for Blakeana, Tatham mysteriously hinted here and there that only a few were destroyed, and the rest sold. If so, there is yet a chance that more of Blake's work will be recovered.

The list of his lost works is extensive. It contains parts of *The Everlasting Gospel* : the last six books of *The French Revolution* ; *Barry, A Poem* ; *The Book of Moonlight* ; *The Book of Enoch* ; *The History of England* (a series of engravings) ; *For Children—The Gates of Hell* ; and *The Bible of Hell*. *The Book of Outhoun* may have been a rejected title for the *Visions of the Daughters of Albion* ; but where is the *Vision of Genesis*, from which Blake read ' a wild passage in a sort of Bible style ' to Crabb Robinson on February 18, 1826 ? These titles remain to tease us ; also Blake's reference to his ' six or seven epic poems as long as Homer, and twenty tragedies as long as *Macbeth*,' though these last may have been written only in Eternity, and never committed to any material medium.[3] Tatham himself said : ' He wrote much upon controversial

---

[1] A. T. Story, *Life of John Linnell*, vol. i. p. 247.
[2] ' Blake was, I think, misled by erroneous spirits ' (*Life and Letters of Samuel Palmer*, p. 302).
[3] ' I now have it in my power to commence publication with many very formidable works, which I have finish'd & ready ' (Letter to James Blake, Jan. 30, 1803—Keynes, p. 449).

subjects,' and adds that his arguments were ' unwarrantable.'   Any one of these books or papers might cast an untold amount of illumination upon many of Blake's obscurest myths.   They may have included the histories of Ariston, Ocalythron, and their strange fellows.   And when we realize how valuable are even Blake's casual jottings in the margins of the works of others, we realize how irreparable was Tatham's destruction or dispersal of his Blake relics.

Meanwhile Blake remained to the world at large a lunatic whose extraordinary works were worth a paragraph or a footnote.   In 1834 Mrs. Hemans found his death-bed was proper material for a poem, *The Painter's Last Work*;[1] but she could not utilize the actual excitement of the moment, and she put ' Eugene ' into that vague and minor ecstasy which characterizes all the work of her school.   In 1835, Bulwer Lytton described the illustrations to the *Night Thoughts* at length, calling them ' one of the most astonishing and curious productions which ever balanced between the conceptions of genius and the ravings of insanity.'[2]   In his occult masterpiece, *A Strange Story* (1861), he referred to them again, though more sympathetically.   In 1847, Robert Southey came across the *Descriptive Catalogue* and the *Poetical Sketches*, which he considered fit material for *The Doctor* (vol. 6, ch. clxxxi.).   In his whimsical and irresponsible work, he could only sneer and gape at ' this insane and erratic genius.'   In the same year, J. G. Whittier mentioned the funeral of the fairy in his *Supernaturalism of New England*.   In 1855 appeared the rare poems of Maria Lowell,[3] some of which were evidently inspired by Blake's work.   The *Song* beginning ' Oh bird, thou dartest to the sun,' merely repeats the lament of Thel, while *Jesus and the Dove* echoes in part *The Little Boy Lost and Found* and *The Little Girl Lost and Found* :

> Then Mary, in her gentle voice,
>   Told of a little child
> Who lost her way one dark, dark night
>   Upon a dreary wild ;
>
> And how an angel came to her,
>   And made all bright around,
> And took the trembling little one
>   From off the damp hard ground ;
>
> And how he bore her in his arms
>   Up to the blue so far,
> And how he laid her fast asleep,
>   Down in a silver star.

In 1857 Ruskin, who may have heard of Blake through Varley,[4] paid the

[1] *Scenes and Hymns of Life.*   Mrs. Hemans added this note : ' Suggested by the closing scene in the life of the painter Blake, which is beautifully related by Allan Cunningham.'   This poem evidently inspired Mrs. Elizabeth E. Eames in America to write another such poem, *Love's Last Work*, which appeared in the *Southern Literary Messenger*, September 1843.   But Mrs. Eames was yet another step from the actual reality : her painter dies upon a ' silken couch ' after having painted his ' wondrous fair ' beloved.   [2] *The Student : A Series of Papers*, vol. ii.

[3] *The Poems of Maria Lowell*; fifty copies privately printed at Cambridge, Massachusetts, 1855.   Maria Lowell was the wife of James Russell Lowell.

[4] Varley predicted the ages of fourteen, eighteen, and twenty-one as especially unfortunate for Ruskin, who, in these very years, met, fell in love with, and lost ' the object of his affections,' thanks to Saturn (see E. T. Cook, *Life of John Ruskin*).

Inventions to Job a high compliment. He considered them ' of the highest rank in certain characters of imagination and expression. . . . In expressing conditions of glaring and flickering light, Blake is greater than Rembrandt ' (*Elements of Drawing*). However, Ruskin was none the less equal to cutting up one of the two coloured copies of *Jerusalem*.

The first real interest in Blake which rose in the outside world came from an American, J. J. Garth Wilkinson. As a Swedenborgian, he was interested in Blake's supernaturalism ; and though he believed that Blake had indiscriminately thrown open the gates of his brain to the ' canaille of the other world,' he could not but admire the poems and designs. As early as 1839 he had persuaded Pickering to publish the *Songs.* for which he wrote a very suggestive preface. In 1857 he published anonymously a book of his own poems, called *Improvisations from the Spirit.* This is a curiosity as being the second book certainly influenced by Blake ; [1] for Wilkinson had been gathering hints from Blake's writings about a new method for snaring inspiration. He believed that Blake's poems were written entirely automatically ; and he found that he could also produce verses in the same way. He explained his method carefully in a terminal note : ' A theme is chosen and written down. As soon as this is done, the first impression upon the mind which succeeds the act of writing the title, is the beginning of the evolution of that theme ; no matter how strange or alien the word or phrase may seem. That impression is written down : and then another, and another, until the piece is concluded.' To ensure the proper inspiration, this act must be preceded by prayer. Though no correction is allowed, ' as a rule, it requires twice as long to copy a poem, as to write one.'

Obviously, poems written without ' fervour,' thought, or correction, and which consequently elevate the rhyming instinct above any other mental factor, can hardly equal Blake's work ! All of Wilkinson's poems, excluding a stray phrase here and there, are quite worthless. One or two indeed seem to strike a rich vein of fantasy in their nonsense, such as the poem entitled *Astrology* ; but it is the very nonsense which gives the poems what little power they have. The plainer the sense, the more blatant the insipidity. The influence of Blake's thought may possibly be traced in *Sand-eating* ; but that is all. Needless to add, the versification is perfectly mechanical, and far from Blakean.

In 1855 Mr. and Mrs. Alexander Gilchrist appeared, fascinated by Blake's pictures, and, to a lesser extent, by the simpler poems. When all but one chapter of the book had been written, in 1861, Mr. Gilchrist died ;

---

[1] Both Rossetti and Swinburne mention C. J. Wells as a poet influenced by Blake. Wells was the friend who sent Keats some roses and received a sonnet in return. *Joseph and his Brethren* (published under the pseudonym of H. L. Howard in 1824) seemed to the Pre-Raphaelites a neglected masterpiece ; therefore Rossetti introduced his name in the supplementary chapter to Gilchrist, while Swinburne gave him a high eulogy in the first pages of his *William Blake.* But elsewhere they do not compare him to Blake, but to Shakspere. The truth of the matter is that *Joseph and his Brethren* stylistically is more like Blake's *Edward III.* than any other writings of either poet ; but the resemblance is never startling. Wells may have been remembering the *Auguries of Innocence* (granting that he had read the *MS. Book*) when he wrote such phrases as

> To me a simple flower is cloth'd with thoughts
> That lead the mind to heaven ;

but the parallel is not convincing. Far more like Blake, in style at least, is Wells's sunset :

> A god gigantic habited in gold
> Stepping from off a mount into the sea.

but his widow and Dante Gabriel Rossetti completed the manuscript ; [1] and the book appeared in 1863, under the title of *Pictor Ignotus*.

This book, with its many illustrations and reprints, at once brought Blake's name before the public. Its fund of original material was invaluable ; for the Gilchrists not only had dug up most of Blake's written work, but had also interviewed his old friends, and had even visited many of the old landmarks.

Yet it had two grave faults. The first was the suppression of Blake's more shocking doctrines, and the second was the inexcusable rewriting of various of the poems by Dante Gabriel Rossetti, in order to 'correct' their metres. *The Tyger* itself was not too sacred to escape. Thus a bad tradition was started, which reached its climax under the editorship of William Butler Yeats and Edwin J. Ellis. The first correct text of the complete lyrics did not appear until 1907, in Dr. John Sampson's edition.

Gilchrist's book was widely noticed. The young Swinburne, using to the utmost his acquaintance with Seymour Kirkup and his own poetic intuition, explained for the first time the real nature of Blake's subject-matter. He was, moreover, the first to insist frankly on the more radical doctrines.

Rossetti and Swinburne soon made Blake a byword among the Pre-Raphaelites. They followed Blake implicitly in his doctrines of the imaginative subject, the determinate outline, and the importance of detail. D. G. Rossetti claimed to discover Blake's influence also on the Scottish painter, David Scott, and the English Theodore von Holst. Yet they could not make Blake sufficiently well known to prevent the controller of the railway bookstalls from banning *The Savoy* for July 1896, under the impression that Blake's *Antaeus Setting Virgil and Dante upon the Verge of Cocytus* was by Beardsley.[2]

Meanwhile George MacDonald must have been reading Blake ; for possibly in his *If I Had a Father* (1882), and certainly in his *Lilith* (1895), Blake's thoughts, his mysticism, his poetry, and even his symbolic methods reappear, somewhat changed but recognizable. The main doctrine of *Lilith* is that salvation consists in an escape from the material world into another containing the eternal and splendid reality of everything which seems to exist here. Death is a sleep on a guarded couch (as in Beulah), from which we are sure to wake ; though whether MacDonald followed Blake in saying that life in this world is the only death, can neither be affirmed nor denied. MacDonald's 'Loves' are Blake's 'Fairies'—or rather the State of Innocence ; while his 'Bags' are those hopelessly lost in Experience. MacDonald's ultimate goal is a golden city—Blake's Jerusalem. Blake's philosophical specialties (double vision, the illusion of Time and Space, 'spiritual forms,' etc.) recur again and again in various quaint phrases. We find the name 'Luva.' MacDonald's symbolic method is startlingly the same : his Bulika is, like Blake's Babylon, the Feminine Lust for Selfhood, symbolized both as a woman and a city.

MacDonald's masterpiece, *At the Back of the North Wind* (1871), while less aggressively symbolic, is none the less written in Blakean terms. The North Wind represents Nature (who is Death) ; the Land of the Hyper-

---

[1] Rossetti's text begins in the middle of the tenth paragraph of chapter xxxix. : 'This last axiom is open to much more discussion than can be given it here.'

[2] W. B. Yeats, *The Trembling of the Veil* (London, 1922, p. 199).

boreans represents Eternity. The little boy Diamond is a mystic, though of a morbid type. His dreams tell very badly upon his health; and when he finally penetrates Nature (walks *through* the North Wind's heart—Blake's ' Northern Gate ') to the realm behind, it nearly kills him : he is unconscious for a week, and his mind is permanently affected. After his experience, he takes to improvising artless (*very* artless) rhymes ' to the tune of the Hyperborean river '—which is obviously another attempt, like Wilkinson's, to catch Blake's method of turning out Songs of Innocence.

Later writers, especially the Irish, show Blake's influence here and there; but usually only in a single thought or image. Francis Thompson had no books but ' Blake and the Bible.' [1] The *Laocoon* epigram, ' Jesus and his Apostles and Disciples were all Artists,' reappears in Oscar Wilde's *De Profundis* : ' The very basis of [Christ's] nature was the same as that of the nature of the artist—an intense and flamelike imagination. He realized in the entire sphere of human relations that imaginative sympathy which in the sphere of Art is the sole secret of creation.' But as the clever borrower goes on, it appears that Christ and his followers were artists mainly because they lived charming lives; which is far from Blake's conception ! Yeats, whose edition of Blake in 1893 was extremely valuable in giving the public the first general idea of the combination of pictures and text in the Prophetic Books, is naturally touched by Blake. The phrase from *Milton* : ' The Poet's Work is Done. . . . Within a Moment, a Pulsation of the Artery,' is adapted to end *The Vision of Red Hanrahan* in *The Secret Rose* : ' for the gateway of Eternity had opened and closed in a pulsation of the heart.' Edwin J. Ellis, collaborator with Yeats in the 1893 edition, was still more deeply influenced. Not only does his volume of poems, *Fate in Arcadia*, echo Blake continually; his *Seen in Three Days* attempts to combine symbolic verse and obscure illustration in the Blakean fashion. We find the cloud-borders, the winged nudes, the vines and snakes copied everywhere. Among other Irish followers of Blake should be mentioned ' A. E.' (*A Candle of Vision*) and James Stephens (*The Demigods*).

Now Blake has conquered the entire English-speaking world, and is an essential factor in everybody's education. One of the younger English poets, while touring America recently, heard a professional thief in New York recasting *The Everlasting Gospel*. But though Blake is known wherever his native language is spoken, his conquest of the world has only begun. In France, Paul Berger has not only written one of the best books on Blake, but is the French centre of the Blake cult. Articles and translations have also appeared by Milsand (1893), Grolleau (1900), Benoit (1906), Cestre (1906), Alfasser (1908), Doin (1912), and Saurat (1920). In Germany, an article on Blake appeared in the *Vaterlandisches Museum* as early as 1811, while in modern times Kassner (1900), Richter (1906), Zweig (1906) and von Taube (1907) have published illuminating essays. In Denmark, Professor Vilhelm Grønbech has made Blake's name well known in a series of lectures, while Niels Moller has translated some of the lyrics. In Sweden, Anders Österling has also translated several of them. It is said that a complete Russian translation of Blake has appeared at Petrograd. In Japan, there is a very wide-spread Blake cult, which began in the Shira-Kamba group of young poets, the name of whose school is

[1] W. S. Blunt, *My Diaries*, ii. p. 182.

derived from their love of the white birch which grows on the mountains where they take refuge from the world.   Soyetsu Yanagi has published a huge book on Blake, with many illustrations ; Sangu has translated several of the lyrics ; and many articles have appeared in the.*Shira-Kamba* and other magazines.

This swift and wide-spread cult of Blake is significant in that, for all his obscurity, and for all his reputed madness, his doctrines are slowly being found valuable by the entire world.   The evils which he attacked are even stronger now than when he wrote ; and at last the world, be-holding the errors, searches for solutions.   Whether or not Blake's solutions are the only ones may well be doubted ; but, at the very least, he has opened the way to fearless discussion, without which these errors will be triumphant everlastingly.

BLAKE'S "VISIONARY PORTRAIT" OF HIMSELF

APPENDIX

APPENDIX

CONTAINING THE COMMENTARIES ON

POETICAL SKETCHES.

AN ISLAND IN THE MOON.

THERE IS NO NATURAL RELIGION *and* ALL RELIGIONS ARE ONE.

SONGS OF INNOCENCE.

SONGS OF EXPERIENCE.

LATER LYRICS.

TIRIEL.

THE BOOK OF THEL.

THE FRENCH REVOLUTION.

THE MARRIAGE OF HEAVEN AND HELL.

VISIONS OF THE DAUGHTERS OF ALBION.

AMERICA : A PROPHECY.

EUROPE : A PROPHECY.

THE BOOK OF URIZEN.

THE BOOK OF LOS.

THE BOOK OF AHANIA.

THE SONG OF LOS.

THE FOUR ZOAS.

MILTON.

JERUSALEM.

THE GHOST OF ABEL.

POETICAL SKETCHES

COMMENTARY

The first six poems are already freed from the ' modern bondage of riming,' [1] being in that extremely difficult and rare form, lyrical blank verse. For parallels we must go to Poe's second poem *To Helen* and to Tennyson's *Summer Night*. Nothing could be more conventional than apostrophes to the four seasons : Spenser had set the example in *The Faerie Queene,* and Chatterton re-enacted the pageant in his *Elegy on Mr. Phillips.* Blake certainly had read the former ; but if there is any influence of the latter, it can be felt only, not seen. The critics agree, however, that in these poems Blake was much nearer the future than the past.

To SPRING. Cf. Milton's translation of Horace's *Fifth Ode*, Lib. I. :

> What slender Youth, bedew'd with liquid odours,
> Courts thee on Roses in some pleasant Cave,
> > *Pyrrha* for whom bind'st thou
> > In wreathes thy golden Hair
> Plain in thy neatness ?

To SUMMER.
Line 12. *Silk draperies.* Mr. H. G. Hewlett, a critic of the surly, genius-denying type, points out that Summer in *The Faerie Queene* (2nd Canto of *Mutabilitie*, xxxix. 2) is ' dight in a thin silken cassock ' (Pt. I. p. 765).

To AUTUMN. A. C. Benson finds it hard to believe that this poem does not include the germ of Keats's *Ode to Autumn* ; but his reference to ' merry summer smiling under the oak ' is difficult to find in either poet.
Line 1. *Laden with fruit.* Hewlett again points out that in *The Faerie Queene* (2nd Canto of *Mutabilitie*, xxx. 3) Autumn is ' laden with fruits.' We know that Blake had read Spenser ; otherwise parallel descriptions of this god would be almost unavoidable. Chatterton, for example, gives Autumn quite the same attributes :

> When golden Autumn wreathed in ripened corn
> From purple clusters prest the foamy wine.

Line 5. R. H. Shepherd (introduction to the *Poetical Sketches*, p. x) points out the same symbol for the months in Tennyson's *Gardener's Daughter*, 195-196 :

> The daughters of the year
> One after one, thro' that still garden passed.

Landor's *Acon and Rhodope* (*Hellenics*), 1847, begins :

> The year's twelve daughters had in turn gone by.

Lines 13-14. Dante in his *Paradiso*, xxx. 67, describes the angelic spirits in the River of Light as ' inebriate dagli odori.'

To WINTER. Here Blake abandoned (if he ever considered) the Spenserian conception of Winter, changing him from a feeble old man to a furious monster. R. H. Shepherd, worried by Blake's excellent and deliberate metre, says (p. xi) : ' Though it opens vigorously, it soon falls into the pseudo-Ossianic grandiloquence of which there is also a taint in several other pieces, and the last three lines, stumbling

---

[1] Surely encouraged by Milton's translation of Horace's *Fifth Ode* (Lib. I.) and Collins's *Ode to Evening.*

and staggering, remind us irresistibly of the same incongruous blending of sublime and ludicrous images (going on halting feet) in Turner's unfortunate *Fallacies of Hope*.' This is a typical example of blaming everything unpalatable in Blake on Ossian, and is thoroughly mistaken.

Line 11. In some copies Blake himself has deleted the second ' in.'

Line 16. *Mount Hecla*, as all the eighteenth century knew, is a volcano in Iceland. Hewlett compares this line to one from Collins's *Ode to Evening* :

> Winter, yelling through the troublous air.

To the Evening Star. This poem, because of three lines, has become one of the best loved in the English language. Of all the critics, only one, Stopford Brooke, has anything against it, and he almost apologizes. ' The metre halts,' he says, ' but it is a boy who is writing.' Others, however, with more knowledge of blank verse, offset this objection. ' Such perfection is not to be matched by any poet of the eighteenth century,' writes H. D. Traill. But Swinburne is not limited by centuries : ' Nothing at once more noble and more sweet in style was ever written.'

What influenced Blake to choose this subject and write as he did ? Ossian's address to the same star (*Song of Selma*) is beneath any comparison. Perhaps Blake, reading *The Faerie Queene*, was attracted by the lines :

> The whyles his Lord in silver slomber lay
> Like to the evening starre adorn'd with deawy ray

(VI. vii. 19, 8-9), and went into a reverie, where his own poem was written. Saintsbury (*Peace of the Augustans*, p. 304, note) calls it Collinsian. But the nearest resemblances come after Blake's time, in the poems of Tennyson and Keats.

Lines 8-10 are the famous ones. The audacity of ' speak silence with thy glimmering eyes ' is incredible in the eighteenth century.

To Morning. Although there are no metrical difficulties in this poem, Stopford Brooke is uneasy. He says (p. 10) : ' If Shelley could have repaired the metre into his own melody, it would be like one of those lyrics of his which embody the nature-myths of the early world. The poem goes back to such lines as those of Shakspere :

> Look where the dawn, in russet mantle clad,
> Walks o'er the dew of yon high eastern hill ;

and it looks forward to Shelley.' Hewlett, as usual the pedant, strives for further damning parallels. Lines 7-8 are ' identical ' with Collins's picture of Cheerfulness in *The Passions* :

> Cheerfulness, a nymph of healthiest hue,
> Her bow across her shoulders flung,
> Her buskins gemmed with morning dew,
> Blew an inspiring air.

Moreover, he finds in line 4 that *Comus* ' supplied the phrase " chambers of the east." ' A comparison will convince the reader, however, that all these quoted parallels are entirely unimportant. They are not close enough to carry conviction of any undue influence.

Fair Elenor. This poem is distinctly of the ' charnel ' school, which was soon to become very popular through the influence of Mrs. Radcliffe's novels. Where did Blake get his inspiration ? Certainly not from Ossian, nor from Walpole's *Castle of Otranto* (I say this in spite of almost every critic, including W. M. Rossetti, Arthur Symons, and Saintsbury), since neither of these works deals with decomposition. The latter indeed describes a skeleton in a monk's costume, but there is no smell of mortality. Mrs. Radcliffe's novels were all posterior to Blake's poem.

The secret is that the charnel atmosphere was always lurking somewhere in English literature. The churchyard was the centre of every town, and, until the

last century, it was invariably in shocking condition.   Shakspere used a considerable amount of charnel accessories ; and Shakspere was Blake's likeliest source
of inspiration.   Stanza 4 is quite similar to

> Shut me nightly in a charnel house,
> O'er-covered quite with dead men's rattling bones,
> With reeky shanks, and yellow chapless skulls ;
> Or bid me go into a new-made grave
> And hide me with a dead man in his shroud.
> —*Romeo and Juliet*, IV. i. 81-85.

> Where bloody Tybalt, yet but green in earth,
> Lies festering in his shroud ; where, as they say,
> At some hours in the night spirits resort.
> —*Romeo and Juliet*, IV. iii. 43-45.

Stanza 16 is still closer to :

> I am thy father's spirit. . . .
> Thus was I, sleeping, by a brother's hand,
> Of life, of crown, of queen, at once dispatch'd.
> —*Hamlet*, I. v.

But perhaps it is unnecessary to go back so far.   ' The fondness of the eighteenth
century for gloom found expression in a number of notable works . . . for example,
Young's *Night Thoughts* (1742-8), Blair's *Grave* (1745), and the less known *Night*
(1782) of Ralph in poetry, and in prose James Hervey's *Meditations among the
Tombs* (1745-6),' writes R. D. Havens.[1] Blake illustrated both Young and Blair
at length, and made one picture for Hervey.   Professor Havens continues, quoting
from Warton's *Pleasures of Melancholy* :

> But when the world
> Is clad in Midnight's raven-colour'd robe,
> 'Mid hollow charnel let me watch the flame
> Of taper dim, shedding a livid glare
> O'er the wan heaps ; while airy voices talk
> Along the glimm'ring wall ; or ghastly shape
> At distance seen, invites with beck'ning hand
> My lonesome steps, thro' the far-winding vaults.

   Blake, then, got his inspiration from such poets ; while Ossian and *Otranto*
are of a different sort.   To the established atmosphere Blake adds nothing ; even
his telling of the story is characteristic of the ' Gothic ' novel, for the mystery is not
explained until the end.   Yet even here Blake found the nice mean between the
purely supernatural and the purely rational, for the words that fall from the dead
head might easily be explained as a hallucination due to Elenor's overwrought
nerves.
   ' Fair Elenor,' happily married, has become the object of a Duke's passion.   He
conceives that the best way to win her is to get rid of her husband.   Elenor, on the
way to the spot of the projected murder, is met by the murderer, who, mistaking
her for a servant, gives her the dead man's head, with an injunction to deliver it
—to herself !   She hurries home with it, and after a lament, whose beauty lifts
one for a moment to another plane, her nerves give way ; the head of her husband
seems to speak ; and the shock kills her.
   Blake, as I have said, added nothing to the established atmosphere ; but what
he wrote was among the very best of its class.   The slow unfolding of the tragedy,
the tense, well-felt emotions, and the general impressionistic treatment of the
whole, plus the seven exquisite lines of the lament, worthy of Deirdre or Iseult,
make the poem one of great power.   To reject it, one must first reject all of its
kind, which is in itself an absurdity.
   Stanza 9.   A reference to *Psalm* xci. 5-6.

---

[1] Raymond D. Havens : *Literature of Melancholy* ; *Modern Language Notes*, Nov. 1909.

Stanzas 11-13. This lament has won praise from critics who could not endure the rest of the poem. Line 45 might have been suggested by Ossian's

> Thou hast fallen in darkness like a star.
>
> —*Fingal*, Bk. I.

Stanza 17 was later echoed by Blake in an epigram against Hayley:

> And when he could not act upon my wife,
> Hired a villain to bereave my life.

What Blake meant by this epigram has been a puzzle to commentators, and will be dealt with in its place. 'Blake's use of *bereave* as a transitive verb is perhaps imitative of the line quoted by him from Chaucer, in his *Descriptive Catalogue*:

> Hath me bireft my beauty and my pith.

(Sampson, 1905, p. 11).

FIVE SONGS. But what is to be said of the five *Songs* which follow? The majority of the critics rapturously quote them, each one dropping the gift of a new superlative upon them. In the efforts to gauge Blake's genius, comparisons have been invoked with Raleigh, Marlowe, Shakspere, Beaumont and Fletcher (particularly Fletcher), Ben Jonson, Webster, Shirley, Milton, Chatterton, Keats, Shelley, Wordsworth, Tennyson, and even Poe. But there are dissenting notes from those who feel the Elizabethan reminiscence more strongly than the poetry itself. Let us confess at once that the parallels are obvious; but that granted (and remember a boy wrote them!), the freshness, the melody, and the handling is of the very highest. This becomes a miracle not to be pooh-poohed, when we consider not only Blake's age, but the Age in which he wrote them. Nothing like them had been done for a century and a half. Blake was reintroducing a truth of ecstasy which had been long absent. After familiarity with Blake and his sources, it seems fairest and truest to admit them 'more directly imitative than his later work; yet this is due less to slavish copying than to an unconscious recognition of the community between his own romantic spirit and that of our older poetry' (Wallis, p. 182).

HOW SWEET I ROAM'D. According to the reliable authority of Malkin (*Father's Memoirs*, 1806), this exquisite lyric was written when Blake was fourteen. It is Blake's first protest against marriage, playful enough now, but later to become quite bitter. The 'golden cage' of line 12 is explained by Quid's song in *An Island in the Moon*: 'Matrimony's golden cage.'

Line 10 'betrays the *fadeur* of the eighteenth century,' according to W. M. Rossetti (note, p. cxv); but this does not taint the poem's beauty in the least.

MY SILKS AND FINE ARRAY. This is the lament of a deserted maiden, in the style of *Come away, Come away, Death* (*Twelfth Night*) and *Lay a Garland on my Hearse* (*Maid's Tragedy*). The third stanza also suggests the Gravedigger's song in *Hamlet*. Saintsbury, Symons, and Thomson also point out that only Chatterton did anything approaching it in the eighteenth century, and he 'was archaic consciously and with intent' (Thomson, p. 244); which certainly cannot be said of this poem. *The Westminster Review* (January 1864), on its dignity as a critic, remarked that it is 'sufficiently remarkable . . . whether the reader recognize or not what Mr. Gilchrist calls its shy evanescent tints or aroma, as of pressed rose-leaves. In spite of its sweetness and harmony, it is, in our opinion, rather the contemplation of a passion than the expression of any personal experience of it.' But perhaps we show a small spirit in quoting such judicious comments.

LOVE AND HARMONY COMBINE. This poem is composed of pure verbal music and clear, delectable images; further comment is unnecessary.

I LOVE THE JOCUND DANCE. 'A simple and pastoral gaiety which the poets of a refined age have generally found more difficult of attainment than the glitter of wit, or the affectation of antithesis,' wrote Malkin (p. 325). ' The opening verses . . . are a diluted paraphrase of a passage in *L'Allegro*,' wrote Hewlett (p. 765), straining unusually hard to prove Blake a plagiarist, but not naming just which passage in *L'Allegro* he referred to.

Line 11. ' A monstrous line, alluding. I believe, to bread,' pompously proclaims A. C. Benson (p. 154).

Line 18. *Kitty.* Catherine Boucher had not met Blake when these poems were written ; but surely it was easy—not to say tactful—to change a ' Polly ' to a ' Kitty ' before sending the poems to the printer.

MEMORY, HITHER COME. This song is surely second only to *How Sweet I Roam'd*, in spite of its reminiscences. The opening lines obviously come from :

> And tune his merry note
> Unto the sweet bird's throat,
> Come hither, come hither, come hither !
> —*As You Like It*, II. v.

The last lines might have been suggested by *Il Penseroso* or by any of the Elizabethans who rhymed ' valley ' and ' melancholy.' Hewlett finds parallels less convincing than ever ; while R. H. Shepherd (p. 22) finds another in the opening lines of Tennyson's sonnet published in *The Englishman's Magazine* of August 1831.

MAD SONG. This poem ' shows that a new birth of prosody had come. . . . For pure verse effect—assisted powerfully by diction, of course, and not to be divorced from thought, but existing independently of it—there are few pieces in English or any language to beat this marvellous thing. And it is very noticeable that its ineffable music is really prosodic, not musical at all. . . . The scheme is very simple, and capable of being defined with rigid accuracy . . . yet, as you read, the thing shifts, outline and texture and shade, like the " rustling beds of dawn " themselves. . . . Nobody in the eighteenth century, not even Chatterton, had yet returned to the true blend of freedom and order in English prosody with such a perfect result as this.'—Saintsbury : *Prosody*, III. 11-13.

I feel fairly sure, yet hazard it only as supposition, that this fascinating shift of metre was due to a musical melody which accompanied the words in Blake's head as he wrote them. There are very few changes of metre as unobtrusive and intangible as this in all English poetry. I can recall but two cases : the Prologue's song in the play within the old play of *Sir Thomas More* (IV. i.) and John Clare's *There's the Daisy, the Woodbine.*

Southey found Blake's poem worth reprinting in his *Doctor* (vol. **vi.** 1847), but as a curiosity only. To some this song would be appropriate in the mouth of Edgar on the heath ; Swinburne says Webster might have signed it ; Symons claims, however, that if it has ' the hint of any predecessor in our literature, it is to be found in the abrupt energy and stormy masculine splendour of the High Priest's Song in *Aella*, " Ye who hie in mokie ayre " ' (*Romantic Movement*, p. 39). Hewlett, naturally, disagrees ; calls the thing ' really a mosaic of reminiscences ' ; then, with a Shakspere *Concordance* open under his left arm, he notes the most unconvincing parallels. The best of these are as follows : lines 5-6, from Milton's *Comus* : ' Ere the blabbing Eastern scout, The nice Morn on th' *Indian* steep, From her cabin'd loophole peep ' ; line 21 from ' I turn thy head unto the east ' (*Faithful Shepherdess*) or ' We must lay his head to the east ' (*Cymbeline*) ; and line 22, ' comforts should increase ' (*Othello*, II. i.).

Line 7. *Beds of dawn.* There has been a good deal of controversy whether ' beds ' is not a misprint for ' birds.' The change was first made by Gilchrist (VI. p. 50),[1] and adopted by all the early Blake editors. Sampson (1905, p. 3) called this change ' violent ' and ' unwarranted ' ; and Saintsbury was also

---

[1] D. G. Rossetti is invariably blamed for this change, which he only endorsed.

amazed : ' The imagery of the poem is atmospheric, and the phrase " *beds* of dawn " for the clouds whence sun and wind issue is infinitely fine ' (*Prosody*, III. 11).   But H. J. C. Grierson (*London Times*, Oct. 9, 1919) defends Gilchrist's change by appealing to rival readings in Blake's works.   ' Does Blake use the epithet " rustling," and the image of birds scorning the earth elsewhere ?   He does, and in a way which gives a definite meaning to the epithet and a precise image.'   Quotations from the *Visions of the Daughters of Albion*, 48-51, and *Milton*, 31 : 28-35, prove conclusively that Blake did think of larks *rustling* in the dawn as they rise to greet it.   However, Blake, who could hear the Evening Star speaking silence with her eyes, was also capable of hearing the clouds rustle when they, too, rise from the earth in the dawn.   But it rather seems that Mr. Grierson is right, since Dr. Keynes records two copies of the *Poetical Sketches* in which Blake himself made the alteration (p. 78).

Line 8.   *Scorn*.   ' If anybody objects to the " cockney " rhyme of " dawn " and " scorn," he may " go shake his ears," which are probably long enough to wave like the reeds that told the story of Midas.'—Saintsbury : *Prosody*, III. 11. Were it not for ' morning ' in line 5, and for a similar false rhyme of ' lawn ' and ' morn ' in the subsequent poem, I should be tempted to believe that ' dawn ' was a slip of the pen, or even a misprint, for ' morn.'

Line 9.   *Vault*.   ' " Vaut " for rhyme has complete justification.'—Saintsbury : *Prosody*, III. 13.

Lines 9-10.   ' There is abundance of evidence, besides what has been given, that the celestial sea forms the floor of the over-world ; our dome being the under side of the pavement, as in these lines of Blake.'—W. R. Lethaby : *Architecture, Mysticism, and Myth* (New York, 1892).   This is the first appearance of Blake's ' Mundane Shell.'

FRESH FROM THE DEWY HILL.   This poem, which is not Elizabethan, is still less of the eighteenth century.   It is sincere, easy, and burns with all the pure fire of a first love.   Berger (p. 242) finds it almost inhuman : ' This is the knight's mute adoration of his ideal lady, the mystic's love for the Virgin who comes down to him from Heaven in a golden nimbus.   But it is not the passion that burns in man's blood, the eternal love of Paolo and Francesca.'   Nevertheless, such was Blake's attitude : on his death-bed he told his wife that ' she had been ever an angel to him.'

Technically, the poem is most remarkable for the rhyming experiments in the first three stanzas—rhymes which Gilchrist (v.) strangely calls ' hackneyed ' !

WHEN EARLY MORN.   This poem is in the same vein as the preceding one, but is weakened by a rather silly last stanza.

Line 1.   Cf. ' While the still morn went out with Sandals gray ' (*Lycidas*, l. 187) and ' Till morning fair Came forth with Pilgrim steps, in amice gray ' (*Paradise Regained*, IV. 426-427).

Line 6.   Already Blake notes the power of Imagination over Nature.

TO THE MUSES.   This, the last of the great poems in the *Poetical Sketches*, deals in the perfect verbal music of Gray.   It is thoroughly of the eighteenth century, and shows what its strict and deliberate technique could produce in a master's hand.   Each effect is subdued, balanced, and perfectly placed.   No critic has passed it by without some word of commendation.   ' In these lines the eighteenth century dies to music.'—Symons : *Romantic Movement*, p. 40.

GWIN, KING OF NORWAY.   This ballad, whose form was taken from Percy's *Reliques*, whose substance is from Chatterton's *Godred Crovan*, and whose imagery is Ossian's, ends with a Blakean moral : that kings who cause war will have much to answer for in the after-life.   This theme embodies the struggle of freedom against feudalism, and therefore is the first of Blake's revolutionary poems. Gordred himself is an early incarnation of Orc, who figures so prominently in the Prophetic

Books, from *A Song of Liberty* onward ; and Gordred's sleep in his cave, from which he is awakened by the cry against tyranny, is quite in the manner of Blake's later symbolism. So we may also assume that this is Blake's first symbolic poem. It was hastily written : words are repeated in close proximity, and there are ' clouds ' enough to sate Ossian himself.

The influence of Percy is limited entirely to the use of the old and virile ballad form. In Blake's day ballads were smooth and sentimental affairs, dealing with the loves of Edwin and Angelina, or with Black-eyed Susan and her Sailor-boy. Percy's collection of the earliest English poetry showed Blake how to use a rougher and gustier metre.

The influence of Chatterton is interesting, since it dates this poem after June 1778, when *Godred Crovan, A Poem*, was included in Chatterton's *Miscellanies*. Godred and Godwin, two of the important characters, remind one of Blake's Gordred and Gwin ; ' the wolf of Norway ' is mentioned, against whom a successful battle is fought.

The unblushing use of Ossianic imagery shows what a tremendous influence Macpherson's poems were then exercising. Blake's sixth stanza is clearly from : ' They came like streams from the mountains ; each rushed roaring from his hill ' (*Fingal*, Bk. I.). L. A. Paton (*Poet-Lore*, Oct. 1893) finds other parallels in *Cath-Loda* and *Temora*. The tenth stanza is from another passage in *Fingal* (Bk. IV.) : ' Like the clouds that gather to a tempest in the blue face of the sky ; so met the sons of the desart, round the terrible voice of Fingal.' Lines 41-42 ' can hardly be irreminiscent of those who " stood silent around as the stones of Loda " in the second *Duan* of *Cath-Loda* '—Saintsbury : *Prosody*, III. 13, note. The eighteenth stanza is again from *Fingal* (Bk. I.) : ' As the troubled noise of the ocean when roll the waves on high ; as the last peal of the thunder of heaven, such is the noise of battle. . . . As roll a thousand waves to the rocks, so Swaren's host came on ; as meets a rock a thousand waves, so Inisfail met Swaran.' The name of Barraton (line 53) is ' probably a reminiscence of " Berrathon " in Macpherson's *Ossian*, a piece from which Blake would also seem to have borrowed the name " Leutha " in the *Visions of the Daughters of Albion* ' (Sampson, 1905, p. 19).

The twenty-sixth stanza alone is worth preserving ; otherwise, this poem is distinctly unpalatable—to modern taste, at least.

AN IMITATION OF SPENSER. Both before and after Blake's day, imitations of Spenser were popular. Pope's youthful *Alley* ; Thomson's *Castle of Indolence* ; John Armstrong's four stanzas written for inclusion in that poem—were early examples. After Blake we find Beattie, Gilbert West, Scott, Byron, Shelley, Keats, and Tennyson all playing with this form. Blake's six spenserians are, in Mr. Sampson's words, ' all different and all wrong ' ; but even so he came closer to the original form than the laureate Warton, whose *Pastoral in the Manner of Spenser* is composed of six-line stanzas !

Line 13. *Leesing nurse.* ' Read with all Blake's editors, leasing nurse, *i.e.* one who holds her charge in a lease or leash ' (Sampson, 1905, p. 22).

BLIND MAN'S BUFF. This is the eighteenth century's cult of the rural, distinguished by the moral (startling enough from Blake !) that ' laws were made to keep fair play.'

Lines 1-2. Cf. :

> When icicles hang by the wall,
> And Dick the shepherd blows his nail.
> —*Love's Labour 's Lost*, v. ii.

The rhyme of ' clothes ' and ' nose ' has excellent authority, the best known being Herrick's :

> When as in silks my Julia goes
> Then, then, me thinks, how sweetly flowes
> That liquefaction of her clothes.
> —*Hesperides.*

A closer parallel, with icicle, rhyme, and all, is in *Mother Goose* :

> Milk-man, milk-man, where have you been ?
> In Buttermilk channel up to my chin,
> I spilt my milk and I spoilt my clothes
> And got a long icicle hung to my nose.

Blake well may have known this rhyme, though the earliest edition of *Mother Goose* yet discovered is dated 1780.

Line 13. Dolly's fall suggests Puck's prank in the *Midsummer Night's Dream*, II. i. :

> The wisest aunt, telling the saddest tale,
> Sometime for three-foot stool mistaketh me ;
> Then slip I from her bum, down topples she,
> And 'tailor' cries, and falls into a cough ;
> And then the whole quire hold their hips and loff
> And waxen in their mirth, and neeze, and swear
> A merrier hour was never wasted there.

Line 49. *Hodge* is, of course, Roger.

KING EDWARD THE THIRD. Blake's admiration for Shakspere went so far as to inspire a historical play on a king to whom scant dramatic justice had been done. The play was never finished ; indeed, we cannot imagine (except by consulting history) what Blake intended to do with his characters, for he had not the slightest sign of dramatic ability. He could not tell an extended story any more now than when he wrote *Jerusalem*. The slender plot of *Fair Elenor* is cleverly arranged ; and *Tiriel* is marred only slightly by its surface meaninglessness ; but aside from these (and possibly the fragment of *The French Revolution*), Blake was quite innocent of the art of knotting and unknotting an episode. *King Edward the Third* is even an exception to the rule that every one can write a good first act. There is absolutely no conflict of ideals or personalities ; the only substitute for these essentials is the bustle preceding a battle. The play leads nowhere ; Blake wisely never tried to finish it.

But granting that *King Edward the Third* is not even the beginning of a drama, we find that it remains a great fragment of poetry. The versification is well sustained, always interesting, and never mistaken. There are many passages of a fine exaltation ; and the terminal chant is one of Blake's very best poems. The imagery throughout is clear-cut and colourful, never running into preciosity or the obscurity of symbolism. From this point of view, *King Edward the Third* is one of the very few close approaches to Shakspere, in spite of a restrained Ossianic chiaroscuro.

The philosophy of the piece is solid, and generously idealistic at times ; but at best it remains adolescent and never plumbs any depths. The main theme is the praise of England and her battles. Patriotism is hymned in a way that Blake never repeated. Liberty also, curiously enough, twice appears, unabashed among royalty, and receives her share of praise.

Another fault of the piece is that it shows no penetrating study of character. The prince and his companions are demi-gods in golden armour rather than mortals. Indeed, the only human being seems to be a sketch of the British grognard, Dagworth ; who is not too cleverly set off against his servant William. William's simple wisdom, however, is apparently designed to expose the errors of his master.

But in spite of its lack of drama and character, *King Edward the Third* is surprisingly Shaksperean. It has been called Miltonic in several essays with much less reason ; in fact, only one line (iii. 290) shows at all the influence of that poet.

Scene I. Line 15. A characteristic thought.

Scene II. Lines 9-10. R. H. Shepherd compares Blake's image to one in Tennyson's *Exhibition Ode*, 1862 :

> Let the fair white-wing'd peacemaker fly
> To happy havens under all the sky.

Lines 10-11. The juxtaposition of ' gold ' and ' silver ' is characteristically Elizabethan ; as in Macbeth's line :

' His silver skin lac'd with his golden blood '
—(II. iii. 119).

Lines 24 *seq.* How Blake's views changed later may be clearly seen by comparing this passage with lines 128 *seq.* of the *Visions of the Daughters of Albion.*

Scene III. ' The scene before Cressy is a modification of that before Agincourt (*Henry V.* Act IV.), the imitation being carried to the point of mimicking Fluellen's Welsh brogue,' writes Mr. Hewlett (p. 763). The Welsh brogue is limited to one phrase of six words.

Lines 116-117. Mr. A. C. Benson finds pleasure in this ' kind of fantastic image belonging to the mystic side of nature ' (p. 154).

Lines 224-231. Precisely this sort of passage had already been burlesqued by Sheridan in his *Critic* (1779) :

Puff : . . . This is one of the most useful figures we tragedy writers have, by which a hero or heroine, in consideration of their being obliged to overlook things that *are* on the stage, is allowed to hear and see a number of things that are not.

Sneer : Yes : a kind of poetical second-sight.

Puff : Yes. Now then, madam.

Tilburnia :   ' I see their decks
' Are clear'd ! I see the signal made !
' The line is formed ! a cable's length asunder !
' I see the frigates station'd in the rear ;
' And now I hear the thunder of the guns !
' I hear the victor's shouts ! I also hear
' The vanquish'd groan ! and now 'tis smoke—and now
' I see the loose sail shiver in the wind !
' I see—I see—what soon you 'll see——'

Governor : ' Hold, daughter ! peace ! this love hath turn'd thy brain :
' The Spanish fleet thou *canst* not see ; because
' —It is not yet in sight ! '

Dangle : Egad, though, the governor seems to make no allowance for this poetical figure you talk of.

Puff : No, a plain matter-of-fact man ; that 's his character.
—*The Critic : or, A Tragedy Rehearsed*, II. ii.

No wonder Mr. Cheney found that Blake's lines ' remind us of the old masters of the drama ' ! (p. 173).

Lines 272-275 anticipate Blake's later thought.

Scene IV. Line 2. Cf. ' Ingratitude's the Growth of · every Clime ' (Dryden's *Don Sebastian*, III. i. ; quoted in Bysshe's *Art of Poetry*).

Line 9. *Is it a little creeping root ?* ' In a single sentence, Blake transports his readers to another world. . . . The words are relentless as a beam of morning light—and suddenly we are aware that this Victory is a painted hag, Liberty cross-eyed, and the rest of our good company not so reputable as they seemed. The flash of revelation was no prepared effect, but came as swift and momentary to Blake as it comes to his readers now. Dagworth makes the only possible answer—answering for the " other soul " in Blake. " Thou dost not understand me, William." William will never understand ' (*Poetry Review*, March-April 1916.)

Scene v. Line 6. *Wons*, a Spenserian word, meaning ' dwells.'

Scene VI., entirely composed of the Minstrel's song, is the climax and the end of *King Edward the Third.* In it Blake celebrates the mythological history of England, according to Geoffrey of Monmouth (I. xvi.). Brutus the Trojan, grandson of Æneas, was supposed to have first settled Great Britain, after conquering the Giants who were its primeval inhabitants. Blake's poem ends with Brutus's prophecy of British naval glory and its liberty. According to Geoffrey (I. xi.), the prophecy came from Diana : ' Ipsis totius terrae subditus orbis erit.' Blake makes Brutus prophesy only Britain's naval supremacy.

When D. G. Rossetti reprinted this poem in Gilchrist, he made so many revisions that he practically rewrote it. I do not think that any one has preferred the revised version.

It is quite possible that Blake's symbolism is to be traced. The island surrounded by the Sea of Time and Space, inhabited only by savage Giants, ' the enormous sons of Ocean,' suggests the Natural Man. Trojan Brutus and his men, fresh from the slaughter of the Greeks (which to Blake later represented the deadly sway of Reason), may well be the immortal part of Man conquering his lower part. ' Their nest is in the sea, but they shall roam / Like eagles for the prey,' certainly implies Man living in this body, but extending his reign far beyond it ; all the more as the Eagle was later to become the symbol of Genius. Even if Blake in 1783 did not consider this as symbolic, he certainly used it later, when he took ' Albion ' as his symbol for Man.

Stanza 7. The comparison of the sensation of prophecy to the sensation of an inrush of sea is also used by Byron in his *Prophecy of Dante* (written 1819) :

> Woe ! woe ! the veil of coming centuries
> Is rent—a thousand years which yet supine
> Lie like the ocean waves ere winds arise,
> Heaving in dark and sullen undulation,
> Float from eternity into these eyes.
>
> —*Canto* II.

Shelley also felt eternity, as seen in prophecy, to be like an ocean :

> And their swords and their sceptres I floating see
> Like wrecks, in the surge of eternity.
> —*Rosalind and Helen*, II. 900-901 ; also *To William Shelley.*

Beddoes, in his turn, wrote :

> Futurity
> Broods on the ocean, hatching 'neath her wing,
> Invisible to man, the century.
> —*Clock Striking at Midnight.*

Line 51. *Prevented,* even as late as the early eighteenth century, was commonly used as meaning ' anticipated.'

PROLOGUE FOR KING EDWARD THE FOURTH. This bit of blank verse expresses the horror and intoxication of war, as a whirlwind of fury from the throne of God, an outpouring of Sin, for which the rulers alone are responsible.

Lines 1-2 were evidently suggested by the *Chorus* in Shakspere's *Henry the Fifth* :

> O ! for a Muse of fire, that would ascend
> The brightest heaven of invention !

PROLOGUE TO KING JOHN. This is the first of Blake's attempts to extend the boundaries of blank verse, by combining all its cadences into a solid block of prose. The poems of Ossian are also printed in prose, though they are quite metrical ; beyond any doubt Blake got his idea from Macpherson. Mrs. Barbauld's *Hymns in Prose* have been suggested as Blake's model ; but this does not seem likely since they are completely non-metrical, even non-cadenced, in spite of her preface explaining that they are. According to Lafcadio Hearn (*Interpretations of Literature,* vol. I. p. 56), Blake's poetical prose, which is ' very much finer than most of Whitman's work,' influenced ' beyond question ' Coleridge's ' one wonderful piece of prose-poetry called *The Wanderings of Cain.* Coleridge got his inspiration from Blake, and passed it on to Bulwer Lytton, who again passed it on to Poe. Thus we may say that Blake's influence indirectly affected most of our nineteenth-century literature of imagination : for there is scarcely any writer of the nineteenth century that has not been a little influenced by Poe.'

A War Song to Englishmen is remarkable only in that it is a dignified bit of patriotic verse. Our own times have taught us what a rare thing this is.

The Couch of Death describes a death-bed vision which overrules the dying youth's previous fear of the God of Justice. There are a few good phrases in this poem, and a great deal of Biblical and Ossianic imitation.

Contemplation describes the struggle of Innocence and Experience. Contemplation is evidently the spontaneous Joy of Life, even the Poetic Instinct, which declares that the world is a wonderful place ; but the youth feels that ' his flesh is a prison, his bones the bars of death,' and that Sorrow has accompanied him all his life.

The melancholy, which later inspired the *Songs of Experience*, here seems conventional and affected. There are two or three ingenious figures and two or three lines of excellent poetry ; otherwise *Contemplation* includes all the faults of this kind of verse.

Samson is a strange mixture of the Bible, Milton, and Ossian. Blake evidently thought well of it, since he selected it as the terminal poem for the *Poetical Sketches*. It certainly is the best of what we may inaccurately call his ' polyphonic prose.' The variety of its cadence, which is not to be found in Ossian, is an imitation of Milton's *Samson Agonistes*.

R. H. Shepherd, Garnett, and Cheney have pointed out various resemblances to Tennyson. The most striking of the parallels are to be found in *Merlin and Vivien*. Blake wrote, ' Thou art my God ! ' and Tennyson caused Vivien in a similar situation to ' Call him her lord, her silver star of eve, / Her god, her Merlin.' Blake wrote : ' Thus, in false tears, she bath'd his feet, and thus she day by day oppressed his soul : he seemed a mountain, his brow among the clouds ; she seemed a silver stream, his feet embracing ' ; Tennyson wrote :

> There lay she all her length and kiss'd his feet,
> As if in deepest reverence and love.
> A twist of gold was round her hair, a robe
> Of samite without price, that more exprest
> Than hid her, clung about her lissome limbs,
> In colour like the satin-shining palm
> Of sallows in the windy gleams of March.

Is it possible that Tennyson once read this anonymous volume of Blake's and then forgot it—but forgot it not entirely ?

Warfare : W. M. Rossetti suggests that this might be a misprint for ' wayfare.'

AN ISLAND IN THE MOON

COMMENTARY

A complete but inaccurate text is to be found in Mr. E. J. Ellis's *Real Blake*, chapter viii.

CHAPTER I

The text begins : ' In the Moon is a certain Island, near by a mighty continent, which small island seems to have some affinity to England, & what is more extraordinary, the people are so much alike, & their language so much the same, that you would think you was among your friends.' EY (I. 187) comment : ' This recalls a verse of Shelley's *Peter Bell* about the

> city much like London,
> A populous, and a smoky city.'

However, the things still remain, and the vanities are the same. This is an early version of ' The Spiritual States of the Soul are all Eternal ' (*Jerusalem*, 52).

The three Philosophers at this time were each endeavouring to conceal his laughter not at them, but at his own imagination. This throws a little light on Blake's own state of mind in company.

CHAPTER II

This, in its brevity, is quite Sternelike. Tilly Lally's name is obviously derived from ' Tilley-valley ! ', the exclamation made famous by Sir Thomas More's wife.

CHAPTER III

As Phebus stood over his Oriental Gardening : i.e., as the sun rose. Is this a quotation from some old play or popular song ?

CHAPTER IV

Mrs. Sinagain must be Mrs. Gibble Gabble. The following speech, ' I 'm sure you ought to hold your tongue,' is spoken by Mrs. Jistagatint.

The end of this chapter is also in the manner of Sterne.

CHAPTER V

Lowering darkness hovered over the Assembly. In *The French Revolution* the clouds are to continue this kind of sympathetic action.

In the first place I think. Cf. ' Je pense, donc je suis ' of Descartes.

CHAPTER VI

Ghiotto : an intentional misspelling to show their unintentional mispronun- . ciation.

In this passage Blake shows his hatred, not so much of surgery (for which, as for any science, he had a great contempt) as of brutal surgeons.

WHEN OLD CORRUPTION FIRST BEGUN. This was suggested by John Gay's *On Quadrille* :

> When as Corruption hence did go,
>   And left the nation free,
> When Ay said ay, and No said no,
>   Without or place or fee ;
> Then Satan, thinking things went ill,
> Sent forth his spirit, call'd Quadrille,
>   Quadrille, Quadrille, etc.

'It may be called Blake's first true symbolic book' (EY, I. 194).   The *dead woman* in the fifth stanza is undoubtedly this mortal flesh.

<h2 style="text-align:center">CHAPTER VII</h2>

A parcel of fools, going to Bristol!   The reader hardly needs to be reminded that the literati were still making trips to Bristol for the purpose of examining the Chatterton manuscripts, to discover whether or no they were modern or ancient.

<h2 style="text-align:center">CHAPTER VIII</h2>

My crop of corn is but a field of tares : 'a line of Chidiock Tichborne's, which Blake may have met with in the *Reliquae Wottonianae*' (Sampson, 1913, p. xxiv).

John Taylor (1694-1761) was a dissenting divine and Hebraist.

Sorrows of Werther (1774) must have been popular at the time.   This is one of Blake's very rare references to German literature.

Vaxhaul and Raneleigh : Vauxhall and Ranelagh, celebrated public gardens.

PHEBE AND JELLICOE.   Though this has more in it of insipidity than simplicity, I imagine that Blake wrote it as a serious poem.   *The Pilgrim* in the 11th line is of course Blake himself, the traveller on life's journey, who cannot stop to join the innocent merriment.

<h2 style="text-align:center">CHAPTER IX</h2>

This drunken chapter is packed full of nonsense verses.   One of them, *I cry my matches as far as Guildhall*, seems to have been a street cry.   *This frog he would a wooing ride* is, of course, a well-known nursery rhyme.

HAIL MATRIMONY, MADE OF LOVE! which is prefaced by the cry, 'English Genius for ever,' was 'perhaps suggested,' both in subject and metre, 'by "He that intends to take a wife," *Pills to purge Melancholy*, iii. p. 106' (Sampson, 1905, p. 55).

TO BE OR NOT TO BE is a song upon 'Thomas Sutton, founder of Charterhouse (1532-1611)' (Sampson, 1905, p. 56).   *Dr. South* and *Sherlock* were Dr. Robert South (1634-1716) and Dr. William Sherlock (1641-1707), dean of St. Paul's, who had a rather famous controversy upon Socinianism.   Sherlock's *Practical Discourse concerning Death* appeared in 1689.

Good English hospitality. 'Old English hospitality. . . . By the bye, this is a phrase very much used by the English themselves, both in words and writings ; but I never heard of it out of the island, except by way of irony and sarcasm,' wrote Smollett in *Humphry Clinker*.   Blake was not sarcastic, and used the phrase in good faith.   Sampson (1905, p. 58) compares Blake's poem with the passage 'Old English hospitality is long since deceased' in Chatterton's *Antiquity of Christmas Games (Miscellanies)*, 1778.   This passage concerns the holiday entertainment of the vassals with food and drink.

<h2 style="text-align:center">CHAPTER X</h2>

This chapter is entirely inspired by contempt for science.

Pestilence: possibly symbolic of the modern curse of science, as Blake conceived it.

Flogiston : Blake's spelling of Phlogiston, the supposed principle of inflammability, a chemical theory accepted by Dr. Priestley.

<h2 style="text-align:center">CHAPTER XI</h2>

The first three songs in this chapter are those which appear later as *Songs of Innocence*, with a few unimportant changes.   Blake thought well of them, since after *Holy Thursday* ' they all sat silent for a quarter of an hour,' while the *Nurse's Song,* as it was later called, is here the song of Mrs. Nannicantipot's mother ; and *The Little Boy Lost* was so overwhelming that ' here nobody could sing any longer till Tilly Lally pluck'd up a spirit & he sung ' a song of quite a different nature.

I SAY, YOU JOE. The substitution of ' tansey ' in line 6 for a more offensive word with the same initial was probably suggested by the same word-juggling in chap. xliv. of Smollett's *Roderick Random.*

LEAVE O LEAVE [ME] TO MY SORROWS must be satirical.

THERE 'S DOCTOR CLASH, a comment on imported music. The final stanza is an entire concert in itself, from the entrance of the conductor to the terminal applause :

> Gentlemen !   Gentlemen !
> Rap !   Rap !   Rap !
> Fiddle !   Fiddle !   Fiddle !
> Clap !   Clap !   Clap !

In the middle of the patriotic song *A crowned King,* the gap in the manuscript occurs ; and here the discovery of Blake's invention for printing was described. The next and last page is the most Blakean of them all. Quid and his wife seem to be Mr. and Mrs. Blake. The text commences :

thus Illuminating the Manuscript. Ay said she that would be excellent. Then said he I would have all the lines engraved instead of printed, and at every other leaf a high-finished print, all in three volumes folio, and sell them a hundred pounds apiece. They would print off two thousand said she, whoever will not have them will be ignorant fools and will not deserve to live.

Then follows a curious passage which is a reference to Hamlet's conference with Polonius (III. ii.), where Hamlet tests how they fool him to the top of his bent : ' Do you see that cloud, that 's almost in shape like a camel ? ' Quid says : ' Don't you think I have something of the goat's face ? Very like a goat's face, she answered. I think your face, said he, is like that noble beast the Tyger.' Blake certainly intended to imply that Quid's fantastic actions were, like Hamlet's, not a sign of madness, but of contempt.

But what follows is still more Blakean, ' " Oh, I was at Mrs. Snickersnacker's and I was speaking of my abilities, but their nasty hearts, poor devils, are eat up with envy. They envy me my abilities and all the women envy your abilities.[1] My dear, they hate people who are of higher abilities than their nasty filthy selves. But do you outface them, and then strangers will see you have an opinion. Now I think we should do as much good as we can when we are at Mrs. Femality's. Do you snap and take me up. I will fall into such a passion ! I 'll hollow and stamp and frighten all the people there and show them what truth is." At this instant Obtuse Angle came in. " Oh, I am glad you are come," said Quid.'

So the manuscript ends.

[1] There is a question here just how the conversation alternates between Quid and his wife. Blake's punctuation was always the most inexpressive thing in his writings.

THERE IS NO NATURAL RELIGION AND ALL RELIGIONS ARE ONE

COMMENTARY

DECORATIONS

THERE IS NO NATURAL RELIGION: *Title-page*. The title is inscribed on a Gothic door. This truth is the gate to Mystical Religion.

Frontispiece. An aged couple sit beneath a tree. Two nude youths stand before them.

Argument. A woman and two children engaged in reading and writing. Instruction by the mother seems to have been to Blake the true method of beginning an education. He repeated the idea on the *Title-page* to the *Songs of Innocence*.

1. An old man, leaning on his staff, looks at his dog.

2. A mother restrains her child, who is reaching after a bird. This design is repeated in Blake's illustrations for Young's *Night Thoughts*.

3. An angel preaches to a bearded man.

4. A 'natural' or idiot (I call him such since he wears the plumed hat which Blake makes the badge of his type in the *Night Thoughts*) plays on a pipe beneath a tree.

5. A child reaches towards a swan.

6. A man reclines under vegetation.

Conclusion. This plate has no decoration except for a few curved lines.

Frontispiece to Part II. A woman inspires a nude youth to rise. The background consists of two Gothic panels.

1. An old man reads.

2. A man asleep.

[3. This plate is lacking. In the facsimile of 1886, Mr. Muir added an aphorism of his own : 'The perceptions of the poetic or prophetic character are not bounded as the perceptions of the senses are.']

4. This plate has no decoration but the usual lines.

5. Two tiny angels fly upward in prayer.

6. A man despairing with fettered ankles.

7. A nude figure rising above clouds.

Application. An old man under a tree describes a geometrical figure with a pair of compasses.

Therefore. A haloed figure (Albion) asleep on a rock.

ALL RELIGIONS ARE ONE : *Title-page*. An angel reveals this truth upon a stone table to an old man with a book in his lap.

Frontispiece. 'The Voice of one Crying,' inscribed under John the Baptist.

Argument. A figure reclines in the grass.

1. Urizen in the clouds ; a design repeated later as the top half of plate 10 in *America*.

2. Above, two youths look upward ; below, sheep feeding.

3. Two old men seated, reading and writing.

4. A man with a staff.

5. Above, Christ seated, surrounded by children. Below, an old man playing a harp. These are the first and last stages of mysticism, as then conceived by Blake.

6. Above, the tables of the Law. Below, Urizen in darkness striding to the right, exploring Urthona's dens.

7. Above, the bust of a man (Christ) appears to two reaching figures. Below are hovering angels.

These decorations are slight commentaries on the aphorisms, showing by contrast the pastoral state of 'Innocence' and the aged despair of 'Experience.' 'Innocence' and 'Experience' here typify Mystical and Natural Religion.

SONGS OF INNOCENCE

COMMENTARY

Introduction. This ' artless ' masterpiece (the adjective is not mine) is peculiarly fitted, by the thought concealed in it, to head the *Songs.* As has been pointed out by another, it ' teaches the very method of the making of such song, and is, in fact, Blake's one great, if brief, Essay on Poetry. . . . First the intention, then the melody, then the words, and finally the recording pen. Do all poets with a purpose allow their songs to grow into existence through this healthful and natural order of change ? Do they not habitually begin with the pen ? '[1] Blake did even more than this. In this poem he declared his divine appointment to write, for the child is at once Jesus and the Spirit of Poetry—a daring identification, which later became the core of his metaphysics. The third stanza distinctly points out that every subject has two sides—Innocence and Experience.

Thus this poem was carefully planned to show : first, the Divine command ; next, the inner revelation of the song's meaning ; then the fitting of words to the wordless melody ; and finally its appearance in visible form.

Line 3. The *cloud* is in the Bible the usual chariot of Divinity.

Line 5. Every one who has loved children will recognize this peremptory tone.

THE ECCHOING GREEN. How far Blake had got from his century is best demonstrated by comparing these beautifully cadenced verses with some lines from Goldsmith (quoted from Oliver Elton's *Survey of English Literature*, I. 22) :

> How often have I blest the coming day,
> When toil remitting lent its turn to play,
> And all the village train, from labour free,
> Led up their sports beneath the spreading tree ;
> While many a pastime circled in the shade,
> The young contending as the old surveyed ;
> And many a gambol frolick'd o'er the ground,
> And sleights of art and feats of strength went round :
> And still, as each repeated pleasure tir'd,
> Succeeding sports the mirthful band inspir'd.

THE LAMB. This poem, whose antitype was to be *The Tyger*, has always been recognized as one of the great poems in English.

THE SHEPHERD. To most of us this poem needs no comment. But Mr. Ellis, no doubt in an effort to justify his statement that ' there is no book of Blake's so difficult to thoroughly understand,' identifies the Shepherd with Tharmas (*Facsimile*, p. 10).

INFANT JOY. This poem, for the simple completeness of thought and the daring of its technique, is to be ranked among Blake's greatest poems. No one else has ever got so entirely the feeling of a mother for her new-born child. Swinburne, for example, invoked all the bells and birds of heaven, all the wells and winds on earth, and ' all sweet sounds together ' to describe *A Child's Laughter* ; but Blake invoked nothing at all, and got a much finer effect.

Only one critic, Coleridge, has found any fault with this poem. He liked it well, on the whole, but felt it not quite perfect. ' For the last three lines I should write, ' When wilt thou smile,' or ' O smile, O smile ! I 'll sing the while.' For a babe two days old does not, cannot smile, and innocence and the very truth of Nature must go together. Infancy is too holy a thing to be ornamented ' (Letter to C. A. Tulk, 1818).

[1] E. J. Ellis : Facsimile of the *Songs of Innocence and Experience*, p. viii.

THE LITTLE BLACK BOY. This poem, which was Coleridge's favourite among all the *Songs of Innocence*, was doubly inspired by the anti-slavery agitation of Blake's times, and by Isaac Watts's *Grace Shining and Nature Fainting* in the *Horae Lyricae* :

> Nor is my soul refined enough
> To bear the beaming of his love,
>   And feel his warmer smiles.
> When shall I rest this drooping head ?
> I love, I love the sun, and yet I want the shade.

The teaching of Blake's poem is that Creation is an act of Divine Mercy, so that by degrees we may learn to bear the beams of Eternal Love. It is worth noting that Blake apparently did not believe in the equality of the negroes and whites (if we may judge by the last stanza). This is one of the few *Songs of Innocence* which are primarily moralistic. Blake deliberately puts the moralizing in the mouth of the mother ; yet, even to her, death is nothing terrible, but rather a release towards a greater happiness.

Lines 16-18. The comparison of the body to a cloud, which hides the light of the soul, is to be found in Dante's *Purgatorio*, II. 122-123 and XXVIII. 90. Shelley also used it in *Adonais*, liv. :

> The fire, for which all thirst, now beams on me,
> Consuming the last clouds of cold mortality.

Lines 27-28. Is the little black boy to stroke the silver hair of the English boy, or of God ? Blake's grammar is ambiguous. The natural inference is that he meant the English boy ; but if he meant God, then the last line of the poem is verified by Blake's dictum in *There is No Natural Religion* : ' God becomes as we are, that we may be as He is.'

LAUGHING SONG. ' The Fairy Glee of Oberon, which Stevens's exquisite music has familiarized to modern ears, will immediately occur to the reader of these laughing stanzas. We may also trace another less obvious resemblance to Jonson in an ode gratulatory to the Right Honourable Hierome, Lord Weston, for his return from his embassy in the year 1632. The accord is to be found, not in the words nor in the subject ; for neither would betray imitation : but in the style of thought, and if I may so term it, the date of the expression ' (Malkin). This passage is reprinted, not because Malkin's parallels are at all like, but to show how far he had to search in 1806 for anything resembling Blake.

SPRING. Mr. H. G. Hewlett, who disliked Blake's work so fervently, found this poem a ' swamp of namby-pamby ' (p. 770). He seems to remain alone in his opinion.

A CRADLE SONG. Some critics feel certain that this poem was inspired by Watts's *Hush ! my dear, lie still and slumber*. There is no more resemblance than there must be between any two cradle-songs.

NURSE'S SONG. Few besides Blake could have written such a successful poem on the delight of being allowed to play a little longer until dusk.

HOLY THURSDAY. For once Blake speaks in his own person.

THE BLOSSOM. This poem is obviously an experiment, and therefore not wholly a success. Plenty of parallels may be found for the false rhymes.

THE CHIMNEY SWEEPER. Even in the lowest degradation to which children can be reduced, they suffer silently, sure that their state cannot last, even though the release be made only by the Angel of Death. This ' broadsheet gone to Heaven ' [1] was inspired by the agitation which was then trying to pass laws against the use of children as chimney-sweeps. It was actually used as propaganda, being ' communicated by Mr. Charles Lamb from a very rare and curious little work ' to James

[1] Elton : *Survey of English Literature*, I. 144.

Montgomery's *Chimney-Sweepers' Friend and Climbing Boys' Album* (1824), for which Cruickshank made some drawings. Lamb changed 'Tom Dacre' in the fifth line to 'Tom Toddy.' In a letter to Bernard Barton, May 15, 1824, Lamb commented on Montgomery's anthology : 'Blake's are the flower of the set, you will, I am sure, agree, though some of Montgomery's at the end are quite pretty ; but the Dream was awkwardly paraphrased from Blake.'

Several critics have pointed out how near Blake's poem is to Wordsworth's style in its homeliness.

Line 3. ''Weep!' is, of course, the child's lisp in pronouncing his cry 'Sweep!' To Blake the pun had its pathetic significance. Lamb certainly remembered this poem when he wrote his *Essay on Chimney-Sweeps* : 'with their little professional notes sounding like the *peep, peep* of a young sparrow . . . poor blots—innocent blacknesses ! '

THE DIVINE IMAGE. This poem was composed by Blake in the New Jerusalem Church, Hatton Gardens, London.[1] This and the succeeding poem were second only to *The Little Black Boy*, in the opinion of Coleridge.

NIGHT. *The Little Black Boy* and *The Chimney Sweeper* dealt with the meaningless cruelty of man to man ; this poem, *Night*, whose very title is symbolic, deals with the cruelty of Nature. Blake promises that 'the lion shall lie down with the lamb,'[2] as did also Shelley, in *Queen Mab*, VIII. :

> The lion now forgets to thirst for blood ;
> There might you see him sporting in the sun
> Beside the dreadless kid.

But Blake does not hope for this Golden Age in this world ; it will obtain only after death, in that 'immortal day.'

This poem is one of the greatest of the *Songs of Innocence*. Something quite like it metrically is to be found in the opening stanzas of Burns's *Jolly Beggars*.

A DREAM. This is an answer, though not a final one, to the problem in the preceding poem. The lost mother-ant is guided home by the glow-worm. Blake might well have meant the mother-ant, whose husband and children are weeping at home, to represent the Emanation. But this speculation is unnecessary.

Could Blake have been influenced in this poem by Mrs. Radcliffe's *Glow-Worm* ? It appeared in the *Mysteries of Udolpho*, which was published in 1794 ; but whether it appeared earlier in some periodical (as was Mrs. Radcliffe's custom) I have been unable to prove. In Mrs. Radcliffe's poem, 'the lines go in a sort of tripping measure, which I thought might suit the subject well enough ; but I fear they are too irregular '—which suggests Blake's metre. Moreover, in her poem the 'vapour of the woods ' (false light) is contrasted with the glow-worm (the true guide) ; which reminds us at once of Blake's *Dream* and also of *The Little Boy Lost and Found*, which is related to the *Dream* by its interior idea.

Bowring's hymn, *Watchman, tell us of the night*, which contains the line, 'Hie thee to thy quiet home,' was not written till 1825.

ON ANOTHER'S SORROW. This expresses exactly what Walt Whitman meant in many passages like the following :

> I become any presence or truth of humanity here,
> See myself in prison shaped like another man,
> And feel the dull unintermitted pain. . . .
> I do not ask who you are—that is not important to me,
> You can do nothing, and be nothing, but what I will infold you.
> —*Song of Myself*, 245, 246.

---

[1] H. N. Morris : *Flaxman, Blake, and Coleridge*, p. 89.
[2] So the text of *Isaiah* xi. 6 is usually quoted. It really reads : 'The wolf also shall dwell with the lamb, and the leopard shall lie down with the kid ; and the calf and the young lion and the fatling together ; and a little child shall lead them.'

Stanza 7. An old Christian theory. ' I am in Heaven, in the Earth, in the Water, in the Air, I am in living Creatures, in the Plants, in the Womb, everywhere ' (Trismegistus : *Pymander*, VII. 47).

THE LITTLE BOY LOST and THE LITTLE BOY FOUND are companion poems. The child, who is Man, is led astray by a marsh-vapour, or false light, which he mistakes for his father (God). God takes pity upon him, appears (though in a human form, in which he is not recognized), and leads him back to his mother. This is one of Blake's favourite themes : the protection of Divine Providence over the Innocent.

The vapour is evidently that referred to by Jakob Böhme in his *Sixth Epistle* (32) : ' For the false light out of imagination ariseth out of the self-will of Nature —namely, from the impression of the properties where the properties do prove one another ; whence self-lust ariseth, and an imagination wherein nature doth modelize and fancy to itself in its own desire the abyss, and desireth to bring itself in its own might, without the will of God, into a dominion and government of its own self-will and rule.'

These two poems end the *Songs of Innocence*. In the earliest copies Blake also included *The Little Girl Lost*, *The Little Girl Found*, *The School-Boy*, and *The Ancient Bard* ; but as soon as the *Songs of Experience* appeared, they were shifted to this second volume. As Blake always changed the order of plates in the *Songs*, to preserve the individuality of each copy, it might be well to explain that I have followed the order which he copied out on a sheet of paper, which was found among his manuscripts ; an order which is followed by all of Blake's later editors and critics, except Dr. Keynes.

DECORATIONS

The designs in the *Songs of Innocence* are almost entirely pure decoration, though once in a while they become a commentary on the text. The Calvert copy, in the Metropolitan Art Museum of New York, is unique in having decorative lines elaborated about each plate : in every case, these added margins seem to spring from the picture itself. The earliest copies are coloured with a rich yet delicate simplicity ; later ones have the text of the poems tinted ; while the latest copies of all are the most gorgeous, gold and silver being freely used. Each copy is usually coloured with an entirely different colour-scheme.

The *Frontispiece* is an illustration to the *Introduction*. The young shepherd drops his pipe at the apparition of the Child.

The *Title-page* bears the words : ' Songs of Innocence, 1789. The Author & Printer W. Blake.' The letters burst into foliage, and are filled with tiny angels, birds, etc. ; a device which is repeated throughout the *Songs of Innocence*. A mother sits in a chair and instructs two children from a book in her lap. We may assume from this, and from *The Little Black Boy*, that maternal instruction was not the education to which Blake objected. Opposite the group stands a broken apple-tree, bearing fruit, and twined with a vine. This is certainly symbolic of Christ embracing what we consider the Tree of Sin.

Introduction. On either side of the text a sort of woody vine twines, leaving four openings on each side, which frame tiny pastoral scenes. These are very difficult to make out ; but after comparing many copies I think I have deciphered them. On the left, from the top down, we see : (1) a thinker in his cloak, leaning on his crook, and discoursing with a sitting woman ; (2) a nude woman dancing ; (3) a plougher ; (4) a mother by a cradle. On the right, in the same order : (1) a bird flying upward ; (2) a woman thinking ; (3) a woman sowing ; (4) a shepherdess with her crook.

THE ECCHOING GREEN, first plate. Above the text: the older folk sit about the trunk of the oak, with children in their laps and on their knees, while in the background, boys are playing at ball. On the left of the text: a boy with a cricket bat. To the right of the text: a boy rolling a hoop. Below the text: vines, grapes, and a bird.

THE ECCHOING GREEN, second plate. To the left of the text: a boy stands on tiptoe in a huge vine to gather the grapes of ecstasy. To the right: another branch of the same vine, from which a boy reaches a bunch of grapes down to a little girl. She is the last of a group which fills the plate below the text; they are evidently the family going home from play. We see the father, mother, and seven children. One boy has a kite, another a cricket bat.

THE LAMB. As usual, the text is framed in a flow of intertwined vegetation. Below the text, a naked child holds out his hands to a sheep. There are also a flock and a cottage embowered with trees in the background.

THE SHEPHERD. Below the text: a shepherd stands on the right with his crook, below a pine which reaches up the side of the plate. He is watching his feeding flocks. In the sky, birds of Paradise are flying.

INFANT JOY. An especially exquisite design. A fantastic plant winds between the stanzas, with a bud to the right; between the text and the title it blossoms into an open, flaming flower, in whose cup a mother shows her baby to a fairy. Blake repeated this design, though not closely, in the 272nd design to Young's *Night Thoughts*.

THE LITTLE BLACK BOY, first plate. Above the text: the black mother beneath a tree, with her child, watch the sun rising just above the horizon.

THE LITTLE BLACK BOY, second plate. Below the text: the Good Shepherd with his crook sits on a bank beneath a tree. The little white boy prays at his knee, while the little black boy stands somewhat behind him. In the background, sheep are feeding. Sometimes a brook is introduced in the foreground.

LAUGHING SONG. Above the text: a table under trees, at which eight children are drinking. One of them, a boy, stands with his back to the reader, lifting a goblet, and waving his plumed hat. The idea of this design is repeated in the 479th illustration to Young; but with the difference that there Blake introduces angels visibly among the feasters.

SPRING, first plate. Above the text: a mother sits under a tree, holding her baby standing in her lap. He stretches his hands towards a feeding flock. Around the text Blake wove some of his loveliest spirals of vegetation (on this and the next plate, wheat), in which are two angels, one reclining, the other piping.

SPRING, second plate. Below the text: a naked child plays with a lamb, while two sheep sit in the back. To the right of the text are two more exquisite spirals of wheat, holding two angels, one dancing, one weeping.

A CRADLE SONG, first plate. Against the first word of the title, in the Calvert copy at least, a tiny figure leans, piping. To the left and right of the text are more tangles of vegetation, in which are many tiny human figures. Whether Blake meant such designs to be symbolic of humanity caught in the lovely webs of what he later called ' this vegetable flesh ' can only be surmised.

A CRADLE SONG, second plate. Below the text: a mother sits in a chair by a large wicker cradle, in which the baby lies. The scene is unusual in being set indoors. Added to this is a sort of Raphaelesque hardness, which in this day is not pleasant.

NURSE'S SONG. The title is embedded in vegetation, through which tiny children play. To the right of the text: a weeping willow trails its branches in the water. Below the text : the nurse is sitting below a tree reading, while in the background children play Snap-the-whip.

HOLY THURSDAY. Above the text : a procession of little boys, two by two, led by two beadles, marches to the right. Below the text : a similar procession of little girls, led by two matrons, marches to the left. All through the interstices of the text is woven a great variety of flowing lines, birds, and children.

THE BLOSSOM. To the right and above the text : a sort of marshy growth, or flame, twines. In it sport six child-angels, two of which embrace ; while an older angel hugs in her lap a baby-angel. This is one of Blake's best designs, and perhaps explains why he retained this poem in his book.

THE CHIMNEY SWEEPER. Below the text : to the right, an angel raises a naked child ; in the centre the naked boys are struck with astonishment, and then embrace ; to the left, they all run off, presumably to go in swimming (l. 16). The ' gesture ' of Blake's pictures is very apt to be clockwise : from left to right above the text, and the reverse below the text.

THE DIVINE IMAGE. Starting below the text, passing between the third and fourth stanzas, and ending above the text, coils an imaginative flame of the type found in *The Blossom*. It is twined with a flowering convolvulus. Above the text : it contains four figures, walking, flying, and embracing. In the lower right corner of the plate, a clothed figure (presumably Christ) raises a naked figure, while a third is still sunk in the sleep of this world. In one copy this little group was tinted to represent a night scene, while light issued from the hands and head of Christ.

NIGHT, first plate. The title stands in a tree, which springs from the lower right corner, before a cave, in which is a lion. Above the cave is a winged figure. To the left of the text : a moon and stars, below which four winged figures fly upward in an ecstasy. For once, the later copies are coloured better than the early ones ; since at first Blake was afraid to represent the deep blues of night, in fear of spoiling the delicate scale of tints which he had been using throughout the book. Yet in many of the later copies the figures are obscured by the colouring.

NIGHT, second plate. Below the text : five angels walk on the greensward. To the left of the text : a tree in which are two more angels. To the right : its foliage. When he used richer colours, Blake introduced stars and gave the angels huge haloes.

A DREAM. Throughout the text is twined the usual foliage with little figures. In the lower right corner stands the glow-worm personified, before a tree-trunk, holding a staff and lantern. Above him the beetle flies away.

ON ANOTHER'S SORROW. To the left of the text : ascending vegetative lines. In them, towards the bottom of the plate, is a piping youth ; above him a climbing figure ; and higher yet are supplicating forms. To the right of the text : a vine with grapes, and a long-tailed bird of the kind found in *The Shepherd*.

THE LITTLE BOY LOST. Above the text : the little boy alone in the forest by night, with huge trees bending ominously over him, reaches out his hands towards a floating triangular flame of white light. Mr. Ellis, for symbolic reasons of his own, claims that this flame is ' just shapely enough to be seen as a little figure head-downwards ' (*Facsimile*, p. xi) ; but neither in the picture he reproduces, nor in the nineteen copies I have seen, have I been able to verify this. The flame is sometimes enclosed in a rayed halo. The text itself is surrounded with six exquisite angels.

THE LITTLE BOY FOUND. Above the text : the boy walks through the forest holding the hand of God, who looks more like our idea of a youthful angel. Sometimes God is given a halo. To the right of the text is an adoring angel.

SONGS OF EXPERIENCE

COMMENTARY

Introduction. Already some of Blake's obscurer symbols have crept unobtrusively into this marvellous poem. The Poet calls upon Fallen Man (whose symbol is the Earth itself) to rise and exert his forgotten control over the visible universe.

Line 5. Cf. *Genesis* iii. 8 : ' And they heard the Voice of the Lord God walking in the garden in the cool of the day.' Any symbolist knows that the Voice and the Word are the same thing. Here, as in the *Introduction* to the *Songs of Innocence*, Blake slyly identified Jesus and the Spirit of Poetry.

Line 9. The stars are the symbol of Reason, because of their scattered, ineffectual sparks of light, and because of their mechanistic motion. Blake believed that man had fallen because he allowed Reason to control him, instead of controlling Reason and subordinating it to the higher power of the Imagination, who is God.

Stanzas 3-4. ' I think ("reasoning rightly in my own division ") I would rather have written these lines than anything in English poetry outside of Shakspere,' (Saintsbury : *Prosody*, III. 15).

Line 14. *The morn* is, of course, the renewal of true light.

Line 18. *The starry floor*, or Reason, roofing Man in from Eternity.

Line 19. *The wat'ry shore* of the dead Sea of Time and Space.

EARTH'S ANSWER. The world answers that it is imprisoned in Time and Space from Eternity, and that it is ruled by Fear and Jealousy, which are other names for Reason. Blake ends Earth's cry with an appeal for Free Love. He did not mention Free Love because of any personal impulses, as we know ; nor was it merely the most conspicuous example of Man's tyranny over himself ; it was, in fact, Man's best road to Eternity, and therefore terminates the poem quite appropriately. A detailed discussion of this doctrine occupies Chapter xv.

Line 7. *Starry Jealousy* was later named by Blake ' Urizen.' He is the Jealous God of Reason, who rules by Prohibition. Blake firmly believed, with Hermes Trismegistus, that ' Nothing in Heaven is servanted, nothing upon Earth free ' (*Pymander*, I. 55). And perhaps he remembered Milton's lines (*Paradise Lost*, IX. 644-645, 654) :

> the Tree,
> Of Prohibition, root of all our woe ;
> . . . our Reason is our Law.

Line 10. *The Father of the Ancient Men* is also Urizen, the God of this world, since, thanks to him, we fell from Eternity into the Creation of Generation.

Stanza 4. Blake did not mean that the acts of love should be performed in open daylight. ' Night ' throughout this book is used symbolically, as the absence of the true Light, or spiritual darkness. George Farquhar had already written, in his *Lover's Night*, how ' His Sun of Beauty shone to light his Breast ' ; and Shelley later was also to call for a light which was not that of a literal day :

> Within my heart is the lamp of love,
> And this is day !
> —*The Two Spirits.*

We can imagine for ourselves what absurdities literalists like G. K. Chesterton have written of Blake's appeal for light ! He was not, however, appealing for love itself, but objecting to the obscurity which hid it, as in that foul doctrine of Comus : ' 'Tis onely day-light that makes Sin.'

In his *Milton*, 22 : 38-42, Blake finally answers the great question, which runs through all the early poems :

> Be patient therefore, O my Sons.
> These lovely Females form sweet night and silence and secret
> Obscurities to hide from Satan's Watch-Fiends Human loves
> And graces, lest they write them in their Books & in the Scroll
> Of mortal life, to condemn the accused.

Line 20. Cf. *Isaiah* xxviii. 24 : ' Doth the plowman plow all day to sow ? '

Line 21. *This heavy chain* is the flesh itself, which prevents the complete union of lovers, who in Eternity are literally made One. Thel also cried : ' Why a little curtain of flesh on the bed of our desire ? ' (l. 127).

NURSE'S SONG. In the *Songs of Innocence* the children were delighted that they could play a little longer at the coming of night ; now we have the Nurse's own thoughts. She sees Experience, or Night, creeping upon them irresistibly ; and remembering her own past, she laments that the Earthly Paradise should not be made more of while it lasts, and that after the Expulsion nothing but hypocrisy should remain.

Line 4. *Green* is one of Blake's rare uses of a colour-word in an unusual sense. He did not symbolize colour, otherwise he would have attached some meaning to it when he painted his books ; which he could not have done, since he coloured each book differently. Blake's use of the word here is ' futuristic '—emotional, and not factual. I can find no deeper reason, nor do I see any reason for expecting one.

Line 6. *The dews of night*. Night, of course, represents Experience. Blake practically always used Water of all kinds with a materialistic meaning, which is thoroughly in accord with Catholic tradition, where the water which one passes through in Baptism represents Death.

Line 7. *Your spring and your day* are easily recognizable as symbols of Innocence.

Line 8. *Disguise*, or hypocrisy, against which Blake had already protested in the preceding poem.

THE FLY. Blake's love of every living thing expressed itself in the doctrine that they are all the works of God, and have God within them.

> Seest thou the little winged fly smaller than a grain of sand ?
> It has a heart like thee : a brain open to heaven & hell,
> Withinside, wondrous & expansive : its gates are not clos'd :
> I hope thine are not ; hence it clothes itself in rich array.
>
> —*Milton*, 18 : 27-30.

Blake interpreted everything in the terms of man—as indeed we all are forced to do—but his recognition of this Anthropomorphism of Nature is sometimes puzzling at first. The human forms that he accords all things were what he called ' spiritual forms.' But personification needs no excuse :

> Thou see'st the gorgeous clothed Flies that dance & sport in summer
> Upon the sunny brooks & meadows : every one the dance
> Knows in its intricate mazes of delight artful to weave :
> Each one to sound his instruments of music in the dance,
> To touch each other & recede : to cross & change & return.
> These are the Children of Los [Poetry].
>
> —*Milton*, 26 : 2-7.

Blake of course was following the usage of his century when by the word ' Fly ' he meant neither the house-fly nor the butterfly, but any bright-coloured flying insect.

Mr. P. E. More, in his *Shelburne Essays* (IV. 229), felicitously contrasts Blake's poem with Gray's on the same subject :

> To Contemplation's sober eye
> Such is the race of man :
> And they that creep, and they that fly
> Shall end where they began.

Alike the busy and the gay
But flutter through life's little day,
In fortune's varying colours drest :
Brush'd by the hand of rough Mischance,
Or chill'd by age, their airy dance
They leave, in dust to rest.

Methinks I hear in accents low
The sportive kind reply :
Poor moralist ! and what are thou ?
A solitary fly.
Thy joys no glittering female meets,
No hive hast thou of hoarded sweets,
No painted plumage to display ;
On hasty wings thy youth is flown ;
Thy sun is set, thy spring is gone—
We frolic while 'tis May.

—' Ode I.'—*On the Spring.*

When we remember that Blake admired Gray's poems enough to make one hundred and fourteen illustrations to them, we may assume that the resemblance of the thought in these two poems is not a coincidence. But Gray merely meant that, in a certain mood, man seems as unimportant as the frailest insect. This is pleasant attitudinizing, which few really take seriously. But Blake did ; and he took it so seriously that he drew the startling inference that if Blake is a fly, then a fly is Blake, which is abundantly axiomatic, and quite defensible. So Blake really reversed Gray's idea, for Gray meant that man was unimportant, Blake on the contrary teaching that a fly is important.

Blake's metre alone is sufficient to place his poem above Gray's ; since he compresses his thought into miniature lines which by their prosody suggest the flitting of the insect. Mr. P. E. More does not agree, however : ' I do not say that Blake is here more successful than Gray ; on the contrary, I am convinced that his method when carried to its extreme is more disastrous to poetry than the most rigid convention of the century ; but the difference of his procedure from Gray's is unmistakable.' The difference is that of an entire age.

THE TYGER. This poem is undoubtedly the best known of all Blake's works, and one of the very great poems in the English language. Every school child knows it, and yet its thought is so profound that it touches everywhere upon the problems of all thinkers. Even in Blake's own day, when most of his poems were quite unknown, this one was circulated everywhere, for it was unforgettable. It was the first thing that Lamb ever heard of Blake's : ' I have heard of his poems, but have never seen them. There is one to a tiger . . . which is glorious ! '[1] Lamb used to misquote this poem with much fervour. Such circulation always causes variants ; and when the authentic text was published, protests appeared in various magazines, giving the lines ' to which we are accustomed.'

Out of the great paragraphs of praise which have been offered up to this poem, we can pick two or three notes of dislike. Rossetti thought the poem so imperfect that when he reprinted it he practically rewrote it. I am glad to record that his emendations have never been accepted. Cestre, looking for madness, found its beginning here : ' Blake a perdu sa sérénité. A partir de ce moment, son esprit se trouble. Il ne conserve assez de lucidité pour concevoir un plan de poème intelligible ' (p. 215). We could as easily accuse Cestre of madness for being unable to perceive the perfectly obvious development in the poem. Mr. Percy Cross Standing, in an article entitled *Was Blake a Poet ?* (*The Catholic World,* July 1905), called this poem ' arrant drivel ! '

The Tyger deals with the immense problem of Evil. It is the same problem which Musset expressed so excellently in his *Espoir en Dieu* :

[1] Gilchrist, ch. xiii.

Comment, sous la sainte lumière,
Voit-on des actes si hideux,
Qu'ils font expirer la prière
Sur les lèvres du malheureux ?

Pourquoi, dans ton œuvre céleste,
Tant d'éléments si peu d'accord ?
A quoi bon le crime et la peste ?
O Dieu juste ! pourquoi la mort ?

Blake could not consider Evil abstractedly. His God was essentially personal; therefore Evil must be his Wrath. 'God out of Christ is a consuming fire,' he wrote elsewhere;[1] and Crabb Robinson recorded that Blake said of Christ, 'He is the only God.'

The problem of *The Tyger* is, quite simply, how to reconcile the Forgiveness of Sins (the Lamb) with the Punishment of Sins (the Tyger). So it is evident that the climax of *The Tyger*: 'Did he who made the Lamb make thee?' is not an exclamation of wonder, but a very real question, whose answer Blake was not sure of. The 27th *Proverb of Hell* distinctly states that 'The roaring of lions, the howling of wolves, the raging of the stormy sea, and the destructive sword are portions of eternity too great for the eye of man.'

Nevertheless Blake found some good in Wrath. 'The wrath of the Lion is the Wisdom of God,' and 'The Tygers of wrath are wiser than the Horses of instruction,' are two other *Proverbs of Hell*. In Iamblicus's *Life of Pythagoras*, he may have come across the sentence: 'It is necessary to purify the woods, in which these passions have fixed their abode, with fire.' Certainly in his Paracelsus he found much praise of wrath:

Destruction perfects that which is good; for the good cannot appear on account of that which conceals it. . . . By the element of fire all that is imperfect is destroyed or taken away (*Preface* to the *Coelum Philosophorum*).

Fire separates that which is constant or fixed from that which is fugitive or volatile (*De Morbis Metallicis*, Lib. II. Tract 1).

The three prime substances are proved only by fire, which manifests them pure, naked, clear, and simple. In the absence of all ordeal by fire, there is no proving of a substance possible. For fire tests everything, and when the impure matter is separated the three pure substances are displayed (*De Origine Morborum*, Lib. I. cap. 1).

Fire is the father or active principle of separation (Third of the *Fragmenta Medica*).

A digression must be made here on the universal use of fire as a symbol of wrath. Blake, as we have seen, used it in his sentence, 'God out of Christ is a consuming fire'; and in *Urizen* he speaks of 'flames of eternal fury.' Böhme, in his fourth Epistle (103), wrote of 'the mystery of the wrath, or fire of God's anger.' In the *Faerie Queene* (II. iv. xxxv. 2) Spenser wrote: 'Wrath is a fire.' Milton also spoke of 'flames, the sign of wrath awaked' (*Paradise Lost*, VI. 58). Blake's association of fire with his Tyger (ll. 1, 6, 8) was due to the old symbol.

Another very old symbol is that of the Forest. The Forest, in Blake, is the world of Experience, where the many sterile errors (dead trees) conceal the path and dim the light. Dante, on his way to Hell, was lost in this identical forest (*Inferno*, I. ll. 1-9). Thomas Vaughan ('Eugenius Philalethes') also began his greatest work, the *Lumen de Lumine*, by losing himself in a forest at night. Shelley's *Epipsychidion* contains several references to this forest: 'the wintry forest of our life . . . struggling through its error . . . the obscure Forest . . . that wintry

---

[1] On a painting in the Tate Gallery. I have not been able to trace the history of this phrase. It used to be much quoted by Calvinists as a proof of the reality of Hell; but it is not to be found in the Bible, as they supposed.

wilderness of thorns . . . the grey earth and branches bare and dead.' Blake was very fond of the symbol. It occurs on the title-page of *The Marriage of Heaven and Hell*, in the margin to the 9th illustration of *Job*, and many other places. It is blown flat in the 6th plate of the *America* and the margin of the 13th illustration of *Job*.

With these two symbols fixed in our mind, we can see readily the answer to the question of the function of Wrath, concealed in the very first lines of the poem :

> Tyger, tyger, burning bright
> In the forests of the night.

Blake intends to suggest that the great purpose of Wrath is to consume Error, to annihilate those stubborn beliefs which cannot be removed by the tame ' horses of instruction.'

But this does not explain whence Wrath came. Blake asks the question characteristically. ' What immortal hand or eye '—that is, what mechanistic force of nature, or what glance of divine vision—dared this creation ? The answer is concealed in the poem. I have already explained the meaning of stars to Blake —that they represented an inferior order of the created world, which is ruled by Reason, or Urizen. In the later books, Blake often depicted Urizen as weeping over the anguish which he has caused, and even terrified at it. Remembering this, we can readily understand the lines :

> When the stars threw down their spears,
> And water'd heaven with their tears.

The Tyger was created in this fallen world of Reason, produced by its mechanical laws ; and his appearance caused Urizen's Aristotelean reactions of terror and pity. The exact moment of his creation is described in *The Four Zoas*, VIII. 439. Reason (Urizen), caught in the clutches of Dogmatic Morality (Rahab), has sunk below even a semblance of human form into that of a dragon (warfare—the ' struggle for life '). It is then that all the beasts appear, as Swedenborg taught, and Urizen in despair realizes that he has fallen to yet a lower plane in his struggle for dominion. But the end of all this evil is nearly at hand. Revolt (Orc) breaks loose, and the Last Judgment hangs over Creation.

The order of the lyric is typical of Blake. He shows the entire process of the tyger's creation. First the ' fire of his eyes ' is gathered from the cosmos ; then the heart is created, the feet forged, and ultimately the brain. This is not unlike the creation of Urizen himself, as described in *Urizen*, *The Book of Los*, and *Milton* (5 : 9-27). Blake probably began the tyger with the creation of his eyes, because the Eye to Blake meant Intellect, as opposed to the Wing of Love. Blake describes the creation by a series of white-hot exclamations rather than by an elaborate description. The effect is one of an intense improvisation ; but an examination of the manuscript shows at once that Blake made a great many corrections *during* the composition of the first draft.

Line 1 ' has a kind of prototype in an expression used by a former translator of Buchanan's *Baptistes*. The writer speaks of

> The fierce wildnesse
> Of the deep-shining yellow Lyonesse.

The two adjectives of the second line represent the Latin *fulvae*. The translator, it deserves to be added, was believed by an editor of 1740 to be Milton. W. B.' (*Notes and Queries*, Sept. 22, 1906.)

Line 3. A letter to Littell's *Living Age* (1863, p. 582) protested against Blake's version of this line : ' certainly this is not the version to which we are accustomed, and seems to us unmeaning. The eye might *discern* but could not *frame* the tiger's symmetry.' Artists, however, do believe that the eye does just that. The suggested emendation was ' What immortal hand on high.'

Line 12. Malkin reprinted this line in 1806 : ' What dread hand forged thy dread feet ? '—which is not only an improvement, but is surely Blake's own emendation. His process of illuminated printing did not allow him to change the text in the *Songs* themselves. Mr. Saintsbury wrote of this emendation : ' It seems to me the *ne plus ultra* of the measure in this direction. It makes almost a seven-*foot* line with pause-syllables after every spoken one ' (*Prosody*, III. 14).

Line 17. Cf. *The Four Zoas*, v. 224 : ' The stars threw down their spears & fled naked away.'

THE LITTLE GIRL LOST and THE LITTLE GIRL FOUND. These poems, which were two of those at first included in the *Songs of Innocence,* teach that Death is a release into the better world of Eternity. They are based upon *Isaiah* xi. 6 (which had also influenced *Night*), Spenser's *Faerie Queene* (Bk. I. Canto III. stanzas 5-7), and Milton's *Comus*, 418-475. Lafcadio Hearn declared that they were ' certainly inspired by the curious belief of the Middle Ages that tigers and other wild beasts could not harm a virgin, and the deeper meaning of the poem is the strength of innocence in its charm' (*Interpretations of Literature*, I. 59-60). But I do not think that Blake needed to go farther for his inspiration than to the Bible, and to Una and her Lion.

Lyca, a little girl of seven, wanders somehow into the sleep of Experience, which is also a desert. The Lion, protector of the Lamb, and also the Angel of Death, removes the little girl to his own land, after divesting her of her ' slender dress,' or her body of flesh. The parents, alarmed at her disappearance, wander in anguish over the desert, till they, too, meet the Lion. But suddenly the great terror, who has removed their child, appears as ' a spirit arm'd in gold '; for they, too, are now dead, and can see that the terror is really a blessing. The awful moment passed without their noticing it. So they follow the Lion, find their daughter unharmed, and live in eternal delight, undisturbed by the wild beasts.

In view of the same rôle of the beasts in *Night*, I cannot agree with some commentators that the seven-year old Lyca wandered forth in search of Free Love, and was destroyed by the beasts of passion.

THE LITTLE GIRL LOST. Stanzas 1-2. These are a prelude, prophesying that all the world one day shall be saved.

Line 12. The name Lyca is derived from the Greek word for wolf, according to Mr. J. C. E. Bassalik de Vries (*Blake in his Relation to Rossetti*: Basel, 1911). This etymology is in direct contradiction to line 50 of the second poem.

Line 15. The aimlessness of Innocence, which leads into Experience.

THE LITTLE GIRL FOUND. Lines 11-12. This was undoubtedly the true fate of the little girl—true, as far as eyes of mortality could perceive. Blake tells us, however, that it was a ' dream.'

Line 27. This is the moment of death, since the Lion actually attacks them here.

Lines 51-52. The conflict of the wolves and the lions over the sheep was Blake's symbol (derived from the Bible) for the conflicts in this world.

THE CLOD AND THE PEBBLE. This poem describes for us the two States of Innocence and Experience, as expressed in unselfish and selfish love. It also teaches that Heaven and Hell obtain within us on this earth, according to the disposition of our own minds. This doctrine is such a universal one that I will do no more than give a list of some references where the same doctrine reoccurs. These are : Omar Khayyám, *Rubáiyát*, stanza lxxi. (2nd ed.) ; Marlowe's *Tragical History of Dr. Faustus*, speeches of Mephistopheles ; Milton's *Paradise Lost*, I. 254-255 ; Böhme's *Aurora*, xx. 85-86, and his second Epistle, 48 ; Thomas Traherne, in his *Dreams* and *The Odour* (*Songs of Felicity*) and *Centuries of Meditation*, I. 36 ; and IV. 37 ; Sir Thomas Browne's *Religio Medici*, I. 70 ; Shelley's *Julian and Maddalo*, II. 174-175 ; his *Queen Mab*, IX. 1 ; and his *Invocation to Misery*, IV ; T. H. Chivers's *Sons of Usna*, III. 3 ; and even in Nietzsche's phrase : ' The idealist is incorrigible ;

if one casts him out of his heaven, he makes an ideal of his hell.' Blake's lines, however, show the closest parallel to some lines from the *Midsummer Night's Dream* :

> Oh ! then, what graces in my love do dwell
> That he hath turn'd a heaven unto a hell.
>
> —(I. i. 206-207.)

> I 'll follow thee and make a heaven of hell.
>
> —(II. i. 243.)

The symbols of the Clod and the Pebble themselves are happily chosen. The Clod is pliable, and has in it the germs of higher life ; and therefore is chosen quite appropriately to represent the unselfish love. The Pebble, on the other hand, is completely dead ; it lies in water, which, as we have seen, is the old Catholic symbol for death, which to Blake meant always materialism.

THE LITTLE VAGABOND. This poem, as a poem, is quite bad, and I have no doubt Blake saved it only for its exquisite decoration. The little vagabond naïvely wishes to unite religion with the joys of life, the latter of which (typified by the ale-house) he quite naturally prefers. While we understand his attitude, we feel that God and the Devil are not quite so easily joined. For once Blake is not convincing. The Marriage of Heaven and Hell is yet to take place.

HOLY THURSDAY. Blake is appalled by the fact that, though there is enough for all, yet the Innocent are starved.

Line 4. Blake always hated organized charities as soulless things which did not—could not—give what was needed most.

Line 8. England was reputed rich among the nations of the world. Blake denies it, since there is such poverty.

Lines 13-14. Wherever the sun of true love and the rain of true charity exist, starvation is impossible.

A POISON TREE. This teaches the danger of suppressed thoughts. Wrath told is wrath destroyed ; but wrath concealed grows into terrible things. ' It strongly suggests, among other things, certain eastern ideas about the unseen influence of revengeful thoughts. . . . The more often that you read the poem, the more often will you make new discoveries in it,' wrote Lafcadio Hearn (*Interpretations of Literature*, I. 59). Blake is certainly within that realm which is condemned as Magic. Yet no explanation of the poem is at all necessary ; though it might be well to point out that the man of wrath never does anything to accomplish his revenge. He is entirely passive—merely lets things go their natural road—and when he finds his dead enemy, his thought was undoubtedly : ' Good ! He had no business stealing in my garden.' Such people never remember that they should not be growing such fruit.

It is possible that Blake was inspired by Chatterton's lines :

> a foule empoysoned leathel tree
> Whyche sleaeth everichone that commeth nere.
>
> —(*First Eclogue.*)

THE ANGEL. The preceding poem dealt with the dangers of wrath when concealed by a man ; this one describes the tragedy of love when concealed by a woman. When Love first comes to her, she cannot resist it, nor can she accept it freely ; so she lives in an anguish of hypocrisy. As a result, her love is driven away. She gathers strength to resist him ; but when he comes again, she is too old.

THE SICK ROSE. This poem is the natural sequel to *The Angel*, for the Rose has always been the flower of love. A symbol equally well known is that of the Worm, or Flesh. Therefore this poem means more than that Love is destroyed by the concealment of sin or the gnawings of conscience ; it means ultimately that love, which is of the spirit, is corrupted by the flesh, in this age of Experience. For the Worm comes only in the night of Experience, and in the storm, which is a Blakean symbol for materialism. Blake believed entirely in the love of the Innocent—the pure-minded—which might, and should, reach bodily expression ; but such love repressed became the torture of a flame, which was as much of a Hell as exists (*Jerusalem*, 52 ; cf. also the *Visions of the Daughters of Albion*, 178-186).

To TIRZAH. At last Blake is deliberately obscure. He felt that one such poem in this book should stimulate its readers to search the other poems for concealed meanings. Since Mr. A. Edward Newton's copy omits this poem and no other, it has been conjectured that this was the last of the *Songs of Experience* to be written.

Tirzah, as we learn from Blake's later works, is the chaste woman, the ensnarer of man, who by hypocrisy and selfishness continues the delusion of our mortal bodies. Her opposite is Rahab, the harlot.

Blake undoubtedly wrote this poem when trying to interpret the unfilial remark of the child Jesus in the Temple : ' Woman, what have I to do with thee ? ' (*John* ii. 4). Blake's conclusion was that Jesus was interrupted in his consideration of spiritual matters by the intrusion of her who bound him into the corporeal world. This is the case with every man. For the mortal body is of the earth, and will return to it, a temporary delusion ; the true body is the spiritual body : a distinction made by Paul (1 *Cor.* xv. 44—which is quoted by Blake in the marginal decoration to this poem).

The sexes were therefore produced by the Fall, and in Eternity will vanish. They sprang from the false emotions of shame and pride ; and they express themselves in cruelty and hypocrisy. But Mercy (Jesus) turned this Death from Eternity into a sleep—we shall awake again. Jesus himself descended to show us the way back : his own ' death ' has set us free from these delusions. ' Then what have I to do with thee,' the continuer of them ?

THE VOICE OF THE ANCIENT BARD. This was originally one of the *Songs of Innocence*. The Bard is the man who retains divine insight. He implores Youth to avoid the dark ways of Experience, and points to the dawn of the true light.

Line 9. Cf. ' Drive your cart and your plow over the bones of the dead ' (2nd *Proverb of Hell*). In other words, do not be misled by the past : ignore it when necessary, but always remembering that there is the richest ground for one's own planting.

MY PRETTY ROSE-TREE. Man is punished for the sin he does not commit. The flower as symbol of sexual indulgence goes back to the Greeks at least. Blake extends it by referring to the wife as a whole tree of flowers which may be legally enjoyed. The sin described in this poem is twofold : first, the sin of repression on the part of the man, and secondly the sin of jealousy on the part of the woman.

Mr. T. S. Perry (*Atlantic Monthly*, April 1875) points out the resemblance of Blake's poem to Goethe's *Gefunden* (' Ich ging im Walde '). Goethe's poem was not written till August 26, 1813.

AH ! SUN-FLOWER. This is another of Blake's supreme poems. The music of it alone has been sufficient to make it unforgettable, though its meaning is concealed far beyond the casual reader's range of vision.

The sunflower, which is rooted in the earth, and whose face is supposed to follow the course of the sun, represented to Blake the man who is bound to the flesh, but who yearns after the liberty of Eternity.

The ' sweet golden clime where the traveller's [sun's] journey is done ' is the west, which in all mythologies is the land of promise. To Blake it was essentially so, since there the Americans had recently established their liberty. A sexual significance is also given the poem by the second stanza. The liberty of the west was always, to Blake, a liberty of the body. Therefore the Virgins of both sexes aspire towards the west. But Blake (we need hardly warn the reader) meant this spiritually, after all; since they 'arise from their graves' or bodies. Eternity can never be wholly attained in the flesh. Love is really only our guide there.

Was Blake inspired by one of the few good lines in Ossian : ' The west opened its gates, the bed of thy repose is there ' (*Carric-Thura*) ? But we must remember that the west had become an ideal place to all Europeans. Shelley also wished to ' follow Love's folding star to the Evening land ' (*Hellas*, 1029-1030).

The Sunflower appears in the 87th design to Young.

THE LILLY. Blake now distinguishes between spiritual love and worldly love. The Lily fears nothing, and is ready to give her entire self. The Rose, on the contrary, puts forth a thorn because she is ' modest '—a deceptive word, which was Blake's final choice after considering ' envious ' and ' lustful.' The ' humble ' sheep was originally called ' coward.' Blake was very fond of such paradoxes, by which he thought to lay bare the inward meaning of such innocent words.

Mr. E. J. Ellis (*Facsimile*, p. xv) considers this ' the most beautiful quatrain in the English language.'

THE GARDEN OF LOVE. Another exquisite poem on the divinity of impulse and the cruelty of religious prohibitions. The priests have turned the garden to a chapel; and where flowers (innocent joys) once grew are now graves (the materialistic bodies acquired in Experience).

THE LITTLE BOY LOST. A child, or rather a person still in the state of Innocence, criticizes established religion by his own intuition. The marvellously compressed first stanza, when paraphrased, means : ' My mind is not large enough to comprehend Divinity. I can only love according to my own measure.' Therefore the child cannot love God more than he can love his brothers, for he is nothing but a little bird living on the crumbs from the Love-feasts of Eternity. The priest cannot allow such an attitude. He sacrifices the little boy to prevent the spread of such thought. The bitterness of the fourth stanza is very Blakean. The priest accuses the little boy of setting up Reason as a judge of the great Mystery. But the fact is that the child was motivated by instinct, not reason ; it is the priest himself who is ' reasonable,' and therefore he can only see Divine Truth as a Mystery.

' As a matter of fact, the religious persecutors seldom burned children under sixteen years of age, except when there was a general massacre of heretics. But the poet uses the figure of the child quite properly for his didactic purpose. In reality he means that in the sight of the eternal power, in the sight of the Supreme Wisdom, we are all like children, and that we are especially foolish in being cruel to each other.' Lafcadio Hearn : *Interpretations of Literature* (I. 62).

INFANT SORROW. Childhood is not all happiness. Even at the moment of birth, the child is accompanied by pain and sorrow. This poem was perhaps suggested by *Sephestia's Song to her Childe* in Greene's *Menaphon*.

THE SCHOOL-BOY. This was originally a *Song of Innocence*. Blake never went to school himself, since flogging affected him so strongly. He was entirely self-educated, and never regretted it. In one of his epigrams he wrote :

> Thank God ! I was never sent to school
> To be flogg'd into following the style of a fool.
> The errors of a wise man make your rule,
> Rather than the perfections of a fool.

He certainly was not advocating ignorance ; he simply felt that self-development was to be placed above the mental bondage to which all school-children submit. Can we not sympathize with those who still go through the terrible mill of instruction ? Would we not rather read the books we prefer in trees, like the little boy depicted on the margin ? That boy is Blake's own explanation that he preferred Education (in the real meaning of the word, which is ' a drawing out ') to Instruction (which is ' pounding in '). Blake's attitude towards schools, far from being ridiculous, is entirely modern.

LONDON. This poem of concentrated wrath is directed against the corruption of civilization by the power of Reason, whose ' mind-forged manacles ' have restricted every natural joy into a terrible agony. The street-cries of the chimney-sweeps are accusations against the Church ; and the death-sigh of the soldier is a stain upon the State (how vividly Blake visualized that stain, as actually running in blood !). Love itself, when so bound, makes the marriage bed a disease-blighted hearse.

Every one of us, at some moment of complete pessimism, has viewed the world in the same way, and has seen weakness and woe in every face. Blake's poem is not only a protest ; it is a picture of a mental state.

A LITTLE GIRL LOST. The young girl, who has given herself freely to love, suddenly sees in the woe of her father's face the sorrow that is to overwhelm her. Blake's protest against the cruelty flung upon such girls is still sadly needed. Such problems produced like lines in Milton :

> Whatever Hypocrites austerely talk
> Of puritie, and place, and innocence,
> Defaming as impure what God declares
> Pure, and commands to som, leaves free to all.
>
> —*Paradise Lost*, IV. 744-747.

Coleridge did not quite like Blake's poem. He wrote : ' I would have had it omitted, not for the want of innocence in the poem, but from the too probable want of it in many readers ' (letter to C. A. Tulk, 1818).

This is Blake's first address to ' the future age.' Later he was to come to the bitter conclusion that his own age could not possibly understand him ; and all his latter works were calculated to appeal to the generations to come.

THE CHIMNEY-SWEEPER. Blake accuses the Church directly for the depraving of these children. Because a child still carries some of his happiness with him wherever he goes is no justification for making him live by such terrible work. The reader who thinks Blake's indignation over-emphasized should read a few of the accounts that were then being published of the cruelties practised upon these helpless victims of civilization. If such accounts are unprocurable, he may turn to his *Water-Babies*, though there he will find none of the worst deeds which the eighteenth century allowed.

THE HUMAN ABSTRACT. This describes the doctrine of Experience : how false virtues arise from selfishness, fear, and weakness ; how they spring up as the Tree of Mystery, or Established Religion. Urizen, as yet unnamed, appears in the margin ; for it is under the reign of Reason only that such a Church could appear.

Stanza 1. This stanza, in a slightly revised form, appears in the later poem, *I Heard an Angel Singing*.

Line 15. These vermin are Blake's usual symbols for priesthood. Cf., for example, the 55th *Proverb of Hell*.

There are two other poems which were intended to be included in this volume, but which never found a place there. *A Divine Image* was engraved ; but it appears printed only on paper water-marked after Blake's death. *A Cradle Song* (*MS. Book*) was never engraved, but was obviously intended as the counterpart of the *Cradle Song* in the *Songs of Innocence*.

A DIVINE IMAGE (the article is significant) is a picture of the God of this World, Urizen. It reveals Satan, as he appears in human form. Blake's interchanging of the adjectives 'divine' and 'human' (for each appears in the image of the other) is well demonstrated here, for the word 'human' appears in every line of the poem.

Stanza 1. Cruelty, Jealousy, Terror, and Secrecy are human qualities, just as much as Kindness, Generosity, Love, and Confidence; therefore a god can be erected out of them.

Stanza 2. As a result, the 'human dress' or the flesh becomes the 'forged iron' of a prison to the soul; the inner form is itself a creator of other forms equally materialistic (since everything is created by the mind); the face conceals its hot passions; and the heart expresses them.

A CRADLE SONG. The poet contemplates a sleeping baby-girl, and sees in her face the foreshadowings of her future power as woman. Already the hypocrisy and 'modesty' of sex springs instinctively within her.

Line 2. The child anticipates the joys she will find in 'night,' or Experience.

Lines 3-4 are very famous. Swinburne called them 'two of the loveliest lines of his writing.'

DECORATIONS

General Title-page. This reads: 'Songs of Innocence and Of Experience, Showing the Two Contrary States of the Human Soul.' The decoration below really refers only to Experience: it depicts the fallen Adam and Eve, clad in vine-leaves, and surrounded by a blast of flame, the 'Furnace of Affliction.' Eve is prostrate, and Adam, in agony, bends over her. They are much younger than usually represented, being no more than a youth and maiden. The lettering itself suggests flame. A bird, symbolic of lost joy, is escaping from the blaze.

Frontispiece. Blake calculated this plate, and the title which follows, as a transition from Innocence to Experience. A youth strides forward, with his back to the setting sun. Upon his head sits a naked, winged child, whom he holds by the hands. In one copy this child has a faint halo. The youth is not only turning his back to the light, but is leaving behind him the flocks of Innocence. On his left is a tree-trunk, over which is growing a vine with scourge-like leaves—the ivy which is found nowhere in the *Songs of Innocence*, but which occurs often in the *Songs of Experience*. He is obviously walking unsuspecting towards trouble, a trouble which we, already in the world of Experience, do not see. We perceive only the clouds of glory which he is leaving.

Title-page. The text reads: 'Songs of Experience 1794 The Author & Printer W. Blake.' The transition is continued. The word 'Songs' still flowers into lovely vines, rejoicing figures, and the like. 'Of' also vegetates—but into the scourge-like plant, which we meet for the second time. The word 'Experience' is without any decoration, and spreads like a bar across the entire page. In Mr. Henry Huntington's copy, this transition is made the more obvious by the gilding of the first word only. Below 'Experience' two children wail by the death-bed of their parents. Their attitude distinctly indicates the Cross. The hard, straight lines of this scene (which is accentuated by the architecture behind them), and the pallid, ghastly colouring are a great contrast to the limpid curves of all the decorations to the *Songs of Innocence*.

Introduction. The text is inscribed in a cloud, against a background of a night sky strewn with stars. Below, a nude female reclines on a cloth, which is spread upon a cloud.

EARTH'S ANSWER. The familiar vines of grapes reappear, but directed downward. Below the text, a mottled snake (which always in Blake's early works represents the priesthood) runs on the ground. This is the Serpent in Eden.

Nurse's Song. The nurse combs the hair of a boy with folded hands. In the majority of copies, the boy looks very unhappy and indignant. In the grape-wreathed cottage door behind sits a little girl.

The Fly. A mother teaches her baby to walk. Behind her a little girl is playing battledore. The shuttlecock was no doubt intended to suggest the Fly. On the mother's left is a barren trunk of a tree.

The Tyger. This, the greatest of the poems, has the worst decoration. A sort of Noah's Ark animal stands beneath the text. Blake did not even try to paint him always in the proper colours.

The Little Girl Lost. The decoration evidently illustrates *A Little Girl Lost*, which is quite another poem. To the right of the text is a slender drooping tree, beneath which a youth and maiden embrace. She points upward at the flight of a long-tailed bird. Neither of them see, in a vine with bell-shaped flowers, the serpent in their Paradise—the priest.

This misplaced decoration accounts for the confusion of some critics over the meaning of the poem.

The Little Girl Found, first plate. She sits on the ground in the forest. Below is a tiger. At least I think it must be a tiger, since in the Palmer copy he is striped with black.

The Little Girl Found, second plate. To the right of the text: a double tree-trunk spirals upward; at its foot are children playing with the lions. An older figure, undoubtedly a parent, is asleep on the grass. This figure is repeated in *America*, plate 9. To the left of the text is a spiralling vine.

The Clod and the Pebble. Above the text: four sheep and two cattle drink from the brook. Below the text are two frogs (one of them leaping) and a duck. There is also a vine, at whose root (in some copies) is the worm.

The Little Vagabond. This bad poem has an unusually fine illustration. It represents the reconciliation of God and the Devil. This latter is a nude youth bowed weeping into the lap of the old man, who comforts him. Around are the oak groves of error. Below the text: a family warm themselves by a street fire.

Holy Thursday. Above the text: a woman stands beneath a leafless tree, and gazes appalled at the corpse of a baby. Behind is a rocky landscape. To the right of the text are large oak-leaves, a mother and two weeping children, and a dead baby wrapped in an oak-leaf. Blake already was using the oaks, of which England has always been so proud, as symbols of the sturdy, flourishing errors which he found on every hand.

A Poison Tree. Beneath the text: a grey corpse lies, arms outstretched, supine, under the leafless boughs of the Tree, which pour down upon him like black rain. This is one of the most effective decorations.

The Angel. Above the text: a mournful, reclining woman thrusts away a naked winged boy, who kneels beside her. To the left of the text is an arrow. The decorative vegetation suggests snakes and scourges. In the Calvert copy, the woman is crowned.

The Sick Rose. The rose-plant entirely circles the text with thorns, rising on the left, and falling on the right, till the Rose itself is bent to earth. In the upper left corner is ' the caterpillar on the leaf.' In the upper right corner are two weeping figures. In the heart of the blossom itself, a human figure is caught by a worm. It shows Blake's lack of observation in that all the thorns point upward. Two copies (the Calvert and the Morgan copies), in defiance of the text, make the Rose a ghastly white.

To Tirzah. Below the text: two maidens raise a reviving naked youth. **An**

old man stands by with a pitcher. On his garments, engraved vertically, are the words : 'It is raised a spiritual body' (1 *Cor.* **xv.** 44). Above are branches of fruit, possibly apples.

THE VOICE OF THE ANCIENT BARD. Below the text : the Bard plays on a triangular harp to a group of people, among whom are children. To the left, behind his back, a little girl sinks weeping into her mother's arms.

MY PRETTY ROSE TREE. This and the two following poems are engraved on the same plate. A girl reclines beneath a tree, disdaining a weeping figure at her feet. These are presumably Mr. and Mrs. Blake. There are also a flight of birds, reeds, and a vine.

AH ! SUN-FLOWER. To the left are decorative spirals and a tiny appealing figure. To the right, the sun is seen setting behind some mountains, below clouds.

THE LILLY. This poem has only a few spirals for decoration.

THE GARDEN OF LOVE. Above the text : a monk kneels and reads by an open grave to two praying children. To the right of the text is the Worm. Below is a grave bound across with briars, representing the 'death' of Experience, a symbol of which Blake was quite fond.

A LITTLE BOY LOST. The pyre blazes smokily in the lower left-hand corner, concealing the Boy himself. The sullen flames ascend on the left of the text. On the right, a tangle of the scourge-like leaves seems to be showered upon a group of people kneeling and weeping in the utmost despair before the pyre.

INFANT SORROW. A mother reaches toward her baby, who flings itself away from her on its bed.

THE SCHOOL-BOY. This is one of Blake's best decorations. Below the text : three boys are playing marbles. To the left of the text, a vine ascends, containing a figure and a long-tailed bird. To the right is a very luxuriant grape vine, in which four boys are vigorously climbing. The top one is comfortably reading : evidently Blake's own idea of the ideal education.

LONDON. Above the text : a little boy leads an aged cripple. This design is repeated in *Jerusalem*, plate 84. To the right of the second and third stanzas, a boy crouches, warming himself before a smoky fire out of doors. Below the text is the Worm.

A LITTLE GIRL LOST. To the right of the text is a tree twined with a vine. In it are to be seen flying birds, a squirrel, and a tiny human figure no larger than the squirrel. When plates such as these were painted carelessly or richly, these miniature figures are often blotted out.

THE CHIMNEY-SWEEPER. Below the text : the little chimney-sweeper passes home with a sack of soot and a brush, in a snowstorm.

THE HUMAN ABSTRACT. Below the text : an old man, instantly to be recognized as Urizen, is struggling in the net of religion, his own weaving. The idea of this design is repeated on the last plate of *Urizen*. The Morgan copy has a sunset on Urizen's right, with a bush holding two big red fruits.

This completes the *Songs of Experience*. The *Cradle Song* mentioned above had no decoration, since it is only found in the manuscript form. *A Divine Image*, however, was actually engraved, though never used by Blake. Below the text : Los, the spirit of Poetry, is forging the Sun upon his anvil. Behind him is the Moon. The usual tiny figures appear in the text. Another decoration which should be mentioned is the terminal vignette in two copies, which is supposed to have been inserted in place of the unwritten *To Tirzah*. This represents a nude youth in prayer borne aloft in an apotheosis by six winged children. This must symbolize earth regenerated.

LATER LYRICS

THE MS. BOOK

Never seek to tell thy Love. The youth terrifies the maiden by telling her frankly of his love. She shrinks away ; and before Love comes into her life, Death claims her. Saintsbury was particularly impressed by the technique : ' Nobody who has an ear can fail to see that . . . the prosodic *unity*, the kinship of the feet, and the wondrous dance that they trip out, are unmistakable. Like the *Mad Song*, it is a thing that you will find nowhere but in English poetry : like that, it shows what English poetry can and may do in the prosodic way. The quintessence of it is almost overpowering, and it carries with it the *beau bouquet de roses franches* which *La Quinte* always has by her to recover her lovers of their ecstasy ' (*Prosody*, iii. 17).

I laid me down upon a Bank. Suppressed love turns men and women to spiritual thorns and thistles. Swinburne, speaking of the second stanza, says : ' The sharp and subtle change of metre here and at the end of the poem has an audacity of beauty and a justice of impulse proper only to the leaders of lyrical verse.' Mr. J. P. R. Wallis, however, while asserting that the first stanza is unequalled before Keats,' and ' almost perfect in its music,' finds the second stanza ' an atrocious verse in crude three-foot anapests ' (p. 192).

I saw a Chapel all of Gold. This chapel is undoubtedly the chapel of love ; but just what the serpent signifies is not entirely clear. In the earliest poems and paintings, the serpent represents Priesthood ; later it came to represent Materialism, which was the religion of the priests ; later still, it was but another word for the Worm, the mortal body itself. All these meanings are connected, of course, and shift into each other. *The Sick Rose* has already taught us that Love is corrupted by the Worm at its heart ; is this but another symbol of the flesh overcoming the spirit ? Or is it a symbol of priesthood polluting the most sacred things of life ?
Lines 15-16. The sty is a cleaner place than the polluted Temple.

I asked a Thief. The triumph of the hypocrite. The ' Angel ' is one of those who figure in *The Marriage of Heaven and Hell*.

I heard an Angel singing. This poem anticipates the stage beyond Innocence and Experience. Here Innocence (the Angel) is Ignorance, while Experience (the Devil) is Cynicism. The symbolism is therefore slightly different from that of *The Marriage of Heaven and Hell*. Both Angel and Devil are wrong ; there is, by implication, a stage beyond both.
Lines 11-14 are revised from the first stanza of *The Human Abstract* (*Songs of Experience*).

A Cradle Song has already been considered under the *Songs of Experience*.

Silent, Silent Night. The honesty of passion defeats itself. This is one of the poems which has found few detractors and many admirers.

I fear'd the Fury of my Wind. This is a delightful bit of cynicism. The youth fears the fury of love, lest it blight love's fragile flowers ; but the tempest never came, and the blossoms were worthless anyhow.

Infant Sorrow. This is the first and longer version of the poem with the same name in the *Songs of Experience*. Blake evidently thought that the first two stanzas, which describe the pathos of the new-born child, were enough.

Here, however, we have the whole life of the child. It is born in sorrow, then gradually learns to turn towards happiness in the ecstasy of friendship (the vine) and of love (the myrtle tree) until baffled by the Priest. But the Priest is a hypocrite, enjoying privately what he denounces publicly. So the youth kills the Priest (defies religion), though only when he is too old to profit by his defiance.

WHY SHOULD I CARE FOR THE MEN OF THAMES. A political poem contrasting the English Thames with the American Ohio.

THOU HAST A LAP FULL OF SEED. The question is asked: why not enjoy love? The question is answered by another: shall the seed be sown in the sand (marriage), since where the ground is rich (where chastity is absent) the weeds would choke the seed?

The meaning of this poem seems to have been generally missed. The sexual significance of the lap full of seed is corroborated by *Ahania*, line 221. Mr. J. P. R. Wallis thinks that Blake was explaining his inability to write lyrics without spoiling them with morals (p. 192); while Berger found the poem an expression of ' his feeling of love for all things ' (p. 320).

IN A MIRTLE SHADE. This is an early form of *Infant Sorrow*. The youth protests that love cannot be bound, even to the lovely Myrtle-tree (his wife). The Father of line 11 is the Priest of *Infant Sorrow*; the terms were used interchangeably in the manuscript of both poems. The last stanza is repeated from the other poem.

TO MY MIRTLE. The second, compressed version of the preceding poem. The first two lines are new ones, introduced to emphasize the beauty of the tree, which nevertheless is so wearying.

TO NOBODADDY. Why is Religion Mystery, so that none dare receive bliss without the sanction of the Church? Because such is Woman's Will? ' To eat the fruit from the wily Serpent's jaws ' was the sin of Eve, and so she is represented in all pictures of the Fall. See also the decoration on *Jerusalem* 9.

' Nobodaddy, a " portmanteau word " for " Nobody's Daddy," antithetical to " Father of All," was Blake's jocular nickname for Urizen, the Father of Jealousy. The same name occurs in *Lafayette* and *When Klopstock England defied* ' (Sampson, 1913, p. 120).

ARE NOT THE JOYS OF MORNING SWEETER. A plea for the honesty and decency of passion.

THE WILD FLOWER'S SONG. This is another version of the ballad *Mary*. Natural delight is crushed out by the world's scorn. Perhaps Blake got his idea from Böhme's use of the same image in the first Epistle (42-45):

When the soul . . . getteth into itself God's *Love-Ens* . . . then . . . it . . . liveth in great patience under the vanity of this world, and yet groweth forth as a fair flower out of the wild earth. . . . The ground of the soul is the divine field; when it receiveth the divine sunshine into itself, a divine plant springeth forth; and this is the new birth, whereof Christ speaketh. . . . And as the body in the stalk must stand in the rain, wind, and storms, in heat and cold, and suffer the sun to ripen it; so likewise must a Christian stand in this thorny world, in the awaked anger of God, in the kingdom of the devil, amongst many wicked men, and suffer himself to be beaten, with scorn and contempt.

If Blake started from this passage, he changed the idea somewhat, for the New Birth is surely the awakening of the love-life.

Line 1. *The forest*: the forest of the night, of error, which is this world.

Line 8. In the state of Innocence (as a seed) the soul is in perfect harmony with the Universe.

Line 9. *The morning*. Possibly Böhme's Morgenroth, but more likely the radiance of Love.

DAY. This is probably a fragment only. It represents the dawn of the day of Revolution. The Sun is Orc-Jesus, clad in Luvah's robes of blood. The rather obvious statement of the first line, ' the sun arises in the East,' really means that Revolution springs up in the realms of passion.

THE FAIRY. The Fairy is natural Joy, who teaches that the marriage-ring is the crown of love ; but the youth who catches and controls the Fairy, instead of being at the Fairy's mercy, has removed the annoyance of the ring.

The 7th plate of *The Gates of Paradise* represents the other side of the story : we see the youth chasing and killing the butterfly-fairies, while beneath is written : ' Alas ! What are these ? the Female Martyr. Is She also the Divine Image ? '

MOTTO TO THE SONGS OF INNOCENCE AND OF EXPERIENCE. This poem was never used in the work for which Blake intended it.

At first, in the state of Innocence, people are unselfish and uncritical ; but when Experience is reached, they begin to order their life consciously, catching and caging ' the Fairies & Elves,' which are the real joys of the natural life.

But then the question of morality is raised, and people at once begin to show their true characters, and ' the Eagle is known from the Owl,' or the genius from the bird of night.

Line 7. *His* : an example of Blake's casual grammar. *His* refers to the poet, who is never directly mentioned, and only symbolized by the eagle in the ensuing line.

LAFAYETTE. Blake never completed his elaborate revision of this poem ; and it certainly was not intended for publication in its present confused and uneven form. However, it has so much beauty that we may be glad we have it even as it is.

It describes the tragedy of the righteous man with the wrong allegiance. Why does Lafayette not renounce the King and Queen, who are the cause of such pestilence and famine, both spiritual and material, and come to the aid of the people ? He himself has seen the corruption of the court (stanzas iv., v.) ; yet foolishly he is ruining himself by protecting it. Who would give up his natural duties to humanity to perform others less human, and without their deserved reward ? We can misplace our pity, as he has done (stanza vii.), but should we sacrifice our new-born child for the dog starving at the gate (stanza ix.) ?

Line 11. *Our Good Queen* : Queen Charlotte, contrasted by her inactivity during times of trouble to Marie Antoinette, whom Blake conceived to have been actively evil. Blake surely intended to change this and the following line, which are interesting as examples of what bad things he could write.

Line 33. *The wintry seas* : symbolic of the uproar of materialism and cruelty preceding and during the French Revolution.

A FAIRY LEAPT UPON MY KNEE. The poet ponders the question of the vanities of the world : of what use are ' patches, rings, pins, necklaces,' and all the other decorations which disgrace the pure form of woman ? The answer is that, since woman's form must be covered for the sake of protection against the elements, the ' fairies,' or artistic pleasure, must sacrifice themselves for her ; however, though they must cover beauty, yet they try to beautify the covering.

MY SPECTRE AROUND ME NIGHT & DAY. This poem has already been dealt with in the text.

Line 1. *My Spectre around me* : cf. ' Reason is the bound or outward circumference of Energy ' (*The Marriage of Heaven and Hell : The Voice of the Devil*).

Line 3. *Far within* : the inner life.

Lines 17-28. Emanation and Spectre have different loves, or worldly interests, which interfere with each other. These must be given up, for they are selfish ; and then Spectre and Emanation can be reconciled (lines 53, 61).

Line 51. Cf. ' Till hard despair wring from the tyrant's soul The iron tears out ' (Isaac Watts : *Horae Lyricae : To Her Majesty*).

Line 54. *The Infernal Grove* : the Tree of Mystery. Cf. :

> Rooting over with thorns & stems
> The buried Soul & all its Gems.
>
> —*Everlasting Gospel*, III. 99-100.

Cf. also Shelley's *Queen Mab*, IX. 191-192 :

> . . . and uproot
> The germs of misery from the human heart.

Cf. also Thomas Vaughan's *Lumen de Lumine* :

We came to an Ancient Majestic Altar ; On the Offertorie, or very top of it, was figur'd the Trunck of an old rotten tree, pluck'd up by the Roots. Out of this crept a snake, of colour white and Green, Slow of Motion like a snayle, and very weake, having but newly felt the Sun, that overlook'd her.

WHEN KLOPSTOCK ENGLAND DEFIED. This poem is quite illegible now, having been pencilled hastily in the *MS. Book* ; so that some of it which Swinburne copied cannot now be read in the original. Unfortunately, he did not copy the whole of it, so that a few lines are now lost forever. This reticence on Swinburne's part was due to the difference of taste in humour between the Georgian and the Victorian periods. *When Klopstock England Defied* is of the same coarse fibre as *An Island in the Moon* ; quite as harmless also.

Klopstock was known as ' the German Milton ' ; Milton was Blake's favourite poet ; therefore we can at once explain the opening line. It was assumed by Swinburne that this poem was written at Felpham, since in Hayley's diary for March 26 and 27, 1803, we find the following entry :

Read the death of Klopstock in the newspaper of the day and looked into his *Messiah*, both the original and the translation. Read Klopstock into English to Blake and translated the opening of his third canto, where he speaks of his own death.

Dr. Sampson points out, however, that this poem refers to Lambeth, while the fourth line was repeated in *Lafayette* ; therefore he assumes that this poem was written about 1793. His 1905 edition of Blake reprints the poem more completely than the 1913 edition.

Saintsbury found this poem very interesting from the technical point of view. ' The miraculous lampoon on Klopstock, which has in considerable part blushed itself off the face of the manuscript . . . is either *Christabel* before *Christabel* and adjusted to *burla* or Butler equivalenced into a wilder state of prosodic puckishness than *Hudibras* itself displays ' (*Prosody*, III. 18).

Line 1. By trying to do what Milton had done.

Line 3. *Nobodaddy* : Urizen-Jehovah.

After line 20 should be inserted a couplet whose reading seems to be :

> That from his body it ne'er could be found
> Till to the last judgment it was bound.

The last four lines are almost entirely illegible. They may read :

> And so feeling, he beg'd me to turn again
> And . . . poor Klopstock now for fun
> Then, ...
> And   .   .   .   .   .

Sideways in the page, as a sort of terminal afterthought, is a last couplet :

> If Blake would do this when he rose up from shite,
> What might he not do if he sat down to write ?

MOCK ON, MOCK ON, VOLTAIRE, ROUSSEAU. A protest against the railings of these two against mystical Christianity. Blake, however, decided later that they were the necessary prelude to the Revolution, and that they did a great deal of good in destroying errors. ' He [Blake] understood the Bible in a spiritual sense. As to the natural sense, Voltaire was commissioned by God to expose that ' (H. C. R., March 1, 1852).

This poem contains an image which has been much commended by various critics. It might have been derived from Webster's *White Devil*, III. 1 :

> As if a man should spit against the wind ;
> The filth returns in 's face.

A closer parallel is to be found in the Buddhist *Sutra of Forty-Two Sections* (quoted by Carus : *Gospel of Buddha*, p. 146) : ' The slanderer is like one who flings dust at another when the wind is contrary ; the dust does but return on him who threw it.'

I saw a Monk of Charlemaine. This poem was eventually divided in two : half appearing as *The Grey Monk* in the *Pickering MS.*, and half as the poem *To the Deists* in *Jerusalem*. Only two stanzas (iv. and xiv.) appear in all three versions.

The Monk is the persecuted Pacifist, who, realizing that War only begets War, preaches non-resistance to Evil, though he well knows that this attitude will ruin his whole life.

Line 1. *Charlemaine* : the state of imperialism.

Line 4. *Infernal* : that is, anti-' angelic.'

Line 33. *Thy father* : Blake often uses the word ' father ' to symbolize the tradition of the past, from which we are sprung.

Line 45. *The tyrant* : Satan.

Lines 53-56. This last stanza is one of Blake's unforgettable quatrains.

Morning. *Mercy* is the death of War.

Line 1. *Western* : freedom.

The Birds. This was apparently an attempt to do something in the style of the *Poetical Sketches* ; but, even with the Blakean metre and rhymes, it seems as though some one else had written it. The two birds represent the Spectre and Emanation readily becoming united in the state of Innocence. The tree probably symbolizes the phallos.

You Don't Believe. ' If the fool would persist in his folly, he would become wise.' Blake tries to prove the unreasonableness of scepticism. Reason recognizes the miracle ; but Newton, the arch-sceptic, questions even the fact. Science says to doubt until the fact is tried ; Jesus says that faith will prove the fact. Blake agreed with Whitman (*Song of the Open Road*) that ' Wisdom is of the Soul, is not susceptible of proof, is its own proof.'

If it is true what the Prophets Write. Blake was very fond of the theory that the Bible was direct inspiration, and that the classics were not so direct, and hence ' derived ' from the sacred writings. That is, the classics were not written from pure inspiration, which Plato called madness, but from inspiration adulterated with reason. Therefore Blake calls them ' stolen from the temple of the Lord.'

Classical art just then was becoming popular, and Blake detested it, even though one of his best friends, Flaxman, was quite given over to it.

This poem was written against this fashion, which to Blake was almost blasphemy. If we have the direct revelation from God, why should we kneel to heathen gods, who were exposed by the prophets ?

Line 4. *I.e.* kneel to them.

Line 5. *Bezaleel and Aholiab* were the craftsmen directly inspired by Jehovah to build the tabernacle and ark (*Exodus* xxxi.).

Line 11. The technique, and not the message, became the important thing.

Line 12. Empire, and not Art (Prophets) governed the land.

Line 13. Selfishness arose.

Line 14. Cf. ' Art degraded, Imagination denied, War governed the Nations ' (*Laocoon plate*).

I WILL TELL YOU WHAT JOSEPH OF ARIMATHEA. This poem means, quite simply, that the inward inspiration can order about the classics at the merest whim. In *The Four Zoas*, VIII. 332, Los, the god of Poetry, is identified with Joseph of Arimathea. According to the old legend, having caught the blood of Christ in the Holy Grail, and having received the body, he left Judea, and brought the true religion to England, at Glastonbury. Blake's first engraving (1773) was inscribed : ' Joseph of Arimathea among the rocks of Albion. This was one of the Gothic Artists who Built the Cathedrals in what we call the dark Ages wandering about in sheepskin and goatskin, of whom the World was not worthy. Such were the Christians in all Ages.' (See *Hebrews* XI. 37-38.)

WHY WAS CUPID A BOY. This poem may go back to chapter viii. of *An Island in the Moon* for its genesis :

They call women the weaker vessel, but I think they are the strongest. A girl has always more tongue than a boy. I 've seen a little crab no higher than a nettle, and she had as much tongue as a city clerk. But a boy would be such a fool not to have anything to say, and if anybody asked him a question he would put his head into a hole and hide it.

Line 17. *Love of war* : that is, blindness to true inspiration.
Line 18. Possibly a reference to the perverse passions of the Greeks, but more probably a reference to their mistaken symbolism.
Line 19. A reference to Niobe—or possibly to Galatea.

NOW ART HAS LOST ITS MENTAL CHARMS. A fragment, in which Blake represents himself as sent to oppose Napoleon's threatened invasion of England by creating works of art so beautiful that France would be under the spiritual dominion of England. Thus war would end. Blake often made references to his theory that physical and spiritual dominion are two different things : that conquest by the sword is nothing compared to conquest by spiritual means. Dr. Sampson quotes in a note to this poem (1913, p. 141), the following passage from the *MS. Book* : ' Let us teach Buonaparte and whomsoever else it may concern, that it is not Arts that follow & attend upon Empire, but Empire that attends upon & follows The Arts.'

I ROSE UP AT THE DAWN OF DAY. Blake condemns money as the Devil. ' He feared nothing so much as being rich, lest he should lose his spiritual riches,' wrote John Linnell to Bernard Barton, after Blake's death.

THE CAVERNS OF THE GRAVE I 'VE SEEN. ' Apparently dedicatory verses to accompany Blake's large water-colour painting of ' The Last Judgment,' executed for the Countess of Egremont ' (Sampson, 1913, p. 144).
Line 1. Cf. Shelley : *On Death* : ' The wide-winding caves of the peopled tomb.'
Line 2. In his edition of Blair's *Grave*.
Line 8. Cf. ' The fires of hell . . . the enjoyments of Genius, which to the Angels look like torment and insanity,' *The Marriage of Heaven and Hell*.
Line 18. *The Atlantic Mountains* are the Lost Atlantis, for which see the Commentary on line 107 of *America*.

TO THE QUEEN. These are the dedicatory verses from Blake's edition of Blair. They are almost unique in being entirely self-explanatory.

THE EVERLASTING GOSPEL. The ideas in this poem have already been discussed. Most of the criticism of this poem has depended on the critics' agreement or disagreement with its doctrines. There has been much talk of Blake's connection with Gnosticism ; but it seems very unlikely that this existed. His only correspondence with the ancient heretics lies in his opposing Jesus to the Creator. But the idea was a common one in Blake's own time. Thomas Paine, in a letter on *The Age of Reason* (Paris, May 12, 1797), wrote : ' It is not a God, just and good, but a devil, under the name of God, that the Bible describes.' Shelley took up the idea in his *Essay on Christianity* : ' According to Jesus Christ, and according to the indisputable facts of the case, some evil Spirit has dominion in this imperfect world.' Blake himself noted in the *MS. Book* : ' Thinking as I do that the Creator of this world is a very cruel Being, and being a worshipper of Christ, I cannot help saying of the Son, Oh, how unlike the Father ! First God Almighty comes with a thump on the head, and then Jesus Christ comes with a balm to heal it.' If Blake had read Mosheim's *Ecclesiastical History* (translated in 1764) or Lardner's *History of the Heretics in the Two First Centuries* (1780), he would have found corroboration of these ideas.

From the literary point of view, *The Everlasting Gospel* is simply a collection of unfinished and unpolished fragments. Some of the couplets are unsurpassable, both rhythmically and from the standpoint of the compression of thought. Others are weak. Still others are audaciously undignified. Whether or not it was actually written before *Christabel,* which wrought such a revolution in English metrics, may never be decided, nor is the point of much importance. Blake had steadily liberated his verse to and beyond the freedom which Coleridge made famous ; and *The Everlasting Gospel* is simply a metrical parallel to the poem which is generally credited with being the first to espouse the new freedom. The metre of one is the metre of the other ; yet the effects are completely different.

Fragment I

Lines 3-4. The doctrine of personal anthropomorphism, that each man makes God in his own image.

Lines 9-12. Cf. *Jerusalem,* 93 : ' Anytus, Melitus, & Lycon thought Socrates a Very Pernicious Man. So Caiaphas thought Jesus.'

Line 14. Cf. *Jerusalem,* 91 : 36-37 :

> Los reads the stars of Albion !   The Spectre reads the Voids
> Between the stars. . . .

Fragment II

Line 7. Cf. *To Tirzah* (*Songs of Experience*) and its Commentary.

Line 11. Cf. Shelley's *Queen Mab* (III. 178), where he calls obedience, ' Bare of all genius, virtue, freedom, truth.'

Line 30. As in *Exodus* ix. 9 ; *Deuteronomy* xxviii. 58-62 ; etc.

Line 31. *The God of this world* is Satan.

Line 32. *He* refers, of course, to Jesus, not to Satan.

Lines 48-49. A typical case of spiritual interpretation. ' Canaanite ' was Blake's own addition.

Line 55. Blake's solitary statement that flesh is sin.

Line 57. *To be worshipp'd* : the sin, not Jesus.

Fragment III

Lines 1-2. ' By the slave-morality of Christianity . . . the impotence which does not retaliate for injuries is falsified into goodness ; timorous abjectness becomes ' humility ' ; subjection to those one hates is called ' obedience,' and the one who desires and commands this impotence, abjectness, and submission is called God ' (Nietzsche, *Zur Genealogie der Moral,* I. 14).

Lines 5-10 are repeated, with slight variations, from II. 3-8.

Line 17. The cleverness of Jesus's preaching has always been ignored as something derogatory. Blake, however, brings his ideal almost to the verge of hypocrisy !

Line 41. ' Bacon, Locke, and Newton are the three great teachers of Atheism or of Satan's doctrine,' Blake told Crabb Robinson. ' Everything is Atheism which assumes the reality of the natural and unspiritual world.' Of course, this assumption is the basis of all physical science.

Line 44. Sir Isaac Newton was a metaphysician as well as a scientist. The statement here attributed to him might have been made by any Deist. It was particularly exasperating to Blake, the mystic, who had known God personally.

Line 62. *The Seraph band*, *i.e.* the ' Angels' as they appear in *The Marriage of Heaven and Hell.*

Line 66. *The Ancient Elf* : Satan.

Lines 75-76. In this famous couplet we reach again the truth hinted in *The Marriage of Heaven and Hell* in the words : that ' those who envy or calumniate great men hate God ; for there is no other God.' Humanity is the greatest of all things ; God is but the highest functions of his life. Nothing, not even God, should be put above Man : when that error is committed, the God, whoever he be, becomes the enemy of society. In the *Descriptive Catalogue* (III.) Blake states the idea remarkably clearly for himself, and asks : ' When separated from man or humanity, who is Jesus the Saviour ? '

It is obvious, however, that though ' all deities reside in the human breast,' Blake distinguishes between God and Man. ' God is Man & exists in us & we in him,' he wrote in his copy of Berkeley's *Siris*. The difference is a subtle one, but none the less clear. Blake found authority for his belief in *Psalm* lxxxii. 6 : ' I have said, Ye are gods '—a passage quoted with approval by the Saviour himself (*John* x. 33-34). *Isaiah* xli. 23 is also possibly to be read in the same light.

The doctrine is an old one, and crops up continually in writings both ancient and modern. Blake's distinction is not always made, however ; particularly in his own century the tendency to exalt Man above God meant simply the denial of God. At other times it became nothing but the old mystical affirmation that God dwells in Man.

A few of these references will not be without interest. ' Osirification ' is dealt with extensively in the Egyptian *Book of the Dead.* When Apollonius of Tyana questioned the Indian sages, he asked ' " what they held themselves to be ? " " Gods," was the answer ' (Philostratus : *Vit. Apoll.* III. 18). The *Pymander* of Hermes Trismegistus contains a number of affirmations : ' For it is Possible for the Soul, O Son, to be Deified while yet it Lodgeth in the Body of Man, if it Contemplate the Beauty of the Good ' (IV. 19) ; ' Man is a Divine living thing ' (IV. 89) ; ' Wherefore we must be bold to say, that Earthly Man is a Mortal God, and that the Heavenly God is an Immortal Man ' (IV. 93) ; ' The Mind, O Tat, is of the very Essence of God ' (XI. 1) ; ' This Mind in Men is God, and therefore are some men Divine ' (XI. 4) ; while in the *Initiation* we learn that ' Certes [Man] deserves admiration, being the greatest of all the Gods ! ' (IX.).

In the seventeenth century, we find the sect of the Ranters teaching this openly, and George Fox in 1649 argued with them in his prison (*Journal of George Fox*). Jakob Böhme announced the same doctrine in his *Aurora* : ' Men are Gods, and have the Knowledge of God, the only Father ' (xxii. 12) ; and other references in his later works are to be found. Thomas Vaughan hinted around the doctrine with his customary reticence : ' Neither should any wonder that I affirme the Spirit of the living God to be in Man, when God himselfe doth acknowledge it for his own ' (*Anthroposophia Theomagica*) ; while S. S. D. D., in notes on the first paragraph of *Euphrates*, quotes words from the mummy-case of Panehemisis : ' The heart of Man is his own God.'

In Blake's day we find Comte's Religion of Humanity. The secret pledge of the Rosicrucians (quoted by E. O. in a note to Eliphaz Lévi's *Paradoxes of the Highest Sciences*, Calcutta, 1883) is probably of the same period : ' Man is God and Son of God, and there is no other God but man.' Cagliostro was accused of the same doctrine : ' " I am that I am," as he is said to have described himself profanely on one occasion ' (W. R. Trowbridge : *Cagliostro*, ch. v.). Saint-Martin proclaimed : ' L'Homme un Dieu ! Verité ! ' in his *Stances sur l'origine et la destination de l'homme*. Swedenborg defined God as the human divine (*Arcana*, 2807 ; *Apoc. Exp.* 1097). In 1811, after Blake had stated his belief several times, the *Prabodha Chandrodaya* was translated, in the last act of which Man is identified with God : ' The eternal God is not distinct from thee ; and thou art not distinct from God, the greatest of beings : but thou appearest to be a separate being in consequence of Maya [error] like an image of the sun reflected in water.'

After Blake, we find Shelley denying God at times, yet struggling towards Blake's idea, as in *Laon and Cythna*, VIII. 6. Whitman's thought played all about the doctrine, but never quite hit it. In the *Song of Myself*, he distinctly states : ' Taking myself the exact dimensions of Jehovah. . . . And nothing, not God, is greater to one than one's self is.'

Lines 79-84. Blake is dealing here in paradoxes. Christ's Judgment is the spiritual revelation of truth ; the mercy of God exists but to bring about such a Last Judgment ; and the revenge is prayer upon the Cross.

Line 88. Jesus admits his mistake in praying for the world, which is error and illusion.

Line 89. This sentence was left unfinished by Blake.

Lines 89-96. A description of the world of generation, which was created when the Soul fell into the sleep of death. Then the soul developed the fibres of the body, and reasoned in doubt over the self-contradictions of the illusions in which it was lost.

Lines 95-96 are repeated, with variations, from *The Gates of Paradise*, 13-14.

Lines 97-98 are revised in the *Auguries of Innocence*, 109-110.

Lines 99-100. In Blake's pictures we often see a grave rooted over with thorns, whose meaning is clearly explained here.

Lines 101-102. Cf. ' Five windows light the caverned Man ' (*Europe*). This couplet may have been suggested by 1 *Cor.* xiii. 12 : ' For now we see through a glass darkly,' which finds a parallel in Trismegistus's *Treatise on Initiation* (XI.) : ' And as for us who are men, we perceive heavenly things as it were darkly through a mist, for thus only does the condition of our human sense permit us to behold them.' But the greatest parallel of all is to be found in Shelley's *Adonais* :

> Life, like a dome of many-coloured glass,
> Stains the white radiance of Eternity.

Lines 103-106 are repeated in the *Auguries of Innocence*, 125-128.

FRAGMENT IV

This fragment is addressed to materialists by Blake's ' Spectre,' or Reasoning power, which is the only part of him that can have converse with such. His questions imply the answer that Jesus taught by Faith from Instinct, not by philosophical rules derived from Reason.

FRAGMENT V

Lines 1-2. The reader should not be surprised to learn that Blake's answer to this question is an emphatic ' No ! ' Mary was not a Virgin, with all the implication of hypocrisy and suppressed desire which is the fruit of chastity. If we ignore the epigram which links her name with that of Joanna Southcott, we can still turn to *Jerusalem*, 61.

Lines 11-12. The idea that the body of Jesus was not subject to pain or temptation of any sort is here denied by Blake. The theory was advanced by the Gnostics ; but Blake was surely attacking the conventional idea of Christ's inability to sin, as a result of supreme purity.

Line 17. The remainder of this fragment is concerned with the sins which

Jesus committed against society and against the Ten Commandments. Cf. *The Marriage of Heaven and Hell*: 'Now hear how he has given his sanction to the law of ten commandments. Did he not mock at the sabbath, and so mock the sabbath's God; murder those who were murder'd because of him; turn away the law from the woman taken in adultery; steal the labour of others to support him; bear false witness when he omitted making a defence before Pilate; covet when he pray'd for his disciples, and when he bid them shake off the dust of their feet against such as refus'd to lodge them? I tell you, no virtue can exist without breaking these ten commandments. Jesus was all virtue, and acted from impulse, not from rules.'

Lines 37-38. Blake later told Crabb Robinson that Jesus had no business to meddle with politics, as they lay out of his sphere.

Lines 47-48. *Righteous law*: that is just, or unmerciful. Cf. Shelley's *Essay on Christianity*: '. . . Jesus Christ proceeds to qualify and finally to abrogate the system of Jewish law. He descants upon its insufficiency as a code of moral conduct, which it professed to be (*Matt.* v. 21, 27, 31, 33), and absolutely selects the law of retaliation as an instance of the absurdity and immorality of its institutions (*Matt.* v. 38).'

FRAGMENT VI

This deals with the Forgiveness of Sins, as applied to the Adulteress. Cf. Blake's remark to Crabb Robinson: 'What are called Vices in the natural world are the highest sublimities in the spiritual world.' Cf. also Nietzsche's semi-truth in his *Götzendämmerung* (IX. 45): 'The criminal type is the type of the strong man under unfavourable conditions—the strong man who has been made sick.'

Blake, following Catholic tradition, identifies the woman taken in adultery with Mary Magdalen. He also identifies the casting out of the seven devils (*Luke* viii. 2) with the forgiving of her sins.

Lines 15-16. The whole world of generation trembles in sympathy with Mary.

Line 29. *Thou Angel of the Presence Divine*: Elohim-Jehovah, the Creator, one of the Seven Eyes of God, who became leprous (*Milton*, 11 : 24).

Lines 31-32. Cf. 'Prisons are built with stones of law, brothels with bricks of religion.' Blake's old idea, based on *Romans* vii. 7-8.

Line 71. Mary's real sin was hypocrisy, which is blasphemy against humanity.

Line 73. Repression of her natural instincts was the cause of her spiritual degradation.

Lines 81-84. In spite of the grammatical obscurity, the meaning is clear enough. *The shadowy man* is evidently a masculine correspondent to the Shadowy Female; in other words, the Natural Man, who desires the body of Jesus for a prey.

Line 93. According to Catholic tradition, Jesus spent the three days between the Crucifixion and the Resurrection in Hell. Blake takes the Descent into Limbo as the descent into this world, where Jesus still feeds on Death, which is the food of Immortality.

FRAGMENT VII

This fragment does not fit with any part of the poem as we now possess it. *This False Christ* evidently refers to a lost description of the Antichrist. Blake ended this brief section with the ' &c ' which always refers to a continuation copied elsewhere. This continuation has never been found. EY and Sampson refer to a line in *Jerusalem*, 12 : 25, which begins with the same words; but no possible connection between the two can be imagined.

FRAGMENT VIII

This couplet, usually called the *Epilogue*, refers to the Antichrist, not to Blake's Jesus.

An additional fragment of *The Everlasting Gospel*, fifty-six lines long, and marked: 'This is to come first,' has turned up. Dr. Keynes (p. 47) prints the opening lines:

> If moral virtue was Christianity,
> Christ's pretensions were all vanity;
> And Cai[a]phas and Pilate men
> Praiseworthy, and the lion's den
> (And not the sheepfold) allegories
> Of God and heaven and their glories.

On the fourth page of the manuscript there is some prose beginning: 'There is not one moral virtue Jesus inculcated but Plutarch and Cicero inculcated before him.' Swinburne saw this manuscript and summarized it, with many brief quotations, in a note (1866, pp. 175-176; 1906, pp. 195-196).

THE PICKERING MS.

THE SMILE. This little poem deals with the war of the sexes. The 'Smile of Smiles,' in which love and deceit mingle, is the woman's attitude; the 'Frown of Frowns' is the man's; while the union of the two produces the smile which is the symbol of perfect union.

Lafcadio Hearn (*Interpretations of Literature*, I. 70) thought that the last smile was the grin of the skull, the laugh of death; but how that can be smiled once 'betwixt the cradle and the grave' he does not explain.

THE GOLDEN NET. The adolescent meets three virgins bearing the symbols of ungratified desire. He pities the situation of the chaste; and the Golden Net, which is Chastity itself, is at once stretched across his heaven.

THE MENTAL TRAVELLER. The meaning of this poem has already been indicated in Chapter XXIII.

Line 5. *The Babe* is Orc, spirit of Revolt.

Line 10. *A Woman Old* is the Shadowy Female, who is Nature in her fallen (materialized) form.

Line 12. Blake was very fond of this image, and often repeated it, as in *Milton*, 24 : 38.

Lines 13-16. The crucifixion of Orc. Revolt is tortured before it breaks loose.

Line 17. Another image which Blake often repeated, as in *Milton*, 17 : 49.

Line 24. This is the story of the *Preludium* to *America*.

Line 41. The grief that was his as Experience has been transmuted into the treasures of heaven, which he dispenses freely to all.

Line 44. The birth of Rahab, the Visible Church. Cf. Swedenborg's *Last Judgment*, 38 : 'Every church at the commencement is spiritual, for it begins from charity, but in the course of time it turns aside from charity to faith, and then from being an internal church it becomes an external one; and when it becomes external, its end is, since it then places everything in knowledge, and little or nothing in life.'

Lines 45-48. The Church is too sacred to be touched or restrained.

Lines 49-52. Whatever doctrine she finds best suited to her, that she adopts, casting out the Truth from whose hearth she sprang.

Line 56. The Maiden, as far as we can define her, is Enitharmon, or Inspiration. Perhaps we might call her, quite simply, Truth. But, at any rate, it is hard to see why her embrace should send the poor man into the horrible desert of Science.

Lines 62-68. The attempt to solve the secret of the world by physical Science. Cf. *Milton*, 28 : 15-18.

> As to that false appearance which appears to the reasoner,
> As of a Globe rolling thro' Voidness, it is a delusion of Ulro.
> The Microscope knows not of this nor the Telescope: they alter
> The ratio of the Spectator's Organs but leave objects untouch'd.

Lines 69-74. Inspiration gradually revivifies the Truth-seeker.

Lines 75-84. These flirtations are the exact parallel of those of Los and Eni tharmon in the first *Nights* of *The Four Zoas*.

Lines 85-86. But when the Truth-seeker is completely rejuvenated, his ideal has become mature.

Lines 87-92. The Ultimate Stage, which is also the State of Innocence.

Line 95. But no state is perfect ! Orc is born again. An illustration of these lines is on the bottom of plate 3 of *The Marriage of Heaven and Hell*.

THE LAND OF DREAMS. The innocent child is a greater master of his dreams and desires than the man. Both recognize the superiority of dream-life ; the child, however, with a faith which in the man is little more than sad fancy.

Blake was also touching upon his theory that thought of the dead is really a communion with them.

This poem recalls the saying of Pythagoras (quoted by Clemens Alexandrinus : *Stromat.* lib. 3) : ' Whatever we see when awake is death ; and when asleep, a dream.'

MARY. This ballad was probably inspired by the attitude of Mary Wollstone craft's friends, when they cast off that lady for practising her ideals of Free Love. Mary of the ballad is condemned for her frank interest in human passion, though she is not shunned until she rises ' to be free ' ; and thereafter no penitence is of any avail.

Lines 21-22 are slightly revised from a poem in Blake's letter to Butts, Aug. 16, 1803.

THE CRYSTAL CABINET. This poem describes the illusion of love. The ' Moony Night ' and the use of the word ' three-fold,' identify it with the state of Beulah, which is the realm of the passions. Within the cabinet, everything is seen other than what it actually is—even the beloved herself is transfigured. The three fold smile and kiss are smiles and kisses which stir body, intellect, and passion— the fourth, Spirit, being omitted. ' The Sexual is Threefold : the Human is Four fold ' (*Milton*, 5* : 5). Their love, then, is not quite perfect ; and the lover endeavours to dominate completely the inmost personality of his beloved ; an attempt which breaks the spell. The beloved has prematurely aged to a woman, while the man sees that he is only a child.

THE GREY MONK is a half of the poem in the *MS. Book, I saw a Monk of Charlemaine*, which has already been discussed.

AUGURIES OF INNOCENCE. A hypothesis as to the projected philosophical structure of this poem has already been advanced.

These aphoristic couplets have precisely the same movement, moral as well as metrical, as those which compose George Herbert's *Charms and Knots* (*The Temple*).

A few parallels to the first quatrain may be mentioned. Miss Evelyn Under hill (*Mysticism*, pp. 305-306) refers to Tennyson's *Flower in the crannied wall*, Henry Vaughan's *Each bush and oak doth know I Am* ; quotes Eckhart : ' The meanest thing that one knows in God—for instance, if one could understand a flower as it has its being in God—this would be a higher thing than the whole world ! ' and then continues : ' Many mystical poets of the type of Wordsworth and Walt Whit man possessed to a considerable extent this form of illumination. It is this which Bucke, the American psychologist, has analysed in great detail under the name of Cosmic Consciousness. It is seen at its fullest development in such cases as those of Fox, Böhme, and Blake.' We might also quote Paracelsus : ' All colours and all elements are present in everything ' (*Phil. to Athen.*, III. 5) ; Traherne's *Centuries* (III. 55) : ' That anything may be found to be an infinite treasure, its place must be found in Eternity and in God's esteem ' ; Shelley's *Hellas* (792) : ' All is contained in each ' ; and Ronsard's *Chanticleer* (I. 6) : ' Dans une mort d'insecte on voit tous les désastres, Un rond d'azur suffit pour voir passer les astres.'

The most remarkable parallels may be found for the individual lines. The first line deals with the world of dead matter, ' the grain of sand.' Blake expanded this idea later in *Milton*, 27 : 36-38 :

> . . . the diamond which, tho' cloth'd
> In ragged covering in the mine, is open all within,
> And in his hallow'd centre holds the heavens of bright eternity.

The Hermetic Museum contains *The Golden Age Restored* by Henry Madathanas (Adrian Mynsicht), whose motto is ' The Centre of the World—a Grain of Sand.' Thomas Traherne, as usual, is most Blakish : ' You never enjoy the world aright, till you see how a sand exhibiteth the wisdom and power of God ' (*Centuries*, I. 27). Shelley's customary echo is to be found in *Queen Mab*, IV. 143-146 :

> . . . every grain
> Is sentiment both in unity and part,
> And the minutest atom comprehends
> A world of loves and hatreds. . . .

The second line of Blake's quatrain deals with matter living as vegetable. Here all the ' nature-mystics ' repeat Blake's thought. We should perhaps remember his own 56th *Proverb of Hell* : ' To create a little flower is the labour of ages.' Gérard de Nerval (*Vers Dorés*) reached the following expression of the same truth :

> Chaque fleur est une âme à la Nature éclose ;
> Un mystère d'amour dans le métal repose.

From Whitman any number of passages parallel to the following from the *Song to Myself* can be remembered :

> I believe a leaf of grass is no less than the journey-work of the stars,
> And the pismire is equally perfect, and a grain of sand, and the egg of the wren.
> And the tree-toad is a *chef-d'œuvre* for the highest,
> And the running blackberry would adorn the parlours of heaven.

Line 3 was echoed by George MacDonald in chapter v. of *Lilith*, which was surely written with some knowledge of Blake : ' Home is ever so far away in the palm of your hand.'

This list of parallels is incomplete and capricious ; no doubt every reader will recall many more.

Lines 21-22. The value of beauty.

Lines 25-28. The anthropomorphism of Nature.

Lines 37-38. These lines are repeated as the ' Keys ' to *The Gates of Paradise*. For explanation, we need only turn to the 55th *Proverb of Hell* : ' As the catterpiller chooses the fairest leaves to lay her eggs on, so the priest lays his curse on the fairest joys.'

Line 42. *The Polar Bar* is the ' Northern Gate ' in *Thel*, the barrier to the realm of the spirit (Urthona).

Lines 67-68. Every sorrow is a spiritual birth.

Line 72. *Waves* of the Sea of Time and Space, which is, of course, outside heaven.

Lines 73-74. Cf. the revenge of the Massacred Innocents in *The Four Zoas*, IX. 250-254.

Lines 93-94. Cf. *Milton*, 43 : 12-15 :

> To cast off the idiot Questioner who is always questioning,
> But never capable of answering, who sits with a sly grin
> Silent plotting when to question like a thief in a cave :
> Who publishes doubt & calls it knowledge : whose Science is Despair.

Lines 103-104. An ambiguous answer, or an appeal to the beauties of Nature, is the only answer which Doubt is worthy of.

Lines 109-110. Cf. *The Everlasting Gospel*, frag. III. 97-98.

Lines 115-116. Cf. Shelley : *Song to the Men of England* :

> And weave your winding-sheet, till fair
> England be your sepulchre.

Lines 125-128. Repeated from *The Everlasting Gospel*, frag. III. 103-106. Elsewhere Blake said : ' I question not my corporeal eye, any more than I would question a window, concerning a sight. I see through it, and not with it.' In Plato's *Theaetetus*, Socrates is accredited with the same idea : ' Which is more correct, to say that we see or hear with the eyes or the ears, or through the eyes and the ears ? ' ' I should say *through*, Socrates, rather than with.' See the Commentary on the poem *To Thomas Butts, Nov.* 22, 1802.

Lines 129-132. To those in Error, God appears as the impersonal light of Truth ; but to those who have achieved the light, he has a form like their own. Miss Evelyn Underhill comments on this quatrain : ' Blake, with true mystic insight, summed up the situation as between the two extreme forms of contemplation ; transcendence and immanence ' (*Mysticism*, p. 424).

LONG JOHN BROWN AND LITTLE MARY BELL. This grotesque ballad might have been inspired by *Novel X* of the *Third Day* of the *Decameron*. The two Rossettis were too shocked to reprint it, but Chesterton comments : ' I have known many cultivated families made happy on winter evenings . . . by wondering what can be its significance ' (page 150).

The symbolism is a little unusual, yet obvious. The Devil represents the Puritan conscience, while the Fairy is the joy of life. In a strain of brutal contempt, Blake retells the old tale of Love denied, and kills off the man and withers the woman to point his moral.

Line 6 is not clear as it is printed. Blake undoubtedly meant the line to read : ' He [the Fairy] laugh'd at the Devil's saying, " Love is a Sin." ' The omission of the *'s* is a common fault.

WILLIAM BOND. This ballad tells of a cure for love. William Bond becomes enamoured of another than his betrothed, Mary Green. He finds no help at church, and falls very sick. Mary appreciates the situation, and offers to release him from his engagement if any one has come between them. William admits this, and Mary falls into a swoon. She is laid on the same bed with William, who suddenly realizes that such a self-sacrificing love as hers is all-compelling. He recants his fault, and confesses that Love does not lie in the dazzle and pride of the sun, but in the gentleness of the moonlight. It will be remembered that the Moon is Blake's common symbol for Beulah.

This poem is written in one of the common ballad metres to be found in Percy's *Reliques*. The use of an obsolete word like ' eyne,' and in particular the method of telling the story by ' striding from peak to peak ' of the action, prove beyond doubt where Blake got his inspiration.

The ballad method of telling the story, added to the simple symbols of Fairies (natural joys) and Angels (spirits of the Church), have given a number of critics immense trouble. One favourite interpretation is that the poem is autobiographical. William Bond is merely a punning name for William Blake. But who is Mary Green, if we are to believe this theory, and why is she not called Kitty Bond ? The theory at once ceases to hold water.

EY pronounce this poem ' undoubtedly among the most difficult in the whole of Blake's collected works ' (II. 19) ; but this may be readily understood when we remember that the simplest poems are always those which fit with the greatest trouble into their system of interpretation.

POEMS FROM LETTERS

To FLAXMAN, 12*th Sept.* 1800. This was written in gratitude for the new friend, Hayley, to whom Flaxman had introduced Blake. It contains a list of names whom Blake considered the most powerful in shaping his mental life. The omission of Swedenborg was surely an oversight.

These verses are in an unusual form : anapestic hexameters.

Line 6. *Shakspere in riper years gave me his hand.* Blake certainly was familiar with Shakspere very early, as the *Poetical Sketches* attest. He means here that he did not appreciate Shakspere's true greatness until later. In *Jerusalem*, 98 : 9, Shakspere appears with Chaucer and Milton among the chariots of the Almighty.

To MRS. FLAXMAN, 14*th Sept.* 1800. A poem wishing that Flaxman and his wife would come to Felpham. *The Ladder of Angels* was painted by Blake as 'Jacob's Ladder.' *The Hermit* is Hayley, and *the Turret* is Hayley's home.

To THOMAS BUTTS, *Oct.* 2, 1800. This is Blake's clearest and most personal description of a mystical vision. Yet even here we must distinguish between Mysticism and Metaphysics, between the conviction and the symbol.

Blake knew quite well that everything beheld by men is seen in human terms. In arranging cosmographies, theorists have always placed man's highest aspects in heaven, and his lowest in hell, and with such success that Shelley pronounced hell to be 'the most perfect possible example of the most fiendish possible crime.' From humanity itself the superhuman is constructed. Blake knew this, so he deliberately represented Eternity as a Man. But his theory was not purely intellectual. The factor which originally determined his symbols was the strong feeling of the human warmth that underlies every part of the phenomenal world.

Blake left a few stray thoughts on the humanity of God. In the Swedenborg marginalia he wrote : 'Man can have no idea of anything greater than Man as a cup cannot contain more than its capaciousness.' Here we may turn to his celebrated dictum : 'Therefore God becomes as we are, that we may be as he is.' Then again reverting to the Swedenborg marginalia, we find the warning : 'But God is a man not because he is so perceived by man but because he is the creator of man.'

The psychological interest of various lines is great :

> Remote from Desire . . .
> And Saw Felpham sweet
> Beneath my bright feet . . .
> All I ever had known
> Before me bright Shone . . .

To THOMAS BUTTS, *Nov.* 22, 1802. The main interest of this poem to commentators has been Blake's vision of the Thistle. In a black mood he sees the thorny flower as a visible expression of the world's meanness and spitefulness. The human equivalent of the Thistle is 'an old Man grey,' with his counsels of despair.

It is perfectly clear that Blake did not confuse the Thistle with the Old Man, nor did he even 'see' the Old Man in the ordinary meaning of that verb. It was a matter of feeling, such as has always been common. The child striking the floor which bumped him and the man cursing his collar-button for its total depravity are the familiar expressions of Blake's kick at the weed.

Mystics have made much of this power of seeing the humanity which lies behind things. Blake's own explanation, and the quotation from Plato which may have furnished him with the phrase, 'through, not with, the eye' have already been cited in the Commentary on the *Auguries of Innocence*, 125-128. We can find many other parallels. Cyrillus (*Contra Julianum*, i. 30*a*) quotes Trismegistus : 'Wherefore the incorporeal vision comes forth from the body to contemplate beauty, lifting itself up and adoring, not the form, nor the body, nor the appearance, but that which, behind all, is calm, tranquil, substantial, immutable ; that which is all, alone, and one, that which is by itself and in itself, similar to itself, and without variation.' In the *Pymander* (I. 30) Trismegistus said, quite simply : 'Everything that is, is double.' Böhme warns us : 'The kingdom of God must be inwardly innate and born within us, else we cannot see with the eyes of eternity into the angelical world' (*Epistle*, IX. 19). Traherne contains many references to Double Vision :

> To walk abroad is not with Eys
> But Thoughts, the Fields to see & prize.

This couplet from *Walking* is echoed in *Sight* and *Consummation* (*Poems of Felicity*) ;

also in the *Centuries*, II. 76 : ' These things shall never be seen with your bodily eyes, but in a more perfect manner. You shall be present with them in your understanding, You shall be in them to the very centre, and they in you, as light is in a piece of crystal, so shall you be with every part and excellency of them.' Thomas Vaughan understood the penetration to the ' Centre,' but, as often happens, he evokes a deceptive parallel : ' Are not the faculties of this Spirit supprest in Man also, when the *Organs* are *Corrupted*, as it appeareth in those that are blind ? But notwithstanding the *Eye* only is destroyed, and not the Visible power, for that remaines, as it is plain in their dreams ' (*Anthroposophia Theomagica*).

In modern times we find, of course, Whitman : ' I do not doubt interiors have their interiors, and exteriors have their exteriors—and that the eyesight has another eyesight, and the hearing another hearing, and the voice another voice ' (*Assurances*) ; also, ' A vast similitude interlocks all ' (*On the Beach at Night Alone*). James Stephens, echoing Trismegistus, or with more likelihood Blake, tells us : ' Everything has two names and everything is twofold ' (*Crock of Gold*, ch. xiii.). But in the works of George MacDonald, we find the direct influence of Blake. As early as 1882 (*If I had a Father*), he represents a sculptor making a statue of Psyche from a painting of a tropical landscape. The sculptor explains : ' Every individual aspect of nature looks to me as if about to give birth to a human form, embodying that of which itself only dreams. In this way landscape-painting is, in my eyes, the mother of sculpture. That Apollo is of the summer dawn ; that Aphrodite of the moonlit sea ; this picture represents the mother of my Psyche.' In the fifth chapter of *Lilith* (1895), the sources of the inspiration is obvious :

' You see that hawthorne ? ' said my guide [a raven] at length, pointing with his beak.
I looked where the wood melted away on the edge of an open heath.
' I see a gnarled old man, with a great white beard,' I answered.
' Look again,' he rejoined : it is a hawthorne.'

Line 14. *Robert*. Blake's beloved younger brother, who died Feb. 1787, and who later told Blake the secret process for publishing the *Songs of Innocence*.

Line 15. *John*, probably the fourth son of James and Catherine. Certainly not the eldest son, who was named James. John, according to Tatham, ' was the favourite of his father and mother ; and, as frequently in life, the object least worthy is most cherished, so he, a dissolute, disreputable youth, carried away the principal of his parent's attachment, leaving the four others, William, James, Catherine, and Robert, to share the interest between them. William often remonstrated, and was as often told to be quiet, and that he would by and by beg his bread at John's door ; but, as is sometimes proved to parents' sorrow, their pet will not be petted into honour nor their darling into any other admiration than their own. John was apprenticed to a gingerbread baker, with an enormous premium, served his apprenticeship with reluctance, became abandoned and miserable, and literally, contrary to his parents' presage, sought bread at the door of William. He lived a few reckless days, enlisted as a soldier, and died.'

Line 31. *Back*, to Hayley.

Line 33. *Theotormon* is Desire. Cf. *Milton*, 6 : 30 : ' Theotormon & Bromion contended on the side of Satan '—Satan being Hayley. But Desire and Reason conspire to make him stay at Felpham.

Lines 35-38. The god of Poetry threatens the poverty and misery of Blake's wife.

Lines 39-40. Blake is afraid that Butts will be the same disappointment that Fuseli had been.

Lines 55-58. This vision was repeated in *Milton*, 20 : 5-14. Blake defies the god of Poetry to do his worst ; claims that he is moved by a yet higher power (' another sun ') ; rejects earthly comforts ; and is rewarded with fourfold vision. From *Milton* we learn the outcome of the struggle : how Los became one with him.

Lines 83-88. *Fourfold vision.* This is one of Blake's familiar terms, and is in reality quite simple. Single vision was pure sensation, such as the scientists (Newton in particular) cultivate; twofold vision added an intellectual appreciation of the object; threefold infused the perception with its emotional value; and fourfold crowned it with mystical insight as to its place in the universe. These four divisions correspond to the Four Zoas: Tharmas guiding single vision; Urizen twofold; Luvah threefold; and Urthona (Los) the fourfold.

This is not very different with the fourfold interpretation of mediaeval symbolism, which allowed four readings to each allegory: literal, moral, spiritual, and mystic. (See the Introduction to *Mediaeval Legends: The Wonderful History of Virgilius*, London, 1893).

To THOMAS BUTTS, *August* 16, 1803. This poem is of interest only for the repetition of its opening couplet in the ballad *Mary.*

GNOMIC VERSES

II. TO GOD. The *circle* is Blake's usual symbol for the everlasting round of Nature. EY, however, think that this epigram ' shows that theology and magic were receiving together a share of contemplation unusually penetrating even for Blake ' (I. 226).

III. Cf. Shelley's *Queen Mab*, IV. 168: ' War is . . . the priest's delight.'

V. LACEDAEMONIAN INSTRUCTION. The Spartans used to make their helots drunk as examples to the younger generation. Blake wishes the young to profit by beholding the misery of a man entangled in theological difficulties.

VI. Advice to the worldly who are persecuting a man of God. To succeed, they must strike at his very life, and not spend their efforts in trivial castigations.

VIII. Child-labour, war, and prostitution. Sampson thinks that this may have been a rejected stanza of the second *Chimney Sweeper.*

IX. SOFT SNOW. The poet is blamed for catching a joy as it flies.

XI. MERLIN'S PROPHECY. When two innocent and truly pure people meet there will be no spiritual winter; but before this can happen the powers secular and spiritual, with their prisons and brothels, must be abolished.

XVI. Possibly a couplet to illustrate Plate 26 of *Urizen.*

XVII. SEVERAL QUESTIONS ANSWERED.

1. If *he* were changed throughout to *she*, these lines would illustrate the decoration to the *Argument* of the *Visions of the Daughters of Albion.*

5. *An Ancient Proverb.* Abolish the church, marriage, and war; and the world will be redeemed.

XIX. This quatrain sounds like a fragment from *I rose up at the dawn of day.*

XX. RICHES. The first two lines of this quatrain were used as lines 34-35 of *The Mental Traveller.*

ON ART AND ARTISTS

III. Surely inspired by an anecdote in Bacon's essay on *Boldness*: ' Question was asked of Demosthenes, What was the chief part of an orator? He answered, Action. What next? Action. What next again? Action.' *Barry,* a poem by Blake on his artist friend, of which this is a fragment, has been lost.

IX. Lines 5-7 contrast the popular attitude towards oil-painting and water-colours.

XXVI. To ENGLISH CONNOISSEURS. 'About the year 1791, Stothard began to study attentively the works of Rubens' (Mrs. Bray's *Life of Stothard*). ' So long as Rubens confines himself to space and outward figure—to the mere animal man with the animal passions—he is, I may say, a god amongst painters. His satyrs, Silenuses, lions, tigers, and dogs are almost godlike; but the moment he attempts anything involving or presuming the spiritual, his gods and goddesses, his nymphs and heroes, become beasts, absolute, unmitigated beasts' (Coleridge: *Table Talk*, July 24, 1831).

XXVIII. Cf. Fuseli's 55th *Aphorism*: 'Commonplace figures were first introduced by the gorgeous machinists of Venice.'

XXIX. ON THE VENETIAN PAINTER. This refers, not so much to the bright colours of the Venetians as to their dazzling effects, which blinded those with real spiritual perception.

XXXI. Written no doubt after hearing some one defend Venetian colouring at the expense of every other artistic principle. Blake always considered colour as accidental, and form (as expressed by outline) the all-important.

XXXIV. Against Stothard. 'Whilst alluding to Stothard's colouring, it may be useful to others here to state that the peculiarly rich brown so often admired in his works was a colour of his own invention, and thus made by himself' (Mrs. Bray's *Life of Stothard*).

ON FRIENDS AND FOES

V. This quatrain has caused much controversy, since Hayley cannot be accused seriously of attempted rape and murder. Blake's own attitude towards Hayley as soon as he left Felpham precludes the possibility of taking this quatrain literally. There are those, however, who have believed that Blake meant just what he wrote at its face value. They absolve Hayley, and accuse Blake of persecution-mania. It is quite possible that Blake was jealous of Hayley; but the murder theory is hard to admit. Nevertheless, two 'hired villains' have been found: the soldier Scofield, and Leigh Hunt.

But all such literal interpretations are in direct defiance of Blake's acknowledged principles of writing. 'To bereave my life' does not, in Blakean terms, refer to actual death. 'He who envies or calumniates, which is murder & cruelty, / Murders the Holy-one' (*Jerusalem*, 91 : 11-12). He called Bishop Watson ' Murderer!' when the Bishop published his wish that Tom Paine had died before writing *The Age of Reason*. Crabb Robinson, on the 13th of June 1826, noted that Blake 'affirmed that he had committed many murders.' Remembering these intentional ambiguities, we must ask what was Blake's 'life' of which Hayley so nearly deprived him? The answer is unexpectedly simple; Blake's 'life' was his art, which Hayley was trying to turn to profitable ends, such as miniature-painting and the like. Blake, after a while, refused to allow his genius to be murdered; and Hayley undoubtedly turned to Mrs. Blake, encouraging her to bring her husband to reason. She, of course, faithfully refused.

George MacDonald, in *David Elginbrod* (ch. lvi.) was nearest to Blake: 'Contempt is murder committed by the intellect as hatred is murder committed by the heart.' Cf. also *Matthew* v. 28.

We do not know, and we probably will never know, who Hayley's friend, the 'villain,' actually was, nor what were his innocent efforts to lead the gentle mystic into the paths of prosperity.

Those who find that the phrase ' to bereave my life' as used by Blake was quite unjustified may find other examples of similar usage in well-known writers. Spenser, in *The Faerie Queene* (II. x. 70) wrote that Prometheus was ' by Love depryv'd of life,' without meaning that Prometheus was killed. Shelley in *The Revolt of Islam* (I. xiv. 5) calls the Serpent ' lifeless,' though he is only exhausted.

Blake's own phrase, with its Chaucerian use of ' bereave ' as a transitive verb, is echoed from his *Fair Eleanor*, line 68.

XXVII. ON CERTAIN MYSTICS. EY inform us (I. 81) that Cosway, the miniature painter, kept a house for the practice and study of magic, and left behind him a considerable bundle of magic formulae.

XXVIII. We lack the beginning of this fragment, which deals with Blake's difficulties with Hayley, with his trial, with Cromek, and with the *Examiner*. Stothard (' Stewhard ') is speaking.

Line 1. *His legs*, referring to Cromek.

Line 2. *Chichester*, where Blake's trial was held.

Line 16. Leigh Hunt's *Examiner* printed two blasting notices of Blake : one, a review of his edition of Blair's *Grave* (Aug. 7, 1808) ; and the other (Sept. 17, 1809) on Blake's exhibition of paintings, Blake being called a lunatic. Blake names himself ' Death,' probably on account of *The Grave*.

Line 19. *Yorkshire Jack Hemp* and *Quibble* are Flaxman and Hayley's lawyer.

Line 21. *Felpham Billy* is Hayley.

Line 24. *Dragoon* is the soldier Scofield.

Line 25. *Daddy* is Dr. Malkin.

Line 32. *Assassinetti* (as the MS. seems to read) is Schiavonetti, who, to Blake's great disgust, engraved Blake's illustrations to *The Grave*.

Line 35. *Screwmuch* is Cromek.

Line 51. *Stewhard* is Stothard.

XXX. Apparently written while Blake was repenting at London of his exasperations.

XXXI. *Bartoloze* is Bartolozzi, a rival engraver.

MISCELLANEOUS EPIGRAMS

These fragments are either inexplicable or sufficiently self-explanatory to need no commentary.

XII. ON THE VIRGINITY OF THE VIRGIN MARY & JOANNA SOUTHCOTT. Blake's disbelief in miracles explains sufficiently his attitude towards the Virgin Birth. Joanna Southcott (1750-1814) was a Methodist servant girl who took to prophesying in rhyme of an imminent Millennium. She claimed to be the woman of the Apocalypse, and at the age of 64 announced herself pregnant of the holy child ' Shiloh ' by the Holy Ghost. Medical opinions varied, but her death proved the pregnancy to have been nothing but dropsy. Nevertheless her sect continued for a few years after her death.

TIRIEL

COMMENTARY

TIRIEL is an early version of *The Book of Urizen*. Many of the same ideas reappear there, though under different symbols.

I

Line 1. *Tiriel* represents the ancient religion of Law empowered by the Curse, now rapidly aging towards death. He has already been cast out by his hated children. His name (with two others) is taken from the tables in Cornelius Agrippa's *Occult Philosophy*, II. xxii.: *Of the tables of the Planets*. Here Tiriel is called the Intelligence of Mercury. Agrippa ascribes to each planet ' an Intelligency to what is Good with a Spirit to what is Evil.' When Mercury is fortunate, he makes one ' grateful, and fortunate to do what he pleaseth : it bringeth gain, and prevents poverty, conduceth to memory, understanding, and divination, and to the understanding of occult things by dreams : and if it be an unfortunate *Mercury*, doth all things contrary to these.'

Agrippa's philosophy was enjoying a revival about this time. *The Conjuror's Magazine* (London, 1792) and Francis Barrett's *Magus* (London, 1801) both contain the same table of names. But *Tiriel* was written before either of them appeared.

Tiriel never reappears in Blake's works ; though in some editions, Thiriel (quite another character) has had his name misspelled ' Tiriel ' throughout.

Line 2. *Myratana* is Tiriel's Inspiration. *The West* has a double meaning to Blake. First it meant Freedom (for there lay America), and secondly the body (for there also lay the Atlantic, in its turn a symbol of the Sea of Time and Space). Both these meanings are used here. Tiriel is therefore a system of thought concerning material things, that once brought some amount of liberty to mankind, but now is outworn.

Line 3. *His eyes were dark'ned* : his vision is lost.

Lines 21-27. The internal rhymes to ' bones ' seem intentional.

Line 24. *Heuxos* suggests the Greek ' εὔξοος ' (well-polished).

Line 29. *O Fire!* Occult philosophers wrote much of the four ' Elements,' of which the Universe is composed. That these were not what is now understood by ' fire,' ' water,' ' earth,' and ' air ' is quite obvious. When we penetrate Agrippa's symbols and paradoxes on the subject (I. v.), it is clear that the philosophic ' fire ' was the principle of Will, which is the soul of all things. The philosophers ' per ignem ' formed a long school. They began with Heraclitus and Zoroaster. The Christians derived from them, feeling justified by *Revelation* xxi. 23. Among the most prominent were Robert Fludd (see his *Apologia Compendiaria*, 1616) and Paracelsus, who wrote : ' whatever lives is Fire ' (*Coelum Philosophorum*, Pt. I. Canon 7). As Blake uses the term, he means to express the inability of the Will to revivify dead Inspiration.

Line 34. *Zazel* was a brother of Tiriel (l. 310), the first to be cast out and enslaved. He was overpowered and made use of, just as Christianity took over many pagan rites and festivals. In Agrippa, he figures as an evil spirit of Saturn. Saturn, when unfortunate, ' hinders buildings, plantings, and the like, and casts a man from honours, and dignities, and causes discords, and quarrellings, and disperses an Army.' *Zazel* also seems to be an apocopated form of Azazel, the first of the demons to fall, according to the *Book of Enoch*. The Lord's accusations and treatment of Azazel are a fair parallel to Tiriel's actions toward Zazel.

Line 43. *Northern fogs*. The North is the realm of pure spirit. Tiriel can see nothing there but obscurity, though later he pretends that there lay his real kingdom.

Line 50. The Inspiration may be killed, but the power of its thought continues.

II

Line 53. The Sun signifies the Intellect, and the Moon the Emotions. This symbolism later was changed, but reappears in the 14th Illustration to *Job*. Tiriel still retains his intellectual faculties, though feebly, while he has no more emotions. This passage suggests somewhat Milton's *Samson Agonistes*, l. 80 *seq*.

Line 56. *Har & Heva* symbolize poetry and painting in a degraded state. Har is the Poetic Genius, as lines 90-100 prove, when compared with the 7th Principle of *All Religions are One*: '. . . the True Man is the source, he being the Poetic Genius.' Since he receives Tiriel, he must be didactic poetry. He sings in a cage, which represents the bondage of poetic laws. His name is the Hebrew for ' mountain,' but now he lives in a vale. He has his mountain, however (l. 320). Heva, one assumes, represents Blake's other art, painting. ' Heva ' is the Latin form of ' Eve '; this pair is evidently intended to suggest Adam and Eve. Both of them are sadly degenerate, being ' as the shadow of Har.' They reappear in *The Song of Los : Africa*. There the Eternals are called the ' sons of Har ' (20, 45) ; and we have a trace of the earlier history of this couple in lines 35-43 :

Till, like a dream, Eternity was obliterated and erased
Since that dread day when Har and Heva fled
Because their brethren and sisters liv'd in War and Lust
And as they fled they shrunk.

The Vales of Har are mentioned three times in *The Book of Thel*.

The oak is always in Blake a symbol for deep-rooted, flourishing error.

Line 57. *Mnetha* is almost an anagram of Athena. She represents the intelligence which preserves Poetry and Painting, though she does not understand them well enough to know their degradation.

Line 74. Har's instinct still tells him the truth. Mnetha, however, is easily deceived.

Line 89. *Heva* is simply misled by Tiriel's age.

Line 90. *Figs* represent fertility and abundance. Cf. 1 *Kings* iv. 25 ; also the 19th Illustration to *Job*. Heva again is misled, imagining fruits where there have been none for a long time.

Line 96. *The North* is the region of the spirit. Tiriel pretends that he dealt with spiritual things, though he really ruled only the West, or the body.

III

Line 105. Poetry is older than religion, being its father. Cf. the 5th Principle of *All Religions are One*: ' The Religions of all Nations are derived from each Nation's different reception of the Poetic Genius, which is everywhere call'd the Spirit of Prophecy.'

Line 115. *The cage of Har* : the laws governing versification.

Line 135. *Woods* : the sterile growth of the errors of theory, where the path is lost and the true light obscured.

IV

Line 142. *Ijim* represents the common people's religion. He is always wrestling with a devil who is not there, for he imagines that there are supernatural forces in natural forces ; in a word, he is an animist (lines 188-198). His name, the only one besides those of Har and Heva which Blake used again, reappears in *The Four Zoas*, VIII. 354, as the 18th name in the generations of Los and Enitharmon. He is the last of the ungenerated, preceding Adam and the rest who descended to this world.

Line 167. Neither heeds the true delights round them.

Line 186. The advanced sects dare not protest against the vulgar insistence on the outward religion.

Line 213. The people (Ijim) cannot believe at first that Law, which they consider true religion, is rejected by their superiors.

Line 215. *It is false & [? as] Matha and as dark as vacant Orcus. Matha* seems to be a corruption of ' Matter,' while *Orcus* is a Latin name for ' Hell.'

V

Line 231. At last Tiriel is empowered to invoke his curse upon his hated sons and daughters.

Line 236. *The five daughters* represent the five senses. They immediately and openly protest against the curse, for Tiriel's reign has been over the West, which is primarily sensuous.

The five senses played a large part in Blake's philosophy. They are not limited to, but rather hindered by, the body. They are the ' chief inlets of Soul in this Age ' (*Marriage* : *Voice of the Devil*). As such, they are catalogued in the *Introductory Lines* to *Europe*. At other times Blake considers them, when closed in by flesh, as obscurers of the ' white radiance of Eternity ' ; as in *Thel*, 122-127, and *The Everlasting Gospel* : ' This life 's five windows of the soul Distort the Heavens from pole to pole.' It is this closing in by the flesh which is about to follow Tiriel's curse.

The fifth sense, the sense of Touch, here represented by Hela, also signifies Sex to Blake. This sense was the only one of the five to escape in part the fall from Eternity, and by sex one may return there. That is the rôle of Hela in this poem ; it is also the explanation of the *Introductory Lines* to *Europe*.

Line 251 *seq. Thirty sons* : cf. the Thirty Cities in *Urizen*, ix. 94 *seq.* Sons, to Blake, always represent accomplishments.

This pestilence is the Death from Eternity into Time ; the Fall ; the closing of the senses from perception of the Infinite ; and the consequent degeneration of all men's acts. The heavenly bodies light them no longer ; the fog arises (? cf. *Genesis* ii. 6) ; and many of the sons are killed outright. (In *Urizen* they merely leave this world.) Four of the senses die to Eternity and the fifth is cursed ; cf. *Urizen*, IVa, ¶¶ 8-11. A still clearer symbol of the same thing is in the 6th Illustration to *Job*, where the four arrows in Satan's hand represent the four deaths, and the vial of boils (traditionally syphilitic) represents the curse upon the fifth.

VI

Line 255. Now that all heresies are killed off, Tiriel expects to return to the innocent state (as he considers it) of Har and Heva. *Hela* (subjected sex) is to be his guide. Her name is that of the Scandinavian goddess of Hell.

Line 260. *The rock* : the stone tables of the Commandments.

Line 282. The tears of hypocrisy.

Lines 294-295. ' An eye for an eye.' Sex refuses to be complacent in her subjection ; therefore she is cursed. She suffers the fate of Medusa, the glory of her womanhood (1 *Cor.* xi. 5) being changed to serpents. (Medusa suffered the same fate for the same sin under the same deity ; Athena, goddess of Logic, like Tiriel, also tried to enforce asceticism by power of the curse.) Tiriel himself is appalled at the effect of his curse.

VII

Line 306. The scorn of those previously rejected.

Line 316. Again the forest of error.

Line 318. *The tygers* are always symbols of God's wrath. See the *Song of Experience* of that name, also the 44th *Proverb of Hell* : ' The tygers of wrath. . . .'

Line 320. Even the high places of poetry are troubled by Hela's cries.

VIII

Line 329. Finally Tiriel admits that his reign holds only over the body (west).

Line 331. At last, when the old religion touches even the lowest part of poetry (however degenerate), he realizes the mistake of his existence.

Line 332. *Mistaken father*, not only of Tiriel, but of all creation, since to the mystic all creation (into this world from the world of Eternity) is bad.

Line 333. Restriction of poetry and the tyranny of logic are alike bad for mankind.

Line 334. Laws should be tested by the individual case, and not imposed arbitrarily upon all. A favourite idea of Blake's, repeated as the last line of *The Marriage* and *Visions*, 109.

Lines 335-350. A summary of Tiriel's whole life.

Lines 335-336. Why, in the first place, is man bound down by flesh ?

Lines 337-338. The father forces the child's brain, while the mother neglects him.

Lines 342-343. Instruction by flogging, preventing self-development.

Line 346. The world brings forth poison by now. Shelley, in his *Prometheus Unbound*, III. iv., prophesied the time when such poison berries would lose all power to harm.

Line 347. Thus was Tiriel forced into becoming a hypocrite. His mistake lay in that he humbled himself to all this oppression, for ' If thou humblest thyself, thou humblest Me ' (*Everlasting Gospel*).

Line 352. Tiriel's last curse is against Har, for being a father, since all creation —especially himself—is evil. But Tiriel is wrong : Poetry was not responsible for the Fall.

ILLUSTRATIONS

The manuscript of *Tiriel* is undecorated, but there are twelve separate illustrations described in Gilchrist's *Life of Blake*. Of all of them, only one seems to cast any light by its symbolism upon the meaning. This is the last picture, where Tiriel is dying, while the vines of the ecstasy of true feeling spring up round him.

The complete list follows :

(1) Tiriel supporting the swooning Myratana and addressing his sons. (2) Har and Heva. (3) Mnetha with Har and Heva. (4) Har asleep, with Heva and Mnetha beside him. (5) Tiriel on the shoulders of Ijim, his daughters kneeling before him. (6) Tiriel cursing his sons and daughters. (7) The death of the sons of Tiriel. (8) Tiriel and Hela. (9) Har and Heva bathing, Mnetha watching. (10) Har and Heva watching Tiriel. (11) Har and Tiriel, with Heva and Mnetha behind. (12) Hela contemplating Tiriel dead in a vineyard.

The 9th is reproduced by Keynes (p. 24) ; the 9th and the 11th appear as plates 4 and 5 in Laurence Binyon's *Drawings and Engravings of William Blake* (London, 1922). The series has been dispersed.

THE BOOK OF THEL

COMMENTARY

Motto. Lines 1-2. We learn only by personal experience.

Lines 3-4. Can wisdom be put in the symbol of love (the phallos) or love in the symbol of wisdom (the brain)? These lines together form one of the deleted lines in *Tiriel*. The symbols are derived from the Bible. In *Ecclesiastes* xii. 6, on the subject of death, the phrase occurs: ' Or ever . . . the golden bowl be broken.' The Rod is often a symbol of generation, as in *Isaiah* xi. 1 and *Psalm* lxxiv. 2.

I

Line 5. *Mne Seraphim.* In the list of spirits in Agrippa's *Occult Philosophy*, II. xxii., from which Blake took the names *Tiriel* and *Zazel*, occurs the name *Bne Seraphim* (the sons of the Seraphim), who represent ' the Intelligencies of Venus.' It is reasonable to suppose that Blake intended to use this name, but made a mistake in the engraving which he could not correct. The change of *Bne* to *Mne* is apparently meaningless. According to Agrippa, ' *Venus* being fortunate, procureth concord, endeth strife, procureth the love of women, conduceth to conception, is good against barrenness, causeth ability for generation, dissolves enchantments, and causeth peace between man and woman, and maketh all kind of Animals and Cattle fruitful; and being put into a Dove-house, causeth an increase of Pigeons. It conduceth to the cure of all melancholy distempers; and causeth joyfulness; and being carried about travellers makes them fortunate.' But in an unfortunate aspect, Venus ' causeth contrary things to all that had bin above said.'

It has also been suggested that Blake started to write *Mnetha*, but remembered too late that he was simplifying his symbolism. *Seraphim*, throughout all Blake's works, are spirits of love and imagination—the beings next to God. Contrasted to them are the *Cherubim*, the spirits of knowledge devoid of love, and hence usually evil.

Line 8. *Adona* is unmistakably derived from *Adonis*. The river is the river of generation flowing from Eternity to this world, which in the epics is named *Arnon* and *Storge*. The lamentations for Adonis were a celebrated part of the antique mysteries which dealt with death and resurrection. In *Paradise Lost*, I. 450, Adonis appears as a river. Thel's problem is the problem of the descent of the soul. Blake did not wish to state too openly the cause of the descent (which, according to the Platonists, was Desire); so he chose names which would suggest it. *Seraphim* are spirits of love; they were taken from a table where they are ascribed to Venus; and *Luvah* (a corruption of ' lover ') later appears as the Zoa who presides over the emotions. Thel's own name is probably derived from a Greek root meaning ' desire,' though (since she approximates the unfallen Prosperine) it may be a softened form of ' Hell.'

Line 10. Thel's lamentation suggests Hermes Trismegistus's *Pymander* (I. 3, Everard's translation): ' What then should a man do, O Father, to lead his life well, seeing there is nothing here true? '

Line 18. Cf. *Genesis* iii. 8: ' . . . the voice of the Lord walking in the garden in the cool of the day.'

Line 22. *The gilded butterfly.* This eighteenth-century artificiality is strangely in place. Conventional as it once was, here it seems to have an unreal lustre which is exquisite. One of the marks of a genius is his revivifying of something killed by over-use.

Line 30. *Har*, as we have seen in *Tiriel*, represents the Poetic Genius. Therefore

Thel lives in his land, the Human Imagination, which is the Bosom of God itself (*Jerusalem*, 5 : 20). But it may be objected that in *Tiriel* Har is degenerate. This is true, but he was not always so : see *The Song of Los : Africa*, 36-48. Thel lives in his original, unfallen realm. It is the state of Innocence, having all the pastoral emblems.

II

Line 52. Thel is in the state of Innocence, where her senses have not yet been closed in by Experience. Therefore she can see clearly the ' spiritual forms ' of natural objects. In Blake's illustration, the Cloud is represented as having a human form, and this does not startle us at all. It is only when Blake treats a Flea in the same way that we wonder. Blake insisted, to the logical extreme, that anything seen through, not *with*, the eye had a human form. (See the *Vision of the Last Judgment* and the letter to Butts, Nov. 22, 1802.)

Line 55. *Luvah* is the regent of the emotions. This is the first mention of any of the Four Zoas. His name is probably a mutation of the word ' lover,' though Blake probably pronounced it with a long u, because of his affection for that letter. Ellis and Yeats derive the name from *luv*, the Hebrew for ' heart.' But the Hebrew actually is ' *leb, lebab*,' in which the b's are sometimes Cockneyized into v's. Moreover, it means only the heart as the seat of the intelligence, not of the emotions. *Luvah*, being the Eastern Zoa, often recurs in the other books ; the only other name which recurs at all is *Har* (see the Commentary on *Tiriel*, 56).

Line 70. *The food of worms* : *i.e.* did Thel exist only to be swallowed up by a physical body ? The worm is a well-known symbol of the flesh: *Job* xxv. 6 ; *Psalm* xxii. 6 ; *Isaiah* xli. 14, etc. Cf. also Blake's *Gates of Paradise*, which begins and ends with the Worm.

III

Line 80. *Art thou a Worm ? . . . I see thee like an Infant.* An identification of the flesh and the worm ; also another example of the perception of the ' spiritual form.'

Lines 88-96. ' No one, before or after him, has ever written anything like the hymn sung by the clod of clay, the *Magnificat* of the earth, mother of men and of all things ' (Berger, p. 262).

Lines 106-107. It is given to spirits to enter this world without becoming generated. So Milton, in the book named after him, descends ; and so many others that never were generated. See, for example, *Jerusalem*, 71 : 50-51.

IV

This fourth section is the one which has puzzled so many commentators. I think it is clear enough, if what has gone before it has been really understood. But some of these comments are strange enough to be repeated.

J. P. R. Wallis (*Camb. Hist. Eng. Lit.*, vol. XI., 1914, p. 186) finds that ' Blake's original conclusion to the argument is lost, for the last section has not any perceptible connection in its context.' J. J. G. Wilkinson (*Songs of Innocence*, 1839, p. 7) calls it ' no inapt description of the ongoings of the Author's mind, and of his immersion in that interior naturalism, which he now was beginning to mistake for spiritualism, listening, as he did, to the voices of the ground, and entering the invisible world through the sufferance of the terrific porter of its northern gate.' Had there been a suggestion that Dürer or Schongauer, or any other imaginative artist, might have been mad, Wilkinson (and many other critics) would pronounce their work a sure sign of their madness ! Garnett (p. 33) says ' the effect of the voice of sorrow upon Thel is answerable to that of the spider upon little Miss Muffet.' J. Milsand, to whom I have already referred, is rash in his very caution : ' Je n'ai pas la prétension de comprendre et je me serais bien gardé de chercher à rendre plus compréhensibles les mystérieux gémissemens que Thel entend sortir de sa tombe. C'est la note insensée qui annonce la folie à venir ' (p. 339). But strangest of all is Muir's remark (Facsimile of *Thel*, 1885) that this section warns Thel ' against the possible consequences of activity born of mere discontent. The curious reader may compare these lines with the morally monstrous scene between Mephistopheles and the angels after the death of Faust.'

It is encumbered by such a clutter of false interpretations and references that the Blake student must work. *Thel* is Blake's simplest Prophetic Book; I leave the reader to imagine what the commentaries on the later books are !

Line 108. *The terrific Porter* is Los, the god of Poetry. Cf. *Milton*, 26 : 16-18 :

> The Souls descending to the Body wail on the right hand
> Of Los : & those deliver'd from the Body on the left hand,
> For Los against the east his force continually bends.

Blake derived his symbol from the *Odyssey* (Book XIII.) : ' Two gates there are to the cave,[1] the one set towards the North Wind whereby men may go down, but the portals towards the South pertain rather to the gods, whereby men may not enter : it is the way of the immortals.' This passage occurs in that strangely moving description of Odysseus's ultimate return to his native land, Ithaca, which he enters through the Cave of the Nymphs. To Blake, the native land of the wandering soul is, of course, Eternity ; and so also Porphyry interpreted it in his famous Commentary on this very passage. Indeed, from Porphyry Blake undoubtedly drew many symbols. The reader may also recall little Diamond's adventure through the Gate of the North Wind.

Homer says nothing of the gate by which Odysseus returns ; like all mystical writers, he leaves something to the intuition of the reader. Odysseus is returning to his original state as an immortal from his wanderings as a mortal ; therefore he enters by the Northern Gate. This gate is the Gate of Ivory, by which Aeneas also returns to the upper world (*Aeneis*, VI.).

We should then expect Thel to descend to earth through the Southern Gate ; but she does not. The reason for this is only to be found in a further study of Blake's symbolism. To him, the Southern Gate was that of the Intellect, through which all souls fall into the world of Generation (the ' grave,' as he calls it here) ; the Northern Gate being its contrary, that of the Imagination, through which all men eventually are raised to the state of gods. (' Osirification ' was the Egyptian term.) Thel is not descending irrevocably into flesh as yet. It has been promised her that she shall enter and return again ; and in the last line, she flees back unharmed to her original Eden. The point is, that she is exploring the earth *through her imagination*. She does not *reason* about it ; she merely perceives it intuitively, and is driven away by an overwhelming fear. When her time comes, she will conquer this fear by her reason ; and once she has passed through this Southern Gate, she will forget how to return.

It is just possible, in this early state of Blake's symbolism, that he did not mean Los (the ' vehicular form ' of the northern god Urthona) to be the ' terrific Porter.' He may have had in mind merely some such guardian as Og or Anak (*Milton*, 31 : 49), who represent a curious psychological inhibition : that terror which attends any change of spiritual state. Such ' dwellers on the threshold ' have been familiar in occult literature for centuries. The first is probably to be found in Hermes Trismegistus's *Pymander*, II. 1.

Lines 110-111. *Where the fibrous roots Of every heart on earth infixes deep its restless twists*. The roots of trees are a symbol of generation, since from roots spring trees, Blake's symbol of our ' vegetative ' flesh. This line was suggested by Young's *Night Thoughts*, v. 1063-4 :

> O the soft commerce ! O the tender ties
> Close-twisted in the fibres of the heart !

---

[1] The Cave is a very ancient symbol for the flesh, and was so used by Blake. See the Commentary on *The Marriage of Heaven and Hell*, plate XIV, ¶ 6.

Blake illustrated these very lines, in his water-colour series to Young's poem, by two nudes embracing in a subterranean twist of roots. The same idea is repeated in a design for the *Hymn to Adversity*, one of Blake's 114 illustrations of Gray's *Poems*.

Line 116. *Her own grave-plot*: her own body.

Lines 122-127 contain a list of the five senses, where (as is customary with Blake) the sense of Touch is represented by Sex. The list, I think, explains itself. The poetic images are pushed practically into symbolism. Thus 120-121: 'Why are weapons of love, "more terrible than an army with banners," hidden in the eye?' Line 122: 'fruits and coined gold' may be the 'mental health and mental wealth' of *I rose up at the dawn of day*, or the golden fruit of the trees in *Love and Harmony Combine*. But this is turning interpretation into pedantry.

Lines 126-127 were deleted by Blake in two copies.

ILLUSTRATIONS

The Book of Thel is very beautifully illustrated. The pictures (all but the last) simply depict the action.

The Title-page shows Thel with a shepherd's crook standing beneath a delicate tree, which arches over the title. She is watching a huge plant, from whose two blossoms issue figures, a tiny male pursuing a clothed female. A bud reaches to Thel's feet. She is watching, in these loves of the flowers, the ecstasy of change in the universe, though the picture may illustrate instead the courtship of the cloud and the dew (lines 59-60): 'weigh my light wings upon balmy flowers,[1] And court the fair-eyed dew, to take me to her shining tent.'

The *Motto* has no decoration.

The third plate (the first of the text) shows the flying delights of the Universe. A male nude soars after an eagle (a symbol of genius [1]); another has a shield and undulant sword, the weapons of intellectual warfare (cf. *Milton*, 2, last stanza of poem); one woman reclines in a spray; another, flying, embraces a flying child. The very letters blossom.

The fourth plate shows Thel and the Lily, as a maiden, beneath a birch-tree. This illustrates line 46: 'The Lilly bowed her modest head.'

The fifth plate has no decoration but a couple of sprigs.

The sixth plate shows Thel, the Cloud (as a flying man), and the Worm (an infant in the Lily's leaf).

The seventh plate shows Thel, the Worm, and the Cloud. Thel, in the shadow of huge plants, sits with her arms crossed upon her breast, watching a baby (the Worm) and a nude girl (the 'matron clay') playing.

The eighth plate alone is enigmatic in meaning; for Blake, just as he hinted in the last section of the poem that he had a hidden meaning, so he made his last picture one to stimulate thought. It represents the serpent harnessed by three children who ride him. This represents the serpent of sex guided by innocence. Blake repeated this idea in the thirteenth plate of *America*, in a water-colour in the Widener collection at Harvard University, and in the fourteenth illustration to *Job*.

---

[1] Cf. the 54th *Proverb of Hell*: 'When thou seest an eagle, thou seest a portion of Genius; lift up thy head!'

THE FRENCH REVOLUTION

COMMENTARY

Title-page. This is autographed ' John Linnell Red Hill 1860.'

Line 3. *Mist* : pestilence, as in *Tiriel*, v.

Line 5. *Mountains* are the high places of human thought. *Vineyards*, which produce the wine of ecstasy.

Line 8. *Five thousand years.* The world is due to last six thousand years, which are nearly up ; therefore we may assume that the first thousand years were passed in the Garden of Eden.

Line 13. *Forty men*, the nobles.

Line 16. On the 17th of June, 1789, the Third Estate called itself the National Assembly.

Line 19. *The Governor* was De Launay.

Lines 26-29. The Poet, for Blake had already decided that ' prophetic ' writings were simply poetry. The serpent is the serpent of materialism.

Lines 29-32. The Prisoner of State, boldly represented by Blake as the Iron Mask, whom tradition asserted to be a brother of Louis XIV. But Blake means more than a literal prisoner. He means that the better part of Royalty (the Eternal Lion, protector of the Lamb) was masked, or made hypocritical, by reasons of state.

Lines 33-35. The Schismatic, who refused to sign papers of allegiance to the Established Church, and who consequently was persecuted (the tower nam'd Bloody). Blake undoubtedly had the Huguenots in mind.

Lines 35-37. The soul who denied the power of the State over the Church (' who refused to be whore to the Minister ').

Lines 38-43. The upholder of Free Speech, or the Agitator, who is confined in the ' tower nam'd Order ' since such people are always suppressed to preserve public quiet.

Lines 43-47. The Good Man, friend to the favourite, turned inevitably (by Destiny) into the Parasite. Therefore he has lost all power for conscientious action ; and, helpless himself, he imagines all conditions equally irredeemable.

Lines 47-51. The Patriot, driven to madness by the hope of liberty. No doubt Blake was commenting on the extreme attitudes struck by many of his radical friends.

Lines 83-88. ' Is it not easy to guess how Blake would have engraved this ? ' Saintsbury, *Prosody*, III. 24.

Line 90. *The Atlantic Mountains.* The obvious reference is to recently liberated America ; but Blake was also thinking of the lost Atlantis, the mountain which had once been a stairway into Eternity. See the ' Commentary ' on *America*, 106-112.

The harvest symbol, which Blake developed with such effect in his last books, refers to the Last Judgment, when all the good of the world will be gathered together for use in Eternity, while the chaff will be cast out and destroyed. Burgundy, of course, wishes no such radical change, being contented with things as they are.

Line 93. *Forests*, the forests of error.

Lines 94-96. He does not wish power or gospel to be derived from any but material things ; Blake, of course, wished the laws established by Materialism to be overthrown.

Line 96. *The Rock of eternity* is the Rock of Ages.

Line 97. *The eternal lion and eagle* appear terrible to Burgundy, for the Lion is the guardian of the Lamb, and the Eagle is the bird of Genius. He can allow neither the Brotherhood of Man nor the Triumph of the Imagination.

Line 113. *The writing of God*, the divine appointment of kings.

Line 114. Necker was actually dismissed on July 11.

Line 127. *The rushing of scales.* Throughout the early poems, as we have seen, the snake is the symbol of the priest.

Lines 130-131 suggest slightly *Job* iv. 12-16.

Line 134. The descent of souls to earth.

Lines 140-150. The slackening of outward ceremony, the disappearance of the hierarchy, the spiritual independence of the people, and the equality of all men before God, seem the end of all religion to the Archbishop.

Line 165. Henri IV., the great popular monarch, precedes the Abbé de Sieyès, thereby antagonizing the militaristic dukes.

Line 175. Blake could not foresee the hypocritical rôle which Orléans was actually playing in Paris.

Lines 183-184. A magnificent image, showing the intellect and the emotions as the two rivers making fertile the great Paradise of the soul. But there should be four rivers of Paradise, according to *Genesis* ii. 10-14 ; and Blake later recognized them all, identifying them with the Four Zoas (*Jerusalem*, 98 : 14-25). But even in this early book, the Brain and Heart are evidently Urizen and Luvah. Are we to assume that as yet Blake had not completed his theory of the Four Zoas, or that he was simplifying it for the sake of the public ?

Line 185. *Feet, hands, head, bosom, and parts of love.* A fourfold division of man later abandoned by Blake. Cf. ' The head Sublime, the heart Pathos, the genitals Beauty, the hands and feet Proportion.'—61st *Proverb of Hell.*

Lines 190-192. This theory that the Brotherhood of Man consists in ' entering the bosoms of each other ' is also expressed in *Jerusalem*, 88 : 3-5. ' When in Eternity Man converses with Man they enter Into each others Bosom (which are Universes of delight) In mutual interchange.'

Lines 211-216. This is one of Blake's compressed accounts of the Fall, which petrified the Universe into its present material form.

Line 213. *Sulphur.* In alchemy, sulphur is the fire extracted from the sun, with which the Great Work is completed. Blake seems to have taken this to mean that ' sulphur ' is the materialized (fallen) form of ' fire,' the original Eternity.

It is difficult to know in what alchemist Blake found his symbol. Cornelius Agrippa's description of it is to be found in his *Occult Philosophy*, I. v. Paracelsus and Böhme both say a great deal ; but I have found nothing in them which point specifically to Blake's usage.

Lines 216-237. An account of the Resurrection of Man, which was about to begin.

Line 218. *Till man raise his darken'd limbs out of the caves of night* : *i.e.* till he transcend his body. The cave is Plato's famous symbol ; for a detailed discussion, see the ' Commentary ' on *The Marriage of Heaven and Hell*, plate XIV.

Line 219. He transcends both Space and Time.

Line 226. *Devour thy labour.* The priest no longer will live on the labour of others, but will work for his own support.

Line 228. *Millions that wander in forests.* The forests of error again.

Line 240. The withdrawal of the troops was requested on July 8.

Line 246. Cf. *London* : ' And the hapless soldier's sigh / Runs in blood down palace walls.'

Line 247. The answer was returned on July 10, and a second refusal followed, July 13. Louis XVI.'s actual threat was to remove the Assembly to some harmless place far from Paris.

Line 269. Not until July 15 was Lafayette given command of the National Guard.

Lines 274-277. One of Blake's most daring images, and, I think, a successful one.

Lines 279-281. An image inspired by Blake's pride in the British Navy, and woefully out of place here !

Line 285. The National Guard left Paris on July 15 by order of the King, after the Bastille had fallen.

Line 306. The New Age is forecasted by the dawn.

THE MARRIAGE OF HEAVEN AND HELL

COMMENTARY ON 'THE MARRIAGE'

Plate I. The title (an obvious reference to Swedenborg's *Heaven and Hell*) signifies the synthesis of all Contraries, Good and Evil in particular. Thomas Vaughan indicated the same purpose in the opening lines of his *Lumen de Lumine*:

> . . . the Sun and Night
> Kisse in a Chequer of mixt Clouds, and Light.

Plate II. The *Argument* is inspired by the 35th chapter of *Isaiah*, which describes the joyful flourishing after man's salvation. The 'perilous path' is the 'highway of holiness' (8); 'the desert shall rejoice, and blossom as the rose' (1); 'for in the wilderness shall waters break out, and streams in the desert, and the parched ground shall become a pool, and the thirsty land springs of water' (6-7); 'no lion shall be there, nor any ravenous beast shall go up thereon, it shall not be found there; but the redeemed shall walk there' (9).

Line 1. *Rintrah* is the wrath of the Honest Man; a good spirit, since wrath is 'wiser than the horses of instruction.' Later [1] we learn that he is one of the four sons of Liberty (Jerusalem) who, though never incarnated, remained with the Poet (Los) to guard personal freedom (the Western Gate).

Line 2. *Swag*: to sink down by its own weight. A rare word, still used colloquially in the South.

Line 10. This also suggests *Exodus* xvii. 1-8.

Line 13. *Red Clay*, the literal translation of the name *Adam*.

Lines 17-18. Cf. *Tiriel*, 348. The whole passage, ll. 337-351, tells the same story from the 'sneaking serpent's' point of view.

Plate III. ¶ 1. *As a new heaven is begun.* Blake refers to his times as the fulfilment of three prophecies.

The first of these was Swedenborg's:

It has been granted me to see with my own eyes, that the Last Judgment is now accomplished; that the evil are cast into the hells, and the good elevated into heaven, and thus that all things are reduced into order, the spiritual equilibrium between good and evil, or between heaven and hell, being thence restored. . . . It was granted me to see all these things with my own eyes, in order that I might be able to testify of them. This Last Judgment was commenced in the beginning of the year 1757, and was fully accomplished at the end of that year.

—*Last Judgment*, 45.

But in Blake's account of this great resurrection of man, Swedenborg finds himself left behind in his own eschatology; his writings, which preserved the divine truths in time of darkness, now being cast off, as the ascended Christ rejected the linen cloths which had protected him in death.

The second prophecy refers to *Genesis* xxvii. 40. Esau, also called Edom (red, earthy, or of blood), had a younger brother, Jacob, who, by aid of a crafty mother, stole their father's dying blessing. When Esau protested, the father prophesied: 'And by thy sword shalt thou live, and shalt serve thy brother; that thou shalt break his yoke from off thy neck.' Esau's descendants, the Edomites, were duly subjected to Jacob's descendants; and one of them, Hadad (1 *Kings* xi.), joined Nebuchadnezzar against Jerusalem. Blake, interpreting the Bible symbolically, now declares that at last the prophecy is fulfilled. Esau, the just man, has at last overcome the crafty Jacob, and need no longer live by the sword.

[1] *Jerusalem*, 72: 10.

The return of Adam to Eden is hardly a fulfilment of a prophecy, for neither in the Bible nor in Catholic tradition did Adam return.   He died outside the gates, his only comfort being the prophecy that the woman's seed would crush the serpent's head (*Genesis* iii. 15).   But Blake takes Adam as the symbol of man, immortal though fallen, and announces that at last he has found his way back.

The references to *Isaiah* refer to a Judgment when the wicked shall be destroyed and the just removed to their proper Paradise.

¶ 2. Blake's theory of the synthesis of Contraries might have been derived from Heraclitus : ' And Heraclitus said that the highest harmony springs from opposites, and all things are in a state of strife ' (Aristotle : *Nicomachean Ethics*, VIII. 2).   Or again, he might have developed it from the Kabala : ' In this Kaba-listic Balance the whole doctrine of the Zohar hangs. . . . Harmony subsists by the resolution of contraries ' (William Batchelder Greene : *The Blazing Star*, p. 37, Boston, 1872).   The great name with which this doctrine is connected is that of Hegel ; but Hegel in 1793 had only just received his theological certificate, which stated him to be of good abilities, but of middling industry and knowledge, and especially deficient in philosophy.

¶ 3. It is worth noting that some years before, Blake had stated in his margin-alia to Swedenborg : ' There can be no Good Will.   Will is always Evil and is pernicious to others.'

¶ 4. Blake, by casting off Good and Evil is quite modern, as well as very ancient. Nietzsche named one of his books *Beyond Good and Evil*, and in Walt Whitman we are quite apt to find passages like the following :

> I make the poem of evil also—I commemorate that also ;
> I am myself just as much evil as good, and my nation is—
> And I say there is in fact no evil.
> —*Starting from Paumanok*, § 8.

Plate IV. *The Voice of the Devil*.   The idea that the body is not a separate thing from the soul is not at all new, and dates back to Xenophanes.   Blake had already hinted at it in Principle 1 of *All Religions are One* : ' The Poetic Genius is the True Man, and the Body or Outward Form of Man is derived from the Poetic Genius.'   Blake may have got the idea from Aristotle's *De Anima*, II. i. : ' The soul must, then, be substance in this sense : it is the form of a natural body en-dowed with life. . . . It is therefore unnecessary to ask whether the body and soul are one, as one should not ask whether the wax and the imprint are one, or, in general, whether the matter of a thing and the thing composed of it are one.' It was probably from this passage that Spenser got the idea for his celebrated lines :

> For of the soul the bodie forme doth take ;
> For soule is forme, and doth the bodie make.
> —*An Hymn in Honour of Beautie*, 132-133.

Milton came to Blake's conclusion : ' That the spirit of men should be separate from the body, so as to have a perfect and intelligent existence independent of it —the doctrine is evidently at variance both with nature and reason.   For the word " soul " (in the Bible) is applied to every kind of living being ' (*Treatise of Christian Doctrine*).   Thomas Taylor, in his anonymous *Vindication of the Rights of Brutes* (London, 1792, p. 6) complained that ' almost every one is now convinced that soul and body are only nominally distinguished from each other, and are essentially the same.'   There are many modern parallels.   Blake's first editor, J. J. Garth Wilkinson, in his correspondence (E. P. Peabody's *Aesthetic Papers*), wrote : ' As the human hand shapes the pen, then writes with it, so the soul forms the body, and then makes active use of the properties resulting from the form.' Thomas Holley Chivers said : ' The body is an outward expression of the soul ' (*Preface* to *Memoralia* : Philadelphia, 1853).   Walt Whitman not only wrote : ' I have said that the soul is not more than the body, And I have said that the body is not more than the soul' (*Song of Myself*), but also: 'Behold! the body includes and is the meaning, the main concern—and includes and is the Soul' (*Starting from Paumanok*, § 14). Shelley in *Queen Mab* (IV. 140) also asserted: 'Soul is the only element,' which amounts to the same thing. And to-day the scientists confirm the poets: 'The psychical (and consciousness) is reality, while matter (and physical process) is a *phenomenon,* the disguise, so to speak, under which the psychical appears when apprehended through the special senses' (Morton Prince: *The Unconscious*, 2nd ed., N.Y., 1921, pp. 130-131). This is precisely Blake's idea, though written in perhaps less happy a style.

This may seem to involve a contradiction in Blake's philosophy. Aristotelean in his belief of the unity of soul and body, he also believed, with the Platonists, in pre-existence. We may well ask how the soul can descend into a body, if the two are really one and cannot exist separate. The answer is unexpectedly simple: Blake believed that the material body was an illusion or error—a part of the soul, but not an essential part.

That Evil may not be Evil in Eternity is an idea which may also be found elsewhere. Blake once told the invaluable Crabb Robinson that 'what are called vices in the natural world are the highest sublimities in the spiritual world' (H. C. R., Dec. 17, 1825). This is because such 'Evil' is strength, not weakness. Turning back to our Paracelsus, we read: 'The Sophists (a race which has more talk than true wisdom) falsely assert that Mercury is cold and of a moist nature, so that they go and advise us to congeal it by means of heat; whereas heat only renders it more fluid, as they daily find out to their own loss rather than gain.' Milton was not unfamiliar with the idea: 'To be weak is miserable' (*Paradise Lost*, I. 157); and even 'All wickedness is weakness' (*Samson Agonistes*, l. 834); and his idea is Blake's, though he uses the words in an opposed meaning. Blake would never have blamed, but pitied, weakness. Thomas Traherne also accepts Energy as the ultimate Paradise: 'Heaven, where the soul is all Act' (*Centuries of Meditations*, II. 73). Shelley repeats this: 'Life is its state of action' (*Queen Mab*, IX. 158). Coventry Patmore, mild as he was, reached the same idea: 'In vulgar minds the idea of passion is inseparable from that of disorder; in them the advances of love, or anger, or any other strong energy towards its end, is like the rush of a savage horde, with war-whoops, tom-toms, and confused tumult; and the great decorum of a passion, which keeps, and is immensely increased in force by the discipline of God's order, looks to them like weakness and coldness. Hence the passions, which are the measure of man's capacity for virtues, are regarded by the pious vulgar as being of the nature of vice; and, indeed, in them they are so; for virtues are nothing but ordered passions, and vices nothing but passions in disorder' (*Magna Moralia*, II.). Nietzsche makes this doctrine a very central one: 'What is good? All that increases the feeling of power—power itself—in man! What is bad? All that comes from weakness! What is happiness? The feeling that power increases—that resistance is being overcome!' (*Der Antichrist*, 2.)

Milton, for all his worship of Reason, seems to imply that, as the Restrainer, it is bad. 'Down, Reason, then!' (*Samson Agonistes*, l. 322), also: 'the Tree / Of prohibition, root of all our woe' (*Paradise Lost*, IX. 644-645).

Plate V. ¶ 2. *The shadow of Desire*. Later Blake used the word *Shadow* as a technical term for restrained desire.

Plate VI. ¶ 1. *This is shown*. 'Oh that I might have my request; and that God would grant me the thing I long for. . . . Then should I yet have comfort . . .' (*Job* vi. 8, 10). But Job is praying for death. Perhaps Blake had *John* xvi. 7 in mind.

¶ 2. *He became Jehovah*. After the crucifixion, the Church worshipped the old God of this world under Christ's name.

A Memorable Fancy. This title is an obvious reference to Swedenborg, who called his visions *Memorable Relations*.

¶ 1. Here Blake anticipated the charge of madness, which later was to become so serious.

¶ 2. The five senses, far from being limited to material use, really can open into the world of Infinity. Cf. the *Introductory Lines to Europe*.

¶ 3. These two septenaries contain a theory already reached by Kant and other contemporary philosophers: that our sense-world probably is an entirely different world from that perceived by beings with other sense-organs. Shelley also reached the idea: 'Some eyed flower whose young leaves waken / On an unimagined world' (*Ode to Heaven*).

Plate VII.   The *Proverbs of Hell*.

1. Blake begins with a common-sense maxim, emphasizing the importance of work. Cf. Proverbs 11 and 41.

2. 'Drive your cart and your plough *over* the bones of the dead,' not awed into leaving them undisturbed, but utilizing the graveyard as the most fertile soil. This is noteworthy, as showing Blake's appreciation of the value of the past. The 9th line of *The Ancient Bard* (*Songs of Experience*) tells the fate of those who wander in such places purposeless: 'They stumble all night over bones of the dead.'

3. The first of the many proverbs (3, 7, 18, 35, 46, 52, 64, 70) teaching the value of excess as a path to wisdom. It eventually became one of Blake's fundamental doctrines that Error, to be cast off, must first be fully recognized. Cf. 'Giving a Body to Falshood that it may be cast off forever' (*Jerusalem*, 12:13); also follow the fate of the Satanic trinity in Blake's *Book of Job*.

5. This teaches the necessity for acting out all one's impulses. It is repeated pictorially in *Europe*, where the plate of the Joys laying down their sceptres before Priesthood is followed by the plate of the Plague. Cf. Proverb 67, also the harper's song, plate XIX of *The Marriage*.

6. This proverb is not so easily explained as it might seem. Comparing it with the 16th and 62nd Proverbs, the worm is merely contemptible in forgiving the injury; but comparing it with a deleted stanza of *The Fly* (*Songs of Experience*): 'The cut worm / Forgives the plough, / And dies in peace. . . .' it appears rather that Blake was upholding the forgiveness of injury.

7. Blake, being a poet, understood the value of wine. It seems that there must have been Prohibitionists in his day, since he advocates dipping them in the river, as a cure by excess. Cf. Proverb 18.

8. Or, 'all things exist as they are perceived.' Blake was an extreme Subjective Idealist, to use the jargon of philosophy. He elaborated this in a letter to Dr. Trusler (23d August 1799): 'The tree which moves some to tears of joy is in the eyes of others only a green thing which stands in the way.' In *The Gates of Paradise* he had already said the same thing, though less happily: 'The sun's light, when he unfolds it, / Depends on the organ that beholds it.' In fact, he made a great point of seeing 'not with, but through, the eye.' Traherne had anticipated it: 'All men see the same objects, but do not equally understand them' (*Meditations*). Henry Sutton, possibly influenced by this very proverb, also expressed the anthropomorphism of nature: 'Man doth usurp all space, / Stares thee in rock, bush, river, in the face. / Never yet thine eye beheld a tree; / 'Tis no sea thou seest in the sea, / 'Tis but a disguised humanity' (*Man*). Bergson also hit upon a tree to point the same lesson.

9. This seems to have been taken from Paracelsus: 'Now, those who give light on earth as torches in the light of Nature shall shine, through Christ, as stars forever' (*Preface to the Hermetic Astronomy*).

10. Blake always felt the eternal world so strongly that he was sure it approved or disapproved of work—especially artistic work—performed in the temporal world. Elsewhere he speaks of his own productions as 'the study and delight of archangels.' So, in the 19th Illustration to *Job* he showed the angels crowding in at the corners to witness Job's triumph. Again he said, more ambiguously: 'The

ruins of Time build mansions in Eternity ' (letter to Hayley, 6th May 1800), implying that all such works are made more perfect in the other world.

12. A wise man's hours, being eternal, cannot be measured by a clock.   Cf.
Milton, 27 : 62–28 : 3 : ' Every Time less than a pulsation of the artery / Is equal in its
period & value to Six Thousand Years / For in this Period the Poet's Work is
Done ; and all the Great / Events of Time start forth & are conceiv'd in such a
Period, / Within a Moment, a Pulsation of the Artery.'   Cf. also the striking
parallel in Walt Whitman's *Song of Myself*, § 44 : ' The clock indicates the moment
—but what does eternity indicate ? '

13. That every injury done to a dumb beast affects the whole Universe is the
doctrine of the body of the *Auguries of Innocence*.

14. A satire on the pedantic poetry of his times.

15. Cf. ' And if we were not weak, / Should we be less in deed than in desire ? '
(Shelley, *Julian and Maddalo*).

16. Cf. ' By the slave-morality of Christianity . . . the impotence which does
not retaliate for injuries is falsified into " goodness " ' (Nietzsche, *Zur Genealogie
der Moral*).

18. ' Sous ces paroles encore, on entrevoit, comme dans un bourgeon fermé,
tout notre xixe siècle, Kant, Fichte, Wordsworth, Chateaubriand, Delacroix, et
Schleiermacher ' (Joseph Milsand, *Littérature Anglaise* : *W. Blake*).

19-20. The hypocrisy of all meanness.

Plate VIII.

21. This proverb must have been inspired by Paul's words : ' By the law is the
knowledge of sin ' (*Romans* iii. 20).   Upon this same text grew one of the Gnostic
heresies : ' Epiphanes . . . wrote a book *On Justice* . . . asserting . . . that the
law, by introducing the distinction of meum and tuum, was the real author of the
sin of theft and adultery ' (Mansel's *Gnostic Heresies*, VIII.) : and in Blake's own
day, just across the Channel, Proudhon was loudly elaborating the text : La Pro-
priété c'est le vol ! '   Blake, however, was less interested in the economic situation
than in the spiritual situation ; and later he developed several other Gnostic ideas.
This proverb sums up a great deal of Nietzsche's wisdom : ' No morality has any
value in itself ' (*Götzendämmerung*) ; and : ' Christianity has lived by distress, it
has *created* distress in order to make itself necessary and eternal.   Consider, for
example, the consciousness of sin ; it remained for the church to enrich mankind
with that state of distress ! ' (*Der Antichrist*).

22-25. ' Everything that lives is holy,' and these things traditionally considered
bad are here justly described as manifestations of God.

26. Extremes resemble each other.   Cf. Fielding's *Tom Thumb*, I. ii : ' Excess
of Joy, my Lord, I 've heard Folks say, Gives Tears, as often as Excess of Grief.'

27. Certain aspects of the world are too great to be understood.   This is Blake's
question asked earlier about the Tyger : ' Did he who made the Lamb make thee ? '
Even at the end of his life he seems to have left the question as definitely insoluble,
when, over the 15th Illustration to *Job* he inscribed : ' Can any understand the
spreading of the Clouds, the noise of his tabernacle ? '

30-31. These proverbs announce that everything has its own appropriate place.
The corollary to these simple truths is the more startling : ' One Law for the Lion
& Ox is Oppression.'

32. Fools may even do good by being excellent discipline.

33. This axiom leads us unsuspectingly toward the doctrine that Imagination
is Truth.

34. Small timid beasts look for causes ; the great ones look for results.

35. A comparison of talent and genius.   This must have been inspired by some
feeling of protest against Fuseli's 14th *Aphorism* : ' Genius without bias is a stream
without direction : it inundates all and ends in stagnation,' or perhaps from the
more sympathetic 47th *Aphorism* : ' Creation gives, invention finds existence.'
Coventry Patmore was somewhat more explanatory in the 25th of his *Aurea Dicta* :

' No great art, no really effective ethical teaching, can come from any but such as know immeasurably more than they will attempt to communicate.'

36. A single thought is infinite, unbound by the laws of Time and Space, therefore it can be said to ' fill immensity.'   Traherne had written the same thing earlier : ' One soul in the immensity of its intelligence is greater and more excellent than the whole world.   The Ocean is but the drop of a bucket to it, the Heavens but a centre, the Sun obscurity, and all Ages but as one day ' (*Centuries*, II. 70) ; and Coventry Patmore repeated it later : ' A moment's fruition of a true felicity is enough, and eternity not too much ' (*Aurea Dicta*, 55) ; but neither of these quotations equals Blake's either in depth or brevity.   It should be remarked that of these three it is very unlikely that any of them had ever read the works of any other.   This is merely an excellent example of mystics talking the same language, and discovering the same truths.

37. Lavater's style, but Blake's character.

38. This proverb anticipates William James's whole theory of pragmatic truth. It states the Truth of Imagination, and is the conclusion drawn from the 33rd Proverb.   Cf. ' I adopt each theory, myth, god and demi-god ; / I see that the old accounts, bibles, genealogies, are true, without exception ' (Walt Whitman : *With Antecedents*, § 2) ; also ' Whatever satisfied Souls is true ' (*Manhattan's Streets*, § 7). Cf. also ' We *cannot* desire any good which is not a reality ' (Coventry Patmore : *Magna Moralia*, 41).

39. Genius should not stoop to the ways of the moneymaker.

Plate IX.

40. The Deity provides for the great of soul, just as he fed Elijah in the wilderness.

41. The normal course of the ordered life : plan, act, profit, rest.

42. This reminds one of the Lavater's 237th *Aphorism* : ' Be certain that he who has betrayed thee once will betray thee again.'   Cf. also *Jerusalem*, 91 : 2-3 : ' The man who permits you to injure him, deserves your vengeance : / He also will receive it.'   George MacDonald, who must have read Blake before he wrote *Lilith*, also noted : ' In this world never trust a person who has once deceived you ' (*Lilith*, ch. xvii.).

43. God rewards no prayers unless some effort is made by man towards their fulfilment.   In other words : ' Prayers plough not.'   Swinburne rather perplexingly calls this ' the fruit of his belief in the identity of body with soul ' ; while EY (II. 67) consider it a reference to the fable of Hercules and the Carter.

44. Wrath is often better than argument—especially with a fool who is easily impressed.   Blake later rediscovered this truth in his conflict with Hayley (see the letter to Butts, July 6, 1803).

45. Beware of the man who never changes his mind, for there he breeds reptiles. Cf. the Harper's song on Plate XIX.

48. This division of the profile into the four elements is typical, not only of Blake's own habit of systematizing, but also of the earlier mystical philosophers. This particular passage may well have been suggested by a passage in Cornelius Agrippa : ' And lastly, in the Soul it self, according to *Austin*, the understanding resembles Fire, reason the Aire, imagination the Water, and the senses the Earth. And the senses also are divided amongst themselves by reason of the Elements, for the sight is fiery, neither can it perceive without Fire, and Light : the hearing is airy, for a sound is made by the striking of the Aire ; The smell, and tast resemble the Water, without the moisture of which there is neither smell, nor tast ; and lastly the feeling is wholly earthy, and taketh gross bodies for its object ' (*Occult Philosophy*, I. vii.).

52. The wisdom of folly.

53. No individual, and no essence, can ever change.   This proverb is used as the 72nd line of *America*.   ' The soul of sweet delight / Can never pass away,' Blake repeated in the 9th and 10th lines of The *Visions of the Daughters of Albion*.

Cf. the first stanza of the *Epilogue* to *The Gates of Paradise* ; also Shelley's ' Soul is not more polluted than the beams / Of heaven's pure orb ' (*Queen Mab*, IV. 150-151).

54. This establishes the Eagle as a symbol of Genius throughout all of Blake's works.   It is an old symbol : ' An Eagle, the emblem from the earliest Christian times of the soul which most aspires to meditate on divine things, and as such adopted for the special cognisance of St. John the Divine ' (A. J. Butler : *Appendix A* to Dante's *Purgatory*).

55. This proverb explains the enigmatic *Keys* to the *Gates of Paradise*.   Cf. also the 29th Proverb.   Thomas Lodge hit upon the same idea in his *Rosalynd* : ' The fairer the rose is, the sooner it is bitten by caterpillers.'   Shakspere used the same figure in the Second Part of *King Henry the Sixth* (III. i. 90) : ' The caterpillars eat my leaves away.'

56. Perhaps suggested by Chatterton's ' meadow flower ripen'd in ages ' (*Narva and Mored*).

59. Another version of Proverb 43.

60. The deep emotions are silent.   Yet cf. Proverb 26.

Plate x.

61. Another apothegm systematizing the human form.   It anticipates the triad of Head, Heart, and Loins, which later figures so prominently in Blake's epics.   However, as it is here, it reappears in *The Four Zoas*, VI. 90-94.

64. This may have been suggested by Lavater's 522nd *Aphorism* : ' Take from Luther his roughness and fiery courage ; . . . mysticism from Fenelon ; . . . from Milton the extravagance of his all personifying fancy ; from Raffaelle his dryness and nearly hard precision ; and from Rubens his supernatural luxury of colour :— Deduct this oppressive exuberance from each ; rectify them according to your own taste—and what will be the result ? . . .'   T. Sturge Moore quotes Flaubert's *Correspondance* (Série ii.) for a parallel : ' Never fear to be exaggerated, all the very great have been so—Michaelangelo, Raphael, Shakspere, Molière. . . . But in order that the exaggeration may not shock, it must be everywhere constant, proportional, in harmony with itself ; if your good folk are a hundred feet high, your mountains must be twenty thousand ; and what is the ideal if it be not that kind of bulking out ? '   Blake had a definite application of this principle in mind, which is made obvious by the proximity of the 61st Proverb.

66. Walt Whitman also said : ' All works shall illustrate the divine law of indirections ' (*Laws for Creation*) ; but the more familiar phrasing is ' Curved is the line of beauty.'

68. ' Where man is not, nature is barren '—of God.

69. A further deduction from the 33rd and the 38th Proverbs.   These three should really be read together.

70. This proverb, which seems at first to be a humorous comment on the whole collection, is very much in the spirit of the age.   La Marquise de Créquy (*Souvenirs*, vol. III.) attributed the same remark to Louis-Philippe d'Orléans, who as a child, on being served some ' rôties à la moelle,' cried : ' J'en veux beaucoup ! j'en veux trop ! '   But Blake also meant it as Thomas Vaughan meant it, when he terminated his description of the River of Pearl, in the *Lumen de Lumine* : ' This is enough and too much, for I hold it not my Duty to insist upon secrets, which are so far from the Reader's Inquiry, that I dare say they are beyond his Expectation.'

Plate XI. ¶ 1. *The ancient poets.*   According to Thomas Taylor in his *Mystical Initiations* ; *or, Hymns of Orpheus* (London, 1787, p. 12), Orpheus was deliberately responsible for this anthropomorphism : ' Orpheus filled all things with Gods subordinate to the demiurgus.'

Plate XI. ¶ 6. *Thus men forgot.*   Cf. Lavater's 398th *Aphorism* : ' Let none turn over books or roam the stars in quest of God, who sees him not in man.'

Plate XII. ¶ 1. The second *Memorable Fancy.*   Many commentators on Blake have pointed out that Blake's surprisingly casual familiarity with the prophets was intended as a satire on Swedenborg. It is also intended as a satire on Paracelsus : ' If your artists only knew that their prince Galen—they call none like him—was sticking in Hell, from whence he has sent letters to me, they would make the sign of the cross upon themselves with a fox's tail. In the same way your Avicenna sits in the vestibule of the infernal portal ; and I have disputed with him about his aurum potabile ' (*Treasury of Treasures*). Blake was also justifying and explaining their visions, and even reproving them for attaching so much importance and awe to them. Blake, who could call up a vision whenever he wished, rather looked down upon those whose abilities were not so well controlled.

¶ 4. *He replied.* This startling doctrine is entirely orthodox. St. Augustine said : ' What ought to be, must be.' Upon *Matthew* xvii. 20 is based the whole theory of Magic. Milton causes his Samson to say : ' They knew not / That what I mentioned was of God ; I knew / From intimate impulse ' (221-223). Shelley's Phantom in *Hellas* cries : ' Yet has thy faith prevailed, and I am here ' (I. 864). Coventry Patmore also approved : ' The power of believing and acting upon self-evidence is true strength of intellect and character ' (*Aurea Dicta*, 117).

Plate XIV.

¶ 1. The tradition that ' the world will be consumed in fire at the end of six thousand years ' antedates Christianity, and was accepted by the early Fathers of the Church, as well as by such people as Luther and Melancthon. It is sometimes ascribed to Elijah (though he says nothing like that in the Bible) and sometimes to Elias the Rabbi.[1] The earliest references seem to be in the *Slavonic Enoch* and the *Epistle of Barnabas* ; after which follow Justin Martyr, Papias, Irenaeus, Tertullian, and Cyprian.

Their theory was, that as the Lord created the Universe in six days and rested on the seventh, so the Universe in turn would labour for six ages, which would be followed by a seventh age, the Messianic Sabbath, or Millennium, after which the last Judgment was to take place. All this was derived from the juxtaposition of the following Biblical texts :

' In six days the Lord made heaven and earth ' (*Exodus* xx. 11).

' And on the seventh day God ended his work which he had made ; and he rested on the seventh day from all his work which he had made. And God blessed the seventh day, and sanctified it : because that in it he had rested from all his work which God created and made ' (*Genesis* ii. 2-3).

' One day is with the Lord as a thousand years ' (2 *Peter* iii. 8).

' There remaineth therefore a rest [keeping of a sabbath] to the people of God ' (*Hebrews* iv. 9).

In Blake's day, the world was commonly thought to have been created in 4004 B.C. Therefore the Second Coming was to be in A.D. 1996. But Blake shifted the date to suit himself.

The ultimate destruction of the world by fire has been announced by prophets over the entire world. See, for example, the Sybils and the Voluspa (*Eddas*).

¶ 2. *A Cherub* is a spirit of knowledge (as opposed to love), whose symbol is the Eye. Cherubim are inferior to the Seraphim (love), whose symbol is the Wing. This Cherub, then, is Reason, with the flaming sword of Prohibition, who drove man from Eden. (Blake never uses the word Cherub in a good sense.) The Tree of Life has often been interpreted as the phallos :[2] so Blake's command is really an exhortation to Free Love, ' an improvement of sensual enjoyment.'[3]

¶ 5. *The doors of perception* are the five senses.

---

[1] Sir Thomas Browne : *Religio Medici*, I. 46, and *Pseudodoxia*, VI. i. Sir Thomas, with the typically casual attitude of the pedant, refers lightly to this Rabbi as a person too well known to need further explanation. But Sir Thomas betrays himself : he did not even know that this Prophecy was once an article in the faith of all Christians.

[2] As in Sir Thomas Browne's *Pseudodoxia*, I. i.

[3] For a more detailed discussion see Chapter xv., *The Fifth Window*.

¶ 6. *The cavern* as symbol of the body was established by Plato in the famous passage in the 7th book of his *Republic* : ' After this, I said, imagine the enlightenment of ignorance of our nature in a figure :—Behold ! human beings living in a sort of underground den : they have been here from their childhood, and have their legs and necks chained, so that they cannot move, and can only see before them. . . . They see only their own shadows, or the shadows of one another . . . on the opposite wall of the cave. . . .' Cf. also Porphyry : ' The Pythagoreans, and after them Plato, showed that the world is a cavern and a den. . . . The theologists . . . were of the opinion that a cave is a symbol of the sensible world, because caverns are dark, stony and humid ' (*On the Cave of the Nymphs*, trans. by Thomas Taylor). Thomas Vaughan used the symbol : ' From this place we moved straight forward, till we came to a Cave of Earth. It was very obscure, and withall darkish, giving a heavy odour like that of graves ' (*Lumen de Lumine*) : also ' The Mercurie, or Mineral liquor (say they) is altogether cold and passive, and it lyes in certain earthly Subterraneous Caverns.' Shelley also uses the Cavern symbol freely, the first example in his works being in the 363rd line of *Alastor*. To Blake the Cavern was specifically the skull, since everything exists in the brain.

The problem of opening the senses is a real one. ' This clarity of [Mystical] Vision may also be enjoyed in regard to the phenomenal world. The actual physical perceptions are strangely heightened, so that the self perceives an added significance and reality in all natural things : is often convinced that it knows at last " the secret of the world." ' (Evelyn Underhill: *Mysticism*, p. 289). Many mystics confirm her. ' But for the present we are less intent to the Vision, and cannot yet open the eye of our Mind to behold the incorruptible and incomprehensible Beauty ' (Hermes Trismegistus : *Pymander*, IV. 16). ' But if God did but once put away that Duskiness, which moves about the Light, and that thy Eyes were opened, then in that very Place where thou standest, sittest, or liest, thou should see the glorious Countenance or Face of God and the whole Heavenly Gate ' (Böhme: *Aurora*, x. 98). ' We are all born like Moses with a veil over the face : this is it which hinders the prospect of that intellectual shining light which God hath placed in us. And to tell a truth that concerns all mankind, the greatest mystery, both in divinity and philosophy, is how to remove it ' (Thomas Vaughan : *Anthroposophia Theomagica*).

Plate xv. The third *Memorable Fancy*.

¶ 2. The Cave having been explained, it is obvious that the Dragon Man, who clears away the rubbish from the cave's mouth, must be a sexual symbol. This is confirmed by the Swedenborgian *Dictionary of Correspondences* : ' Dragon, in a good sense, signifies the same as serpent ; viz. the sensual principle.' There is only one other use of the Dragon as a sexual symbol in Blake's works ; that is in *Milton*, 10 : 2. Elsewhere it means the Worm at war.

¶ 3. The word Viper occurs only once elsewhere in Blake, and then with a different meaning. Here, since he ' folds around the rock,' he is obviously Reason, ' the outward Circumference of Energy.' The precious stones and metals are hardened truths, whose dead glitter attracts so many to the Snake. In *America*, Orc (Revolt) is called the Viper.

¶ 4. The Eagle, who ' causes the inside of the Cave to be infinite ' is the Genius. Cf. Proverb 54. These birds create works of art, which elsewhere Blake called ' mansions in Eternity.'

¶ 5. The Lions of flaming fire represent the wrathful guardians of the Lamb (Imagination) who in their revolutionary fury melt the fixed metals of Reason ' into living fluids,' in preparation for new forms.

¶ 6. The Unnamed Forms, which cast these metals, are the ungenerated, whom Blake later named Rintrah, Palamabron, Bromion, and Theotormon, the four sons of Jerusalem who guard the Western Gate (*Jerusalem*, 72 : 10). There is no need to explain them here, except to say that they are spiritual forces which assist the poetic spirit.

¶ 7. In the expanse, the Abyss of the Five Senses, are the men who receive this 'excess of delights' of the creative spirits ; in their charge the immortal works take on the contracted, outward form of books, and are classified into libraries.

Plate XVI.

¶ 1. *The weak in courage.* This proverb is the 49th *Proverb of Hell.*

Plate XVII. The fourth *Memorable Fancy* is completely explained in Chapter XIV.

Plate XXIX.

¶ 3. *Passed all the planets till we came to saturn.* Blake's astronomy is at fault ; he should have known that Uranus lay beyond Saturn. Not until 1845 was Neptune, the eighth and most outward planet, discovered. Blake probably selected Saturn because of its meaning to Jakob Böhme (*Aurora,* xxvi. 1-3), where we learn that it 'takes its Beginning and Original *not* from the *Sun* ; for it has in its Power the *Chamber* of Death, and is a Drier up of all Powers, from whence Corporeity exists.'

Plate XXIII. The fifth *Memorable Fancy.*

¶ 3. The extraordinary colours of the Angel seem to be a satire on Raphael's blush of propriety : ' Celestial rosie red, Love's proper hue ' (*Paradise Lost,* VIII. 619). Can Byron have read *The Marriage of Heaven and Hell ?* If not, how can we explain the 61st stanza of his *Vision of Judgment ?*

> When Michael saw this host, he first grew pale,
> As angels can ; next, like Italian twilight,
> He turn'd all colours—as a peacock's tail,
> Or sunset streaming through a gothic skylight
> In some old abbey, or a trout not stale,
> Or distant lightning on the horizon *by* night,
> Or a fresh rainbow, or a grand review
> Of thirty regiments in red, green, and blue.

Plate XXIV.

¶ 3. What was the *Bible of Hell,* which Blake promised the world ? Apparently the idea remained in his mind all his life. Rossetti catalogued an uncoloured work (Sec. A, No. 2) : 'A Naked Man touching a Ram as he recedes. Daringly designed.' On the back Blake has written in title-page form, ' The Bible of Hell, in Nocturnal Visions Collected. Vol. I. Lambeth.' Perhaps Blake intended to gather together all his short Prophetic Books into one collection, to be called ' The Bible of Hell.' *Urizen* and *The Book of Los* would have stood for *Genesis* ; the *Song of Los* would continue the tale of creation ; *The French Revolution, America,* and *Europe* would represent the historical books ; the *Visions of the Daughters of Albion* would replace the *Song of Solomon* ; *The Marriage of Heaven and Hell* would be an excellent substitute for *Proverbs* ; *Ahania,* which retells the Crucifixion, would summarize the *New Testament* ; while *Tiriel* and *Thel* would have to be inserted as purely literary works, such as *Job* and *Ruth.*

If this were Blake's intention—and I think it quite probable—he abandoned it, to recast all these books into one great epic. *The Four Zoas,* which was also *A Dream of Nine Nights.* This, however, was not intended for the world.

But there are other possibilities. On the 18th of February, 1826, Blake read to Crabb Robinson ' his " Version of Genesis," for so it may be called, as understood by a Christian Visionary. He read a wild passage in a sort of Bible style.' This seems to be lost. There does exist an eight-page manuscript of Blake's, sold recently at the sale of the H. Buxton Forman Library, which is entitled : *Genesis /* *The Seven Days / of the Created World* (water-marked 1793). The handwriting (as Mr. Arthur Symons declares, whose statement seems accurate, judging from the facsimile of the first page in the Sale Catalogue) is clearly Blake's ; but this poem, for all the corrections made in his hand, cannot have been composed by him. It is a stilted eighteenth-century bit of blank verse metaphysics ; and Mr. Robert Hillyer suggests that Blake copied it from Hayley's dictation. By no stretch of the imagination could it be called ' wild ' or ' in a sort of Bible style.'

Blake's last attempt at the *Bible of Hell* was probably the *Genesis* in Mr. Henry Huntington's library. Here Blake used the text of the Bible unchanged, restricting his own ideas to the decorations and the chapter headings.[1] A detailed description of this will be found in Chapter XXIX., *Illustrations to Others.*

¶ 4. This proverb, which had already been used in the 334th line of *Tiriel*, was to do duty again as the 108th line of the *Visions of the Daughters of Albion.*

It is interesting to discover that the influence of Swedenborg on Thomas Lake Harris, the occultist, caused the latter to dictate under inspiration a book superficially not dissimilar to *The Marriage of Heaven and Hell.* This was his *Song of Satan* (N.Y., 1858), issued as an Appendix to the *Arcana of Christianity.* Under the influence of Swedenborg, Harris also descended into a visionary hell where 'the Evil Genius appeared as a man of leaden aspect, much like the portraits of Lord Byron. He was accompanied by a youthful Spirit resembling greatly the published pictures of John Keats; a third Spirit presented a likeness to the engravings of Milton' (p. xiii.). The first Spirit, however, was not Byron; on being accused of deception, he turned into Wordsworth, then into Thomas Moore. Harris was not too comfortable in this Hell of poets (all of whom recited verses on every occasion); nor did the publication of his book add to his reputation, even among his followers.

COMMENTARY ON *A SONG OF LIBERTY*

1. The Eternal Female is Enitharmon, Poetic Inspiration (also Space). She groans in child-birth. A spiritual force is about to appear in the world of matter.

2. This shows that Blake was describing the American Revolution.

3. *France's dungeon* is the Bastille.

5. Rome's keys are St. Peter's.

7. Enitharmon's child is Orc, the spirit of Revolt.

8. These mountains, of which we hear more in *America*, are lost Atlantis, the path to the world of Eternity, now barred out by the Atlantic Ocean, the deluge of Materialism. Part of this verse is repeated verbatim, *America*, 108. In this place, halfway between the Temporal and the Eternal, Orc stands to be judged by Reason, or Urizen, who is jealous of his power.

10. Orc is cast out by Urizen. Rejected from the mental world, he falls into a physical manifestation—Revolution.

13. *The western sea* is America. Both west and water are symbols of the body. Just as historically the first Revolution of the times appeared in America, so spiritually it began in the body, by upsetting the laws (especially the sexual laws) which had subjected it.

14. The material aspect of the body (the sea) at once rushes away.

15. As a result of this transcending of the body, Reason is dethroned. The 508th design for Young's *Night Thoughts* (IX., 1851) was evidently connected with this idea; there we see a similar fall also involving, to our surprise, an elephant.

16. *Urthona's dens* are the lowest part of the spirit. Urthona, the only name mentioned in this poem, may come from Ossian's character 'Urthono';[2] from 'earthern, with sonorous vowel changes . . . or . . . Ur and Thon, original clay.'[3] Since his symbol is earth, it may simply be 'Earth-owner.' He is the regent of the world of spirit, the highest of the four Zoas. Los, the spirit of poetry, is only his temporary form in this world.

18. Urizen (Reason) is here definitely identified with Jehovah of *Exodus.* As we have seen, in verses 9-10, he is a jealous god (cf. *Exodus* xx. 5); and now he issues the Decalogue. Blake obviously wished to suggest the fall of Lucifer.

19. Orc's station is in the east (passions) where the light of the New Day is rising.

20. He spurns the clouds of curses (obscurantism) and the stony law (the tables

---

[1] Water-marked 1826.   [2] Hewlett, p. 779.
[3] W. N. Guthrie: *Sewanee Review*, Oct. 1897, p. 490.

of the ten Prohibitions), loosing the horses of instruction from darkness, and crying that the eternal strife of the Lion (guardian of the Lamb) and the Wolf (the traditional enemy of the sheep) shall cease.

Chorus. Let the Church no longer curse the joys of man, nor the State (his ' accepted brethren ') build the structure of society. Nor shall the filthy repressions of Religion ' call that Virginity which wishes but acts not ' (cf. *Marriage*, plate v). Restif de la Bretonne, in a note to his autobiography (*M. Nicolas*, 1796), also felt nothing but contempt for ' ces prétendus moraux, qui font consister toute la vertu dans l'abstinence de l'amour.'

For everything that lives is Holy !—with emphasis on the word ' lives,' since errors and negations have no real existence. Blake repeats this line as the 215th of the *Visions of the Daughters of Albion*, the 71st of *America*, and the 574th of *Night II. of the Four Zoas*. By it Blake means little more than that God is All. In his notes on Lavater, he was more specific : ' Everything on earth is the word of God, and its essence is God.' Cf. Milton's *Treatise of Christian Doctrine*, ' There remains but one solution of the difficulty—namely, that all things are of God.'

ILLUSTRATIONS

The decorations of *The Marriage* and the *Song of Liberty* are for the most part simple illustrations of the text. Several pages, which are completely covered with the text, have the spaces between the words and at the ends of the lines filled with tiny figures of trumpeting men, horses, plants, even miniature landscapes.

The *Title-page* illustrates the last episode of *The Marriage* : the embrace of the Angel and the Devil. This takes place in ' the Cavern,' or within the outer shell of the earth, on whose surface are the forests of error, where tiny human figures walk and lament.

Plate II. The joys of Innocence. A youth in the Tree of Life hands down to a girl the grapes of ecstasy. This repeats, with an added sexual significance, the decoration of the second plate of *The Ecchoing Green* (*Songs of Innocence*). The fifth design for Grey's *Ode on a Distant Prospect*, is another version of this plate.

Plate III. Above the text : the liberated soul bathes in the flames of Hell. Below, Enitharmon gives birth to Orc, the spirit of Revolt. This is the birth of the Babe in *The Mental Traveller*, line 95.

Plate IV. Below the text : the ' Good and Bad Angels ' struggle for a soul. Blake repeated this picture as a fresco and as a colour-print. The Bad Angel, blind, and chained in the flame of passion, hovers over the Sea of Time and Space ; from him the Good Angel, entirely free, snatches the infant soul. A thin barrier of cloud between the two Angels indicates that they belong to different worlds. Of course these Angels are *not* the forces of Good and Evil. They are ' pale Religion's lechery,' the spirit caught in the flame of unsatisfied desire (cf. the same symbol in the 6th plate of the *Visions of the Daughters of Albion*) ; and the spirit of Freedom, which is true Innocence.

Plate V. A naked youth, with cloak, sword, and horse, falls into flames. The fall of Orc.

Plate X. The Devil (Orc, now on earth) dictating his Proverbs.

Plate XI. Above the text : the ' spiritual forms ' of nature are seen : the sun appears as a god ; a stream as a nude girl ; and a plant as a baby. In Miss Amy Lowell's copy (Keynes, G) the cave is already closing in on the scene. As a separate picture, this bears the title : *Death and Hell teem with Life*. Below the text, the child Orc flees from Urizen.

Plate XIV. A woman in flames hovers over a nude male corpse. She is the Emanation (the Imaginative portion of man) trying to rouse the material portion.

Plate XV. Below the text : an Eagle soars with a serpent : Genius uplifting

Nature (or controlling Priesthood). This picture might well illustrate the *First Canto* of Shelley's *Revolt of Islam*.

Plate XVI. The five Giants who formed this world (the five senses) crouch in darkness.

Plate XX. Below the text is the apparition of the Leviathan in the Sea of Time and Space, which is described on plate XVIII. Above him is the tiny figure of William Blake in the root of the oak. Beneath this scene is a motto usually painted out : ' Opposition is True Friendship.' It is quite clear in the J. P. Morgan copy. Blake probably inserted it as a *Proverb of Hell*, which he thought of too late to insert in its proper place ; and then obliterated it, because it seemed to imply that the strife of nature was true friendship to men. Cf. Henry More's *Second Lash* : ' Better are the wounds of a friend then the kisses of an enemy.'

Plate XXI. The newly resurrected man, with the skull (cavern) beneath his feet. This was a favourite idea of Blake's, and is repeated in *America*, Plate VIII ; and in the celebrated *Death's Door* in Blair's *Grave*.

Plate XXIV. Nebuchadnezzar, Man maddened and brutalized until he tries to live by the things of this ' vegetable world ' only. He is introduced again as the 299th design for Young's *Night Thoughts*. This picture is ' without doubt derived from Plate 146 of *The Bible Commentary* (Richard Blome, 1703) which was probably drawn by G. Freeman and engraved by some Dutch or Flemish engraver, as is the case with most of the plates in the same volume. This fact appears to me interesting, as I know of no other instance in which Blake has borrowed an attitude or an idea,' wrote Mr. Frederick York Powell in *The Academy*, Jan. 16, 1875. I have been unable to see this volume.

VISIONS OF THE DAUGHTERS OF ALBION

COMMENTARY

The Argument is spoken by Oothoon.

Line 1. *Theotormon* (later one of the four sons of Los) is Desire. His name may be derived from the Greek *Theo* (God) plus the Hebrew *Torah* (doctrine).

Line 4. *Leutha,* as we learn from *Milton,* 9 : 28-30, is the regent of sex under Satan : she may be called Puritanism. It is therefore possible that her name is a feminized form of ' Luther.'

Line 5. Gathering a flower as symbolic of the sexual act is very old. However, in Neoplatonic writings, this symbol of desire also becomes symbolic of the descent of the spirit into generation. Thomas Taylor, in his *Eleusinian Mysteries* (1790), wrote as follows : ' The design of Prosperina, in venturing from her retreat, is beautifully significant of her approaching descent ; for she rambles from home for the purpose of gathering flowers, and this in a lawn replete with the most enchanting variety, and exhaling the most delicious odours. This is a manifest image of the Soul operating principally according to the natural and external life, and so becoming ensnared by the delusive attractions of sensible forms.'

VISIONS. Line 1. *The daughters of Albion* : oppressed womanhood.

Line 2. *America* : freedom in the realm of the body (west).

Line 3. *Oothoon* is the being descended to this plane of existence. She reappears often in the later books. Her name seems to have been built upon Blake's favourite vowel, the long *u*.

Line 5. *Marigold.* Blake's choice of flower is beautifully significant. Its name is a contraction of ' Mary's gold,' which implies that Oothoon's act is both incorruptible (since gold cannot rust) and innocent (since Mary was the mother of God). Moreover, this flower is supposed to open only to the rays of the sun itself.

Line 6. *Nymph.* Oothoon, being completely innocent, sees the ' spiritual ' or living form of the flower. As the west (body) is a watery region, the form is that of a water-goddess. Later, in *Jerusalem,* 13 : 28, we read of sixty-four thousand nymphs which guard the Western Gate. This symbol was undoubtedly suggested by Thomas Taylor's translation of Porphyry's *Cave of the Nymphs,* § 4 : ' For we particularly call the Naiades, and the powers that preside over waters, Nymphs ; and this term also is commonly applied to all souls descending into generation.'

Line 16. *Bromion* (later another of Los's four sons) represents Reason in this world. The tragedy of the soul here is to be torn between Desire and Reason. But in the tragedy of the descent into generation Bromion also represents Karma, the laws of Fate, which snare the wandering soul. His name is evidently derived from *Bromius* (or Bacchus). Cf. Taylor's *Eleusinian Mysteries* (p. 113) : ' Bacchus is the evident symbol of the partial energies of intellect, and its distribution into the obscure and lamentable dominions of sense.' Bromius is specifically the descended Bacchus in the Mysteries (see M. Ouvaroff: *Essay on the Mysteries,* London, 1817, p. 101). Bacchus eventually becomes the Saviour ; but Blake believed that the Greeks placed their highest hopes in Reason, and accordingly he identified the two.

Mr. H. G. Hewlett derived the names of Oothoon, Theotormon, Bromion, and Leutha from names of Ossian's characters : Oithona, Tonthormod, Brumo, and Lutha (p. 779).

Lines 21-22. He controls all Theotormon's life : the four compass points represent the four Zoas, which constitute the soul of man, being subjected to Bromion through his possession of Oothoon.

Lines 27-28. Oothoon and Bromion are forced by society to marry each other. 'Marriages of this kind are downright prostitution,' wrote Tom Paine in his *Reflections on Unhappy Marriages* ; which explains Blake's paradoxical use of the word 'adulterate.'

Bound back to back. Milton had made popular the image of two corpses chained together, but Blake's image was probably influenced, if not inspired, by the *Zohar* (*Idra Suta*, § 997) : ' It is the doctrine of the Kabala, that the woman, as originally conjoined with the man, back to back, in one complex person, is necessarily evil ; because misplaced, if for no other reason. When the man and the woman are separated from each other, the woman ceases to be evil. The woman becomes positively good as soon as she is brought into communication, face to face, with the man ' (William Batchelder Greene : *The Blazing Star*, p. 93).

Lines 31-32. The World under Reason. Theotormon, in his sorrow, sees that the slavery both of negroes and of children (which institutions were then being violently attacked by philanthropists in Blake's day) are due to selfish and sanctified custom, whose outward expression is in these fierce blasts of passion.

Lines 41-42. Blake's sympathetic analysis of the lovers' psychology is here worthy of notice.

Lines 46-59. In her lament Oothoon points to the coming of day which is saluted by all nature. This is the light of moral revolution, the wisdom she has learned from experience. The materialists (or shall we say ' Deists ' ?) had imposed mental limitations upon her by their false teaching that the body completely encloses the soul.

Line 58. *An eye* : the symbol of the cherubim (knowledge), as opposed to the seraphim (love). The Eye is at times a symbol of the Accuser : here, as well as in *Paradise Lost*, vi. 846-852.

Line 59. *The Eastern cloud* : the focussed obscurity of passion.

A sickly charnel house. Luvah (the eastern god of passions) punishes men for their sins. ' That living creature [or Zoa] on the left [east] of the throne gives to the seven Angels the seven vials of the wrath of God, with which they, hovering over the deeps beneath, pour out upon the wicked their plagues ' (*MS. Book : Last Judgment*). The night of Oothoon's passion has become a place of the dead joys—Milton's corpses chained together.

Lines 63-74. Even the beasts of nature are something more than ' sensible organs,' for, though they share the five senses in common, yet each acts diversely, according to interior promptings, which we name instinct, and which Blake called God. Is man to be less than the beasts, by limiting himself to what he calls ' natural morality,' ignoring the divine commands within him ?

Lines 75-81. For these instincts are pure. ' How can I be defiled when I reflect thy image pure ? ' is the defence of all rejected lovers.

Line 79. The lamb and the swan are symbols of innocence.

Line 80. *Red earth* is a literal translation of the name ' Adam,' the flesh, which is the bank of the waters of life. *The wings* are the symbol of the Seraphim (love) which Blake had already connected with Innocence in *Thel* (line 5).

Lines 83-97. Theotormon's answer is one of bewilderment. Where in the mental world are Joys to be found and Sorrows to be avoided ? What is the function of a thought, and what will it bring back to the soul ?

Lines 99-110. Bromion's woe, which ' shakes the cavern,' or disturbs the whole physical life, seeks a solution in science. He tries to reach the infinite through the microscope and telescope. He is in error ; cf. *Milton*, 28 : 15-18 :

> As to that false appearance which appears to the reasoner
> As of a Globe rolling thro' Voidness, it is a delusion of Ulro.[1]
> The Microscope knows not of this nor the Telescope : they alter
> The ratio of the Spectator's Organs but leave Objects untouch'd.

---

[1] *Ulro* is Blake's technical word for Maya, the illusion of this world ; or, specifically, matter.

Therefore Bromion's answer to Theotormon is entirely rational and false.   There are no intellectual warfares, he thinks, but only those of the physical sword and fire ; no sorrows but those of poverty ; no joys but those of riches.   One law binds alike the lion and the ox (cf. *Tiriel*, 334, and the last line of *The Marriage of Heaven and Hell*) ; and Hell awaits the transgressor.

Lines 114-115. In answer, Oothoon blames Urizen (now for the first time named), the evil Creator, the false god of Reason worshipped by this world, who endeavours to make all men rational like himself.   Cf. *Genesis* i. 26.   Urizen's name is composed of the two words ' Your Reason ' (W. B. Guthrie, in *The Sewanee Review*, Oct. 1897).

Lines 116-127. He is wrong, for each joy, each individual, exists separately and distinctly.

Lines 119-120 are repeated in *The Four Zoas*, II. 597-598, with the substitution of the serpent for the ape.

Line 120 was probably suggested by the obscene sixth chapter in Taylor's *Vindication of the Rights of Brutes* (1792)—a book which Blake could hardly have avoided seeing, since it attacked his friends.

Lines 128-131 describe the way in which ' religion ' is imposed upon innocent man.

Lines 132-143. The consequent binding of woman ' in spells of law to one she loathes.'   Blake's attack on marriages not made in heaven is very fine.

Line 139. *Cherubs* : rational beings.

Line 141. Her sin is continued in the premature corruption of her child.

Lines 144-155. Each animal follows its own instincts, till even the worm teaches man to ' take his bliss.'

Lines 152-153 are repeated in *The Four Zoas*, VIII. 488-489.

Lines 156-172. Oothoon contrasts true Innocence with the hypocrisy of Modesty. She blames her own sex for its dissembling.   Passions are universal, and therefore should be honest.   Milton also condemns ' dishonest shame / Of nature's works, honor dishonorable ' (*Paradise Lost*, IV. 313), and describes woman so corrupted :

> Expert in amorous Arts, enchanting tongues
> Perswasive, Virgin majesty with mild
> And sweet allay'd, yet terrible to approach,
> Skill'd to retire, and in retiring draw
> Hearts after them tangl'd in Amorous Nets.
> —*Paradise Regained*, II. 158-162.

Blake adapts the figure of the nets in line 163.   Swift also vented his bitterness against such women :

> Where never blush was call'd in aid,
> That spurious virtue in a maid,
> A virtue but at second-hand ;
> They blush because they understand.
> —*Cadenus and Vanessa.*

Lines 173-177. Oothoon insists on the honesty of her innocence, and celebrates it, even though she is suffering from her frankness.

Lines 178-186. This is one of the most direct, most terrible, and yet most dignified attacks upon chastity ever made.   ' That is the average experience of the average man who restrains desire,' comments Mr. C. Gardner (*Vision and Vesture*, p. 34).   Shelley also bewailed those forced :

> To nurse the image of unfelt caresses
> Till dim imagination just possesses
> The half-created shadow.[1]

This passage might seem to have been directly inspired by line 186 of the *Visions.*

[1] This is to be found among Shelley's ' Fragments.'   He later changed and weakened it, for *The Cenci*, II. ii. 141-143.

Line 187. *Father of Jealousy*, or Urizen, the codifier of the Decalogue. Many times Blake identified Urizen with the Jehovah of *Exodus*.

Line 190. Desire, cast out, becomes only a Shadow. Later Blake applies this symbol both to Ahania and Enion.

Lines 192-197. Oothoon condemns Theotormon's error, which is Jealousy.

Line 199. *Girls of mild silver or of furious gold* : a classification of feminine temperament repeated in *William Bond*.

Lines 205-212. All evil beings avoid the sun ; therefore Oothoon invokes it to shine on her loves.

Lines 214-215 are repeated in *The Four Zoas*, II. 572-574. 'Everything that lives is holy ' is also to be found as the last line of the *Song of Liberty*, and as line 71 of *America*.

Line 217. *Shadows* of suppressed desire. See the *Commentary* on plate v of *The Marriage of Heaven and Hell*.

ILLUSTRATIONS

The decorations of the *Visions of the Daughters of Albion* are the last of Blake's simple illustrations, although already the symbolic character is highly developed. In his next book, *America*, he conceived the book not only as a consecutive poem, but as a consecutive picture-book, whose fundamental meaning was that of the poem, but which did not necessarily coincide with the text at any given point. In this book, however, Blake had not yet developed his systematizing of expression so far.

Frontispiece. The frontispiece represents the marriage of Oothoon and Bromion, who are chained back to back in a cave, while Theotormon weeps at the threshold. In the background is the Sea of Time and Space, over which a terrible sun is setting among clouds. Sometimes this plate is inserted at the end of the book.

The Title-page shows Urizen as the avenger of Society pursuing Oothoon across the Sea of Time and Space, and drawing in his wake the tempest of Materialism (water). Above, various spiritual forms are despairing among the clouds. Urizen's passage upsets by its sheer wake a circling dance of Joys. The storm beats down two colossal figures (which may instead be cliffs). But across the whole page is swept the rainbow of hope, the promise of God, which might be explained as apotheosized water. Below Blake inscribed : ' The Eye sees more than the Heart knows.' Blake certainly meant by this that he could not understand the facts of this world. He could not believe the cruelty and prejudice which he saw everywhere ; they are, in the words of the 27th *Proverb of Hell*, ' portions of eternity too great for the eye of man.' Another explanation has been made [1] that Blake did not always understand what his visions signified, but nevertheless recorded them, and then put this motto on the title-page as a warning to the reader that he was not responsible for his work.

The Argument is decorated with a nude woman, who, with hands crossed upon her breast, kisses a tiny flying figure which emerges from a flower. In the background is a sunrise. This is obviously Oothoon and Leutha's marigold ; and yet this picture illustrates not so much the *Argument* itself as another quatrain of Blake's :

> He who bends to himself a Joy
> Doth the wingèd life destroy ;
> But he who kisses the Joy as it flies
> Lives in Eternity's sunrise.

The colouring of this book is generally not very interesting ; but in one copy at least—that owned by Miss Amy Lowell—Blake certainly made his paint express the force of the text. This particular picture, which is generally a charming pastoral

---

[1] EY, II. p. 353, and Berger, p. 51.

scene, there becomes intense, electric, almost unpleasant; the sunrise pours its rays of terrific yellow and orange across the whole page, every inch of which seems to quiver with passion.

Plate 4. Around the title various figures float in clouds and shoot arrows downward. This design seems to have been suggested by the lines of Isaac Watts:

> A flight of demons sit
> On every sailing cloud with fatal purpose;
> And shoot across the scenes ten thousand arrows
> Perpetual and unseen, headed with pain,
> With sorrow, infamy, disease, and death.
> The pointed plagues fly silent through the air,
> Nor twangs the bow, yet sure and deep the wound.
> —ISAAC WATTS: *Horae Lyricae, To Milio.*

Below the text Oothoon and Bromion lie exhausted after their sin, entirely exposed to the arrows which are directed at them from above.

Plate 5. Between lines 39 and 40 a nude man coloured grey (negro : south : reason) has sunk on the earth overcome with fatigue, leaving his pickaxe in an excavation. This represents Bromion, the materialist, baffled in his attempt to solve spiritual problems by physical means.

Plate 6. Theotormon's eagle rends Oothoon's bosom, while she is stretched upon a cloud. The idea of this design is repeated in *America*, plate 15 ; and in Blake's illustration to Young's *Night Thoughts*, VIII. 77.

Plate 7. Theotormon sits in despair on the rocky shore of the Sea of Time and Space, while above him hovers Oothoon, chained in the green-black flame of her unsatisfied passion. In the distance the sun sets. In the illustrations to Dante, Blake represented Paolo and Francesca in such a flame ; another example is to be found at the bottom of the 4th plate of *The Marriage of Heaven and Hell.*

Plate 8. Below line 143 Oothoon, in a long robe, lies prostrate.

Plate 9. Theotormon, nude in the clouds of night, scourges himself, while gazing at the figure of Oothoon, who passes, weeping. In the copy owned by Mrs. W. Emerson, the rays of a rising sun are bursting from behind a cloud ; but neither sees it.

Plate 10. The despairing Daughters of Albion. There are four of them, though their number is not always clearly distinguishable. In the epics, there are twelve Daughters.

Plate 11. Oothoon, appearing in a flame and cloud to the weeping and terrified Daughters, who wail in an embrace of fear beside the Sea of Time and Space. As human beings are placed halfway between the temporal and the eternal, we seldom find them entirely submerged in the ocean.

AMERICA : A PROPHECY

COMMENTARY

Preludium.

Line 1. *The shadowy Daughter of Urthona* is Vala (*The Four Zoas*, VII. 626), or Nature fallen into a material form. She is ' shadowy ' because she is an illusion ; a Daughter, because she is a sensorial expression ; and a child of Urthona, because the mind creates its own *milieu*—the world is our own imagining. Urthona is the spiritual portion of man : his temporal form is Los, the genius of poetry.

Orc is the spirit of passionate Revolt. He was born from the heart (*The Four Zoas*, v. 37), and his name is actually an anagram of *Cor*, or ' heart ' (W. M. Rossetti, p. cxxi).

Line 2. *Fourteen suns* represent fourteen years, which mark the change in his life about to take place, and explain his epithets : ' hairy Youth ' and ' Terrible Boy.'

Line 3. *Iron* is the metal of spiritual warfare (*Jerusalem*, 97 : 11). What food Orc got was wrested from the world by such combat.

Line 4. *Female.* Nature is essentially passive ; the problem of every artist is to make her productive.

Lines 5-6. While Nature remains a mystery, she is armed with Pestilence.

Line 7. The cloud of ignorance is the only hindrance to her fertilization.

Line 9. She cannot speak (or, in the other symbol, become fruitful) until the Genius dominates her. Cf. the 68th *Proverb of Hell* : ' Where man is not, nature is barren.'

Line 11. The tale of the binding of Orc is told at length in *Urizen*, VII. §§ 1-7, and in *The Four Zoas*, v. 79 *seq.* Los (poetry), jealous of Orc's boyish affection for his mother, Enitharmon (inspiration), binds him on the rock of Jealousy. Later, repentance on the part of Los is unavailing ; for when he returns to release Orc, the fetters have become one with the boy and the rock (*The Four Zoas*, v. 143-175). Release follows, however, in this *Preludium.*

Lines 12-17. Though the body of Orc (the actuality of revolt) is bound, his spirit is abroad : his fire, as sublime forces, penetrates the other three elements. In the form of passion (serpent) he investigates the basis of spirit (pillars of Urthona) ; in imagination he embraces Vala herself in the spiritual region (Canada—north) of America. The Eagle, as we have seen, is the Genius ; the Lion is Divine Wrath, protecting the Lamb ; and the Whale is a similar symbol of the realm of Water.

Line 19. *Red eyes* are given by Ossian to practically every one of his heroes.

Lines 21-22. These are repeated in *The Four Zoas*, VII. 625, 629.

Line 24. Orc puts forth his strength to overcome Nature, and finds her joyful to accept his strength. Her mystery vanishes, and for the first time she smiles.

Line 27. Nature recognizes her salvation in Revolt.

Line 28. *Darkness of Africa*, the night of Reason (south).

Line 29. The great function of Deity is to descend to raise.

Lines 30-34. In America, throughout its whole extent, she sees Orc in the sublimest symbols.

Line 37. *Eternal Death.* It is one of the deep mystical doctrines, recognized by all Christian mystics, and magnified by Taoists and Buddhists, that only by Death of Self (the forsaking of the torments of selfishness) can salvation, or unity with the Godhead, be attained.

A Prophecy.

Line 1. This line recurs as the last line of *Africa.*

Line 4. Among all these famous names, the only one who need detain us is

Tom Paine, on account of his brief but deep friendship with Blake. ' Early in the year 1792, Paine lodged in the house and book-shop of Thomas " Clio " Richman, now as then 7 Marylebone Street. Among his friends was the mystical artist and poet, William Blake. Paine had become to him a transcendental type ; he is one of the Seven who appear in Blake's " Prophecy " concerning America (1793). . . . It is difficult to discover from Blake's mystical visions how much political radicalism was in him, but he certainly saved Paine from the scaffold by forewarning him (Sept. 13, 1792) that an order had been issued for his arrest. . . . I may add here my belief that Paine also appears in one of Blake's pictures. The picture is in the National Gallery (London) and is called " The spiritual form of Pitt guiding Behemoth." The monster jaws of Behemoth are full of struggling men, some of whom stretch imploring hands to another spiritual form, who reaches down from a crescent moon in the sky, as if to rescue them. This face and form appear to me certainly meant for Paine ' (M. D. Conway : *Writings of Thomas Paine*, III. p. 7). Blake's saving of Paine was even more dramatic : on hearing his friend telling of a speech, Blake realized the danger, and warned him to leave England at once, not even returning to his lodging. Paine luckily took his advice, and escaped to France that night, while the officers were actually waiting, as Blake suspected, at his lodgings. Paine never returned to England ; therefore on the night of Sept. 13, 1792, occurred the last meeting of Paine and Blake.

Line 14. *Eastern cloud* : not only because England was literally east of America (for Blake need not have mentioned so obvious a fact), but because the English reaction was one of purely unreasoned emotion. Blake never mentions a point of the compass without reference to its symbolic meaning.

Line 16. Symbolic of the political persecution at home.

Line 21. Urizen's place is now in the zenith.

Line 24. *A Wonder* is Orc.

Line 28. *Heat but not light*, a common metaphysical conception of the flames of hell.

> — hell
> Where in dark places, fire without light doth dwell.
> —DONNE, *Eclogue*.

> The fire of hell this strange condition hath,
> To burn, not shine, as learned Basil saith.
> —HERRICK, *Hesperides*.

> Yet from those flames
> No light, but rather darkness visible.
> —*Paradise Lost*, I. 62-63.

To the Angel of Albion, Orc is a Demon. Blake has reverted to the paradox of *The Marriage of Heaven and Hell*, that the Angels are all Stand-patters, and the Devils the original thinkers. Orc is a demon of this Hell. He is lawless and impulsive : therefore his flames show heat (passion) but not light (reason), since he is fighting against Urizen. Similar flames occur in the fourth *Memorable Fancy* of *The Marriage*, *Urizen*, III. § 5, and l. 49 of *The Book of Los*.

Line 30. *The Stone of Night* is the Mosaic table of the Ten Commandments. Urizen set up this Stone in the South, or Intellect (*Europe*, 94-96). Such a table is naturally sacred ; which explains the Temple in line 36.

Lines 31-34. This absurd astronomical theory was entirely original with Blake ; and since he never repeated it, he cannot have been very proud of it. Mars is evidently a symbol of the passionate heart of Man, which once was all-inclusive ; but from which the Poetic Instinct (the Sun) was divided in the course of Creation. The three planets originally revolving about Mars would have been Mercury, Venus, and the Earth.

Line 37. The resurrection of man to liberty.

Lines 42-48. Repeated in *The Four Zoas*, IX. 667-673.

Lines 49-50. The Sun and Moon (Poetry and the Passions) are redeemed.   These lines are repeated in *The Four Zoas*, IX. 822-823.

Line 51. The Lion, according to the Bible, is the protector of the Sheep, while the Wolf is their traditional enemy. The strife of the world is very aptly symbolized by warfare between these two.

Line 54. The serpent is a very old symbol of eternity. Blake's use of the serpent as a symbol varies only too often.

Line 55. Cf. *Revelation* xii. 4. *Enitharmon*, as we shall see later, represents, among other things, Space. Orc is leading mankind from Time and Space to Eternity and Infinity; therefore he may be said to devour her children. To Albion's Angel this seems like death. Enitharmon's name is an anagram of Anerithmon (numberless), according to W. M. Rossetti (*The Academy*, April 15, 1878). W. N. Guthrie, however, thought that ' Enitharmon from (z)enith and harmon(y) is intelligible ' (*Sewanee Review*, Oct. 1897).

Line 59. For the details of this myth, see *The Four Zoas*, VII. 152-165.   Revolt, bound, is forced by Reason (Urizen) to assume a hypocritical form (the serpent) in established religion (the Tree of Mystery). Orc then becomes the Shadow (suppressed desire) of woman (Enitharmon); he is then the serpent which tempts Woman to eat of the Tree of Good and Evil.

Lines 61-62. The *ten commands* are the Decalogue. Again Urizen is identified with the Jehovah of *Exodus*.

Line 63. *Religion* signified to Blake only outward religion, which is of itself bad.

Line 71. Repeated from *A Song of Liberty*.

Line 72. Repeated from the 53rd *Proverb of Hell*.

Lines 73-75. *Man is not consum'd* because he is eternal; the flame of Revolt, far from annihilating him, purifies him into the precious metals.

Lines 76-102 are spoken by the Angel of Albion, as is evident from line 103.

Line 76. The *Thirteen Angels* are, of course, the thirteen Original States of the Union.

Lines 80-83. Diseases, repressions, and errors, cannot thrive in America. The first two of these are characteristic weapons of the *Old Testament* Jehovah.

Line 83. *The stubbed oak.* The English oak represented to Blake thriving, stubborn errors which had overspread his native land. In *Jerusalem* such groves become very prominent, especially in connection with the Druids.

Line 90. The *Eternal Viper* is Orc. His birth (appearance in the material world) is described. He is said to have ' devoured his parent,' because he has annihilated Space for the Infinite.

Lines 107-112. These brief and beautiful lines hint at a legend which Blake never elaborated. The Lost Atlantis was to Blake a pathway to Eternity which was overwhelmed in the Deluge of Time and Space (or, specifically, the Atlantic Ocean). Blake referred to it again in *A Song of Liberty*, 8 ; and in the lines *The Caverns of the Grave I 've Seen* :

> . . . Above Time's troubled fountains
> On the great Atlantic Mountains
> In my Golden House on high. . . .

The sources of the story of the Lost Atlantis are to be found in a passage from Plato's *Timaeus* and his unfinished *Critias*. Nine thousand years before Solon, a nation living beyond the Straits of Gibraltar grew so powerful that it tried to subdue the whole Mediterranean, but was defeated by Athens ; and some time later, the entire island on which it lived was destroyed. ' In those days the Atlantic was navigable ; and there was an island situated in front of the straits which are by you called the Pillars of Hercules ; the island was larger than Libya and Asia [Minor] put together, and was the way to other islands, and from these you might pass to the whole of the opposite continent which surrounded the true ocean. . . . Now in this island of Atlantis there was a great and wonderful empire. . . .' Plato then describes its attempt to dominate the world, and its defeat by Athens, after which the wrath of heaven was roused against this proud people ; their island, ' when afterwards sunk by an earthquake, became an impassible barrier of mud to voyagers sailing from hence to the [outer] ocean.'

Reading this, with a mind attuned to Blake's symbolism, we see that to him it was but another symbol of the defeat of the Imagination by Reason (Athens), with the subsequent wrath of Urizen destroying, not only the island itself, but the way to Eternity. By just this method the Jehovah of the *Old Testament* punished mankind for any attempt of theirs to raise themselves to a higher sphere.

But to understand Blake's conception of the Lost Atlantis thoroughly, we must also consider Bacon's *New Atlantis* (an unfinished work published posthumously in 1627). In those days the Lost Atlantis was identified by many with America. Bacon accepted this idea, but changed the catastrophe. ' But the *Diuine Reuenge* ouertooke not long after those proud Enterprises. For within lesse than the space of one Hundred Yeares, the *Great Atlantis* was vtterly lost and destroyed : Not by a great Earthquake, as your *Man* saith ; (For that whole Tract is little subject to Earthquakes ;) But by a particular Deluge or Inundation. . . . But it is true, that the same Inundation was not deepe ; Not past fourty foote, in most places, from the Grounde ; So that, although it destroyed Man and Beast generally, yet some few wild Inhabitants of the Wood escaped. . . . They of the Vale, that were not drowned, perished for want of Food, and other things necessary.' Then, about 1900 years before Bacon's time, a certain King Solamona reorganized the remains of Atlantis into such an ideal order that whatever visitors came generally preferred to remain forever. ' What those few that returned may haue reported abroad I know not. But you must thinke, Whatsoeuer they haue said, could bee taken where they came, but for a Dreame.'

Bacon's description was preferred by Blake, since it allowed him to identify the catastrophe with the Deluge of Time and Space, from which only those escaped who lived in the high places. It also allowed him to identify the Island itself with a definite place on the globe. America, therefore, was the body itself, submerged (though not deeply) in the Flood of materialism.

The Americans, then, meet in the regions of the high places of the body, which is a pathway to Eternity.

It might not be out of place to note that modern anthropologists claim to have identified the Lost Atlantis with Crete, which very early reached a high stage of civilization. The legend of Theseus and the Minotaur is undoubtedly an allegory of its destruction by the Athenians.

Ariston is the man who through his passion defies convention ; his palace is probably the one later called ' Los's Halls ' (known to Plato as the ' World of Ideas '). According to Herodotus (VI. 61-66), Ariston, whose name in Greek signifies ' best,' was a king of Sparta who cheated his friend of his bride. The son of this union was Demaratus, one of Sparta's most famous kings. Blake identified the stolen bride with Pleasure (Ahania), who is properly the emanation of Urizen (*Four Zoas*, frag. 3). Since Ariston was true to himself, Blake represents him building a Gothic (' pinnacled ') palace in Atlantis. But since Ariston was not true to his friend, this palace was not on the Atlantean mountains, but in a forest (error), even though it was the ' forest of God.' For after all, Ariston was not only a Greek (reason : therefore associated with Urizen), but a Spartan (militarist) ; therefore later he shudders at Los's truthful song (*Song of Los : Africa*, 4).

Line 110. *Archetype* : a ' stupendous original.'

Line 117. Boston was the first city to defy England. Boston's protest here, however, is not against taxes on tea, but against the degradation of man.

Lines 124-125. One of Blake's attacks on organized charity. Cf. Coleridge's *Table Talk* (August 14, 1833) : ' I have never yet known a trader in philanthropy who was not wrong in heart somewhere or other. Individuals so distinguished are usually unhappy in their family relations,—men not benevolent or beneficent to individuals, but almost hostile to them, yet lavishing money and labour and time on the race, the abstract notion.' Something of this sort certainly inspired Blake ; probably the idea that such charity could not give the very thing—personal sympathy—which was most needed. Instances of Blake's own charity, which were a real sacrifice to him, are to be found in all his biographies.

Line 130. They throw off all disguise, all pretence at dominion.

Line 142. Sir Francis Bernard, governor of Massachusetts from August 1760 to July 1769, was so distinguished for his avarice and double-dealing that when he was recalled to England (who promised never to send him back), Boston gave over the day to public rejoicing. His governorship antedated the Revolution by several years ; but, on the strength of his being a contributory cause, Blake includes him as a symbol.

Line 155. The *Atlantic Mountains*. Albion's hosts try to cut America off from Eternity.

Line 157. *Forty millions* : *i.e.* fourfold, therefore affecting all of Man's faculties. The zeros, to Blake as to Swedenborg, meant—nothing.

Line 174. *The Atlantic* is always symbolic of the Sea of Time and Space.

Line 176. It is a well-known principle in Magic that a curse, warded off, returns upon its author. England's persecution of America reacted badly upon herself ; the oppression propagated a similar oppression in her own land.

Line 186. York and London, or Church and State.

Line 193. England's very poetry is infected. The Bard's brain becomes enclosed in flesh, and he 'reptilizes.' This might be a reference to William Whitehead, who, as Laureate, was obliged to take England's part against America. His attitude is now very amusing : it sounds like pure blindness or hypocrisy. He represents Britannia as barely able to suppress the rising tear at her cherished children's attempt at matricide ; he claims that they are bringing inevitably upon themselves an unfortunate but well-deserved punishment ; that nowhere but under England's rule is to be found true liberty ; and therefore he cannot imagine why those enthusiasts are revolting. In fairness to Whitehead, we must admit that he did not burst forth into the fashionable rodomontades of blind hatred ; his position undoubtedly forced him to write as he did.

Line 196. In Blake's early poems, priests are very apt to be symbolized as snakes, since they teach Good and Evil, which was the doctrine of the original Serpent in the Garden of Eden. See the decoration to *The Little Girl Lost* (first plate) ; *Tiriel*, line 348 ; *The French Revolution*, lines 126-127 ; also Blake's characterization of Bishop Watson's argument as 'Serpentine dissimulation !' (Watson marginalia, page 3.)

Lines 199-203. The frightened priesthood leaves the 'daughters of Albion' free to love as they will—which is the opening of the Gates of Paradise.

Line 201. *Long-drawn arches* : *i.e.* Gothic.

Line 205. Finally Reason himself is roused—for Reason is always the last thing to be roused in such matters.

Line 216. He is roused too late ; he cannot quench the American Revolution. But he can conceal the truth about it from Europe for twelve years—the time which elapsed between the American and the French Revolutions.

Line 218. The French Revolution.

Line 222. *The five gates*, or the five senses, which can look out upon Eternity. See the introductory lines to *Europe*.

Line 225. But the 'doors of perception' are 'cleansed' by the fires of Orc ; and everything appears to man 'as it is, infinite.' Cf. plate 14 of *The Marriage of Heaven and Hell*.

The pages of the first version of *America* are published by Keynes, pp. 459-463. The first page, except for a few unimportant verbal changes, was re-engraved as plate 5 ; the fourth was used without being re-engraved as plate 15. Plates B and C, however, were discarded.

B, 4. *Reveal the dragon thro' the human* : reveal his real thirst for war through his outer appearance of humanity.

B, 4. *When the moon shot forth* : when the universe was disrupted. Cf. *Jerusalem*, 49 : 19 : ' In one night the Atlantic Continent was caught up with the Moon.'

B, 18-19. Cf. *The Four Zoas*, VII. 638-639.

B, 21. *Sotha* : see the Commentary on *Europe*, 186.

C, 2. *Twelve demons* : the signs of the Zodiac. The English forces are the rulers of Time, but not of Eternity.

C, 14-17 are repeated in *The Four Zoas*, VI. 307-310, with a slight change of symbols. This passage is interesting as showing an early reference to Man's four-fold nature.

Among Blake's papers there has also been found a sheet which seems to have been originally intended as a page of *America*, but which, as far as we know, was never used. Only two copies (both coloured) have been found. It was probably to have followed plate 6 (which ends with line 29). The omitted text is as follows :

> As when a dream of Thiralatha flies the midnight hour :
> In vain the dreamer grasps the joyful images, they fly
> Seen in obscured traces in the Vale of Leutha, So
> The British Colonies beneath the woful Princes fade.
>
> And so the Princes fade from earth, scarce seen by souls of men,
> But tho' obscur'd, this is the form of the Angelic land.

This is interesting, in view of its references to dreams, from which Blake derived so much inspiration. (See Chapter XXVIII., ' *Spirits* ' and their ' *Dictation*.') Thiralatha is a ' secret dweller of dreamful caves ' (*Europe*, line 186), evidently a Muse, or ' daughter of Beulah ' ; yet not a bearer of true dreams, since she is connected with Leutha, the regent of sex under Satan (error). Blake wished to imply that, as the false dream fades and cannot be remembered, so the British colonies under the mistaken rule of their Princes are vanishing from the Reality of Eternity.

DECORATIONS

This book, as we have said, marks a new epoch in Blake's method of expression. The change is also reflected in the decorations, which no longer illustrate, nor even comment upon, the text of the same page. Blake's new idea was that the pictures should of themselves tell a consecutive story, as well as the text : the same story, to be sure ; but entirely detached. Therefore when the meaning of the picture is actually the same as the meaning of the text which it surrounds, the coincidence is pure accident. *The Gates of Paradise* had tried telling a story without text (in the first edition—explanatory verses were added later) ; here the text and pictures appear together though independent. When Blake wrote Trusler (Aug. 23, 1799), claiming that children understood his books, he surely meant that they followed the pictorial sequence somehow.

Of all the Prophetic Books, *America* is the most splendid. Its masterful, free execution places it second only to *Jerusalem*. The exultation of the text is reflected in the pure strength of the colouring, which Gilchrist described as ' sometimes like an increase of daylight on the retina, so fair and open is the effect of particular pages.' Never again did Blake quite attain the same brilliancy, the same sensitiveness to broad sweeps of tonality, which intensify each other as the pages are turned.

Plate 1. *Frontispiece.* Urizen, a titanic manacled angel, sits in the breach of the wall of the flesh, in his despair refusing to let pass into *this* world a daughter of Beulah (or Muse) with her infant joys. A cannon upon the ground suggests the remedy. Evidently the scene is laid on the eternal side of the Northern Gate.

The stone wall, as symbolic of the wall of flesh, was repeated in the illustration to Young : ' This mould'ring old Partition Wall thrown down ' (III. 660).

Plate 2. *Title-page.* 'America a Prophecy.' An old man and a woman sit back to back reading the Books of Law, completely ignoring the little Joys which try to distract them. Below: in the black tempest of materialism, many men lie dead. An Emanation (imaginative portion of man) strives frantically to revive one of them with kisses. Below is inscribed: 'Lambeth Printed by William Blake, in the year 1793.'

Plate 3. *Preludium.* The first two plates showed the present state of man in his mental bondage and death. At last Orc, the Spirit of Revolution appears. Los (Poetry) and Enitharmon (Inspiration) are appalled at his crucifixion on the Rock of Jealousy, under the Tree of Mystery. The tree is continued down the left of the page; its roots suggest human torsoes, or 'vegetated' mankind. Below the roots crouches a sullen man, beside the Worm of mortality.

Plate 4. Orc, liberated at last, emerges from the earth in a sun-burst. His head is barely above the ground as yet. All about him are sprouting vines and wheat.

Plate 5. *A Prophecy.* The flames of Revolution break out, even between the lines of the text. A flying nude blows immense fires from a trumpet. Below, a naked family flees from the conflagration of their dwelling. Above, a man soars with broken and dropping fetters. Birds dash to and fro, bewildered in the smoke. The letters of the title are entwined with wheat (plenty) and the scourge-vine which figured so prominently in the *Songs of Experience.* It is notable that Blake recognized the evils of Revolution, though he thought them more than cancelled by its benefits. In the middle of the page is the flaming trumpet of revolt; below is destruction (of material things); above is liberation (of spiritual things).

Plate 6. Above, War as a dragon chases Urizen with his books of Law. Below, men cower, naked among their prostrate errors (the forests of the night). These fallen trees, as symbolic of errors overthrown, appear later in the margin of the 13th illustration to *Job.*

Plate 7. *A Last Judgment.* 'Whenever any individual rejects error and embraces truth, a Last Judgment passes upon that individual' (*MS. Book: Last Judgment*). The spiritual trinity is rejecting the material trinity. In the group above the text, the central figure is about to cast down a figure whom he carries, bound, upon his back. To his right is the angel with the uneven balances (Blake's balances are seldom even, as he did not believe in absolute justice); to his left is the angel with the flaming sword which was the weapon of Christ ('I come to bring, not peace, but a sword'). Below the text, two figures are falling into flames. The central one, upside-down (the loins, or lowest instincts, predominating) falls encircled by the serpent of materialism. On his right falls a man with his hands to his head—mistaken intellect. Therefore we may assume that the third figure, about to be cast down, represents the region of the heart—wrong feeling.

Plate 8. The Last Judgment is followed by a Resurrection (as also in the 16th and 17th illustrations to *Job*). A nude man gazes upward. (Cf. plate 21 of *The Marriage* and the top portion of *Death's Door* in Blair's *Grave.*) Below the text are the symbols of misdirected humanity, above which the man has risen: a fantastic thistle, a lizard catching a fly, a toad, and a tiny snake.

Plate 9. Beneath a drooping birch, whose branches are filled with exquisite Birds of Paradise, a youth and a maiden sleep with a ram. The sun rises behind them (in some of the coloured copies). They are Har and Heva (Poetry and Painting) asleep on their fleeces (*Tiriel*, line 124), but about to awake in the new dawn. The idea of this plate is repeated in the 3rd plate of *Africa.*

Plate 10. But this state of Innocence in the rebirth of man is not perfect. Hidden in his clouds, Urizen broods over the Sea of Time and Space. This design is repeated from the first *Principle* of *All Religions are One.*

Plate 11. Man, as the new-born infant, lies almost lost in the riches (the wheat-field) which surround him.

Plate 12. Orc springs upward, clad only in his flames. Man, we assume, awakes from the sleep of the previous plate.

Plate 13. Innocence. Above, the youth soars from the earth on the back of a swan. Below, the joys of Innocence guide the serpent of nature in the night of the passions (Beulah). The original sketch for the lower part of the plate is in the Widener collection at Harvard University. Other versions of it occur on the last plate of *Thel* and the 14th illustration to *Job*.

Plate 14. Innocence, however, is only the first stage of the new life. Experience, which is the death of the senses, follows. An old man on crutches is blown into the door of a tomb which opens downward. The landscape is represented by a few barren trees. This is the ' Death's Door,' which also figures in *The Gates of Paradise*, plate 17 ; and in Blair's *Grave*.

Plate 15. Below the text, man is seen, drowned in the Sea of Time and Space, just as he was drowned in *The Gates of Paradise*. His body is being devoured by the monstrous inhabitants of that ocean. Above is the woman who has escaped the Sea by indulging her instincts (Oothoon). She is torn by the Vulture of Remorse.

Plate 16. Below the leafless Tree of Mystery, Rahab teaches the ' Natural Religion ' of the Serpent (who appears between her knees) to a youth, who holds his hands in prayer towards her, and rests his arm on the book of the Law. She is Woman beguiling the youth with materialism, under protection of the priesthood (snake), beneath the shade of Mystery. The 163rd illustration to Young represents the worship of the Serpent under the sterile Tree of Mystery.

Plate 17. The result of their union is the anguish of generation. Among the flames of desire, ignoring the grapes of ecstasy which they contain, souls cower in anguish. On the left, they are actually passing into the ' vegetative ' forms of the flesh—are becoming trees.

In the later books, Blake hardly ever refers to the material world without calling it ' vegetable.' Like many of his symbols, this appeared in his pictures before it appeared in his writings. He pictures it again in the next plate ; in the 79th, 215th, 258th, and 495th illustrations to Young ; in *Milton*, 11 ; and in *Jerusalem*, 15, 45, and 74. Blake certainly made the symbol his own ; yet we can find other uses of it. Dante's human forest of suicides (*Inferno*, XIII.) was derived from the story of Polydorus (*Aeneid*, III.). Henry More says Plotinus surmised 'that the most degenerate souls did at last sleep in the bodies of Trees, and grew up merely into *Plantal life*' (*Immortality*, III. i. 2). Thomas Vaughan, in the *Postscript* to his *Aula Lucis*, refers mysteriously to his ' living a tree.' Shelley, in his very Blakish fragment, *The Triumph of Life*, finds Rousseau grown into a tree, beneath which he watches the triumphal passage of a Shape (evidently Urizen), with another (Orc) bound to his chariot wheels.

Plate 18. The Earth, as a woman, weeps and prays to the void of Nature. Her hair streams like water over the precipice. Behind her, human forms have grown into a small forest. On her bowed head, a tiny figure is seated, reading ; on her back, one prays, and another stands with a book ; at her thighs, still another reclines under a tree ; in the folds of her garments two weep and embrace.

Below the text, ' Finis ' appears in a tangle of thorny, fantastic flowers, and the serpent ; tiny figures are wandering through the branches.

The rejected plate shows, above the text, a woman overcome with grief beneath a sterile tree. On the left, a nude woman is reaching towards her dream, who appears as an infant flying towards her, and kissing her lips.

The text of *America* ends with the Revolution still in the process of consummation. The pictures, however, end with the state of Experience as yet unrelieved. Both text and illustrations were to be continued in the next book, *Europe*.

EUROPE: A PROPHECY
COMMENTARY

Introduction.

Lines 1-5 The five senses. The fifth one (Touch or Sex) is not actually named by Blake, for here his secret doctrine lay.

Line 6. Man will not pass out into Eternity through the 'fifth window,' since he persists in allowing hypocrisy to dominate love.

Line 7. This was taught Blake by a 'natural joy' (Fairy).

Line 13. A warning that *Europe* contains an explanation of Creation.

Line 14. *Leaves of flowers.* The prophecies of the Cumean Sybil were written on leaves of trees (*Aeneid*, VI. 74). Blake's mysterious books, being illuminated, may more appropriately be said to have been written on petals.

Lines 15-16. Imagination and love explain all things.

Lines 17-18. This world is not dead; it is eternal. But it is encrusted with illusions (matter, Ulro) which obscure its truth to eyes of flesh. Man must be 'tipsie' on poetry, before he can escape seeing with (not through) the eye.

Line 20. This line, as Blake engraved it, runs:

> Wild flowers I gather'd; & he shew'd me each eternal flower:

Line 24. *Dictated.* An early use of Blake's 'dictation' jargon; surely his meaning is clear enough here.

Preludium.

Line 1. The agony of creative Nature. This *Preludium* continues the *Preludium* of *America*.

Line 2. *Her snaky hair.* The fallen Vala evidently shares the curse of Hela (*Tiriel*, 295).

Enitharmon in this book represents in particular the female aspect of things, as separated from the male (Eve divided from Adam, Space divided from Time). She is evil only when she tries to dominate the male.

Lines 4-7. Nature calls upon Space to produce other sons than Orc (Revolt); for Nature is weary of travail.

Lines 8-11. Nature sees·her existence in Matter as nothing but an endless struggle for existence; and therefore bewails it. Her roots are in Heaven, her fruits in earth, because 'every Natural Effect has a Spiritual Cause, and not a Natural: For a Natural Cause only seems' (*Milton*, 26 : 44-45).

Line 11. The birth of the Shadowy Female is described in *The Four Zoas*, VII. 315. Her parents are Los's Spectre (poetic logic) and Enitharmon's Shade (suppressed spiritual desire).

Lines 12-15. She conceals herself in the most material forms (water); yet still the Sun, Moon, and Stars (Poetry, Emotions, and Reason) impregnate her with their light. This stanza contains a complete anticipation of the theory of the Four Zoas; the Sun, Moon, and Stars being Urthona, Luvah, and Urizen; while the Shadowy Female herself represents Tharmas.

Line 23. Enitharmon (Space) is begged not to stamp spatial forms upon the offspring of Nature. Cf. Marcus Aurelius.

Line 28. 'Who shall bind the Infinite?' is the motto on the first sketch for the Creator (frontispiece of *Europe*), in the *MS. Book*, page 96. Urizen (Reason) is the one who shall circumscribe it with his laws; but the Divine Mercy shall enter it as the incarnated Christ. The divine Babe shall understand and redeem Man, who is the babe of Eternity. Cf. *Jerusalem*, 56 : 5-9:

> He who is an Infant, and whose Cradle is a Manger,
> Knoweth the Infant sorrow: whence it came, and where it goeth:
> And who weave it a Cradle of the grass that withereth away.
> This World is all a Cradle for the erred wandering Phantom,
> Rock'd by Year. Month, Day & Hour . . .

Lines 28-30. Nature sees Christ himself about to assume his mortal form; and knowing that in him lies the salvation of all, including herself—' even Tree, Metal, Earth and Stone ' (*Jerusalem*—99 : 1)—she silences her complaint.

A Prophecy.

Lines 1-4. Cf. Milton's *Hymn to the Nativity* :

> It was the Winter wilde
> While the Heav'n-born childe
> All meanly wrapt in the rude manger lies. . . .
> No War, or Battails sound
> Was heard the World around. . . .

By this cross-reference Blake undoubtedly meant to identify his ' Secret Child ' with Jesus. This is the mystical birth, when all wars seem to cease ; the beginning (but only the beginning) of the Mystic Way. As Blake makes Jesus descend through the ' orient gates,' it is evident that this is another reference to Sex as a door to Eternity, for the East is always the realm of the passions. This theory had already been anticipated in lines 5 and 15 of the *Introduction*; while following lines confirm it.

Line 5. Enitharmon (now as Inspiration) sees her sons and daughters (poetic thoughts) meeting in the ' crystal house ' (the pure heart—cf. *The Crystal Cabinet*).

Line 7. *Los* (Poetry), *possessor of the Moon* (Enitharmon, or Inspiration), rejoices in the night of the Passions (which later is to be named ' Beulah '). This is always a time of inspiration.

Lines 9-28. Los, seeing trouble ahead, calls his sons to war on the old usurper Urizen with song. See the commentary on line 43 below.

Line 10. The spiritual portion of man (Urthona) is at rest, thanks to the coming of the Christ.

Line 11. But this rest is dangerous, since the Reason (Urizen), set free, is attempting to usurp the throne of Urthona (North).

Line 24. Orc (Revolt) is the first child of Poetry and Inspiration (Los and Enitharmon). Every true poet always has been somewhat of a radical in some form.

Line 30. *The Immortal Fiend* is Los.

Line 35. When Enitharmon's voice is heard apart from her husband's, the error enters unconsciously. Her false doctrine is one which is calculated to assert the Female Will over the Male. This is a separation of the sexes, which is bad ; for ' in Eternity woman is the emanation of man ; she has no will of her own ; there is no such thing in Eternity as a Female Will ' (*MS. Book : Last Judgment*).

Enitharmon's doctrine is the false one that sexual indulgence is sin. This doctrine, enforced, gives woman the desired domination.

Line 36. *Rintrah* we have already met in the *Argument* of *The Marriage of Heaven and Hell*. He is Honest Wrath. *Palamabron* is Pity. These two, both sons of Los, are later to play a very important part in *Milton*. There Palamabron is identified with Blake himself.

Lines 38-39. The common doctrine of man's death, which is to be followed by life in a Paradise, which (according to Blake) was really only an allegory of a state in this life.

Line 43. *Eldest-born* : a typical inconsistency of Blake's—the sort of thing which prevents one's drawing up any accurate theogony. Line 25 told us that Orc was the first-born ; now we find it is Rintrah. Revolt (Orc) is naturally the first child of any poet ; yet Wrath (Rintrah) precedes Revolt. Blake indicates his inconsistency at once by calling Rintrah ' second to none but Orc.' Later, the four sons of Los do not include Orc at all : they are Rintrah, Palamabron, Theotormon, and Bromion (*Milton*, 23 : 11-12) ; even in the *Four Zoas*, VIII. 351-361, that very complete genealogy omits Orc. Yet other passages in the same poem deal at great-length with his legend.

Blake did this, I think, deliberately ; so that commentators in the future would be baffled by the inconsistency of the myths, and therefore be obliged to seek more deeply for Blake's intentions. He was quite justified in his theory, since spiritual states like Orc and his brethren may be the children of a variety of other spiritual states ; and in turn they may be the progenitors of various sets of emotions. To say that Rintrah (Just Wrath) should always be produced by one set of parents only is absurd.

Line 46. *Elynittria*, the bride of Palamabron, the correct feminine attitude towards sex ; here identified with Diana, the goddess of natural purity (' silver-bowed queen') ; in *Milton* to be identified as Mrs. Blake. She is mentioned once in *Jerusalem*, 93 : 5 ; and from *The Four Zoas*, VIII. 357, we learn that she is the second daughter of Los and Enitharmon. Otherwise she is not mentioned in Blake's works.

Line 49. *Ocalythron* is the emanation (bride) of Rintrah. She appears twice elsewhere (*Milton*, 8* : 19 and *Jerusalem*, 93 : 5), in connection with Elynittria ; in the catalogue of *The Four Zoas*, VIII. 357, we learn that she is the first daughter of Los and Enitharmon. She is evidently the spirit of Female Jealousy.

Lines 50-51. *The King of Fire, Prince of the Sun* is Rintrah. Fire is the symbol of wrath ; and as the eldest son of Los, the Sun-god, he is the prince of the Sun.

Lines 55-56. Secure in her domination, Enitharmon (Inspiration) sleeps from the birth of Christ to the end of the eighteenth century. Man all this while is in illusion—possibly a reference to the doctrine of the Pythagoreans, which was being revived in Blake's day ; as for example, by Saint-Martin : ' If this world will seem to us, after our death, as nothing but magical illusion, why do we regard it otherwise at present ? ' (*Œuvres Posthumes*, I. 209). But the sleep in this error is to end with the American Revolution and (incidentally) with Blake's own teachings.

Lines 60-67. The American Revolution.

Line 62. A reference to *America*, 177-179.

Lines 66-70. The confusion caused in Europe by the reaction upon themselves of England's oppression of America is a matter of history. But cf. *A Song of Liberty*, §§ 15-17. Blake's inner meaning is simply that a revolution in thought causes a downfall of the original system of thought.

Line 69. *As the stars arise from the Salt Lake, i.e.* as Reason emerges from the dead sea of materialism. This cannot be a reference to the Salt Lake of Utah, which had not yet been discovered.

Lines 71-93. The ancient system re-establishes itself, with increased tyranny. This is the building of the ' Serpent Temple,' of which a picture may be found on the last page of *Jerusalem*. It is the old Serpentine Temple of the Druids at Avebury in North Wiltshire, to which Charles Lucas wrote an anonymous poem (published at Marlborough in 1795). Though its existence had always been known, it was not until 1743 that Dr. William Stukeley discovered its serpentine shape. A passing reference was made to this temple in *America*, line 36. It represents the Druid (materialistic) religion, which is the sacrifice of others, and not of the self. This is the religion of all unredeemed men. The Serpent to Blake meant, fundamentally, Materialism. An extension of this meaning is in his use of the Serpent to represent Priesthood (the Serpent teaching Good and Evil, thus driving man from Eden ; also we must remember the materialism of the Church in Blake's own day).

Line 72. *The Fiery King* is Urizen.

Line 75. *Verulam* was the seat of Bacon, the materialistic philosopher, who was one of Blake's pet aversions, since he was responsible for the contemporary rule of Science.

Line 77. *Oak*. We have already explained Blake's use of the oak as symbolic of Albion's spreading, stubborn errors.

Line 79. Urizen is the ' Starry King ' : these twelve pillars represent the Zodiac ; the everlasting Karmic round upon which his reign is built. Cf. Shelley's *Prometheus Unbound*, III. iv. 116-117 :

> . . . a dome fretted with graven flowers
> Poised on twelve columns of resplendent stone.

Jakob Böhme also makes much use of these twelve colours.

Lines 80-85. *The Deluge* of the Time and Space. This is the final period of the Fall, known as Experience.

Line 83. *The ever-varying spiral ascents*, or Jacob's Ladder, as we learn from one of Blake's finest pictures.

Line 86. *Thought chang'd the Infinite to a Serpent*: Logic changed Eternity to Nature. The symbol of the snake with his tail in his mouth is a very old one, to which Blake specifically refers in his own comment on his *Frontispiece to Night the Third* of Young's *Night Thoughts*: 'Eternity is represented by its usual symbol —a serpent with its extremities united.' But this symbol was not satisfactory to Blake: for it interpreted Eternity, which is progress, as the Everlasting, a dull round, incessantly repeating itself. This was the old and false idea of Eternity, as symbolized by early thinkers, whom Blake conceived to be materialistic. In his 257th illustration to Young, he carefully distinguished his conception from the early one: above the Everlasting circle of Nature stands Man, a straight line pointing upward. Young's lines are:

> Nature revolves but Man advances. Both
> Eternal: that a Circle, this a Line.
>   —*Night Thoughts*, VI. 692-693.

Lines 86-87. *That which pitieth to a devouring flame.*—Cf. 'God out of Christ is a consuming fire.' Urizen turns the Lamb to the Tyger.

Lines 88-89. The *forests of night* are, of course, errors. These, by dividing (which is always the progress of error) split into separate worlds: the creation of the solar system.

Line 89. *Like an ocean*: the Deluge again.

Line 90. Within the flesh Eternity is still to be found.

Line 92. *An Angel*: the conventional law-bound Angels of *The Marriage*. Man should be, of course, a God.

Line 93. *Heaven a mighty circle turning*. Astrological fatalism: the highest seems to be nothing but the mechanical laws of reason.

God a tyrant crown'd. Jehovah-Urizen.

Line 94. *The ancient Guardian* is Urizen. 'Ancient' is used in the sense of 'former': Urizen has since usurped the North.

The southern porch is his rightful realm of the intellect.

Line 96. *The Stone of Night* is the Decalogue, the ten prohibitions engraven on the stone tables.

Line 97. *Purple flowers and berries red*: Deadly Nightshade.

Lines 98-99. The closing of the brain within the skull.

Lines 100-101. The things of the spirit (north), placed beneath the feet, become a vortex of destruction.

Line 102. *The Stone of Night*, the Decalogue, was enshrined in the Serpent Temple (*America*, 30, 36).

Line 104. The *brazen book* is Reason's code of charity, which turns philanthropy into a dead silence (*The Four Zoas*, VII. 109). Such philanthropy is false, since it deals only with material things, and cannot give what is most needed; sympathetic understanding. It resembles, in exteriors only, the charity which Paul praised (1 *Cor.* xiii.) as brass resembles gold. Against this sort of charity Boston's Angel spoke his bitterest words (*America*, 124-125). See also Blake's fifth illustration to *Job*.

Line 114. *A vast rock* is the Stone of Night.

Lines 118-119. Prospective Revolution already tortures Albion's Angel. To seek release, he must establish the facts about mankind. This he is unable to do.

Lines 122-123. The hypocrisies of the Judge become part of him.

Lines 129-130. Palamabron and Rintrah are honest spirits; but under the domination of Enitharmon they attack Orc instead of Albion's Angel. (Good

Emotions, in fact, are often found on the wrong side.   In *Milton*, 7 : 8-11 we shall see Rintrah not only entering into Satan, but even fighting against Palamabron !

Line 131. Cf. ' The things that are Evil love Bondage and Slavery ' (Hermes Trismegistus : *Pymander*, I, 10).

Line 144. He attempts to pass a final judgment upon man by invoking the past.

Lines 145-149. Sir Isaac Newton's discoveries in science place man definitely in the world of matter.   This is obviously death.   But in the very moment of the triumph of Error, its Fall begins ; for once formulated, it can be recognized as error, which immediately destroys it.

Line 150. The old error of Enitharmon revives.   She does not know that the world is changing.

Lines 157-188. Enitharmon arouses four pairs of sons and daughters : Manatha-Varcyon and Ethinthus ; Antamon and Leutha ; Theotormon and Oothoon ; and Sotha and Thiralatha, who correspond to the Spirit, the Reason, the Emotions, and the Body. (These divisions later become the four Zoas.)   All the names appear elsewhere, but apparently with changed meanings.   Manatha-Varcyon shifts his sex in *The Four Zoas*, VIII. 358.   Leutha changes her consort for Bromion. Rintrah, Palamabron, Theotormon, and Bromion are later grouped together. For a detailed discussion of each personality, see the Commentary below.

Line 157. *Ethinthus*, since she is ' Queen of Waters,' must be a sensorial (female) spirit of materialism.   She is mentioned twice outside of *Europe*.   Once she appears as the eighth name in the catalogue of the daughters of Los and Enitharmon (*Four Zoas*, VIII. 358).   The second reference is an ambiguous mention in *Jerusalem*, 12 : 26.

Line 163. ' Begin [a reverie] with this line . . . and see how it flickers with the light of many symbols ' (W. B. Yeats : *Ideas of Good and Evil* ; *Symbolism of Poetry*).

Line 166. *Manatha-Varcyon* appears outside of *Europe* once.   He appears as the seventh daughter of Los and Enitharmon (*Four Zoas*, VIII. 358).   His flames, eagles, and wings indicate that he is Inspiration ; but Inspiration ' of false delusion ' for the present, at least.

Line 169. *Leutha*, the regent of sex under Satan, is mentioned in the *Visions of the Daughters of Albion* : *Argument*, 4-5, and *Prophecy*, 4-10 : in *The Song of Los* (*Africa*), line 28 ; *The Book of Los*, line 2 ; *The Four Zoas*, VIII. 357 ; several times in *Milton* ; and twice in *Jerusalem*.   She is the goddess of female hypocrisy, attended by the dogs that killed Actaeon.   She is associated with Antamon.   She is the fourth daughter of Los and Enitharmon.

Lines 173-174. This suggests a line of Baudelaire's in his *Harmonie du Soir* : ' Les sons et les parfums tournent dans l'air du soir.'

Line 180. *Antamon*, the fifth son of Los and Enitharmon, is the artist (*Milton*, 27 : 13-18) attracted by Leutha.   He is responsible for the *Koran* (*Song of Los : Africa*, 28-29).   There is also an obscure reference in *Jerusalem*, 83 : 28.

The seven churches of Leutha are the seven churches founded by the Apostles, who were already spreading the error of Enitharmon (Puritanism) after the death of Christ.

Line 181. Oothoon, Blake's Magdalen, figures too prominently in the *Visions of the Daughters of Albion*, to need further elucidation.

Line 183. Cf. *Milton*, 27 : 62-63 :

> Every Time less than a pulsation of the artery
> Is equal in its period & value to Six Thousand Years.

Line 184. *Theotormon* is the jealous lover, separated from his beloved (Oothoon).

Line 186. *Sotha*, the ninth son of Los and Enitharmon, is a musician (*Europe*, line 187 ; *Four Zoas*, IX. 683), who falsely inspires to battle (*Europe*, line 188 ; *Song of Los : Africa*, 30).   Here he and his bride are invoked to win Orc over.

He also appears obscurely in *America*, cancelled sheet B, 20, and in *Milton*, 27 : 21.

Thiralatha, his bride, has already appeared in cancelled sheet D of *America*, where she represents a false dream of inspiration. In *The Song of Los : Africa*, line 31, her name shifts to ' Diralada ' ; and then she vanishes forever from our ken.

All these names of the children of Los and Enitharmon seem to have been chosen solely for their sound values.

Line 187. *The horrent Fiend* is Orc.

Line 189-191. Enitharmon, not knowing she is in error, and therefore never suspecting what Orc may do, welcomes him.

Lines 192-194. Even in her night, the Poet and the spirits of Poetry, mistaken though they be, revel in the moonlight. Blake was undoubtedly referring to his works produced before his new revelation, which inspired *The Marriage of Heaven and Hell*.

Lines 195-196. But Passions (east) bring the new light ; and all the erroneous spirits flee.

Line 199. The French Revolution.

Line 204. *The ruddy tide* is a strange backsliding to the phraseology of the eighteenth century.

Line 206. *Then Los arose* : Blake's reference to his own new period of inspiration at Lambeth.

DECORATIONS

Again Blake retells the story of the text by his series of pictures. He does not follow the poem closely ; he depicts independently the various stages of Error which lead towards Revolution ; or, mystically, the transition from the state of Experience to the New Birth.

In the Palgrave copy (British Museum), the pictorial sequence is made clearer by certain fragments of poems written under several of the illustrations. These are not in Blake's handwriting ; nevertheless I have no doubt but that he was directly responsible for their insertion. As we know from the *MS. Book*, Blake was apt to quote just such fragments under his sketches—it may be that they were his original inspiration. It is easy to imagine some friend buying this copy of *Europe* —asking what the various pictures meant—and noting the poems in the margin. Moreover, the majority of these quotations are obviously taken from Bysshe's *Art of English Poetry*, a book which we know Blake possessed.[1] And lastly, the quotations are so apposite that they help considerably in interpreting the course of the illustrations. Therefore it seems worth while to print them in full.

Blake varied the order of his plates, in accordance with his usual custom ; but since he could not shift the text, and since there are only two full-page illustrations besides the *Frontispiece*, the rearrangements make little difference in the story of the pictures.

Plate I. *Frontispiece*. This is one of Blake's most famous pictures. He drew it from a vision which persistently hovered over the top of his staircase at Lambeth.[2] On his death-bed he coloured a copy of it in the excitement of ecstasy, abandoning it only to draw a picture of his wife. His choice of subject at such a moment is significant ; for he was not merely leaving mementoes—he was actually testing his powers to discover his worthiness of entering at last the Eternity of Imagination. The first sketch appears on page 96 of the *MS. Book*.

It represents Urizen (Reason) as the Creator with his dividers. Creation, though evil, is always a work of Art ; Urizen therefore appears appropriately as the Great Architect, since Architecture is the Art nearest Science. (Cf. *Milton*,

---

[1] In the *MS. Book*, Blake recorded using Bysshe in a fortune-telling experiment, with pleasing results. The poems quoted in *Europe* follow Bysshe's misquotations.

[2] J. T. Smith : *Biographical Sketch*.

24 : 55-56.) This picture illustrates *Proverbs* viii. 27 ; *The Book of Urizen*, vii.
§§ 7-8 ; and also the following, quoted from the British Museum copy :

> In his hand he took the Golden Compasses, prepared
> In God's eternal store, to circumscribe
> This Universe, and all created things.
> One foot he center'd, and the other turn'd
> Round through the vast profundity obscure,
> And said, thus far extend, thus far thy bounds
> This be thy just circumference, O World !
>
> —Milton [*Paradise Lost*, vii. 226-231].

Urizen is intended beyond all doubt, since he is creating with his left (material)
hand.

Blake's Creator-Scientist corresponds precisely to Dr. Robert Fludd's ' Simia
Naturae.' The first plate of Fludd's *Utriusque Cosmi . . . Historia* (1617) shows
the Ape of Nature chained to the Great Mother, seated upon this earth, and applying dividers to a globe inscribed ' Arith[metic].'

Plate II. *Title Page.* ' Europe a Prophecy Lambeth Printed by Will: Blake
1794.' The design consists of the Serpent of Materialism, whose circular folds
suggest the Everlasting of Nature. This Serpent is the result of the Creation of
the preceding plate.

A very spirited ink-sketch owned by Mr. J. P. Morgan is an earlier, rejected
design for the title. Under the single word ' Europe ' appears Urizen with his
Book, riding upon the serpent as on a chariot. Above him, three flying figures
point out the way. Below are the words : ' Lambeth Printed by Will. Blake :
1794.' Blake seems to have abandoned this excellent design since he thought it
might have obscured the course of the pictures.

Keynes (p. 139) reproduces a water-colour sketch for the title-page (dated 1794),
which is that of the final version, except for the addition of a nude youth struggling
against the Serpent.

Plate III. *Introduction.* This plate is undecorated.

Plate IV. *Preludium.* Above the text : a grinning, naked figure in a cave way-
lays with a dagger a foot-traveller. This represents Man, the pilgrim through life
towards a spiritual goal, waylaid by the evil of the world. The first sketch appears
in the *MS. Book*, page 97. On the reverse of the title-page of the British Museum
copy is quoted Ann Radcliffe's poem, *The Pilgrim*, from her *Mysteries of Udolpho*.
(This poem does not appear in Bysshe.)

Below the text : a man falls upside down (the man dominated by lust) ; also
a bat-winged head wrapped in a serpent. This little medallion was preceded by
several sketches in the *MS. Book*. A larger version of it appears in the illustration
to Young's *Night Thoughts*, vii. 798.

Plate V. As a result of the ambush of evil, ' Horror, Amazement, and Despair
appear.' A flying male nude strangles two others ; above, another escapes.
The nudes are coloured ' futuristically,' and the drawing is distorted to intensify
the emotional effect. Blake's quotations are both from Bysshe :

> He views with horror next the noisy cave
> Where with hoarse din[s] imprison'd tempests rave,
> Whose clam'rous Hurricanes attempt their flight
> Or whirling in tumultuous Eddies fight.
>
> [Sir Samuel Garth : *The Dispensary*, vi. 104-107.]

> This orb's wide frame with the [1] convulsion shakes,
> Oft opens in the storm and often cracks.
> *Horror, Amazement*, and *Despair* appear
> In all the hideous forms that Mortals fear.
>
> [Sir Richard Blackmore : *Prince Arthur*, vi.]

---

[1] *The* should be *this*. Here Blake follows Bysshe's misprint.

The Boston Museum of Fine Arts possesses the original water-colour of this plate. There is no text: where it should be, two nude women, crowned with flowers, float blissfully among airy clouds. One reaches towards the nude who is escaping from the conflict below. This nude is of a cinnamon colour; those being strangled are respectively green and blue. This picture is dated 1793.

Plate vi. *A Prophecy.* The comet shaking the evils, which she presages, from her hair. She is represented as a clothed woman, floating horizontally. In the lettering, various joys of Innocence appear; it is these she is dooming. To the right of the text, a pensive figure sits in a globe.

> He like a Comet burn'd
> That fires the length of Ophiuc[h]us huge
> In th' Arctick Skye, and from his horrid hair
> Shakes Pestilence and War.
> > [*Paradise Lost,* ii. 708-711.]

> As the Red comet from Saturnius sent
> To fright the nations with a dire portent . . .
> With sweeping Glories glides along in air
> And shakes the sparkles from his [1] blazing hair.
> > [Pope's *Iliad,* iv. 101-102, 105-106.]

> Comets, importing change to times and states,
> Brandish your golden tresses in the Skies.[2]
> > [Shakspere: *1st Henry VI.* i. i. 2-3.]

> Like some malignant
> Planet that lowrs
> upon the world.[3]
> > [Nicholas Rowe: *The Fair Penitent,* iii. i. 6-8.]

All but the quotation from the *Iliad* are to be found in Bysshe.

Plate vii. Enitharmon (Inspiration) awakes Orc (Revolt). She lifts a mantle from his prone, sleeping form, while he buries his aureoled head in his arms. In the background is seen the 'enormous revelry' of Enitharmon's children. This evidently illustrates line 191 (on plate xvii): 'Arise, O Orc, and give our mountains joy of thy red light!' The poem in the British Museum copy is:

> Forms without body [4] and impassive air. . . .
> Thin shades the sports of winds are tosst
> O'er dreary plains, or tread the burning coast.
> > [Dryden: *Aeneis,* vi. 409.]

Plate viii. War naturally follows the awakening of Revolt. He appears as a dark, scaly, crowned nude, with a sword in his left (material) hand. Beneath his feet, flames flow downward. He is attended by two exquisite angels. Though he turns his back on them, War is inevitably followed by Pity and Compassion. EY suggest that this is the 'ghost' which Blake saw at Lambeth (Gilchrist, ch. xiv).

> O War! thou Son of Hell,
> Whom angry heavens do make their minister.
> > [Shakspere: *2nd Henry VI.* vii. 33-34.]

This quotation is not in Bysshe.

---

[1] Pope wrote *its.*

[2] So Bysshe misquotes. The passage really runs:

> Comets, importing change of times and states,
> Brandish your crystal tresses in the sky.

[3] Bysshe gives the lines correctly:

> Like some malignant Planet,
> Foe to the harvest and the healthy year,
> Who scowls averse, and lours upon the World.

[4] Dryden wrote 'bodies.'

Plate IX. War is followed by Famine. This full-page illustration represents two women about to devour a dead child, for whom the cauldron is already steaming. Such cannibalism was not allegory, but fact: it had been true in Ireland, within the century, when Swift wrote his *Modest Proposal.*

> Famine so fierce that whats denied mans use
> Even deadly plants and herbs of pois'nous juice
> Will Hunger eat [1]—and to prolong our breath
> We greedily devour our certain Death.
>
> [DRYDEN: *Indian Emperor*, IV. ii.]

Plate X. The horror of invasion. An old man helplessly repels the enemy (as yet unseen), while his daughter clasps his knees in abject terror:

> Thus Deluges descending on the Plains
> Sweep o'er the yellow year, &c.
>
> [DRYDEN: *Aeneis*, II. 409-410.]

The poem is extracted from the taking of Troy.

Plate XI. The harvest blighted. Through curving stalks of wheat, two nudes, male and female, fly madly, blowing spiral horns, from which the sooty scales of mildew are scattered.

Plate XII. To the left of the text: a flame-breathing, crested serpent rampant. This is the Infinite transformed by Reason to the Everlasting. For once, Blake illustrates a line which appears on the same plate.

Plate XIII. As a result, Outward Religion usurps the gothic throne of the Gospel of Jesus. The priest sits, triple-crowned, with bat-ears and bat-wings, the book of Prohibitions in his lap, and his feet concealed in a cloud. Before him, two Fairies (natural joys) throw down their fleur-de-lys headed wands.

Plate XIV. The results of Prohibition are easily guessed. 'He who desires but acts not, breeds pestilence' (5th *Proverb of Hell*). When the lover disappears, the prostitute appears, 'and blights with plagues the marriage-hearse.' The city is smitten, and the Bell-man passes, announcing the coming of the death-carts. One maiden implores heaven: another sinks dying into the arms of her lover. Upon a door in the background are the words made famous as the quarantine sign in the Great Plague of London: 'Lord Have Mercy On Us.' The British Museum copy is inscribed 'Plague,' and has inscribed beneath it the following verses (not in Bysshe):

> The midnight clock has toll'd, and hark! the Bell
> Of Death beats Slow!—heard ye the note profound?
> It pauses now, and now with rising knell
> Flings to the hollow gale the sullen sound.
>
> [WILLIAM MASON: *Elegy on the Death of Lady Coventry*, 1760.]

Plate XV. Between the lines of the text are flies, spider-webs, oak leaves, and other offspring of corruption. Below the text, a figure agonizes, bound tightly in a scurf-like net. Such is the spiritual fate of the youth who in the previous plate were smitten with the diseases of Experience.

> Them to a Dungeon's depth I sent, fast [2] bound,
> Where stow'd with snakes and adders now they lodge
> [Two Planks their Beds, slippery with Oose and Slime]
> The rats brush o'er their faces with their tails,
> And croaking Paddocks crawl upon their limbs.
>
> [DRYDEN: *King Arthur*, III.]

Plate XVI. But now literal prisons appear, the manifestation in the physical world of the spiritual state. Politics add their horrors to those of War and Priest-

---

[1] Dryden's version: 'Wild Hunger eats.'   [2] *Fast* should be *both.*

hood.   A nude youth, chained by the ankles in a stone-cell, despairs as his monstrous jailor ascends the steps to depart.

IMPRISONMENT

This is all my world—I shall nothing know,
Nothing hear, but the Clock that tells my woes,
The Vine shall grow, but I shall never see it,
Summer shall come, and with her all delights,
But Dead cold Winter still inhabit here.[1]
                [BEAUMONT and FLETCHER : *Two Noble Kinsmen*, II. ii. 44-49.]

This passage is not in Bysshe.

Plate XVII. Again we see scattered all through the text the smaller parasitic lives : snails, caterpillars, gnats, spiders, serpents, moths, and even a few birds lost among them.   But the remedy is at hand ; for high in their midst appear the first jets of flame—Revolution—which will consume all these vermin entirely.

Plate XVIII. And suddenly, in a splendid burst of brilliant colour, Revolution, as a conflagration, overwhelms the old structure of things, of which only one vestige, the base of a classic [2] pillar, remains.   A man drags his family from the furnace. The idea of this group is repeated from the 5th plate of *America*, and reappears again in the 3rd illustration to *Job* :

FIRE

Th' impetuous flames with lawless power advance,
On ruddy wings the bright destruction flies,
follow'd with ruin and distressful [3] cries.
The flaky Plague spreads swiftly with the wind
And gastly desolation howls behind.
                [SIR RICHARD BLACKMORE : *Prince Arthur*, III.]

---

[1] Again a misquotation from memory.   Perhaps in this case the text was changed to make the prisoner more pitiable by being placed in solitary confinement.   The original is as follows :

                . . . . This is all our world ;
We shall know nothing here but one another,
Heare nothing but the Clocke that tels our woes.
The Vine shall grow, but we shall never see it ;
Summer shall come, and with her all delights ;
But dead-cold winter must inhabite here still.

[2] Classic, *i.e.* Reason.   [3] *Distressful* should be *amazing*.

THE BOOK OF URIZEN

COMMENTARY

The Book of Urizen was originally called *The First Book of Urizen*, but in the later copies, Blake carefully obliterated the word 'First.' The *Second Book* was undoubtedly that one ultimately known as *The Book of Ahania*, which continues the story.

Preludium, Line 1. *Primeval Priest*: Urizen, since he is responsible for the Net of Religion.

Line 3. *In the North*, the region deserted by Urthona.

Line 6. Another reference to 'dictation.'

Chapter I. Line 1. Already Reason has become divided by contemplating its desires. *Shadow*: cf. *The Marriage*, plate 5: 'And being restrain'd, it by degrees becomes passive till it is only the shadow of Desire.'

Line 2. *Unprolific*: pure Reason is never creative.

Line 8. Division is the great method of Creation.

Line 21. *A self-contemplating Shadow*. Cf. *Jerusalem*, 29 : 37 *seq.* for a clearer exposition of the same idea.

Line 23. *His vast forests* ' of the night,' or, error.

Lines 28-33. Storms, seas, clouds, snows, hail, and ice are all forms of water.

Chapter II. Line 36. *Globes of attraction*: *i.e.* Eternity was One, untroubled by separated powers. These globes later appear in the form of hearts, around which Selfhoods are formed.

Line 58. In Eternity all these events happen simultaneously; and even in Urizen's cycles of time, deeds are bound to recur. This battle with fire is the battle with Orc, who is yet to be born, but who has been born before. For the details of this battle, see *The Four Zoas*, VII.

Lines 65-67. The foundation of the firmament, corresponding to *Genesis* i. 2, 6. Urizen could not create light nor darkness, for there had always been light, and he himself was darkness.

Line 68. *Books form'd of metals*. Cf. Paracelsus: *Economy of Minerals*, ch. ii.: ' So, then, the element of water is the mother, seed and root of all minerals.'

Line 76. *The Book of eternal brass*: of false charity. A selection from it is to be found in *The Four Zoas*, VII. 109-129.

Lines 78-79. These Christian virtues are Blake's own ideals, but Urizen expects to enforce them by law! The result has been Nietzsche, who despises such artificial 'virtues,' and not without reason. Only when they are spontaneous are they admirable.

Lines 80-84. Urizen's error: that his ideal can be attained only in one way.

Chapter III. Line 92. After this line, Dr. Sampson has unaccountably omitted a line which has never been printed. Lines 91-93 should read:

> In whirlwinds of sulphurous smoke
> And enormous forms of energy
> *All the seven deadly sins of the soul*
> In living creations appear'd.

The italicized line is the omitted one.

Line 97. Eternity, the limitless, is broken into limits.

Line 109. The wrathful flame, not the flame of revelation. Cf. Commentary on *America*, line 28.

Line 127. The Eternals stand on the brink of the Sea of Time and Space, where they behold the earth.

Line 137. The division of Poetry and Reason.

Chapter IV. There are two fourth chapters. The first one, which occupies one plate only, was apparently written as an afterthought, as a necessary preparation for the Changes of Urizen.

Chapter IVa. These Changes of Urizen have particularly impressed many critics. Blake himself thought well enough of them to repeat lines 183-253 almost verbatim in *The Four Zoas,* IV. 208-246 ; while lines 206-253 reappear, much compressed, in *Milton,* 5* : 10-27.

Line 178. *Sulphur,* in alchemy, represents a derivative fire. Blake uses it to symbolize the torments of Intellect.

Line 186. The lake of the Indefinite (Udan-Adan).

Line 197. The Skull. Cf. *Europe,* lines 98-99.

Line 198. *His fountain of thought.* Cf. *Jerusalem,* 77 : ' Is the Holy Ghost any other than an Intellectual Fountain ? '

Line 241. The *Throat* represents the last of the four senses ; the fifth, Touch, is Sex, which was never wholly bounded by the flesh.

Lines 247-248. His right hand seizes upon the North (spiritual region) ; his left upon the South (his own kingdom). As a result, he faces the West (the body) and turns his back upon the East (the passions).

Chapter V. Line 260. Urizen, being an Eternal, cannot be killed.

Line 278. Inspiration fades.

Line 285. *Pity* is Enitharmon.

Line 294. The division into sexes.

Line 322. Cf. ' And Pity no more could be / If all were as happy as we ' (*I heard an Angel singing, MS. Book*).

Chapter VI. Lines 331-334. Poetry and Inspiration separated, Inspiration becomes cruelly coy.

Lines 335-337. Poetry, no longer self-sufficient, builds upon *Pity,* not upon Love.

Line 340. *Sick,* with the first appearance of lust.

Line 341. *The Worm* is a symbol of the Flesh, which appears simultaneously with lust. Orc (Revolt), brought forth by Space, is to appear in the physical manifestation of War.

Line 347. *The Serpent* is merely the more dangerous form of the Worm.

Lines 355-357. In the anguish preceding the birth of Revolt, things begin to take on human aspects.

Line 364. *The Human Shadow.* Revolt (Orc) is suppressed desire.

Line 365. *Delving earth.* Revolt always rises ' from the soil.' Cf. the illustration on the fourth plate of *America.*

Chapter VII. Line 388. The iron Chain of Jealousy.

Line 392. *The Rock,* of the ' Stone of Night.' Orc is at first bound to the Decalogue.

Lines 395-398. But even so, all ' dead ' things begin to grope towards life again at his voice.

Lines 402-409. Cf. *Proverbs* viii. 27 : ' When he prepared the heavens I was there ; when he set a compass upon the face of the deep ' ; also *Paradise Lost,* VII. 226-231 :

> . . . and in his hand
> He took the golden Compasses. . . .
> One foot he center'd, and the other turn'd
> Round through the vast profunditie obscure
> And said, thus farr extend, thus farr thy bounds,
> This be thy just Circumference, O World.

This is the moment pictured in the famous *Frontispiece* to *Europe.*

Line 410. *The garden of fruits* is Eden, notorious for its apples.

Line 414. This *enormous race* is catalogued in *The Four Zoas,* VIII. 351-361.

Chapter VIII. Lines 430-437. The four elements appear. *Thiriel* has nothing to do with *Tiriel*, in the early book of that name. He represents Air, his name probably being an apocopated form of ' etherial.'

Line 440. Cf. ' The all-miscreative brain of Jove ' (Shelley, *Prometheus Unbound*, I, 448).

Line 445. *Shadow* : again suppressed desires, but this time emerging as Religion.

Line 464. *A Female* : that is, Urizen's religion is entirely passive, negative ; *embryonic*, because it is not well-developed enough to be productive.

Line 465. *Wings of fire* : *i.e.* genius or love.

Line 468. Cf. Shelley, *Queen Mab*, VI. 69-71 :

> Religion . . . prolific fiend,
> Who peoplest earth with demons, hell with men,
> And heaven with slaves !

Chapter IX. Line 469. Each city is a son of Urizen.

Lines 470-484. The ' creation ' of man ; consisting of shrinkage and solidification into material forms.

Line 479. *Streaky slime*, the Net of Religion.

Lines 485-488. The seven days of Creation, according to *Genesis*.

Line 489. So in *Tiriel*, line 251, thirty sons survive the Curse, ' to wither.' But Tiriel's other seventy sons are killed outright ; Urizen's sons escape from the earth. Much of *Urizen* shows a great parallelism with *Tiriel*, v.

Line 495. Death appears on earth.

Line 498. *Tombs* of desire.

Line 503. The first civilization rises in Egypt. See the Commentary on *Ahania*, 162.

Line 512. *Fuzon*, the fire-elemental, born lines 436-437. *Ahania* tells of his subsequent attack on Urizen.

Line 514. *The pendulous earth* : cf. ' the pendulous round earth,' *Paradise Lost*, IV. 1000.

Line 516. *The salt ocean* : the sterile Sea of Time and Space.

DECORATIONS

In its completest form, *Urizen* has twenty-eight plates. Their designs retell the story of the book, following it so closely that for the most part, the pictures are actual illustrations. Nevertheless Blake, in his effort to make each copy individual, pursued his usual policy of changing the order of the plates as much as he could. Since ten of the twenty-eight are full-page illustrations without text, a good deal of rearrangement was possible, all the more so since Blake did not care whether the pictures followed each other in the proper order. He felt safe in doing this : first, because, as the pictures were clearly illustrations, their meaning is not obscured by such shifting ; and secondly, because the ' states ' which they represent are eternal, and therefore continually happening everywhere. Thus Blake, by confusing the temporal order, probably felt that he was referring his myth to eternity more effectively.

However, the full-page illustrations are not the only plates which are shifted. Parts of the text itself may be occasionally transposed. Apparently some plates were added later : such as the rare fourth plate, also probably the seventh and tenth plates. The eleventh plate is commonly placed between the ninth and tenth. Mr. W. A. White's late copy (water-marked 1815) is a fine example of an elaborate rearrangement. No less than three of the plates *with text* (5, 15, and 9) are out of their normal place. The order is as follows : 1-3, 4, 10-12, 5, 15, 14, 9, 7-8, 16-17, 19-22, 13, 23, 25-27, 24, 28. The rare fourth plate is omitted.

In the absence, then, of any standard order, I have taken the liberty of rearranging the plates myself, so that they tell their story as clearly as possible. I have followed the order of the text as given by Sampson, and inserted the full-page illustrations in the places for which they seem originally intended. The numbers in parentheses refer to the plates as numbered by Dr. Keynes.

Plate 1 (1). *Title-page.* 'The Book of Urizen. Lambeth. Printed by Will. Blake 1794.' In the early copies 'First' is inserted before 'Book'; but later it was erased from the plate, and the void which it filled was painted over with the bough of a tree. The decoration represents Urizen writing his books. He crouches beneath the barren Tree of Mystery (described in *Ahania*, ch. iii.), eyes closed, writing with both hands in two books, a third book beneath his feet, and the Decalogue erected behind him.

Plate 2 (2). *Preludium.* Enitharmon floating in Space with the infant Orc. Below, the green flames of vegetation burst downward.

Plate 3 (3). Los in the flames of inspiration. He gazes inward, and holds his arms in the cruciform position, striding forward with the right (spiritual) foot. The use of right and left, as referring to spiritual and material aspects, is used fairly consistently throughout *Urizen*, but not always. For example, Urizen, on the title-page, is displaying his right (spiritual) foot, though he is in a materialistic act.

Plate 4 (4). Humanity in the black rain of materialism. These first four plates introduce the characters; the story begins with the fifth plate.

Plate 5 (5).

> Lo! I unfold my darkness, and on
> This rock place, with strong hand, the Book
> Of eternal brass, written in my solitude

(lines 75-77). Urizen, his head streaming with light, opens the book with both hands. Its pages are splotched with colours.

Plate 6 (6). As a result of this promulgation, a trinity of Eternals fall headlong into fires. They are entwined with the serpents of Materialism. Dimly behind them are to be seen the faces of Urizen's armies driving them out. These same faces drive Adam and Eve from Eden, in the illustrations to *Paradise Lost*. The central figure is 'crucified upside-down.' In some copies the two side figures are painted out; but they were not erased from the plate, since they appear in late copies. This plate suggests the lower half of Plate 7 in *America*; but the meaning is entirely different. That represented a casting out of errors; this, a Fall into Materialism.

Plate 7 (16). Los falls also:

> And a fathomless void for his feet:
> And intense fires for his dwelling

(lines 138-139). This plate suggests Blake's illustration to the *Night Thoughts*, IX. 137-138: 'Conflagration . . . chained in caves.'

Plate 8 (9). Urizen shut in by his petrified world. A rock presses upon his head. His eyes are closed, and he is trying to rise. In one copy, at least, his eyes are open.

Plate 9 (7). Los in his anguish.

> Los howl'd in a dismal stupor,
> Groaning! gnashing! groaning!

These lines (144-145) are on the same plate!

Plate 10 (8). Urizen's embryo as a skeleton; the First Age. This illustrates lines 199-207.

Plate 11 (10). Los trying to rise in the petrific darkness. He faces inward, and his arms again suggest the crucifixion. His head and hands are buried in the rock which he is trying to lift. This plate is often placed before the tenth, so that the

Changes of Urizen may not be interrupted. I have not done so, for the sake of preserving the normal order of the text.

Plate 12 (11). To the left is the partially clothed skeleton of Urizen in flames, with a chain at his feet; to the right Los howls, hammer in hand. This illustrates line 254: ' In terrors Los shrunk from his task.'

Plate 13 (12). Urizen, completed, swims through the black waters of materialism. Cf. lines 262-266.

Plate 14 (14). Urizen (in Mr. W. A. White's copy, his beard is clearly visible), having lost all sense of direction, tries to penetrate the rocks (clouds ?) below him.

Plate 15 (13). Urizen is now divided, and we see his cast-out emanation, Ahania. This incident is to be found in *The Book of Ahania*, lines 38-43 :

> She fell down, a faint shadow, wandr'ing
> In chaos and circling dark Urizen,
> As the moon anguish'd circles the earth,
> Hopeless ! abhorr'd ! a death-shadow,
> Unseen, unbodied, unknown,
> The mother of Pestilence.

She is represented as pushing clouds aside, possibly with a suggestion of the moon behind her right hand.

Plate 16 (15). The Eternals, horrified at Creation, separate themselves from it. ' They began to weave curtains of darkness ' (line 326). Four Eternals, two young and two old, lean over, a young one spreading the curtain between them and the earth with his left hand. Above them is an Eagle, the sign of genius. In the Muir facsimile, one of the Eternals and the Eagle are painted out, but are still visible. In the Hooper copy, they are completely obliterated. In some copies, the veil of darkness seems more like a shell of rock.

Plate 17 (18). Los in the world of matter. He strides forward with his left foot, but his right hand is upon a rock, as though to rend it away. His left hand holds the hammer which rests on a rock. His arms repeat the cruciform position.

Plate 18 (17). The creation of Enitharmon, illustrating lines 307-312 :

> The globe of life blood trembled,
> Branching out in roots :
> Fibrous, writhing upon the winds :
> Fibres of blood, milk, and tears :
> At length in tears & cries imbodied.

Enitharmon is evolving around the incandescent globe, over which her hair streams. Both she and it are marked with strange veins, the ' fibres,' which stream out into the void.

Plate 19 (19). Enitharmon, now completed, hovers before the despairing Los, from whom she turns away. There are generally fires beneath her feet. This illustrates lines 313-314 :

> A female form trembling and pale
> Waves before his deathy face.

Plate 20 (20). The birth of their child, Orc.

> Delving earth in his resistless way,
> Howling, the Child with fierce flames
> Issu'd from Enitharmon

(lines 365-367). The child, in a great swirl of flame, dives diagonally downward.

Plate 21 (21). The jealousy of Los, illustrating lines 378-389. The sun is setting. Enitharmon is being hugged by her boy. Los, hammer resting upon his anvil, gazes at them with anguish in his eyes. The Chain of Jealousy hangs from an iron band about his chest.

Plate 22 (22). Urizen sits in fetters, tears pouring from his closed eyes. A halo surrounds his head. Evidently this refers to line 449 : ' And he wept, & he called it Pity.' Upon a drawing for this plate in the Forman sale was written, probably in Blake's hand :

> Frozen doors to mock
> The world ; while they within torments uplock.

Plate 23 (23). But now Urizen, ' craving with hunger ' arises :

> Urizen explor'd his dens,
> Mountain, moor, & wilderness,
> With a globe of fire lighting his journey ;
> A fearful journey, annoy'd
> By cruel enormities, forms
> Of life on his forsaken mountains

(lines 415-420). He strides, left foot first, with the globe in his right hand, among the mountains. A lion faces him : the lion, defender of the lamb, who appears to Urizen as a cruel enormity.

Plate 24 (24). The four elements, his first sons, are born :

> First Thiriel appear'd,
> Astonish'd at his own existence,
> Like a man from a cloud born ; & Utha
> From the waters emerging laments ;
> Grodna rent the deep earth howling
> Amaz'd ; his heavens immense cracks
> Like the ground parch'd with heat ; then Fuzon
> Flam'd out, first begotten, last born

(lines 430-437). Thiriel, the air-elemental, alone has completely emerged ; the others are still partly involved in their elements. The sun is setting behind the sea.

In the British Museum copy, only the first two sons, Thiriel and Utha, are visible. The eighth print in the small Book of Designs shows Utha alone, the sun having set completely behind a horizon of hills.

Plate 25 (25). The birth of Urizen's three daughters, the logical division of man into the Head, Heart, and Loins :

> His daughters . . .
> From monsters & worms of the pit

(lines 439-440). They emerge from the coils of a winged Worm, on the surface of the Sea.

Plate 26 (26). ' The Dog at the wintry door ' (line 448), as typifying the cruelty of Urizen's creation. Near the howling dog, a boy clasps his hands in anguish.

Plate 27 (27). The creation of the Web of Religion (lines 451-457) :

> Cold he wander'd on high over their cities
> In weeping & pain & woe ;
> And where-ever he wander'd in sorrows
> Upon the aged heavens,
> A cold shadow follow'd behind him,
> Like a spider's web, moist, cold, & dim.

Urizen flies inward, trailing his right foot behind. The flow of his garments is the Net itself :

> And where-ever he travel'd a dire Web
> Follow'd behind him, as the Web of a Spider dusky & cold,
> Shivering across from Vortex to Vortex, drawn out from his mantle of years,
> A living Mantle adjoined to his life & growing from his Soul.
> —*The Four Zoas*, VI. 241-244.

Plate 28 (28). Urizen, caught in his own net, sits resigned, revealing his left foot.   An early version of this plate is to be found in the decoration of *The Human Abstract* (*Songs of Experience*) ; but there, Urizen is struggling against his bonds ; here, he has given up the hopeless fight :

> Himself caught in his own Net, in sorrow, lust, repentance.
> —*The Four Zoas*, VIII. 178.

THE BOOK OF LOS

COMMENTARY

Chapter I. Line 1. *Eno* is Enion, the Earth Mother, the emanation of the Senses. The identity of Eno with Enion is proved by a comparison of *The Four Zoas*, I. 193 *seq.* with *Jerusalem*, 48 : 18, 30 *seq.*

Line 2. *The chariot of Leutha* is the body, which is the vehicle of the Emotions.

Line 3. *The day of thunders*, the day of the Fall.

Line 4. *The eternal Oak*, as we have seen, is symbolic of the error of the world.

Line 7. *O Times remote!—i.e.* Eternity.

Line 26. Cf. ' I proclaim Simha, the annihilation of egotism, of lust, of ill-will, of delusion. However, I do not proclaim the annihilation of forbearance, of love, of charity, and of truth' (Buddha, quoted from Paul Carus : *Gospel of Buddha*).

Line 27. *The flames of desire*; cf. *Urizen*, III. § 4.

Line 31. *The Eternal Prophet* is Los.

Line 49. *No light from the fires!* See the Commentary on *America*, line 28.

Line 55. *Egypt*, a state of Empire, warring against the true arts.

Chapter II. Line 77. Cf. the fall of Lucifer.

Chapter III. Line 103. *The Lungs*. During the Deluge of Time and Space, ' all in whose nostrils was the breath of life, of all that was in the dry land, died' (*Genesis* vii. 22): that is, died from Eternity into Mortality. The lungs are the first organ to set up communication with the new element; in Swedenborgian symbolism, they correspond to Understanding.

Line 106. *The Polypus* later becomes the symbol for growths in the Sea of Time and Space.

Lines 122-128. The creation of Light, corresponding to *Genesis* i. 1-4.

Chapter IV. Line 149. *An Orb*, the Sun of Poetry.

Lines 171-176. Cf. Shelley : *Queen Mab*, VII, 108-112 :

> I . . . created man ;
> I planted him in a Paradise, and there
> Planted the tree of evil, so that he
> Might eat and perish, and my soul procure
> Wherewith to sate its malice.

Line 172. The four rivers of Eden.

Line 174. The creation of Adam.

DECORATIONS

The Book of Los has the fewest and most poorly decorated plates of any of the Prophetic Books.

Plate 1. *Frontispiece.* Eno crouches upon a stony slab, lamenting.

Plate 2. *Title-page.* ' The Book of Los Lambeth Printed by W. Blake 1795.' Below the title, Los crouches, with his back to the spectator, completely enclosed in the Rock of Eternity.

Plate 3. In the O of the title, ' Los,' Urizen crouches in his Net of Religion, which spreads out below, ensnaring a youth and a maiden. Above ' Chap. I' a robed figure reads the Book of Law.

Plate 4. No decoration whatever, not even the usual flowing lines.

Plate 5. Below the text of the right-hand column, Los kneels in a cloud, his arms in the cruciform position, gazing at the immense Sun which has just been launched upon the Deep.

THE BOOK OF AHANIA

COMMENTARY

This book was undoubtedly suggested by the first part of Plato's *Philebus*.

Chapter I. Line 10. *This Demon of Smoke*. To Fuzon, the god of Fire, Urizen seems nothing but an exhalation. See the Commentary on *Jerusalem*, 5 : 48.

Line 21. *The broad Disk*: Urizen's shield against Passion.

Line 23. *Mills*: the processes of logic. But logic is not a good protection against passion.

Line 32. Ahania, Urizen's emanation, is Pleasure.

Line 38. *Shadow*: suppressed desire.

Line 43. Pleasure, separated from Reason and then suppressed, breeds spiritual disease.

Line 45. That Luvah later replaced Fuzon in Blake's symbolism is proved by the identity of their symbols. Cf. *Jerusalem*, 62 : 28.

Line 48. *The Sun*: Christ as the Sun is one of Böhme's great symbols.

Chapter II. Lines 55-60. A reference to *Urizen*, 13-17.

Line 61. The Serpent of Materialism.

Line 71. Cf. *Jerusalem*, 52 :

> When Satan first the black bow bent
> And the Moral Law from the Gospel rent,
> He forg'd the Law into a sword
> And spill'd the blood of mercy's Lord.

Line 72. *A poison'd Rock*: the Decalogue. Thus Moral Virtue is the weapon against Passion made by Reason from its conquest of Matter.

Line 75. *Lust-form'd*. Matter is the result of Generation.

Line 84. *Tygers* of wrath.

Chapter III. Line 100. *The dead corse*: Fuzon is not dead, as we shall see. No immortal can be killed.

Lines 111-122 were rewritten in *The Four Zoas*, VII. 29-39. The growth of the Tree of Mystery is also described in *The Human Abstract* (*Songs of Experience*) and *Jerusalem*, 28 : 14-19.

Line 112. *His Book of Iron*: the doctrine of War.

Lines 119-122. Religion grows so rapidly that it almost ensnares Reason himself. He is forced to depart, leaving the Book of Iron (the doctrine of War) in its keeping. Cf. ' The priest promotes war.'

Line 125. Repeated in *Jerusalem*, 28 : 19.

Lines 126-129. The Crucifixion of Passion by Reason upon the Tree of Mystery, which is the Church.

Chapter IV. Lines 132-137, a reference to *Urizen*, 186-187.

Line 148. *The Eternal Prophet* is Los ; for Time is the promise of Eternity ; Poetry the promise of Heaven.

Line 152. *The Shapes* are the ' spectres,' the product of suppression and division. They are wandering spiritual fragments which the Poet tries to save by giving them human forms. They are the shadows which drew Theotormon's attention from his beloved Oothoon. The later epics describe the process of Incarnation at length. See *The Four Zoas*, VIII. 205-214, and *Milton*, 27 : 1-43.

Line 158. *Forty years*. The Israelites wandered forty years in the wilderness before reaching the Promised Land ; Christ fasted in the wilderness forty days.

Line 162. Africa, the materialized form of Reason, appeared in *Urizen*, 503. The next continent to be civilized (or the next realm of Man to be materialized) is Asia, the realm of the Passions.

Chapter V. Line 170. *No form*: Pleasure is given no outward expression.

Line 206. *His harvests*. Urizen's function in Eternity is to harvest the immortal Bread of Thought. This process is described at length in *The Four Zoas*, IX.

Line 221. Reminiscent of the poem in the *MS. Book*: *Thou hast a lap full of seed*. See also the Commentary on *The Four Zoas*, IX. 319.

Line 226. *Science*: not the ordinary meaning of the word, but ' knowledge.' Blake did not disbelieve in this, the true meaning of the word. He never casts out Urizen's province ; he merely protests against its domination over the other provinces. ' What is the life of Man but Art and Science ? ' (*Jerusalem*, 77).

DECORATIONS

The Book of Ahania, like *The Book of Los*, is very meagrely decorated.

Plate 1. *Title-page*. ' The Book of Ahania Lambeth Printed by W. Blake 1795.' The shadowy form of the outcast Ahania parting clouds in her wandering. The idea of this design is repeated from the 15th plate of *Urizen*.

Plates 2-4. No decoration.

Plate 5. The fallen yellow-bearded Urizen in anguish. Blood spouts from his neck. (It is possible that this represents fallen Albion.)

The frontispiece reproduced by EY is not in the only known copy of *Ahania*.

THE SONG OF LOS

COMMENTARY

Africa.

Line 2. *Four harps*: Blake's books of the four continents.

Line 4. *Ariston* is one of Blake's most obscure characters. See the Commentary on *America*, 112.

Line 9. *The children of Los* are the prophets.

Line 10. The black skin of the African was due to his inability to endure the sunlight otherwise; which was a sign of decadence.

Line 15. *Shrunk beneath the waters*: entered the state of Materialism.

Line 16. *Chaldaea* signifies to Swedenborgians the profanation of the Truth. It contained Babylon. It was Abram's native land (*Genesis* xi. 31). Blake says that he 'fled in fires' from it, meaning that in the fire of inspiration he fled from natural error.

Line 17. As the world becomes divided, the Everlasting Gospel becomes divided. The four systems of philosophy are now taken from Los's sons, not from Los himself. Wrath produces Brahminism, Pity produces Greek thought, Reason produces Hebraic law (line 17), and Desire produces Christianity.

Line 18. Hermes Trismegistus was one of the great sources for mystical theologists; but in *Jerusalem*, 91 : 34, Blake rejected his work as being a step towards the Indefinite.

Line 19. Blake's dislike of Greek philosophy has already been commented upon. He found it was based upon Reason, and only too often openly antipoetic, besides being completely non-mystical. His attitude was endorsed by many of the early thinkers.

'Pythagoras could not be called a wise man, because the Egyptian priestcraft and wisdom were not perfectly taught, although he received therefrom many mysteries and arcana.'—PARACELSUS: *Aurora Philosophorum*, ch. iii.

'Upon the foundation, therefore, of human or mundane wisdom, was the Philosophy of the Grecians erected.'
—ROBERT FLUDD: *Mosaicall Philosophy*, Bk. II. Sec. I. ch. i.

Line 20. *The sons of Har* are the human race. Har was the Poetic Genius himself in *Tiriel*; and from him all humanity was derived.

Line 28. *Antamon*: see the Commentary on *Europe*, 180. For *Leutha*, see Commentary on *Europe*, 169.

Line 30. *Sotha and Diralada*: see the Commentary on *Europe*, 186.

Line 32. These four types of buildings symbolize the four states of Man in his decadence: Churches represent the fallen Spirit; Hospitals the sick Body; Castles are the dwellings of the prudent; and Palaces the settings for the Passions.

Line 36. *Har and Heva* are Poetry and Painting, in the early Prophetic Book, *Tiriel*.

Line 48. *Newton and Locke*. 'Bacon, Locke, and Newton are the three great teachers of Atheism, or Satan's doctrine' (Blake, as quoted by Norton, p. 19). Locke was notorious for having denounced poetry as idle and pernicious. 'The pith of my system is to make the senses out of the mind, not the mind out of the senses, as Locke did' (Coleridge: *Table Talk*, July 25, 1832).

Line 52. This, the last line of *Africa*, is repeated as the first line of the *Prophecy* of *America*, which continues the story.

Asia. Line 3. *Web* of Religion.

Line 4. *Den* of the body.

Line 9 *seq.* This philosophy might well have been quoted from Urizen's Book of Brass.

Line 38. *His Books of brass, iron, and gold* : *i.e.* of charity, war, and economics.

Lines 44-47. Both the Natural Man and the Imagination are destroyed under Urizen's reign.

Lines 55-58 describe a Last Judgment.

DECORATIONS

The Song of Los is decorated with something of the old splendour of *America* and *Europe.* In at least a few of the copies, Blake was using some technique of his own invention : his paints are ground coarsely, with the admixture of some oily medium, though it might better be described as water-colour. The effect is curiously successful.

Plate 1. *Frontispiece.* A man, draped from the waist down, kneels with his back to the spectator, before a classic altar, in worship of the dark, mottled sun of Reason. In the background is the dim outline of a mountain.

Plate 2. *Title-page.* 'The Song of Los   Lambeth   Printed by W. Blake   1795.' An old man, clad in white, reclining in a rocky landscape with his hand upon a skull, gazes upward. This evidently illustrates the lines :

> For Adam, a mouldering skeleton,
> Lay bleach'd on the garden of Eden :
> And Noah, as white as snow,
> On the mountains of Ararat.

Plate 3. ' Africa.' In this title, the immense serpent of Materialism is twined. Below line 5, Har is sleeping by his ram (cf. *America*, plate 8). To the right, a butterfly escapes from its cocoon.

Plate 4. Below the text : Har and Heva fleeing from their corrupted home. To the right of the text, a bat-winged female in flight.

Plate 5. A full-page illustration of the ' Lillies of Havilah,' in whose cups, beneath a night of stars, the King and Queen of the Fairies (Natural Joys) are resting.

Plate 6. ' Asia.' Below this title, Man in his cave tries to resuscitate his Emanation. In the lower right-hand corner, a nude male crouches in despair.

Plate 7. On the right of the text : a nude male falls upside-down. To the left of the text are boughs of a tree.

Plate 8. A full-page illustration of Los launching the Sun, which he has just finished, upon the Void. Naked, he kneels in a cloud, leaning on his hammer, and gazes at the Sun below him.

(The 9th plate in Mr. Huntington's copy does not belong to the book at all. It is the plate commonly known as ' Glad Day.' Albion, as a nude youth, stands on the mountain-top with his arms in the cruciform position. Under the print is sometimes engraved :

> Albion arose from where he labour'd at the Mill with slaves :
> Giving himself for the Nations, he danc'd the dance of Eternal Death.)

THE FOUR ZOAS

COMMENTARY

The quotations from *The Four Zoas* have been made, as far as possible, from the original manuscript; and therefore the reader will note many discrepancies when they compare these quotations with the printed texts. So far only two editions have been published: the Ellis and Yeats edition of 1893, and the Ellis edition of 1906. The second edition contains many corrections of the first, though with some new and surprising variations. Mr. Ellis and Mr. Yeats are to be congratulated in making Blake's complete works accessible to the public; indeed, the present knowledge of Blake is largely due to their efforts. On the other hand, we cannot condemn too strongly the complete lack of editorial responsibility, which has resulted in the worst editions of any poet ever issued.

Mr. Ellis and Mr. Yeats have admitted, and even defended in advance, their disregard of written and engraved texts. They have culminated the bad tradition (started, it is true, by no less a person than Dante Gabriel Rossetti) of revising Blake's text to suit their own theories of versification. But the changes which cannot be so explained are too numerous to be laid against even the hastiest transcription from the manuscript. As an example chosen at random, we shall quote the opening lines of *Night the Eighth*. Blake wrote:

> Then all in great Eternity Met in the Council of God
> As one Man Even Jesus upon Gilead & Hermon
> Upon the Limit of Contraction to create the fallen Man
> The fallen Man stretch'd like a corse upon the oozy rock
> Wash'd with the tide pale overgrown with weeds
> That mov'd with horrible dreams hovering high over his head.

The Ellis-Yeats version of this (repeated in the 1906 edition) is:

> Then all in great Eternity, *which is called* the council of God,
> *Met* as one Man, even Jesus, upon Gilead and Hermon,
> Upon the limit of contraction, to *awake* the fallen Man.
> The fallen Man stretched like a corse upon the oozy rock,
> Washed with the tide, pale, overgrown with *the waves,*
> *Just* moved with horrible dreams, *and waving* high over his head.[1]

Sometimes these changes are even more serious: as when they pervert the meaning of a whole passage. 'Man is a worm renewed with joy' (IX. 624) is far from Blake's own version: 'Man is a Worm wearied with joy.' The very names do not escape. 'Aha' (VIII. 359) may be explained as a glaring misprint for 'Adah'; but the substitution of 'Tiriel' throughout for 'Thiriel,' though involving a sad confusion of two characters, could only have been intentional.

Unfortunately, these editions, bad as they are, are the only ones yet given the public. I have chosen the second (Ellis, 1906) as the later, the more correct, and the more accessible; and to this the line references are made.

NIGHT THE FIRST

At the head of this *Night* Blake quoted from *Ephesians* vi. 12 the following passage in the Greek: 'For we wrestle not against flesh and blood, but against principalities, against powers, against the rulers of the darkness of this world, against spiritual wickedness in the high places.'

Line 1. *The Aged Mother.* Blake's original idea seems to have been to make his epic the great cry of Nature (or Vala, as he named her). He chose her name

---

[1] None of these changes are noted in the long list of *Verbal Emendations*; though elsewhere (II. 300) this list is guaranteed to be complete.

from Scandinavian mythology. The oldest Edda, the 'Voluspa,' is the vision of a Vala who is the guardian spirit of the earth, and the earliest of all prophetesses. Odin himself consults her, having raised her by a magical song from her death-sleep; whereupon she prophesies on the grave of the Huns the eventual destruction of the world by fire. *The Four Zoas* was intended to be just such a prophecy. But unfortunately Vala came to play such a small part in the spiritual wars that Blake removed her name from the title-page and erased it from the first line.

His other choice for Prophetess was Enion, who could more properly be called the 'Earth Mother,' since she represents the Generative Instinct. As 'Eno' (another name of hers—see Commentary on I. 193), she had opened *The Book of Los* with a lament. As Eno she was to open this book. Blake, however, erased her name. Nevertheless the epithet 'Mother' identifies her.

Line 6. *Four Mighty Ones*: the Four Zoas. Blake gives a marginal reference to *John* xvii. 21-23: 'That they all may be one; as thou, Father, art in me, and I in thee, that they also may be one in us: that the world may believe that thou hast sent me. And the glory which thou gavest me I have given them; that they may be one, even as we are one: I in them, and thou in me, that they may be made perfect in one; and that the world may know that thou hast sent me, and hast loved them, as thou hast loved me.' The appeal is clearly for a harmony of the Zoas.

Line 8. Blake gives a marginal reference to *John* i. 14: 'And the Word was made flesh, and dwelt among us (and we beheld his glory, the glory as of the only begotten of the Father), full of grace and truth.' Blake quotes in Greek the phrase 'among us.'

Line 9. For the names and positions of the Four, see VI. 276-277.

Lines 11-13. Blake is deliberately confusing his names here. *Urthona* is the ultimate name of the Spirit of Man; his form on Earth is *Los*, the god of poetry. Poetry is the temporal form of the Spirit.

Line 14. *The Auricular Nerves*: through which the appeal of Poetry is made.

Line 16. *Daughters of Beulah*: Blake's muses. *Beulah* is a Hebrew word meaning 'married,' which Blake selected because of his theory of the sexual nature of inspiration.

Line 20. *Tharmas*, the western Zoa, represents the Body and the senses. His name was undoubtedly derived from Tamas (Tama, or Tamasee), the Hindu name for Desire. Blake had been reading the *Bhagvat-Geeta* (London, 1785), and had been so impressed by it that he made a water-colour drawing of *The Brahmins— Mr. Wilkin translating the Geeta* (No. 84 in Rossetti's list of Blake's paintings). In Lecture XIV of this book is a description of the three 'Goon': '*Satwa* truth, *Raja* passion, and *Tama* darkness; and each of them confineth the incorruptible spirit in the body' (p. 107). From other references to the Goon, it appears that they correspond almost precisely to the three lower Zoas: Satwa being Urizen, Raja being Luvah, and Tama being Tharmas. The fourth and highest Zoa, Urthona, is the 'incorruptible spirit' in the passage quoted above. Needless to say, Blake thought more highly of the Goon than the Brahmins: he desired a harmony of the four Zoas; they sought the subjection of three to Urthona.

Line 21. His delights are gone. *Enion* is his mate, the Earth Mother, the generative and maternal instinct. The senses have lost touch with the Earth Mother.

Line 23. Selfishness (jealousy) has brought the consciousness of sin.

Line 25. *Jerusalem* is liberty. *Tirel* is a name never used again; all we can certainly say is that it is not a reference to *Tiriel*.

Line 27. Tharmas (the senses) has pitied, not loved, Enitharmon (space); yet Space has entered into him, and he cannot cast it out. Pity produces shame, hence it is not a good substitute for love, which produces sympathy. Therefore Tharmas is ashamed of the Emanations.

Line 34. *A shadow in Albion*: a cast-out desire of man.

Line 35. She must see the eternal Tharmas to live.

Line 39. She, too, has perceived sin, and therefore is fallen.

Lines 41-42. Sometimes the Senses perceived the act of generation as a purpose (flower) and sometimes as an end in itself (fruit).

Line 46. Analysis (the function of Urizen) is the Curse. Joy felt is lovely; analysed, it soon becomes horrible.

Line 56. The Body condemns the generative Instinct as diabolic though beautiful.

Line 58. The conflict divides (in a further Fall) the Reason (or Spectre) of Tharmas from him. Analysis is thus cast out; but becomes dominant and proud of its strength. The *loom of vegetation* is the means by which the physical body is formed.

Line 72. Reason soon discovers the generative instinct (Enion) hidden in the dark places of the mind (Cave).

Line 82. The Seventh Day of the creation.

Line 83. Reason defies and threatens the Generative instinct with his power of judgment. Accusation is the great sin, in Blake's mind. This is always a spectral function.

Line 96. The generative instinct thought to hide her sins under a 'veil' of modesty; but in doing so she only uncovers the sins of the Body.

Lines 97-98. I have not been able to find these lines in the manuscript.

Lines 99-102. A description of Beulah, where the Females sacrifice themselves for the Males. All things live by the death of others—the mystical death of self-sacrifice, of course.

Line 103. Therefore Enion sacrifices herself (suppresses herself), though in error, for the masculine Reason.

Line 105. *A tabernacle of delight.* The decoration on page 21*b* shows a nude crowned woman, with a tabernacle covering her loins. The 'death' of the Eternals is a descent into flesh.

Lines 106-110. The suppression of the generative instinct has a terrible effect. Tharmas, though innocent, has to submit to the Circle of Destiny, the laws of cause and effect, praying meanwhile for the complete reunion of his personality when the day of darkness is over. For the Circle of Destiny, see lines 122, 210; also the proverb: 'Where man is not, nature is barren'—the mind creates its own universe. Tharmas sets the Circle in motion.

Line 111. *The sea* is the sea of Time and Space. Tharmas is a 'corpse,' because this is death.

Line 112. *Her filmy woof*: the loom of Vegetation.

Line 113. *His feet*: the lowest part of his person. Enion's self-repression allows the Spectre (the Reason) to grow and assume a personality of its own.

Lines 114-116. The anguish of self-analysis in desire. Cf. *The Mental Traveller.*

Line 118. *Her Shadow* is the form she will wear during her absence from Eternity (her sleep in Beulah).

Line 123. Space solidifies in the process of generation.

Line 125. *Shadow* of suppressed desire, which is to solidify eventually into the material body.

Line 143. Enion still feels self-justified.

Line 145. Reason still blames Enion for their mutual Fall.

Line 151. So they struggle, infecting each other.

Line 155. They infect each other.

Line 161. From the sorrow of their struggle is born Los and Enitharmon. Poetry and Inspiration are always born of woe. For the earlier part of their story, see VII. 277-295.

Lines 169-172 (a later insertion). But the gods watch over them all this while, from Gilead (the Hill of Witness) and Hermon (Lofty). Hermon is the Northern Limit (Spirit) of the Promised Land.

Line 173. Enion as the Earth-Mother. She produces the world of vegetation.

Line 182. *They sulk*: Los and Enitharmon.

Line 185. The Poetic Instinct is originally ascetic ; repulsing, and nearly killing, the Generative Instinct, though its life comes from her.

Line 193. *Eno* (anagram of 'Eon,' or emanation) is Enion, as a Daughter of Beulah. The moment of Time, which is equal to all created time, and the atom of space whose centre opens to Infinitude, is the work of Love (Poetry), which reveals Infinity and Eternity within everything. Cf. : ' To see a world in a grain of sand.' Undoubtedly this revelation comes during the first moment of love. Cf. *Jerusalem*, 48 : 18, 30 *seq.* This passage was probably suggested by Henry More's *Divine Dialogues* (London, 1668) : ' The Thread of Time and the Expansion of the Universe, the same Hand drew out the one and spred out the other.'

Line 194. The world's history is to last 6000 years ; then will follow the final 1000 years, the sabbath of the chosen. See the Commentary on *The Marriage of Heaven and Hell*, plate XIV.

Line 209-210. They limit the Circle of Destiny (Karma, in Oriental phraseology) to Space, and name it Ulro (or Maya).

Line 217. The gate of the tongue : the ability to express oneself.

Line 218. Here Los and Enitharmon obviously become William and Catherine in their early married life ; but at the same time they symbolize every young poet and his Inspiration, which are not yet in accord.

Line 225. *Prophecy*, or Poetry.

Line 231. In Blake's last version, he ended *Night the First* here, deleted line 232, wrote *Night the Second* in the margin, and inserted line 233 to introduce lines 234 *seq.*

Line 232. *Nine years* : according to Swedenborg (*Arcana*, 2075), nine signifies conjunction.

Line 239. Catherine sees the world's great struggle, and reproves William for not flinging himself into it, and for repressing her.

Line 245. Enitharmon's song is the voice of Inspiration. When Albion is fallen into the sleep of death, and Reason is off guard, then Passion (Luvah) and Nature (Vala) literally go to his head. ' Why does Enitharmon appear as Vala (Material, not Spiritual, beauty) ? ' Passion, seizing the Horses of Instruction, sees that Jealousy is the cause ; for all these joys were ' Once born for the sport & amusement of Man, now born to drink up all his Powers.'

Line 249. This incident (Passion directing the light of Reason) is often referred to as one of the most crucial moments of the Fall. It may have been suggested by Plato's famous symbol of the chariot, in the *Phaedrus*.

Line 263. This suggests that this was written by the sea at Felpham.

Line 265. Los is shocked at her condemnation of jealousy.

Line 267. *I die not* : he refuses to sacrifice himself for her. Cf. the voice of Jesus : ' Every kindness to another is a little death in the Divine Image ' (*Jerusalem*, 96 : 27-28).

Line 273. He blames Enitharmon for Vala's rejection of Albion for the lost Luvah.

Line 276. Los and Enitharmon live in the faith of the Incarnation. They must struggle ('in stern debate') until One becomes All ; and his Crucifixion will be blamed upon Enitharmon.

Line 283 is repeated by Ellis from line 273.

Line 284. Los also foresees Passion entering Nature, and the wars that will result.

Line 289. *Lamps* : The stars.

Line 290. He believes that they exist only in the material body : the watery expanse of Tharmas.

Line 293. Enitharmon unfortunately calls upon Reason (Urizen) to answer Los.

Line 301. *The Wandering Man* is Albion (Humanity).

Line 302. *The one* : Luvah.

Line 304. So the terrible reign of Urizen begins.

Line 306. *The Prince of Light* is Urizen.

Line 308. Reason approves of the Poet, but not of Inspiration ; and he gives the Poet dominion over Nature and Passion.

Line 324. Reason, repulsed, reveals himself as the destroying god opposed to Jesus.

Line 327. The dominant idea of the Eighteenth Century.

Line 334. *The bright Sun* is the eternal sun of Imagination and Poetry.

Line 335. *The blue shell* is the sky, the shell of the Mundane Egg.

Line 336. Los, having rejected Reason, is again united to Enitharmon.

Line 340. The bread and wine of love.

Line 344. Passion and Nature are abandoned ; yet they are watched over by the Saviour.

Line 349. *Luvah's robes of blood* are the Incarnation.

Lines 356-358. The eternal round : the descent into the Void of this world because of the cravings of the Generative Instinct and the return to the golden feast of Eternity.

Line 359 repeated Fragment I. 38.

Line 369. The marriage song of the Poet and Inspiration is the song of Revolution—in its bad aspect, as well as the good.

Line 387. The lament of the Earth Mother over the Cruelty of Nature, the struggle for existence.

Line 403. *The golden tent* is the dwelling of the Good Shepherd.

Line 404. *Eternal Death* : Nature, which is Death from Eternity.

Line 406. *The Palm Tree* is the symbol of martyrdom : *the Oak* of stubborn Error, and hence of Weeping.

Line 407. Albion sinks still farther from Eternity, having passed below Beulah, into the world of Generation.

Lines 408-410. This moment is repeated in *Jerusalem*, 23 : 24-28 and 48 : 1-4.

Line 410. *The Rock of Ages* is the outward limit of stoniness, where Man must rest. This line is marked ' End of the First Night.'

Line 411 begins page 9*a*. Possibly this page was intended as a substitute for some other, or perhaps it belongs in another place. However, the sequence is clear enough.

Line 415. *Shiloh* is the site of the Tabernacle, and often used to indicate the Messiah.

Line 418. *Gilead*, the Hill of Witness.

Line 419. The Seven Eyes of God chosen to protect Albion are the seven various aspects of Man which have been successively worshipped as the supreme God. The first Six fail, but the Seventh, Jesus, is successful. The whole list will be found in VIII. 392-400, in *Milton*, 11 : 17-29 ; while in *Jerusalem*, 55 : 31-33, a mysterious Eight is added, which is the essence of the Individual. The engravings for Job are based upon these seven.

The seven aspects of God, which are implied in each other, and yet may be considered distinctly, are derived from *Revelation* iv. 5 : ' And there were seven lamps of fire burning before the throne, which are the seven Spirits of God.' In *Revelation* v. 6, these seven are gathered together in the figure of Jesus : ' And I beheld, and, lo, in the midst of the throne and of the four beasts, and in the midst of the elders, stood a Lamb as it had been slain, having seven horns and seven eyes which are the seven Spirits of God sent forth into all the earth.' A reference in the Old Testament may be that in *Zechariah* iii. 9, of the seven-eyed stone.

Jakob Böhme laid great stress on the seven aspects of God, which resolve into an analysis of the creative act. Blake, however, used them to symbolize the stages of the passage through Experience.

For a detailed discussion of Blake's conception of each of the Seven, see the Commentary on VIII. 392-400.

Line 423. *Mount Ephraim*, according to Swedenborg (*Arcana*, 5354) signifies the intellectual principle of the Church, as opposed to the spiritual and celestial, hence being the lowest of the three.

Line 425. This line is also marked ' End of the First Night.'

Line 426. Page 9*b*, which begins with this line, is written entirely with pencil. Very evidently it was not intended to be inserted here; but as it was probably another version of some part of the quarrels of Los and Enitharmon, it is hard to say just where it should go, though it surely belongs in the *First Night*.

Line 429. *These gates* : the head, heart, and loins. This whole passage represents the coyness of the woman towards the man, as well as the uncertainty of inspiration towards the poet. Blake's symbolism here becomes somewhat obscure : Enitharmon herself generally represents Inspiration; but now, the Emanation has taken that rôle. As Inspiration is to be obtained in love, Enitharmon's modesty excludes the Inspiration by closing all the three gates of sympathy.

Line 435. However, neither Inspiration nor Freedom (Jerusalem) can be killed, for they are Eternals.

Line 438. *The Living creatures* are the Four Zoas, caught in the wheels of Logic.

Lines 442-445. This passage means, quite simply, that all men, organized in the Invisible Church, form a single, living body. It was suggested by a passage in the *Timaeus*, 68 D.

Line 447. *Gilead*, the Hill of Witness.

Line 449. *Shiloh*, the site of the Tabernacle.

Line 451. *The Gate of the Tongue*, or Poetry.

Line 455. *Beth-Peor*, a Moabite town west of the Dead Sea, given to Reuben.

Line 459. Albion having fallen into his sleep of this world, Reason and Passion remain awake. Reason has already tried to make a pact with Poetry, but has failed ; now he tries the same with Passion. Reason wishes to reign over the Spirit, while Passion is to assume Reason's former throne. But naturally Passion refuses to be advised by Reason.

This whole episode may well have been suggested by Satan's conspiracy with Beelzebub (*Paradise Lost*, i.). ' We have here a development of the Miltonic scene ; more precise directions, more complex movements, a different meaning, but the same general lines. And the same fall into the abyss overtakes the adventurers, at once in Blake . . . but in Milton only as the grand termination of the battle in Heaven ' (Saurat, pp. 16-17).

Line 463. *The North*, the spiritual realm, which Urizen desires.

Line 464. *The South*, Urizen's realm, which he is abandoning in favour of Luvah. Reason is to usurp the soul ; Passion to take Reason's place.

Line 465. *The Universal Tent* is the dwelling of the Spirit.

Line 466. *The chariots of the morning*, drawn by ' the horses of instruction.' See the Commentary on i. 249.

Line 470. *Jerusalem*, or Freedom.

Lines 479-480. *Anak, Sihon, and Og* were three giant kings who at various times opposed the Israelites on their way to the Promised Land, and who were totally destroyed with their kingdoms as a result. Passion considers the offspring of Liberty as just such enemies.

Line 491. At the noise of the combat of Reason and Passion the Spirit is stopped in his work.

Line 495. *He is divided* : the two remaining parts are his Spectre (Los) and Enitharmon, who is now Pity.

Lines 497-501. Pity is harboured in the realm of the body, but is suppressed by Enion, the generative instinct, who here is symbolic of the modern Sex-Religion. To-day ' Enitharmon remains a corse ' in this world—Pity is killed—by the cruel selfishness of this jealous religion which sacrifices everything to itself. ' Such a thing was never known in Eden,' comments Blake. EY, for reasons they can best explain, insert a ' before ' after *known*, thus making nonsense of the passage. Obviously the murder of Enitharmon did not take place in Eden !

Line 502. The result of the division of the Spirit comes speedily. Urthona's

Spectre, Los (Poetry), flees to the Generative Instinct for Inspiration ; and at once becomes a Serpent (Materialistic).

Line 505. ' The Sons of War,' the people of this world, drive Poetry downward, far into the world of the Body, into the ' caverned Rock ' of the material skull.

Line 509. Now that Urthona is divided, Reason can without opposition usurp the spiritual throne. He does so, leaving Man helpless beneath the assaults of Passion.

Line 513. The result is a still greater Fall of them all.

Line 515. *The Man's exteriors are become indefinite* : that is, there is now no limit to Man's ability to wander in error, away from the central Truth. ' Truth has bounds, Error none.'

NIGHT THE SECOND

This *Night* was originally the first ; but later Blake erased the word *First* and wrote a preceding Canto.

Line 1. *His Couch of Death* : this world.

Line 2. *Outward to Self.* This phrase distinguishes between the Selfhood and the essential Individual, which is the kernel of every living thing. The Self, or Selfhood, is always used by Blake in an evil sense : it is the outward husk of errors which becomes Satan.

Line 5. Man, in pure weariness, yields to Reason.

Line 9. *The Feast of Eternity.* Urizen has not yet fallen. This *Night* was written originally as *Night the First* ; and this inconsistency escaped revision.

Line 13. *The golden porches* are the senses.

Line 18. The Fall is not only downward, but outward—the symbols are practically the same ; for we not only picture God as above, but also as within. The Void is boundless Error, which now is nearly about to absorb all Existence itself.

Line 23. Reason realizes the danger, and in pure self-protection builds, with the aid of Passion and Nature, the Mundane Shell, which is the coating of matter over everything. Sometimes it is symbolized as the sky itself. This Shell is the limit fixed to the Fall, the protection against Non-Existence.

Lines 38-65 were added marginally in the late revision. They are in the style of *Jerusalem*, yet they must have been written before ; since in the same list of Albion's daughters (*Jerusalem*, 5 : 41-44) Blake substituted Gwiniverra for Boadicea.

Line 38. This line is Blake's clearest description of the process of Creation. The material world is ' what is within now seen without.'

Line 39. *Tyburn* : the site of the gallows. *Oxford* : the place of dead instruction.

Line 40. *Druid Temples* : the religion of Selfhood, which sacrifices the blood of others to the Self.

Line 41. *The Atlantic Mountains* : the Lost Atlantis, pathway to Eternity.

Lines 42-44. Albion now divides into the fourfold division. ' Man anciently contain'd in his mighty limbs all things in Heaven & Earth ' (*Jerusalem*, 27) ; but in his Fall they were separated. The sun and moon (Urthona and Luvah) fly upward, the stars (Urizen) fall, while all the peoples of the earth flee from Albion's loins (Tharmas).

Lines 45-46. The wreck of spiritual liberty, as typified by the Archbishop's Palace at Lambeth.

Line 49. *The Severn.* Plenty of battles were fought on this river, any one of which would explain Blake's symbolism ; but he probably preferred the drowning of Sabrina and Estrildis by Gwendolin (Geoffrey of Monmouth, II. iv.).

Line 53. *Reuben slept on Penmaenmawr* : Reuben is the vegetated (incarnated) Man of the lowest animal type. He was the first son of Jacob, and was cursed for incest. Levi is the Priest with his ' instruments of cruelty ' (*Genesis* xlix. 5), Jacob's third son. The significance of Penmaenmawr (north-west of London) is difficult to guess ; but by Blake's changing of *Gilead* to *Snowdon* (*Four Zoas*, I. 447), we know that the latter is the English equivalent of the ' Hill of Witness.'

Line 54. Their four senses (excluding touch) become materialized : they see as externalities what are really portions of themselves. Cf. *The Four Zoas*, VIII. 554 *seq.*

Line 55. The internal world seems exterior ; and they are lost in its wilderness.

Line 56. They seem like separate beings.

Line 57. *The daughters of Albion* are the natural functions of Man. Their particular rôle is that of weaving the body. There are twelve of them, named after characters in Geoffrey of Monmouth's *History of England* ; except for Boadicea (for whom Gwiniverra was substituted in *Jerusalem*), who came from Milton's *History of England*. As these twelve daughters do not appear as distinct individuals until later, specific commentary on each is to be deferred.

Line 58. That is, removing the garments of Spiritual Beauty from the delights of nature—the ' golden demons that none can stay ' (Letter to Butts, Nov. 22, 1802). This cross-reference to these lines composed ' above a twelvemonth ago ' probably dates this insertion.

Line 59. Their course is towards the East—the passions.

Line 63. *Babylon* is always the worldly city, as opposed to Jerusalem, the city of God. The reference here is of course to the Babylonian Captivity.

Line 64. *Nimrod*, the first monarch, the ' mighty hunter.'

Line 65. That is, while Reason sat enthroned in Stonehenge, the famous temple. Blake called modern Puritanism ' the Druid Religion,' because both are based on the sacrifice of our neighbours to our God.

Line 66. Here the description of the building of the Mundane Shell is continued.

Line 71. *Ulro* is Blake's name for the world of matter, where the ' dead ' (or in our phraseology the *living*) lament without ceasing.

Lines 72-79. Passion is tormented in the fires supplied by Nature.

Lines 83-85. The Worm (flesh) becomes the Serpent (materialism).

Line 91. Nature is limited by the Sea of Time and Space. Drowned in matter, she is tiny enough to be endured.

Line 98. The delights of Nature taken from Passion.

Line 102. The mental state of the man blind to Eternity : a blind memory (or chaos) of incoherent love and hate.

Line 104. Passion restricted is no longer Love.

Line 105. Cf. ' Reason says, " Miracle " : Newton says " Doubt " ' (*You Don't believe*). Originally, Reason recognized the Supernatural ; but in his fallen state he does not.

Line 107. *The Human Delusion* : the Divine Vision.

Line 108. *From bondage of the Human Form* : though there is no other God. Cf. *The Divine Image* (*Songs of Innocence*).

Line 114. Nature herself fades during her separation from Passion ; and in this fading Passion finds rest.

Line 117. When this is accomplished, then Commerce, Universities, and other fixed institutions arise.

Line 122. The earth is still infinite.

Line 126. *Families* : these always seemed to Blake a symbol of selfishness extended beyond the physical bounds of the individual body.

Line 128. Astronomy : the obtaining of laws from the physical sun.

Line 136. The pyramids are surely intended to suggest Egypt.

Line 142. Cf. the *Frontispiece* to *Europe*.

Line 143. Justice (the scales) is torn from the weakness of Love.

Line 156 *seq.* This division of Eternal Unity into the Temporal Many may have been influenced by a passage in Porphyry's *Auxiliaries to the Perception of Intelligible Natures* (II. 39) : ' It is not proper to think that the multitude of souls was generated on account of the multitude of bodies ; but it is necessary to admit that, prior to bodies, there were many souls, and one soul [the cause of the many]. Nor does the one and whole soul prevent the subsistence in it of many souls ;

nor does the multitude of souls distribute by division the one soul into themselves' (Taylor's translation, p. 228).

Thus Albion remains whole in his sleep, though all these things are part of himself.

Line 161. That is, many a false aspect of delight (the lyre, or Greek art) is erected as a prison-grating against Eternity.

Line 166. The building of the Palace of Reason, the world of Science. Architecture is the most scientific of the arts, and well chosen as the manifestation of Urizen's creative power.

Line 168. *A line*: the horizon.

Line 173. *The twelve sons* are the signs of the Zodiac.

Line 175. Urizen's three daughters, of whom we shall hear much later (VI. 5 *seq.*; VII. 92 *seq.*; and IX. 100 *seq.*), are the rationalistic division of Man into the Head, Heart, and Loins.

Line 179. *The western wall*: the barrier against Freedom.

Line 181. Ahania, or Pleasure. As yet, Urizen allows her to dwell in his halls.

Line 194. *Brass*: the metal of false charity.

Line 204. Already Pleasure appears separated from Reason.

Lines 209-210. The mistake of all the Zoas with their Emanations. Cf. I. 229, which, as Blake (not Ellis) wrote it, reads:

> She drove the Females all away from Los,
> And Los drove all the males from her away.

Lines 229-230. The illustration for these lines occurs on 69*b* and in *Jerusalem*, 62. Vala can only behold the lowest parts of Passion, wandering in torture through non-expression.

Line 232. Nature is unable to recognize true Passion.

Line 236. The Poet and his Inspiration find joy in all these things.

Line 239. They recognize Reason as their enemy; and they think that if they can divide Pleasure from Reason, they can overcome him.

Line 247. Christ's Incarnation is the climax of the work of Creation.

Line 256. *The world of Tharmas* is always a watery one, since water is the symbol of matter.

Line 263. When human passion was debased, Jesus himself put on the body (robes of blood) to enact his own Passion.

Lines 266-267. The stars themselves, the karmic round, the rule of Reason, bind Man from falling farther. Plato's *Timaeus* (38) mentions these 'vital chains' of the stars; and Blake's 454th design to Young's *Night Thoughts* illustrates the word: 'That Pow'r / Whose Love lets down these silver Chains of Light.'

Line 290. Their attack begins by drawing the voice of Generation to the ear of Pleasure.

Lines 295-300. See the Commentary on v. 121-141.

Lines 302-382 symbolize the struggle of the Poet with his Inspiration, of which he is not yet master (l. 332). They also symbolize the conflicts of the young married couple.

Line 324. Inspiration often appears as Pleasure or the Generative Instinct.

Line 326. In the days of Innocence.

Lines 328-335. Spiritual Beauty vanishes when she sees the Poet mistaking Pleasure for herself.

Lines 340-341. The Poet dies in the absence of Inspiration, but is revived by her song.

Line 348. The *nine bright spheres* are the seven planets known in Blake's day, and the sun and moon. They symbolize the Spirit, the Passions, and the Intellect.

Line 367. The *weeping babe* is the Secret Child, Jesus.

Line 383. Thus the young poet tries to crush out the Generative Instinct, and even Pleasure.

Line 384. *A vortex* is a Thought, or a system of thought, which becomes a nucleus of action, and draws all other things into it. They must pass through it till the vortex has worked out its energy.

Line 386. *And thus she wails from the dark deep*: *i.e.* the despair of Enion, the Earth Mother. Ahania alone hears it (line 419).

Line 395. Her heavens are false charity, her earth warfare, her passions apparent death, and her inspiration disease.

Line 397. This splendid passage is in a fine Biblical style, and may have been suggested by the passage on Wisdom in *Job* xxviii., though in no sense is it an imitation. Cf. L. C. Saint-Martin's *Oeuvres Posthumes*, I. 213: 'Never persuade yourself that you possess wisdom in virtue of mere memory or mere mental culture. Wisdom is like a mother's love, which makes itself felt only after the labours and pains of childbirth.'

Lines 419-424. Pleasure hears the voice of the tortured Earth Mother; and at the knowledge of such misery, Pleasure can never rest again.

NIGHT THE THIRD

Line 11. Pleasure protests against Reason's gloomy consideration of the Future. And Reason does not escape from his troubles till he gives up worrying (IX. 181).

Line 14. *A Boy*: Orc, or Revolt.

Line 20. Nature shall be brought forth by Space.

Line 22. Passion shall be the seed of Time.

Line 32. Cf. I. 466. When Passion guided the Horses of Instruction, which should have been guided by Reason, an important part of the Fall took place.

Line 35. *The wine-press of Luvah*: War.

Line 50. Man now worships his Shadow, or cast-out desires. In this shadow appears Luvah, his Passions, who torments him, and then leaves him spiritually diseased. Cf. Shelley's *Laon and Cythna*, VIII. 6:

What then is God ? Some moonstruck sophist stood
Watching the shade from his own soul upthrown
Fill Heaven and darken Earth, and in such mood
The Form he saw and worshipped was his own,
His likeness in the world's vast mirror shown.

Omar's soul was also in this state when he found

Heaven but the vision of fulfilled desire
And Hell the shadow of a Soul on fire.

Line 54. *Wat'ry*, or materialistic.

Line 82. *Cover'd with boils*: the cursing of the fifth sense, Touch or Sex. Cf. the 6th Illustration to *Job*. Cf. also the *Vision of the Last Judgment*: 'That Living Creature on the left of the Throne [*i.e.* Luvah] gives to the Seven Angels the seven vials of the wrath of God, with which they, hovering over the deeps beneath, pour out upon the wicked their plagues.'

Line 97. *Like a serpent*: Nature has become materialized.

Lines 105-107. Man closes the gate of Freedom in the realm of the body.

Line 113. Reason, furious at the victory of Passion over Man, exerts his authority and casts Pleasure out from his palace.

Line 136. The offspring of Reason flee in horror, not towards the Rational and Spiritual realms, but towards the Carnal and Passionate.

Line 139. Materialism (the Sea) becomes triumphant.

Line 146. Pleasure falls into flesh (the caverns of the grave) and generation (the places of human seed).

Line 155. Tharmas (the body) is generated as the result.

Line 179. The Body, now materialized, hates Enion, the generative instinct.

Line 181. She, in her turn, plunges into materialism—the cold billows of Time and Space.

Line 182. *Entuthon Benython* is the valley of Abstract Philosophy.

Line 207. Only a voice now remains of the Generative Instinct.

Line 209. Pleasure follows the Generative Instinct to the verge of destruction (Non-Entity).

NIGHT THE FOURTH

Line 7. At a glimpse of Poetry, the Body recalls his love.

Line 24. Cf. the epigram :

> What is it men in women do require ?
> The lineaments of gratified desire.
> What is it women do in men require ?
> The lineaments of gratified desire.

Line 26. *My Son* : Los. Cf. I. 491 *seq.* and VII. 282 *seq.*

Line 29. The Body itself demands a higher world than its own world of Matter.

Line 35. Los here repeats the words of Canute. Blake was very fond of utilizing incidents from sacred and English history in this way.

Line 39. A reference to the First Commandment, to identify Urizen with Jehovah. The young Poet thinks himself above Good and Evil.

Line 43. The Poet thinks himself even greater than the Spirit from which he came.

Line 50. Inspiration loves the world of Matter, forgetting that though Urizen ordered it, it is properly the realm of Tharmas.

Line 56. Just when the Poet thinks himself supreme, the Body intervenes, and snatches away Inspiration.

Line 63. When Enitharmon, Los's Emanation, is taken from him, all that remains is the Spectre, the logical part of the Poet.

Line 70. The Body commands Poetic Logic to find Inspiration.

Line 76. *The Spectre of Urthona* is Spiritual Reason. See the Commentary on VII. 217.

Line 88. *Vortex*, see Commentary on II. 384.

Line 90. Los's Spectre recalls his old life under a new symbol.

Line 99. The division of Urthona into Los and Enitharmon.

Line 100. *And call'd it Love* : though it was only Pity (*Urizen*, V.).

Line 106. The Poet and Inspiration separated by Generation.

Line 113. See the Commentary on I. 249.

Line 114. A reminiscence from *Hamlet* (I. v. 15-16) :

> I could a tale unfold whose lightest word
> Would harrow up thy soul.

Line 119. *This son of Enion* : Los himself (see lines 105-106 *supra*).

Line 120. The Body tells the Poet that Reason must be limited, or the Generative Sense will never be happily united again to the Body.

Line 122. The Body gives Inspiration to the Poet.

Line 129. Now the Body thinks itself triumphant.

Line 130. The Passions have fallen to the World of Generation.

Line 131. The Body thinks that the Spirit is a product of physiology, since Los (the Poet) was apparently born of the Body.

Line 146. Yet the Body, though it thinks itself God, prefers being man ; the humility of Tharmas helps him to see clearly. For the Gods, as we shall learn, should never put themselves above Man. Cf. IX. 706.

Line 147. *Science* : to Blake, the state of knowing (scientia).

Line 148. The State of Innocence.

Line 150. The Poet must create a universe of imagination, or die in spirit.

Line 179. The Logic of the Poet, or Los as the Time-God, creates Time as a limit to Reason.

Line 187. The chain of Time hurts Inspiration as much as it hurts Reason.

Line 201. *The Prophet of Eternity* is Time, or Los.

Line 210. *A lake, bright shining and clear* : Udan-Adan, the Indefinite.

Line 253. Cf. *John* xi. 21 : ' Then said Martha unto Jesus, Lord, if thou hadst been here, my brother had not died.'

Line 254. Cf. *John* xi. 22 : ' But I know, that even now, whatsoever thou wilt ask of God, God will give it thee.'

Line 266. *A polypus* : human society.

Line 270. Cf. *John* xi. 23 : ' Jesus saith unto her, Thy brother shall rise again.'

Line 271. Jesus limits the extent of Opacity and Contraction : Opacity to the Divine Light, and Contraction from Infinity. Thus he mercifully limits the Fall. And thus Blake came to the paradox that Jesus is the creator, not only of Adam, but of Satan.

Line 275. *The starry Wheels* (Blake's later reading for ' the deeps beneath,' which Mr. Ellis preferred) are the system of Reason, astrological fatalism.

Line 276. *Eternal Death* : that is, this world, which is Death from Eternity.

Line 277. *The seventh Furnace* corresponds to the seventh Eye of God, who is Jesus. Cf. *Jerusalem*, 11 : 5-13 and 48 : 45. This is the Divine Mercy, which (in another symbol) fixes the limits of the Fall.

Line 287. One of the Eternal laws.

Line 293. Los's mad dance of triumph.

Page 27*b*. At the bottom of this page, written very illegibly in pencil, are the words : ' Christ's Crucifixion shall be made an Excuse for Executing Criminals.'

NIGHT THE FIFTH

Line 12. *Shrunk into fixed space* : that is, into temporal bodies.

Line 17. *But all the Furnaces were out* : all the poetic inspiration derived from the Body is gone, leaving the two hopelessly materialized.

Line 37. Orc, the Revolt against such terrible conditions, is born from the heart of Inspiration.

Line 42. Orc is but a lower form of Luvah (Passion) ; and all fear him.

Line 43. Reason tries to keep Revolt in ignorance. Passion, not recognizing their kinship, attacks Revolt with the weapons of Reason.

Line 46. The cry against Nature, who is blamed for the situation.

Line 59. *The Enormous Spirit* : Poetry (Los).

Line 63. Material Beauty (Vala) is to be born of Spiritual Beauty (Enitharmon).

Line 75. Poetry fears his own death in the outburst of Revolt, but Inspiration nurses her child.

Line 76. *Golgonooza* is Los's City of Art, built in opposition to Udan-Adan, the Indefinite, which corresponds to Adam, the Natural Man. The root of the name seems to be ' Golgotha '; since all Art is self-sacrifice.

Line 77. *Luban* (not *Laban*) is mentioned eight times by Blake : *The Four Zoas*, v. 77 ; vii. 430 ; and viii. 34 ; *Milton*, 23 : 49, 26 : 24, and 27 : 21, and *Jerusalem*, 13 : 24 and 13 : 25. It is the gate into Golgonooza, the City of Art, built by Los on the Limit of Translucence, where the Tree grows. Here Enitharmon's Looms of Cathedron are placed. The Spectres of the Dead wail outside, till they are snared by Theotormon (Desire) and Sotha; then they have mortal bodies woven for them on the looms, so that they may again take on the human form which they have lost. In *Jerusalem*, the position of Luban is moved from the circumference to the centre of Golgonooza.

Line 79. The story of the Jealousy of Los varies slightly here from the earlier versions. In the *Preludium* to *America*, Orc was fourteen when he finally broke loose from his bonds. In *The Four Zoas* the motivation is slightly clearer, for Orc has already reached the age of potency before he is bound.

Line 85. The Chain of Jealousy.

Line 113. *Storgeous* : an adjective derived by Blake from ' storge,' meaning Parental Love, used by Blake in preference to the more violent word, ' incestuous.'

Lines 121-141 might have been suggested by Thomas Vaughan's *Anthroposophia Theomagica*: 'Spirits (say the *Platonicks*) when they are *in sua patria*, are like the Inhabitants of green Fields, who live perpetually amongst *Flowers* in a *Spicie oderous Aire*: but here *below, in Sphaera Generationis*, they mourn because of darknesse, and solitude, like people lock'd up in a *Pest-house*. . . . It is miraculous to consider how she struggles with her chaines when Man is in Extremity, how she falsifies with Fortune; what pomp, what pleasure, what a Paradise doth she purpose to herself? she spans Kingdoms in a Thought, and injoyes all that inwardly, which she misseth outwardly. In her are patterns and Notions of all things in the world. If she but fancies herself in the midst of the Sea, presently she is there, and hears the rushing of the Billowes: she makes an Invisible voyage from one place to another, and presents to her self things absent, as if they were present. The dead live to her, there is no grave can hide them from her thoughts. Now she is here in dirt and mire, and in a trice above the Moon:

> Celsior exurgit pluviis, auditque ruentes
> Sub pedibus Nimbos, & caeca Tonitrua calcat.'

Line 129. Cf. the Printing House in the third *Memorable Fancy* (*Marriage of Heaven and Hell*, plate xv.); ' In the third chamber was an Eagle with wings and feathers of air: he caused the inside of the cave to be infinite. Around were numbers of Eagle-like men who built palaces in the immense cliffs.'

Line 147. *Entuthon Benython*: the Valley of Abstract Philosophy.

Line 156. Poetry and Inspiration, though the parents of Orc are unable by themselves to unchain him.

Line 164. Neither the force of pure Spirit nor the animal forces of Passion by themselves can unchain Revolt.

Line 173. *Herbs of the pit*. The Spirit revives them by natural objects. Cf. the rôle of the wild thyme in *Milton*, 35-54: 'The Wild Thyme is Los's Messenger to Eden.'

Line 175. Not to be understood literally.

Line 177. *Dranthon*. This is Blake's single use of this name. Its significance is only to be guessed by the context. Evidently it is the place of Enitharmon's repentance. At the sight of the agony of Revolt Bound, Inspiration feels again her heart open: she begins to view Nature again, and she realizes the miserable plight of Pleasure.

Line 179. Nature is conceived in Space. She is born VII. 315.

Line 200. *Nine virgins*: the sun, moon, and seven planets once composed the harmony of the spheres.

Line 209. Reason realizes that, because he did not give his services to the Lord of Mercy, his whole realm is darkened.

Line 219. *Light* is Urizen, and hence the first of created things. Jakob Böhme taught the same doctrine under the symbol of Sophia.

Line 224. Cf. *The Tyger* (*Songs of Experience*): 'When the stars threw down their spears.'

Line 226. Under the rule of Reason, the Passions and Nature faded.

Line 240. Passion (Luvah-Orc) may be born of Inspiration.

NIGHT THE SIXTH

' The journeys of Urizen in the sixth Night of *Vala*, his explorations through the dark world of Urthona, are strongly reminiscent of Satan's travels through outer Hell and Chaos. As Satan meets his family at the gates of Hell, Urizen comes unawares upon his three daughters. . . . Then the whole of Night VI. is hardly more than a splendid paraphrase of Milton's description of the voyage through Chaos ' (Saurat, pp. 17-18).

A less close parallel is that of Dante's meeting the three Furies at the gate of Dis. But Blake did not follow the ideas either of Milton or of Dante. Urizen's three daughters are Eleth, Ona, and Uvith : the division of Man into the Loins, Heart, and Head (for Urizen sees Man upside-down). Eleth, the Loins, pours out the water of Matter (10) from her iron pail (101) ; like the ' Shadowy Female ' (another symbol of the Loins), she is clad in the clouds of mystery. Ona, the Heart (whose name we have already met as *A Little Girl Lost* in the *Songs of Experience*, where she sacrificed herself for love), ' draws all into a fountain ' at her ' rock of attraction '—the function of the Passions. Uvith, the Head, divides the water of Matter into her four rivers of Paradise (18) ; she is Queen of the Waters, since with her hands she moulds it to its shape—the function of the Mind of Man. These daughters appear very seldom in Blake's writings : *The Book of Urizen*, 439-440 ; *The Four Zoas*, II. 175 ; VI. 5 *seq.* ; and VII. 95 *seq.*

Line 2. The river of Matter, of which Reason can never drink enough.

Line 6. The three-fold division prevents his sating himself ; for the proper balance of Head, Heart, and Loins always prevents a further Fall.

Line 9. *That Name* : Eleth, which might be an anagram of Lethe.

Line 22. At the sight of Reason, the three shrink to the limit of Death (rocky forms), while the Water of Matter, or (in this world) of Life, dries up immediately.

Line 38. A reminiscence from the curse of Tiriel.

Line 43. The three worship the Body as God.

Line 49. *Froze to solid were his waves* : Reason solidifies and kills the world of Matter.

Line 54. The Body cannot withstand Reason, but always fights it.

Lines 60-61. In the ' struggle for life,' Body still destroys Body, but its fecundity is insuperable. *Fishes* are the lowest form of animal : those who alone can live in the Sea of Time and Space.

Line 82. The poet observes the ' Struggle for Life ' with ' cruel delight.'

Lines 90-92. The fourfold division into Sun, Moon, Stars, and Earth.

Line 97. *The regions of the Grave* : this world.

Line 99. After this line Blake wrote :

> Not so clos'd up the Prince of Light now darkened wand'ring among
> For Urizen beheld the terrors of the Abyss wand'ring among
> The Ruin'd Spirits once his Children & the Children of Luvah.

But as these lines repeated in part lines 87-88, he deleted them ; then forgot to insert anything to explain his shift of subject from men in general to Urizen. The *He* in line 103 obviously refers to Urizen, however.

Line 103. *Women* : the war of the Female Will.

Line 113. *Dishumaniz'd Men* : men fallen into the state of beasts.

Line 121. To such men, the voice of the law of the Universe is thunder, comprehensible only as wrath.

Line 150. ' Truth has bounds, Error none.'

Line 160. Reason, entering the world of the Passions, dies, but is soon reborn.

Line 164. *His books* : his laws.

Line 168. *The cloths* represent the dogmas which conceal truths and often are mistaken for what they merely enfold.

Line 193. Reason looks for a place to stand, but he cannot transcend himself.

Line 201. *Vortex*. See Commentary on II. 384.

Line 210. A sudden reversion to the Personification of the Eighteenth Century.

Line 224. Reason, unable to find any bounds to Error, decides to be content for the while with organizing what he has explored.

Line 228. The attempt to reform the world by Religion.

Line 233. *The living wheels* of the constellations.

Line 241. *A dire web* : the spider-net of Religion. Cf. *The Book of Urizen*, 451 *seq.*

Line 250. *For every one open'd within into Eternity at will* : Heaven is within each of us ; but Religion hides it from us.

Line 261. *Four caverns*: the four Zoas, now prisoned in unexpansive rocky caves.

Line 263. Orc, who represents Luvah (the Passions), now is bound in the realm of Reason.

Line 264. The cave of Reason is in the realm of the Body.

Lines 266-268. Blake indicates here the misplacement of the Four Zoas. The Spirit still dwells in his proper place, the North, but is locked in solid blackness from the rest. Reason is moving towards his realm. The realm of the Passions is void, Orc (Luvah) being chained in Reason's realm. Meanwhile the Body dwells everywhere, seeking for the immortal form of the Earth Mother, but can find nothing but foul water (Matter).

Line 289. In reaching the 'state' of Revolt (Orc), Urizen has at last reached the realm of the Imagination, but he is soon opposed —for the first time with any success.

Line 295. Urizen can see only the lowest aspects of Spirit.

Lines 309-311. The Spirit's armies are the armies of Time (fifty-two, the number of the weeks); they are led by four of Reason's own sons, the elements (see *The Book of Urizen*, 430-437; these are not included in the twelve sons mentioned in *The Four Zoas*, II. 173 *seq.*). Urizen was bound to Time and Space in *Night the Fourth*; Time and Space now oppose his invasion of Eternity and Infinity.

Line 314. Reason cannot exist against the Spirit, but has to retire into the Web of Religion.

Line 322 reads: 'In their progressions & preparing Urizen's path before him.'

NIGHT THE SEVENTH

Line 1. The Spirit (now, of course, divided) cannot withstand Reason and his Religion.

Line 5. Reason confronts the forces of Revolution, which are still held in check. The flames are those of Youth, the hotter for restraint.

Lines 10-12. The scales of Justice consumed by the Oil of Mercy.

Line 14. The instruments of agriculture represent the tillage of mankind itself; in *Night the Ninth*, they are used by Urizen and his sons, but in *Milton* by Los.

Line 18. Reason does not quite dare to deal with Revolution.

Line 22. Inspiration, it will be remembered, was the mother of Revolution.

Line 26. Revolutionary ideas, nevertheless, fly over the world.

Line 29. *The Book of iron* is the Code of War.

Line 31. *A deadly Root*: Mystery, which is the Outward Church of Reason's Religion. The Spirit must always remain a Mystery to Reason.

Line 34. Like the deadly upas-tree.

Lines 37-39. Reason himself barely escapes from his Church; and he leaves the Code of War in its shade. Warfare remains the property of worldly Religion, and not of Reason.

Line 44. Reason cannot comprehend Revolution.

Lines 44-68. The fires of Genius always look to the Angels 'like torment and insanity.'

Line 74. *In torture.* Reason suffers as much as Genius (for Blake always considers the Genius as a Revolutionist).

Line 78. The Head, Heart, and Loins feed Orc with the bread of Materialism, which elsewhere (VIII. 73) is identified with the fruit of the Tree of Mystery.

Line 109. *The book of brass* is the code of false charity, which outwardly resembles true charity, as brass seems to be gold.

Line 113. To bring the desire of Inspiration within the Outward Church.

Line 116. That is, let the logical part of the Spirit overcome the Poet.

Lines 130-134. The embryo of the Shadowy Female (materialized Nature).

Line 145. Reason maddens Revolution.

Line 147. The light of Reason, when stolen by Revolution, becomes Wrath.

Orc remembers his former existence as Luvah. This is one of the many references to the time when Luvah guided the Chariot of Light. See the Commentary on I. 249.

Line 150. Revolution recognizes that the Paradise promised by Reason is non-existent.

Line 151. Reason now realizes that Revolution is Passion.

Line 152. Revolution, maddened by Reason, begins to assume the form of hypocrisy, the only way in which he can get free. Thus Reason turns even Revolution into evil.

Line 163. Revolution, now disguised, is the Serpent in the Tree of the Knowledge of Good and Evil. Reason, by directing Revolution, intends to make the highest part of Man fall, and so become subject to Reason.

Line 167. His thoughts flow downward, and break futilely over Mystery.

Line 184. Inspiration is lost to him.

Line 210. Suppressed spiritual desire appears in Religion.

Line 216. As a result, Plagues appear. Cf. the fifth *Proverb of Hell* : ' He who desires but acts not breeds Pestilence.'

Line 217. *The Spectre of Urthona*. Blake's psychology here becomes very subtle, and hardly capable of definite adumbration. Both the advantages and disadvantages of his symbolic system are now demonstrated. Urthona, it may be remembered, is the Spirit whose manifestation in this world is the double being of Los and Enitharmon (Poetry and Inspiration). At present Los and Enitharmon are divided, and appear as Spectre and Shadow, or Poetic Logic and Suppressed Spiritual Desire. But all these characters exist and melt into each other : for they are psychological states, which always are shifting. In the last analysis, we have Urthona (Spirit), the Spectre of Urthona (Spiritual Logic), Los (the Poet), the Spectre of Los (Poetic Logic), Enitharmon (Inspiration), and the Shadow of Enitharmon (Suppressed Inspiration). Yet all these are playing the part of two— Adam and Eve ; and it may be remembered that Adam and Eve were originally One. The Spectre of Urthona can sometimes be defined as Metaphysics ; and the Spectre of Los as Poetic Technique.

The advantages of Blake's symbolic method is that it allows him to deal with the overtones of psychology, which are ruled out from ordinary allegory. The disadvantage is purely a literary one : those readers who look for a consecutive story are baffled hopelessly by the instability even of the characters.

Line 219. Metaphysics seeks to possess the secret of Inspiration.

Line 230. *Sweet delusions of Vala* : The Poet promises his Inspiration delight in Natural Religion.

Line 239. Albion, seduced by Nature (in her unfallen form), caused her to bring forth Reason, ' the first born of generation.'

Line 246. Then Vala divided into a double form ; Passion and Nature.

Line 249. Man is cast out from Eternity, but finds solace and forgetfulness in the state of Innocence.

Line 255. Passion and Reason conspire against the State of Innocence. For the details of this conspiracy, see I. 459-490.

Line 259. Poetry and Inspiration are born when Reason and the Passions begin their warfare.

Line 263. That is, bound to flesh through the Passions, who smote the Central Humanity and then assumed his throne.

Line 265. *The fiery south* : when Revolution is enchained in the cave of Reason.

Line 268. The Church of Mystery is considered a refuge from the storms of this world, until Eternity is found again.

Line 279. *The manhood* : Albion.

Line 282. *A female bright* : Albion was divided when his Passions were separated from him.

Line 286. Then the Spirit fell into the realm of Generation.

Line 289. The Spirit, now divided as Los and Enitharmon, are brought forth by the Earth Mother.

Line 300. Nature must be submitted to the domination of the Genius (Revolution), and the body (Selfhood) must be destroyed, before Eternity can be regained.

Line 315. Nature in a material form ('the Shadowy Female') is brought forth by the Shadow (Suppressed Desire) of Enitharmon (Space), her father being the Spectre of Urthona (Metaphysics).

Line 321. The breaking of Enitharmon's heart symbolizes Pity, which must exist as long as Matter exists.

Line 325. *A Cloud she grew* : the Materializing spreads rapidly, till many of those in this world sink lower yet ('through the bottoms of their tombs'), without ideals ('female counterparts').

Line 329. *In dreams of Ulro* : in illusions of Matter.

Line 330. *Her* : the Shadowy Female, who is Vala in a fallen form. (See VIII. 252.)

Line 333. Los and Enitharmon become yet more entangled in Mystery.

Line 334. Reason enters Los's very heart.

Line 337. Enitharmon confesses her seduction ; Los readily forgives her.

Line 340. The Spectre speaks, trying to establish his Selfhood—promising that in his domination, salvation will be found.

Line 361. *This fourth Universe* : that of Spirit.

Line 370. Inspiration is not to be won by any power of Logic.

Line 371. Nevertheless, the union with the Spectre (the first act of being made whole) 'opens the Centre' into Eternity ; and with the inspiration derived from Divine Mercy, the City of Art is built.

Line 372. Thomas Vaughan's Commentary on the 'Centre' is of great interest. 'Again he that enters the centre shall know why all influx of fire descends—against the nature of fire—and comes from heaven downward. He shall know also why the same fire, having found a body, ascends again toward heaven and grows upward' (*Lumen de Lumine*).

Line 377. Cf. *Revelation* xxi. 1: 'And I saw a new heaven and a new earth : for the first heaven and the first earth were passed away ; and there was no more sea.'

Line 379. The worlds of the Head, Heart, and Loins are continuous from the world of the Spirit.

Line 380. *A limit twofold* : the limits of Opacity from the Divine Light and of Contraction from Infinity. See the Commentary on IV. 27.

Line 384. At last Blake reaches the story of the Fall, as told in *Genesis*. It is to be noticed that the eating of the Apple is here only the climax of Error, while in the Bible this sin is the first and only cause of the Fall. But Blake, in common with many others (notably the Gnostics and Jakob Böhme) read other meanings into the Biblical symbols : all the acts of Creation were divisions and separations from the original Unity, and therefore evil ; the sleep of Adam, during which Eve was divided from him, was obviously representative of a further Fall ; the coats of skin which they put on after the expulsion were surely meant to be the mortal flesh ; and so on. Creation, then, was not caused by the good God, but by an inferior deity, whom Blake calls Urizen, or Reason, or Law—whose character is entirely similar to the Jehovah of the Pentateuch.

It was an old doctrine of Blake's that the division of the entire universe into the black and white of Evil and Good was a false system preventing any real valuation of the universe, which is essentially holy. This was *The Voice of the Devil* who had spoken so valiantly in 1793. Therefore we must not be surprised to find him endorsing *Genesis* completely when he says that the final sin is the eating of the fruit of the Tree of the Knowledge of Good and Evil. Not of the Knowledge of Evil only, but of both ; for Good only exists by its antithesis to Evil. This Knowledge is Law, by which we know Sin and Justice. Many of the *Proverbs of Hell* are based on this doctrine, as for example : ‘ Prisons are built with stones of Law, brothels with bricks of Religion.’

I think that it must be fairly clear from line 163 that Orc was intended to be Enitharmon’s tempter, but that Blake forgot to introduce him here.   Revolt, hypocritically concealed in the Church, leads Inspiration to the doctrine of Virtues and Vices.

Line 385. A reference to *Romans* vii. 7-9 : ‘ . . . I had not known sin but by the law : for I had not known lust, except the law had said, Thou shalt not covet. But sin, taking occasion by the commandment, wrought in me all manner of concupiscence.   For without the law sin was dead.   For I was alive without the law once : but when the commandment came, sin revived, and I died.’

Line 386. *Without ransom.*   An attack on the doctrine of vicarious atonement. Cf. *Jerusalem*, 61 : 17-19 :

> . . . Doth Jehovah Forgive a Debt only on condition that it shall
> Be Payed ?   Doth he Forgive Pollution only on conditions of Purity ?
> That Debt is not Forgiven !   That Pollution is not Forgiven !

Line 388. *Despair* is the inevitable result of the judging by Good and Evil. Cf. the words of Bildad to Job (xxv. 4) : ‘ How then can man be justified with God ?   or how can he be clean that is born of a woman ? ’

Line 391. She believes that Los will surmount this test triumphantly ;   and hopes that in his victory he will demonstrate the reality of the superphysical.   But Good and Evil touch nowhere on the Eternities ;   Los eats of the fruit, and is himself given over to despair.

Line 397. *Six thousand years* : the time allotted to Creation, whose end Blake claimed was very near.   Then the material world is to be consumed, and the sexes united forever.

Line 398. The Logic of the Spirit is troubled at ‘ the spectres of the dead,’ which symbolize the triumph of Reason over men in this world.

Line 399. *Without a counterpart* : that is, without an Emanation, or Ideal.

Line 407. *For without a created body the Spectre is Eternal Death* : by binding Reason in a material body, he is limited.   Therefore, he is no longer *Eternal* Death.

Line 408. The limit of the Fall has now been reached ; the mazes of Error begin to disentangle themselves ; and out of their long sufferings in the State of Experience, Los and Enitharmon begin to see clearly.

Line 412. They turn their eyes inward at last ; and Enitharmon sees in her broken heart the Divine Vision of Mercy.   This is the conception of Jesus.

Line 413. *Luvah's robes of blood* : the flesh created by the Passions—the Incarnation.   This is not actually the Nativity ; which takes place, VIII. 256.   Jesus is still inward, though in the form of a man.

Line 423. Inspiration cannot yet believe the Divine Mercy ; convinced of her sins against the Christ, she is sure that he will destroy her as an example.

Line 430. *Luban* : see Commentary on v. 77.

Line 437. Los feels a desire to make ‘ embodied semblances ’ (works of art) by which the ‘ dead ’ may come to share their community of delight.

Line 440. *A world of sacrifice* : the world of art is essentially this, both spiritually and practically.

Line 441. Art is a comfort to the suppressed instincts.

Line 443. At last Poet and Inspiration are in accord.

Line 448. *Piteous forms* : inspirational ideas, which must be caught by the Poet, or else they vanish at once.

Line 450. *Moderate fury.*   The adjective recalls the innumerable warnings of the Alchemists that the Fire must not be too hot.

Line 452. In the work of Art is the justification of their lives, and even their life itself.

Line 457. Los draws the fire of his inspiration from the intellectual warfare of ideas, and from the enchained passions of humanity.

Line 461. Reason now is used as the firm foundation for Art.

Line 463. Heaven itself is the page on which he paints. Cf. the *Descriptive Catalogue* (xv.): ' Leave out this line and you leave out life itself ; all is chaos again, and the line of the Almighty must be drawn out upon it before man or beast can exist.'

Line 464. It may be recalled that Mrs. Blake helped her husband to colour some of his books.

Line 469. *The Spectres view'd the immortal works,* etc. Mankind, in contemplating Art, become what they behold, reposing with the Ideal.

Line 471. Los has discovered the true means of warfare, which overcomes the enemy by converting him, and which strives for life, not death. No longer does he try to destroy or subjugate ; he comprehends, idealizes, and synthesizes, until he feels only pity and love, rather than hatred. First Rintrah (Just Wrath) and Palamabron (Pity) are won to his side, and enter again the State of Innocence.

Line 478. The Poet refuses to suppress any human aspect.

Line 484. *Soft silken veils* : flesh.

Lines 486-495. This passage was inserted in the margin, and Blake forgot to make the transition clear. *His immortal spirit* refers to Los, not to Tharmas. Reason, also made Innocent (an infant), is conquered.

Line 489. *Thiriel* (so spelled by Blake, and not to be confused with Tiriel) is the element of air (the ' Memory of Nature '). See the Commentary on VII. 730-731.

Line 490. Reason becomes Honest Wrath. Air becomes Pity.

Line 495. This line ends one version of the *Seventh Night*. The triumph of Urizen immediately after this passage which describes his conversion was obviously not intended by Blake to be inserted here. It is marked ' Beginning of the Seventh Night.' Blake wrote two versions of the *Seventh Night*, and never combined them.

Line 496. Mystery as the Sphinx.

Line 497. *The Shadow* is Orc, at whose bondage Reason triumphs.

Line 499. *The Time of Prophecy.* Prophecy, as we have seen, is synonymous with Poetry. Reason now thinks that he has attained to the supreme gift, and is Lord of all.

Line 504. *A God and not a Man* : the continual mistake of the Zoas. Harmony is only obtained when they are ' servants to the infinite & Eternal of the Human form ' (IX. 372).

Lines 507-510. Child-labour and slavery as the results of commerce.

Line 512. *A temple in the image of the human heart* : the religion founded on sex : those who set up Chastity as the ultimate ideal are worshipping Sex.

Line 513. *Wondrous workmanship* : an image of the Phallos, as represented in the illustration.

Line 518. *Plays at disguises* : the worship of those who mistake their own sublimated sexual impulses for divinity, and thence create the laws of Moral Virtue.

Line 521. The Sun itself (symbol of the Spirit) is compelled to serve this religion.

Line 535. The resulting warfare.

Line 555. *My crystal form* : Enion.

Line 562. *The Demon* is Tharmas.

Line 572. *In thee* : in Los, whom she does not recognize. Repressive measures terrify Inspiration during the time of Revolution.

Line 583. Cf. *Isaiah* xxi. 11.

Line 589. *The broad oak* : these trees represent the growth of error.

Line 614. *The nameless shadowy vortex* is Fallen Nature, the material world. Blake retells the story of the *Preludium* to *America*. Revolution has at last reached manhood ; he breaks loose and bends the material world to his desire.

Line 637. *The northern drum* of the Spirit.

Line 655. But Revolution is far from good in its immediate effects. The Crucifixion is enacted : the Passions are nailed to the Tree of Generation.

Line 667. The Industrial Revolution.

Lines 685-686. ' The sound of harps which I hear before the sun's rising ' (letter to Hayley, Jan. 27, 1804).

Line 702. Revolution, entering the material world, loses his divinity. Nothing remains but the Serpent—such is the course of even the justest war.

Line 707. The destruction of Matter is the salvation of Nature.

Lines 714-715. The rage of the Body in warfare is destroying Reason altogether.

Line 716. The Body mistakes the world of Matter for the Earth Mother herself.

Lines 720 *seq.* The Body remembers its ancient Eden, which is to return (IX. 535 *seq.*).

Lines 730-731. *The air*, the greatest of the elements, here represents the Memory of Nature, where the entire Past, Present, and Future are completely recorded. This theory figures in most of the magical authors. One legend tells that all lost things are to be found on the other side of the moon ; here Astolpho found the lost wits of Orlando. Blake seems to have combined this theory with his common symbol of the Moon, which is Beulah, the realm of Love. For the theory of the air, see Agrippa's *Occult Philosophy*, I. vi. : ' It remains that I speak of Aire. This is a vitall spirit, passing through all Beings, giving life, and subsistence to all things, binding, moving, and filling all things. Hence it is that the Hebrew Doctors reckon it not amongst the Elements, but count it as a *Medium* or glew, joyning things together, and as the resounding spirit of the worlds instrument. It immediately receives into it self the influencies of all Celestiall bodies, and then communicates them to the other Element ; as also to all mixt bodies : Also it receives into it self, as if it were a divine Looking-glass, the species of all things, as well naturall, as artificiall, as also of all manner of speeches, and retaines them.' For such reasons, Paracelsus called Air 'the cloister of the Invisible Fates.' Cf. also Thomas Vaughan's *Anthroposophia Theomagica* : ' The thing to be now spoken of, is Air. This is no Element, but a Certain miraculous *Hermaphrodit*, the *Caement* of two *worlds*, and a Medley of Extremes. It is natures Common Place, her Index, where you may finde all that ever she did, or intends to do. This is the worlds *Panegrick* : The Excursions of both Globes meet here, and I may call it the Rendezvouz. In this are innumerable Magicall Forms of Men and Beasts, Fish and Fowls, Trees, Herbs, and all Creeping Things. This is *Mare Rerum invisibilium*, for all the *Conceptions in sinu superioris Naturae* wrap themselves in this *Tiffany*, before they imbark in the shell. It retaines the species of all Things whatsoever, and is the Immediate Receptacle of Spirits after Dissolution, whence they passe to a *Superior Limbus*. I should amaze the Reader if I did relate the severall offices of this *Body*, but it is the *Magicians Backdoor*, and none but Friends come in at it.' It is extremely interesting to learn that William James, in his endeavour to account for Mrs. Piper's phenomena, came to the theory of a Cosmic Memory, the reservoir in which records of all things are stored. See also the Commentary on *Jerusalem*, 16 : 61-69.

Line 736. Inspiration and Pleasure, combined with Generation, hid the Passions in the form of Revolution.

Line 766. *The living soul* : ' Man looks out in tree & herb & fish & bird & beast ' (IX. 554).

Line 777. Fallen Nature clings to Beulah as the social system clings to the Decalogue.

Line 781. A reference to the raising of Lazarus, *John* xi. 23.

Line 789. Those who fall below the state of man become Satans, or Errors. Possibly, however, Blake meant that the wisdom of the Past becomes the error of the Present.

NIGHT THE EIGHTH

Line 2. The Eternals, when in harmony, always take the form of One Man, Jesus. *Gilead* is the Hill of Witness. *Hermon* (' lofty ') marks the northern (spiritual) limit of the Promised Land.

Line 7. Two winged immortal shapes, the guardians of the Passions and of the

Body, representatives of Beulah. See the illustration to *Jerusalem*, 14. They cannot represent the Cherubim of the Ark, since the latter are symbolic of Reason.

Line 14. *Pointed at the top* : *i.e.* Gothic.

Lines 18-19. Sneezing and a nose-bleed are traditional signs of resuscitation. Blakes changes the latter into the bitterest kind of tear.

Lines 20-22 take the story back to the Conception of Jesus in lines 408-421 of the previous *Night*.

Line 22. *Zion*, the heart of Jerusalem.

Line 25. *Ulro's Night* : the world of Matter.

Line 29. Inspiration flows freely to the Poet.

Line 30. Those who have materialized and are worshippers of Reason are the subjects for Art (Golgonooza) when Inspiration opens the way through Pity.

Line 35. Mortal bodies are woven by Inspiration upon her looms ; so that by giving human, though temporary, forms to the wandering ghosts, she can raise them from the despair of a lower existence.

Line 39. Jesus (divine love) enters Art.

Lines 55-56. Each ghost is given a body best fitted to his capacity.

Lines 58-61. Again we reach a confusion of symbolic figures, blurred for the purpose of being more subtly definite. Jesus (Love), Luvah (the Passions), and Orc (Revolution) are at the same time three aspects of the same Eternal State, and coexist in time. Reason is puzzled to see a Divine aspect of the Passions, though Revolution (War) is obviously a bad aspect ; he is amazed to learn that Peace and War, however different, are both forms of Passion.

Line 74. *Uvith*, the third daughter of Urizen, representing the Intellect divided from the other two parts of Man. She works out the Knowledge of Good and Evil in her ' kneading-trough,' the skull ; while Fallen Nature feeds it to Revolution.

Lines 90 *seq.* Blake is certainly more successful than Milton in describing artillery.

Line 94. *The Synagogue of Satan* is the school of the Ten Commandments. Henry More, in his *Divine Dialogues*, II. 182 (London, 1668), also contrasted the ' Synagogue of Satan ' with the Temple of God.

Line 100. *A shadowy hermaphrodite* : the opposite of the Eternal Man. The Hermaphrodite preserves both sexes, a combination of unsynthesized contradictions ; Eternal Man blends the sexes till both disappear in a single harmony. Reason never intends a contradiction, which is doubt ; yet always produces it.

Line 103. *Hiding the Male* : the Female Will being predominate. According to *Milton*, 37 : 38-40, this is the religion whose innermost motive is warfare.

Line 107. *The gates of death.* Urizen's armies have fallen so far that they are completely bestialized. Only by passing through rebirth (the gates of death) can they rise into some semblance of humanity.

Line 136. Reason will sacrifice anything whatsoever to itself.

Line 146. *The King of Light* : Urizen.

Line 150. *The murderer* : Urizen.

Line 165. The source of every joy. Cf. : ' Energy is Eternal Delight ' (*The Voice of the Devil*).

Line 166. *Allegoric.* This word is practically always used by Blake with a bad meaning to represent the mistaking of a symbol for the reality behind it.

Line 168. Reason at last sees that Matter (the Shadowy Female) is the very basis of his whole system.

Line 173. As a consequence there follows the Fall of Outward Religion ; all the evil forces feed on its scattered doctrines ; and Reason himself is snared in it at last.

Line 185. *A Universal Female form* : Jerusalem, or Liberty, the Emanation (Inspiration) of all on earth.

Line 188. The Conception of Jesus. The Forgiveness of Sins is to be born of Freedom.

Line 197. *Looms* : where bodies are woven. *Forges* : where poetry is written —where truths are beaten into permanent forms.

Line 198. *Tirzah and Rahab.* Tirzah is the prude, Rahab is the harlot. One represents the repressed life, the other the abandoned life. As ' Tirzah ' was the name of the central city in Samaria, we may identify Blake's character with the Woman of Samaria. Rahab is, of course, the harlot who saved Joshua's spies in Jericho (*Joshua* ii.), whom Blake often identified with Mystery in *Revelation*. These two also help weave the body ; for together they represent all the Daughters of Albion (VIII. 322). The *mills* represent the processes of logic. *Beelzeboul* is Beelzebub.

Line 202. The Poetic Genius (the Human Imagination) creates all the glories of the visible universe and gives the wandering Spectres bodies, that through them they may rise again.

Line 212. *The Arnon* is the southern boundary of Israel, separating it from Moab and flowing into the Dead Sea. Thus the Spectres cross from the state of pure Reason into the Holy Land of the Human Form.

Line 214. *The dread Sleep* of Ulro : the illusion of Matter.

Line 214. *Og and Sihon* were two giant kings who opposed the Israelites in their way to Canaan, and who were utterly destroyed. Og ruled Bashan, in the North ; Sihon ruled the Amorites in the South.

Line 215. The Spirit and the Reason under Satan combine in building the Mills of Logic to strip off the flesh, which is the means of salvation of these spirits ; and then the Spectres are exposed, unredeemed, to the divine vengeance, which is that of Urizen.

Line 217. Sex, in its two aspects of Restriction and Licence, combine in torturing the Spectres. It provides Veils of hypocrisy and ignorance—a contrast to the frank veil of the flesh.

Lines 221-226. The Void of the Indefinite, in the realm of Abstract Philosophy, contains the Satanic Mills. The Indefinite and the Abstract feed the Outward Church, and are formed of the agonies of the victims of the Laws of Reason.

Line 230. The Harlot-Church, Mystery, is always the enemy of the Christ ; but her efforts to destroy him only destroy Mysteries which are her own work.

Line 233. Jesus dies endlessly in the flesh.

Line 236. *The ends of Beulah* : Beulah will vanish when all is perfect in Eternity. ' It is curious to notice that the more inspired his utterance the more passionately and dogmatically Christian even this hater of Churches becomes. . . . This is the doctrine of the Incarnation in a nutshell : here St. Thomas himself would find little to correct ' (E. Underhill : *Mysticism*, pp. 127-128).

Line 248. Satan (Error of Selfhood) is born from the Hermaphrodite of Doubt and Self-Contradiction.

Line 256. The Nativity.

Line 259. The birth of Jesus is both mystical and literal : in the symbols preserved by the Church (' Mystery's woven mantle ') and in the flesh (' the robes of Luvah ').

Line 263. The fragment which appears on page 73*a* of the manuscript is an early version of this passage. In this particular line, Blake originally had Jesus confronting Urizen, who was changed to Satan.

Line 264. Jesus invades his enemy's territory, facing him even in Abstract Philosophy, on the heights of Amalek, the extreme South (Reason) of the Holy Land.

Line 267. Jesus is to be condemned by the Synagogue of the Ten Commandments.

Line 268. He is charged with murder and robbery. Cf. *The Everlasting Gospel*, v. 39-40 and 43-44.

Line 269. *Number'd among the transgressors.* So Isaiah prophesied (liii. 12) ; see also *Mark* xv. 28 and *Luke* xxii. 37.

Line 271. The twelve are the Sons of Albion, who in *Jerusalem* are named after those involved in Blake's own trial. They symbolize the cruelty of man to man.

Line 275. *Vala.* In the court there appears against Jesus ' Mystery, Babylon the Great, the Mother of Harlots and Abominations of the Earth ' (*Revelation* xvii.). She is the goddess of Nature, the Church which is Materialism, the Seductress of the whole world.

Line 280. In the state of Error, the beauty of Nature is the highest possible achievement, and may even destroy Error. Many who are otherwise complete Materialists have experienced something of the mystical union through Nature.

Line 282. The Law creates Nature from the Knowledge of Good and Evil.

Line 287. The real form of Nature is hidden within Illusion : ' an outside shadowy Surface superadded to the real Surface ' (*Jerusalem*, 83 : 47), which is to be rent by the Divine Imagination.

Line 290. These daughters of the Holy Land become in *Jerusalem*, 67, quite simply the Daughters of Albion. They represent Female Cruelty in sex. They appear in the double form of Rahab and Tirzah (Licence and Repression) ; but eventually they appear as Rahab only, because Repression is merely the reverse aspect of Licence.

Line 294. Because Man does not live up to the Female Ideal of Repression, the Daughters bind his love down, turning what should have been Love into Lust.

Lines 295-299. They shut the senses from their normal perception of the Eternal.

Line 300. *Seven furnaces* : the Seven Eyes of God, now become places of torture.

Lines 304-305. *Manasseh* and *Ephraim* were the two sons of Joseph, from whom great races were descended. *Kanah* is in the north (spiritual region), the boundary brook between Manasseh and Ephraim.

Lines 306-312. Mahlah, Noah, Hoglah, Milcah, and Tirzah were the five daughters of Zelophehad, and represent the five senses, and particularly Man fallen into a purely sensorial existence. Zelophehad had no sons (*Numbers* xxvi. 33), and his five daughters were the cause of Moses' law that daughters should inherit when there were no sons (*Numbers* xxvii. 8). Mahlah, the name of the first daughter, means ' disease.' *Ebal* was famous for the curses delivered from it ; *Lebanon* for its forests (errors) ; and *Sinai* for its Laws.

Line 314. *Shechem* : the murdered lover of Dinah (*Genesis* xxxiv.).

Line 317. Jesus descends into the lowest passions to redeem them.

Line 320. The Crucifixion of Love which is Forgiveness on the Tree (Good and Evil) of Mystery (Materialism).

Line 322. The Daughters sometimes appear as twelve (the Daughters of Albion) ; sometimes as five (the senses), and sometimes as one (Rahab).

Line 325. Liberty (or Spiritual Beauty), seeing the Divine in Man killed by Materialism, flees, appealing at once in her despair both to Poetry and to Reason for pity.

Line 329. She worships Death, where she thinks the Divine is to be found.

Line 332. Here Los plays the part of Joseph of Arimathea. He preserves the form of the Divine in the hour of darkness. Later, according to a legend accepted by Blake, Joseph of Arimathea was to bring Christianity to England.

Line 333. Cf. *Matthew* xxvii. 60 : ' And laid it in his own new tomb. . . .' Poetry, when once ' despairing of the Life Eternal,' built a philosophy for himself by which he could exist in this world. Now, knowing that the Divine is slain by men, he conceals in his philosophy the last vestiges of the Divine. This is, in a way, Blake's own apologia for his symbolic system.

Lines 336-338. The revealed heart of Jesus is shown to contain all his Enemies, even in their worst forms.

Line 341. After the Divine Death, the Poet cannot hate, but must pity, those who knew not what they did.

Line 345. *Shadowy prophet* : ' shadowy,' because he is but the reflection of the Spirit ; ' prophet,' because he is a poet, whose works are all prophecies of Eternity.

Line 346. Cf. ' As all men are alike, tho infinitely various ; so all Religions : and as all similars have one source the True Man is the source, he being the Poetic Genius ' (*All Religions are One*, 7).

Line 349. Even the Spirit may sin against Jesus by reason of Pride. Blake suggests here the identity of Los with Lucifer.

Lines 351-361. This catalogue is intended to cover all human types and their history, culminating in the perfection of the sexes as embodied by Milton and Mary. The catalogue starts in Eternity and ends on earth. It has little value in calculating a theogony, since Blake invariably left all such ' allegorical ' matters either vague or contradictory, in fear that they should be taken literally. For example, Orc, the most famous of the sons of Los, is omitted, and not by accident. (See the Commentary to *Europe*, line 43.) Orc, after all, is a form of Luvah, not of Urthona. Any parents or offspring must be accepted for the moment only : as we have said before, psychological states may be born of a variety of conditions ; therefore Blake often represents them as being born in many various ways. They are not subject to the Laws of Urizen—One Cause, One Effect.

Though many of the names in this catalogue are never used again throughout all Blake's works, we can sketch the broad outlines of their development.

The first four sons of Los—Rintrah, Palamabron, Theotormon, and Bromion—should be already familiar to the reader. They were never generated (*Jerusalem*, 71 : 50) ; they never fled during the Fall, but remained with their father Los to guard the wall of Freedom (*Jerusalem*, 72 : 10-13). Each is a dim reflection of a Zoa : Rintrah (Wrath) of Urthona ; Palamabron (Pity) of Tharmas ; Theotormon (Desire) of Luvah ; and Bromion (Reason) of Urizen. Their four Emanations are the first four Daughters, who will be described later.

After these first four follow ten names of a lower order, only three of whom are mentioned elsewhere. They are all aspects of the creative faculty. Antamon, the oldest, moulds and circumscribes the human body (*Milton*, 27 : 13-18) ; he is often attracted by the false doctrines of sex (*Europe*, 180) ; and for this reason wrote the Koran (*Africa*, 29). Ananton, the second of the ten, is not mentioned elsewhere. Ozoth guards the delights of Vision, hiding them from the worldly rich, but revealing them to the poor (*Milton*, 27 : 29-39). Ohana, the fourth of the ten, again is not mentioned elsewhere. Sotha is a singer (*Europe*, 187) who helps Theotormon to snare the wandering Spectres (*Milton*, 27 : 21), and who gave the northern races their code of war (*Africa*, 30). The rest of the ten : Mydon, Ellayol, Natho, Gon, and Hurhath, are nothing but names to us.

Next follows a series of five names representing the fallen states, which terminate in the appearance of Man. They are Satan (the error of Selfhood) ; Har (Poetry fallen from its state of Innocence) ; Ochim, of whom nothing more is known ; Ijim, who represents the mad brutality of the Common People (in *Tiriel*) ; and Adam (Man completely in the realm of Nature). These represent the limit of the Fall : Satan being the limit of Opacity, Adam the limit of Contraction.

The next twelve names, from Reuben to Benjamin, are the names of the twelve sons of Jacob, in the order of their birth. They represent the spread of mankind into various races ; for from them the tribes of Israel were descended.

The rest of the names are completely modern. David and Solomon represent the great monarchs ; Paul, Constantine, Charlemaine, and Luther represent the four great Churches (*Milton*, 23 : 31-32) ; while Milton ends the list as the great poet.

The list of the Daughters is rather less complicated and more obscure. The first four are the Emanations of the first four sons. They are Ocalythron, who seems to represent Female Jealousy ; Elynittria, the ideal wife ; Oothoon, the Magdalen ; and Leutha, the puritanic doctrine of sex. Till now Leutha had been considered the Emanation of Antamon, but with his relegation to a lower order, she became the Emanation of Bromion. She shares with Elynittria the attributes of Diana, dividing between them the admirable and the cruel aspects of that goddess.

Only two of the next four are mentioned elsewhere, but from the attributes ascribed to those we know, we may assume that they represent the four elements, as their names indeed suggest.   Elythiria represents Air, which was the first element (*Urizen*, 430-432) ;   Enanto the Earth ;   Manatha Varcyon the element of Fire (*Europe*, 166-168) ;   and Ethinthus the element of Water (*Europe*, 161).

The remaining ten are a strange medley.   Moab and Midian are to be explained by *Numbers* xxv., where the Moabite women seduced many Israelites to the worship of Baal-peor ; where Zimri the Midianitish woman introduced a great plague among them.   Adah was one of Lamech's wives, the mother of Jabal and Jubal (*Genesis* iv. 19) ; from her sons' attributes of the pastoral life and music, she probably represents the State of Innocence.   (Zillah, Lamech's other wife, was omitted because, according to Swedenborg, *A.C.* 333, she represented only the external church, Adah being the internal.)   Tullah and Caina are names unknown to me ; though perhaps the latter represented to Blake the nameless wife of Cain.   Naamah was the sister of Tubal Cain (*Genesis* iv. 22) ; and from her brother's attributes of the blacksmith, she may represent the State of Experience (for Tubal Cain is often unfairly blamed as being the first maker of weapons), or she may instead represent the spiritual life, since Urthona is a blacksmith.   Tamar (*Genesis* xxxviii. 6) certainly represents the evils of a disappointed maternal instinct, since after the sin of Onan she acted as a harlot.   The list culminates in three familiar names : Rahab, the harlot ; Tirzah, the repressed woman ; and Mary, who was neither, but lived her life instinctively and innocently (*Jerusalem*, 61).   For a revised list, see *Jerusalem*, 62 : 8-12.

Lines 362-366, 382-389.   These lines contain, much compressed, and used in a highly symbolic manner, a brief reference to Blake's quarrel with Hayley, which recurs, much expanded, in the first pages of *Milton*.   Therefore these lines date this portion of *The Four Zoas*, 1803.   It is, of course, just possible that Blake wrote these lines before the quarrel, foreseeing what might happen in just such a situation ; and rewrote them later in the *Milton* to fit the situation when it had arisen.   We can be sure that here Blake did not intend them to be connected with his own life, but to be interpreted purely as a bit of the history of Eternity.   Nevertheless, the personal element intrudes.   Satan is Hayley ; Palamabron is Blake.

The Error of Selfhood condemns Pity and upsets his poetical work (the instruments of ploughing are used in *Milton* as symbols of the work of Poetry).   Pity, joined with Wrath, cuts Error from the world of Art.   However, Error is not deserted by Inspiration ; she pities him and protects him in the days of Revolution.   Then Error, aided by the arts of Reason, seduces all mankind (the twelve sons of Jacob) from the Inspirational Life, and the Nations are divided.

Line 374.   This is Blake's condemnation of the psychology of association.   Cf. *Jerusalem*, 73 : 42-43.

Line 275.   Error can never be redeemed, because in Eternity it must cease to exist.   Cf. ix. 157.

Lines 376-380.   When the Passions, as Revolution, descended into material warfare, they became Error.   Inspiration preserved Revolution in this form because Inspiration had been his mother.

Lines 380-387.   Error, aided by Reason, and profiting by the mistake of Revolution, would have dominated the world, but that Pity, aided by Wrath, called him to a valuation.   Wrath, being foreign to Error, triumphs.

Lines 388-391.   Wrath and Pity cut off and cast out the world of Error from the city of Art : Satan and his companions fall away, and now exist as this Earth. They did not fall into complete annihilation, however, because Divine Liberty saves them with mantles of flesh from falling farther.

Lines 392-400.   Here Blake enumerates the Seven Eyes of God, who watch over all those in this world.   They represent the necessary course of Experience, and were divinely instituted so that the revolving of their cycle would inevitably bring Man back to the Saviour.   The *Illustrations to Job* are based on this cycle.

The first of the Seven is Pride in the Selfhood, which leads Man to become successively the Executioner, Judge, and Accuser of all those who do not follow his holy example. After these four States, Man falls into the State of Horror at the results of his acts; then follows the State in which he discovers the nature of his Evil. Evil recognized is cast out, and so Man reaches the Seventh State, in which the Truth is revealed.

Blake chose the names for these seven States from the Bible, the last five being names given God in various places. (Elohim, Shaddai, and Pahad do not appear in the English versions, being translated as ' the Lord,' ' God,' etc.) It may seem strange that the first two names, those of Lucifer and Molech, should appear as names of Eyes of God, and Lucifer was certainly never worshipped by the orthodox. Molech, however, was actually set up as a god by Solomon (1 *Kings* xi. 7), and the Israelites often followed his example (*Jeremiah* xxxii. 35, etc.).

The first of the Seven is Lucifer (*Isaiah* xiv. 12) who, according to tradition, was the first to fall from Eternity. He represents Pride—the Selfhood which unconsciously usurps the central power. He proved an inadequate god, as his pride forbids him to sacrifice his Selfhood, and so overcome error.

The second is Molech, the Executioner, to whom Men sacrifice others, even their own children, but never their Selfhoods. He proves inadequate because he is too impatient with humanity.

The third is Elohim (a plural name, meaning ' Judges '). After Execution follows Judgment; but even this is insufficient to right the world. Once we begin judging mankind, the task is endless. The Elohim grow weary and faint.

The fourth is Shaddai (' all-powerful '), the Accuser. But he is angry, and hence proves no god for Humanity. (In reality, Shaddai seems to have been a god of fertility (*Genesis* xxviii. 3; xxxv. 17; xlviii. 4; xlix.; etc.), who was worshipped by the patriarchs before Moses, according to *Exodus* vi 3.)

The fifth is Pahad (or rather, Pakhad), the god ruling by Terror (*Isaiah* ii. 10, 19, 21, etc.). Terror is the natural consequence of inverted ' justice,' and Pahad proves inadequate because terror is blind.

The sixth is Jehovah, whom Blake identified with Urizen, the god of Law and Reason. To escape from Pahad, Man naturally applies his reason to the problem of the laws which bring about such terrifying results. But Law, sooner or later, gets corrupted. Jehovah proves insufficient because he becomes leprous.

The last, of course, is Jesus, who breaks the whole cycle of Cause and Effect by forgiving sins, that they may have no more consequences, and by sacrificing, even to false ideals, the Selfhood which leads one into the State of Lucifer.

It is just possible that Blake intended the Seven Eyes of God to correspond to the Seven Deadly Sins : a theory which is suggested by his use of the Four Cardinal Virtues in *Milton*, 28 : 49 as the pillars of Satan's Throne. But the lists of Eyes and Sins do not correspond very closely; while the correspondence of four of them (Lust, Envy, Covet, and Wrath) to the four Zoas, in the opening lines of the *Book of Los*, gives us a much more useful classification.

In *Milton* and *Jerusalem*, a shadowy Eighth Eye is added : the essence of the Man himself; which cannot be found easily.

This doctrine of Blake's is developed from an astrological theory in Paracelsus's *Interpretation of the Stars*. (In the quotation, ' astrologer ' means ' a guiding star.') ' There are four astrologers of the elements, two of the stars of men and animals respectively, which make six; and then one of the superior star; which is the seventh. Besides these there remains yet another astrology born of the imagination in man, superior to all the rest, and standing eighth in order.'

How Blake interpreted this is clear : Lucifer is a fallen form of Urthona; Molech of Tharmas; Elohim of Urizen; Shaddai of Luvah; Pahad of the animals; Jehovah of men; while Jesus is the ' superior star '; and the ' shadowy Eighth ' is Man himself.

Line 401. Los tells all this to the Church of Moral Virtue that it may be converted (destroyed to another form) and allow Freedom; but the Church will not hear.

Lines 404-406. Moral Virtue, rejected by the Man of Vision, appeals to Reason.

Line 410. Reason welcomes Moral Virtue, and at once feels a blow struck at his life.

Line 415. Natural Religion. Reason begins to work upon Fallen Nature.

Lines 416-424. The fall of Urizen below human form is due to the old law : ' He became what he beheld.' Observing the world of matter, he becomes a brute. This transformation may have been suggested by *Paradise Lost*, x. 511-515.

Lines 438-447. Creation of the animals. This was the time when the Tyger was created.

Line 452. Reason discovers that by himself he had not been able to keep to a human form ; the Divine Imagination always had given him unsuspected strength.

Line 454. Revolution rises against the horrible creation.

Line 457. To combat Revolution, Reason ' forgets his wisdom ' by accepting stereotyped dogmas.

Lines 460-463. Both Body and Spirit are afflicted : the Body rages fruitlessly, while the Spirit begins to organize society (' a vast fibrous form '—the Polypus).

Lines 464-469. The Poet and his Inspiration begin to take on material forms.

Lines 470-473. Body and Spirit combine forces in the Poet, because of Inspiration, Fallen Nature, Revolution, and Reason.

Line 474. *The nameless Shadow*: Fallen Nature (' the nameless Shadowy Female ').

Line 475. *Made permanent*. ' Giving a body to Falshood.'

Lines 478-485. The Body flees from itself, trying to escape the voice of outcast Pleasure, which is now Sin, though she speaks of Heaven itself. She looks to Reason for help.

Line 496. *The murder'd one* : Albion.

Lines 500-513. A symbolic picture of fallen Man. He is blind to the glories of the Spirit, the Passions, and Reason (500-501) ; he is involved in War (502-503) ; by his corrupted imagination he creates constantly the lower forms of life (503-506) : he is almost dead in the Sea of Time and Space (506-509).

Line 514. *The strong Eagle* : the flights of Genius.

Line 520. *The Lion* : guardian of the Lamb.

Line 522. *The pale Horse* : Instruction.

Line 536. Pleasure laments the fall of Man : the Earth Mother replies that Man *is* the Universe.

Lines 529-530. This was the attitude of Thel.

Line 534. A reference to the parable of the Wise and Foolish Virgins (*Matthew* xxv. 6) : ' And at midnight there was a cry made, Behold, the Bridegroom cometh : go ye out to meet him.'

Line 539. The Generative Instinct finds her hope in her own disappearance, which will take place in Eternity.

Line 543. Cf. *Matthew* xxii. 30 : ' For in the resurrection they neither marry, nor are given in marriage, but are as the angels of God in heaven.'

Line 547. *Invisible*. The increase of spiritual knowledge draws the saint from the view of his fellow-men. The material body will gradually be put off for the spiritual body.

Line 548. *The caverns of the grave* are this material world.

Line 554. *So Man looks out*. This splendid passage means more than that all Creation groans to be delivered ; and more than that Man sees all things in terms of himself. It means that the exterior world *is* Man, separated from him by the Division which was the Fall. Cf. *Jerusalem*, 27 : ' Man anciently contain'd in his mighty limbs all things in Heaven & Earth.' Blake refers this to an ancient tradition of the Jews ; but it is also to be found in Jakob Böhme. From Man, not from God, nor yet *ex nihilo*, was the Universe formed. Cf. also Shelley's *Queen Mab*, II. 211-212 : ' There 's not one atom of yon earth But once was living man,' etc.

Line 557. Even now, by power of his Imagination, he moves at will through the Universe. Cf. the Commentary on v. 121-141.

Lines 561-562. Here Blake denies the principle of the famous Smaragdine Table, the basis of all occultism, according to which the superiors govern the inferiors. See also the Commentary on *Jerusalem*, 90 : 34.

Line 567. *Forget & return.* When Man has escaped from his body, he may forget his former woes, and allow himself to be drawn again into the material world. The purposelessness of Reincarnation is clearly indicated.

Lines 578-580. A return to lines 332-334. This indicates the chaotic state in which this night was left.

Line 581. *Two thousand years*: the time, speaking broadly, between the death of Jesus and the coming of Blake's doctrines.

Night the Ninth, being the Last Judgment

Lines 1-3. The Poet and Inspiration build the city of Freedom over the few doctrines which remain to them after the crucifixion of Love by the world. These doctrines appear to them to be really dead.

Line 5. The death to this world.

Line 8. Los appears for the moment as the Angel of Death destroying the universe. (Cf. Blake's design for the *Night Thoughts.*) In his agony he tears down the visible symbols of the Spirit and the Passions, not knowing that by destroying the symbols he is opening the way to their eternal reality. But Jesus is the real Angel of Death.

Line 10. *The fires of Eternity* are those which were predestined to destroy the material universe. Cf. *The Marriage of Heaven and Hell* (plate XIV.) : ' The ancient tradition that the world will be consumed in fire at the end of six thousand years is true, as I have heard from Hell ' ; also see the Commentary for the prophecies.

Line 14. Cf. *Revelation* vi. 14 : ' And the heaven departed as a scroll when it is rolled together ; and every mountain and island were moved out of their places.'

Line 19. The lines dealing with the retaliation of the oppressed upon their oppressors were inserted later, to explain *Revelation* vi. 9-10 : ' And when he had opened the fifth seal, I saw under the altar the souls of them that were slain for the word of God, and for the testimony which they held : And they cried with a loud voice, saying, How long, O Lord, holy and true, dost thou not judge and avenge our blood on them that dwell on the earth ? ' Blake interprets this lust for revenge as almost entirely automatic and inevitable : the breaking out of the passions temporarily suppressed by death. The ghost of the gentle Abel cried for blood with precisely the same reaction.

Lines 24-31. At this terrible moment, only the logical parts of the very highest remain ; they cling together in fear.

Lines 32-33. All the errors begin to be destroyed.

Lines 33-35. The material aspect of Orc (the serpent) also begins to vanish. His own flames—those of Intellectual Revolution—are consuming the earth, as at the end of *America*.

Line 70. *Blood* is always associated by Blake with material life. At last this bursts forth from the crucifixion which is itself and deluges all persecutors.

Lines 74-79. This universal catastrophe is a characteristic of all Apocalypses. Blake gives it meaning by representing it as the destruction of all worldly tyrants.

Line 83. The flames spare nothing : even in *Jerusalem* they find materialism to be destroyed.

Line 92. *A horrible rock* is the Rock of Ages (I. 410). It is horrible only on account of the Fall ; for it was forsaken when Reason gave instruction to be guided by the Passions.

Line 93. See the Commentary on I. 249.

Line 97. Albion begins to awake, though it be only to lamentation.

Line 123. *O Prince of Light* : Urizen. Albion calls upon Reason to end the strife of the world, and laments his separation from Pleasure.

Line 137. At the failure of Reason to allay the strife, Albion begins to see more clearly. At first he cannot recognize Reason at all in his form of the Dragon ; but he is soon disabused.

Line 142. Reason, by circumscribing the Passions, keeps them in a perpetual heat. Cf. the third *Proverb of Hell* : 'The road of excess leads to the palace of wisdom.'

Line 144. Man threatens to ignore Reason, if Reason will not work for Man. Urizen in his debased form cannot be accepted.

Line 151. *War is energy enslav'd* : it is the inability to express. It is Luvah bound by Urizen. See the Commentary on line 142.

Lines 156-160. Error (Satan) can never be redeemed, because he is an illusion, and must perish when the Truth appears. The Outward Church (Mystery, or Rahab) will be consumed in so far as it is Error ; but will be redeemed in so far as it is merely Sin. For even the harlot is not wholly bad, as Blake reminds us in line 159 (*Joshua* ii. 18). Though the Church rules in a land of heathen, sometimes it secretly protects the Chosen.

Line 167. Reason as Corrupt Civilization.

Line 181. See Commentary on III. 11.

Line 187. As soon as Reason renounces his authority over the other three Zoas, he resumes his ancient Apollonian form.

Lines 194-199. This curious passage suggests that at the moment of such tremendous rejuvenation, Pleasure cannot exist, through sheer ecstasy. The recognition of new power brings overwhelmingly the thought of the tragedy of the world, which is to be set right by that power.

Line 200. The Head, Heart, and Loins guard the memory of Pleasure.

Line 212. True Pleasure prepares for comfort, knowing that she cannot exist always.

Line 229. Now all things reveal themselves in their true forms, with all the marks of suffering which they have undergone. The Eternity within each one expands so rapidly that it bursts the shell of matter (the circumference imposed by Reason), and this shell vanishes into Non-Entity.

Line 251. The Massacred Innocents rage against their murderers. Even the babes feel the automatic release of passions cut off by death.

Line 264. Each man sees in his victim the crucified Saviour.

Line 271. Cf. *Revelation* i. 7 : 'Behold, he cometh with clouds ; and every eye shall see him, and they also which pierced him : and all kindreds of the earth shall wail because of him.'

Line 278. Cf. *Revelation* iv. 2 : '. . . and, behold, a throne was set in heaven, and one sat on the throne.'

Line 279. Cf. *Revelation* iv. 4 : 'And round about the throne were four and twenty seats : and upon the seats I saw four and twenty elders sitting, clothed in white raiment, and they had on their heads crowns of gold.'

Line 280. The Four Zoas. Cf. *Revelation* iv. 6 : '. . . and in the midst of the throne, and round about the throne, were four beasts full of eyes before and behind.'

Line 289. Mere vision is not sufficient for consummation. All the nations must yet undergo a final harvest and vintage, to make the Bread and Wine of Eternity. This takes seven days : the reversal of the Seven Days of *Genesis*.

Line 290. The FIRST DAY : the ploughing and sowing.

Line 302. Cf. *Isaiah* ii. 4 : '. . . and they shall beat their swords into plowshares and their spears into pruning-hooks : nation shall not lift up sword against nation, neither shall they learn war any more.'

Line 319. Cf. Plato's *Timaeus* (42) : 'When he [the Creator] had given all these laws [of reincarnation] to his creatures, that he might be guiltless of their future evil, he sowed some of them in the earth, and some in the moon, and some in the other stars which are the measures of time ; and when he had sown them he committed to the younger gods the fashioning of their mortal bodies.'

Line 342. After this labour, Pleasure revives at last.

Lines 352-355. The Resurrection of the (spiritual) Body.

Line 356. At last Revolution has run his course, and now may be subdued to his place as a servant of Man.

Line 361. Orc and the Shadowy Female are now regenerated to their original forms of Luvah and Vala.

Line 363. Passion and Nature are ordered to their place : the Loins. They obey, and find themselves in Eden.

Lines 364-372. The holiness of Man, above any of his functions, any gods whatsoever.

Line 373. The Passions and Nature re-enter the State of Innocence, which is Eden, the Lower Paradise.

Line 381. *Those upon the couches* : the Eternals, for this is the night of the First Day. *Dreams of Beulah* are true (inspired) dreams.

Line 389. Cf. Pope's *Essay on Criticism* (172-173) :

> Not so when swift Camilla scours the plain,
> Flies o'er th' unbending corn, and shines along the main.

Line 391. Nature awakes at the voice of Passion, which, however, she does not recognize. Possibly Blake intended to suggest the unfallen Psyche and the invisible Cupid.

Lines 406-407. Cf. *Psalm* xc. : ' They are like grass which groweth up. In the morning it flourisheth, and groweth up ; in the evening it is cut down, and withereth.'

Line 408. The redeemed Vala is also reminiscent of the innocent Thel.

Line 417. The Immortality of Nature.

Lines 452-454. These lines recall one of Blake's favourite designs, to be found in the second plate of *The Little Girl Found* (*Songs of Experience*), the ninth plate of *America*, and the third plate of *Africa*.

Line 461. The sleep of Vala in Eden is to be contrasted with the sleep of Adam (*Genesis* ii. 21). Adam had no dreams, and in his sleep Eve was divided from him ; Vala, however, dreams true dreams, and wakes to find the Palace of Passion. The reason for the contrast is that Vala's sleep is natural ; but Adam's was cast on him during the Fall by the Elohim.

Line 480. Water, as usual, represents the Sea of Time and Space. But the redeemed Vala does not suffer from her immersion ; on the contrary, ' her eyes were open'd ' to the world of matter. She can see the unredeemed, though they cannot see her.

Line 504. Though her call seemed to go unheeded, yet the simple sight of the misery of the Body and the Generative Instinct was enough to redeem them. The two children are Tharmas and Enion.

Line 525 is a sort of ethereal echo of VII. 717.

Line 554. Though the redemption of Nature, the Body, and the Generative Instinct was true, yet to those in Eternity these lower functions can appear only as a dream.

Line 563. This torrent from heaven is not one of the woes mentioned in *Revelation*. What seems a woe to the human harvest is to those in Eternity only a nocturnal storm which is necessary for the grain.

Line 564. The SECOND DAY : the Reaping.

Line 565. Cf. *Revelation* x. 6 : ' And sware by him that liveth for ever and ever, who created heaven, and the things that therein are, and the earth, and the things that therein are, and the sea, and the things which are therein, that there should be time no longer.'

Line 572. Cf. ' All Creation groans to be delivered ' (*Vision of Last Judgment*).

Line 576. Cf. *Revelation* xiv. 14-16 : ' And I looked, and behold a white cloud, and upon the cloud one sat like unto the Son of man, having on his head a golden crown, and in his hand a sharp sickle.   And another angel came out of the temple, crying with a loud voice to him that sat on the cloud, Thrust in thy sickle, and reap : for the time is come for thee to reap ; for the harvest of the earth is ripe. And he that sat on the cloud thrust in his sickle on the earth ; and the earth was reaped.'

Line 587. The THIRD DAY : the Resurrection and Reunion of the Earth Mother and the Body ; and the welcoming of Albion to the Feast of Eternity.

Line 590. Death to mortals is the painful rebirth.

Line 595. *A golden Moth* : in Greek philosophy, the butterfly was the parallel symbol.

Line 600. All things are renewed, for all are immortal.

Line 613. *Over the ruin'd worlds, the misty tomb of the Eternal Prophet.* Los, strictly speaking, has vanished, for he was only the temporal form of Urthona.   He appears only once more ; and then his change is emphasized : ' Los, who is Urthona ' (line 798).   Therefore the worlds are called his tomb, since there he died into his higher form.

Line 619. The female is still separate from the male.

Line 624. *Man is a Worm wearied with joy.*   Mr. Ellis's substitution of *renewed* for *wearied* gives an entirely false turn to the passage, which is explaining how Man can fall from Eternity.

Line 629. See Commentary on line 319.

Line 632. *Windows* of the five senses.

Lines 634-636 have a marginal reference to *Ephesians* iii. 10 : ' To the intent that now, unto the principalities and powers in heavenly places, might be known by the church the manifold wisdom of God.'

Line 647.. The FOURTH DAY : the Threshing and Winnowing, by which all the chaff is blown into the Sea of Time and Space.

Lines 667-673, which in *America* were given a literal sense, are now taken spiritually.   Death is the great liberator.

Line 683. *Sotha,* it will be remembered, gave a Code of War to Odin (*Africa,* 30) ; and therefore is a symbol of the northern races who enslaved the Africans.

Line 691. Cf. *Revelation* xiv. 17-19 : ' And another angel came out of the temple which is in heaven, he also having a sharp sickle.   And another angel came out from the altar, which had power over fire ; and cried with a loud cry to him that had the sharp sickle, saying, Thrust in thy sharp sickle, and gather the clusters of the vine of the earth ; for her grapes are fully ripe.   And the angel thrust in his sickle into the earth, and gathered the vine of the earth, and cast it into the great winepress of the wrath of God.'

Line 693. Cf. Paracelsus's *Philosophy Addressed to the Athenians* (I. 10) : ' Before all creatures were made, the work of separation began.   When this had commenced, afterwards every creature emerged and shone forth with its free will ; in which state all will afterwards flourish up to the end of all things, that is, until that great harvest in which everything shall be pregnant with its fruits, and those fruits shall be reaped and carried into the barn ; for the harvest is the end of its fruit, and signifies nothing else than the corporeal destruction of all things.   The number of those fruits is, indeed, almost infinite ; but the harvest is one wherein all the fruits of creation shall be cut down and gathered into the barn.   No less marvellous will be this harvest, the end of all things, than was stupendous at the beginning that Mysterium Magnum.'

Line 698. *The Bulls of Luvah* represent the Passion that makes the Sun of Poetry move through the Stars of Reason.   In the most ancient astrologies of Assyria and Babylon the solar Bull ploughed the heavens, and the furrow was the Zodiac.

Line 706. The great lesson learned by the immortals. Cf. the *Descriptive Catalogue,* No. 3 : ' These Gods are visions of the eternal attributes, or divine names, which, when erected into gods, become destructive to humanity. They ought to be the servants, and not the masters, of man or of society. They ought to be made to sacrifice to Man, and not man compelled to sacrifice to them ; for when separated from man or humanity, who is Jesus the Saviour, the vine of eternity ? they are thieves and rebels, they are destroyers.'

Line 708. *His crown of thorns* : obviously intended to suggest the relationship between Christ and Luvah, but also to indicate his former circumscription.

Line 713. The FIFTH DAY : the Vintage. The wine-press represents war. The ultimate world-war foretold in all Apocalypses seems to the Eternals like a village festival. Blake also emphasizes the agony of the human grapes, whose outer skins are being burst, that all the best that is in them may mingle in the wine of brotherhood.

Line 722. *Human families* : the family always seemed to Blake nothing but an extension of the Selfhood. Cf. *Jerusalem*, 27 :

> Is this thy soft Family-love,
>   Thy cruel patriarchal pride ;
> Planting thy Family alone,
>   Destroying all the World beside ?

However, this must be understood in a special sense ; for Blake certainly never advocated anything like the Platonic Communism. It was the jealousy and the competition between families as social units that he deplored, and nothing more.

Line 723. Cf. *Revelation* xiv. 20 : ' And the winepress was trodden without the city, and blood came out of the winepress, even unto the horse bridles, by the space of a thousand and six hundred furlongs.'

Line 727. ' Excess of sorrow laughs. Excess of joy weeps ' (26th *Proverb of Hell*).

Line 748. Cf. *Paradise Lost*, II. 621 : ' Rocks, Caves, Lakes, Fens, Bogs, Dens and Shades of Death.'

Line 755. As usual, all these animals are intended to *suggest* symbols to the reader. They represent the hosts of minor evils which accompany war. Cf. Sir Thomas Browne's *Pseudodoxia*, II. 7 : ' For Pestilence is properly signified by the Spider, whereof some kinds are of a very venomous Nature. Famine by Maggots, which destroy the fruits of the Earth. And War not improperly by the Fly ; if we rest in the phansie of *Homer*, who compares the valiant *Grecian* unto a Fly.'

Line 763. *Naked in all their beauty* : *i.e.* in their spiritual forms.

Line 765. Cf. *The Mental Traveller* : ' Catches his shrieks in cups of gold.'

Line 773. Urthona, with his limp and his hammer, suggest the fallen Vulcan. The Zoas are reassuming their ancient attributes : Urthona has a hammer for he is the ' Maker ' (which in the old sense meant the Poet). Tharmas is a Shepherd, since he is the God who rules the realms of Innocence.

Line 783. *Quite exhausted* : Passion, when given free play, always wears itself out.

Line 795. Man casts out the Passions for the woe they have caused, until Eternity is perfect, when they will find their places.

Line 800. The Sea of Time and Space gives up its ' dead.' Cf. *Revelation* xx. 13 : ' And the sea gave up the dead which were in it. . . .'

Line 803. The SIXTH DAY : the Grinding of the Corn and the Making of the Bread. This final work is accomplished by the profound (' dark ') Spirit. After the bitter wars of Experience, its philosophy is educed. The Body furnishes the winds which move the wheels.

Line 821. The bread of Experience is made : the truths which are to be the food of the future are completed and laid away. Then the Spirit, freed from its labours, takes its repose in the deeps, ' in the night of time.'

Line 823. The SEVENTH DAY, which is the Sabbath of Eternity.

Line 846. Urthona, the Spirit, is at last one : no longer ' divided from Enitharmon—no longer the Spectre Los.' Poetry has vanished, and is replaced by the Instinctive Life itself. But no time is a time of complete repose; the joy of 'intellectual Warfare' still remains, and will always remain.

Line 851. *Sweet Science*: Knowledge (from scientia); not 'the 'doubt and experiment' of Newton and Locke. Art and Science correspond to the Seraphim and Cherubim.

FRAGMENTS

(A). This page (69) was possibly to be inserted before page 8 (line 385). The catchword is ' Enion '; moreover, line 38 of the fragment and line 359 of *Night the First* are the same. More likely, however, this was a page from an earlier version which was destroyed.

It describes the confusion which attended the Fall.

Line 12. *The Mighty Father*, from his attributes, must be Tharmas.

Line 29. The birth of Luvah is surely the birth of Orc. The Passions, born of Space, are named War.

Line 35. This bridal feast is that described in i. 340 *seq.*

(B). This page (70) is a fragment of the myth of Rahab, a portion not eventually included in the completed poem. It represents the trouble of the Established Church (who is identified with Natural Religion) over the sorrows of out-cast pleasure and of out-cast Generative Instinct. But her secret sympathies only produce mental strife; until the Church condemns its own humanitarianism.

(C). On page 71*a* occurs one fragment; on the verso (71*b*) occur several notes for various passages. All were rejected.

The fragment on 71*a* concerns the creation of the Hermaphrodite of Contradiction and Doubt, also of his Emanation. Blake later denies that these Devils had any Emanations, which probably accounts for his rejection of this portion.

Line 3. *Ahana* is probably a slip of the pen for *Ahania*. All the Zoas are seeking the wrong Emanations (Ideals).

Line 4. *The shady bride* must be the Shadowy Female.

Page 71*b* contains several notes for the union of the Spectre of Tharmas with Enion (*Night the First*, 151-161).

(D). Page 72 was torn up, but saved for the sketch on the verso. It deals with the struggle of the Spectre of Tharmas and Enion, and was little changed when incorporated into *Night the First*.

(E). This page (73*a*) contains an early version of *Night the Eighth*, lines 263-410. This account is very much compressed: it omits the account of Rahab in the Synagogue (which was added marginally in the later version); the song of the females of Amalek; the generations of Los and Enitharmon; the quarrel with Hayley; and the appointment of the Seven Eyes of God.

REPETITIONS

Proof that *The Four Zoas* was not intended to be given the public is to be found in the fact that Blake later utilized long passages of it for the two later epics. He also repeated a few lines from the earlier books. Such repetitions are never quite literal. For example when Blake retold the forging of Urizen's body he varied the refrain in *The Four Zoas* as follows:

> A first Age passed, a state of dismal woe. . . .
> And a second Age passed over. . . .
> And a third Age passed, a state of dismal woe. . . .
> And a fourth Age passed over and a state of dismal woe. . . .
> And a fifth Age passed and a state of dismal woe. . . .
> And a sixth Age passed of dismal woe. . . .
> And a seventh Age passed over, and a state of dismal woe. . . .

In the passages repeated in the later books, many symbolic names are added, and often lines are inserted. Sometimes a whole passage is reduced to a couple of lines ; or a couple of lines may be expanded to a whole passage.

A list of these repetitions, with a few of the more important parallel passages which were entirely rewritten, follows.

NIGHT THE FIRST

29-32, 38-39, repeated in *Jerusalem*, 22 : 1, 10-12, 14-15.

46-50, repeated in *Jerusalem*, 22 : 20 24.

192-193. Cf. *Jerusalem*, 48 : 30 *seq.*

203-207, entirely rewritten in *Milton*, 30 and 31.

408-410. Cf. *Jerusalem*, 48 : 1-4.

442-446, repeated in *Jerusalem*, 38 : 17-21.

491-493. Cf. IV. 89-94 ; VII. 282-284.

500-501, revised in *Jerusalem*, 80 : 23-24.

NIGHT THE SECOND

61-62. Cf. *Jerusalem*, 5 : 41-44

72-79, repeated in *Jerusalem*, 7 : 30-36.

364-366, repeated from the *Visions of the Daughters of Albion,* 214-215.

389-390, repeated from the *Visions*, 119-120, with the substitution of *serpent* for *ape.*

NIGHT THE THIRD

44-103, repeated, with unimportant changes, in *Jerusalem*, 29 : 33-82, omitting lines 47-48 (deleted in *The Four Zoas*), 72-76, 84, and 91-92.

NIGHT THE FOURTH

208-246, repeated almost verbatim from *Urizen*, 183-253.

253, repeated in *Jerusalem*, 50 : 11.

260-262, repeated in *Milton*, 30 : 25-27.

277. Cf. *Jerusalem*, 48 : 45.

280-283, repeated almost verbatim from *Urizen*, 254-261.

NIGHT THE FIFTH

56-66, rearranged in *Jerusalem*, 40 : 32, 38-42.

83-91, revised from *Urizen*, 378-389.

NIGHT THE SIXTH

236-257. Cf. *Urizen*, 451 *seq.*

307-310, repeated from *America*, cancelled plate C, 14-17.

NIGHT THE SEVENTH

29-39, rewritten from *Ahania*, 111-122.

110-124, repeated in *Jerusalem*, 30 : 30-31.

618-621, remembered from *Tiriel*, 222-225.

653-697, repeated in *Jerusalem*, 65 : 5-55, with a few added lines and names of places.

723, repeated IX. 536.

NIGHT THE EIGHTH

78, revised from *America : Preludium*, 3.

111, revised, became *Milton*, 4 : 6.

192, repeated in *Milton*, 11 : 28.
200-201, repeated in *Milton*, 23 : 63-64.
205-214. Cf. *Milton*, 34 : 24-31.
293-315, repeated in *Jerusalem*, 67 : 44–68 : 9.
345-346, repeated in *Milton*, 20 : 15-16.
382 *seq.*, retold, much expanded, in *Milton*, 6 and 7.
392-400, rewritten in *Milton*, 11 : 17-27.
488-489, revised from the *Visions*, 152-153.

NIGHT THE NINTH

99-112, repeated in *Jerusalem*, 19 : 1-14.
667-673, repeated from *America*, 42-48.
740-768, repeated, with some rearrangement, and the omission of three lines and the addition of eight lines, in *Milton*, 24 : 3-41.
822-823, repeated from *America*, 49-50.

DELETIONS

According to his custom, Blake planned to omit a great deal of what he originally wrote. Many of these deletions are indicated, and we have good reason to believe that more would have been crossed out, particularly in the later *Nights*. In the editions hitherto printed practically all Blake's discarded passages have been retained. The following list indicates those lines which Blake marked for rejection.

NIGHT THE FIRST

Lines 66-96 ; lines 127-135 (preceded by the deleted couplet : ' He spurn'd Enion with his foot, he sprang aloft on Clouds / Alighting in his drunken joy in a far distant Grove ') ; lines 142-153 ; lines 159-161 ; lines 169-181 ; line 232 ; lines 274-282.

NIGHT THE THIRD

Lines 28-29 ; lines 47-48.

NIGHT THE SIXTH

After line 99 follow the deleted lines : ' Not so clos'd up the Prince of Light now darken'd wand'ring among / For Urizen beheld the terrors of the Abyss wand'ring among / The Ruin'd Spirits once his Children & the Children of Luvah.'

NIGHT THE EIGHTH

Lines 10 (from ' but other wings ') through line 14 ; lines 200-201.

FRAGMENT E

Lines 19-28.

THE ILLUSTRATIONS TO *THE FOUR ZOAS*

The illustrations which surround the text of *The Four Zoas* prove beyond doubt that Blake never intended his poem to be given the public during his own days ; and they also prove that he anticipated a time when our present prudery would exist no longer. Quite a number of the sketches (for few of them got beyond that stage) are of a *naïveté* commonly found in primitive art, but which the modern age unhesitatingly calls indecent.

The connection of so-called obscenities with the deepest mystical philosophies has often been noted, particularly in the case of the Antique Mysteries (cf. Iamblicus : *De Myst. Aegyp.* IV.) ; and many explanations, some partly right, none entirely wrong, have been given.

The monograph which might be inserted here, however, is unnecessary. Blake's intentions are perfectly clear. He was obviously too pure a soul to indulge in such drawings for their own sake ; nor did he intend to excite others by them. Therefore they cannot be called ' obscene ' with any accuracy whatsoever.

These drawings are exactly parallel to various passages in the *Visions of the Daughters of Albion.* They are equally frank, and equally dignified, with the same slight veil of poetical symbol drawn over them. Blake intended now, as then, to expose the pitifulness of human vices, in order to condemn their causes. Pure himself, he could gaze clear-eyed on impurity, feeling neither scorn nor anger. Courageous beyond any man of his or our times, he could practise his doctrine that the exposure of evil is sufficient to destroy it—when, of course, it is really evil. We may add that Iamblicus gives exactly the same reasons for the displays in the Antique Mysteries, calling them a cure.

But it must be added that Blake's drawings, though sufficiently frank, are not realistic pictures of orgies. The symbol, as usual, comes to his aid. The scene of the women gathering phalloi in the woods is obviously not literal. Blake's sense of beauty always gives his designs the dignity of his own decency.

Unfortunately John Linnell, to whom the manuscript was left, did not share Blake's faith in a cleaner future ; and not being able to tolerate even the frankness of a female nude, he utilized the eraser freely. The effect of his expurgations are ludicrously opposed to his intentions ; the smeared blanks in the designs leave too much to the imagination, as may often be seen by tilting the page so that a shadow fills the grooves made by Blake's pencil.

With *The Four Zoas*, Blake abandoned his earlier scheme of retelling the story by means of the series of pictures. Epics are too long to sustain a symbolic sequence of designs. Most of the pictures, therefore, are nothing but illustrations of the text on the same page, though many give symbolic commentaries ; while others seem to be pure decoration. The unfinished character of many leave their meaning in doubt, while the deletions of John Linnell plus those of Time are a constant source of difficulties.

Page 1*a*, *Title Page.* A trumpeting angel descends to a cauldron of tortured human forms. He is evidently calling them from the Hell of this world to a higher life by the doctrines in the book.

1*b*. Man in this world, as seen from Eternity. A sleeping male nude, viewed from above. This is inscribed ' Rest before Labour.'

NIGHT THE FIRST

2*a*. Enion as the Earth Mother in her Cave.

2*b*. A young archer kneeling on the Worm, and aiming at something below him. Such archers have already appeared as spirits of affliction (as in the *Visions of the Daughters of Albion*, plate 3) ; and the steed of this one renders his function unmistakable.

3*a*. The sleeping Spectre of Tharmas, ' a shadowy human form winged ' (I. 59).

3*b*. Tharmas weeping over the Sea of Time and Space (I. 106).

4*a*. Enion suckling the children Los and Enitharmon (I. 168).

4*b*. Enion with flaming hair and serpent legs, ' half Woman & half Spectre ' (I. 155).

5*a*. Los and Enitharmon as children playing while blind Enion stumbles after them (I. 186).

5*b*. Los and Enitharmon floating through the Forest of Error (I. 219).

6*a*. Los and Enitharmon floating—a very vague sketch (I. 218).

6*b*. Los striking Enitharmon (I. 265).

7*a*. This sketch is so vague indeed that its subject is uncertain. It seems to be a sleeping serpent with a human head.

7b. 'Bright souls of vegetative life budding and blossoming.' Three women exult ; two tiny figures fly upward (I. 364).

8a. Enion floating in despair (I. 386).

8b. A very vague sketch, containing a descending angel.

9a. One of the deleted sketches. Jerusalem, a nude female, hides with a gesture of modesty behind a rock, while on the left a grotesque sort of god descends.

9b. Enitharmon lies upon her back, about to give birth to Orc. This picture resembles the lower half of plate III. of *The Marriage of Heaven and Hell.*

Pages 10*a* and 10*b* have no decoration.

Night the Second

Page 11*a*. Albion reclines with open eyes (II. 1).

11*b*. A woman flies downward ; presumably a spirit engaged in building the Mundane Shell.

12*a*. A vague sketch of a figure with poles.

12*b*. The monstrous forms engendered by the tortures of chastity (Luvah in the fires of Vala). 'Deform'd I see these lineaments of ungratified desire.' They are respectively : a winged fairy with an exaggerated kteis ; a bat-winged woman flying and embracing a huge phallos ; a monster with crane's head, bat wings, serpent legs, and a prominent kteis ; and a many-breasted, serpent-necked woman-dragon (II. 112).

13*a*. Albion and Rahab. His form is wasted ; he draws a veil from her figure while she smiles at him.

13*b*. Woman visiting Youth in his dreams. She kneels over his naked, impassioned form. This sketch is partly deleted.

14*a*. A crouching male nude weaves a net (II. 158).

14*b*. To the left, a female torso, partly erased.

15*a*. A woman kneels in despair before a man, chained to a rock, who does not recognize her.

15*b*. The despairing Daughters of Albion. One group has been erased.

16*a*. A design of which nothing can be distinguished.

16*b*. No decoration.

17*a*. The Perversion of Woman through Abstinence. Nude women kneeling and uprooting what may be mandrakes or possibly phalloi ; in either case, the plants are a symbol of the sexual desire. To the left, a woman stands with a basket of flowers (?) on her head.

17*b*. Enion falls headlong, wailing (II. 386).

Night the Third

18*a*. Ahania bowing before the startled Urizen (III. 2).

18*b*. The Perversion of Man through Abstinence. A seated Silenus turns to embrace a struggling woman, but is prevented by the vicious acts of two other men.

19*a*. Two small boys, partly erased, point with glee to an obliterated figure or figures.

19*b*. A winged and spurred Cupid sits on the back of a man who is attempting to turn a woman on her back. This sketch is mostly obliterated. The commentary of this and the following designs on the accompanying text, which describes Albion's worship of the Cloud of Luvah, with the resultant diseases, is perfectly clear.

20*a*. A nude woman lying on her back arouses the passions of a man who stands at her head.

20*b*. A woman excites two children to lust. To the left, a woman pursues a winged phallos.

21*a*. For the most part, the rest of the text is copied on proofs of Blake's illustrations to Young, which occupy the obverse of each page.   As these illustrations have nothing to do with *The Four Zoas*, they will be omitted from this list.

21*b*. Urizen preaching his religion of abstinence ; but above him, to the left, Enitharmon stands, with a tabernacle covering her loins (I. 105).

22*b*. Enion floats separated from Tharmas by a curl of flame.   Both are in agony (III. 179).

NIGHT THE FOURTH

23*b*. Tharmas in agony beats his breast till it bleeds (IV. 7).

24*b*. Enitharmon swept away on a wave of Tharmas (IV. 56).

25*b*. Enitharmon, crouching in fear, repels the kneeling Los.

26*b*. Urizen forming into a globe (IV. 208).

27*b*. Christ seated, pulling a boy upon his lap.   Behind the boy is another child.

NIGHT THE FIFTH

28*b*. Enitharmon prostrate before Los (V. 5).

29*b*. Los watching the embrace of Orc and Enitharmon (V. 81).

30*b*. Los and Enitharmon appalled at the crucifixion of Orc (V. 170).

31*b*. A figure pulling at a net ; behind, a man kisses a woman.

32*b*. A full-page illustration.   Los, with the sun on his head, faces inward, while two figures float in a circle about him.   Two other figures sit below.   Then four subordinate figures may well represent his four sons : Wrath, Pity, Desire, and Reason.

NIGHT THE SIXTH

33*b*. One of Urizen's daughters falls forward with her head between two rocks (VI. 22).

34*b*. A monster encountered by Urizen (VI. 117).

35*b*. The three daughters of Urizen asleep beneath the sterile tree of Mystery.

36*b*. Urizen, globe in hand, explores the dens.   This design is adapted from the 23rd design of *The Book of Urizen* (VI. 283).

37*b*. No text.   A nude female, either Jerusalem or Enitharmon, descends.

NIGHT THE SEVENTH

38*b*. A supine male nude, with an erection, symbolized as flames in the verses. This is Orc, though he is not in his customary cruciform position (VII. 20-22).

39*b*. Whatever decoration once was on this page has since been cut off.

40*b*. Enitharmon (?) and the Starry Wheel.   She lies prone on a cloud, holding the wheel, which has seven stars—the Seven Eyes of God.

41*b*. A crouching man points downward.

42*b*. In the centre of the page, between lines 363-364, is a large sketch of Enitharmon, kneeling and holding her breasts.

43*a*. No decoration, though this page is the verso of half of Blake's engraving of the *Trial of Elenor*.

43*b*. This page contains, over the engraving, the following lines :

> The Christian Religion teaches that No Man is indifferent to you but that Every one is
> Either your friend or your enemy, he must necessarily be either the one or the other
> And that he will be equally profitable both ways if you treat him as he deserves.

44*a*. No text : the other half of the engraving.   In the lower left-hand corner is a sketch of a man with a dagger about to stab a kneeling woman.

44*b*. No decoration.

NIGHT THE SEVENTH (second version)

45*b*. A reclining man and woman. She is weeping, while a third figure flees away.

46*b*. Vala as the ' howling Melancholy ' (VII. 775) ; she is flying naked through space.

47*b*. The worship in Urizen's temple. Three figures bow before the phallos (VII. 516).

48*b*. The prester-serpent (VII. 603).

NIGHT THE EIGHTH

49*b*. A Spectre fallen below the human form ; he appears as a sort of bug with a man's face, surrounded by flames.

50*b*. Albion reclining in sorrow.

51*b*. A kneeling woman repels the Starry Wheel which is rolling upon her.

52*b*. A reclining male nude. Behind him a woman stands, leaning back into the arms of a man.

53*b*. Ahania wailing in her cloud. A Cupid with his bow sits on her back (VIII. 481).

54*b*. Enion drawn into her vortex (VIII. 538).

55*a* is covered with text, and has no decoration ; the verso is the full-page engraving of the Rising Christ from the *Night Thoughts*.

56*b*. Full-page sketch of the Saviour parting the clouds (VIII. 400).

NIGHT THE NINTH

57*b*. Three laughing women (? the daughters of Urizen) knotted somehow into a group.

58*b*. Albion lamenting. This is a repetition of the sketch on page 50*b* (IX. 94).

59*b*. The Female in Eternity (IX. 218).

60*b*. The State of Innocence. A man leaning on a stick speaks to a nude woman in a lily (the ' Lilly of Havilah '). She touches his brow.

61*b*. The Sense of Sight begins its redemption. As a giant still half buried in Matter (cf. the 60th illustration to Dante), it beholds a flying spirit (drawn across the text) ; while a tiny shepherd strides along.

62*b*. The Wine-Press of Luvah. A man and woman are trampling the grapes, while a turbaned dancer sleeps with her hand on a tambourine, and a flutist sits above her (IX. 740).

63*b*. The wasted form of Albion awaking (IX. 614).

64*b*. Vala in the river, while Tharmas on the bank bends over (IX. 480). Drawn over this sketch is another : a man on the ground strikes with a sword at a flying form.

65*b*. Mystery as a Harpy, of classical conception. On her back is a figure with whip and goblet.

66*b*. A Seraph, as an old man's face surrounded by four wings.

67*b*. The Soul as a woman waking in the grave.

68*b*. The Soul as a woman, leaping from the tiny globe which is this world.

FRAGMENTS

69*a*. An old man with a rope.

69*b*. Vala sees the flaming feet of Luvah pass by (II. 229).

70*b*. A full-page sketch of Los endeavouring to embrace the struggling Enitharmon.

71. No decorations on either side.

72*b*. Enion half Spectre (I. 155).

73. No decorations on either side.

MILTON

COMMENTARY

Blake intended *Milton* to be fifty pages long, but none of the three copies known to exist is complete. The British Museum and the Huntington copies contain forty-five pages only, while the New York copy omits the *Preface*, but adds the missing five pages. These ' extra pages ' have never been printed in the order which Blake intended. In the Ellis-Yeats edition, they are renumbered at the whim of the editors, and all subsequent editions have followed their numbering, and not Blake's. As these pages contain Blake's final ideas for his epic, they cannot be treated as extraneous matter.

In *The Four Zoas* we found a few English names used with symbolic intent; but now they begin to overwhelm us. Generally they are either self-explanatory, or practically incomprehensible. Blake used familiar names (such as *Oxford* and *Tyburn*) in their familiar sense; he used others (such as *Lambeth* and *Felpham*) with purely personal meanings; or he used them according to their relations to the points of the compass. The difficulty of understanding most of these English names is due to the growth of London during a century, so that its physical aspect has entirely changed. The bathing pools of boys are now dingy rows of tenements. The poetical facts being gone, the symbols are meaningless. But in *Milton* we find comparatively few obscure places.

As several passages are repeated from *The Four Zoas*, the reader will refer to the earlier Commentary for their explanation.

Plate 1. *Title-page.* The motto is from *Paradise Lost*, I. 26.

2. *Preface. The Stolen and Perverted Writings.* It was once a common theory that all heathen religions were heresies from the original Jewish religion. To Blake, Religion was Art, and therefore all heathen art was perverted from true Inspiration, which was Christianity. He could point to the Muses, who were called by the Greeks themselves the ' Daughters of Memory '; he could cite Plato's ejection of poets from the Republic, and his classification of Inspiration as a form of madness. Rome, through the voice of Virgil, had preferred Empire to Art (*Aeneid*, VI. 847 *seq.*—a text referred to on the *Laocoon plate*); and Empire was in Blake's mind as definitely opposed to Art, as War is to Peace. In the Bible, however, he found the poets and prophets accorded due reverence, and Inspiration set up as the ultimate authority. Therefore, classic art was necessarily second-hand, being based on the Memory of some original Inspiration—which could be no less than the Bible. On the 7th water-colour to Dante, Blake referred again to ' The Poetry of the Heathen Stolen & Perverted from the Bible, not by Chance but by Design, by the Kings of Asia & their Generals, the Greek heroes, & lastly by the Romans.' Blake's violence on this point was at least partially due to Thomas Taylor's assertion that the exact contrary was true. But Blake had Milton on his side. Cf. *Paradise Regained*, IV. 336-340 :

> Our Hebrew Songs and Harps in *Babylon*,
> That pleas'd so well our Victor's ear, declare
> That rather *Greece* from us these Arts deriv'd—
> Ill imitated, while they loudest sing
> The vices of thir Deities, and thir own.

Homer & Ovid, Plato & Cicero. Blake had much more sympathy for these authors than we might expect. He admitted their greatness, but attacked their philosophy. Moreover, as great masters, they were the more likely to be imitated, and hence to ' oppress art.' Therefore Blake here ' drives his plough over the bones of the dead.' We hardly need to point out Blake's many approving references to

Homer: the largest of which is the little essay *On Homer's Poetry*, and the least known of which is the marginal comment on Bishop Watson on heathen savages: '. . . Likewise Read Homer's Iliad. He was certainly a Savage in the Bishop's sense. He knew nothing of God in the Bishop's sense of the word & yet he was no fool.' Tatham records: 'He was very fond of Ovid, especially the Fasti.' The *MS. Book* contains the following note: 'Apuleius' Golden Ass and Ovid's Metamorphoses and others of the like kind are fable; yet they contain vision in a sublime degree, being derived from real vision in more ancient writings.' Of Plato, we know Blake read much: *Urizen, Ahania*, and *The Four Zoas* were obviously influenced by him. Blake felt that Plato was not so much wrong, as that he did not see deeply enough. Therefore, in the 199th design to the *Night Thoughts*, the library of 'wisdom shallow' contains volumes inscribed: 'Plato, de Animae Immortalitate,' 'Cicero: de Nat: Deor:' 'Aristot: Respub:' 'Plutarchis: Chaer:' and 'Lock on human under.' On an unpublished fragment of *The Everlasting Gospel*, he wrote: 'There is not one moral virtue Jesus inculcated but Plato and Cicero inculcated before him.'

Shakspeare & Milton were Blake's idols; yet they, too, he thought, dealt too much with the materialistic world and its virtues and vices.

Satanic Mills: the grinding, non-creative processes of logic.

I will not cease from Mental Fight. Cf. Nietzsche's *Götzendämmerung*, IX. 38: 'And warfare prepares a man for freedom. For what is freedom? The Will to be responsible for oneself. . . . The free man is a warrior!'

Jerusalem: spiritual freedom. Cf. Shelley's *Queen Mab*, IV.: 'A garden shall arise in loveliness / Surpassing Fabled Eden.'

BOOK THE FIRST

3:1. *Daughters of Beulah!* These are the 'Daughters of Inspiration,' as opposed to the classic 'Daughters of Memory.' After the attack on the Classics which we found in the *Preface*, we hardly should expect such a classical opening!

3:5-7. This is Blake's explanation of the 'reality' of his 'visions.' Those who still find it irrational should compare Cowper's *Poetical Epistle to Lady Austen* (Dec. 17, 1781), which may have influenced this passage:

But when a Poet takes the pen,
Far more alive than other men,
He feels a gentle tingling come
Down to his finger and his thumb,
Derived from Nature's noblest part,
The centre of a glowing heart.

3:10. *The False Tongue* is the voice of Satan, the Accuser. His doctrines are 'vegetated' into the Flesh.

3:14. *Death Eternal* is not *everlasting* death, but death *from* Eternity into Time and Space.

3:15. Jerusalem is the Bride (Emanation) of the Lamb (*Revelation* xxi. 9-10).

3:17. *One hundred years.* Milton actually died in 1674; therefore the centenary of his death came in 1774, not in 1804. Blake never troubled about being too accurate about such details.

3:19. *His Sixfold Emanation*: his three wives and his three daughters. Blake believed that Milton had not solved the problems of sex, that he had not lived in perfect harmony with his family, and therefore that they still remained divided from him. So Milton is 'unhappy tho' in heaven'; and he must return (though not in flesh) to redeem his error.

3:20. *Her to redeem*: i.e. his Emanation, considered as one. *& himself perish.* Self-sacrifice is mystical death. Cf. *Jerusalem*, 96:27. This is far different from passing into Non-Existence, which can be done only by Satan. The great sacrifice of Christ was not in the Crucifixion, but in the Nativity. Buddha's great sacrifice was in refusing to enter Nibbana before his work on earth was completed. Milton's sacrifice is entirely comparable.

3 : 25. The Bard's song extends from this line to 11 : 44.

3 : 26. *Three Classes* of Mankind exist in this world of Time ('Created by the Hammer of Los'). They are the Reprobates, who correspond to the Devils of *The Marriage of Heaven and Hell*; the Elect, who correspond to the Angels; and the Redeem'd, who are midway between the other two. Cf. *Milton*, 25 : 31-37, where a complete explanation is given. Man, however, is really fourfold, as will appear in Eternity, when all these Classes are merged into a new Class (*Milton*, 3* : 5).

Page 5*, followed by *page* 3*, should come between pages 3 and 4. These 'extra pages' were numbered by Blake 3 and 4; the *Title-page* and the first page of the poem being numbered 1 and 2. (The *Preface* is omitted from the copy with the 'extra leaves.')

5* : 1. *Enitharmon's Looms* are the looms of Cathedron, on which she, as goddess of Space, weaves the flesh. *When Albion was slain upon his Mountains, i.e.* when Man fell; for which see *The Four Zoas, passim.*

5* : 2. *Through envy*: Urizen's desire for undue power.

5* : 6. This desire for domination created a 'Selfhood,' and shut Urizen from communion with the other Eternals. For the details of this story, see *The Book of Urizen*, *The Book of Los*, and *The Four Zoas*, IV. 165 *seq.* Blake retells the story here, as it is the great prelude to all the Felpham sufferings. The Fall must precede the Redemption. However, Blake compresses this account into the barest outlines.

5* : 8. *Druid*: Moral Virtue; the sacrifice of others, not of the Self.

5* : 10-27 are compressed and revised from *The Book of Urizen*, 206-253.

5* : 28-36. The birth of Enitharmon, and the separation of Los's Spectre. See *The Book of Urizen*, 285 *seq.*; and *The Four Zoas, passim.*

5* : 38-39. More of the familiar story. Los and Enitharmon create bodies (on 'the Looms of Generation') as an act of mercy toward wandering spirits, who thereby can rise again. They also create Art ('Great Golgonooza').

5* : 40. *Orc* and *the Shadowy Female* (Revolution and Materialized Nature) are their first children. For the rest of the family, see *The Four Zoas*, VIII. 351-361, and Commentary.

5* : 41. *Satan* (Error) is now made the last of Enitharmon's children; a characteristic and deliberate inconsistency of Blake's. Satan is immediately identified with Urizen, which causes still greater confusion. *The Miller of Eternity* must be Satan (cf. 'these dark Satanic Mills,' *Milton*, 2); while *Prince of the Starry Wheels* is a conventional epithet for Urizen. This identification has been made before (see Commentary on *The Four Zoas*, VIII. 263). Error is essentially shifting, *Refusing Form*, because once it is given a definite Form, it is recognized as Error and is cast out.

3* : 1-3. But at present Error is so mingled with Truth that mankind must be thoroughly worked over in a Great Harvest before Satan can be eliminated. This Harvest is described at length in *The Four Zoas*, IX. The characters are somewhat changed. There Urizen did the ploughing himself (IX. 309); but in *Milton* the Plough is Rintrah's (Just Wrath), the Harrow is Shaddai's (Accuser), and they are guided by Palamabron (Pity).

3* : 6-7. Los speaks. Cf. *The Poison Tree* (*Songs of Experience*).

3* : 8 contains in one septenary all of James's Pragmatism.

3* : 9-14. The Poet admits that the function of Urizen-Satan has a place in the universe, though a low one.

3* : 11. *Pantocrator*: an instrument for making copies. *Newton* and *Locke*, the arch-scientists, need no explanation.

3* : 18. Satan, being an illusion, cannot enter Eternity.

3* : 21. Here begins the building of Golgonooza by Los; or shall we say, the artistic works of Blake ? *South Molton Street* was Blake's address after leaving Felpham. All such work is self-sacrifice, as Blake well knew ; therefore he inserted *Calvary's foot* as an explanation of his English terms.

3* : 22. *Their Cherubim.* Blake always used Cherubim, whose symbol was the Eye of Knowledge, as practically synonymous with the term ' Spectre.' These always have to be subdued, or ' sacrificed.'

3* : 23-28. The instruments of spiritual warfare (the tygers of wrath and the arrows of desire) are prepared.

3* : 24. *All colours of precious stones.* These may be the breast-plate of Aaron used as a body-armour ; or it may simply be spiritual sensation transmuted into colour : as in Jakob Böhme's *Aurora*, XII. 142-145 :

' In this Rising up the Armies or Companies of *all* the Angels of the *whole* Heaven become triumphant and joyful, and that melodious *Te Deum Laudamus* (We Praise Thee, O God) rises up.

' In this rising up of the Heart, the *Mercurius* in the Heart is stirred up or awakened, as also in the whole *Salitter* of Heaven there rises up in the Deity the *miraculous*, wonderful and fair beautiful Imaging of Heaven, in several manifold various Colours and Manners, and each Spirit presents itself in its own peculiar Form.

' I can compare it with nothing but only with the most *precious* Stones or Jewels ; as *Rubies, Emeralds, Topazes, Onixes, Sapphires, Diamonds, Jaspers, Hyacinths, Amethysts, Beryls, Sardiusses, Carbuncles,* and such like.

' In *such* Manner and Colours, the Heaven of God's Nature shows or presents itself in the Rising up of the Spirits of God : And now when the Light of The Son of God *shines* therein, then it is like a bright clear *Sea*, or the Colours of the abovementioned Stones or Jewels.'

3* : 26. Cf. the letter to Butts, April 25, 1803 : ' If a man is the enemy of my spiritual life while he pretends to be the friend of my corporeal, he is a real enemy ; but the man may be the friend of my spiritual life while he seems the enemy of my corporeal, though not *vice versa.*'

3* : 27. *Druidical Mathematical Proportion.* Blake might quite as easily have said ' Greek,' ' Egyptian,' or ' anti-Christian.' *Druidical* is a technical phrase for the reasonable religion, which would reduce even the divine Human Form to mathematical proportions.

3* : 28. *Displaying Naked Beauty.* Cf. the Laocoon plate : ' Art can never exist without Naked Beauty displayed.'

4 : 1. *The spiritual Four-fold London* : fourfold, because it is now taken as a symbol of fourfold Man.

4 : 3. *Albion's four Forests,* the growths of error which have overspread Man's four divisions (Zoas).

4 : 6 is revised from *The Four Zoas*, VIII. 111.

4 : 12. These are the four chief sons of Los who were never generated. Rintrah represents Wrath ; Palamabron is Pity ; Theotorm[on] is Desire ; and Bromion is Reason (as in *Jerusalem*, 54, illustration). See the Commentary on *The Four Zoas*, VIII. 351.

4 : 13. For the final Judgment of Man.

4 : 14. Lambeth : where Blake wrote most of his minor Prophetic Books.

4 : 15. Here his Vision began ' the foundations of Jerusalem ' ; but here also the Visions later abandoned him.

4 : 16. *Oak Groves.* Trees generally represented errors to Blake ; the British Oak came to represent the most stubborn of them, especially from their connection with the Druid religion. Cf. Sir Thomas Browne's *Pseudodoxia* : *To the Reader* : ' What roots old age contracteth unto errors, and how such as are but acorns in our younger brows, grow Oaks in our elder heads, and become inflexible unto the powerfullest arm of reason.'

4 : 20. A reference to the Archbishop's palace at Lambeth.

4 : 25-26. A reference to the idea that the unfallen Man once contained all things, but that in his Fall they became separated from him.

4 : 35-5 : 1. *And woven*, through the subsequent line, is obliterated in the New York copy, probably to avoid a repetition of the idea. Here Tirzah, the repressed woman, is seen aiding in the work of Generation.

5 : 4-5. The last half of one line and the beginning of the next line are obliterated in all copies. This lacuna probably contained some reference to the fourth Class, which is the synthesis of all three in Eternity.

To destruction: in the worldly sense only. *Follow with me my plough* is an exhortation to the reader to follow the path of the poet. It is repeated 6 : 20.

5 : 5. *Of the first class was Satan.* Here the story of the Felpham quarrel begins. A compressed version appears in *The Four Zoas*, VIII. 362-367, 382-389. In *Milton*, however, Satan is 'generated' into the form of Hayley; a spirit 'of the first class,' the Elect, who consider themselves saved, and yet 'they cannot Believe in Eternal Life Except by Miracle' (25 : 34).

5 : 6. Hayley's attempts at poetry.

5 : 7. *Palamabron* is Blake's name throughout this incident. The reader should have no difficulty in tracing the main outlines of the quarrel; remembering, however, that this is not literal 'allegory,' but a spiritual interpretation, where forces appear, though no one actually represented them in the world of flesh.

5 : 19. Work under Hayley disturbs Blake's own creative powers.

5 : 20. *The Gnomes* are Earth-spirits, comparable to the Fairies of the earlier poems. This proves that Blake believed that much of his inspiration came from natural forces.

5 : 34. Blake shows Hayley that he cannot work if Hayley interferes. Hayley blames Blake in return.

5 : 36. *Los* throughout this incident represents Blake's higher self.

5 : 42. Blake's higher self commands him to submit to Hayley, keeping his own creative work separate from the work which was bringing in remuneration.

6 : 7. Hayley finds the work he has given Blake quite disrupted with Blake's own ideas.

6 : 11. *His left sandal*: a symbol of the greatest humiliation. The feet are the lowest part of the body; and, as we shall see in the *Job*, the left represents the materialistic aspect of things, while the right represents the spiritual. We must interpret this to mean that Blake was very sorry to have abandoned the work he was doing for Hayley in such confusion, and tried to repress his creative instincts. 'But Rintrah also came.'

6 : 24. Blake, incapable of working either on his own things or on Hayley's, spends a day in thinking it over. This process is symbolized by the act of ploughing.

6 : 27. *Jehovah* represents the logic of the situation; *Molech* represents the unnatural sacrifice of Blake's own 'children'—his Art.

6 : 30. *Theotormon & Bromion* represent Blake's concern for his wife in the two aspects of natural love and a husband's logic. They fight against Blake's artistic independence, fearing that Catherine may be miserable.

6 : 32. *Michael*, the leader of the heavenly hosts, and the enemy of Satan (*Revelation* xii. 7), does not appear again in Blake's writings. Undoubtedly he represents Spiritual Warfare.

6 : 33. *Thulloh* appears nowhere else in Blake. He represents the natural sympathy between Blake and Hayley.

6 : 34. *Rintrah* is Wrath, who stirs the various mental forces now at work in Blake's mind to an appreciation of the situation. He is 'of the reprobate,' that is, of the third and highest Class of mankind, a 'devil' condemned by Satan and all his angels, the 'elect.'

6 : 39. Wrath kills Blake's sympathy for Hayley and urges Spiritual Warfare 'to arise.'

6 : 40. *Enitharmon* represents Catherine's higher aspect; her lower appears under the name of Elynittria.

6 : 41. Blake conceals from Catherine his loss of sympathy for Hayley.

6 : 42-43. Catherine tries to reconcile the two men, deploring the mental conflict (Michael). *She form'd a Space*: her function as goddess of Space; probably to be translated, ' She made allowances.'

6 : 47-48 repeated *Jerusalem*, 9 : 29-30, which continues: ' That Enthusiasm and Life may not cease.'

7 : 2. *Druids & Bards*: the two contrasting types.

7 : 5-6. Cf. John Marston's *Malcontent*, IV. iv.:

> *Malevole*: Now God deliver me from my friends!
> *Pietro*: Thy friends?
> *Malevole*: Yes, from my friends; for from mine enemies ile deliver my selfe.

7 : 10. *Judgment.* Blake makes an appeal against the situation; and is blamed for his wrath—even though Hayley also ' flam'd high & furious.'

7 : 12. Hayley is admired for his firmness; ' till it became a proverb in Eden.' This proverb, ' Satan is among the Reprobate ' (the third Class), was of course quite false. Cf. the letter to Butts, July 6, 1803: ' As if genius and assurance were the same thing ! '

7 : 20-29. Hayley infuriates Blake the more by accusing him of conventional crimes against friendship: ' of ingratitude, of malice.' (In so doing, Satan masquerades as Jehovah, though remaining the Accuser.) The idea that one should sacrifice one's very nature to Friendship, in order to imitate an inferior nature, was terrible to Blake. See 35 : 4-6. He had hoped for a sympathy that would rise above ordinary social standards; yet Hayley had not only done his best to hinder Blake's own creative work (' perverting the Divine voice in its entrance to the earth ') with warnings of poverty and the like; but now, at the first sign of disagreement, he had fallen back on the hollowest names of selfish virtues.

7 : 30-35. Hayley's wrath, being repressed ' beneath his own mildness,' burns inwardly, blackening everything against the Divine Vision of true sympathy. He falls yet lower in the spiritual scale. Blake's theories about the repression of such emotions may be found in the *Proverbs of Hell* and in *The Poison Tree* (*Songs of Experience*). *Ulro* is a technical word for the illusion of Matter.

7 : 40. *The east*: the realm of the passions. Hayley's passions are entirely overwhelmed by this ' opakeness ' to the Divine Light.

7 : 46. *Science*: scientia, ' knowledge.' As Hayley was unable to understand Blake's wrath, so he cannot understand his own. Blake had really mourned over the death of their friendship (6 : 45); but Hayley separates wrath and pity.

7 : 50. *The seven mountains*: the Seven Churches.

7 : 51. *The Covering Cherub* is the symbol of Doctrine which once guarded the truth (as the Cherubim guarded the Ark), but now it has become a False Doctrine, since it is mistaken for the Truth formerly concealed within. Specifically, the Covering Cherub often represents the Visible Church, as opposed to the Invisible: the Militant warring against the Triumphant. We shall often meet this symbol. It is derived from Ezekiel's lament over the prince of Tyre's errors (xxviii. 14-16): ' Thou art the anointed cherub that covereth; and I have set thee so: thou wast upon the holy mountain of God; thou hast walked up and down in the midst of the stones of fire. Thou wast perfect in thy ways from the day that thou wast created, till iniquity was found in thee. By the multitude of thy merchandise they have filled the midst of thee with violence, and thou hast sinned: therefore I will cast thee as profane out of the mountain of God; and I will destroy thee, O covering cherub, from the midst of the stones of fire.' Cf. also *Exodus* xxv. 20. The False Doctrine descends upon the oppressors of Israel: Rome, Babylon and Tyre.

8* : 1. Blake and his wife now recognize Hayley as no poet acting from divine impulse, but as a logical person acting from rules, and endeavouring to dominate all those who are really higher than himself. Satan is now openly identified with Urizen. ' It is a grand piece of poetical intuition on Blake's part to set Milton to fight Urizen, since " Los & Enitharmon knew that Satan is Urizen " and since in *Paradise Lost* the real Adversary and Pursuer of Satan is the poet himself' (Saurat, 22).

8* : 2. In the wars of Body and Intellect (Tharmas and Urizen), Revolt (Orc) sided against Urizen, and gradually got great power over him. Among other things he caused the fall of Urizen's Net of Religion (*Four Zoas*, VIII. 171); this success and the others followed only when Orc wedded the Shadowy Female (when War entered the Material World). Thus Urizen was drawn down into Generation by the two. Cf. also *The Four Zoas*, VII. 244 and 785-789.

8* : 3. Enitharmon, as Inspiration, is lost and aged when she tries to enter the realm of Satan ; as Catherine Blake, she is ineffectual in her attempts to reconcile the two men.

8* : 12-13. Blake cannot agree with any of Hayley's fundamental rules of life. His theories of Church and State are equally impossible.

8* : 14-18. *Elynittria* is the lower aspect of Mrs. Blake. Evidently she did not share her husband's views regarding Free Love. Even she is tainted with Satanic selfishness! Her arrows of jealousy (cf. 9 : 38) kill inspiration. The *deadly fading Moon* is symbolic of their married life (Beulah), suffering from its restriction.

8* : 19. *Ocalythron* is a spirit of Female Jealousy. She is one of Blake's most obscure characters. See the Commentary on *Europe*, 49.

9 : 1. *Eon* is another word for ' Emanation.' *He* refers to Satan. Albion's emanation is Jerusalem (Freedom).

9 : 4-5. Love and Inspiration end, where executions begin.

9 : 8. Here Hayley is lost in the eternal symbol, Satan. Satan's Druid sons are all those who follow the philosophy of which Hayley was the exponent. Everywhere they sacrifice Humanity to their own system of life.

9 : 14. *The Unutterable Name* is the name of God never pronounced aloud, the Tetragrammaton.

9 : 16. The great problem of injustice on earth. *The Innocent* are, in general, the Human Victims of line 8, and specifically Blake himself.

9 : 17-21. The answer is that, if the guilty were condemned at once, they would have no chance to work out their errors, and hence would be cut off from Eternity forever. The innocent, who cannot be so cut off, must be sacrificed to them. Thus Jesus was sacrificed to Satan. Meanwhile the guilty must be born and reborn until they have attained wisdom.

9 : 18. Cf. *Jerusalem*, 96 : 23-28.

9 : 28. *Leutha* represents simultaneously Hayley's Inspiration and the conventional, false doctrine of sex. It is not likely that she can be identified with any person then existing in the world of space and time. Hayley's wife was dead ; his illegitimate child had just died ; while he himself was in straitened circumstances ; therefore it is not likely that he had begun the harem, whose tradition (quite probably false) has been often mentioned.

The importance of sex in matters of inspiration has already been dealt with. Blake now tries to explain Hayley's spiritual failings by referring them to a lack of any sense of the higher functions of love. The little we know about Mrs. Hayley indicates that her life was not what could be called happy ; for which Blake, with ourselves, blamed the husband.

9 : 29. *The Serpent* is the Everlasting of Nature.

9 : 37. We must take Leutha, then, as Hayley's Inspiration. He also wanted to be a poet (Leutha loved Palamabron) ; but his Inspiration was not of the right sort, and he failed. Blake symbolized this as jealousy between Elynittria (his own Inspiration) and Leutha. Since Leutha cannot be identified with any one, we cannot interpret this passage as an attempt at a vulgar liaison, frustrated by Mrs. Blake. Blake was not writing literal allegory, but spiritual interpretation.

10 : 2. The essential antagonism between the two ; another reference to Hayley's oppression of Blake's creative work.

10 : 3-5. *This is to prevent* : *i.e.* Blake's creative work. She is responsible for Hayley's friendship to Blake for this very purpose. Cf. the epigram :

> Of H——'s birth this was the happy lot :
> His mother on his father him begot.

Had Hayley been less passive, and spiritually more aggressive, he would have understood Blake much better.

10 : 9. When Blake was exhausted with his own work, he should have had rest. But Hayley's Inspiration insisted on utilizing Blake's powers for other work, until they revolted.

10 : 12. *Those living creatures.* This identifies the horses that drew the harrow with the Four Zoas themselves.

10 : 15. *A bow of varying colours.* Leutha is not seen in her real form ; otherwise, as a visible Error, she would have been cast out. She appears therefore as a rainbow, the promise of the Lord. But the rainbow is only apotheosized water, and water is the symbol of death. In her most exalted moments she cannot change her nature.

10 : 23. As usual, the flames of creative genius seem like the torments of Hell to the ' angels.'

10 : 25. The Assyrian conception of the Sun (which to Blake meant Poetry) ploughing its way through the Stars (which meant Reason) seems to have fascinated Blake. Usually, however, Luvah (Passion) guides the Plough ; but now Satan does so, with destructive results.

10 : 28. *Dark fires* : devoid of light (wisdom).

10 : 29. *The Serpent* : the system of Materialism.

10 : 31. The Earth Spirits themselves fight against Materialism and finally function no more.

10 : 35. *The Living Creatures* : the Four Zoas, who are the horses of the Harrow.

10 : 38. Leutha appears in her real form, but is rejected, and takes refuge in Hayley's subconscious mind. She emerged from his head, because she is a form of intellection, and is not of the heart.

10 : 39 is quoted from *Paradise Lost* II. : ' . . . and call'd me *Sin,* and for a Sign / Portentous held me.'

10 : 42. Hayley's one influx of true Inspiration (Elynittria) must have come in the period preceding the birth of his illegitimate son. At first he was intoxicated by his adventure, but at once he repented, ' being most impure, self-condemn'd to eternal tears,' till he cast out even his normal sex-life (Leutha).

10 : 49. See the Commentary on *Jerusalem,* 42 : 32-34.

11 : 1-2. As a result, Satan has become a Spectre, while his Emanation, Leutha, is cast out, and sick almost to non-existence.

11 : 4. *The Sick-one* is Satan.

11 : 5. *Individual Law* : One Law, drawn from the character of a single personality ; ' let all obey my principles of moral individuality ' (7 : 26).

11 : 8. *The Spectre of Luvah* : the reasoning portion only of the god of the Passions. When Albion fell, Luvah defied Urizen's offer to share the supreme power, smote Albion, then rose to fight Urizen. Cf. *The Four Zoas,* I. 459 *seq.*

11 : 10-11. That is, the Sin was not begun in the world of Time, nor will it end until the two Eternities of the Past and of the Future close in over the Present ; when Time, ' the parenthesis in Eternity,' is obliterated.

11 : 13. Enitharmon often plays the part of goddess of Mercy in this world, by protecting spirits from immediate judgment, that they may have time to work out their errors. Satan is protected by Space from the boundlessness of Infinity ; a limit is put to Error, which otherwise would extend everywhere. This is an explanation of all Creation.

11 : 17. *Six Thousand Years* : the time allotted to the created world, according to a prophecy derived from the Bible. See the Commentary on *The Marriage of Heaven and Hell*, plate XIV.

11 : 18-26. This list of the Seven Eyes of God is slightly rewritten from *The Four Zoas*, VIII. 392-400. See the Commentary on that passage.

11 : 31. *The Transgressor* is another term for the Reprobate, the third of the Three Classes of Mankind. Cf. H. C. R., 17 Dec. 1825 : ' What are called vices in the natural world are the highest sublimities in the spiritual world.' Cf. *The Four Zoas*, IX. 264.

11 : 35. *The Fatal Brook* : Tyburn.

11 : 36. Liberated Sex endeavours to convert Conventionalized Sex.

11 : 40. Conventionalized Sex, in the embrace of Pity, gives birth to the Illusion, Death. Cf. Shelley's *Queen Mab* : ' How beautiful is Sleep, / Sleep and his brother Death.'

11 : 41. *Rahab*, licence in sex, is the mother of *Tirzah*, sex suppressed. *Her sisters* are the Daughters of Albion.

11 : 42. See the Commentary on *Jerusalem*, 57 : 7.

11 : 45. *The Bard ceas'd*. His song began 3 : 25.

12 : 5. *Vegetative power* : the power of the flesh.

12 : 12. *Ulro* : Matter.

12 : 14. *Eternal Death* : death from Eternity. The descent into the world of Time and Space always seems like death to the Eternals. When knowingly performed, it is also a process of *mortification*, of self-sacrifice. Cf. Shelley's *Prometheus Unbound*, III. iii. 113 : ' Death is the veil which those who live call life.'

12 : 15. *Gods of Priam* : self-expression by means of War.

12 : 17. *The sleeping body* is Albion.

12 : 20. *The grave* and all similar terms are symbols of the world of the flesh. Cf. the 4th section of *Thel*.

12 : 22. *Self-annihilation* : self-sacrifice.

12 : 23. *Unannihilate* : with his Selfhood (Selfishness) not completely gone, with his life therefore not made whole.

12 : 28. *My Emanation* : the sixfold soul of his wives and daughters. Milton is not made whole, since he is still divided. Cf. the Commentary on 3 : 19. By finding his Emanation, he will relieve the world from that false ideal.

12 : 29. ' He spoke of Milton as being at one time a sort of classical Atheist ' (H. C. R., Dec. 17, 1825).

12 : 30. *I in my Selfhood am that Satan*. Selfhood (or selfishness) is always error. Blake believed firmly that the Individuality is immortal ; distinguishing between the Individuality (or Humanity) and the Selfhood, which is its outer coating of error. Here Blake becomes almost Buddhist ; but the Buddha refused to say whether the individual soul survived or not. However, there are plenty of Buddhist texts which seem to distinguish between the Individual and the Self-hood : ' The Truth is the immortal part of mind. Establish truth in your mind, for the truth is the image of the eternal. . . . Learn to distinguish between Self and Truth. Self is the cause of selfishness and the source of sin ; truth clings to no self ; it is universal and leads to justice and righteousness. . . . The consciousness of self dims the eyes of the mind and hides the Truth ' (quoted from texts in Paul Carus's *Gospel of Buddha*).

12 : 31. When the Emanation is outcast, only a Spectre remains. When the Imagination is rejected, Logic is triumphant. Milton's theology was entirely rational, hence an Error (Satan). The Creative faculty (Furnace) is always Hell to the Spectre.

12 : 35. *The graves of the dead* : physical bodies. Cf. Paracelsus : ' All putrefaction is essentially and excessively cold ' (*De Tartaro*, II. ii. 7) ; ' Putrefaction takes away the acridity from all corrosive spirits of salt, renders them soft and

sweet, transmutes their colours, separates the pure from the impure, and places the pure higher, the impure lower, each by itself' (*De Natura Rerum*, VII.).

12 : 36. *Beulah* stands between Eternity and Time. To those in Eternity it is a place of sleep; to those in Time it is the great source of all Inspiration. Here Milton finds *his own Shadow*, which is the illusory vehicle, becoming in its lowest form the physical body. Till now, ' Shadow ' had meant suppressed desire; but in *Milton* it takes a new meaning. Cf. the poem to Butts, Oct. 2, 1800: ' And saw Felpham sweet. . . . / And in her fair arms / My Shadow I knew / And my wife's Shadow too,' where the meaning is obviously the same.

It is possible that this idea was suggested by Porphyry's *Auxiliaries to the Perception of Intelligible Natures* (I. 32): ' Moreover, in its egress from the body, if it still possesses a spirit turbid from humid exhalations, it then attracts to itself a shadow, and becomes heavy; a spirit of this kind naturally striving to penetrate into the recesses of the earth ' (Taylor's translation, p. 216).

12 : 37. *Hermaphroditic*: that is, containing the unsolved contradictions of his sexual doctrine. Emanation and Spectre not being one, the forms of both sexes are distinct ' in one wonderful body.' This is the paradox which Milton is to solve.

12 : 39. *Twenty-seven-fold*: his error extends everywhere, throughout all the ' Twenty-seven Heavens and all their Hells ' (16 : 24). They represent all the false religions which the earth has accepted. A list of them is given 37 : 35-43. These religions stand between Eternity and ' this earth of vegetation on which now I write.'

12 : 41. *The Seven Angels of the Presence* are the Seven Eyes of God. Cf. 11 : 27.

14 : 1. Here Blake describes the psychological state in which the Mortal communicates with the Eternal, and *vice versa*. Cf. Swedenborg's *Heaven and Hell*, 440: ' . . . A man is brought into a middle state betwixt sleeping and waking, during which he knows no other than that he is perfectly awake, forasmuch as all his senses are as lively as ever, his sight, his hearing, and what appears still more strange, even his feeling; nay, this last is at such a time more exquisite than at others. In this state I have seen angels and spirits to the life, have heard them speak, and, what will be thought still more wonderful, have touched them, though the material body then bore no part therein. . . . Into this state I have been brought only three or four times.' Blake seems to have been very familiar with this state. See Chapter XXVIII. See also Iamblicus: *De Myst. Aegypt.*, III. 7.

14 : 4. *His Sleeping Body*. When Milton entered Beulah, his Spiritual Body (1 *Cor.* xv. 44) sank into sleep; at this moment he entered his Shadow.

14 : 5. *An Eighth*: to the Seven Eyes of God is to be added each man's own individuality. Needless to say, on this earth Man adds his own Essence to the various Principles which he worships. See the Commentary on *The Four Zoas*, VIII. 392-400.

14 : 8. *The Polypus* is Blake's symbol for a growth of Material Thought in the Sea of Time and Space; generally it is a symbol of human Society. See the Commentary on *Jerusalem*, 67 : 35-37.

14 : 9-16. A description of Milton's condition when he enters the world of flesh. Cf. the Commentary on 14 : 4. *The Couch of death* is his resting place in Beulah; *his real and immortal Self* is his Individuality; *but to himself* refers to the Shadow on earth.

14 : 22. *Its own Vortex*. Cf. the Cartesian vortices. Everything is an Active Principle, which draws all other things to itself (hence the law: ' he became what he beheld '). Once such a Vortex is passed through, it takes its place in the Universe (as Imagination becomes the Sun, Love the Moon, and Intellect the Stars).

14 : 32. *Thus is the earth one infinite plane*. See Commentary on 28 : 15.

14 : 33. *I.e.* to the man beneath the state of Inspiration (Beulah), and confined to this earth.

14 : 34-35. Thus we have passed through heaven, but have not yet passed through earth.

14 : 36. Milton's first sight in his descent is that of Man outstretched in the same death which Milton is now entering.

14 : 42. Cf. *The Four Zoas*, VI. 199-203. In the confusion of descent, all sense of direction is lost. Things which are below heaven soon appear above the earth.

14 : 46. Cf. John Dyer's *Ruins of Rome*, 40-42 :

> Towers
> Tumbling all precipitate down dashed
> Rattling around, loud thundering to the Moon.

. 14 : 49. *The left foot* is the very lowest part of the body ; since left is always inferior to right, the first being material, the second the spiritual. This left and right symbolism is very ancient ; and was developed to a very great extent in Blake's illustrations to *Job*. Blake means that the spirit of Milton entered him through exterior means (such as books) and not by interior communion.

When the spirit of the unredeemed Milton enters Blake (that is, when he absorbs the spirit of the older poet), Blake sees the dark cloud of Puritanism which has spread over Europe.

14 : 51-16 : 3. When Milton enters Blake (for Blake believed that the thought of a dead person was actual communion with that person—see letter to Hayley, May 6, 1800), Milton realizes his error. He learns that when he lived here in the body (not for sixty, but for sixty-six years, in reality), he was made a poet (beholding the Three Heavens of Beulah—which include the three visions granted to man on this earth, but excluding the ultimate fourfold vision) for the purpose of correcting his sexual theories (' To Annihilate the Self-hood of Deceit & False Forgiveness / In those three females whom his wives, & those three whom his daughters / Had represented and contain'd ') ; so that at last he might be made whole ' by the giving up of Selfhood.'

The Maclagan-Russell text at this point unfortunately omits the single line on page 15, which is essential to the sense of the sentence ; and numbers page 16 as 15.

16 : 4. *Human* ; or, in more common phraseology, ' Divine.'

16 : 5. *Till the Judgment*, which occurs on page 44. A Last Judgment is the exposure and destruction of an error.

16 : 8. *Dividing*. His error is repeated numberless times in the cruelties of the sexual doctrines of the Puritans.

16 : 11. Milton's first wife was Mary Powell (1625-1652), by whom he had his three daughters : *Ann* (1646-1678), who was a handsome cripple ; Mary (1648-1674), who appears to have been the meanest of the three daughters ; and Deborah (1652-1727), who was the only one to continue Milton's line. There was also a son, John (1651-1652), who, on account of his early death, was not considered by Blake. Milton had courted and married Mary Powell in a month. He soon realized that they were completely incompatible ; indeed, he wrote his first divorce pamphlet during their honeymoon. Four years after her death, he married Katherine Woodcocke (?-1658), whose only offspring was Katherine (1657-1658), also omitted from Blake's symbolism on account of her early death. Milton loved his second wife deeply, as his last sonnet testifies. Five years after her death, in desperation against the meanness and mismanagement of his three daughters, he married Elizabeth Minshull (1630-1727), who does not appear to have been much more than a housekeeper. She and the three daughters survived him.

Blake lays the blame on Milton for being unable to cope with the women in his house ; and that they turned out so badly was to be explained by Milton's own inhuman austerities. They were, quite literally, expressions of Milton's own attitude towards life.

Blake names them after the brotherless daughters of Zelophehad (*Numbers* XXVI. 33), adding Rahab, to make the sixth. (See the Commentary on *The Four Zoas*, VIII. 306.)

16 : 13. When Milton became blind, his daughters used to take down his poems from his dictation.

16 : 14. *The Rock Sinai* : Milton was of the Old Testament tradition, whose ultimate expression was reached in the Ten Commandments, delivered upon Mount Sinai. Blake always took these ' ten Negations ' as opposed to the teachings of Christ, who forgave the very sins which the Commandments denounced. In the ultimate sense, therefore, Milton was not Christian (for all his being a poet) ; and his error, which is Puritanism, must be solved.

16 : 16. These are the names of various mountains which circumscribe the Promised Land. Of course, they are not to be found in ' the Desarts of Midian.' Midian is a State of spiritual whoredom, a following after false sexual doctrines ; Blake derived his symbol from the Midianitish woman who brought the plague to the children of Israel (*Numbers* xxv. 6-18).

16 : 20. Hostile countries surrounding the Promised Land.

16 : 21-23. The Earth is the petrifaction of the Human Imagination.

16 : 24-26. It contains all the familiar errors : the twenty-seven religions with their Heavens and Hells ; the Chaos which is the result of imperfect Memory ; and the Ancient Night which is the Void of Non-Entity.

16 : 27. *The lark*, in this poem, becomes the symbol of poetic inspiration. Cf. 31 : 29. Perhaps this was suggested by *Ecclesiastes* x. 20.

16 : 29-30. Descending from Eternity, one passes outward to Error ; ascending towards Eternity, one passes inward to the City of Art.

16 : 31-33. The Poet is terrified at Milton's advance, for his Inspiration announces that, while they will be freed, Error will also be unloosed over mankind.

16 : 35. *Like roots of trees* : like fibres of flesh (vegetation). In short, the flesh itself limits the advance of the great spirit. It will be remembered that the flesh is woven on Cathedron's looms by Enitharmon.

16 : 36. *The immortal Man* : Milton.

17* : 1. These two names complete the list of the four Zoas who behold the progress of Milton.

17* : 2. The Shadowy Female is materialized Nature.

17* : 12. *Writings* : the philosophy of Experience.

17* : 18. *Rahab & Tirzah* : the two forms of false sexual doctrine : Licence and Repression.

17* : 25. The Shadowy Female (Vala) is the Emanation of Orc (Luvah) ; their story is one which Blake never tires of repeating in new forms. Passion, when degraded to this world, is Warfare, the Revolt of Youth ; Nature on the same plane is the world of Matter. When the two are united, warfare enters the world of Matter. The union is destructive to both, and therefore very terrifying to them ; though they are destroyed only to rise in their higher forms of Luvah and Vala. War, in short, always burns itself out, and consumes Materialism in the process. This conflagration is, in Blake's terms, a ' Consummation.'

17* : 26. Orc is angry that Nature should assume definite form.

17* : 30. *Satan* or Error.

17* : 37. *Covering Cherub* : see Commentary on 7 : 51.

17* : 39. *Oothoon & Leutha* : symbolizing the true and the false doctrines of sex ; one opening into Jerusalem, the other into Babylon.

17* : 42. The conflict between two sexual ideals is not delightful to the Material World.

17* : 47. *His rocky Couch* : see *The Four Zoas*, v. 101, for the binding of Orc.

17* : 51. We return to Milton's voyage. Urizen opposes his progress. We are now to see Milton's own reason struggling with Reason itself.

17 : 6. Blake's geography is obviously symbolic. The Arnon is not near Mahanaim, much less ' on the shores of Albion.' The Arnon is the river of generation on whose banks the Spectres put on the flesh (*The Four Zoas*, viii. 212). Later, Blake renames it ' Storge.'

17 : 7. *Mahanaim* was the spot where Jacob wrestled (*Genesis* xxxii.).

17 : 9. Reason baptizes Milton with the water (death) of his religion.

17 : 10. *The red clay of Succoth.* Of Succoth clay Hiram had various utensils made for the Temple (1 *Kings* vii. 46). Milton is giving Reason a form (cf. the labours of Los).

17 : 14. *Beth Peor*, a place of erroneous doctrines of sex. Here the Israelites followed the sins of the Moabites (*Numbers* xxv. 3).

17 : 15-18. The four Zoas in their normal position.

17 : 19-20. But when the Passions tried to direct Reason, Man died from Eternity.

17 : 21. All shrank and fell.

17 : 22-23. Logic is now ruined by wrath ; Love has faded to nothing ; the Body is overwhelmed in the Sea of Time and Space ; and the Spirit is locked in frigid blackness.

17 : 25. *The Universe of Los and Enitharmon* : the realm of Poetry. The ' Centre ' is the throne of God, where the ' intellectual fountain ' breaks forth ; it is the residue of the Divine Imagination which has not been petrified into fixed form.

17 : 26. Milton tries to reach the very core of Man, but Reason opposes his path.

17 : 28. Standing in the West (realm of the Body) the twin false attitudes toward sex (licence and repression) watch the strife.

17 : 29. Cf. *Jerusalem*, 43 : 41-43.

17 : 31. *The river* is the Arnon (17 : 6). The false doctrines of sex try to tempt Milton to re-enter the life of generation.

17 : 32-34. The old religions of doubt and cruelty appear before Milton, tempting him with their magnificence. For a list, see 37 : 35-43.

17 : 35. *Entuthon*, or Entuthon-Benython, the realm of abstractions.

17 : 36–18 : 6. This song of seduction promises Milton the glory of the Old Testament patriarchs, if he will but follow its strict morality. This was, quite literally, the ideal of the English Puritans. The song also pictures the state of fallen man.

17 : 36. *Ephraim*, Joseph's younger son, who nevertheless was blessed with the right hand, since from him the greater race was eventually to come. Milton's generation is to be this younger and greater race.

17 : 37. *The Beautiful Amalekites* : these formed a race successively smitten by Israel, Gideon, Saul and David. The sound of their name, with its overtone of Love (amare), caused Blake to use them as a symbol of youth smitten by Puritanism. *The fires of youth* : the flames of Orc. See *The Four Zoas*, v. 101.

17 : 39. *The banks of Cam* : where Cambridge University is situated.

17 : 40. *Rephaim's Vale* : where the Philistines spread, till they were smitten by David (2 *Samuel* v. 18).

17 : 41-43. References to the early part of *The Four Zoas*. Pleasure is cast out (III. 134) ; the Generative Instinct has withered to a mere voice (III. 207) ; and Nature has become a torturer (II. 73).

17 : 44. Therefore the Repressed Sex triumphs.

17 : 46. *The Grecian Lyre* : in æsthetics, this is Realism ; in religion, it is the triumph of the Intellect over the Spirit. Cf. Blake's marginalia to *Siris* : ' The Whole Bible is fill'd with Imagination & Visions from End to End & not with Moral Virtues ; that is the baseness of Plato & the Greeks & all Warriors. The Moral Virtues are continual Accusers of Sin & promote Eternal Wars & Dominency over others.'

17 : 47. *Natural Religion* : Rousseau's term, which Blake applied to all Intellectualized religions, particularly to the contemporary religions. His first book of illuminated printing was an attack on Natural Religion.

17 : 51. *Horeb* : the desert about Sinai. Here Man is enclosed in the physical body.

17 : 58. *Hand, Hyle,* and *Coban* are three of Albion's monstrous sons, born as a result of the Fall. In general, they represent the cruelty of Man to Man ; or War. They belong to the symbolism of *Jerusalem,* rather than to *Milton* ; and their inclusion proves this page to be of comparatively late date. *Hyle* has been identified with Hayley. *Hyle* is the Greek term for Matter.

17 : 59. *Scofield* is another monstrous Son of Albion ; he is easily identified with the soldier who attacked Blake at Felpham. *Reuben* is the materialized Man.

17 : 60. *Two lovely Heavens* : the separated sexes.

18 : 2. *Three Heavens* : of the Body, the Intellect, and the Emotions.

18 : 3. *Ephraim & Manasseh* : the two sons of Joseph (*Genesis* xli. 51-52).

18 : 6. *Hazor* : a city overcome and burned by Joshua (*Joshua* xi.).

18 : 7-10. Milton, having encountered Urizen, has given him a form—has created a logical philosophy.

18 : 10-14. Milton in his threefold division (Elect, Redeem'd, and Reprobate —see the Commentary on 3 : 26). The *Mortal Part,* or Shadow, which is frozen in the Law (Horeb being an alternative symbol for Sinai) is the Elect (18 : 20) ; the *Redeem'd Portion,* or Spectre, at present is giving Falsehood a form ; while the *real Human,* or Humanity, is the Reprobate at the core of his Personality : ' he was a true Poet, and of the Devil's party without knowing it ' (*Marriage of Heaven and Hell,* plate vi.). When he finds his Emanation, he will be fourfold and complete.

18 : 15. Blake speaks.

18 : 19. Of the many references in the New Testament, 1 *Corinthians* xiii. 2 is the nearest to this passage.

18 : 20-24. As Blake uses ' redounding ' with its early meaning ' overflowing,' this passage should be clear. Blake casts off the reasoned part of Milton's philosophy (the *Spectrous Body* or the *Cherub*) ; this portion remains in the world of Time and Space, and preserves Milton's entire work (as, in *The Marriage of Heaven and Hell,* plate iii., Swedenborg's erroneous writings preserved the true doctrines unwittingly).

18 : 23. *The Great Consummation* is the Last Judgment.

18 : 25. *Albion's sleeping Humanity* : his inmost self.

18 : 27-42. The gist of this passage is that everything opens within into Eternity. Milton, as a poet, entered the Centre ; but he went too far and entered the realms of Abstract Philosophy ; and so ' fell through ' the heart of Man.

18 : 27. Cf. *The Fly* (*Songs of Experience*). Cf. also Jakob Böhme's *Aurora,* XXVI. 68 : ' The clear Deity stands everywhere hidden in the Circle in the Heart of the whole Deep.'

18 : 31. A Platonic doctrine.

18 : 32. *Beyond the skies* : outside man. This was Milton's error : seeking God away from Humanity.

18 : 33. *Og & Anak.* These two, with Satan and Sihon, constantly appear as Accusers, and workers at the Satanic Mills. They appear twice in *The Four Zoas* (I. 480 and VIII. 214) ; and many times in the other two epics.

According to the Bible, Og was the giant king of Bashan, and Sihon was the king of the Amorites ; both were destroyed by Moses on the way to the Promised Land (*Numbers* xxi.) Anak was the supposed ancestor of the Anakim, another race of giants, cut off by Joshua (*Joshua* xi. 21) on the way to the Promised Land.

In Blake's symbolism, Og and Anak are the ' guardians of the threshold.' They guard jointly the gates of the heart and the brain in nature (*Milton,* 31 : 49) as well as in man (*Milton,* 18 : 33). Though they are of the Satanic forces, the Divine Mercy has placed these giants between the two worlds of Imagination and Matter, to prevent a further fall, ' bending the Laws of Cruelty to Peace ' (*Jerusalem,* 49 : 56).

Blake associates Og and Sihon as the fabric of the starry Mundane Shell (*Milton,* 37).

The four together probably correspond in some way to the Zoas.

18 : 46. *The Watchers* are the Seven Eyes of God.

18 : 47. *The Shadowy Eighth* is the sleeping Humanity of Milton.

18 : 48. The Eight are driven by the wrath of the Eternals over the Fall into the material world.

18 : 49. *Three wide gates* : in the brain, heart, and loins (18 : 38).

18 : 50. *Ulro* : the illusion of Matter.

18 : 51. *Rintrah & Palamabron* : Honest Wrath and Pity.

18 : 53. *Reuben & Gad* : the first and seventh sons of Jacob. See *Joshua* xxii. 11 *seq.*

18 : 57. *An old Prophecy*, apparently *not* recorded elsewhere than in Eden.

18 : 61. *Orc* : ' the fires of youth ' (17 : 37).

19 : 1. *Udan-Adan* : the region of the Indefinite.

19 : 2. *Satan* : Hayley again, whose poetry obviously belongs to this region.

19 : 3. *Shadow* : used in the old sense of Repressed Desire, and not in the new sense of Body. (We may conjecture this page to have been one of the earliest.) When Hayley's logic is asleep, his sympathies awake, and *vice versa*.

19 : 7. *The vast breach* : the destruction caused by Milton's fall ' thro' Albion's heart ' into Puritanism. Milton's reascent is to be through the person of Blake (his errors are to be corrected by Blake) ; therefore Milton, being fallen, has to enter Blake through the foot.

19 : 11. Since, in fact, Man *is* the Universe.

19 : 12-14. Cf. Plato : ' The true order of going is to use the Beauties of Earth as steps along which one mounts upward for the sake of that other Beauty.'

19 : 15-19. *Ololon*, though she does not know it, is the eternal form of Milton's erring Sixfold Emanation. Ololon first appears as a river of spiritual riches ; but after that she is always a woman. When Milton descends to seek her (though not knowing it is she he must find), she is similarly moved to descend, with the same high motives, and the same ignorance as to her true relation to Milton. Those interested in psychological curiosities should compare Ololon with Thomas Vaughan's *River of Pearl* (*Lumen de Lumine*, v.).

19 : 20. Cf. the Commentary on 10 : 25. In this Moment all the rest of the epic's action takes place.

19 : 20-27. Ololon's lamentation, when heard on earth, is inspiration for the finest poetry. What is woe in Eden is immense delight on the more woeful earth. The moment when this inspiration is heard is at dawn. For the peculiarly inspired character of that hour, see Chapter XXVIII. Cf. also Blake's letter to Hayley, Jan. 27, 1804 : ' The distant approach of things mighty and magnificent, like the sound of harps which I hear before the sun's rising.'

19 : 28-30. Los and Enitharmon (as manifested in Blake and his wife) are in the world of Generation ; they hear the lamentation vaguely.

19 : 31-36. The Poet who rejected Milton now realizes that Milton was more than a mere lyrist—he came to correct errors. Now Los hears the appeal of the outcast (' those whom Milton drove down into Ulro ') and he sees the cloud of Puritanism spreading over Europe.

19 : 33. *The Bard* is he who sang from 3 : 25 to 11 : 44.

19 : 37. *Four Suns* : the Four Zoas.

19 : 40. *Southward* : toward the place of bondage, where Orc is chained.

19 : 46. *The Transgressors* are the Martyrs (Reprobate).

19 : 47. *Is Virtue a Punisher?* The question which condemns all Puritanism, besides most of Milton's theology.

19 : 51. *Six Thousand Years*, the time allotted to Creation. See the Commentary on plate XIV. of *The Marriage of Heaven and Hell*.

19 : 52-57. Both she and Milton knew by instinct that the cycle was ended, and that they were appointed to raise the Universe. But no hope can be given that she will raise Milton ; with such a hope the Great Sacrifice would be no sacrifice.

19 : 56. A reminiscence from *Matthew* xxviii. 20.

20 : 4-14. When Blake was turning the material universe into a means for spiritual progress (binding on his sandals—cf. 19 : 12-14), which took place in

Lambeth, the god of Poetry came upon him and entered him (inspiring the Lambeth books). Then Blake knew that he was a poet and that he could not ever be anything else (' 'Twas too late now to recede '). Los now takes Blake to his ' supreme abode,' the city of Art, which is Golgonooza.

20 : 15-16 are repeated from *The Four Zoas*, VIII. 245-246.

20 : 22. All error is destroyed ; but nothing else. Whatever seems to vanish from the earth has in reality taken its place in Eternity.

20 : 31. Honest Wrath and Pity are not big enough to appreciate at once the arrival of Blake, whom they see as a new force of terrible potentialities. They remember the errors created by Milton, and see those errors repeated in Blake's ' fibrous left Foot black.' They know Blake's intention to unchain the forces of Revolution (Orc), and fear that in doing so he will also loose upon mankind all the old errors (Satan) of natural forces (the giants Og, Sihon & Anak).

20 : 36. *The Shadowy Female* : Nature in her form of Matter.

20 : 38. The Daughters of Inspiration, fearing the freedom which would come from the triumph of Desire (Theotormon), are creating false philosophies for self-protection.

20 : 39-60. The condition of contemporary religion. Puritanism is the cause. As a reaction against it, the spirit of licence raised up Voltaire, while the spirit of restraint raised up Rousseau, who, though destroying superstition, also destroyed the last vestiges of belief in Inspiration and in anything beyond abstract virtues. Even Swedenborg's visions of the Conjugal Life and of the World of Matter were overcome by the popular errors of the Church of Moral Virtue (Rahab), so that ' he has written all the old falsehoods' (*Marriage of Heaven and Hell*, plate XXII.). Finally Honest Wrath raised Whitefield ; Pity raised Wesley ; and the Methodist movement revived the Christ in the heart.

20 : 39. Milton is blamed for Puritanism, since he was its greatest exponent.

20 : 51-52. One of the oldest errors, refuted in *The Marriage of Heaven and Hell*.

20 : 53. Cf. the *Siris* marginalia, quoted in the Commentary on 17 : 46. *Trojan Gods* are deified heroes. Cf. the letter to Hayley, May 28, 1804 : ' As the French now adore Bonaparte and the English our poor George, so the Americans will consider Washington as their god. This is only Grecian, or rather Trojan, worship, and perhaps will be revised in an age or two.'

20 : 55. For an account of George Whitefield (1714-1770), John Wesley (1703-1791), and the birth of Methodism, see Chapter II. Of course, neither Whitefield nor Wesley were killed in the attacks of the mobs ; but they often stood in great danger of it ; and some of their followers were not so lucky as they.

22 : 1-2. Blake did not believe in the ordinary conception of miracles. ' The manner of a miracle being performed is in modern times considered as an arbitrary command of the agent upon the patient, but this is an impossibility, not a miracle ; neither did Jesus do such a miracle. Is it a greater miracle to feed five thousand men with five loaves than to overthrow all the armies of Europe with a small pamphlet [?] Look over the events of your own life & if you do not find that you have both done such miracles & lived by them you do not see as I do ' (from Blake's marginalia in his copy of Bishop Watson's *Apology for the Bible*). Cf. Sir Thomas Browne's *Religio Medici*, II. 11 : ' Now for my life, it is a miracle of thirty years, which to relate, were not a History, but a piece of Poetry.' Cf. also Walt Whitman's *Miracles*, which begins : ' Why ! who makes much of a miracle ? / As to me, I know of nothing else but miracles.'

22 : 4. *Twice sounded* : in the American and French Revolutions.

22 : 6. The American Revolution. Orc is at last released.

22 : 10. *The Covering Cherub* : see Commentary on, 7 : 51.

22 : 12. ' How long sacrifice our highest inspirations to the false doctrine ? '

22 : 16. *Gwendolen & Conwenna* are the first and last of the twelve Daughters of Albion, who represent the cruelty of Woman to Man. Though the Daughters

appear as early as *The Four Zoas*, II. 61-62, they belong in reality to the symbolism of Jerusalem.

22 : 18. *Bowlahoola* is the assimilative system (Digestion) ; or in general, the Laws of Physiology. It is below the Head, Heart, and Loins, and does not open into Eternity. The root from which the name was derived is 'bowel.'

22 : 33. *The falling Death* : Milton. As Milton has entered into Blake, there is a natural confusion between the two.

22 : 39-44. The answer to Blake's question throughout the *Songs of Experience* : what is the reason for feminine hypocrisy ? It exists in order to protect love, while love is still called evil. *Spectrous* and *Vegetation* are almost synonymous terms for this fallen world.

22 : 45-46. A vision of the sacrament of Eternity. See *The Four Zoas*, IX.

22 : 49. 'God never makes one man murder another, nor one nation' (Blake's marginalia to Bishop Watson).

22 : 55. This seems to have been a belief not uncommon in Blake's day. Cf. Burns's *Death and Doctor Hornbook* : 'Sax thousand years are near-hand fled.'

22 : 56. *The Elect* : Milton died self-justified, and therefore is of the 'Elect' ; but in Eternity he learned that he was really a Transgressor, and has returned to earth in Blake's form.

22 : 60. *The Sun of Salah* : evidently the material sun. This is Blake's only use of the word 'Salah,' which seems to have no relation to the Biblical characters of that name. 'The dead Sun is only a phantasy of evil Man' (Swedenborg marginalia). *Udan-Adan* is the lake of the Indefinite.

22 : 62. *Twelve Sons* : the Twelve Tribes of Israel. *The thousand years of sorrow* refer to the Blake-Hayley quarrel (5 : 14).

23 : 2. Apparently a list of the twelve sons was to follow, but it was not completed as in *The Four Zoas*, VIII. 369-371. Manazzoth, however, is a name not met elsewhere in Blake, and not at all in the Bible : we must assume that it, as well as Menassheh (lines 6 and 20), is a peculiar spelling for Manasseh.

Blake considered the division into tribes as further fruit of the Fall from the original Unity. Tirzah, who is restrained sex, here represents the Jewish marriage-system.

23 : 9. Three of the Zoas have fallen ; Los does not seem to realize that he, the Fourth, is also fallen from his original station, when he was known as Urthona.

23 : 10. *My four mighty ones* : his four principal sons (*Four Zoas*, VIII. 351-352), who were never generated, but remained with Los to guard the West against further flights from Eternity (*Jerusalem*, 72 : 10-13). These four sons are dim reflections of the Zoas : Rintrah (Wrath) of Urthona ; Palamabron (Pity) of Tharmas ; Theotormon (Desire) of Luvah ; and Bromion (Reason) of Urizen.

23 : 14. Blake believed each nation was one person in Eternity, therefore he often personifies them. In *The Four Zoas*, VIII. 358, we find Moab and Midian among Los's daughters.

23 : 17-19. Blake's account differs from *Genesis*. There Joseph, far from being an infant, was aged seventeen ; he wore a coat of many colours, not emblematic needlework ; and he was sold to Ishmaelites, not to the Amalekites. The two essential symbols of Joseph's life were the stripping off of the coat and the selling into Egypt. As Joseph's position is the West (*Jerusalem*, 72 : 3), he must represent the body, stripped of all covering of its sins (as in *The Four Zoas*, VIII. 215) and sold to slavery under the Intellect (Egypt—south).

Jakob Böhme, in his great commentary on *Genesis*, *The Mysterium Magnum* (III. 65), has nothing to say of the significance of Joseph's coat. Swedenborg (*Heavenly Arcana*, 4677) claims that the coat represents 'truth of the natural,' in particular, 'the appearances of truth, whereby the spiritual of the natural is known and distinguished.'

23 : 20-21. The sons of Joseph led the nations to spiritual whoredom.

23 : 26-33. An explanation how error arose from the teachings of Christ. The

raising of Lazarus was the climax of the miracles of Jesus. It was the triumph over death. This symbol of immortality, however, was misunderstood, and so rose 'into the Covering Cherub,' which is the false intellection, that nevertheless preserves the Truth in times of darkness by circumscribing it. The Covering Cherub is the literal interpretation of the mystical symbols. From it rose the four Churches of Paul, Constantine, Charlemaine, and Luther: Theocracy, Imperialism by divine right, the Militant Church, and Sectarianism.

23:27. *The Vehicular Body of Albion*: the temporal symbol of Man.

23:36. *Bowlahoola & Allamanda*: Digestion (Law) and the Nervous System (Commerce).

23:46. Wrath and Pity are Rintrah and Palamabron themselves.

23:48. Blake has entered Golgonooza.

23:49. *Luban* is the place in Golgonooza where the merciful looms of Cathedron are erected. There the wandering Spectres are snared by the children of Los, and given bodies, that they may rise through this assumption of the human form. Satan waits outside Luban. Cf. *The Four Zoas*, VIII. 205-219.

23:63-64 are repeated from *The Four Zoas*, VIII. 200-201.

23:65. *The double drum* probably refers to the kettle-drums; but Blake may have been remembering faintly Dryden's ' The double double double beat / Of the thundering drum ' (*Ode on St. Cecilia's Day*).

23:75. Cf. *All Religions are One*: Principle 7.

Plate 24, in the New York copy, is placed after plate 26.

24:3-41 is rearranged and expanded from *The Four Zoas*, IX. 740-768, of which see the Commentary. The additions are lines 1-2, 8-10, 15, 17-18, 21-24.

The Wine-Press of Los is War, situated in the realms of the passions (east); begun by Passion and finished by Reason. Here they ' trample out the vintage where the grapes of wrath are stored.'

24:8-10. A pun seems to be the origin of this image in Blake's mind. Another unconscious pun will be found in 14:48. Warfare is the ' printing-press ' because it writes the history of the world.

24:42-46. *Allamanda* is the nervous system and its five senses, where ' the Sons of Los labour against Death Eternal ' by endeavouring to change sensorial impressions of the dead world of Matter into living Vision. The reader will recall Blake's ability to see ' through, not with, the eye.' The artist thus ' cultivates ' the land outside of Golgonooza. Allamanda is also called *the Sense of Touch*, because that sense is both the highest and the lowest of the senses. In the acts of love, it is capable of the highest ecstasy; but in ordinary life, it convinces us most firmly of the reality of the exterior world.

The False Tongue is false doctrine, flesh, or touch.

24:50. *Theotormon* (Desire) is here enslaved to the Mills (logic) of Satan.

24:52. *Oceans*: water (death of matter).

24:53. A reference to the Creator and his work in Plato's *Timaeus*. Blake identified Plato's God with Urizen. See the Commentary on *The Four Zoas*, IX. 319.

24:55-63. The meaning of this passage is to be found only when the four arts are related to the Four Zoas. Poetry, of course, is the function of Urthona-Los; Architecture, ' which is Science,' of Urizen, who is the architect of the Universe; then Painting, which apparently deals with the external world, must be the function of Tharmas; while Music, which is pure Emotion, is the function of Luvah. On this earth, however, Poetry reaches its highest form in Religion; the Emotions are curbed by Laws; the treatment of the Body appears as Physic and Surgery; while Architecture remains as Science.

The division of these Sciences into Bowlahoola and Allamanda means that they are all functions of human physiology, in its two functions of assimilation and perception.

25:3. *The Rhine*: a focus of the Napoleonic wars.

25 : 8-11. The old order will be completely changed before the war is over.

25 : 14. The old error.

25 : 20. *In caves :* within skulls, etc.

25 : 21. All Nature, as well as all Mankind, is to be redeemed.

25 : 22. *The Awakener :* Milton-Blake.

25 : 30. Since the Fall from the Fields of Eternity.

25 : 32-37. In his classification, Blake characteristically inverted the Methodist order, placing the Elect as those not yet ready for Consummation, while the Reprobates (or Transgressors) are of the very highest class. Line 34 shows clearly enough what Blake thought of Revival conversions; and when he wrote 'New Birth' he meant it in the most literal sense—that of a new incarnation.

25 : 38-39. Error must be changed from an indefinite form, which might overspread the earth, into fixed forms. Thus it is not only cut off from Eternity, but is manageable.

25 : 48-49. *Lambeth* contained the Archbishop's Palace, where in 1804 we may imagine that the Holiness of War was being preached ('given to the detestable Gods of Priam'—see the Commentary on 20 : 53). In Lambeth was also the famous mad-house, Bethlem. Blake places here all those suffering from the 'classical' philosophies of moral virtues. Lambeth thus becomes a symbol of the unregenerated earth, thanks to its famous buildings.

25 : 50. *Tirzah* here becomes Omphale. Hercules is, of course, the strong man subjugated beneath that monstrosity, the 'Female Will.'

25 : 51. A reference to the famous 'Choice of Hercules.'

25 : 66. All the rest of Book I is a description of the Universe from the Poet's point of view.

25 : 66–26 : 12. The Universe as seen through the 'double vision,' in its human forms.

26 : 2. Spirit in Nature.

26 : 13-22. Reincarnation. Souls descending to birth in the body descend through the south, the region of the intellect (Urizen), those who are returning from the body rise in the north, the region of the spirit (Urthona). During this period of war, Los confronts the realms of the Passions, fighting against them to save the realm of the Body.

These two Gates are evidently those in Homer's Cave of the Nymphs (*Odyssey*, Bk. XIII.) of which Porphyry wrote a celebrated explanation. See the Commentary on *The Book of Thel*, line 108.

26 : 23-25. *Allamanda* is the Nervous System ; *Golgonooza* is the City of Art ; *Luban* is the place of generation ; *Udan-Adan* is the Indefinite ; *Entuthon Benython* is the Abstract.

26 : 26-30. Souls unclothed by flesh, who nevertheless have fallen from Eternity, wander formless, being 'meer passion & appetite.' The Sons of Poetry redeem them from this indefinite state by giving them mortal bodies.

26 : 31. The Body.

26 : 38-46. The bodies given these Spectres are in accordance with their spiritual capabilities ; for everything has a spiritual cause, and not, as it seems, a natural cause.

27 : 3. A quotation from Theseus's celebrated speech in the *Midsummer Night's Dream*, v. i. 12-18 :

> The poet's eye, in a fine frenzy rolling,
> Doth glance from heaven to earth, from earth to heaven ;
> And, as imagination bodies forth
> The forms of things unknown, the poet's pen
> Turns them to shapes, and gives to airy nothing
> A local habitation and a name.
> Such tricks hath strong imagination.

The passage in *Milton* is Blake's commentary on Shakspere. However, he was not wholly pleased with Shakspere's calling these things airy *nothing*' (Gilchrist, ch. xxxv.).

27 : 13. *Antamon*, one of the vaguest of Los's sons, here appears in the function of the painter, circumscribing the indefinite Spectre with a bounding outline ; after which the flesh is made for it. Cf. *The Ghost of Abel* : ' Nature has no Outline, but the Imagination has.'

27 : 21-28. The entering of the Body. *Theotormon & Sotha* are the two sons who snare the wandering Spectres, that they may be circumscribed by Antamon, and then take on the flesh. If the Spectres cannot be lured by ' soothing forms,' they must be terrified by animal forms, from which they recoil into ' Human lineaments.'

The device of revealing to some the animal forms of the Cock, and to others the Lion, is explained by the magical antipathy between these two animals. This is mentioned in Camerarius's *Symbola*, Pliny's *De Sacrificiis et Magia*, Proclus, and Sir Thomas Browne's *Pseudodoxia*. Blake, however, probably found the tradition in Cornelius Agrippa : ' As *Proclus* gives an example in a spirit, which was wont to appear in the form of a Lion, but by the setting of a Cock before it, vanished away, because there is a contrariety betwixt a Cock and a Lion and so the like consideration ' (I. xliii.). Agrippa refers thrice again to this peculiar antipathy (I. xlviii. ; I. liv. ; III. xxxiii.).

27 : 29-43. The windows of the Body. This passage is an expansion of the line ' To see a world in a grain of sand.' This poetic vision is given to the poor and not to those full of the love of money. Blake is not excluding the rich *per se* : ' Works of art can only be produced to perfection where the man is either in affluence, or is above the care of it ' (*Vision of the Last Judgment*).

27 : 44-61. Time. The Sons of Los also build Time ; for Los, as the Sun-god, is master of Time.

27 : 48. Inspiration is conceived in less time than a moment. Cf. *Europe*, 183 : ' Between two moments Bliss is ripe.'

27 : 62-28 : 3. An expansion of 27 : 48. Cf. also the 36th *Proverb of Hell* : ' One thought fills immensity.'

28 : 4-20. Space. To the artist, the world exists as it is perceived. Perception depends upon the perceiver. The world, as conceived by the scientist, is nothing but abstract law, with no relation to human instinct, and is therefore false.

' Thus is the earth one infinite plane ' (14 : 32). Blake was very fond of *obiter dicta* upon this subject. ' He declared his opinion that the earth is flat, not round, and just as I had objected the circumnavigation, dinner was announced. But objections were seldom of any use ' (H. C. R., Dec. 10, 1825). Almost equally amusing is the anecdote retold by Gilchrist (xxxv.) and Palmer (*Life and Letters*, p. 245) : ' Some persons of a scientific turn were once discoursing pompously and, to him, distastefully, about the incredible distance of the planets, the length of time light takes to travel to the earth, &c., when he burst out, " 'Tis false ! I was walking down a lane the other day, and at the end of it I touched the sky with my stick." ' In this he was bolder than Sappho, if we may credit her choriambic quoted by Herodian : ' I do not think to touch the sky with my two arms.' Possibly Blake had been reading Philostratus's *Life of Apollonius of Tyana* (II. 5) : ' A man who has his station upon this vast and mysterious engine ought to express clearer views about heaven and the sun and moon, which I dare say you fancy you could touch with a stick, from our vantage of proximity to yonder heaven.'

28 : 21-22. Everything contains Eternity in its centre. Cf. Thomas Vaughan's *Lumen de Lumine* : ' Every natural body is a kind of black lantern ; it carries this candle within it, but the light appears not : it is eclipsed with the grossness of the matter.'

28 : 23-26. This globule is the light of Poetry itself, which is enclosed in the physiological processes.

28 : 29-31. Every man is the crucifixion of the fires of youth upon the flesh.

28 : 32-45. The present state of the Four Senses (the fifth, Touch, being excluded for reasons given below). Blake identified these Four Senses with the Four Zoas : the Eyes belonging to Urizen, the Nostrils to Luvah, the Ears to Urthona, and the Mouth to Tharmas (*Jerusalem*, 12 : 59-60). The fifth, Touch, is a universal sense, which has not fallen like the other four, but is merely diseased. Eternity can still be attained through it.

In the Eyes (Reason) Sleep appears as death, which is an error. In the Nostrils (Emotions) the Saviour set the twin limits of the Fall : the limits of opacity to the Divine Light and of contraction from Infinity. But in the Ear (the realm of Poetry) the material universe is created day after day, as a barrier against further death. The Tongue (the Body) is closed since the Fall : that is, the Body is drowned in the Sea of Time and Space.

28 : 34. Error is the Reason of Revolution ; and Revolution is the god of the Passions in the world of Generation.

28 : 47. Redemption by Poetry.

28 : 49. The four Cardinal Virtues are the pillars of Satan's throne.

28 : 51-57. The opposed influences of Inspiration and of the false doctrines of sex. *The black Woof of Death* is Tirzah's abstract philosophy.

28 : 58. *Zelophehad's Daughters* were five in number, and had no brothers (*Numbers* xxvi. 33). To Blake they symbolized life fallen into a purely sensorial existence.

28 : 60. *The River* of Matter (which is always signified by water). From the Eternal point of view, it is a pleasant stream known as the Arnon. In this world, it seems like a limitless ocean.

28 : 65. *The Elohim* are the gods of Creation, who together form one of the Seven Eyes of God. In the Bible ' Elohim ' is usually translated as though it were singular, and not plural.

BOOK THE SECOND

Plate 30. At the top of this page are written in reversed writing three mottoes : ' How wide the Gulf & Unpassable ! between Simplicity & Insipidity ! Contraries are Positives. A Negation is not a Contrary.'

30 : 1-31 : 7. This is Blake's famous description of Beulah, the realm between Eternity and this world. To the Eternals it is a place of rest from intellectual warfare ; and here all the tenderer joys that could not endure the full blaze of Eternity come for protection. To the inhabitants of this world, Beulah, far from being a place of rest, is the source of all inspiration. Even the sorrows of Beulah seem like intense joy on this still more sorrowful plane.

The germ of this passage is to be found in *The Four Zoas*, i. 203-207, 260-262.

30 : 1. *Contrarities are equally True* in Beulah, because here they achieve a synthesis before passing into Eternity. This synthesis is brought about by the power of Love (for Love is essentially of this plane, there being no sexes in Eternity ; see *The Crystal Cabinet* for Love as an illusion).

30 : 5. The moon is the symbol of Beulah, since the moon reflects the light of the sun, and makes it endurable to the eyes of those on this earth.

30 : 25. *Wings* are always the symbol of Love.

31 : 10. The coming of the **Lord** indicates a Last Judgment, therefore the tender-hearted weep.

31 : 17. Even the Four Elements wail. They are the physical reflections of the Four Zoas : the Gnomes (Earth) being descended from Urthona, the Fairies (Air) from Urizen, the Genii (Fire) from Luvah, and the Nymphs (Water) from Tharmas.

31 : 25-26. *A Corporeal Strife in Los's Halls.* Everything is found in Los's Halls. Everything is used in the labours of Art. See 5 : 20 *seq.* for Palamabron's servants, the Gnomes.

31 : 28-63. This celebrated passage has been universally admired, with the one exception of T. Sturge Moore (page 200). Blake is writing pure poetry: yet for its symbolism, see the Commentary on 35 : 48.

31 : 49. *Og & Anak.* See the Commentary on 18 : 33.

32 : 1. The Divine Voice confronts Tirzah (the Daughter of Rahab-Babylon) with the error of her jealous limitation of love. Because of her attitude, Milton finally 'abstracted himself from Female loves'; and she must now relent, giving her maidens to her husband (after the fashion of Rachel) lest she herself die.

32 : 14. *The Sixfold Female*: Milton's Emanation.

32 : 22. Then Freedom shall no longer be harlotry.

32* : 1. Milton's sleeping Humanity begins to awake and recognize his past errors.

32* : 4-5. He denounces the strife between his Reason and his human instincts. These lines are obviously a quotation from *My Spectre Around Me* :

> My Spectre follows thee behind.
> He scents thy footsteps in the snow,
> Wheresoever thou dost go
> Thro' the wintry hail and rain.

32* : 8. *Hillel, who is Lucifer.* Hillel was the celebrated Jewish scholar who died about B.C. 10, and who anticipated many of Christ's teachings. Consequently he is likened to the morning star (Lucifer) which precedes the sun.

Blake represents Lucifer, or Hillel, plotting with the six other Eyes of God against Satan, the god of this world. Blake had evidently been reading Thomas Vaughan's *Anthroposophia Theomagia* (1650), on pp. 31-32 of which occurs the following passage: 'The first in this plot was *Lucifer*; *Montanus* tells me his name was *Hilel*. He casts about to Nullifie that which God had Inacted, that so at once he might overreach him and his Creature. This Pollicy he imparts to some others of the *Hierarchy*, and strengthens himself with Conspirators. *But there is no Counsel against God*. The mischief is no sooner hatched but he and his Confederates are expell'd from *Light* to *Darknesse*, and thus Rebellion is as the sinne of *Witchcraft*, a Witch is a Rebel in Physicks, and a Rebell is a Witch in Polliticks: The one acts against *Nature*, the other against *Order*, the Rule of it: But both are in League with the *divel* as the first Father of *discord* and *sorcerie*.'

Vaughan apparently took 'Hilel' for the name of some evil spirit; Blake understood his error, but adapted it for the sake of the deeper truth he could wring from it.

32* : 10. *We*: that is, the Seven Eyes. They are talking of themselves, not of Milton or of any human being. Men are Individuals; these Gods are States, through which men pass. The States are debased and made definite by Satan, while Divine Mercy adapts them to Humanity. They can change from one to another—or rather, man can pass from one to another.

The Individual Identity can never die, but it can assume forms which may be destroyed, and enter states which may change. Yet the Eternal Form (the Platonic Ideal) cannot be destroyed, and the States also 'remain permanent forever' (*Jerusalem*, 73 : 43). Thus the Identity, the Form, and the State are the three eternal factors, all indestructible, yet all shifting through various errors. Thus the Identity may appear contracted into a Selfhood, and assume a physical form. The physical body is destroyed by death; but the spiritual body never dies. The Selfhood will also be destroyed, while the Individual lives on.

32* : 11. *Druids*: the State of cruel Holiness which sacrifices others, but not the self.

32* : 13-15. To the right of these lines is engraved: 'as multitudes. Vox Populi,' with the Hebrew for 'multitudes' preceding the English.

32* : 18. Space is a 'Satanic' illusion.

32* : 24-29. Milton's self-sacrifice does not mean annihilation of his Identity (as he thought), but only of his Selfhood.

32* : 33. Love is only a part of the Imagination.

32* : 35. In other words, Reason is always transcending itself.

32* : 36-38. Cf. Wordsworth's *Valedictory Sonnet to the River Duddon* : ' The Form remains, the Function never dies.'

32* : 42. *The Linen Clothes* : the symbols which preserved the Divine Truth in darkness are recognized as nothing but symbols—the reality is elsewhere.

34 : 1. Inspiration (the Songs of Beulah) comfort Ololon by helping reveal her error.

34 : 8-16. A new classification of Humanity ' in its repose,' corresponding to the four sons of Los. To the old classification of Head, Heart, and Loins, Blake adds a fourth, the Digestive System (Bowlahoola—see 23 : 67). The place of Beulah is, of course, the Head, since from the brain descends all inspiration (3 : 5-9) ; Alla is a new name for the Heart ; while Ulro is divided into the Sexual and digestive functions. Alla, Al-Ulro, and Or-Ulro are names never used again.

34 : 17. There is no Gate opening from Bowlahoola. See 18 : 38-39.

34 : 19. Ololon descends to the lowest state, the state of the physical world. She is not actually incarnated, we may assume ; but she becomes visible to Blake's imagination (36 : 26). Perhaps this, according to Blake's doctrine, was quite as real an incarnation as we ourselves suffer, since ' the Satanic Space is delusion ' (36 : 20) and matter is only an error.

34 : 20. *The Martyrs* are all of fallen humanity.

34 : 23. In this lowest state, in the realm of Logic (23 : 48), Contraries seem mutually exclusive.

34 : 24-31. A description of this world of Generation, rewritten from *The Four Zoas*, VIII. 207-214. Matter is a sort of parasite growth, divided into the Twenty-seven Religions. Within it, the Five Senses and Enion (or possibly Vala in her fallen form of the Shadowy Female) weave sexual bodies for the spiritual forces which they lure by songs of delight down the river of parental affection (such is the meaning of ' Storge ') into the Dead Sea of Time and Space.

34 : 30. *The River Storge* (*which is Arnon*) : Blake here notifies us of a change of symbol.

34 : 32-39. A passage repeated without important changes from 17 : 15-21, for the sake of keeping the symbolism clear in the reader's mind.

34 : 41. *The Chasms* are those spaces deserted by the shrunken soul of Man, between the Egg and the outer arcs of the four Circles. On page 32 Blake inscribed a careful diagram of these four Universes (or Zoas) and the Mundane Egg.

34 : 42. *Southward & by the East.* The course of Milton in this world lay midway between Reason and Passion, as Blake carefully shows us in his diagram.

34 : 50. *They said* : *i.e.* Ololon, who is plural, as also in 35 : 18.

35 : 2. *War & Hunting*, the search for, and conflict with, Ideas is the life of Heaven.

35 : 7-17. These names will be recognized as the names of Zelophehad's five daughters (*Numbers* xxvi. 33) plus the name of Rahab : which represent Milton's Sixfold Emanation. See the Commentary on 16 : 11. The Looms are the Looms of Generation.

35 : 18-25. The City of Art cannot be seen by Immortals till they have passed through the Experience of Matter ; but those in Matter already can see it.

35 : 18. *They* : Ololon again, and not the Daughters of Zelophehad.

35 : 31-41. This is the moment of Inspiration. To the Immortals, it appears like the reunion of an Individuality, when the feminine inspiration confesses her error and submits to the masculine portion. In modern psychology, this would be explained as the Subconscious (Emanation) working out its problems unperceived by the Conscious (Spectre), then presenting them to the Consciousness. The breach of Ololon's descent opens the way to the Truth which is in Heaven.

35 : 42. For another description of the Moment of Inspiration, see 27 : 62–28 : 3.

35 : 48–36 : 12. The Lark and the Wild Thyme are symbols peculiar to *Milton*.

Wild thyme is mentioned nowhere else outside of this book, and the Lark but once, and that merely in a catalogue of birds (*The Four Zoas*, I. 178). They were undoubtedly inspired by actual observation of nature at Felpham. The Lark is the first bird to sing in that early morning hour, which has from classic times been sacred to visionaries (see Chapter XXVIII.); and the Thyme is the first flower to shed its perfume (31 : 51). They represent the joyful reaction of man to the reception of inspiration; that heightening and transfiguration of the senses which follows mystical insight (as at the very end of *Milton*).

This exultation is of great spiritual importance to Blake: here the material earth ends (16 : 27), and man can then communicate with Eternity. This mood preserves the Seven Eyes of God from slumbering in any of the twenty-seven religions (35 : 63-65); in other words, it eternally quickens Man's religious sensibilities, and prevents them from being killed by dogma.

Blake, however, distinguishes carefully between the Lark and the Wild Thyme. The first is ' a mighty Angel,' the second ' a mighty Demon.' There would be no reason to think that ' Demon ' were uncomplimentary, did not Blake specially add: ' Terrible, deadly, & poisonous his presence in Ulro dark.' The key to this obscurity lies in the fact that the Lark is a bird free to come and go, while the Wild Thyme is a vegetable, rooted in matter. But at such a moment, both good and bad reveal their inner divinity, the Lark by its song, the Thyme by its perfume.

35 : 50. *The two Streams* are readily explained by their courses: one fountain of Life reaches Eden through the Body (the western gate), while the other (the emotions) runs through all dogmas, passing them eventually to reach the city of Art.

35 : 59. Here Luvah (the emotions) was buried and rose from the dead. Luvah, it may be remembered, is often associated with Christ.

35 : 62. Luther's religion was the last great religion, and therefore the first to be passed through on the way to Eternity. For the complete list, see 37 : 35-43.

35 : 66. The Lark nests at the eastern gate, because of his emotional quality.

36 : 14-15. Inspiration must come to men in a form that is capable of giving birth, or producing; otherwise the suppressed creative spark is fatal to the one who receives it.

36 : 17. Ololon, being twelve years of age, is at last old enough to be fruitful.

36 : 20. Here ends the description and analysis of the Moment of Inspiration which began 35 : 31.

36 : 21. Blake suddenly realizes the purpose of his stay at Felpham.

36 : 22. *My Vegetated Portion*: Blake's physical body.

36 : 31. *My Shadow of Delight*: his wife.

37 : 6-12. When the voice of the outcast Woman is heard, all the Miltonic philosophy is at once presented to Blake's mind, and its error made manifest.

37 : 8. *The Covering Cherub*, which guards the Ark, is the symbol of the dogma protecting the truth, yet which is false if mistaken for the truth. See the Commentary on 7 : 51.

37 : 10. The old distinction of the true Identity and the false Selfhood. See the Commentary on 12 : 30.

37 : 11. *The Wicker Man of Scandinavia*: a symbol of the ' Druidic ' religion, which sacrifices others, and not the Self. This is the Druidic image, referred to in Cæsar's *Commentaries* (VI. 16): ' Others use huge figures, whose wicker limbs they fill with living men and set on fire, and the men die surrounded by flames.'

37 : 15-39 : 4. Blake sees Milton's errors in their complete organization. They contain all the errors ever made. They are divided into the twelve Gods of Ulro and the twenty-seven false Churches of Beulah.

The twelve Gods (Baal, Ashtaroth, Chemosh, Molech, Dagon, Thammuz, Rimmon, the trinity of Osiris, Isis, and Orus considered as one, Belial, Saturn, Jove, and Rhea) are all the old, false mythologies. Their names are taken from the list in *Paradise Lost*, I. 392-521. Being Error, they are Satan. Each is fourfold, since each is a deformed reflection of Humanity. They are reflected, therefore, as forty-eight : as the twenty-seven districts of Og and the twenty-one of Sihon. Og is comprehended in the constellation Orion, Sihon in Ophiucus ; for all are of the starry (Urizenic) region—products of Reason. Orion represents the fifteen southern constellations plus the twelve constellations of the zodiac ; Ophiucus represents the twenty-one northern constellations. Blake chose these particular two, since Orion was the Giant slain by Diana, the goddess of chastity, while Ophiucus was the Giant in the deadly embrace of the twin serpents of Good and Evil (see the *Laocoon* plate).

The Twenty-seven Churches are not the worship of twenty-seven gods, but twenty-seven ways of worshipping God, which have been sufficiently formulated to interfere with direct communion. They are dogmas ; and each is named after the man who founded it. Each has its own heaven and hell ; and each heaven must be passed before Eternity can be reached. The first nine names give the line of Adam through Lamech, according to *Genesis* v. ; these are the antediluvian Giants (also known to Blake as the Ancients), in whom vision and will were equally balanced ('Hermaphroditic' in the good sense). The next eleven names continue the line, from Noah to Terah, according to *Genesis* xi. ; with the addition of 'Cainan the second,' after Arphaxad, according to *Luke* iii. 36. These are the 'Female-Males,' in whom the will was concealed within the vision. The last seven names continue with Abraham through the great religious leaders down to Luther, the 'Male-Females. . . . Religion hid in War,' or, in other words, Rahab and the Dragon. (A picture of this state will be found on *Jerusalem*, 75.) But with Luther the end has not come, for the twenty-seven are a cycle : 'And where Luther ends, Adam begins again in Eternal Circle' (*Jerusalem*, 75 : 24). And in Blake's own day, were they not returning to Adam, the Natural Man, in Rousseau's philosophy ; and was it not an age of giants ?

Blake followed Swedenborg in believing that each of these persons signified a church ; that these churches are grouped together into larger churches ; and that every church at last turns into its opposite error. But only the first of his groups (the Antediluvians) corresponds with Swedenborg's. Swedenborg had four large churches, beginning respectively with Adam, Noah, Moses, and Jesus. Blake has three, beginning with Adam, Noah, and Abraham. Jesus does not appear at all, his religion being the Everlasting Gospel, which all the others try in vain to approximate. Blake's three groups probably represent Man upside down : Adam to Lamech teaching the religion of the Loins, Noah to Terah that of the Heart, and Abraham to Luther that of the Head.

The twelve Gods are Error (Satan), the twenty-seven heavens are their Churches, and the forty-eight starry regions are the active results of the teachings (the 'Cities of the Levites'), and the source of modern society ('the Heads of the Great Polypus').

See also the Commentary on *Jerusalem*, 39 : 13.

37 : 34. *The Druid Albion* is Humanity in his primeval, unillumined states : the Twelve false Gods are the children of his Reason.

37 : 35-43. This passage is repeated in *Jerusalem*, 75 : 10-20, with a few added lines.

37 : 45. *The Covering Cherub* is the Logic derived from Emotion ('the Spectre of Luvah').

37 : 56-60. The starry regions touch upon Art ; but none can reach Eternity by thinking to pierce the Mundane Shell : all must descend into the four regions represented by Los, Bowlahoola, Allamanda, and Entuthon Benython—that is, through Poetry (which is of the Spirit), the flesh of the Body, the nerves of Emotion, and Abstract Philosophy : these four corresponding to the Four Zoas.

39 : 9. Satan, who triumphed over Palamabron, now is about to be vanquished by Milton. We can no longer identify Satan with Hayley ; but nevertheless he

still represents Hayley's type: the self-righteous man who is the source of all error.

39:16. This passage recalls forcibly Walt Whitman's *City Dead-House*: ' But the house alone—that wondrous house—that delicate fair house—that ruin! / That immortal house, more than all the rows of dwellings ever built! '

39:28. *The Eastern porch of Satan's Universe*: the emotions which lead towards intellect.

39:29-49. Blake might easily have set himself up as the leader of a new sect; this passage explains why he did not. He had seen every sect before him begin well and end badly; or, to quote Swedenborg: ' Every church at the commencement is spiritual, for it begins from charity, but in the course of time it turns aside from charity to faith, and then from being an internal church it becomes an external one; and when it becomes external, its end is, since it then places everything in knowledge, and little or nothing in life ' (*Last Judgment*, 38). The search for truth always ends in the worship of dogma and the dogma's creator. Therefore Blake, rather than set himself up in the name of truth, sacrificed himself that the truth might progress.

39:46. *The Natural Heart*: that is, the heart that does not know God because of Nature (matter) which surrounds it. Rousseau's ' Natural Man ' taught Deism, which to Blake was Atheism.

39:51. *I am God*: or Jehovah. The God of Justice, as opposed to Mercy; the Accuser, not the Forgiver.

40:11. *The Lake of Los*, of which we have never heard before, is the Lake of the flames of annihilation. It is not a place of torment.

40:19-20. Satan-Jehovah is the ' I am that I am,' or the religion of things as they are. Any vital change is terrific torture to him.

40:22-27. This passage may have been suggested by Satan's appearance in *Paradise Lost*, II.:

> . . . God-like imitated State; him round
> A Globe of fierie Seraphim inclos'd
> With bright imblazonrie and horrent Arms. . . .
> Toward the four winds four speedy Cherubim
> Put to thir mouths the sounding Alchymie.

40:29. Sin and Death are Satan's chief followers in Blake's illustrations to *Paradise Lost*.

40:30. We have noted many times how the Starry Heavens represent astrological Fatalism, or the rule of Karma, in Blake's system.

40:32-52. At the clear vision of Error, Man begins to rise, but is not yet strong enough. The gist of the geographical symbols is that Man now covers all his regions, and treads their errors under foot.

40:35. These four pillars represent the Four Zoas. In *Jerusalem*, 74:3, Verulam and York are substituted for Bath and Legions.

40:53-54. Reason and the Poet struggle at the River of Generation.

40:54. The Ploughman, the Artificer, and the Shepherd are respectively Urizen, Urthona, and Tharmas. The omission of Luvah, the Weaver, is not clear.

40:61. *Tho' seen in fallacy outside*: since it is error to believe in the exterior world, which is really interior.

42:1. At last Milton stands face to face with his erring Emanation; and he sees the Truth (' Eternal Form ') within her.

42:4-5. Milton as he appeared in the flesh.

42:6. *Orc* is a form of Luvah; he is Luvah as the revolting energies of youth.

42:9-11. Those who attack Conventional Religion are apt to cast out with the errors a portion of Truth; and this portion (in Milton's case, Ololon herself) gives life to all the errors associated with it.

42:17. As Milton is opposed by Satan, so Ololon is opposed by Rahab.

42:20-22. Cf. 37:43.

42 : 25-26. On earth the errors are known by the names of Truth ; in Eden they shall be errors no more, and therefore will deserve the names falsely given them on earth.

42 : 30. The only things which can be annihilated are Errors, Negations, Prohibitions, and other such illusions.

43 : 3. Reasoning cast off for Faith.

43 : 4. Realism cast off for Imagination.

43 : 5. *Bacon, Locke & Newton* are the arch-scientists.

43 : 8. This line proves that Blake felt bitterly the scoffs (we cannot say ' accusation ') of madness.

43 : 14. A picture of this person, waylaying the Pilgrim on his way of Faith, is to be found in *Europe*, plate IV.

43 : 23-24. Another attack on Realism in poetry.

43 : 27. *Which Jesus rent* : a reference to the rending of the veil of the temple at the climax of the crucifixion.

43 : 30. Ololon, already feeling the union with Milton which is not yet accomplished, speaks of the errors within herself, the ' Six-fold Miltonic Female ' or Emanation, as another person.

43 : 33. *Our Sexual* : our generated portion.

44 : 3-6. As soon as Ololon attempts the supreme sacrifice of herself, her errors divide from her Truth, and become reconciled in Milton. See the Commentary on 42 : 9-11.

44 : 7-11. When Ololon is reunited with Milton, then the process of reunion continues. The Seven Eyes of God with the Individuality which made the Eighth become fused as Jesus.

44 : 12-15. The garments of Jesus have often been a subject of symbolism. See, for example, the *Pistis Sophia*, Book I. Blake's conception is that all history itself is only the garment of the Deity, a garment of spiritual warfare.

44 : 18. *The Immortal Four* are, of course, the Zoas.

44 : 24. At the climax of the vision—the reunion of God with Man—Blake is overcome, and he returns to himself. This is accurate description of mystical psychology.

44 : 28. *My sweet Shadow of delight :* his wife.

44 : 29-30. See the Commentary on 35 : 48.

44 : 31-32. The Poet, united with his Inspiration, hovers over London.

44 : 32. *Oothoon* : Blake's Magdalen—here as pity for the sufferings of restrained womanhood.

44 : 36—45 : 1. Wrath and Pity behold all things preparing for the Last Judgment.

THE ILLUSTRATIONS TO *MILTON*

Title-page. Milton, in his spiritual form as a nude youth with a Christ-like beard, strides forward with his spiritual (right) foot, and with right hand oustretched, into the pillar of smoke which is his Shadow (12 : 36). He is descending to Eternal Death (*Milton*, 12 : 14). In the New York copy, light flames start up beneath his feet.

Inscribed : ' Milton a Poem in 2 Books. The Author & Printer W. Blake. 1804. To Justify the Ways of God to Men.' In the New York copy, it reads apparently ' in 12 books ' ; in the Huntington copy, it might read either way ; but the British Museum copy reads definitely ' in 2 Books.'

Plate 3. *Milton Book the First.* Milton as a descending star sheds his rays on the sleeping spiritual forms of the bread and the wine. These forms appear as a male (?) and female whose respective right and left feet touch. One rests on a couch of wheat, the other on a couch of grapes.

Plate 5*. To the right of the text : crouching nudes. Below the text are flames.

Plate 3*. Below the text, an illustration to lines 4-5 : ' Here the Three Classes of Men take their Sexual texture woven. / The Sexual is Threefold ; the Human is Fourfold.' Before a sort of Druidic Acropolis, three women with the spindles and distaffs of Generation stand or crouch in despair. A fourth, without such instruments, crouches in despair at the extreme left.

Below line 14 is a row of Druidic rocks and a Druidic gate (as in plate 4) with the moon seen rising through it.

Plate 4. Between lines 26 and 27, a picture of Man in the state of Druidism (Experience). He appears as a traveller riding through a barren country lighted by a new moon and large stars. He is passing a titanic Druid gate or trilithon made of three immense stones ; and before him stands a balancing rock.

Plate 5. Between and to the right of the text : fine vague lines suggesting birds, vines, and nudes. Such lines are to be found on practically all the other plates not described here.

Plate 8. No text. Los and Enitharmon regard with horror the flaming Orc, who stands on a block of stone. (The Poet and Inspiration before the sacrifice of the flames of youth upon the Druid altar.)

Plate 8*. ' An aged Woman raving along the Streets ' (line 4). Aged Enitharmon flees in horror before a gate.

Plate 9. In the New York copy, painted across the text, is the rainbow of Leutha (10 : 14) stretched from the upper left corner to the right.

Plate 10. Tiny nudes fly through the text. In the Huntington copy; the rainbow of Leutha is painted across the text.

Plate 12. Cain flees from the corpse of Abel under a tree. There is a similar design in *The Ghost of Abel*, beside Jehovah's first ' Adam.' In the New York copy, Cain is given a gold halo ; probably the halo of martyrdom.

Plate 13. No text. Milton preparing to descend. This picture is an illustration of 12 : 13 : ' He took off the robe of the promise & ungirded himself from the oath of God.' He stands aureoled and nude upon a dark globe, with the robe in his left hand and the girdle in his right. He looks upward in the dark, while a dark sun sinks behind him.

In the New York copy, his aureole is of dark silver, while the sun is of a very dark gold. In the British Museum copy, light is reflected upon the under side of his arms and hands very effectively.

Plate 14. To the right of the text : a mother and child ; beneath them a startled figure. Below line 46 is a tiny miniature of plate 29, representing the star of Milton ' Descending perpendicular, swift as the swallow or swift, / And on my left foot, falling on the tarsus, enter'd there ' (lines 48-49). Separated by a tangle of fibres from this picture of Blake is a mourning figure, which may represent his wife.

Plate 15. Blake as a nude youth strides upward and inward (*i.e.* with his back to the reader), and grasps Urizen by the beard in order to dethrone him. Urizen is identified by the tables of the Law to which he clings in anguish. Above him dance in an arc the liberated senses, represented as four maidens and a youth playing upon musical instruments. In the New York copy, a golden sun rises behind the youth's feet.

Plate 16. Above the text : Milton's three wives sit on a couch and turn their faces from his three daughters, who are dancing before them.

Below the text : Los, as a tree-man (vegetating), and Urizen, whose head emerges above the ground, oppose Milton's path (lines 35-36).

Plate 21. Blake turns from binding his sandal (on his *right* foot, in contradiction to the text), and sees Los stepping from out the Sun close behind him. This plate illustrates 20 : 4-8 : '. . . what time I bound my sandals / On, to walk forward thro' Eternity, Los descended to me : / And Los behind me stood : a terrible flaming Sun : just close / Behind my back : I turned round in terror. . . .'

Plate 23. From this plate onward, the tiny decorative nudes, vines, etc., become larger and more distinct. Here we distinguish a snake-limbed woman, a man flying from her in despair ; a man gazing upward ; a woman bound by a vine ; and a kneeling woman.

Plate 24. Below line 24 is a procession of the vermin of the Wine-press (lines 12-22) : we see a caterpillar, spider, cricket, worm, and others.

Plate 26. Below lines 15 and 43 are stretches of Albion's icy mountains.

Plate 27. Below line 43 a spiral ; to the right of the text, birds.

Plate 28. To the right of the text : four floating nudes. Below the text, a stretch of dark earth. 'End of the First Book.'

Plate 29. No text. Blake, as a nude youth, falls backward, while a flaming star (Milton) descends to his left foot. This plate is inscribed : 'William.' Blake is advancing towards the right—towards the material realm. Three stone steps are behind him.

This picture is an enlargement of part of a design on plate 14 ; and it has a complement on plate 33.

Plate 30. *Milton Book the Second.* The descent of the sons and daughters of Ololon. Above the text : two falling nudes ; below it, two flying females ; to the right, one ascending figure. In reversed writing, above the text : 'How wide the Gulf & Unpassable ! between Simplicity & Insipidity ! Contraries are Positives. A Negation is not a Contrary.'

The British Museum copy adds a border of very tiny ascending and descending figures.

Page 32. Below the text : a map of the Four Zoas, as four interlacing circles. (Cf. the xivth Illustration to *Job.*) The circles are named, and given compass points : Urthona is North, Luvah is East, Urizen is South, and Tharmas is West. This evidently illustrates 19 : 37-39 : ' But all the Family Divine collected as Four Suns / In the Four Points of heaven, East, West & North & South, / Enlarging and enlarging till their Disks approach'd each other.'

Upon these four circles is drawn the Mundane Egg, representing the shrinkage of life in this world. The upper half of the Egg is marked ' Adam,' the lower half ' Satan.' Flames burst from Satan and enter Adam ; flames surround the Zoas.

A line, inscribed ' Milton's Track,' passes from the lower right, into the design through the intersection of Urizen and Luvah, passes through the very centre of the design, and stops on the point in the centre of Adam.

There have been various attempts to ascribe different colours to the Zoas, but the diverse colourings of the three copies of this plate seem to disprove any such symbolism. In the New York copy, Urthona is a red brown ; Luvah and Tharmas are both of a greenish grey ; Urizen is a dark violet ; and the Egg is a bluish white. The Huntington copy is coloured practically the same. The British Museum copy, however, colours all the Zoas brown, and the Egg blue.

Plate 33. A full-page reversal of plate 29 ; inscribed ' Robert ' and not ' William.' He sinks backward while a flaming star descends upon his *right* foot. *Four* stone steps are seen behind him and he advances towards the left, or spiritual region. In all the copies, the colouring is distinguished from that of plate 29 by an emphasis on cold blues, rather than pinks and yellows.

Robert Blake was William's beloved younger brother, who died so tragically —and who inspired William with the idea of Illuminated Printing. On the 6th of May 1800, Blake wrote to Hayley : '.Thirteen years ago I lost a brother, and with his spirit I converse daily and hourly in the spirit, and see him in my remembrance, in the regions of my imagination.' This picture is further evidence of his belief that his brother brought him inspiration. The correspondence of left and right feet in the material and spiritual worlds is a symbolism which is most important in the interpretation of Blake's *Job*.

Robert is not mentioned in *Milton* ; nevertheless, Blake did not think it out of place to insert this tribute to his dead brother's influence.

Plate 35. In the Huntington copy, this page is tinted to suggest a sun rising behind the lower right corner.

Plate 36. Below the text is a scene inscribed : ' Blake's Cottage at Felpham.' The cottage (rather simplified from the original) is in the background ; Blake is walking in the garden and Ololon descends towards him. This illustrates lines 16-20.

It has been stated that Blake represented himself naked ; but this is certainly not true in the New York and the Huntington copies ; while it is extremely doubtful in the British Museum copy.

Plate 37. In the Huntington copy, this plate is tinted to suggest a sun rising from the centre of the lower edge of the page.

Plate 38. A full-page illustration of the Moment of Inspiration, as seen by the Poet. He lies in the arms of a woman on a rocky shore just above the reach of the Sea of Time and Space. The woman's head is on his bosom, while his own head is thrown back to behold the descent of the Eagle of Genius. In one of the three copies of *Milton*, the sexual nature of the moment is clearly indicated ; an indication which is suppressed in a second copy ; and only hinted in the third.

Plate 39. In the Huntington copy, yellow sun-rays radiate from the upper left-hand corner.

Plate 41. The Forgiveness of Sins. Milton, as an aureoled nude, stands upon a dark bank, upholding Ololon, who kneels, bent forward with shame.

Plate 42. Below the text : the Forest of Error. A male nude hides behind a tree from a serpent with two heads, one of which is a wolf's.

Plate 43. ' To bathe in the waters of Life : to wash off the Not Human ' (line 1). Above the text six figures float with their hands entwined above their heads. In two of the copies, these figures are floating in flames ; in the Huntington copy, merely in a brilliant atmosphere.

Plate 44. Below the text : Oothoon weeps over her Human Harvest (lines 32-33). She floats in a cloud, extending her left hand, from which falls rain upon a field of green wheat.

Plate 45. The Soul in the ultimate ecstasy. She stands as a woman (lightly veiled in a delicate green) uplifting her arms between two many-winged Seraphim of love.

Dr. Keynes (p. 159) describes this plate as ' a sprouting stalk in the form of a naked woman with arms straining upward ; on either side an ear of human corn.'

A sketch for the central figure is in the possession of Mr. W. A. White. In place of the Seraphim are masses of vegetation, indicating that this ecstasy can take place in the flesh. (Cf. Blake's note in Swedenborg : ' this, Man can do while in the body.') On the back of this sketch is written : ' Father & Mother, I return from flames of fire tried & pure & white.'

JERUSALEM

A TABLE OF BLAKE'S FOURFOLD CORRESPONDENCES IN 'JERUSALEM'

NORTH	EAST	SOUTH	WEST	
Urthona (Los)	Luvah	Urizen	Tharmas	The Four Zoas
Blacksmith	Weaver	Plowman	Shepherd	Their callings
Spirit	Emotions	Reason	Senses (Body)	Their meanings
Poetry	Music	Architecture	Painting	Their Arts
Friendship	Love	Hunger	Lust	Their Desires
Nadir	Centre	Zenith	Circumference	Their places
Breadth	Inward	Height & Depth	Outward	Directions
Iron	Silver	Gold	Brass	Their Metals
Enitharmon	Vala	Ahania	Enion	Their Emanations
Spiritual Beauty (Inspiration)	Natural Beauty (Nature)	Pleasure (Sin)	Generative Instinct (the Earth Mother)	Their meanings
Rintrah	Theotormon	Bromion	Palamabron	The Four Sons of Los
Wrath	Desire	Reason	Pity	Their meanings
Ocalythron	Oothoon	Leutha	Elynittria	Their emanations
Jealousy	The Magdalen	Puritanism	Toleration	Their meanings
Eternity (or Golgonooza)	Beulah	Bowlahoola	Generation	The Four Worlds
Sun	Moon	Stars	World	Their symbols
Gods	Men	Matter	Vegetation	States
Earth	Fire	Air	Water	Elements
Gnomes	Genii	Fairies	Nymphs	Elementals
Humanity	Emanation	Spectre	Shadow	Divided Man
Head	Heart	Stomach (Bowels)	Loins	The Body
Ears	Nostrils	Eyes	Tongue	The Senses
Europe	Asia	Africa	America	Continents
Scotland	England	Wales	Ireland	British Isles
Edinburgh	London	Verulam	York	Cities
Pison	Euphrates	Gihon	Hiddekel	Rivers of Paradise

COMMENTARY ON *JERUSALEM*

To understand the *Jerusalem*, the reader must have a fair knowledge of Blake's technical vocabulary. I have been obliged to assume such a knowledge in the reader; otherwise this Commentary would be about three times as large as the poem itself. Nevertheless, each term is explained on its first appearance; and the general character of the meaning of any obscure passage is outlined.

For the most part I have omitted explanations of the geographical symbols, whenever such explanation is not covered by one simple statement. The references to places in the Holy Lands are clear enough: they may usually be divided into sacred and profane places, while the more familiar names are immediately self-explanatory. Blake assumed that his readers would have a considerable knowledge of the Bible; I have tried to lighten their task by explaining the more obscure references. The references to places in the British Isles are extremely difficult to explain at times, for only too often Blake read into them purely personal meanings; and when their symbolic meanings have been exposed, they usually were not worth the labour involved.

Plate 3. *To the Public*. Blake obliterated certain words on this plate, and never inserted any substitutes. By comparing various copies, I have been able to complete the poem and some of the prose, while a word here and there from the other lacunae indicates the general trend of the omissions. This has been possible because the words are not entirely obliterated in some copies. The restored words are indicated by italics.

'My former Giants & Fairies having reciev'd the highest reward possible, the *love* and *friendship* of those with whom to be connected, is to be *blessed*: I cannot doubt that this more consolidated & extended Work, will be as kindly reciev'd. The Enthusiasm of the following Poem, the Author hopes *that all will think* —— —— *or engraving when he* / —— *?and the Ancients* —— —— *to their* —— —— / —— —— —— —— *I have* —— —— *acknowledge* ——*for my* /—— —— ——; *for they ?are wholly ?accursed in their ideas.* I also hope the Reader will be with me, wholly One in Jesus our Lord, who is the God *of ?Fire* and Lord *of ?Love*,' etc.

'Therefore *Dear* Reader, *forgive* what you do not approve, & *love* me for this energetic exertion of my talent,' etc.

> 'Reader! *lover* of books! *lover* of heaven.
> And of that God from whom *all hymns are given*,' etc.

After 'Digestion or Sleep' Blake's cancelled text continues: '*I fear / the ?best in Jesus whom we* —— —— —— —— —— / When this Verse,' etc.

3 : 1. *Three years slumber*: at Felpham.

3 : 2. *My former Giants & Fairies*: epics and lyrics.

3 : 7. *The Author hopes*: the obliterated passage probably contained contemptuous references to his rivals.

3 : 9. *God of Fire and Lord of Love*: the synthesis of Moses and Jesus (see heading for chapter i.), the joint approval of wrath and love, of the Old and New Testaments.

3 : 21. *The wondrous art of writing gave.* It was a common belief in the eighteenth century that writing began as the result of the revelations at Mt. Sinai. Thus Defoe wrote in his *System of Magick* (ch. vii., *ed.* Scott, p. 183): 'The first knowledge of letters to write by, and to read upon, was dictated to Moses from mount Sinai, by the immediate revelation of Heaven.' Previously, of course, the Egyptians had used picture-writing; but sometimes the question of Moses's priority became a trifle nice. However, we find Bishop Percy asserting in his *Miscellaneous Pieces Relating to the Chinese* (London, 1762, vol. i. p. 29): 'It is certain that the most exact inquirers have not been able to trace the use of *alphabets* earlier than the time of Moses.'

3 : 31. *Every thing is conducted by Spirits.* Writing poetry is as natural a

function as eating or sleep, which also have spiritual causes. Cf. *Milton*, 26 : 44-45 : ' And every Natural Effect has a Spiritual Cause, and Not / A Natural : for a Natural Cause only seems : it is a Delusion.' So Blake interpreted Milton's doctrine : ' Millions of spiritual Creatures walk the Earth / Unseen, both when we wake and when we sleep ' (*Paradise Lost*, IV. 677-678).

3 : 32. *When this Verse* : the first Free Verse Manifesto in English.

3 : 33. *A Monotonous Cadence* : cf. Edward Bysshe's *Art of English Poetry*, Section VII. : ' Blank verse is where the measure is exactly kept without Rhyme ; Shakespeare, to avoid the troublesome Constraint of Rhyme, was the first who invented it.'

3 : 34. *Derived* : possibly a mistake for *delivered*.

3 : 35. *The modern bondage of Rhyming* : cf. the *Introduction* to *Paradise Lost* : ' Rime being no necessary Adjunct or true Ornament of Poem or good Verse in longer Works especially, but the Invention of a barbarous Age, to set off wretched matter and lame Meeter. . . . This neglect then of Rime so little is to be taken for a defect, that it is rather to be esteem'd as an example set, the first in *English*, of ancient liberty recover'd to Heroic Poem from the troublesom and modern bondage of Rimeing.'

CHAPTER I

4 : 10. *A black water* : materialism—the Sea of Time and Space.

4 : 14. *Thy Emanation* : Jerusalem, or Freedom.

4 : 17. Cf. the *Auguries of Innocence* : ' But doth a Human form display / To those who dwell in realms of Day.'

4 : 22. *The perturbed Man* : Albion.

4 : 23. *Shadow* : desire.

4 : 26. *Daughters* : effects.

4 : 27. Cf. *Matthew* iv. 4 : ' Man shall not live by bread alone,' etc.

5 : 4. *The starry wheels* of the Satanic Mill of Logic.

5 : 10. *Udan-Adan* : the Lake of the Indefinite.

5 : 12. *The Vale of Entuthon-Benython* : the Philosophy of Abstractions.

5 : 16-26. Blake speaks.

5 : 22. *The Selfhood* : the selfish and illusory shell round the eternal Humanity in every one. Cf. the Commentary on *Milton*, 12 : 30.

5 : 24. *Golgonooza* : the City of Art.

5 : 25, 27. These are the names of the Twelve Sons of Albion. In general, they represent the Cruelty of Man to Man. In detail, they represent the Crucifixion Upside-down of man in the flesh ; therefore their names are given in reverse order, the lowest (eldest) coming first. Their table (based on a study of the maps) is as follows :

	NORTH	EAST	SOUTH	WEST
Loins (Executioner)	Hyle (bad Art)	Coban	Hand (bad Science)	Gwantok
Heart (Judge)	Brereton	Peachey 71 : 45	Slayd	Hutton
Head (Accuser)	Bowen 71 : 4	Scofield 71 : 38	Kox 71 : 42	Kotope 71 : 44

(The reader is warned, however, not to expect too much correspondence between this table and that of the twelve Sons of Israel (16 : 28-58), who are a higher order of being). During Albion's fall, his sons are separated from him ; later they re-enter his limbs. In Eternity they are not bad at all : Blake gives a description of their immortal state on plate 71.

The names of several of the Sons have been identified with those concerned in Blake's trial for high treason ; and if we could get a complete list of them all, we should probably find that all but the first two sons—or even those as well—bear the names of actual men. The Twelve divide into the Satanic Trinity : the fourfold Accuser, Judge and Executioner. The last four (separated from the others in line 27) represent the Accuser. Blake puts the Executioner before the others, as a satire on their Justice. The Twelve constitute the infernal Court of Justice, opposed to the Mercy of Jesus.

Hand, the eldest and most important of the sons, who at times absorbs all the others, is the Spectre, Reason (36 : 23). His symbols are the Wheel (logic), the Rock (matter) and Egypt (mathematics). His name is probably to be explained by the antithesis between Wings and Hand (vision versus mechanism) in lines 7-8 of *The Tyger*.

Hyle, who often works side by side with Hand, is the bad Artist, also the Puritan who would set up his own standard of morality for everybody else. His name in Greek signifies ' Matter ' ; and its resemblance to ' Hayley ' is unmistakable.

Coban (also spelled Koban) is the desire for domination. His son is Nimrod, the first king.

Gwantok (Gwantock, Guantock, Gwantoke, Kwantok) and *Peachey* are judges ; as John Quantock, J.P., and John Peachey, J.P., they appeared on the bench at Chichester.

Brereton (Brertun) is also a judge ; he was William Brereton, J.P., at Petworth. From his association with *Slayd* (Slaid, Slade) we may assume that the latter was another Petworth magistrate, though ' Slayd ' may be derived from ' slay.'

Hutton (Huttn, Hutn) is notable only as the father of the seven from Enoch to Adam (7 : 24). Enoch is the seventh name from Adam in *Milton*, 37 : 36. Blake reversed the order in the case of Hutton, to show that these seven revolve in a perpetual circle.

Scofield (Schofield, Skofeld, Skofield, Scofeld) is the Natural Man as Accuser. He absorbs the remaining three of the Twelve (7 : 47). He is identified with Adam several times. His name should already be familiar as that of John Scholfield (so Blake spells it yet again in his letter to Butts, 16th August 1803) by whom Blake was accused.

Kox (Kock) is described as the Noah of the Flood of Udan-Adan, the Indefinite. He is trooper Cock, Scofield's friend, who also testified to Blake's utterance of treasonable remarks.

Kotope and *Bowen*, the last of the Twelve, may be conjectured to have been further witnesses induced by Scofield to testify against Blake ; though the latter may be Thomas Barton Bowen, a name on the Law List of the times as practising on the Home Circuit and Sussex Sessions. Scofield, Kox, Kotope, and Bowen, however, are closely associated, being given points of the compass. Scofield is East, the Accuser from passion ; Kox is South, the Accuser from Reason ; while Kotope, who is West, would be the Accuser from Irresponsibility (or the promise of reward) ; and Bowen, who is North, the Accuser through moral reasons—his sense of duty to his fellows, or his disapproval of the poet. But the original Bowen must have said a good word for Blake ; since his reward in Eternity is great. As the last in the list of sons, he is the one nearest Eternity, and eventually he inherits all the north (71 : 46).

Four of these names (Hand, Hyle, Coban, and Scofield) appear for a moment in *Milton* (plates 17 and 22) ; and none of them appears in *The Four Zoas*. The spelling of the names varies very much ; and since these variations often occur in consecutive lines, we must suppose them wilful.

Each of the Sons had his Emanation ; for which see the Commentary on 5 : 40-44.

It is perhaps worthy of mention that Rabelais is supposed to have used the names of people he had encountered in lawsuits, etc.

5 : 27. The fourfold Accuser wars against the Poet.

5 : 28. *The eastern gate* : of the emotions.

5 : 32. They enter the Poet's life by Reason, and are defeated by power of the Spirit. Cf. *Milton*, 26 : 16-17.

5 : 34. The two sexes in their various creative functions : the Male creates weapons of war and the instruments of peace ; the Female creates the Veil of Vala —material nature.

5 : 38. As we shall see, Blake named the Twelve Daughters after women in the mythological history of England.

5 : 39. Their work is to control the physical functionings. See the Commentary on 3 : *Every thing is conducted by Spirits.*

5 : 40-44. The Twelve Daughters of Albion represent the Cruelty of Woman to Man. They are the living forms of the female Will, which subjects Man to feminine standards of conduct. Thus they are the goddesses of Lust and Chastity, who weave and embroider the material body. Blake distinguishes their work from that of the Looms of Cathedron (though not very clearly), because the Daughters of Albion try to perpetuate the state of Generation in selfishness ; while Enitharmon creates bodies that, by passing through them, wandering spirits may escape through Ulro into Generation and upward.

These Daughters may unite into One, as Rahab, the false, worldly religion ; sometimes they appear as two : Rahab (licence in sex) and Tirzah (repression of sex).

The names of the Twelve Daughters were taken from the mythological histories of England by Geoffrey of Monmouth and Milton. Blake adopts the spelling sometimes of one, sometimes of the other, and sometimes uses his own.

Gwendolen, the emanation of Hand, is the most important of them all. As Hand is really a lower form of Urizen (Reason) so she is a lower and selfish form of Ahania (Pleasure). Once she seems to have absorbed all her sisters, as Hand absorbed all his brothers (34 : 52). She is the leader of the others, knowingly preaching falsehood to them (82 : 17). She is named after Guendoloena, Corineus's daughter, who married Locrine, but was deserted by him for Estrildis after the death of Corineus. When Locrine was killed in battle, Guendoloena drowned Estrildis and her illegitimate daughter, Sabrina, in the Severn ; reigned for fifteen years ; then retired to Cornwall when her son was able to take her place (Geoffrey, II. iv.-vi.). Thus Gwendolen also represents Jealousy.

Cambel, the emanation of Hyle, is the false inspiration of the bad poet. She is really another form of Leutha (Puritanism). In this capacity she directs the building of the Mundane Shell. She is probably named after Kambreda, a daughter of Ebrauc (Geoffrey, II. viii.). In *Jerusalem* she is twice identified with Boadicea (whose story Milton took from Dion and added to Geoffrey's account). As Boadicea, Cambel represents the dominant Female Will, of which Blake disapproved as heartily as Milton. 'For *Boadicea* and her Daughters ride about in a Chariot, telling the tall Champions as a great encouragement, that with the *Britans* it was usual for Women to be their Leaders. A deal of other fondness they put into her mouth, not worth recital ; how she was lash'd, how her Daughters were handl'd, things worthier silence, retirment, and a Vail, then for a Woeman to repeat, as don to hir own person, or to hear repeated before an host of men. *The Greek Historian* setts her in the field on a high heap of turves, in a loose-bodied Gown declaming, a Spear in her hand, a Hare in her bosome, which after a long circumlocution she was to let slip among them for lucks sake, then praying to *Andate the British Goddess*, to talk again as fondly as before' (Milton, Bk. II.). Milton rejects this story, however, as a fabrication of foreigners to prove that ' in *Britain* Woemen were Men, and Men Woemen.'

Ignoge, the emanation of Coban, is another figure representing the baffled desire for domination. She is named after Ignoge, the daughter of Pandrasus, King of the Greeks, who was married as a hostage to Brutus (Geoffrey I. xi.).

Cordella, the emanation of Gwantok, is named after Cordeilla (Shakspere's Cordelia), the daughter of Leir, whose story hardly needs retelling, save that in Geoffrey, Cordeilla commits suicide (II. x.-xv.).

Mehetabel, the emanation of Peachey, is named after Methabel, a daughter of Ebrauc (Geoffrey, II. viii.).

Ragan, the emanation of Brereton, is another daughter of Leir, who quarrelled with her father (Geoffrey II. xi.-xii.). She is the spirit of cruelty (11 : 21).

Gonorill, the emanation of Slayd, is named after the other daughter of Leir, Gonorilla; who also judged her father too harshly (Geoffrey, II. xi.-xii.).

Gwinefred, the emanation of Hutton, is the most obscure of them all. She does not appear either in Geoffrey or Milton, and may well have been a name which Blake invented to complete his list.

Gwiniverra (Gwinevera), the emanation of Scofield, is the faithless wife of the unworthy husband which Scofield, the Natural Man, must have been. In the history of Britain, however, she is the wife of King Arthur. Being left in charge of his kingdom with Mordred, she allowed herself to be corrupted by him, then in despair took the veil (Geoffrey, IX. ix.-xi. i.). Geoffrey spells her name 'Guanhumara,' and Milton, 'Guenever.'

Estrild, the emanation of Kox, represents the secret sin of the woman. She is named after the princess Estrildis who was captured by Locrine and hidden by him in a subterranean chamber, where she bore him the illegitimate Sabrina. Both mother and daughter were drowned by Guendoloeña, the lawful wife, after Locrine's death (Geoffrey, II. ii.-iv.).

Sabrina, the emanation of Kotope, therefore represents the fruits of secret sin, unjustly punished. The Severn, in which she was drowned, was named after her.

Conwenna, the emanation of Bowen, is named after the mother of Brennius and Belinus, who fought each other continually, until she persuaded them to stop (Geoffrey, III. vii.). Therefore she represents the Mother of Hatred.

The Twelve Daughters thus represent the course of Feminine Error. Beginning with Selfish Pleasure (Gwendolen), it passes through Restriction (Cambel). Capture (Ignoge), and Disastrous Submission (Cordella)—this is the region of the Loins. The four daughters in the realm of the Heart (Mehetabel, Ragan, Gonorill, and Gwinefred) are all probably forms of Hatred of Custom. The last four (Head) represent the Faithless Wife (Gwiniverra), the Secret Sin (Estrild), its consequences (Sabrina), and Motherhood of Evil (Conwenna). But this whole course leads upward (from south of Loins to north of Head), Motherhood being the logical end of Selfish Pleasure.

From their appearance here (*Jerusalem*, 5 : 40-45), when five unite as Tirzah and seven as Rahab, the Daughters seem to be a combination of the five senses (who restrict sex) and the seven virtues (who encourage sex); but Blake, if this were his idea, did not develop it elsewhere.

The Twelve Daughters appear once in *The Four Zoas*, II. 61-62, where their names are given in a list, whose order varies from that in the *Jerusalem*. Boadicea is substituted for Gwiniverra. The only specific reference to them in *Milton* is 22 : 16, where Gwendolen and Conwenna (the first and last Daughters, therefore intended to comprise them all) appear as the Covering Cherub's garment, 'woven of War & Religion.'

5 : 40-41. The five who become Tirzah, goddess of the restraint of sex, may represent the five senses.

5 : 42. *Rahab* is the goddess of Moral Virtue. *The Covering Cherub* is her false religion created by mistaking the symbol for the truth which it conceals.

5 : 48-53. Cf. Paracelsus's *Philosophy Addressed to the Athenians* (III. 3): 'Every body or every tangible substance is nothing else but coagulated smoke. . . . As long, therefore, as it is driven and disturbed, so long the thing grows, but

when the ebullition ceased the smoking also ceases. . . . All bodies will at last pass away and vanish in smoke, and will be terminated only in smoke.' Cf. also Jakob Böhme's *Six Theosophic Points* (II. 29) : ' Thus you are to understand what this Worlds Substance is : a *Coagulated* Vapour or Cloud out of the Eternall Aether ; which thus hath a Completion or product *like* the Eternall.'

5 : 55. *The Immortal Form* of Albion, which is sleeping in Beulah.

5 : 67–6 : 4. The division of Los. In his pity over the plight of Freedom, his Inspiration is separated from him, ' for Pity divides the Soul ' (*Urizen*, 287).

6 : 6. His reason curses the poet for his interest in mankind.

7 : 5. *The smoke* which is Vala (Nature).

7 : 11. *He drinks* : *i.e.* Albion.

7 : 14. *Thy stolen Emanation* : if this refers to the quarrel with Stothard over the *Canterbury Pilgrims*, it would date this page not earlier than 1806.

7 : 18-26. All this means, quite simply, that a cruel race of men has peopled the earth.

7 : 19. *Nimrod* was the first king. According to *Paradise Lost*, XII. 24 *seq.*, he upset the original pastoral existence through ambition, hunting men (instead of beasts), and finally built Babel out of pride. ' A mightie Hunter thence he shall be styl'd / Before the Lord, as in despite of Heav'n.'

7 : 22. *Constellations* represent the mechanistic laws of Fate.

7 : 30-36 is repeated from *The Four Zoas*, II. 72-79. Passion is tormented in the fires supplied by Nature.

7 : 42-44. The Natural Man is the father of all generated men.

7 : 44-49. The first eight Sons (the fourfold Judge and Executioner) are caught in the false feminine standards of war and religion ; the fourfold Accuser remains outside even such standards.

7 : 56. *Tenfold* : the meeting of the five senses of the Spectre with those of the Emanation ? Or merely a number of joy ? Cf. *The Four Zoas*, IX. 346.

7 : 61. *Self-annihilation* is regeneration, since it destroys the false Selfhood, and reveals the Eternal Humanity. Cf. Buddha's doctrine : ' Self is death and truth is life. The cleaving to self is a perpetual dying, while moving in the truth is partaking of Nirvana which is life everlasting.'

7 : 63. *The Religion of Generation* is the religion of this world of generation : Materialism.

7 : 63-67. The errors of religion conceal within them the truth, which they thus protect until the Last Judgment. Blake has often expressed this doctrine under the symbol of the Covering Cherub. Thus the whole visible universe becomes the symbol of the invisible ; and error arises only when we mistake the symbol for the reality.

7 : 68. *The Dead* : those in this world despise the Saviour.

8 : 3. *My Mace* : Los's weapon with which to protect Albion.

8 : 12. Reason (the Spectre) must be submitted to the Poet.

8 : 22. *His prey* : Albion.

8 : 32. *Uncircumcised* : Circumcision is used by Blake as another symbol of the sacrifice of the Selfhood.

8 : 34. *Triple form* : divided into Head, Heart, and Loins.

8 : 43. *Condens'd* when they should expand.

8 : 43. *Hand has absorb'd all his Brethren.* Accuser and Judge unite as the Executioner.

9 : 1-6. The appearance of physical war.

9 : 14-16. The suppression of genius and all self-expression.

9 : 18. Against this brutal folly, Los begins his spiritual warfare, forming his weapons from human misery.

9 : 29-30. Repeated from *Milton*, 6 : 47-48. Though the Poet may not yet be creating forms of Truth, he is at least giving a body to Falsehood, so that it can be recognized and destroyed.

9 : 34. *Erin* replaces America in the *Jerusalem* symbols, since America was now definitely not a part of England. Erin lies to the west, and is also separated from England by the sea. Therefore Erin represents the Body.

10 : 7-16. The rationalistic philosophy.

10 : 10. *An Abstract which is a Negation* : a Law which is a Prohibition.

10 : 20-21. These famous lines were probably suggested by Horace's :

> Si quid novisti rectius istis
> Candidus imperti ; si non, his utere mecum.

10 : 37-59. The Spectre sees himself as a sinful man before the God of strict Justice, to whom all sins must be sacrificed. These sins arise from the same impulses which bring the poet his inspiration (Enitharmon).

10 : 54. Creation in the flesh is an act of Mercy, though the Spectre cannot understand this.

11 : 2. Vision operates in the moment of time and the grain of matter. Cf. *Milton*, 28 : 1-3, 21-22.

11 : 6-7. *He might feel* : *i.e.* the Spectre. Thanks to the works of poetry, Reason cannot attack mankind without realizing the pain it is causing. Cf. *Milton*, 40 : 19-20.

11 : 8-12. At last the poet produces perfect works, which are led by his defence of the Body (Erin).

11 : 22. Reuben is the vegetated Man. His incest and consequent curse (*Genesis* xlix. 4) represented to Blake the love for the Earth Mother, who is goddess of Generation.

11 : 24–12 : 3. Nature is only the reflection of Eternity. If Vala's existence is admitted she becomes ' a devouring worm '—the grave of mankind ; but as a dream, she is beautiful. Cf. Saint-Martin : ' If this world will seem to us, after our death, as nothing but magical illusion, why do we regard it otherwise at present ? The nature of things does not change ' (*Œuvres Posthumes*, I. 209).

12 : 5. The Finger of God touches the Seventh Furnace, as in *The Four Zoas*, IV. 275-279, and in *Jerusalem* again, 35 : 1-6 and 48 : 44-45. The Seventh Furnace is the Seventh Eye, Jesus. The touching coincides with the fixation of the double limit to man's fall—Satan and Adam, the limits of Opacity and Contraction.

12 : 13. Stating untruths in order to disprove them.

12 : 25–13 : 29. This description of the building of Golgonooza has been approved by some critics and censured by others. Though Blakean throughout, it is certainly reminiscent of the fourfold cities of Ezekiel and John, with a touch of medieval (possibly Spenserian) romance.

12 : 26. *Ethinthus* is the eighth daughter of Los and Enitharmon (*The Four Zoas*, VIII. 358). She appears in *Europe* as the Queen of Waters, and therefore must be a spirit of materialism.

12 : 38-42. A reference to the Lambeth period of inspiration.

12 : 45-50. Like the cities of Ezekiel and John, Blake's city is fourfold throughout. These four correspond to the Four Zoas. As usual we can chart Golgonooza only by the use of the fourth dimension, since its circumference, zenith, nadir and centre open alike inward into the four worlds of Eden, Beulah, Generation and Ulro.

For correspondences, consult the Table at the head of the Commentary.

The Bulls of Luvah guard the Spirit ; the Wheels of Tharmas guard the Emotions ; the Lions of Urthona guard the Intellect ; and the Cherubim of Urizen guard the Body. Apparently Blake intended to utilize the four beasts of Ezekiel for these guardians ; but he substituted Wheels for the Eagles. The Wheel usually stands for Urizen ; but in this case the discrepancy is noted in line 12 : 51.

Each of these regions has four gates opening into the four worlds of Eden, Beulah, Generation and Ulro. Eden is Eternity itself (for Golgonooza represents the Imagination, which is Existence, and which is not bounded by Eternity) ; Beulah is the same as we have always known it ; while the distinction between

Generation (living material forms) and Ulro (minerals) is new. Blake has abandoned for good the classification into Beulah, Alla, Al-Ulro, and Or-Ulro (*Milton*, 34 : 8-18).

In the centre of Golgonooza is Luban, where the Looms of Cathedron are placed.

12 : 51-52. Golgonooza, however, is not perfect as yet. The realm of the Body is still afflicted by the fatalism of Science ; its gates are closed until the Last Judgment ; while the Gates of Eternity are frozen solid.

12 : 55-56. Cf. Thomas Vaughan's *Anima Magica* : ' Circumferences dilate, and Centres contract ; Superiours dissolve & Inferiours coagulate.'

13 : 6. *Cherubim* : these forms of logic are the same which guard the Tree. They are Prohibition, which closes the Western Gate against indulgence in the joys of the Body.

13 : 17. To the perversion of the emotions Blake ascribed all diseases. Cf. the *Vision of the Last Judgment* : ' That living creature on the left of the Throne gives to the seven Angels the seven vials of the wrath of God, with which they, hovering over the deeps beneath, pour out upon the wicked their plagues.'

13 : 24. *Luban* : see the Commentary on *The Four Zoas*, v. 77.

13 : 26-29. The four elements guard the various gates.

13 : 30. Outside the City of Art lies the universe of the scientists.

13 : 32. *The Twenty-seven Heavens* : the various false religions of the earth, repeated on 75 : 10-20 from *Milton*, 37 : 35-43, of which see the Commentary.

13 : 36. Eternity can be achieved in two ways : by expansion, until the universe is included in oneself ; and by searching the centre of oneself.

13 : 37. A slight shift in symbols. Formerly the Stars formed the wheels of logic ; but now (possibly through the influence of the astrologer Varley) the empty spaces between them take their meaning.

13 : 38-40. A recapitulation of symbols belonging to the material world : the Platonic Cave of the skull ; the Rock of moral law ; the Tree of Mystery ; the Lake of the Indefinite ; the Forest of Errors ; the Marsh of Despond ; and so on. These symbols are a combination of those in Virgil's *Aeneis*, vi., and Dante's *Inferno*.

13 : 43. *The Salamandrine men* are probably men who live in continual wrath.

13 : 44-45. Creation is an act of the Divine Mercy, because by the fixation of form it prevents a further Fall. Cf. Jakob Böhme, *Six Theosophic Points*, vii. 28 : ' And therefore hath God introduced the Soul into Flesh and Bloud, that it might *not so easily* be capable of the fierce wrathfull Substance ; also it hath its Joy the while in the Sun's Looking-Glasse, and rejoyceth it self in the *Sydereall Essence*.'

13 : 50. The Voids of Error, the Solids of Matter, the Clouds of Ignorance, and the Waters of Time and Space.

13 : 52. A summation of everything exterior to Golgonooza.

13 : 59. *Six thousand years* is the limit of Time. See the Commentary on *The Marriage of Heaven and Hell*, plate xiv.

13 : 60–14 : 1. Everything exists in Eternity, except errors. Even Matter has its eternal form ; and everything, living and dead, is to be redeemed. Cf. Paracelsus's *Coelum Philosophorum*, ii. : ' The earth with its frigidity is a coagulation and a fixation. . . . For the house is always dead ; but he who inhabits the house lives. If you can discover the force of this illustration you have conquered.'

13 : 62-63. These things also exist under the Twenty-seven Heavens of the false religions, which are always being elaborated by the aspiring Logic of earth-inhabitants.

14 : 1. Cf. Paracelsus's *Philosophy Addressed to the Athenians* (ii. 17) : ' There is no frail or fading thing in the whole world which does not substitute in its place something which is eternal.'

14 : 2. *The Cherub* is the cruel Logic with the flaming sword which prevents sexual freedom. *The Serpent Orc* is the revolt of youth still suppressed and made to take on a hypocritical form.

14 : 3. *The Dragon Urizen* is brute Reason debased below any semblance of humanity, and fallen into a form of War.

14 : 4-6. *Tharmas the Vegetated Tongue*. The materialized Body is a false doctrine (Tongue) composed of false thinking, false emotions, and false sensations.

14 : 7-9. Symbols of the materialized Body. *The wat'ry flame* is the torture of Lust (see the Commentary on the illustration of plate IV. of *The Marriage of Heaven and Hell*) ; *dark roots and stems* are forms of Vegetation, or flesh (cf. *The Everlasting Gospel*, III. 99) ; the *Forest* is the forest of error ; and the *seas of sorrow* are those of Time and Space.

14 : 10-14. *The Four Females* are the four emanations of the Zoas. Pleasure, the Earth Mother, and Material Beauty fade and vanish ; but Spiritual Beauty still lives, though apparently separated from the Poet.

14 : 15. Creation, the act of Divine Mercy, is performed by the Poet and his Inspiration ; since by giving a form to Falsehood they can eventually destroy it.

14 : 16-26. A description of Blake's own works. Their appeal is triple : through the senses, through the intellect, and through the spirit ; but the fourth gate (of Bowlahoola) is closed—no way of entering Golgonooza is opened to those who serve only the belly-gods.

14 : 29-30. Possibly suggested by *Ephesians* iii. 18 : 'That ye may be able to comprehend with all saints what is the breadth, and length, and depth, and height' ; but changed to conform with 12 : 55-56—the 'centre' is too important in mystical psychology to be omitted. See Ouspensky's *Tertium Organum* for a development of fourth dimensional theory in connection with mysticism.

14 : 31-34. Freedom appears through the emotions (eastward) in the realms of Abstract Philosophy. She seems almost an illusion (a cloud) though she is borne by the Daughters of Inspiration.

15 : 4. *The Polypus* is the constrictive and devouring symbol of rationalistic society. See the Commentary on 67 : 35-37.

15 : 6-7. The four divisions of Man are : (1) the Humanity, which is the immortal essence of his Individuality, now asleep ; (2) the Emanation, which is his inspiration, now an outcast ; (3) his Spectre, or Reason, which now dominates him ; (4) the Shadow, withered yet cruel, of his denied Desire. They correspond to Urthona, Luvah, Urizen, and Tharmas.

15 : 11. Bacon, Newton, and Locke are the three arch-scientists, who are responsible for the reign of Reason.

15 : 20. As in *Ezekiel* i. 16.

15 : 22. *Death* : the mystical death of self-sacrifice.

15 : 23. *Cutting the Fibres* : freeing Man.

15 : 26. From Noah to Abram, there was no promise of redemption.

15 : 27-28. When the promise of redemption came, Abram changed his name to Abraham, and fled from the errors of Chaldea. Then Reuben, the Vegetated Man, will (for the symbol belongs to all ages) reunite himself with Humanity.

16 : 4. Trees always represent growths of error.

16 : 8. *Theotormon* : Desire.

16 : 9. *Palamabron* : Pity.

16 : 11. *Rintrah* : Wrath.

16 : 26. Cf. *The Vision of the Last Judgment* : 'While we are in the world of mortality, we must suffer—the whole Creation groans to be delivered.'

16 : 28-60. This assignment of the various counties of Great Britain among the twelve Sons of Israel is not too important in the understanding of *Jerusalem*, and poetically is the worst place in the book. The division of Ireland (promised, but omitted here) will be found 72 : 17-27.

In general, this passage means that mankind, when divided, fled from the wars of Eternity, and overspread the earth as separate nations. This fleeing of the twelve sons of Israel has often been mentioned before (*The Four Zoas*, VIII. 369 ; *Milton*, 22 : 62 ; etc.), but never with any elaboration of detail. They 'fall' as the Sons of Israel ; then, after working out their salvations, they return as the Twelve Tribes of Israel. There is a slight difference between the names of the Sons and the names of the Tribes, since the tribe of Levi became scattered through the other tribes, while Joseph's two sons (Ephraim and Manasseh) founded the two tribes which replace the names of Levi and Joseph (*Numbers* ii.). In *Revelation* vii. the tribe of Dan does not appear, being replaced by the tribe of Levi. Blake is sometimes careless in his lists : he confuses the Sons and the Tribes, omits Gad in favour of Levi, etc.

The Tribes of Israel and their compass-points are given in *Numbers* ii. On the basis of this, Blake constructed his map of Ireland (72 : 17-27), which, unlike the maps here given, represents the state of salvation. His arrangement is as follows :

	NORTH	EAST	SOUTH	WEST
Head	Dan 72 : 4	Judah 72 : 4	Reuben 72 : 3	Joseph 72 : 3 (Ephraim)
Heart	Asher	Issachar	Simeon	Gad (Manasseh)
Loins	Napthali	Zebulun	Levi	Benjamin

However, clear as this seems, there is possibly some confusion in the south. Reuben (in spite of 72 : 3) may correspond to Hand (south of Loins), if we acknowledge 34 : 36 and 90 : 25 to indicate that ; but then again, Levi rules the provinces governed by Hand on the map of England (16 : 45 and 71 : 11-12).

But the maps on plate 16 represent the confusion of the Fall. Few Sons rule their rightful provinces. In England, the four chief 'Gates' (or Heads) are characteristically dispersed. Dan (the Spirit) is cast down to the south-west (loins of the Body) ; Judah (the Emotions) is just above him (loins of the Body) ; Reuben (Reason) is enthroned in the east (the Emotions) ; and Joseph alone keeps his place in the west (Body). Yet all four still 'keep their heads' sufficiently to share the northernmost provinces. Just below these northern provinces is Simeon (sentimental Reason) who owns vast tracts. The positions of the other sons are very much confused, and not of much importance in understanding *Jerusalem*. Further trouble comes when we discover that the positions of the Sons varies in the maps of Scotland and Wales. Zebulun (loins of the Emotions) is assigned to the islands, and so is cut off from the others. In Scotland, the northern land *par excellence*, Dan (head of North) is shrunk almost to nothing.

For further information, see the Commentary on 72 : 17-27.

16 : 61-69. This celebrated passage means more than that everything is contained in Art, or in Eternity. Blake is retelling quite clearly one of the most persistent of all occult theories. This is the theory of the 'Cosmic Memory,' in which all images and events of the Past and the Future are preserved. Soothsayers and clairvoyants claim to penetrate this Memory ; and by beholding those Ideas which are descending to birth on the material plane, they can foretell the future. This theory is to be found in Indian, Greek, Egyptian, Celtic, and Jewish thought. It is the 'Perfect Land' of the Egyptian mysteries, it is Plato's World of Ideas, it is the 'Yesod' (Archetypal World) of the *Kabalah*, the 'Astral Plane' (or 'Light')

of later occultists, and the 'Akashic Records' of Theosophy. Shelley describes it (*Prometheus Unbound*, I. 195-202):

> For know there are two worlds of life and death:
> One that thou beholdest; but the other
> Is underneath the grave, where do inhabit
> The shadows of all forms that think and live,
> Till death unite them and they part no more;
> Dreams and the light imaginings of men,
> And all that faith creates or love desires,
> Terrible, strange, sublime, and beauteous shapes.

Blake claims this doctrine is to be found in both Testaments (16 : 68-69) and identifies the 'Cosmic Memory' with the Divine Imagination. See the Commentary on *The Four Zoas*, VII. 730-731.

17 : 1-15. Poetry is the weapon to subdue the worldly logic of the Sons; but Logic alone should approach the feminine ideals, lest the Poet himself be seduced by them. Neither Spectre nor Emanation should triumph or be destroyed.

17 : 18. Logic must be subdued by the Poet, lest it destroy Inspiration.

17 : 26. Cf. 43 : 35-36. The 'love' of hypocrites is invariably selfish and destructive.

17 : 33. Cf. *Milton*, 30 : 'Contraries are Positives. A Negation is not a Contrary.' This passage is a restatement of Blake's doctrine that salvation consists in the synthesis of Contraries; while Satan is the great Negation, which has no real existence.

17 : 36. *If thou separate*: Los addresses his Spectre.

17 : 46. The *Worm* is a new symbol, whose significance may be guessed by its association with graves. It represents Man, fallen to the very lowest point. He no longer possesses Head, Heart, and Loins; he has fallen into the fourth state (Ulro, or Bowlahoola), and is only a blind 'devouring stomach.'

17 : 48-58. The birth of Enitharmon, as related in *Urizen*, 307 seq.

17 : 59. 'Demand of the Accuser if he be the healer in things physical or spiritual.'

17 : 60. Error and Falsehood always refuse 'explicit words,' taking refuge in vague generalities.

17 : 62-63. The Poet discovers that he can use the forces of evil as well as good. Cf. *The Four Zoas*, 42b (margin): 'The Christian Religion teaches that No Man is indifferent to you but that Every one is / Either your friend or your enemy: he must necessarily be either the one or the other / And that he will be equally profitable both ways if you treat him as he deserves.'

18 : 1. The story now changes from the conflict of Los and his Spectre to the lamentations of Jerusalem and Vala over Albion.

18 : 1-3. See the Commentary on 13 : 36. *Identity* means Selfhood.

18 : 6. Ashamed of the works of Freedom.

18 : 7. The works of genius have a material form, but their spirit is that of Freedom.

18 : 8. *Three Immense Wheels*: The Accuser, the Judge, and the Executioner; the Satanic Trinity.

18 : 11. The cry against Freedom is the necessary prelude to the further Fall which Albion is about to undergo. The spokesman for the Twelve Sons are Hand and Hyle (18 : 36); they are the Rational Man and the Bad Artist.

18 : 15. *Transgressors*: the geniuses. Sometimes called the Reprobate. They correspond to the Devils of *The Marriage of Heaven and Hell*.

18 : 26. *The Perfect*: called in *Milton* the Elect. They are the opposite of the Transgressors, and correspond to the Angels of *The Marriage of Heaven and Hell*.

18 : 34. *Parents*: Albion and Brittannia. See the Commentary on 36 : 28.

18 : 39. The Rational Man absorbs all the other types of mankind: and the Polypus of the social system appears.

18 : 41. Bad Art and the Lust for Dominion are the Emissaries of War of the Rational Man. They tear themselves away from the body of Mankind.

19 : 1-14. Repeated with practically no changes from *The Four Zoas*, IX. 99-113. Line 8 is added.

19 : 16. *Eon* : or Emanation.

19 : 20. *The Twenty-four* : the Sons and Daughters, who are now divided into Spectres and Emanations.

19 : 26. *Seven diseases* : see the Commentary on 13 : 17.

19 : 27. *Luvah in his secret cloud* : the Emotions are hidden.

19 : 28. *The Friends* : the Zoas and the Cities of Albion.

19 : 36. Man's senses are closed, and his emotions are darkened.

19 : 37. Man enters Beulah—the first state below Eternity.

19 : 42. *Havilah* represents the State of Innocence. Its symbols are the Lilly, the Sun, and the Fairies. Blake probably chose the name partly for its connotation of Avalon. It was a region full of gold, north of Eden and was watered by Pison, the first of the four streams of Eden (*Genesis* ii. 11). Plate VII. of *The Song of Los* is a full-page picture of the Lilly, with Oberon and Titania in its cup.

19 : 43-44. These lines connect Havilah with Beulah, the place from which all Inspirations come.

20 : 1. *Lambeth*, unfallen, is the place of inspiration ; fallen, it is the place of the Palace of the worldly religion and the Bedlam of rationalism.

20 : 5. Freedom and Nature begin to feel a certain enmity.

20 : 19. *Thy shame* : Nature begins to see Jerusalem as a sinner.

20 : 26. *The Veil of Vala* is an important symbol in this epic. It represents the veil of Matter which hides the inner, eternal beauty of Nature. Freedom is now ensnared in this Veil.

20 : 30. The loves of Albion and Vala are recounted in *The Four Zoas*, VII. 239-254. There, as a result of the union, Vala and Luvah are divided, and Urizen is born ; but this story does not seem to be followed here. Albion's rending the Veil and possession of Vala is a symbol of nature-mysticism.

21 : 1. Albion is smitten with diseases, which he attributes to his former Freedom and intercourse with Nature.

21 : 4. This is a reminiscence of the boils of Job.

21 : 6-10. Albion laments his division into the visible universe.

21 : 10. Tharmas, Urizen, Urthona, and Luvah.

21 : 11-12. Albion expects to find redemption in hypocrisy.

21 : 14. *Gwendolen & Ragan* : selfish pleasure and cruelty.

21 : 16. Their higher aspects wither at the death of the Emotions.

21 : 28. The Bad Artist cries out against the fruits of Albion's loves ; the Rational Man tortures them, because they caused the Emotions to be deified by Man.

21 : 42-47. Killed by the cruelty of Man to Man, the Daughters are preserved in Arks of Oak (error) and become the inspiration of War itself (as the Ark of the Lord was carried before the Hebrew armies). Dead in eternity, the Daughters are reborn as doctrines of this world, adding the bitterness of their false sexual standards to the cruelty of Man to Man.

22 : 1, 10-12, 14-15, 20-24 repeated from *The Four Zoas*, I. 29-32, 38-39, 46-50.

22 : 2. Nature herself was crucified until the Hunter of Men utilized her in his warfare.

22 : 3. *Nimrod* : see the Commentary on 7 : 19.

22 : 26-32. Albion thinks that Freedom must be hidden, and that Nature must sacrifice him, since he has killed his own Emotions.

22 : 33. Jerusalem speaks from Love (Moon—Beulah).

22 : 34-35. The Wheel (mechanistic logic) as opposed to the Wing (of Love, of the Seraphim).

23 : 7. Jerusalem begins her answer to Albion in the middle of the line.

23 : 10. *Eternal Death* : Freedom is willing to sacrifice herself for Man by dying from Eternity into the bosom of Nature.

23 : 20. The Veil of Vala is cast into the Sea of Time and Space, where it snares the souls of the ' Dead ' in forms of matter.   The story of the Veil is continued 59 : 2.

23 : 24. This moment, when Albion is falling below Beulah into Generation, is repeated from *The Four Zoas*, i. 406 *seq.*, and recurs 48 : 1.   At this spot is the Oak of Error and the Palm of Triumph.

23 : 29-33. The materialistic religion : God is separated from Man, and Nature is a curse.

23 : 40 is repeated from 21 : 49.

24 : 4. Druidic worship.

24 : 10. Imagination had fled from the brain, love from the loins.

24 : 29. This suggests the Potter of Omar Khayyám.

24 : 34. *The Synagogues* of the Ten Commandments (Moral Law) as opposed to the Churches of Jesus (Moral Lawlessness).

24 : 42-50. All was once the land of God.

24 : 51. Jesus is imprisoned in the death of the Emotions.

24 : 52. ' Sooner murder an infant in its cradle than nurse unacted desires.' Cf. the Commentary on 13 : 17.

24 : 56. Men, in assuming the right to judge, which properly belongs to God alone, have slain Man.

25 : 4. *The Oaken Groves* (living errors) of the Druids.   *The Dragon* is the symbol of War.

25 : 8. Cf. *Matthew* x. 29 : ' Are not two sparrows sold for a farthing ? and one of them shall not fall on the ground without your Father.'

25 : 13. To forgive sins, one must blame the state and not the individual.   One must blame the anger, and not the man who is angry.   For he will pass out of anger ; but anger is eternal.   This is simply Blake's way of saying : ' Hate the sin, but love the sinner.'

25 : 16. *Ulro* : the error of Matter.

Plate 27. *To the Jews.*   Blake's references to the Kabalah cannot be traced to any one volume, but to the general Kabalistic philosophy.   He identifies Albion with Adam Kadmon (Swedenborg's Grand Man), and implies other parallels.   These he takes as proof that originally all religions were one, and points to the similarity of the ruins of the aboriginal temples all over the earth.

It is very difficult to discover just what Blake knew of the Kabalah, partly on account of the scattered nature of the works comprised under that title, and partly because Blake might have absorbed a great deal of Kabalistic doctrine through Agrippa, Paracelsus and Vaughan without ever seeing the original sources.   Perhaps he had also read Henry More's *Conjectura Cabbalistica.*   Many of the Kabalistic doctrines differ from Blake's, while those which do not could easily be explained as parallels.   But from this page of *Jerusalem* we must assume that he knew something.

Blake rejects wholly the idea of the Ain Soph (the unknowable abstract God) ; ' for when separated from man or humanity, who is Jesus the Saviour ? '   The very essence of Blake's philosophy is that God is knowable and human.   The Ten Sephiroth are entirely ignored in Blake's work.   We might compare Kabalistic Emanations with Blake's, but a close inspection shows them to have been quite different.   In the Kabalah, the Sephiroth emanate from the Ain Soph in a chain which endeavours to bridge the unbridgeable space between God and Matter.   Blake avoids that difficulty by calling Matter an error, and saying that all true things are part of God.   He has no Emanation at all in the Kabalistic sense : his Eternity was divided many times ; and not, as it were, thinned out.

But the Kabalistic theories concerning Man are quite Blakean.   Albion, as we have seen, is the Adam Kadmon, in whose limbs all things were formerly contained. ' For the Zohar . . . the world is a " disguised humanity " and all that interests a man is man. . . . The form of man comprises all that is in heaven or on earth, and prior to its manifestation no form could subsist. It is the perfection of faith in all things and the absolute form of all. . . . There is even a certain withdrawn and inconceivable sense in which man through Sephirotic mediation brings the *latens Deitas* into manifestation, and as all things exist and subsist for man, so the problem of evil in the universe is solved in his interest, as it is the condition of his development ; while with a Catholic comprehensiveness which has no parallel in any sacred literature, the scheme of human existence is regarded by the Zohar with an optimism strange in its profundity, from man's pre-existence in the archetypal world to the beatific vision, the absorption and the eternal nuptials which await him ' (A. E. Waite : *The Doctrine and Literature of the Kabalah*, pp. 208-209).

In the Kabalah we can also find the Four Worlds : reincarnation ; the original unity of the sexes ; the Seven Eyes ; and the eventual salvation of all things.

Was Britain the Primitive Seat ? According to British mythology, Joseph of Arimathea brought the Holy Grail to Glastonbury, and there founded Christianity.

Albion was the Parent, etc. When Albion fell, he divided into rational men (Druids) ; and during the sleep of death, various forces (the Elohim) created False Religion, the Natural Man, and the world of Matter. Cf. the *Vision of the Last Judgment* : ' He is Albion, our ancestor, patriarch of the Atlantic Continent, whose history preceded that of the Hebrews, and in whose sleep, or chaos, Creation began.'

The poem describes the original state of Innocence (stanzas i.-vi.), contrasts it with the present state of Experience (vii.-xiv.), and promises Redemption (xv.-xxii.).

Lines 25-26 are revised from 12 : 25, 27-28.

Line 56. Salvation is to be found within.

Line 75. The Reason is not to be destroyed, but reclaimed.

Line 77. *Family-love.* As a family is only the extension of a man's personality, so his promotion of that family at the expense of others is a sin of selfishness.

Humility, according to Blake, was hypocrisy. ' If a man is master of his profession, he cannot be ignorant that he is so.' Also cf. *The Everlasting Gospel*, III.

CHAPTER II

The order of the plates of this chapter in this commentary follows the standard order as usually printed. Blake's revised order (28 : 33-41 ; 43-46 ; 42 ; 29-32 ; 47-50) is followed in the synopsis given in Chapter XXVII., *The Ultimate City*.

28 : 6. The conviction of sin.

28 : 7. Cf. H. C. R., Dec. 17, 1825 : ' What are called vices in the natural world are the highest sublimities in the spiritual world.'

28 : 15. *A deadly Tree* : the Tree of Mystery, for which see *Ahania*, 109-129, and *The Four Zoas*, VII. 29-39. This is the sterile Tree of Puritanism.

28 : 19. Like the deadly upas-tree.

28 : 21. *Twelve Altars* : to the twelve Gods of Ulro—see *Milton*, 37 : 20-34, where they are identified with the Twelve Sons. The Gods themselves would be condemned by their own laws.

29 : 1. The setting of the sun.

29 : 4. Cf. *Ezekiel* i. 26.

29 : 9. *The Reactor* : Satan.

29 : 10. Evil must be revealed through its works.

29 : 18. *Ephratah* : a place of the Ark. Cf. *Psalm* cxxxii. 6 : ' Lo, we heard of it at Ephratah ; we found it in the fields of the wood.'

29 : 28. *Two Immortal forms* : Los's Spectre and Emanation. The Powers of Poetry have fled from Man's brain, though the Poet remains his friend.

29 : 29. Cf. *Job* i. 15-19.

29 : 33-82. Repeated from *The Four Zoas*, III. 44-103, with a few verbal changes and the omission of lines 47-48, 72-76, 89, 91-92. For the meaning of this passage see the Commentary in *The Four Zoas*.

30 : 6. *A Shadow*: suppressed desire.

30 : 11. *The Sexual Religion*: Urizen's temple of Chastity, where the phallos is worshipped (*The Four Zoas*, VII. 511-529).   *Uncircumcision*: selfishness.

30 : 13. *Their Humanity*: Los himself.

30 : 14. *Urthona's Spectre*: Los.

30 : 16. The Spectre and Emanation are united in Los by divine Mercy.   The Spectre was divided 6 : 1 ; the Emanation, 17 : 49.

30 : 18. *Feminine Allegories*: false doctrines, where the symbol is interpreted wrongly in favour of the Female Will.

30 : 26. *The Twenty-eight Cities*: see the Commentary on 39 : 13.

30 : 28-32. The practice of the doctrines of Urizen's 'Book of Brass.' Lines 30-31 are repeated from *The Four Zoas*, VII. 110, 124.

30 : 33-40. The highest aspect of Man is above Sex. 'For in the resurrection they neither marry nor are given in marriage, but are as the angels of God in heaven ' (*Matthew* xxii. 30).   But now Man has embraced Nature ; he is falling from Beulah into the next lower world, Generation, whence he can only be released by a destruction of Error.

31 : 2-6. The Poet, in hopes of saving Man, examines his soul throughout.

31 : 7-27. He sees all the ' Minute Particulars '—all the little tendernesses and impulses of the personality, which in the last analysis are the essentials of the individual—degraded and despised ; while the ' Universal Form ' has fallen from a living thing to a barren Abstraction.   Los cannot see who commits these sins ; for Satan is not to be revealed until the fruits of his ways are evident.

31 : 24. *A building of Luvah*: the Tower of London, far from being a piace of cold justice, is a creation of the passions of Man.

31 : 25. *Bethlehem*: Bedlam.

31 : 44. *Thy Wife*: Freedom will not be bound.

31 : 50-56. Man in the grip of Nature is fighting his Passions with the aid of Reason.

31 : 57-66. Nature blames Freedom for Albion's condition.

32 : 3-14. The Poet cannot penetrate to the interior of Albion's impulses, where Satan is hidden ; but he sees that Man has become ingrowing, instead of expanding outward to Eternity.   He rises to work, but the Sons bear him to the Death-Couch in Beulah.

32 : 15. This line is repeated from plate 27.

33 : 2. Albion is now definitely in the world of Generation.   Blake identifies Chaos with Memory, in contrast to the Eternity of the Imagination.

33 : 5-16. Rational Religion.

33 : 26. *Albion's Emanation* in Generation is not Jerusalem, but her Shadow, Vala.

33 : 28. *Sexual Reasoning Hermaphroditic*: the doubt of self-contradiction.

33 : 30. *Autumn ripeness*: decay, though Albion takes it for a time of harvest.

33 : 31. Nature appearing from Chaos seems a new thing.

33 : 36–34 : 1. The false doctrines drawn from the delusions of Nature.

33 : 41. Nature is the result of the Emotions.

33 : 48. Material Beauty claims to be the only beauty.

33 : 49. Nature claims the Human Form itself is her own creation.

34 : 7-8. Albion believes that the Sun of Imagination, the Moon of Love, and the Stars of Reason are all products of Nature.

34 : 15. See the Commentary on 30 : 33-40.

34 : 20-21. Reason (the Starry Heavens) has not yet left Albion.

34 : 23-40. The Poet laments over the cruelty of Nature.   Albion, in submitting to her control, has violated the great law that Man shall rule Woman.

34 : 27-28. Cf. 1 *Corinthians* xi. 3, 8, 9 : ' But I would have you know, that the head of every man is Christ ; and the head of the woman is the man ; and the head of Christ is God. . . . For the man is not of the woman ; but the woman of

the man.   Neither was the man created for the woman ; but the woman for the man.'

34 : 31. *Create a Female Will* : submit to a lower influence.

34 : 36. The Rational Man is only another form of the Natural Man.

34 : 37. *Merlin* is the Prophet (or Poet) submitted to the Feminine Will. According to the old legends, Merlin was seduced by Nimuë, the Lady of the Lake (Matter), who enclosed him forever in a rocky tomb, though he could never wholly die.

34 : 40. *Weight & Distance* : Gravitation and Space.

34 : 43. The Vegetated Man sleeps, seemingly dead to Eternity ; but Los gives him his physical limitations, when the Emotions are divided.

34 : 46. The Emotions are divided into three : the cold intellectual passion ; the hot revolutionary passion of the heart (Orc) ; and the blind passion of the loins.

34 : 47. Reuben's first sense to be limited by Los is that of smell (Nostrils : Emotions).   Mankind flees from his apparition, but is overtaken by his fate.

34 : 52. The Twelve Daughters, comprised in the form of Gwendolen (selfish pleasure), divide into the two forms of Rahab (sexual licence) and Tirzah (sexual restraint).

34 : 53. *His Eyes* : Reuben's second sense to be limited (his Reason).

34 : 55-58. All things are as we behold them.   If Man sees the world as the World of Generation, it is his own shame that he sees.

35 : 1-2. Jesus places the limits of Opakeness and Contraction (of Blindness and Narrowness) in Man's bosom, lest Man fall beyond into Ulro, the realm of lifeless matter, and thence into Non Entity.   The limit of the Fall is thus fixed by Divine Mercy ; now Man must work out his errors.   This is the moment when the Hand of God touches the Seventh Furnace which is Jesus (12 : 5, also *The Four Zoas*, IV. 275-279).

35 : 5. Suggested by *Daniel* iii. 25 : ' He answered and said, Lo, I see four men loose, walking in the midst of the fire, and they have no hurt ; and the form of the fourth is like the Son of God.'

35 : 9-10. All Eternity must pass through Jesus for worldly condemnation.

35 : 13. *Be permanent, O State !*   By fixing the State, Jesus releases the Individual.   Error (Satan), made definite, and fixed into a certain form, can be transcended and escaped.

36 : 1-20. The Poet fixes the form of the Vegetated (materialized) Man.

36 : 1. *Tirzah* : repressed sex.

36 : 2. *Eyelids* : intellect. *Nostrils* : passions.   These were bound on plate 34.

36 : 4. *The Moon of Ulro* : Love in the material world.

36 : 5-6. His senses (*Tongue*) are bound.

36 : 13. *Ear* : The last of the powers of perception to be bound is that of spiritual perception.   Reuben's four senses are now closed from Eternity.

36 : 23-24. Reason stands between the Flesh and the Imagination.   Here, as often elsewhere, Blake gives the interpretation of his symbols in the form of a simile.

36 : 26. *They change their situations.*   The usurpation by each other of the various thrones of the Zoas occupies a large part of *The Four Zoas*.   They should never try to dominate each other.

36 : 28. *England, who is Brittannia.*   Cf. the *Vision of the Last Judgment* : ' The good woman is Brittannia, the wife of Albion, Jerusalem is her daughter.'

36 : 29. Reason dominates the Emotions ; the Emotions (as Orc) are bound in the realm of Reason.

36 : 32. *Four Elements* : Earth is North, Fire is East, Air is South, and Water is West, according to 13 : 26-29.

36 : 34. The Laws of Chance are discovered in the rational universe.

36 : 38. *The Atlantic Continent* is the Lost Atlantis, the stairway to Eternity. See the Commentary on *America*, 107-112.

36 : 39. The *Sea* of Time and Space.

36 : 40-41. When the Vegetated Man is circumscribed by the Poet, he is seen to be the Fallen Imagination exploring the three stages of Matter.

36 : 48. Cf. the Laocoon plate : ' Art can never exist without Naked Beauty displayed.'

36 : 49-55. *Death* : life in this world. Illusions are real, as long as they are believed, and have the most dreadful consequences, until Man is released from them by the power of the Divine Imagination. *Length, Bredth, Highth*, the three dimensions, represent the delusion of Space.

37 : 1. *One* : Los.

37 : 7. All the Fall does not take place in Time, which lasts only six thousand years. Man leaves Eternity for eight thousand years ; Los for eight thousand and five hundred years (83 : 52). After Time ends, there are yet things to be done before Eternity is achieved ; presumably there were also acts which took place between the beginning of the Fall and the beginning of Time.

37 : 8. *His Spear* : the phallos.

38 : 11. *The Divine Similitude* : or Ideal.

38 : 17-26. Cf. Swedenborg's *Arcana Cœlestia* : ' The whole Heaven is a Grand Man (Maximus Homo), and it is called a Grand Man because it corresponds to the Lord's divine Human ; and by so much as an angel or spirit or a man on earth has from the Lord, they also are men. . . . All things in the human body, in general and particular, correspond most exactly to the Grand Man, and as it were to so many societies there.' 38 : 17-21 are repeated from *The Four Zoas*, I. 442-446, of which see the Commentary.

38 : 28. Blake speaks.

38 : 45-54. Verulam, Canterbury, York, and Edinburgh seem to be a fourfold symbol ; but in *Jerusalem* these symbols shift too often to be definitely explained. In 46 : 24 we find another similar group, but with London substituted for Canterbury ; and in 57 : 1 yet another, where Bath is substituted for Verulam. Verulam was Bacon's title ; while Canterbury and York are England's two archbishoprics.

38 : 55-39 : 11. The Northern Gate of the Imagination, which opens into Eternity, through Beulah. *Tyburn*, the place of the gallows, is an obvious symbol. Tyburn Tree stood near what is now the Marble Arch, Hyde Park. On the earthly side of the Gate is the Mill of Logic, the Sea of Time and Space, and the Religion of Moral Virtue. When Urthona (the Spirit) passes through this Gate, he becomes Los (the Poet). Man now flees definitely through this Gate into Ulro.

39 : 13. *The twenty-eighth* : in the list of cathedral towns and cities. Los corresponds to Edinburgh (north). The names of the first seven in the list are given 40 : 48-61 ; the next seventeen, who are contained in Bath (the seventh), are named 46 : 3-19 ; the last four, who sum up the other twenty-four, and who represent the Zoas, are named 46 : 24.

These twenty-eight Cities evidently correspond to the twenty-seven Religions, if we add to the latter the name of Milton, which is given in *The Four Zoas*, VIII. 356. The list begins with Selsey (or Chichester, where Blake was tried for treason), which corresponds to Adam (or Scofield, 7 : 42), and ends with northern Edinburgh, who corresponds to Milton (or Bowen, the Head of the north). Thus the list should represent a rise of mankind from Adam ; and such was Blake's idea in *The Four Zoas*. (Swedenborg's very similar list of churches represented a Fall.) But in *Jerusalem*, Blake has cast aside the idea of progress on this plane : the individual may progress, but the state never. Therefore he omitted Milton, joined Adam on again after Luther, and thus got the symbol of the everlasting round of Nature.

Blake's list of Cities does not correspond exactly to the twenty-seven dioceses of his time. Apparently he made London and Canterbury interchangeable, and added Edinburgh and Verulam (which, as St. Albans, actually became a diocese in 1875).

Hand, Hyle, Coban, and Scofield are assigned Selsey, Winchester, Bath, and

Ely, respectively (71 : 11, 20, 26, 38), to indicate what forces are necessary for the salvation of that state which each city represents.

For further information about the Cities, consult the Commentary below under their names.

40 : 4. *The four*: the last four of the list of cities.

40 : 4-5. Line 4 evidently ends with the word ' Chariot,' which must have been carried over into line 5 by some carelessness in the engraving.

40 : 7. *Sixteen pillars*: the inspired books of the Bible. See the Commentary on 48 : 7.

40 : 21. *The Twenty-four*: the cities of Albion, excluding the Four mentioned, 40 : 4.

40 : 22. *The Living Creatures*: or Zoas. *The third procession*, that of the Body.

40 : 32, 38-42. Rearranged from *The Four Zoas*, v. 56-61.

40 : 33. *The Merciful*: Jesus.

40 : 41-42. *Eon*: Emanation. Cf. *The Marriage of Heaven and Hell*: ' The man who never alters his opinion is like standing water, and breeds reptiles of the mind.'

40 : 45-61. This list of cities is completed 46 : 1-24.

40 : 48. *Selsey* (Chichester). The original see was Selsey, but was changed to Chichester in 1075. The site of the old cathedral is now a mile out to sea. Blake was tried at Chichester; therefore it comes in the place of the Accuser, and corresponds in the list of Religions to Adam, the Natural Man. In the state of salvation (71 : 11) the Natural Man is ruled by the Rational (Hand).

40 : 53. *Winchester* represents that state saved by Art (here by Los ; in 71 : 20 by Hyle).

40 : 57. *Bowlahoola & Allamanda*: the digestive and nervous systems of Man, which together represent his entire physiology. Winchester is obliged to descend into Generation.

40 : 61. *Salisbury* must have been associated in Blake's mind with the Druid remains on Salisbury Plain, to which he refers very often. *Bristol* he early associated with Chatterton (*Island in the Moon*). The Polypus seems to have reached no farther than this city (67 : 37).

41 : 1. *Bath*, where the healing springs issued from the earth, represents the healing Power of Nature—in the broadest sense, the Body. But complete reliance on the Body tends to Materialism. Therefore Bath is both ' the best and worst in Heaven and Hell ' ; Blake promptly warns the Materialists that within the Grain of Sand a Gate opens. Being the Body, Bath speaks from the western porch (45 : 2). He is once beheld in vision to contain all the others (45 : 37-39).

41 : 4-14. ' Poplar (near the East India Dock in the East of London) and Bow (a part of the same district), and then further towards the east " to Malden and Canterbury," means to transfer the Divine Vision into the regions of the emotions, to speak only to the heart instead of to the intellect, and to make religion an affair of mere feeling. . . . The reasoning power first attempted to analyse religious faith in a spirit of love and in the highest regions of the human soul. But he took a triple octave—twenty-four—which he tried to reduce to twelve ; he wished to divide the Bible into two parts, and to see in it only the book of the twelve tribes, otherwise the Old Testament, thus upholding the religion of Jehovah instead of the eternal Gospel of Christ. Casting Jerusalem forth to Poplar, Bow, Malden, and Canterbury, he endeavours to make Christ's teaching a purely emotional thing, quite independent of the intellect, and therefore to be believed or rejected according as each man is inclined. The shuttles of death, singing to Islington and Pancrass, round Marylebone to Tyburn's river (from north to west) mark the progress of Materialism (the western region). The black net of melancholy and the meshes of despair closely woven over the west of London signify that all the purely vegetative and physical part of human life is really dead, and that man can only obtain true life through the Divine Vision. This Divine Vision, Jerusalem, would have perished utterly,

if there had been no other regions of the spirit. But she found a refuge in Lambeth, a quarter of the south where the prophet lived, and where there is still some light. There, beneath the southern and consequently luminous Surrey hills, which are the highest peaks of our little human intelligence, she stayed her course and rested ' (Berger, pp. 231-233).

I suggest that ' reducing twenty-four to twelve ' means eliminating the Emanations (inspirations) of the twelve.

41 : 15-22. ' To see a Heaven in a Grain of Sand.' Blake found the gate through Nature to Eternity in Lambeth. When all other spirituality is dead, one can always find it in Nature. Cf. Jakob Böhme's *Six Theosophic Points*, III. 52 : ' Thus also is to be seen in the Metals, which outwardly are a *Grosse Body* of Brimstone Mercury and Salt, wherein the vegetation standeth or consisteth, and in their inward ground they are a clear *bright Body* wherein the incorporated Light of Nature of the divine Efflux *shineth* : In which Glance or Lustre a Man understandeth the Tincture and great Power, how the hidden Power maketh it self visible.' Blake connects this with sex-mysticism, which is an approach to Eternity through the body of the beloved (Oothoon).

42 : 3-4. A reminiscence from *Urizen*, VIII. 3.

42 : 18. *From Dover to Cornwall* : the southern coast.

42 : 29-31. See the Commentary on 35 : 1-2.

42 : 32-34. The Divine Mercy gives visible form to those powers which Man has cast out ; thus Woman is created, and Jesus himself may follow Man into the realms of Ulro.

42 : 35. A contradiction (in symbols only) of *The Book of Los*, 79 : ' Truth has bounds, Error none.'

42 : 47. The Rational Man and the Bad Artist are to destroy the Poet.

42 : 48. *The Twenty-four* : Albion's cities.

42 : 55. The outcome of the attack of Hand and Hyle is not described ; presumably, they could not reach Los.

42 : 63. *Rahab* : the worldly religion of Moral Virtue.

42 : 76. *The Serpent Temples* of the Druids. See the Commentary on *Europe*, 71-93.

42 : 78-81. The Mundane Shell is the Veil of Vala (Matter).

43 : 2-3. The Four Zoas in their fallen aspects.

43 : 6. They saw the Freedom of the Body prevented by the laws of Reason. The following line repeats the same idea under a new symbol. Human sacrifice formed a part of the ceremonies of the ancient Mexican religion.

43 : 8. *Rooty Groves* : the Druidic groves of Oaks.

43 : 16. The twenty-seven false religions. See the Commentary on *Milton*, 37 : 15.

43 : 23. *Minute particulars* : see the Commentary on 31 : 7-27.

43 : 31-32. Slightly revised from *Milton*, 35 : 2-3.

43 : 37. Oshea (Joshua) and Caleb were the only two remaining of all the Israelites who left Egypt (*Numbers* xxvi. 65). They were apparently great friends, and there is no record of any contest between them ; but Blake, using them as symbols of the men who *should* be the greatest friends, allows them to fall out.

43 : 41. ' Opposition is true Friendship ' (*Marriage of Heaven and Hell*).

43 : 43. ' God never makes one man murder another, nor one nation ' (Blake's marginalia in Watson's *Apology for the Bible*).

43 : 46-47. This passage refers to Richard Brothers's theory that the English were the Lost Tribes of Israel, and therefore due to inherit all the blessings prophesied in the Bible. Richard Brothers (1757-1824) was a religious fanatic who raised some excitement in 1794-5 by various striking prophecies, some of which (notably the violent death of Louis XVI.) came true. Unfortunately for himself, he foresaw equally violent changes in England ; was tried for treason ; but was sent to a mad-house.

His name still lives, however, as the first to propose the theory of Anglo-Israelism

—a belief which later was held by over two millions of English and Americans. The beginning of Brothers's theory came when he discovered himself to be the Slain Lamb in *Revelation* (among other things), and consequently of the line of David. Then he began telling his privileged followers that they, too, were Jews, which pleased them immensely. As his followers increased, so did the numbers of the elect, until it seemed that most of the English must be included. William Bryan, an ardent convert, addressed his *Testimony of the Spirit of Truth* (London, 1795), ' To the Children of Israel, wherever scattered, under the Multitude of Names, which Christendom is divided into,' and said ' Ten years ago the Lord was graciously pleased to communicate to my mind, in a peculiar manner, the following particulars, *viz.* that there were many Jews, who were not known to be Jews, or called by that name ; that very many of those called *Christians*, are the true descendants of Jacob . . . that the greatest number of the inhabitants of this land (*called Great Britain, &c.*) are Israelites, of the tribe of Benjamin, that there are some of Judah, and some of Levi ' (pp. 7-8).

Brothers's theory was not finally completed until 1822, when he issued for the benefit of his few faithful followers *A Correct Account of the Invasion and Conquest of this Island, by the Saxons, so interesting to, and so necessary to be known to the English Nation, the Descendants of the greater part of the Ten Tribes of Israel.* This work is generally considered the beginning of Anglo-Israelism.

Blake, as usual, did not accept such theories exactly, either as to spirit or detail. He was willing to admit, for symbolic reasons, that the English were the children of Jerusalem (Freedom), thus taking advantage of the popular agitation. But he really believed that England was the synthesis or ' melting pot ' of the nations. Specifically, these nations were, of course, fourfold : the giant Britons (west), the Saxons (north), the Normans (east), and the Romans (south), who together formed the English (90 : 1-6).

43 : 47-50. Evidently inspired by the rhyme in *Jack and the Bean-Stalk* :

> Fa, Fe, Fo, Fi, Fum !
> I smell the blood of an Englishman.
> Be he live, or be he dead,
> I 'll grind his bones to make me bread.

43 : 51. *Scofield & Kox* : Blake's own accusers.

43 : 60. See the Commentary on 13 : 38-40.

43 : 65. *A Wicker Idol* : the Druidic idol in which men were burned. See the Commentary on *Milton*, 37 : 11.

44 : 1, 6. *The Wings* of Love opposed by the Wheels of Logic. Man cannot be redeemed but through his own will and wisdom.

44 : 21. *The Ulro* : matter, or error.

44 : 26. *In Erin's Land towards the north.* The religion of Ulro springs from a combination of the body and the spirit.

44 : 28. *They* : the Cities, which are now fallen into Ulro.

44 : 36. *The Gate of Los* : see the Commentary on 38 : 55.

44 : 38. Friendship comes from intuitive sympathy. See 88 : 3-10.

44 : 39-40. The Emanation (intuition) in every man is free (Jerusalem) ; the physical laws which seem to cause such friendships are only the Shadow (suppressed desire) of such Freedom, regulated by Reason.

45 : 3. Bath, the healing power of Nature, appropriately wails over the restriction of the Senses, closed by the Sea of Time and Space.

45 : 13. *Selfhood* : see the Commentary on *Milton*, 12 : 30.

45 : 19-22. The enslavement in Egypt, and the release under Moses.

45 : 30. *Oxford* : see Commentary on 46 : 7.

45 : 38-40. This joining of the Cities into two forms (one containing the first six and the last four, the other the remaining eighteen who appear as Bath) represents the Cities in the two aspects of Spirit and Body.

46 : 1-24. This completes the list begun 40 : 48-61.

46 : 5, 18. *Lincoln* and *Norwich* are twice associated (5 : 10, 21 : 39).

46 : 5. *Durham & Carlisle* are again associated in *Milton*, 40 : 43.

46 : 6. *Ely*, here described as Los's Scribe, is in Cambridgeshire, where Los has his eternal station (39 : 12).

46 : 7. *Oxford*, as one might expect, is mentioned in connection with Cambridge no less than five times. He is an eloquent Bard, here, as in 45 : 30. Perhaps this is to be explained by Blake's letter to Hayley (Jan. 27, 1804): '. . . my much admired and respected Edward, the bard of Oxford, whose verses still sound upon my ear like the distant approach of things mighty and magnificent, like the sound of harps which I hear before the sun's rising.' This bard has never been identified. Oxford's association with Oothoon (*Milton*, 11 : 42, *Jerusalem*, 83 : 28) and with the Tree of Life (45 : 30, 46 : 7) is to be explained by the fact that Rosamond's Bower was in Oxfordshire. (It is sometimes difficult to distinguish between City and County, when Blake gives no clue, as elsewhere.)

46 : 12. Rest in love, until the Last Judgment.

46 : 14-15. The Last Judgment is represented by a final harvest of the Nations, from which the Bread of Philosophy is made (*The Four Zoas*, IX.). See also the Commentary on *Milton*, 3* : 1-3.

46 : 18. *Chester* is twice associated with Benjamin (63 : 12, 90 : 15).

46 : 25-28. The time will come when a family will be a man's worst hindrance. In such a time, Jesus brings no peace, but a sword (*Matthew* x. 34-36); 'And a man's foes shall be they of his own household.' Cf. also lines 81-82 of the poem on plate 27.

47 : 3. The Emotions are separated from mankind, and break into war. Soon they will turn the places of religion into the places of the sacrifice of others.

47 : 6. *The Wicker Man*: see the Commentary on *Milton*, 37 : 11.

47 : 11. The illusion of Matter is created by the Reason of those in this world.

47 : 17. Cf. Dante's 'Abandon hope!' over the gates of Hell. We have already had Albion's last words once before, in 23 : 26.

48 : 1-4, 30 *seq.* and 45 are rewritten from *The Four Zoas*, I. 408-410, 192-193, and IV. 277.

48 : 4. *Surrounded with a Cloud*: concealing the inner sense under a veil of symbol.

48 : 7. *Sixteen pillars*: the inspired books of the Bible, according to Swedenborg (*Arcana Cœlestia*, x. 325).

48 : 13-17. Beulah (Love) is a mild repose from the splendours of Eternity (Imagination).

48 : 14. Repeated from *Milton*, 30 : 1.

48 : 18. Enion awakes Freedom in Love.

48 : 28. *An aged, pensive Woman*: Enion, maternal love, the Earth Mother, and often the Generative Instinct. In *The Four Zoas* (I. 193) she is renamed Eno when she opens Time and Space into Eternity.

48 : 35. *A Rainbow* always represents a watery (material) illusion.

48 : 36. The Moment becomes eight thousand and five hundred years, which is the length of Los's existence outside of Eternity (83 : 52). The Moment of Inspiration is equal in value to all time.

48 : 37. Every second century produces a great genius.

48 : 45. See the Commentary on 12 : 5.

48 : 47. Freedom at last is wholly separated from Man.

48 : 51. *Erin*, the Body.

48 : 56-58. Now Man must sacrifice his opinions and his works (his Children) if he wishes to keep his friends; for no toleration remains.

49 : 10. *The Gigantic roots*: the Wicker Man of Scandinavia.

49 : 15. *Havilah*, or the Eden of Innocence, is materialized into the visible sun.

49 : 19. *The Moon* is supposed to have been a part of the earth at one time; Blake identifies it with the Lost Atlantis.

49 : 24. *Polypus* : the social system based on Materialism.

49 : 47. *Shiloh*, the site of the Tabernacle, represents Inspiration direct from God. The soul is female towards God (the Masculine Emanation) but male towards all other kinds of Inspiration (Daughters of Beulah). See the note on the illustration to plate 96.

49 : 51. A reminiscence from *Psalm* cxxi. 6 : ' The sun shall not smite thee by day, nor the moon by night.'

49 : 53. The gesture of the cross enclosed in the circle.

49 : 54. The Mundane Shell is the Tomb of Man.

49 : 56. *Og & Anak* : see the Commentary on *Milton*, 18 : 33.

49 : 58. *Divine Analogy* : the Swedenborgian correspondences, or the Kabalistic Macrocosm and Microcosm.

49 : 58-59. The heathen giants, in the tears of the repentant Balaam, give their powers to the two steadfast friends. See the Commentary on 43 : 37.

49 : 60. *Surfaces* of matter, beneath which Man is bound.

49 : 61. The twenty-seven heavens and hells are forming to shut Man from Eternity. See the Commentary on *Milton*, 37 : 15.

49 : 66. *To the State.* The States are moods and attitudes, through which any Individual may wander. These are to be blamed for Iniquity, and not the Man who is in them ; for the Man will pass beyond them. We must blame the Anger ; not the Man who is angry, for Anger is eternal, yet it is not an essential part of any individual.

49 : 67. *Death* : the life in this world, which is Satan (Error).

49 : 73. Cf. *Ezekiel* xxviii. 14 : ' Thou art the anointed cherub that covereth : and I have set thee so : thou wast upon the holy mountain of God ; thou hast walked up and down in the midst of the stones of fire.'

49 : 77. Creation as an act of Mercy.

50 : 3. *The Twelve Gods of Asia* : for their names see *Milton*, 37 : 20-34.

50 : 11. Cf. *The Four Zoas*, iv. 253 and Commentary.

50 : 20. *Stars* : Reason.

50 : 22. The lovely illusion of the Body contains the Reason.

50 : 27. Cf. *Ephesians* iv. 26 : ' Be ye angry, and sin not : let not the sun go down upon your wrath.'

Plate 52. This attack on Deism (' the Religion of Nature ') and Militarism is so clearly written that it needs hardly any explanation.

Man is born a Spectre. Cf. Thomas Vaughan's *Anthroposophia Theomagica* : ' We are all born like *Moses* with a Veil over the Face : This is it, which hinders the prospect of that Intellectual shining Light, which God hath placed in us ; And to tell you a Trueth that concernes all Mankinde, the greatest Mystery both in *Divinity* and *Philosophie* is, *How to remove it.*'

Vegetated Spectre : embodied reason.

Prophecied of Jesus : among them Virgil (*Pastoral*, iv.), Hermes Trismegistus and the Sybils.

The poem consists of the second half of the poem in the *MS. Book*, of which the first half was copied into the *Pickering MS.* The Monk represents the follower of Jesus, martyrized under Charlemaine, or imperial power.

Line 17. *The black bow* of material warfare, as opposed to spiritual warfare.

For further notes on this poem, see the Commentary on *I saw a Monk of Charlemaine* among the ' Later Lyrics.'

CHAPTER III

53 : 1. *Vehicular Form* : the Poet is the temporal form of the Spirit.

53 : 4. *Albion's Tree* : the Church of Mystery, founded on Moral Law.

53 : 10. *Seven-fold* : Los's Furnaces are the Seven Eyes of God.

53 : 12-13. Repeated from *Milton*, 23 : 58-59.

53 : 22. *The Twenty-four* and *the Four* are the twenty-eight cathedral cities.

54 : 5. Repeated from plate 26.

54 : 11. Seeing his sons give themselves over to the Passions, Albion is filled with hatred.

54 : 21. The Temptation in the Wilderness.

54 : 25. *Arthur* was the first English king. With Merlin and Bladud he forms a Trinity : Merlin represents the enslaved Imagination, Arthur the enslaved Logic, and Bladud (who founded Bath) the enslaved Body, or Senses.

54 : 27. Albion tries to regain his Emanation, but she opposes him with Reason (stars) and War (dragons). Nevertheless, the vision of Freedom united with Nature appears, though in torment.

55 : 1. The Eternals see Albion still in Beulah, as a result.

55 : 11. *That Veil*, of the flesh.

55 : 13. *The Serpent* of Materialism.

55 : 14. To limit to Generation.

55 : 15. The selling of Joseph as an example of family hate.

55 : 22. The legend of this symbol seems to be lost.

55 : 27. A reminiscence from *Judges* v. 20.

55 : 31. For the Seven Eyes of God, see the Commentary on *The Four Zoas*, VII. 392-400.

55 : 37. The mind of man has complete control over his body.

55 : 55. *The Living Creatures* are the Four Zoas.

55 : 57. *The Indefinite*, or the abstract.

55 : 58. *By his own Works*, and not by a comparison of his principles with the common standards.

55 : 62. This doctrine is often interpreted as meaning attention to detail at the expense of general composition. As a matter of fact, it is merely the cult of the *mot juste*, with all the accuracy of thought and feeling which such a cult implies.

55 : 64. The Infinite, as opposed to the Indefinite.

55 : 66. On self-sacrifice, and not on abstinence.

56 : 8. Man is nothing but the baby of Infinity.

56 : 10. Cf. ' Between two moments, bliss is ripe,' *Europe*, 183.

56 : 18-19. The Sun (Imagination) shall be the chariot of spiritual warfare ; the Moon (Love) a ship bearing us over the Sea of Time and Space.

56 : 26. The Daughters of Albion reply.

56 : 27-28. Pleasure has fallen to all-but-senseless matter ; the Imagination has become the worm which is Man.

56 : 42-43. St. Paul's, with its classic appearance, is the church of the Moral Virtues. Round the Cross stand the three Marys as mourners of crucified Man : mourning, although feminine standards have murdered their Saviour and have smitten two of them.

57 : 7. *Rosamond's Bower*, where Love hides from Satan's Watch-fiends, was the subterranean labyrinth in Blenheim Park (Oxfordshire) supposed to have been built by Henry II. for his mistress, Rosamond Clifford. See also *Milton*, 11 : 42, and *Jerusalem*, 83 : 28.

57 : 12-15. Man refuses to face the warfares of the world, and is caught and mutilated by his own Past (the Dead) ; nevertheless his Reason rises untouched. Finally Man reaches the Rock of Ages itself ; and at last resting there, the centre of things opens and reveals the divine vision.

58 : 1. But Man is not yet saved. Vision is not enough to release him, while all the forces of the world revel misdirected. Albion's first vision of Truth is of the misery of the world, due to the cruelty of the Female Will, which tortures Man under its selfish standards of morality. This Female Will appears sometimes as One, Rahab, the Church of Moral Virtue ; sometimes as two, Rahab and Tirzah, sexual excess and restraint ; and sometimes as the Twelve Daughters.

58 : 2. *Gwendolen* : selfish pleasure.

58 : 11. *The Hermaphroditic Condensations* : the contradictions of Lust and Chastity are divided.

58 : 19. By definitely dividing the sexes, the Male can then dominate the Female again.

58 : 22. Reason's temple of the World of Matter.

58 : 26. *Ungenerate* : not descended to the world of Generation ; but not necessarily in Eternity.

58 : 29. Rationalism encloses the Imagination.

58 : 30. The Bad Artist encloses Love.

59 : 2. See 23 : 20 *seq.*

59 : 5. The Poet makes Matter the wall of Man's tomb, between the Oak and Palm which grow at the entrance to Beulah.

59 : 10-21. Cf. *Milton*, 17 : 15-25 and 34 : 32-39.

59 : 22. The Looms of Generation are between the Spirit and the Body, near the descent (towards Beulah).

59 : 23. The Poet's works are in the realm of Reason, since his Spectre helps him at his labours.

59 : 28. The Daughters of Los weep at their task of weaving bodies, but it is a necessary work for salvation.

60 : 1. *Eastern heaven* of the passions.

60 : 2. Man's Reason is really Emotion.

60 : 10. The Song of the Lamb.

60 : 11. *The stems of Vegetation* : the phallos.

60 : 12-21. Freedom and Innocence once overspread the whole earth.

60 : 18. *Nimrod's Tower* : the Tower of Babel.

60 : 21. *The Four Rivers* : the Four Zoas.

60 : 45. *Vala* : Nature.

60 : 60. *The Stars* of fatality.

61 : 1. This plate, inserted at a late date, represents the Conception of Jesus in the Divine Vision. Blake did not believe in miracles in the ordinary sense ; and he ascribes the conception of Jesus to the Holy Ghost, because Mary ' ignorant of crime in the midst of a corrupted age ' (as he describes her in the *Vision of the Last Judgment*) yields to the impulse of true desire, which is a command from God. Being ignorant of ' sin,' Mary sins in the world's sense ; but there is no impurity in her. ' O felix culpa ! '

61 : 2. *Elohim Jehovah* : God as Judge and Redeemer together. The term is used thus again in *The Ghost of Abel*, 52.

61 : 7. Cf. *Job* iv. 17 : ' Shall a man be more pure than his Maker ? '

61 : 11. If she had been without desires herself, she could not know how to forgive others.

61 : 17. Cf. H. C. R., Dec. 7, 1826 : ' He spoke of the Atonement : said, " It is a horrible doctrine. If another man pay your debt, I do not forgive it," etc., etc., etc.'

61 : 20. *Of the Gods*, of the Heathen.

61 : 25. As in the Lord's Prayer : ' And forgive us our debts, as we forgive our debtors.'

61 : 31-33. Euphrates, Gihon, Hiddekel, and Pison are the four rivers of Eden.

61 : 35. *Another voice* : that of Nature (Vala).

61 : 48. The Nativity.

61 : 49. The Crucifixion.

61 : 50. Jesus speaks.

61 : 52. Repeated from line 3 of the *Epilogue* to *The Gates of Paradise*.

62 : 7. Shall Jesus be born of Nature ?

62 : 9-12. A purely spiritual genealogy, invented by Blake himself. *Cainah* was apparently his name for Cain's Wife ; *Ada*, *Zillah*, and *Naamah* were wife, daughter, and grand-daughter of Lamech ; the latter being the aunt of Noah, whom she married (according to Blake).

62 : 14, as in *John* xx.

62 : 16 is quoted from *Job* xix. 26.

62 : 18 is quoted from *John* xi. 25.

62 : 20-21. The Passions and Nature are also to be redeemed ; but first they must be created into a definite State, that they may put it off.

62 : 25-28. The journey through the wilderness to the Promised Land. The pillars of Cloud and Fire become the delusion of Nature and the tortures of Passion.

62 : 30-34. The old warfare between Passion and Reason.

63 : 1. *Jehovah*, the Father, about to be born as the Son, Jesus. Cf. *John* x. 30 : ' I and my Father are one.'

63 : 5-6. During the Terror in the French Revolution, Christianity was officially denied. The Passions (Luvah) slew the true Doctrine (Tongue).

63 : 7. Nature (as Natural Religion) then takes her revenge.

63 : 9. *Thor & Friga* : the Scandinavian gods of War and Love.

63 : 11. *The Chariot Wheels filled with Eyes* : the warfare of Reason (Eye, Cherubim). This is reminiscent of the splendid passage in Milton's *Paradise Lost*, VI. 749-755.

> . . . Forth rush'd with whirl-wind sound
> The Chariot of Paternal Deitie. . . .
> . . . As with Starrs thir bodies all
> And Wings were set with Eyes ; with Eyes the Wheels.'

63 : 12. Reuben and Benjamin, as the oldest and youngest of Jacob's sons, one cursed and one blessed, though of the same father, are often associated by Blake.

63 : 14. *The Fairies lead the Moon* : natural joys lead Love.

63 : 16. Christ is born of Mary (the Victim of social order, since she has given birth to an illegitimate child).

63 : 21. *The Looking Glass of Enitharmon*. Blake uses a very old symbol, which describes Nature as the Mirror of Deity. Cf. the *Vision of the Last Judgment* : ' The world of imagination is the world of eternity. . . . The world of Generation, or vegetation, is finite and temporal. There exist in the eternal world the permanent realities of everything which we see reflected in this vegetable glass of Nature.' This Platonic symbol is constantly referred to in Spenser's *Fowre Hymns*. Cf. also Jakob Böhme's *Six Theosophic Points*, I. 13 : ' It is like a Looking-Glass, which is a retainer of the Aspect of Nature, yet it doth not comprehend Nature, neither does Nature comprehend the shimmering Glimps or Reflexion in the Looking-Glass ; and thus the one is free from the other ; and yet the Looking-Glass is really the retainer or *preserver of the Image*.' Cf. also Thomas Vaughan's *Anthroposophia Theomagica* : ' God in love with his own Beauty frames a glass, to view it by reflection.'

63 : 23. *The Divisions of Reuben* are the dividings of the Nations.

63 : 40. Los thought it a mirage.

64 : 3. *Cherubim* are forms of Reason.

64 : 6. With the formation of the World of Matter, Man himself becomes a Worm, feeding on death.

64 : 13. *Thyself Female* : Man is so obsessed with feminine ideals that he is become female in spirit.

64 : 15. The Pope is taken as the chief enforcer of the Female Will. *Arthur*, the first king, enforces his rule.

64 : 25-30. Reason and Nature become one, and appear as the Hermaphrodite of unsolved contradictions, or Doubt.

65 : 1-4. The two worlds of Natural Religion and Christianity are at last opposed. The Passions are cast into the fire of Wrath, Man is pitied (and separated from his Passions), while Christ is crucified.

65 : 6-55. This passage is repeated from *The Four Zoas*, VII. 653-697. Lines 9 and 33-36 are added, also a few names. See the *Four Zoas* Commentary.

65 : 9. *A poisonous blue* : the woad.

65 : 33-36. The press-gang and the navy.

65 : 58. *Drinking his Emanation* : feeding on Nature.

65 : 59-60. Reason gets its inspiration solely from the mistakes of others.

65 : 66. The Body spreads its delusion subtly as a perfume.

65 : 70. Nature has become the Holy Place of Reason.

66 : 2. Stonehenge, as Natural Religion.

66 : 15. The persecution of the French by the English during the Revolution.

66 : 19-21. The sacrifices of the Daughters (works) of the Poet.

66 : 22-34. The sacrifice of the Poet himself.

66 : 30. The death into this world, as Baptism.

66 : 41-43. The Divine Vision becomes the torture of wrath, then the Wheel of fatality, and finally disappears.

66 : 45. Man's brief year.

66 : 46-56. In the world of Generation, men appear separated ; yet they are bound together in the Polypus of the present social order.

66 : 58. *The Mountains* represent those on earth who rise above it.

66 : 67. The Intellect and the Emotions having succumbed to the world of Generation, only the Body and Spirit are left to protest.

66 : 70. *The Dove & Raven*, sent out during this Deluge of the Sea of Time and Space.

66 : 74-81. The Sun is Imagination, the Moon is Love, the Stars are Reason, and the Earth is the Senses.

67 : 2-8. See the Commentary on 58 : 1.

67 : 16. *The bloody Veil* : the tortured body.

67 : 24. *Tirzah* : restraint in love.

67 : 35-37. This is surely a loose description of the spreading of the Roman roads across Great Britain. Their centre really was at London, and not Verulam : Blake evidently changed the place for symbolic purposes. He mentions only those roads going south and west. The Polypus's head is in Reason (Verulam), its heart in Cruelty (Salisbury Plain), it progresses towards order (south) and materialism (west), and it reaches even to Art (Bristol, Chatterton's city—though this was not a Roman city ; a Roman road, however, went past its site, from Bath to Caerwent).

67 : 42. *A golden pin* : the phallos.

67 : 43. Tirzah suffers with the rest.

67 : 44–68 : 9 is repeated from *The Four Zoas*, VIII. 293-315, with the addition of lines 67 : 51, 58, half of 67 : 61 and 68 : 1-2. See *The Four Zoas* Commentary.

68 : 18. *O Double God of Generation* : Hermaphroditus ? *Molech* was the national god of the Ammonites, to whom children were sacrificed. *Chemosh*, the national god of the Moabites, was a similar deity.

68 : 30. The sacrifice of one's child is the sacrifice of one's works.

68 : 41. *The Twelve Stones* : the altars to the twelve gods of the heathen, for which see *Milton*, 37 : 20-34.

68 : 42. A physical symbol.

68 : 51. *Uzzah* (Uzza) was smitten by the Lord for touching the Ark (1 *Chron.* xiii. 10).

68 : 53. *A beautiful Daughter* : Tirzah.

69 : 1. All men become of one type : Hand, the Rational Man.

69 : 11. *Leah & Rachel* : Jacob's two wives (*Genesis* xxix. 20-28).

69 : 19-25. Beulah, the state of Love.

69 : 26-27. Cf. ' Brothels are built with bricks of Religion.'

69 : 30-31. Such love causes a descent from the world of the Poet. Beulah is below Eternity : Love is inferior to Friendship. Blake repeats this doctrine in 86 : 42.

69 : 32-37. The ruin of love when controlled by Reason.

69 : 38. *The Infernal Veil*: flesh, which becomes the centre of the religion of Rationalism.

69 : 42-44. But in reality, Mundane love is of the spiritual body (circumference). (See 12 : 55.) It includes every aspect, and is not limited to the sexual act.

70 : 1-16. *Hand*, the Rational Man, is the type of mankind in the world of Generation. His three heads represent the contradictions of the impulses of his Head, Heart, and Loins, though (as Bacon, Newton, and Locke) each is directed by Reason.

70 : 6-7. Disbelieving that Contraries can exist together.

70 : 17. *Rahab* (Moral Virtue) is his inspiration. She is threefold, as she dominates Head, Heart, and Loins ; and thus is the antithesis of Beulah.

70 : 25. *A threefold kiss* is a reminiscence from *The Crystal Cabinet*.

70 : 31. Moral Virtue is only the shadow of Nature.

70 : 32. Reason (stars) has left Man.

71 : 1-49. The vision of the Twelve Sons and Daughters of Albion in their Eternal State. The southern part of Great Britain is given to the Loins, the central part to the Heart. The four Sons of the Head, however, are distributed according to their four 'gates': Bowen is in the North ; Scofield in the East ; Kotope is in the West (overlapping both Heart and Loins) ; while Kox (also overlapping Heart and Loins) is in the centre of the South, since, as the Head of Reason (or Law) he is the inmost impulse of generation.

71 : 6-9. An elaboration of the symbols of 12 : 55-56. The Circumference is the Body, the Centre is the Emotions.

71 : 10-49. For the characters of the Sons and Daughters, see the Commentary on 5 : 25-27 and 40-44. Blake gladly demonstrates that the 'unnatural consanguinities and friendships' which Albion feared (28 : 7) are the great Virtues of Eternity.

71 : 50-53. Wrath, Pity, Desire, and Reason live in the Body and the Spirit. They are the ungenerated Four, which make the Twelve into the Sixteen of Eternity. The generated Twelve are Albion's Sons.

71 : 57-59. The Poet dares not address Man in his fallen state, lest Man turn his back on the Divine Imagination.

72 : 1-4, 17-27. The completion of the list of counties begun 16 : 28-60. This map of Ireland, however, represents the ideal state, as contrasted with the confusion indicated on the maps of plate 16. The Tribes (the matured forms of the Sons of Israel) have at last found their proper stations. See *Numbers* ii.

This map must be read clockwise. Beginning in the east, Judah, Issachar, and Zebulun represent the head, heart, and loins of Luvah. In the south (reading clockwise, east to west) are Reuben, Simeon, and Levi ; for according to Urizen, head, heart, and loins are distinct, though equally important. In the west (Body) we get the crucifixion upside-down : Ephraim, Manasseh, and Benjamin (reading from south to north) are the head, heart, and loins—the loins predominating. In the north, Dan, Asher, and Napthali interlace somewhat, to represent the 'wheels within wheels'—the head, heart, and loins being equally important, as in the south, but not carefully separated. It is worth mention that each of these northern divisions have one county touching upon Lough Neagh.

Though the number of counties ascribed to each compass-point varies, each has approximately the same amount of land. Each Tribe has one-third of the counties ascribed to his compass-point, taking them in the order given by Blake ; the only exception being in the west, where there are but five counties : Galway alone here being assigned to Ephraim.

72 : 5-9. *The Sixteen Gates* are described 12 : 61–13 : 19. On each of the four walls of Golgonooza are four gates, opening into Eden, Beulah, Generation, and Ulro. But all the gates opening from the Body are closed till the Last Judgment.

72 : 9. See the Commentary on 71 : 50-53.

72 : 10-16. See the Commentary on 71 : 50-53.

72 : 32. A list of the Thirty-two Nations is given 72 : 38-42.

72 : 43. The Nations are islands, separated from each other only by the Sea of Time and Space.

72 : 50. ' St. Teresa was his delight ' (*Life and Letters of Samuel Palmer*, p. 245).

72 : 51. *Hervey*, author of *Meditations among the Tombs*, on which Blake painted an allegorical picture.

73 : 16. *Albion's Tomb* is the sky, whose constellations are divided between Og and Anak, the guardians of the Threshold. (In *Milton*, 37 : 51-55, Sihon is substituted for Anak.) Stars represent Reason ; therefore this line means that they read the Fate of Man by Reason, ignoring the two higher spheres of Imagination (Sun) and Love (Moon).

73 : 22. *Luvah's World of Opakeness* : the materialized world, Vala (Nature) being the emanation of Luvah (the emotions).

73 : 24. *Of the Elohim* : a Creator himself.

73 : 27-28. For these two limits, see the Commentary on *The Four Zoas*, IV. 271. Now Los is partially identified with Jesus. *Peleg & Joktan* : see *Genesis* x. 25. This line means simply that Adam and Satan are instinctive enemies.

73 : 48-49. Rewritten from *Milton*, 26 : 31-32.

73 : 52. Cf. H. C. R., 10th Dec. 1825 : ' I have conversed with the Spiritual Sun —I saw him on Primrose hill.'

74 : 2. In order to arrange these Four Sons of Los in agreement with the symbols of the next two lines, they should read : Bromion, Theotormon, Palamabron, and Rintrah.

74 : 3. Blake speaks.

74 : 20-21. This legend was never told in its entirety. In *Milton*, 22 : 61–23 : 1, we learn that they fled in the ' thousand years of sorrow, of Palamabron's Harrow & of Rintrah's wrath & fury.'

74 : 23. The four extra sons are the ungenerated Rintrah, Palamabron, Theotormon, and Bromion.

74 : 24-26. Bad art and philosophy.

74 : 27. See the Commentary on 72 : 5-9.

74 : 33. Woman is seduced by Man's physical form.

74 : 47. See the Commentary on *Milton*, 39 : 1.

74 : 54. *Dinah*, the woman whose lover, Shechem, was killed (*Genesis* xxxiv.). Erin represents the Body ; Shechem and Dinah are but a lower form of Theotormon and Oothoon.

75 : 2. *Bath*, the Body, possesses the Imagination, Logic, and Senses of the Fallen Man. See the Commentary on 54 : 25. According to Geoffrey of Monmouth, II. x., Bladud, the son of Hudibras, founded Bath ; and this fact furnished Blake with his symbolic significance. Milton's *History* (Book II.) gives his life as follows : ' *Bladud* . . . built *Caerbadus* or *Bathe*, and those medcinable Waters he dedicated to *Minerva*, in whose Temple there he kept fire continually burning. He was a man of great invention, and taught Necromancy : till having made him Wings to fly, he fell down upon the Temple of *Apollo* in *Trinovant*, and so dy'd after twenty years Reigne.'

75 : 3. *Twenty-seven fold* : according to the Twenty-seven religions.

75 : 10-20 is repeated from *Milton*, 38 : 43.

75 : 24. These religions circle endlessly.

75 : 27. Repeated from plate 27.

Plate 77. From ' We are told ' to ' incoherent roots ' is a summary of the philosophy of Puritanism ; to which Blake contrasts his philosophy as an artist.

An Intellectual Fountain. Cf. Jakob Böhme's *Theoscopia*, ii. 13 : ' The Great Love of God is come to help . . . as a *new* fountain of *divine* Unity, Love, and Rest.'

Art & Science : Art and Knowledge, Seraphim and Cherubim.

The blank verse shows Jesus striving against Puritanism (or Natural Religion), and being overcome by it.

Line 1. *South* : this is an intellectual vision.

Line 2. The flaming wheel of Religion.

Lines 3-4. In Blake's designs, the normal ' current ' of ' Creation ' is clockwise ; the lower half only being visible to mortal eyes. Therefore ' from west to east ' is against this current of life. It opposes Nature, and is called ' Natural Religion ' ; in the name of Jesus it crucifies Jesus.

Lines 7-8. Imagination and Love are nearly destroyed.

Line 11. Man has ' vegetated ' ; his life is a span.

Line 15. As at the gate of Eden.

CHAPTER IV

78 : 1-9. The Poet protects Man against the cruelty of Reason and Puritanism.

78 : 10-20. The Spectres then attack the Body (Erin) by its forty-two gates (counties), hoping to destroy its freedom ; having already made Nature the supreme goddess, and formed her into the Church of Moral Virtue. This passage may be summed up in the line from the preceding page : ' Opposing Nature, it is " Natural Religion " ! '

78 : 17. *The Concave Earth* : the flesh, which surrounds *Golgonooza*, the City of Art, and reaches to *Entuthon Benython*, the region of abstractions.

79 : 3. *Heshbon* : an Amorite city destroyed by the Israelites (*Numbers* xxi. 25).

79 : 17. The small island of England is taken as symbol of Man, shrunken and rocky, surrounded by the Sea of Time and Space.

79 : 20. For the list of Counties, see 16 : 35-51.

79 : 54. *Cherubim & Seraphim* : Science and Art in the Lost Atlantis.

79 : 59. Here the Cherubim are the guardians of the Ark. Reason protects Divinity.

79 : 71-72. The sexes, once separated, war together against mankind.

80 : 1. The Net and the Tree are Matter and Mystery.

80 : 4. *A worm going to eternal torment* : the Puritanical conception of Man.

80 : 12. Vala sings. Nature is no longer free.

80 : 13. *Flames* : of everlasting corruption.

80 : 14-15. If once Nature be found not true, her power over Man will be gone.

80 : 16. *My Father* : Luvah. Emanations are at once the daughters, sisters, and wives of their Zoas.

80 : 19-23. When the Passions were conquered by Man, they were revived by Nature, who then took her revenge on Man.

80 : 23-24. A reminiscence from *The Four Zoas*, i. 500-501.

80 : 31. Nature calls for Jesus to spend himself in the emotions, and not to waken Man. Should he do so, she believes that the Emotions would be murdered, and she would be an outcast illusion ; but she is wrong.

80 : 36. *A Dragon form* : War.

80 : 39. *Cambel & Gwendolen* : Restricted Sex and Selfish Pleasure.

80 : 43. *The Four Forests* : Albion's fourfold errors.

80 : 45. *The Stones of power* : the twelve Druidic altars. See the Commentary on 23 : 21.

80 : 48. *Serpent Temples* : Druidic temples. See the Commentary on *Europe*, 71-93.

80 : 52. Error always refuses to ' take definite form,' and hides among abstractions.

80 : 57. A development in the story of the first two Sons of Albion and their emanations begins here. Hand and Hyle, the Rational Man and the Bad Artist, are drawn to each other's emanations, Gwendolen and Cambel, or Selfish Pleasure and the Female Will. The Rational Man is now attracted to the Female Will (or restricted sex), while the Bad Artist indulges in Selfish Pleasure. As a result,

both give the doctrine of Jesus a debased interpretation ; and both are debased in turn.

80 : 65. To make Freedom appear inconsistent with Christianity.

81 : 2. Selfish Pleasure as the seducer of Merlin.

81 : 9. Selfish Pleasure claims to have destroyed the lust for mere physical beauty (Reuben) and to have brought Man back to the State of Innocence, which is spiritual infancy.

82 : 17. *So saying* : this evidently refers to the poem in the design on plate 81, rather than to the speech of 80 : 83–82 : 9, which is only the development of the doctrine of Gwendolen's falsehood. In the design, Gwendolen points to the following truth :

> In Heaven the only Art of Living
> Is Forgetting & Forgiving,
> Especially to the Female.

Behind this, in deep shadow, is the falsehood, the implied corollary of the truth :

> But if you on Earth Forgive,
> You shall not find where to Live.

82 : 19. The left hand is the material hand.

82 : 20. Forgetting that every Lie contains its Truth within it.

82 : 22-44. The falsehood of Selfish Pleasure, which the Poet desires to destroy.

82 : 32. *This Tree* of Generation.

82 : 33. The Flesh is a covering for sin ; by laying the soul naked, it may be convicted of sin. See *The Four Zoas*, VIII. 210-216.

82 : 47. Man, having sunk to the form of a mere baby, now becomes the Worm, which has neither Head, Heart, nor Loins, but is only a devouring Stomach. He is in the lowest state, that of Ulro, or Bowlahoola.

82 : 49. *Herself perfect in beauty* : she is the complete ideal.

82 : 51. Restricted Sex is jealous of Selfish Pleasure.

82 : 55. *The Seventh Furnace* is Jesus.

82 : 56-69. The Poet draws Restricted Sex into his Furnace, to show her the analysis of the Rational Man. She tries to form Hand, her beloved, according to her own principles ; but instead of a Man, Hand also sinks into the Infant, then to the Worm.

82 : 64. See the illustration on plate 17 of *America*.

82 : 70-77. At this horrible sight, both Selfish Pleasure and Restricted Sex begin to sacrifice themselves, in order to give the Worm ' a form of love '—some semblance to humanity.

83 : 5. The Spirit, in his fall, divided into the Poet and his Inspiration. Los and Enitharmon, falling still further, enter the world of Generation as the children of Tharmas and Enion (the Body and the Generative Instinct). See *The Four Zoas*, I.

83 : 13. The Crucifixion of the Flesh on the Tree of Moral Virtue.

83 : 27. *Oothoon* is Blake's Magdalen. See the Commentary on 57 : 7.

83 : 28. *Antamon* : see the Commentary on *Europe*, 180.

83 : 40-41. According to the various scientific theories.

83 : 52. The allotted extent of time is only Six Thousand Years. But the labours of Los both antedate and follow time.

83 : 67. Inspiration appears separated in a material (watery) form.

83 : 79. Cf. *Milton*, 19 : 3.

83 : 82. *The Dogs of Leutha* (Puritanism) are those which destroyed Actaeon.

84 : 17. The Rational Man demands the sacrifice of children (ideas and works).

84 : 18. *Chemosh* : the Moabite god, to whom children were sacrificed.

84 : 28–85 : 2. In fear lest they be destroyed, the Daughters weave a whole

religion out of Pleasure's falsehood, with which the Worm (man) is surrounded as in a false paradise.

85 : 1. This allegory is surely the false doctrine elaborated by Enitharmon in *Europe*.

85 : 3. False though this is, the Poet accepts it, hoping to bring the Materialized Man back from his wanderings through it.

85 : 6-9. Time is the active Male, Space is the passive Female. Together they parent all history, which is a debased copy of the events of Eternity.

86 : 2. *Three-fold*, as Beulah, with the three gates of the Head, Heart, and Loins opening into Eternity.

86 : 19. Cf. *Revelation* xxi. 2 : 'And I John saw the holy city, new Jerusalem, coming down from God out of heaven, prepared as a bride adorned for her husband.'

86 : 42-43. Cf. 69 : 30-31.

86 : 45. *Erin* : the Body.

86 : 50. As in 83 : 67. This separation of the Poet and his Inspiration and their desertion of Enion (their mother in this lower form) is told in *The Four Zoas*, I.

87 : 6. *Overgrown in roots*, or vegetation (matter).

87 : 12. Inspiration, divided from her master, tries to dominate him.

87 : 16. Cf. 81 : 6.

88 : 3-10. Cf. 44 : 38 and 71 : 16.

88 : 7. *The Human Four-fold Forms* : the Zoas.

88 : 18. 'And Bladud' should have been added, to complete the Trinity. See the Commentary on 54 : 25.

88 : 23. *Sussex* : Felpham. Though Inspiration seemed separated from Blake there, yet almost by force it came to him eventually.

88 : 31. Love.

88 : 37. The Spectre speaks.

88 : 43. *Want* : *i.e.* 'lack.'

88 : 48. In the City of Art, in the Indefinite, and in the Abstractions of Reason.

88 : 51. Inspiration, divided from the Poet, wastes all his efforts in her own emotions.

88 : 56. See 75 : 3. Freedom seizes the poisonous doctrines of Moral Virtue.

88 : 58. *Hermaphroditic* : self-contradictory.

89 : 1. The sexes were divided by the sacrifice of Christ (see 42 : 32). Christ's sacrifice (his whole life on earth) is symbolized by the fourfold instruments of the Passion. Yet Christ's power is not universal ; and those untouched by his miracle live in the wars (wine-press) of contradictions.

89 : 6-7. The Pharisees, Scribes, Presbytery, High Priest, Priest, and Sadducees. The collective nouns *Pharisaion* and *Saddusaion* (Pharisees and Sadducees) were apparently invented by Blake, who thought that they represented some organized body.

(In his illustrations to Young's *Night Thoughts*, Blake represents the seven heads of the Beast on which Rahab rides as those of the Judge, the Warrior, the King, the Pope, the Cardinal, the Bishop, and the Priest.)

89 : 9. The Antichrist appears, and the Last Judgment is about to begin. For the Covering Cherub, see the Commentary on *Milton*, 7 : 51. As a Dragon, he is a form of War.

89 : 13. He is a distorted reflexion of the Christ whom he opposes. The Christ, during his three days in the grave, threw off the flesh ; the Antichrist absorbs it.

89 : 14-15. In each of his four divisions of Head, Heart, Loins, and Bowels, he holds the children of Israel (divine ideas) in captivity.

89 : 15. *Gihon* is the southern (intellectual) river of Eden (*Genesis* ii. 13).

89 : 19. *The Dragon of the River* : the Leviathan. (See the 15th illustration to *Job*.) The Leviathan, with his many coils (from which his name is derived) represents the devouring round of existence in Time and Space.

89 : 21. *Twelve ridges of stone* : the Druid altars to the Twelve Gods of Asia.

89 : 25. The river of Generation (Arnon, or Storge), which flows into the Dead Sea of Time and Space, is the product of his love (heart). Blake identifies it with Pison, the first river of Eden (*Genesis* ii. 11), which should water the region of Havilah (innocence).

89 : 30. *Generalizing Gods* : the gods of Abstract Principles—abstracted from Humanity.

89 : 35. *Hiddekel* is the third river of Eden (*Genesis* ii. 14), which flows westward (the Loins).

89 : 38. *Euphrates*, the last of the four rivers of Eden, runs east (the emotions) (*Genesis* ii. 14).

89 : 43. Freedom cannot be destroyed ; therefore she is hidden away in the lowest region, Bowlahoola.

89 : 50-51. The Giants' Causeway taken as poetical proof that giants lived here before the Sea of Time and Space overwhelmed us.

89 : 52-53. The appearance of Rahab and the Dragon : Moral Virtue in the form of War. For other descriptions, see *Milton*, 37 : 43, 42 : 22, and *Jerusalem*, 75 : 17.

89 : 58. *Alla* is the state just below Beulah (*Milton*, 34 : 12).

89 : 60. To ' burst the bottom of the grave ' is to descend below human form.

90 : 1. The Masculine and the Feminine are respectively the Spectre and Emanation of Man (the Humanity). The sexes are now losing touch with the Humanity, taking his life into themselves.

90 : 1-6. See the Commentary on 43 : 46-47.

90 : 11. The Sublime and the Pathetic as the Masculine and Feminine in the world of Art. In degenerate art, the Pathos is apt to conceal the truth, which is at once terrible and sublime.

90 : 14-27. The various Sons and Daughters of Albion draw their delight from their torture of the Emotions ; meanwhile they separate the material universe from materialized man.

90 : 27 is repeated from 5 : 34.

90 : 28-38. Los begins to see clearly the errors of the world, and one by one he announces them. No Individual should claim, either for himself or for his inspiration, the absolute authority in matters temporal or spiritual which we attribute to the symbols of sacred characters.

90 : 34-38. It is a self-contradictory blasphemy to claim that the Christ could be born in material form from a Virgin. The very fact of such a birth proves that Christ has entered Satan (illusion) ; and he must cast it off again, or illusion would conquer reality. But such a descent is necessary, if Man is to be saved.

90 : 52-54. When an Individual sets himself up as the Infallible Authority, he has cast out his finer instincts—separated into Male and Female. And when one of these divisions claims a like Authority, it is a fall from the Truth of Eternity into Error.

90 : 55-56. The contradiction of Puritanism.

90 : 58-66. The reaction of the Deists into Natural Religion.

91 : 5. Tell them to obey their deepest instincts, to live their real lives, and not be hypocritical, pretending to accept a system of ethics which is at variance with themselves, especially when they are cruel to others. (For the significance of ' murderers,' see line 10 and the Commentary to the 5th Epigram *On Friends and Foes*.)

91 : 7-12 is expanded from the fifth *Memorable Fancy* in *The Marriage of Heaven and Hell*.

91 : 18. *Children* : thoughts and works.

91 : 21. Must see it completely.

91 : 32-33. The stupendous labour of the Intellect.

91 : 34. *The Smaragdine Table of Hermes* was reputed to be one of the oldest of magical documents, and is of great authority. To this day all occultism is based

upon its philosophy. It was supposed to have been discovered by Alexander the Great, written in gold upon an emerald tablet in the sepulchre of Hermes Trismegistus, beneath the head of that sage.

This document is so short that it may be quoted in full :

It is the truest and most certain thing of all things.

That which is above is as that which is below, and that which is below is as that which is above, to accomplish the one thing of all things most wonderful.

Ascend from earth to heaven and descend again to earth and thou wilt have accomplished the potency of things superior and of things inferior.

The sun was its father, its mother the moon, it was borne in the winds' belly.

It is the strong power of every power, for it overcomes all things subtle and penetrates all things gross.

Thence proceed many marvellous adaptations which were established in this wise.

It is thus the world was created.

For this reason men call me *Thrice-Greatest* because I have three parts of the philosophy of the whole world.

This is all I have to say concerning the mystery of the one thing.

In rejecting this, Blake rejects all Occultism, which he conceived to be an indefinite Abstraction and a physical work created by Reason, the Spectre, without spiritual significance.

91 : 36. Cf. ' But thou readst black where I read white.' The Poet can see the Light which shines, however dimly, in Reason ; the Spectre wastes his time in the empty spaces between these crumbs of Truth.

91 : 38-39. Leviathan and Behemoth are two monsters mentioned in *Job*, which Blake takes to represent the warfare in the Sea of Time and Space, and in the flesh of man. They reappear on the 15th plate of the illustrations to *Job*. Cornelius Agrippa (*De Occult. Phil.*, II. v.) calls ' Beemoth ' and Leviathan ' two chief of the divels.' They play important rôles in *Enoch*, II. lx. 7 *seq.*

91 : 44-52. The Poet masters his Reason, giving it its proper place to regulate (' a separate space '), and not allowing it to interfere in matters of Faith, Art, or Love. Yet he releases its intellect (Eye) and spirit (Ear).

91 : 50. To ' alter a Ratio ' means to extend the knowledge of Reason until a new system is formed. The paradise which the Spectre thought was so near is shown to be an illusion ; and the complete extent of knowledge (' his starry heavens ') something too vast for any intellect to grasp.

91 : 54-57. At the same time Blake emphasizes the importance of the Intellect. ' Men are admitted into heaven, not because they have curbed and governed their passions, or have no passions, but because they have cultivated their understandings. The treasures of heaven are not negations of passion, but realities of intellect, from which all passions emanate, uncurbed in their eternal glory. The fool shall not enter heaven, let him be ever so holy ' (*Vision of the Last Judgment*). Cf. the *Fo-Sho-Hing-Tsan-King* : ' Ignorance was the root of all evil.' Cf. Thomas Vaughan's *Euphrates* : ' And here I doubt not to affirme, that the Mysterie of Salvation can never be fully understood without Philosophie.' Cf. Milton's *Second Defence* : ' You therefore who wish to remain free, either instantly be wise or as soon as possible, cease to be fools.' Cf. Oscar Wilde's *De Profundis* : ' The supreme vice is shallowness.'

92 : 1. *Briton, Saxon, Roman, Norman* : west, north, south, east,

92 : 1-6. Albion's children return to his loins ; the scattered Nations are becoming one in England.

92 : 7-11. Inspiration will have no separate existence from the Poet when the perfect nation, or Man, is finally produced. The looms of Generation will cease to work. Inspiration thinks that her union with Los will be her own death.

92 : 13-14. When Man awakes from his sleep of death and enters Eternity, the sexes will no longer be separated. See the Commentary on 30 : 33. This is not annihilation of either sex, but union, which is the mystical death of Selfhood.

92 : 15-27. Then all the miseries of this world will exist only in ' the shadows of Possibility,' where they will remain as a warning.

93 : 2-16. Spiritual Beauty cannot understand the meaning of Wrath and Pity, who are no longer commanded by her. She fears that their own natures will drive away their ideals ; and she remembers a time (the time when Satan-Hayley drove the Poet's Plough) when Pride met Pride, and all poetry fled.

93 : 8. *Genesis* xxx. 14-16. Mandrakes were supposed to be aphrodisiacs.

93 : 13. The Imagination was Wrath in that day.

93 : 18. *This Waking Death* : the Covering Cherub.

93 : 23. *Deus* : the Latin for ' God ' ; hence ' Empire.'

93 : 26. In the triumph of Error, in the coming of the Antichrist, lies the signal for the Resurrection and Judgment.

94 : 7. *England* : Albion's Emanation.

94 : 13. *Erin*, the Body, is the watcher at the Tomb.

94 : 18. The Six Thousand Years are finished.

95 : 16-18. Man compels the Four Zoas to labour for him.

95 : 19-20 is repeated from 30 : 14-15.

95 : 22. Albion is united with his Emanation.

96 : 1-2 is repeated from 95 : 21-22.

96 : 6. Cf. Henry More's *Second Lash* : ' For God doth not ride me as a horse, and guide me I know not whither myself ; but converses with me as a friend.'

96 : 8. With the resurrection of Man, the consequences of his errors do not cease immediately. The Selfhood is his Selfishness, in the form of the Covering Cherub.

96 : 13. Man now recognizes that Creation, as well as Redemption, was an act of Mercy.

96 : 29. *The Cloud* is the Covering Cherub.

96 : 35. At that moment, when Man sacrifices himself for his friends, the evil illusion vanishes ; and what he thought to be torture is the ultimate source of life itself. Cf. the 85th illustration to Dante.

97 : 5. *In my hearing* : Blake again testifies to the reality of his Vision.

97 : 6-11. In every act of the glorified Albion, the four Zoas move in fourfold repetition.

97 : 12-15. Albion's Bow is a weapon of spiritual warfare. It is the symbol of love in Eternity, of the united sexes.

98 : 1. *Each* : of the Zoas.

98 : 6. With one Arrow (deed) of Love, the selfish Reason is slain.

98 : 9. Science and Art in Eternity.

98 : 11. All the works of Eternity are perfect, containing both the ' sexes,' both Sublimity and Pathos (90 : 11).

98 : 12. The fourfold division of Man is according to his Zoas.

98 : 15. The Four Rivers are other symbols of the Zoas. There were originally Four Rivers in Eden (*Genesis* ii. 10-14).

98 : 44. Nature itself (the Serpent) is saved, ' even Tree, Metal, Earth & Stone,' since ' one hair nor particle of dust, not one can pass away ' (14 : 1). ' Everything has as much right to Eternal Life as God, who is the breast of Man,' Blake wrote in his copy of Thornton's *Lord's Prayer*. ' All things are Immortal, Matter, Life, Spirit, Soul, Mind, whereof every living thing consisteth ' (Trismegistus : *Pymander*, xi. 79). ' If therefore . . . the whole microcosm is to be healed, then the corporeal coagulated balsam should be united with the spiritual celestial balsam and the discord between the elements of the sun should be reconciled, so that the superfluous elements may be separated from the fixed predestined element and altogether die out and leave their fixed element, as their inhabitant, alone ' (Paracelsus : *Archidoxis*, x. 9). ' If all things are not only from God, but of God, no created

thing can be finally annihilated ' (Milton : *Treatise of Christian Doctrine*).   ' For my own part, I fear not to say, that Nature is so much the business of Scripture, that to me, the Spirit of God, in those sacred Oracles, seems not onely to mind the Restitution of Man in particular, but even the Redemption of Nature in Generall ' (Thomas Vaughan : *Euphrates*).   In modern times we find Shelley's *Prometheus Unbound* : ' Man, one harmonious soul of many a soul. . . . Where all things flow to all, as rivers to a sea.'   Also Walt Whitman : ' I swear I think now that everything without exception has an eternal Soul ! / The trees have rooted in the ground ! the weeds of the sea have ! the animals ! / I swear I think there is nothing but immortality ! ' (*To Think of Time*) ; ' Nature and Man shall be disjoin'd and diffused no more ; / The true Son of God shall absolutely fuze them ' (*Passage to India*).

From the quotations above, it will be seen that Blake is absolutely in agreement with occult theory.   The common source of this theory (aside from Nature-mysticism) is probably *Romans* viii. 21 : ' The creature itself also shall be delivered from the bondage of corruption into the glorious liberty of the children of God.'

98 : 46. *Priam* : War.

98 : 53. *The Spectrous Oath* of Allegiance.

99 : 3. ' After the passing away of the present creation, a new Mysterium Magnum may supervene ' (Paracelsus : *Philosophy addressed to the Athenians*, II. 12).

99 : 4. ' Thereupon follows the greatest arcanum, that is to say, the Supercelestial Marriage of the Soul, consummately prepared and washed by the blood of the lamb, with its own splendid, shining, and purified body. . . . The body will receive and embrace its soul ; since the body is affected with extreme desire for the soul, and the soul is most perfectly delighted with the embrace of the body ' (Paracelsus : *Aurora of the Philosophers*, XIII.).

ILLUSTRATIONS TO *JERUSALEM*

Plate 1. *Frontispiece.*   The Poet entering the Man's inner life (31 : 2-4).   Holding his globe of fire in his right hand, he passes inward, right foot first, through a Gothic door, which opens on darkness.

Plate 2. *Title-page.   Jerusalem, The Emanation of the Giant Albion*, 1804.   *Printed by W. Blake, Sth. Moulton St.*   Five of the Daughters of Beulah soar in various attitudes of ecstasy and despair.   They are six-winged, as the Seraphim ; and in these wings are the four symbols of the four states of Man : the Sun, Moon, Stars, and the Earth.   Between the letters of the title are birds and butterflies.

Plate 3. *Sheep.   To the Public.   Goats* (cf. *Matthew* xxv. 32).   The blanks in the text are filled with decorative lines.   A Daughter of Beulah floats to the left of the couplets.

Plate 4. *Jerusalem.   Chapter I.*   Above the title is written in Greek : ' Moses and Jesus,' signifying Blake's synthesis of the two Testaments.   Jerusalem (Freedom), as a nude woman, points out the new moon of Beulah (Love) to two nude children who follow her through the air.   These children, and two others below them, are escaping from the heavily-draped Rahab (Moral Virtue) who clutches the fifth, an unwilling youth, by the head.   Behind him appear the flames of Affliction.

Plate 5. To the right of the text : five women ascend from flames.

Plate 6. Los at his anvil, while his Spectre, as a fantastic bat, hovers over him (6 : 4-7).

Plate 7. To the right of the text : three decorative nudes.

Plate 8. A Fairy (or Natural Joy), as a nude woman, drags the bleeding Moon of Love after her, through the Valley of Logic (63 : 14).

Plate 9. On this plate are three strata of decoration, separated by the text. They represent the State of Innocence, the Fall, and the State of Experience. Innocence is represented by a piping shepherd, a flock, and a kneeling figure playing with a leopard. The Fall shows Woman turning her back on despairing Man, to receive the Apple from the jaws of the Serpent. The last design, Experience, shows the corpse of the giant Albion bewailed by the five senses, while in the background rise the huge stars of Reason.

Plate 10. No decoration.

Plate 11. A woman with a swan's head, neck, and wings wades in a river by a gloomy shore. Behind her a fish is seen in the water. She is a semi-satirical symbol of the brainless woman, who concerns herself entirely with Time and Space (water). She is the ' Female Will ' whose head is that of the Spectre on Plate 71.

Below the text : a nude woman, in jewels and flames, flies toward the spiritual regions (to the left). She represents Inspiration (an Emanation), in contrast to the half-animal figure above, who faces in the other direction. This lower figure has been conjectured to be an Indian squaw ; in which case she would represent the Inspiration of the Body (west).

Plate 12. To the right of the text : a vertical row of decorative figures : a woman in contemporary dress, with winglike growths on her arms ; below her a nude man upside-down (with loins elevated over heart and head) applying compasses to the globe ; below him, a woman indicates a point on the globe.

Plate 13. To the right : vine-leaves and tendrils. Below them a woman tries to catch a bat.

Plate 14. To the right are the Sun, Moon, and the planets, among which Saturn is identified by his rings.

Below the text : Inspiration visits the Poet in his sleep. She appears as Enitharmon beneath a Rainbow (83 : 67, 86 : 60). The background of stars, clouds, and a new moon indicates the state of Beulah. At the head and feet of Los are very small kneeling angels.

Plate 15. Abraham, the Prophet, fleeing from the errors of Chaldea (15 : 28). He is opposed by the vegetating Man, Reuben.

Plate 16. No decoration.

Plate 17. No decoration.

Plate 18. Jerusalem and Vala, each beneath a Moon of Beulah, sleep in harmony, one crowned with the lilies of spiritual beauty, the other crowned with the roses of material beauty (19 : 40-44). Their emanations rush forth to embrace between them. A similar design occurs in the margin of the 19th illustration to *Job*. To the right of the text are falling figures.

Plate 19. The escape of Albion's children. Some rush madly above the text, hand in hand ; others ascend to them, to the right of the text ; while below lies Albion's corpse, crushing three of the Sons. He is bewailed by the Four Senses, beneath a setting sun. The current of this design runs contrary to the normal current of the universe (19 : 1).

Plate 20. The text is divided by various horizontal rows of figures, representing Albion's released children. Two flying figures meet face to face ; three moons and two stars and a comet ; figures drag burning wheels and stars ; a row of flames ; four old men drag flaming stars, followed by a flying female ; and two comets.

Plate 21. Hand, both as Accuser and Executioner, scourges three Daughters of Albion (21 : 29-30).

Plate 22. Above the text : the Spectre and Emanation separate in flames. Below the text : the Angels of Forgiveness embrace above the flaming and intercogged wheels of Punishment, which are half sunk in the Sea of Time and Space (22 : 34-35).

Plate 23. To the right of the text : Jerusalem and Vala, as two winged fairies.

Below : a winged female is clogged in mire ; to the left is a flowering plant ; and above is a festoon of intestines.

Below : three giant figures are encased in rock ; and below them, multitudes of nudes, in the same plight.   Mankind buried in matter.

Plate 24. The Moon, a crescent containing the winged head of a Seraph, sails as the Ship of Love over the Sea of Time and Space (56 : 18).

Below line 11 : the Daughters of Albion weave the bowels.

To the right of the text : Gwendolen (Selfish Pleasure) kneels horrified at the sight of the bowels (Bowlahoola).

Plate 25. The Body of Albion, supported by three of the Daughters of Albion. His limbs still contain the heavenly bodies : his right leg is marked with the sun and the morning star ; his left leg is marked with the moon and the Pleiades ; Orion's Belt girds him ; and his right shoulder is marked with another star.   One of the Daughters in tears is winding a clue of ' vegetation ' from his navel.

Plate 26. No text.   Freedom (Jerusalem) is aghast at the awful vision of the Rational Man (Hand).   Both characters are labelled with their names.   The picture is inscribed :

> Such visions have appear'd to me
> As I my order'd course have run :
> Jerusalem is named Liberty
> Among the Sons of Albion.

Plate 27. *To the Jews.*   No decoration.

Plate 28. *Jerusalem.   Chap.* 2.   The King and the Queen of the Fairies (natural joys) embrace in the Lilly of Havilah (the state of Innocence).   Below them is the Sea of Time and Space.   A design with similar subject appears in *The Song of Los.*

To the right of the text are queer sea-animals and shells.   One of them, a man with his head caught in a shell suggests the influence of the fantasies of the elder Peter Bruegel.

Plate 29. To the right of the text : a nude, ecstatic woman in flames (reminiscent of the last plate of *Milton*) ; below her figures fall and despair.

Plate 30. Los's Spectre and Emanation being received by him (30 : 16).

Plate 31. Two women (' Minute Particulars ') fallen ; one is dead, the other is entangled tightly in a net.

Plate 32. Vala (Nature) in her veil moves towards a cathedral with Roman dome and cross ; she questions Jerusalem, who stands nude with two nude girls before a Gothic cathedral.   A nude, flying away, tries to attract one of Jerusalem's daughters.

Plate 33. An old man ploughing with human-headed monsters.   This probably represents Urizen guiding the Bulls of Luvah in the work of Generation.

Plate 34. No decoration.

Plate 35. The birth of Eve.   Christ, with pierced hands and feet, hovers in flames above Adam, from whose side Eve emerges.   This represents the Divine Mercy changing Death into Sleep, by separating the sexes (42 : 33).

Plate 36. Los hammering the Sun upon his forge, while a man turns away in woe.

Plate 37. Between the Oak and the Palm, Christ receives the falling body of Albion (48 : 1-4).   Below them is a winged globe.

Below the text : Man reposed on the Rock of Ages, with his Spectre hovering above.   The sun and moon shine fruitlessly.

Plate 38. On both sides of the text : vegetation, entangling forms of people.

Plate 39. A bat-winged man on a flying horse draws a threefold bow. This probably represents the Covering Cherub, smiting the Head, Heart, and Loins. The bow (which appears as three parallel bows) has been conjectured to represent motion.

Below the text : a dark sun is setting.

Plate 40. The grapes of ecstasy ; two friends gather them in delight.

Plate 41. Below the text : the titanic figure of Hyle is sunk in despair, holding a scroll, on which is written reversed :

> Each Man is in his Spectre's power
> Until the arrival of that hour
> When his Humanity awake
> And cast his Spectre into the Lake.

A small figure reads the scroll.

The Humanity is, of course, the deepest essence of the Individual ; but the Lake is not so easy to identify. It is probably the ' Lake of Los that ever burneth with fire ' (*Milton*, 40 : 10-12). The flames of such a Lake would be those of annihilation, not of torture.

Plate 42. Six nudes stand on each other's shoulders to reach a bunch of grapes.

Plate 43. To the right of the text : clouds and a praying woman.

Plate 44. A winged Ark floats over the Sea. It represents Love, the refuge of the Man of Imagination (Noah) during the Deluge of Time and Space. Two angels guard it.

Below the text is an open-mouthed serpent, whose body ends in leaves and fruit ; probably implying that Nature can be transmuted into some fruitful end.

Plate 45. The tragedy of Lover and Beloved. Oothoon, as a nude woman, flies away, raining her sorrows as from a cloud and leaving Theotormon, who vegetates in despair.

To the right of the text : a watersnake and a fish. Below line 2, one fish swallows smaller fish. These and other marine animals represent the ' Struggle for Life ' in the Sea of Time and Space.

Plate 46. The Sage and his Inspiration as Elijah in the chariot of flame, whose structure is composed of the Serpent of Nature. It is drawn by the human-headed Bulls of Luvah, whose spiralling horns terminate in hands. On their backs sit winged monsters, possibly Gnomes.

Plate 47. Albion, his feet on the Sea of Time and Space, turns his face from Jerusalem and Brittannia. One of them, falling, appeals to him ; the other stands on her shoulders.

Plate 48. To the right : birds, butterflies, etc.

Plate 49. Erin beneath Albion's Tree.

Plate 50. Hand sitting on Albion's cliffs (70 : 1-16). Two of his three heads are crowned ; from his neck emerges the Giant Brood, unfolding from each other in flames, as they rush over the land. The first emanation is two-headed ; from him evolves two more, the last of which points to the right. These three are Bacon, Newton, and Locke. The crowned heads weep. Below Hand, the sea breaks on the rock. Behind him, on the left is a crescent moon and eyed lightning ; on the right, clouds, a setting sun, and a comet.

Plate 51. No text. Vala, Hyle, and Scofield. Vala sits crowned and sceptred upon a stone throne, her head bowed ; Hyle sits on the ground, his head sunk below his knees in an agony of despair ; Scofield in flames, walks towards the right (the material side) with chains dragging from wrists and ankles.

Plate 52. *To the Deists.* No decoration.

Plate 53. *Jerusalem. Chap. 3.* Beulah, mercifully veiling the Sun of Eternity from our eyes. She is crowned with the threefold crown of the three states which she commands; her outer wings contain the Moon and the Stars. Like her Daughters on the title-page, she has the six wings of the Seraphim of Love. She is throned high above the Sea of Time and Space upon the Sunflower of the Desire for Immortality. The Sun glows behind her, but we can see only its rays.

To the right of the text: Friendship and Love—one man supporting another; while a third man reaches down to drag a woman from the Sea of Time and Space.

Plate 54. Between the outer flame and ' This World ' (inscribed ' Reason, Wrath, Desire, Pity ' as N., E., S. and W.) float nine nudes. This division of the world occurs only in the Fall, when Urizen has usurped the throne of the Spirit, and when Luvah (as Orc) is bound in the realm of Reason. It corresponds to the four ungenerate Sons of Los: Bromion, Rintrah, Theotormon and Palamabron.

Below the text, a giant with four heads is tormented by a cloud of flies. In the background are four large stars. He represents the four senses, buried and tortured by the pests (or even pestilences) in the realm of Reason (stars).

Plate 55. No decoration.

Plate 56. Web-like lines to the right.

Plate 57. The triumph of the worldly religion. York and London, as two women from whose hands influences stream, soar over the top of a circle, which contains their names and a sketch of St. Paul's. The background is studded with stars. The circle is continued below the text, beneath which is the fallen Jerusalem, with influences streaming from her breast. Just above her, within the circle, is a tiny Gothic cathedral. She has a star above her head.

Plate 58. The Spectre, a fantastic bat, hovers over Man, as a skeleton in the flames of corruption (generation).

Plate 59. Three Daughters of Los at the spinning wheel.

Plate 60. To the right of the text: flames and a nude woman in prayer.

Plate 61. To the right of the text: birds.

Plate 62. Luvah (the Passions) in his agony. Above the text: his head, bound with the snake of Nature, and rayed with a sort of peacock glory, peers over the stone wall of the flesh, which he clutches in agony, as though to tear it down. Below the text: his feet are seen flaming, while Vala, as a tiny nude, wonders at them. This evidently illustrates her cry in *The Four Zoas*, II. 229-230:

> I see not Luvah as of old, I only see his feet
> Like pillars of fire travelling thro' darkness & non entity.

Another design for the same incident appears in *The Four Zoas*, 69b.

Plate 63. Beneath an eclipse of the Moon (Love), Woman is caught in the folds of the Worm.

Plate 64. In the death of this world, Woman devotes herself to the Scroll of the Law; but when she sleeps, her emanations are released; and are seen issuing from her in a wing-shaped projection.

Below the text, a sage reposes and reads.

Plate 65. To the right of the text: the Chain of Jealousy.

Plate 66. To the right of the text: a female nude is carried by another nude in a mounting flame. This may represent a victim borne to the sacrifice.

Plate 67. A male nude chained and stretched as on a rack.

Plate 68. No decoration.

Plate 69. Rahab and Tirzah, the former with her cup, the latter with her flint knife and a scalp, dance naked around a naked victim. Above the Druidic rocks in the background glow the moon and stars.

Plate 70. A Druid trilithon of immense size, through which is seen a new moon. Three women follow the road beneath the gate. They probably represent the Head, Heart, and Loins (Urizen's daughters) passing through the State of Experience.

Plate 71. The Emanation exhausted beneath a tangle of fibres ; at her feet is the Spectre, half bat and half swan.

Plate 72. Between the flames and the World, two angels weep. The World is inscribed : 'Continually Building, Continually Decaying, because of Love & Jealousy.'

Below the text is the Serpent of Nature, with an inscription in reversed writing : ' Women the comforters of Men become the Tormenters & Punishers.'

Plate 73. Los hammering the half-disc of the Sun on his Anvil.

Plate 74. Reuben, the Vegetative Man, enrooting. Vegetation springs into the earth from his hair, ear, hand, and groin.

Plate 75. The Forgiveness of Sins and the Brotherhood of Man, as opposed to the Warfare of Moral Virtue. The first is represented by a row of Angels in a series of interlocking circles, which ' enter each other's bosoms,' as it were. The second is represented by Rahab and Tirzah entwined by the Dragon of War, whose coils are covered with the interlocking circles of Cause and Effect. This is a repetition of the idea of the design on plate 22 under another form.

Plate 76. No text. The Crucifixion. This is one of Blake's most celebrated designs. For feeling, it ranks among the greatest Crucifixions ever painted. Mystically, it represents the Dark Night of the Soul. Its converse appears in the 90th illustration to Dante.

Albion (so named in some of the copies) stands in the cruciform attitude, facing inward, and adoring Jesus upon the Cross. It is Man beholding the torture and death of his highest faculties. The sun has set, and there is barely the faintest glimmer on the horizon—just enough to outline the huge dead trunk of the Tree of Moral Virtue. The faint light still emanating from Christ barely illuminates the Man below.

The various copies of this plate differ greatly. In some, the light is so increased as to make all the details perfectly clear. In the Morgan copy, the Tree bears four Apples ; in General Stirling's copy, many Apples.

Plate 77. *To the Christians.* To the right of the quatrain, the Reader, as a tiny figure, winds up the clue of thread.

Plate 78. *Jerusalem, Chap.* 4. A dark-rayed sun sets over the Sea of Time and Space. Upon the rocky shore sits Egypt as a nude man with a fantastic, melancholy bird's head.

Plate 79. To the right of the text : birds, leaves, and grapes.

Plate 80. To the right of the text : Gwendolen (Selfish Pleasure), caught in the folds of the Worm, tries to mould it ' into a form of love ' (82 : 74). Below her is Cambel.

Plate 81. Gwendolen (Selfish Pleasure) instructing her sisters. With her left hand closed behind her back, she points to a motto inscribed on a cloud :

> In Heaven the only Art of Living
> Is Forgetting & Forgiving
> Especially to the Female.

Hidden behind this, as Gwendolen's hand is hidden, is the Falsehood :

> But if you on Earth Forgive
> You shall not find where to Live.

Cambel, directly addressed by Gwendolen, assumes the attitude of the Medicean Venus; behind her, the other ten Daughters rise from the depths, expressing consternation.

Plate 82. The Worm.

Plate 83. To the right of the text: two figures in a cloud.

Plate 84. London, as an old, crippled beggar, is led through the streets of Babylon by a child (84:11). This decoration is repeated from *London* in the *Songs of Experience*. In the background is a Gothic cathedral; showing that the true faith always finds its altar, even in Babylon.

Plate 85. The work of the Male and Female, which continues though they are separated and their faces turned from each other. Man is in Beulah (Love), as the Moon, Star, and Cloud are behind him. The Woman is the Emanation, and behind her is the haloed and rayed Sun of the Imagination. In the sky between them is a comet. She is weaving the Vine of Friendship, part of which comes from the Man, and part from another Man who is not seen. Cf. 'Man is adjoin'd to Man by his Emanative portion' (44:38).

Plate 86. No decoration.

Plate 87. Enion trying to catch Enitharmon who escapes holding the hand of young Los. Ahania mourns in one corner; while the aged Tharmas laments Enion's absence in another corner. They wander over the deserts of Man's four-fold nature (87:1).

Plate 88. No decoration.

Plate 89. To the right: Los and Enitharmon reach to each other above the Tree (*The Four Zoas*, VII.).

Plate 90. No decoration.

Plate 91. Albion asleep between the rays of Jehovah and Jesus. Jehovah is represented by his customary symbol, the six-pointed star; Jesus is represented by an ear of wheat as a vortex.

Plate 92. Jerusalem (so labelled) sits before the Druidic gates of Babylon, and weeps. About her feet are the faces of her sacrificed children.

Plate 93. The Accusers point downward to the black flames of wrath and punishment. Upon them is written: 'Anytus Melitus & Lycon thought Socrates a Very Pernicious Man. So Caiphas thought Jesus.'

Below the text lies their victim, the soul as a nude woman, reclining peacefully in a flame-lapped sarcophagus.

Plate 94. Above the text: the downfall of the three Accusers.

Below the text: Brittannia awakening on Albion's bosom (94:20). In the Background are Druidic trilithons. This design recalls the title-page to *America*.

Plate 95. The resurrection of Man. Albion, as a nude youth, rises inward and upward in the flames of his wrath (95:5). An old man's face is beneath his left hand, symbolizing the illusion of his aged body, which he leaves to vanish in the grave (cf. previous design).

Plate 96. To the right of the text: God raising the Soul (as a nude woman). At the end of each epic Blake always represents the Soul before God as a woman. Cf. Coventry Patmore's *Aurea Dicta*, XXI.: 'No writer, sacred or profane, ever uses the word "he" or "him" of the soul. It is always "she" or "her"; so universal is the intuitive knowledge that the soul, with regard to God who is her life, is feminine.'

Plate 97. The Poet advancing inward towards Eternity. He dances upon a rocky cliff, holding his globe, which is now a blazing sun. He is still in Beulah, as is proved by the Moon and Star in the sky. With the exception of the position of the left hand, this figure is repeated from page 6 of the water-colours illustrating Young's *Night Thoughts*.   It recalls forcibly Blake's letter to Butts (22nd Nov. 1802) : ' I have conquered and shall go on conquering.   Nothing can withstand the fury of my course among the stars of God and in the abysses of the Accuser.'

Plate 98. The Worm with a Dragon's head : Man in his lowest form advancing to war.

Below line 55 is a row of the offspring of war : the snail, toad, moth, inch-worm, spider, worm, and flies.

Plate 99. *The End of the Song of Jerusalem.*   Below the text : God and the Soul in the ecstasy of an embrace, entirely surrounded by fire.   This represents the ultimate union.

Plate 100. No text.   Urthona, with hammer and tongs, stands before the Serpent Temple, which is evidently copied from the Serpentine Druid Temple at Avebury in North Wiltshire.   Blake, however, gives the Temple two tails and no head— presumably he saw the original ruins and did not grasp completely its original plan.   He also omits the altar in the central coil.

On Urthona's right is his spectre, Los, flying inward with the sun.   On his left, his emanation, Enitharmon, weaves the dark garment of the flesh against a background of Moon and Stars (Beulah).

THE GHOST OF ABEL

COMMENTARY

Line 2. *Outline*: as in Painting.

Line 3. *Tune*: as in music.

Lines 7-8. Cf. *Genesis* iii. 15: 'and her seed; it shall bruise thy head, and thou shalt bruise his heel.'

Line 12. Cf. *Job* xvi. 18: 'O earth, cover not thou my blood, and let my cry have no place.'

Line 14. *The Elohim*: the Creators—distinguished from Jehovah, who is the 'Father.' Cf. H. C. R., Feb. 28, 1852: 'Whoever believes in Nature, said Blake, disbelieves in God. For Nature is the work of the Devil. On my obtaining from him the declaration that the Bible was the Word of God, I referred to the commencement of Genesis—In the beginning God created the Heavens and the Earth. But I gained nothing by this, for I was triumphantly told that this God was not Jehovah, but the Elohim; and the doctrine of the Gnostics repeated with sufficient consistency to silence one so unlearned as myself.'

Line 15. *Prince of the Air*: cf. *Ephesians* ii. 2: 'the course of this world, according to the prince of the air.' This prince commonly signifies the devil; but to Blake he represented the tendency of acts to repeat themselves. Blake accepted the occult doctrine that 'air' is the cosmic memory of Nature. Cf. Cornelius Agrippa's *Occult Philosophy*, I. vi.: 'Hence they say it is, that a man passing by a place where a man was slain, or the Carkase newly hid, is moved with fear and dread; because the Aire in that place being full of the dreadfull species of Man-slaughter, doth, being breathed in, move and trouble the spirit of the man with the like species, whence it is that he comes to be afraid.' See the Commentaries on *The Four Zoas*, VII. 730-731, and *Jerusalem*, 16: 61-69.

Line 18. As in *Exodus* xxi. 24: 'Eye for eye, tooth for tooth.'

Line 26. Jehovah is revealed.

Line 28. Cf. *Hamlet*, I. ii. 185: "In my mind's eye, Horatio.' This is not only interesting as another explanation of Blake's own visions, but as an interpretation of the ghost in *Hamlet* as well.

Lines 33-34. Cf. *Psalms* xxxiv. 18: 'The Lord is nigh unto them that are of a broken heart; and saveth such as be of a contrite spirit.'

Line 44. *Thou human*: God is also Man, therefore Satan has power over him.

Line 45. Probably inserted at the re-engraving. The Druid religion is Satan's.

Line 47. A condensation into one line, of Satan's speech to Christ in the Prologue to Shelley's *Hellas*.

Line 50. *Torment*: of Experience. The States are eternal; but one can always pass out of them.

Line 52. *Elohim Jehovah*: the good Creator as distinguished from the bad. The bad created the world of matter, while the good works through the Creative Imagination.

Line 53. *Death, O Holy!* The Mystical Death of the Selfhood; self-sacrifice for others by forgiveness.

Line 54. *Eternal Fire*: Wrath, or Hell.

THE ILLUSTRATIONS TO *THE GHOST OF ABEL*

All but the final illustration on the last of the two plates of this little drama are tiny initial or terminal designs, which fill all the spaces left blank by the text.

Round the title. Floating and adoring figures.

Seen by William Blake. To the left is Eden, represented by a lion and a stag ; to the right, The Expulsion from Eden, where an angel drives a despairing form upon a thorny path leading to the left.

Jehovah's first *Adam !* To the right : Cain flees from the body of Abel, as in plate XII. of the *Milton.*

Jehovah's second *Adam !* To the right : the serpent approaches the fruit.

Lines 6-9. To the left : Adam and Eve under the well-laden Tree.

Enter the Ghost of Abel. To the right : a floating figure.

Lines 14-17. To the left : a man reclining under a tree beholds a descending vision.

Lines 22-27. To the left : Adam and Eve under a barren tree, which probably is the Tree of Mystery.

Lines 30-31. To the left is Abel in Eternity, a figure bowed and yet radiant.

Lines 33-38. To the left : the Druidic sacrifice. A naked man sacrifices a youth who is bound upon a stone altar.

Abel sinks down. To the left : a descending figure.

Lines 42-47. To the left : a seated and a flying man argue with uplifted hands. The arguments of error.

Lines 48-50. To the left : Adam and Eve under the serpent-bound Tree.

Below the text : Adam flung in grief upon Abel's corpse, while a wailing figure, inscribed ' The Voice of Abel's Blood,' floats horizontally above them. Below this picture is the inscription : ' 1822 W. Blakes Original Stereotype was 1788.'

ABBREVIATIONS

BENSON, ARTHUR CHRISTOPHER : *Essays.*   London and New York [1909].

BERGER, P. : *William Blake, Poet and Mystic.*   New York, 1915.

BROOKE, STOPFORD A. : *Studies in Poetry.*   New York, 1907.

CESTRE, CHARLES : *La Révolution Française et les Poètes Anglais.*   Paris, 1906.

CHENEY, JOHN VANCE : *That Dome in Air.*   Chicago, 1895.

CHESTERTON, G. K. : *William Blake* (The Popular Library of Art).   London and New York [n.d.].

CUNNINGHAM, JAMES : Life of Blake (*Lives of the Most Eminent British Painters*). London, 1830.   Reprinted in Symons, pp. 389-433.

EY.   *The Works of William Blake,* edited by Edwin John Ellis and William Butler Yeats.   London, 1893.

GARNETT, RICHARD : William Blake, Painter and Poet.   (*The Portfolio Monographs.*)   London and New York, 1895.

GILCHRIST, ALEXANDER : *The Life of William Blake.*   London, 1907.

H. C. R.   HENRY CRABB ROBINSON : *Diary and Reminiscences.*   London, 1869. The parts relating to Blake reprinted in Symons, pp. 251-306.

HEWLETT, H. G. : Imperfect Genius : William Blake.   *The Contemporary Review,* October 1876 and January 1877.

KEYNES, GEOFFREY : *A Bibliography of William Blake.*   New York, 1921.

MALKIN, BENJ. HEATH : *A Father's Memoirs of his Child.*   London, 1806. The parts relating to Blake reprinted in Symons, pp. 307-329.

MILSAND, JOSEPH : *Littérature Anglaise et Philosophie : W. Blake.*   Dijon, 1893.

MOORE, T. STURGE : *Art and Life.*   London [1910].

MORE, PAUL ELMER : *Shelburne Essays,* Fourth Series.   New York and London, 1906.

MS. Book, also known as the *Rossetti MS.* : a notebook of Blake's filled with sketches, poems, and prose.

NORTON, CHARLES ELIOT : *William Blake's Book of Job.*   Boston, 1875.

ROSSETTI, W. M., *ed.* : *Poetical Works of William Blake* (The Aldine Edition). London, 1911.

SAMPSON, JOHN, *ed.* : *The Poetical Works of William Blake.*   Oxford, 1905.

SAMPSON, JOHN, *ed.* : *The Poetical Works of William Blake . . . with the Minor Prophetic Books.*   Oxford, 1913.

SAURAT, DENIS : *Blake and Milton.*   Bordeaux, 1920.

SELINCOURT, BASIL DE : *William Blake.*   London and New York [1909].

SHEPHERD, R. H., *ed.* : *Songs of Innocence and Experience.*   London, 1868.

STOKES, FRANCIS G., *ed.* : *The Marriage of Heaven and Hell.* London and New York, 1911.

SWINBURNE, ALGERNON CHARLES : *William Blake.* New York, 1907.

SYMONS, ARTHUR : *William Blake.* New York, 1907.

TATHAM, FREDERICK : The Life of William Blake, published in *The Letters of William Blake.* London [1906].

THOMSON, JAMES (B. V.) : *Biographical and Critical Studies.* London, 1896.

TRAILL, H. D., *ed.* : *Social England,* Vol. V. London and New York, 1896.

UNDERHILL, EVELYN : *Mysticism, A Study in the Nature and Development of Man's Spiritual Consciousness.* New York, 1911.

WALLIS, J. P. R. : *The Cambridge History of English Literature,* Vol. XI. Cambridge, 1914.

WICKSTEED, JOSEPH H. : *Blake's Vision of the Book of Job.* London and New York, 1910.

WILKINSON, J. J. GARTH, *ed.* : *Songs of Innocence and Experience.* London, 1839.

INDEX

CPSIA information can be obtained
at www.ICGtesting.com
Printed in the USA
BVOW09s1031251017
498626BV00019B/741/P